OFFICE WITHOUT POWER

Tony Benn, who first entered Parliament in 1950, has been the Labour MP for Chesterfield since March 1984. He was elected to the National Executive Committee of the Labour Party in 1959, and was the Chairman of the Party in 1971–2. He has been a Cabinet Minister in every Labour Government since 1964, holding the positions of Postmaster General, Minister of Technology and Minister of Power. From 1974–9 he was Secretary of State for Industry, later Secretary of State for Energy and one-time President of the Council of Energy Ministers of the European Community. He contested the leadership of the Labour Party in 1976 and in 1988.

He is the author of nine previous books, including *Arguments for Socialism, Arguments for Democracy, Fighting Back* and *Out of the Wilderness,* the first volume of Diaries which was published to great critical acclaim in 1987. He holds four Honorary Doctorates from British and American Universities. He is married to Caroline, and they have four children and five grandchildren.

D1353099

TONY BENN
Office Without Power
DIARIES 1968–72

ARROW BOOKS

Arrow Books Limited
62-65 Chandos Place, London WC2N 4NW

An imprint of Century Hutchinson Limited

London Melbourne Sydney Auckland Johannesburg
and agencies throughout the world

First published in Great Britain by Hutchinson 1988
Arrow edition 1989

Printed and bound in Great Britain by
The Guernsey Press Co Ltd
Guernsey, C.I.

ISBN 0 09 963450 3

List of Illustrations

Cartoon Acknowledgments

Franklin, *The Times*, 27 May 1968 (page 69); Garland, *Daily Telegraph*, 27 May 1968 (page 72); Cummings, *Sunday Express*, 8 October 1972 (page 457).

Contents

This book is dedicated, with love,
to my life-long friend and partner in socialism, Caroline,
and the family, who went through it all too.

Acknowledgments

This second volume of my Diaries could not have been prepared for publication without the effort and advice of a formidable team of people.

Sheila Hubacher and Ruth Hobson bore the brunt of the transcription of the Diaries and began the task of editing the raw material.

Ruth Winstone, as Editor, was responsible for researching and preparing the book for publication and overseeing the project at every stage.

I must also record my deep appreciation to Century Hutchinson, who have undertaken the publishing of the whole series, which will run into several volumes, reflecting the most interesting periods of my political and ministerial life.

In particular, I would like to thank Richard Cohen, who has always expressed his confidence in the project, and Kate Mosse, who gave detailed attention, encouragement and advice throughout.

Editor's Note

This Volume represents only a third of the original Diary dictated by Tony Benn over five years, in both Government and Opposition. The guiding consideration when making such substantial cuts was to preserve as much as possible of the inherent balance between Benn's interests and activities as a member of the Cabinet, as a leading Labour Party figure and as a constituency MP. Within this framework, particular issues obviously prevail: the arguments over expenditure cuts during 1968, for example, and the protracted and profound differences over the Common Market which savagely divided the Labour Party in 1971 and 1972. Recurring passages have therefore been edited to reflect the contemporary significance of the discussions and decisions taken, whilst reducing repetition and excessive detail.

The absolutely raw Diary, with all its quirks of transcription from audiotape to the written word, in future will be available for those intent on examining the minutiae which did not survive the blue pencil, or for those wishing to follow every development of a particular theme.

A diary of this kind inevitably involves a generation gap. What does Pinkville mean to readers born during the years of the Vietnam War? Or UCS, on everyone's lips in 1971? The choice of footnotes and chapter notes is, in this sense, largely intuitive and does not attempt to provide a comprehensive political background. Appendices give full details of the Labour Government, Shadow Cabinet and National Executive Committees between 1968 and 1972; biographical notes of leading figures – both political and personal – appear in the Principal Persons at the end of the book.

Since the late Sixties, there has been a revolution in political language. Because of the unique nature of a published Diary, contemporary usage has been retained: leading women politicians are therefore described in the notes and text as Chair*men* and the Soviet Union is referred to in explanatory links as Russia, as was common at the time.

Ruth Winstone
July 1988

Introduction

This second volume of my political diary opens in January 1968 on a Labour Government enjoying an enviable parliamentary majority of ninety seats. By the close, in October 1972, the Labour Party is firmly entrenched in its customary role of Opposition, bitterly divided over the Common Market and with little apparent prospect of forming another administration.

The pages thus span a period of rapid political reversal, chronicling the decline of a Government which experienced office without power, and charting the subsequent sharp radicalisation of the Labour movement as a whole, a process which undoubtedly played a crucial part in Labour's surprising Election victory during the Miners' strike in 1974. The first weeks of 1968 witness the Cabinet and Government wrestling with a package of expenditure cuts, insisted upon by the then Chancellor of the Exchequer, Roy Jenkins: this followed the devaluation of the pound the previous autumn, and the cuts were opposed by other sections of the Party. *Office Without Power* details these discussions for the first time, taken from extensive notes in Cabinet and National Executive meetings.

Internationally, 1968 was the year in which the USA and Europe were in turmoil: protests against the Vietnam War reached a climax, and students were engaged in demonstrations against state bureaucracy, demonstrations which were interpreted as popular disenchantment with politics. But these movements were not confined to the West. In the same year in Czechoslovakia, Dubcek launched his experiment in liberalisations – twenty years ahead of Gorbachev – which was to end so tragically with the invasion by Soviet troops. Yet it is still possible to detect – in my private talks with Soviet and Eastern European ministers during official visits – the first stirrings of *perestroika* and *glasnost*.

At the other extreme, Milton Friedman was working on his theories of monetarism in Chicago, and the Conservative Party, already under his influence, was moving towards its 1970 Selsdon Park Conference where monetarist ideas were officially endorsed. But this diary records that, even before 1970, the Labour Cabinet too had been warned that the control of money supply had to be included in its economic policy, thus also marking the end of the predominance of Keynesian economics in Britain's two leading political parties.

Another aspect of the shift in basic thinking related to the trade union movement, which came under fierce attack from many quarters in the late 1960s and early 1970s, being widely criticised in the press and blamed for the economic problems of the country as a whole. Harold Wilson persuaded himself that it would make him popular if he were to legislate against the unions, loosening the bond linking them with the Party. He hoped this would allow him to project Labour as the 'natural party of government'. Barbara Castle was given the task of preparing the White Paper – 'In Place of Strife' – and of introducing the legislation. But the Cabinet itself was advised only after the basic work had been done, and the outline well-leaked to the press. Thus Ministers were forced into the position of having to accept the Paper: it became nothing more than an issue of confidence in the Prime Minister. Along with others in the Government, I was initially sympathetic to some of the proposals, despite the way in which they had been introduced. I did not appreciate the full significance of what the trade unions were to see as a betrayal of their interests, undermining their strength and threatening to destroy the Party as well.

As Minister of Technology my departmental responsibilities extended to the aircraft, shipbuilding, motor, machine tool, computer and nuclear industries, as well as to regional policy. All of this presented me with the immensely complicated problems of trying to sustain and rejuvenate our manufacturing base and check the downward drift towards de-industrialisation. It became clear that these problems could not be solved by the policies that the Cabinet had accepted, and which I had previously worked so hard to implement. This is why in the 1980s – when these same policies were being advocated by the SDP and even the Labour leadership – I remained quite unconvinced that they could work: all my efforts in the period covered by this diary to bribe and bully businessmen into co-operating with us, while following the demands of market forces, had simply not produced the results we had hoped they would.

It was during the period 1968–72 that my own radicalisation took shape, and I began, while still an active Minister, to formulate policies which were more explicitly democratic and socialist. My weekend speeches infuriated the Prime Minister, Harold Wilson, but found an echo in the mood of the Party which was increasingly anxious about the Cabinet's loss of direction.

When Labour was defeated in June 1970 and the Tory government began to apply its Selsdon Park philosophy against trade unions and 'lame duck' industries, a fresh impetus was given to shop floor activity. Freed from the restraints of loyalty to a Labour Government, this was matched by a return to a socialist analysis and debate within the Party. As Shadow Front Bench Minister I was intimately involved in the campaigns to defend the victims of Conservative industrial policy, such as the workers at Rolls Royce and UCS.

The political issue with the greatest long-term significance during this time was Britain's membership of the Common Market. I felt that a decision of such constitutional importance could not be contemplated without the explicit consent of the electorate in a general election or referendum. This view initially found no support when I put it to the Shadow Cabinet and the National Executive. During the long and protracted argument about Europe which followed – and which is included here in detail because of its importance – it became clear that a group of pro-European Labour MPs would never accept an adverse Conference decision on this question, and had therefore decided that if their dream of an enlarged Common Market conflicted with their membership of the Labour Party, then the Party would have to be sacrificed. It was this commitment that ultimately led to the formation of the SDP in 1981.

Out of office I was much freer to speak my mind, and I took every advantage of this during my year as Chairman of the Party. My priorities as Chairman were to work for a new and more radical programme for the next election, to try to restore a close working relationship with the TUC, and to open up the whole question of Party democracy. It was therefore during 1972 that 'Labour's Programme for Britain' was drawn up as the basis of our next manifesto, that the TUC–Labour Party Liaison Committee got under way, and that the debate began on the democratic reforms in the Party which would make the Leadership and MPs more accountable to the membership.

More generally, I concluded that we needed far-reaching democratic reforms in the structure of the state, of industry, finance and the mass media, a view which guaranteed opposition from all those who enjoy power and who rightly suspected that what I was urging might strip them of that power.

Writing a diary, even allowing for gaps and errors, and keeping contemporary archives in order, has been a valuable discipline. It has provided a useful historical perspective against which it has become easier to understand the situation in which the people of this country now find themselves.

Since this is a political, not a personal, account, the most obvious omissions relate to the work done by Caroline and the family who have been, and remain, unfailing friends and advisers, often critical but always loyal. They made it possible to withstand the intense and often hostile pressures to which those who hold my views in the Britain of yesterday and today are continuously subjected.

Tony Benn
July 1988

1

Retrenchment and Retreat
January–December 1968

The most serious problem confronting the Labour Government in 1968 was the mounting pressure for further public expenditure cuts, and early in the New Year a succession of Cabinet meetings was held to consider the situation.

The City of London had been urging these cuts since devaluation in November 1967 and at the National Economic Development Council the industrialist Sir Kenneth Keith complained that there was no sense of urgency, a view reinforced by the Confederation of British Industry. It was left to George Woodcock, General Secretary of the Trades Union Congress, to warn of the public opposition there would be to health and education cuts.

It was also clear to Ministers that defence expenditure would have to come under review, the crucial issues here relating to our commitment East of Suez and to the defence equipment budget, notably the proposed purchase of fifty American F-111 aircraft which had been ordered to replace the TSR-2 after Labour came to power. Concorde was again under threat. The prospect of these cuts in foreign commitment and defence caused considerable anxiety to the Foreign Office and the Ministry of Defence in particular.

The first stage of the drama in 1968, as far as the Ministry of Technology was concerned, was that my officials arranged a meeting at which I would discuss some of these matters with Denis Healey, Minister of Defence. Officials in the two Departments were keen that I should go along with the MOD strategy and that I should support the purchase of the F-111s.

Wednesday 3 January 1968

Denis was surrounded by some of his senior people who were in a very angry mood, and his language was full of f... this and f... that. He said that the defence cuts were mad; that they were just being done to make it possible to introduce prescription charges; that the whole thing was crazy. He did not intend to offer or accept any reduction in the F-111 commitment. He was also strongly in favour of retaining Polaris. I asked him about Concorde and warned him that if cancelled, this might lead to the cancellation of the Anglo–French military package. He thought that Concorde should go but if I supported the F-111, he was prepared to let others take the lead on the Concorde issue. This was really very crude politicking and I listened attentively and left without any sort of commitment.

In the evening we went to the Crossmans where we had dinner with Tommy Balogh, Peter Shore and Barbara Castle. We started with a great gripe about the absolute exclusion of Cabinet Ministers from important decisions.

Barbara is very departmentally orientated and is terrified that her major road programme is going to be cut by Roy Jenkins. We managed to get her off that and agreed that a small group of five Ministers – that is to say Harold in the chair, the Foreign Secretary, the Lord President, the Chancellor and the Secretary of State for Economic Affairs – should form an inner Cabinet (which would be politically balanced, as it happens), and that other Ministers should be invited to come along as and when it was necessary to air their views on particular issues. But it is unlikely that Harold will agree to this, Harold now being full of euphoria about his success last December in preventing the South African arms deal and not feeling sufficiently threatened to call in his friends.

I am simply not prepared to accept the Treasury's right to dart into individual Ministers' Departments and find savings to suit their particular policies. Whether or not this argument will survive tomorrow, I do not know. I put forward some powerful alternatives to the educational and health cuts proposed, and Caroline is working with her Comprehensive Schools Committee Group to give me an alternative list of proposals that would reduce Government subsidies to private education and save as much without affecting the school leaving age, which is absolutely essential for comprehensive reorganisation.

It was an enjoyable evening but it became clear that Dick believed he had established a relationship with Roy that was as good as his relationship with Harold. This transfer of loyalty should make Harold pretty anxious. Roy is, of course, sitting pretty.

One forty-five, and all my red box still to do. What a life!

Thursday 4 January

The Cabinet met in an icy atmosphere, every Minister realising that he would have to defend his departmental estimates. The Chancellor opened with a severe warning about what could happen if things went wrong.

There had already been a general agreement that we should be out of our Far Eastern bases by either 1970/71 or 1971/72, and possibly earlier from the Persian Gulf. George Brown argued strongly in favour of 1972 and in this he was supported by George Thomson and Jim Callaghan,

Fred Peart, Denis Healey, Cledwyn Hughes, Willie Ross and Michael Stewart. On the other side were Roy Jenkins, Dick Crossman, Barbara Castle, Peter Shore, Gerald Gardiner, Tony Crosland, Lord Longford, Patrick Gordon Walker, Ray Gunter, Tony Greenwood and Dick Marsh.

I said that I had never supported the idea of East of Suez very enthusiastically. I thought the Cabinet had not yet realised how isolated Britain was: we were locked out of the EEC, our US link was weakening and we would just have to look after our own interests. For my part I could see little credibility in a lame duck military presence on borrowed money and the best thing to do was to speed up the withdrawal.

We went on to discuss our military hardware. The Chancellor led in favour of a substantial cut and although he detailed the Phantoms and one or two other possible cuts, the whole debate centred on the F-111.

Here Denis Healey made the most formidable case in favour of the F-111, calmly and quietly, and with considerable power of argument. He said that our ground troops and our air force in Europe were much smaller than those of the French and the Germans and that the particular contribution we could make was strike reconnaissance by having fifty F-111s which were the only aircraft capable of penetrating into Eastern Europe. He said this was the cheapest way of doing it and he drew attention to the offset purchases by the US in Britain which would help to meet the foreign exchange costs.

After that the argument began building up for and against. Roy Jenkins was the first to speak and he said that here was a clear saving that could be made in foreign currency and he was prepared to accept the fact that the cancellation charges would be slightly more expensive in the coming year.

I was the last to speak and by the time I was called, the vote was ten in favour of keeping the F-111 and nine against, with mine really being the decisive vote. My heart was in my boots and I knew what this would mean in terms of relations with the Ministry of Defence.

I started by saying I found it an extremely difficult issue to deal with. Two factors inclined me strongly towards the Defence Secretary. The first was on defence planning grounds: we had just reached a most important decision that would move us back towards Europe and for the first time since 1940 we were thinking of the defence of these islands in an uncertain period. We didn't even know what the American role in Europe would be. The second factor that inclined me towards the Defence Secretary was the offset, although I agreed with the Chancellor that it meant that we were simply walking up a down escalator. But we had other things, such as the Rolls Royce RB-211 engine for the American Airbus, which might be prejudiced and might involve a loss of many thousands of millions of dollars in exports.

However, there were other arguments which pushed me in the opposite direction. First I recalled that at least one of the reasons for the F-111 had been our East of Suez position and that as late as March we had thought of stationing thirty-six F-111s in Europe and only fourteen East of Suez. The case, therefore, for going to fifty F-111s in Europe would need to be made out, and it had not been.

The decisive argument for me was that it was inconceivable that we could change our defence role and maintain the same hardware purchases. If the F-111 were to continue, we should have to knock off other bits of hardware: either the Polaris submarine fleet, the Harrier, which was the most advanced aircraft produced in Britain and had considerable export potential, or the British military capability to build complete aircraft on our own. If we abandoned this capability, it would mean we would be committed for ever after to buying American or French military aircraft. Therefore, if there was a hardware choice – and I thought there was – and if, as a responsible Cabinet Minister, I accepted that we had to make a choice, I had to come down against the F-111. It was the last contribution and it left the Cabinet divided ten–ten.

Denis Healey then wound up and he directed much of his speech to me. He said he thought my arguments were fallacious, particularly with regard to the alternatives, and he might be prepared to find other savings.

We were left with the Prime Minister throwing in his vote against the F-111, so that, seen one way, Harold Wilson and I decided that issue between us.

As soon as it was done, George Brown said it would make his job a great deal more difficult in talking about our maintenance of a capability to help Australia, New Zealand, Singapore or Malaysia and he thought that as it had been such an evenly balanced vote, the Defence Secretary should be allowed to produce a paper inviting the Cabinet to reverse its decision and to accept alternative savings. I strongly agreed that any Minister whose programme was being decided for him by the Cabinet should have this right. I must say Denis behaved with great strength of character and did not allow this critical decision against him – on the vote of the Prime Minister, who had supported him through-out – to affect his composure in any way.

The Cabinet broke up at 7.30 and I went back to my office and summoned John Stonehouse and Ronnie Melville. I told them that the discussions we had been having on the package must be regarded as absolutely secure and only to be made available on a 'need to know' basis. I asked them to prepare three short papers for Cabinet for use by me as an aide-mémoire: one on the independent British military aircraft capability, one on the Concorde and one on the Harrier. I also decided to send out a minute to the same effect to everybody who had been involved in any of these discussions. For added security, I did not tell them what had happened in the Cabinet and said that we had simply had a general discussion.

I got home at 10.10 and had a word with John Silkin on the phone. He told me that he had had lunch with the Left and they were preparing their own package of cuts and wanted to put down their own amendment. If allowed to do this, they would probably support the Government on a vote of confidence. He said that two or three of them would be perfectly happy to be expelled from the Party in order to frighten us and stir up the Party against the Government. This, of course, is exactly what Denis Healey and the other expulsionists in the Cabinet would like to see happen and John Silkin's position is going to be very difficult.

I heard by indirect methods that George Brown had sent telegrams to all the Ambassadors in the Six, asking for an assessment of the reaction of the Governments concerned if we did cancel Concorde unilaterally. Every single one of them reported unfavourably on the idea and the Ambassador in Bonn, Frank Roberts, said it would be the worst single blow short of withdrawing our troops unilaterally from Germany. He said it would confirm all the French suspicions about us being bad Europeans and would destroy our credibility as a technological partner. What is interesting about the telegrams is that they did not come to Mintech from the Foreign Office. We heard about them because the Intelligence Department at the Ministry of Defence thought it would be interesting for Ronnie Melville to see them. In fact, we have virtually had to spy on the Foreign Office. This is a very curious way for the Foreign Secretary to behave.

Friday 5 January
At 10 to the Nuclear Policy Committee, a top secret committee which I attend by virtue of my control of the Atomic Weapons Research Establishment at Aldermaston. Last year Denis Healey asked for authorisation to go ahead with the hardening of the warheads and the acquisition of penetration aids to make Polaris more effective against the Russian anti-ballistic missile system. Solly Zuckerman had been very agitated about this and had come to see me to say that he thought if we did this, it would be the end of the Labour Government as the extra cost could be so great. I had come out earlier against the hardening, although the Atomic Energy Authority had told me that if they didn't harden, it would be impossible to ensure employment for the necessary skilled team at Aldermaston.

This Committee had been called as part of the Defence Review. Harold Wilson reminded us of the background and then Roy Jenkins opened up the question of abandoning the Polaris programme altogether. He said that the economies would be well worthwhile, though he did recognise that now the F-111 had been cancelled the case for the Polaris might be stronger. George Thomson, Michael Stewart, George Brown and Jim Callaghan all supported the existing programme of Polaris and so indeed did Harold, leaving Roy to make the running.

I argued that since it was easy to stop the Polaris programme at any time, but extremely difficult to restart it once you stopped it, the best thing to do was to keep it going as it now was and then either to vary it upwards by hardening and having the penetration aids, or downwards by re-equipping the Polaris missiles with the conventional warheads instead of nuclear warheads, both options involving extra cost but both being possible. Since the running costs of Polaris are only about £20 million a year, this seemed to me to be a reasonable insurance policy. I did, however, oppose the hardening of the missiles and believed the proposed enquiry into Aldermaston should go ahead on the basis that we did not harden.

The Cabinet met at 2 to deal with the rest of the Chancellor's paper. On education the big debate centred around the proposal made by Roy Jenkins, with which Pat Gordon Walker agreed, that the school leaving age should not be raised to sixteen on the date planned. Roy wanted it deferred by three years. This led to an extremely tense discussion. Pat Gordon Walker introduced it by more or less agreeing to what Roy had asked for and said, 'I am suggesting this in place of the cuts in university expenditure because the universities represent such an influential body of opinion.'

George Brown exploded, 'May God forgive you. You send *your* children to university and you would put the interests of the school kids below that of the universities.' It took some time to restore order. George then continued his attack, in which he said that education was the basis of class in Britain and if we denied these kids the opportunity of staying in school for an extra year, we would be perpetuating class distinctions.

Michael Stewart made a really excellent speech also in favour of raising the school leaving age, as did Ray Gunter who said that we were critically short of technicians in exactly the group that would benefit by an extra year at school. Fred Peart and Frank Longford supported it, as did Jim Callaghan, on the grounds of his own experience, and George Thomson and Tony Crosland who said the date had been fixed to meet a specific demographic situation and could not be altered easily.

In favour of postponement were Roy, of course, Pat Gordon Walker, whose arguments were quite disgraceful, Dick Marsh, who didn't see it mattered, Denis Healey, who was obviously trying to get his own back for the cuts in the F-111, Cledwyn Hughes, for no very clear reason, Gerald Gardiner, which was really rather surprising and Willie Ross, who gave no particularly strong argument. Tony Greenwood was in favour of postponing too and Dick Crossman, Barbara Castle and Peter Shore were so vague in their comments as to suggest that they didn't give much priority to this. Harold Wilson indicated that he was in favour of postponement for two years.

I said that I had a direct departmental interest because, of course, my industries were customers of the universities and the school system, and that there were too few science and technology candidates, too many of them staying at university doing soft and pure research and too few going into industry. I also pointed to the danger of the brain drain which was taking 40 to 50 per cent of our annual output and said that these considerations had led me to believe that there should be economies in the university sector.

It also seemed to me quite scandalous that, faced with the need for economy, we should economise on the state system while continuing to supply £7 million a year under the direct grant system. I said the really important thing about raising the school leaving age was not just the money that it made available for comprehensive reorganisation, but that for the first time ever, school teachers throughout the country would have to take seriously the extra year and wouldn't just be able to shovel the majority of children on to the labour market at fifteen. But the argument went against and the raising of the school leaving age is to be postponed by two years.

We then moved on to prescription charges. Roy said he wanted the prescription charges restored at half a crown [twelve and a half pence] an item. Kenneth Robinson said he well understood the need to save the money but thought that if you put a shilling [five pence] on the insurance stamp, this would meet the whole cost without having to go for those who were actually sick.

I strongly supported Kenneth's view, which I had come to independently, but unfortunately it was a tiny minority view. Peter Shore proposed a compromise under which we would have some increase on the stamp, with half a crown per item charged and a number of exemptions which he thought might be done under the aegis of the doctor so as to avoid the awful business of having refunds. Harold supported this, no doubt after a private agreement beforehand, and it was left that we would investigate it. Only Barbara Castle and I were opposed to this compromise.

Finally, as the last item of the day, we came to Concorde. George Brown reported on his chairmanship of the meeting that had been held to discuss this and said it was divided between those Ministers who wanted Concorde cancelled and the Attorney-General, who had said it couldn't be done without enormous financial damage, and myself who had taken the same view. George said he had consulted the

Ambassadors and even though their advice was very strongly against cancellation, he thought on balance we should cancel.

The Attorney-General then came in and gave the arguments in favour of continuing which were based on the £200 million damages we would probably be bound to have to pay the French in two or three years' time if we cancelled.

I pointed out that Concorde was the most advanced aircraft project in the world and it was three to five years ahead of the United States in supersonic work. I said if it was cancelled our position as a partner with any other country in an international technological project would become quite impossible, that it would undoubtedly force us out of the Airbus project and effectively destroy the British aircraft industry which would then have no civil aircraft projects left. I don't think any of these arguments carried weight with the Cabinet but when I came on to the legal arguments people listened. I said I would have no hesitation in recommending unilateral cancellation in eighteen months' time when the plane had flown and we would have an idea as to whether or not anyone would buy it. 'Therefore,' I said, 'I would suggest that I should say to the French now that we believe that summer 1969 would be the moment to decide whether or not to go on with Concorde and that if they do agree to these conditions, whether they were prepared to implement them or not in the summer of 1969, it would greatly strengthen our case if ever in the future the matter came to the International Court.'

Tuesday 9 January

Drove myself to the office in my own car because of the snow and from 10 to 11.45 we had a conference following up the Cabinet meeting at which it was decided to go ahead with Concorde but to try to get some agreement with the French on airline commitment by the summer of 1969.

After that, Ronnie Melville stayed on to tell me a bit more about the F-111 and the Ministry of Defence position. First he said that Sir James Dunnett, the Permanent Secretary at the MOD, wanted an opportunity to apologise to me for Denis Healey's behaviour at the end of last week.

I replied that I had known Denis for many years and neither his language nor his approach had in any way influenced me. But obviously it had greatly shaken the officials of the Ministry of Defence, and they were keen that I shouldn't have been so alienated that I would desert the F-111. Ronnie also told me that Denis is fighting for 100 per cent of his programme, and that the Ministry of Defence realise that there will have to be a fall-back position and are trying to persuade him to work one out.

I think what is really going on is an alliance between Ministry of

Defence and Ministry of Technology officials to try to persuade Denis to recognise that he is not going to get everything he wants; and to try to drive me towards Denis, particularly in favour of a major purchase of the F-111, even if it is a little bit less than fifty.

At 4 the Cabinet met again for a further session on the survey of public expenditure. We began with roads and poor Barbara Castle was absolutely at the end of her tether. Her voice was rising with emotion as she explained the consequences of what Roy Jenkins was proposing and in the end a compromise which will affect a large chunk of her programme was agreed.

Then we had an amusing session on Home Office economies whereby Roy, because of his expert knowledge, has suggested a number of cuts which poor Jim Callaghan, his predecessor at the Treasury and successor at the Home Office, would have to carry out. Jim said, 'Now that Roy Jenkins has left the Home Office, he is proposing serious cuts, and I'm the one who has got to carry these cuts through so that the reforms which I, as Chancellor, financed for Roy will come to a stop.' This had a ring of truth about it. He stuck his toes in on the reduction of the strength of the police force and there was a flare-up in which Dick Crossman, always ready for a row, said it was intolerable that a Minister should decline to carry cuts through. The atmosphere was very unpleasant.

We came on to Technology and I took the opportunity of making the first speech I had ever made to Cabinet about Mintech's purpose. I said that we were talking about the fifth year of a new department, and I was trying to make a number of shifts. First, a shift from defence to civil projects; second, from aerospace and nuclear to other engineering; third, from intra-mural to extra-mural research; and fourth, a shift from research itself, wherever it was done, to development and production technology. I said that in effect we were trying to turn off the taps – the defence tap, the aerospace tap, the nuclear tap and the intra-mural research tap.

My policy did require cuts and this would free money and resources, qualified scientists and engineers, but there was one developing side, one tap that we were trying to turn on, and that was technological support for industry which was growing now after three years' preparation.

I got a lot of support for this, and then Harold stepped in smartly. He said he thought the support for civil technology was immensely important and that that shouldn't be cut, but I would have to find the money elsewhere in my budget, and he indicated that the defence research was the obvious candidate. This is going to shake the Department to its roots, because it will have to come out of Farnborough and other defence establishments, but it has got to be done, and on the whole, if I can find almost all he wants, it shouldn't be too bad.

A query was waiting for me back at my office. Sir John Mallabar, Chairman of Harland and Wolff, has discovered that his new dry shipbuilding dock – which was to have cost £10.5 million – is now to cost £13 million and unless the Treasury give him the money, he says he is going to resign the chairmanship and cancel the orders for the big Esso tankers that he had got in the autumn. This is putting a gun at our head and with the present review of public expenditure, I don't think I can help him. But it meant another big headache.

Wednesday 10 January

Another very cold day and I went this morning to Sir Jules Thorn's factory at Enfield to see his work on colour television and fluorescent lamps. Thorn, the Managing Director of Thorn Electrical Industries, has been bullying me for three years to go and visit one of his factories and he devoted about one third of the total time we spent together complaining that I had not been before, that I was staying too short a time, and pleading with me to come back again next month or go and see another factory almost immediately. I have obviously got no good will out of the trip and from that point of view it was a waste of time.

Thorn is an astonishing man. He started in the late Twenties or early Thirties selling lamp bulbs and now has an enormous business employing 50,000 people. His technique is rather interesting because it is unusual for Britain. Almost all his technical progress is based on licencing agreements from big American companies, most of whom have large shareholdings in his Thorn Electrical Industry. Sylvania have provided the basic technology and machinery for his lamps; General Telephones have got a shareholding and he has very recently signed an agreement with Bendix under which they have management control of the joint company, and he has 51 per cent of the shares. This is exactly how the Japanese have got on. It means, of course, that he is not at all interested in exporting to the Soviet Union because the American shareholders would not permit it.

From a personal point of view, I must say I came away liking him rather less. I overheard him shouting at his chauffeur, and when the phone rang in the research labs while we were there, he picked it up and bawled in a most offensive manner at some poor woman who had innocently rung through.

I came back at 3.30 and went straight to see Denis Healey at the Ministry of Defence, with his Private Secretary and William Knighton present. William had worked out a memorandum showing how you could get a mix of defence cuts and Denis was totally different from the last meeting. No doubt he had been told by his Department that he had insulted me; anyway, he wanted my support. We left it that he would complete the paper for Cabinet on Friday. By then, of course, George

Brown and George Thomson will have reported from their Asian trip and it is perfectly evident that in Malaysia and Singapore there had been a huge explosion when they heard of our intention to withdraw. Harry Lee, the Prime Minister of Singapore, cabled to say that he wanted to see Harold at Chequers this weekend and threatened appalling things, including the withdrawal of the sterling balances. This will create a serious problem and it is going to involve very tough bargaining. But it really isn't for us to defend Malaysia and Singapore.

Thursday 11 January

Cabinet at 2.30 and it went on for four and a half grim hours. We began with a discussion about the Race Relations Bill which Jim Callaghan is introducing, although he took it over from Roy Jenkins. It extends the protection of the Race Relations Act to employment and housing and we had some difficult decisions to take. The first related to whether the Act should apply to owner-occupiers selling their houses or not, and we decided that it should.

The next – and much more difficult – problem was whether the Crown should be bound by the Act. I was strongly in favour of this but Mr Purnell, my Assistant Secretary in charge of security, had given me a warning brief to the effect that if the Crown was bound by the Act, there would have to be exemptions dealing with security. The problem here is that security is based on loyalty and loyalty is based upon nationality and nationality tends to preclude foreigners; and any foreigner who is coloured, even if he comes from the Commonwealth, will feel that he has been adversely treated because he is coloured and not because of his foreign origins. The Ministry of Technology security department has responsibilities for the whole of the Civil Service and for policing about five hundred defence firms which handle classified information and whose employees have to be screened by us. In the end we agreed the Crown should be covered by the Act subject to provisions that still have to be worked out.

After that we dealt with the Chancellor's devaluation package and went through a large number of points. At the end of the most enormous argument, we decided to restore prescription charges to half a crown with special exemptions for the elderly, expectant mothers, children and for those on social security benefits generally.

Everybody was in favour of cutting down local authority spending, for the obvious reason that other people's spending looks easier to cut than one's own.

Friday 12 January

Frank Kearton came to see me at 9.45. He certainly is the one industrialist who has stuck loyally by the Government over the last three and a half years.

At 11 I went to the first Cabinet of the day. George Brown was back, having flown overnight from New York, where he had had discussions with US officials about the impact of our proposed measures on US interests.

We had a long discussion about the extravagant level at which British diplomats lived abroad, and the cost of Embassies in the light of our likely withdrawal of military forces. Harold Wilson pointed out that it wasn't necessary to have massive political intelligence when you hadn't got the power to make use of the information, and he urged that we group our Embassies and concentrate almost entirely upon commercial work.

Tony Crosland introduced his paper in which he said it was time we had a look at the total switch of resources; how they should be divided between civil and military and then between taxation and cuts in public expenditure. He said he thought the Chancellor was asking for too much and it would be better if he asked for fewer cuts and was prepared to raise more revenue by taxation. George Brown supported Tony. He said the Chancellor really had to justify what he was asking for. Having been challenged in this way, Roy said that he would do his best.

I was so tired after four consecutive nights staying up till 2 or 2.30 that I had a short sleep during the lunch hour.

At 2.30 Cabinet met again and George Brown reported on his previous day's talks with the Americans. He said that he had worded his telegram to the Prime Minister deliberately. In the telegram he began by saying that he had had 'a bloody unpleasant' talk with Secretary of State Dean Rusk. He repeated the substance of the telegram which was that it had been the most awful experience of his life. Rusk, although a courteous Southern gentleman, had spoken to him more strongly than he had ever known. He had been really disgusted that Britain was turning its back on its responsibilities and he felt like saying to George Brown, 'Why don't you act like Britain?' Rusk also said that the whole thing had the 'acrid aroma of a fait accompli'.

George said he had discharged his obligation to the Cabinet in a way he thought they would have expected of him, as strongly as the Lord President (Richard Crossman) would have presented it – there was a strong note of contempt in that phrase – but having done so he had felt so physically sick that when it was over he had gone back to the Embassy and had not been able to speak to anybody. For his part he felt the Government was doing irreparable damage which would probably never be put right. He recognised that in saying this it might be against his own interests, but he did believe that if we agreed to stay in the Far East until 1972, and do what the Americans wanted us to do – which was to put no fixed date on withdrawal from the Middle East and to keep the 'bird', by which he meant the F-111 – then he thought we might possibly salvage something.

The Americans didn't seem too concerned about the Far East, as, after the Vietnam war was over, they intended to police the Far East from their bases in Okinawa and elsewhere, but they were desperately concerned about the Gulf. George said that he had come to the conclusion that this was the end of an era. He thought that there was a real risk that America would go isolationist and Rusk had said to him, 'Scratch any American and underneath you'll find an isolationist.' George spoke very movingly.

One senior American had asked him, 'George, as I understand it, you won't be in Asia; you won't be in the Middle East; and you won't be in Europe. What I want to know is where will you be? And what equipment will you have, to do what you say you have to do?'

This had obviously deeply upset George. His lunch with Secretary of Defence Robert McNamara had been painful because of their old and long friendship. He didn't think they were too upset about the F-111 decision although George felt it necessary to keep the F-111 in order to discharge our obligations. He said that our position would be quite untenable without the F-111 since nobody would believe that our European capability would be of any assistance at all to the Middle East or Asia after our withdrawal. He finished up by making a forceful plea to the Cabinet not to take a disastrous decision to withdraw early but to try to salvage our reputation. It was one of the most brilliant speeches he has ever made and it was delivered without a note.

Harold, who followed him, struck exactly the wrong note. Whatever he may have thought of George, who was highly emotive and emotional, George was chronicling the end of an era and from that point of view made a deep impression on me. Harold said there were a lot of counter-measures that we could take against the Americans and that if they were difficult with us, we would be able to withdraw our portfolio of investments. It was a sort of classic Harold misjudgment of the situation based entirely on economic terms; George was full of contempt and made no secret of it.

Then Jim came in and said he thought Harold had played our economic power against the United States very skilfully over the last three and a half years but he thought we were now seriously facing the possibility that the Americans would write us off altogether.

Roy thought that we couldn't go on as we had done over the last three and a half years, and that if we tried to we would get the worst of both worlds.

Tony Crosland said that of course the Americans never had the slightest hesitation in using their power and making their decisions in their own national interest, and what he regretted was that we had never done the same.

Then we came to Michael Stewart, who was in favour of staying *later*, and said that the United States and Britain were twin pillars of world peace and we had to take account of that.

Denis Healey said that he was in favour of staying later on the basis of British interests. We couldn't save by removing the forces earlier and an orderly withdrawal would require four years and not three.

Frank Longford said he was in favour of staying later, having switched his view after listening to George Brown.

Dick Crossman and Dick Marsh were in favour of coming out earlier. Dick Marsh said he didn't really think you would get an orderly Gulf anyway.

Then we had Pat Gordon Walker, who rather surprisingly came out for withdrawing earlier, followed by Ray Gunter who said the same.

After that we moved on to defence hardware which meant the F-111 again. Harold Wilson reported that this morning he and Denis Healey had seen the Chiefs of Staff at Number 10, who had come in by the back door so as not to be the subject of press comment. Harold stressed the fact that they had not come to put pressure on the Government but to point out that the morale of the forces would be very gravely affected by a faster run down.

Well, that was just by way of introduction, and Denis began an interminably long speech on his F-111 paper which must have lasted forty minutes.

Harold asked, 'How do we know that if we sent the F-111s into Europe to bomb airfields, the Russians won't think that this is a nuclear attack?' Denis said this was no greater risk than Phantoms which also carry nuclear weapons.

Harold then asked what the chances were of getting through the Soviet anti-ballistic missile system, to which Denis admitted that the Soviet air defence would be about 100 per cent effective in the 1980s. So then Harold asked how many planes the Americans had lost in Vietnam against more primitive missiles and Denis said 1 per cent of all the sorties they had undertaken: they had lost 762 aircraft last year.

Harold asked about other reconnaissance capabilities and Denis said it was very secret but the United States were now using cameras on satellites and that this information would come in too late to be of any use.

Finally the vote began to shape up. Frank Longford, who had made it plain internally and to the press that he was going to resign over the postponement of the school leaving age, said with incredible naïvety that he had been opposed to the cancellation of the F-111 but Denis

Healey had very kindly arranged for him to see a technical expert in his own Department and he had been convinced and was now going to vote *for* the F-111.

At that moment I thought it would mean that the Cabinet vote would shift but Cledwyn Hughes said that his view had changed the other way, and so did Pat Gordon Walker.

Roy Jenkins deployed an extremely skilful argument against Frank Longford. He had made it known that he was against the school leaving age postponement and he had found this the most difficult and painful thing of all to do; but he didn't see how, if the raising of the school leaving age was to be postponed, that during the years of postponement we should be making the maximum purchase of American aircraft. It was impossible by this time for Frank Longford to change his vote back but he did make himself look very stupid and his loss from the Government will not be a serious one.

In the final line-up, with the exception of those three people who switched their views, there was no change and when I was asked my view I simply said 'Chancellor', meaning that I was against the F-111. The vote was as follows. For the F-111: Denis Healey, George Brown, Michael Stewart, Frank Longford, Jim Callaghan, Ray Gunter, Dick Marsh and Willie Ross; plus George Thomson who clearly was for it and had been before, and had sent telegrams to confirm it, ie nine in favour of the F-111. Against it were: Harold himself, whose view was unchanged, Roy Jenkins, Peter Shore, Tony Greenwood, Barbara Castle, Gerald Gardiner, Dick Crossman, Tony Crosland, Cledwyn Hughes, Fred Peart, Pat Gordon Walker and myself, making twelve.

Although I had last-minute doubts, it would have been inconceivable to have made these savage domestic cuts and not to have cut our defence. This really was 1951 all over again with Harold Wilson being confirmed in his view that you couldn't spend more on defence than you could afford and at the same time accept some social service cuts. So everybody had to compromise. It wasn't the old Bevanite line-up at all. It was a shattering experience to do this because it is an irreversible decision which will affect the future of this country over the next ten or fifteen years and probably for ever.

Also, as one would expect in an intensely interesting policy discussion of this kind in Cabinet, a thing we never normally have, the character of the people concerned did come out. Denis behaved with enormous courage and dignity in the face of a shattering blow, quite as great for him as devaluation was for Jim Callaghan; George Brown was emotional, sensational but immensely powerful in personality; Crosland rather niggling; Jim Callaghan trying to be weighty but without substance; Harold never quite equal to the occasion. I don't know what it is about Harold, but he always falls two or three points below par. Roy was very effective: I must say my opinion of Roy rose – I don't regard him as having any principles but today in argument, getting all that he wanted from his colleagues, he was very impressive.

Monday 15 January
Cabinet at 10. When we got there, the Prime Minister handed round two telegrams from Lyndon Johnson about the current review of public expenditure. It concentrated on two things: first, our projected withdrawal from the Far East and the Middle East by 1971, which filled him with dismay; and second, the proposal to cancel the F-111. Johnson warned us in the strongest terms that this would be a catastrophic decision and would affect the offset arrangement that had been reached under the original agreement. I have often heard of American pressure upon British Cabinets, but this was extremely direct and it is much to our credit that we ultimately resisted it.

Then Harold reported on his talks with Harry Lee over the weekend. He said Lee had been almost hysterical and incoherent for large parts of the discussions, although he calmed down over dinner. He had threatened to withdraw the sterling balances and it had been very difficult to make sense of what he was saying. Lee kept repeating, 'This is the end of 150 years' association.' But he had left Harold in no doubt of his view.

George Brown raised the question of a letter to the Treasury from the Governor of the Bank of England, Sir Leslie O'Brien, pointing out the dangers that might come as a result of some pressure on sterling through a premature withdrawal. Roy was unable to identify the letter. Later he made enquiries and then said that Sir William Armstrong had spoken to Sir Leslie, who had said that this letter did not indicate that he had a view on the date of withdrawal and that indeed, speaking for himself, he preferred the earlier date of 1971.

In the end Harold made a proposal that we should compromise on December instead of March 1971. This would be some concession to Lyndon Johnson and to Harry Lee, and the Cabinet agreed without taking a vote.

Over lunch, Pen Piercy, one of the Department's Under-Secretaries, came to say that British Motors and Leyland had agreed very late last night to merge their two companies into one. This is a fantastic achievement, and it all began in my house in November 1966 when George Harriman and Donald Stokes came to discuss the future of Rootes and I put it to them that they ought to consider merging.

At 3.30 the Cabinet met again and we had a session on the cuts package as a whole. George Brown warned us once more of the historic decisions we had taken and what a tragedy they were.

After another round of discussions, going over much of the same ground, we went through the draft statement paragraph by paragraph. On the school leaving age Tony Crosland spoke for sixty seconds in support of a reconsideration and Harold said that, although he was reluctant to reopen the package since it had been very carefully constructed, he was ready to take the vote on those who were in favour of reopening it. The list of honour was George Brown, Michael Stewart, Tony Crosland, Fred Peart, Frank Longford, Ray Gunter, George Thomson, Jim Callaghan and myself. That made only nine and wasn't a majority and so it was confirmed that raising the school leaving age to sixteen should be postponed by two years.

The scandal of it all was that if Gordon Walker had voted to reopen it, that would have been ten and we might have just done it. As for the rest, they were silent: Dick Crossman, Peter Shore, Barbara Castle, Tony Greenwood. It really was rather disgraceful. Still, that is politics.

Home at 9 and settled down very quickly to the phone because I wanted to try to brief a few friendly journalists about the Industrial Expansion Bill and the significance of the Kirillin visit which begins tomorrow.

One of the enduring achievements of the Labour Government was the negotiation of a series of technological agreements covering trade and technology with the Soviet Union and other Eastern European Governments. Harold Wilson, who had a long experience of East-West trade in the Fifties and early Sixties, was one of the driving forces behind this movement, although in fact both the French and German Governments were engaged in more active negotiations with Eastern Europe than we were and, in truth, we always lagged behind them.

Kosygin had already come to London for discussions to start this process but the practical work fell to me as Minister of Technology in direct negotiations with Academician Vladimir Kirillin, the Chairman of the State Committee for Science and Technology of the USSR. Kirillin was a scientist and an engineer whose field of expertise was in the development of superconductivity. In practice he was an unpolitical person and I think, for him, these links were primarily of technical and industrial interest. However, from the outset, I saw them as an opportunity to develop direct connections with the countries of Eastern Europe and encourage the operation of détente, in which I profoundly believed.

A serious obstacle to the developing of these links was the strategic arms embargo, code-named COCOM, imposed by the United States. American influence was exerted by banning the supply of parts to any British company that exported to the Soviet Union without getting 'End-use' certificates which complied with the COCOM embargo list.

In the discussions that took place with the Russians, the question of COCOM continually arose and the other Eastern European Governments with which I had to negotiate repeatedly told me that the French and the Germans took a much less rigid approach to COCOM restrictions than we did and that as a result of this Britain lost out on a number of trade opportunities. I never entirely supported the COCOM list except in respect of the supply of weapons and this question never arose.

Khrushchev once commented of COCOM that if its rules were strictly applied trouser buttons made in America would not be allowed to be sold to the USSR because they would hold up the trousers of the Red Army and thus contribute to their plans to attack the West.

Tuesday, 16 January

I greeted Kirillin at the plane and we went to have a cup of coffee together in the VIP suite. I deliberately didn't make a speech of welcome to him on the spot as I feel that he is an old friend now and we don't have to have all the formalities. Mikhail Smirnovsky, the Ambassador, Kirillin, Mme Santalova (the interpreter) and I travelled in Kirillin's car to his hotel. In the car, I told him that it was a historic day on which he was arriving in Britain as the cuts would end our world role and bring us back to Europe.

I tried to underline the political importance of Russian friendship at this moment. We were an isolated country whose relationships with the United States were now somewhat strained and who had been locked out of Europe, and therefore Soviet friendship was of great importance. I said that I knew the Prime Minister attached a lot of significance to *his* visit to Moscow next week.

He stressed that he now only did a five-day week and when I asked him about his programme, he said he was particularly keen on Thursday, which was his free day. We had an amusing chat about *The Black and White Minstrel Show* which my people had arranged for him to visit on Friday night. This seemed to me most unsuitable for him to see, but he really did want to go and I think the reason is that they don't have this type of entertainment in Russia.

At 11.15, Otto Clarke came in in a state of great excitement and said that Field Marshal Harding, Chairman of Plessey, wanted to see me; it was pretty evident that Plessey intended to bid for ICT,* which would put me in a very difficult position.

Ten minutes later, Harding, Henry Grunfeld, the President of Warburg's bank, and Sir Eric Roll, the Chairman of Warburg's, came to see me. I used strong language in trying to frighten them off. I said that we had devoted three years of effort in trying to establish a viable British computer corporation, that we were determined to get it, and that £25–£30 million of Government money was involved in it. I also

---

* International Computers and Tabulators Ltd was a major British computer firm which had been provided with financial support by the Ministry of Technology since 1965. When it merged with English Electric in 1968, it became known as ICL.

hinted that there were very large orders involved, and even went so far as to say that we were large purchasers of telecommunications equipment and didn't intend to see Plesseys frustrate our policy in this way. I pointed out that ICT simply wouldn't exist if it hadn't been for Ministry of Technology support in the early days and that I took a most unfavourable view of what they were proposing to do.

I went to the House at 2.30 for the Prime Minister's statement on cuts. The House was packed and Harold started off at a rattling pace and got through in forty-five minutes. It was an agonising statement for him to make with his background and I felt very sympathetic, after the agony we had been through. Heath muffed it as he always does and, of course, the entire bloc of the Left led by John Mendelson, Stan Orme, Eric Heffer and Jim Dickens* all rose to their feet to protest. But the House mainly listened to it quietly.

I hurried away from the House and at 4 Kirillin and his delegation came to the office. We got through our meeting in about twenty minutes. I think he wanted to go and see the Tower of London.

Later Ron Vaughan drove me to Newbury for a meeting. Of course, it was the first public meeting since the cuts were announced and I was a bit nervous but I presented the story as best I could. Although the audience was made up of the Party faithful and included a lot of very high-quality people from the Atomic Energy Authority who tend to be rather on the Left, I was heard with sympathy.

I didn't get a single question about the prescription charges but a couple of critical questions about the school leaving age. Quite frankly, it was a repugnant decision, and I was able to use that word because Harold had used it himself.

Wednesday 17 January
At 10.30 Mintech began the plenary talks with Kirillin and it was a fruitful two hours. I started by stressing that we didn't want to intervene in any relationships which might be established between the State Committee and the CBI, and indeed any individual company. Kirillin entirely endorsed this and he reported on the arrangement that had been made with the CBI during their time in Moscow.

I then added a number of other subjects that interested us: information technology, educational technology, colour television, where we obviously have a motive in trying to weaken their links with the French, the non-conventional methods of food production, and materials research. The final proposal we made was transport technology. Kirillin accepted most of these proposals and then we went on to

* Labour MPs for Penistone, Salford West, Liverpool Walton and Lewisham West respectively.

other suggestions of ours, including mining machinery and construction engineering.

Afterwards I had a talk with Harry Slater who told me that the security people had made a big effort to try to stop the technology agreement on the grounds that it would lead to a lot more Russians coming to this country, but he had driven them off. This obstruction never came to me, of course – but Harry Slater said it would have done if there had ever been a serious likelihood that the security objections would succeed.

I went to lunch at the Embassy and had quite a talk to Smirnovsky. I stressed the great political importance that we attached to this agreement so that he would go back to Moscow and make it clear, in advance of Harold Wilson's visit, that we did regard this as a major change in the direction of our policy. I spoke and welcomed Kirillin again. I said that we had done what Wilson and Premier Kosygin asked us to do, that no two Prime Ministers had ever had such cooperative Ministers, and that as soon as we had completed our work, the Prime Minister had decided to go to Moscow, and we wished that Prime Ministers always took the same rapid action in response to ministerial initiatives!

Then to Lancaster House where we had a formal dinner at which I made a speech saying how politically important this venture was, how Britain was changing its role in the world and was going to make sacrifices to concentrate on its industrial efforts. Our links with the Russians were very important in this context and there was a great background of sympathy and affection in Britain, dating back to the war and beyond, for the wonderful courage and ability of the Russians.

Kirillin himself was, as always, charming and delightful and altogether this is going to be a big success story.

The news coverage tonight is about the BMH/Leyland business. Donald Stokes has very kindly and generously said that we had something to do with it and I am anxious to see that some aspect of Mintech's involvement should be reported in the press.

Thursday 18 January
Cabinet at 10 and after a short discussion about parliamentary business we went on to discuss Europe. A lot of people said what I strongly believe: that we shouldn't go on hanging about in the ante-chambers of Europe with plans, waiting to be rebuffed. I urged that we should pause and reflect what our view should be. Harold complained to George, in the nicest possible way, that he had been worried by the Byzantine diplomacy that had been going on designed, primarily, to isolate the French, which had succeeded in annoying the Germans, worrying the Italians and which had divided the Six into the Five, then the Five into

the Four, the Four into the Three, and had, generally speaking, failed. George was embarrassed by all this but he is like a chicken who goes on running after its neck has been wrung.

Friday 19 January

I took Kirillin to see the Prime Minister at midday and we had half an hour's friendly talk. Harold looked very worried because there is a huge row brewing over the leadership. Apparently he made a very bad speech in the House yesterday and all the papers are now effectively calling for Roy Jenkins to take over.

The only thing of any interest that emerged was that Harold said when he goes to Moscow next week he intends to raise with Kosygin the question of the COCOM list, the strategic embargo.

At 3.30 I met Kirillin in the front hall and we came upstairs and signed the agreement. I had got the Foreign Office to agree that this should be signed in the Ministry of Technology and I regarded this as a big scoop because I want to develop our own foreign policy and not find that we are just an agent of the Foreign Office. It was really enjoyable and there were a number of newspapers there. Kirillin was friendly and kept saying to the press how much he enjoyed our cooperation.

I went home, collected Melissa, and took her to the Victoria Palace with Kirillin and most of his delegation to see *The Black and White Minstrel Show*.

Tuesday 23 January

I went straight to Victoria Station this morning and met Mr Verdet, the Rumanian First Deputy Premier. After all the warnings about this dark, swarthy, mysterious man of whom the British Embassy in Bucharest knew practically nothing, I found a most agreeable person of about forty-six who had never been outside a Communist country in his life. He had come from Bucharest by train which had taken forty hours and I took him to the Savoy Hotel. We got on very well and he has an excellent sense of humour.

Wednesday 24 January

I had Ronnie Melville in, extremely anxious about the report which is coming out next month on the Bristol Siddeley affair[1]. Apparently, Sir Reginald Verdon-Smith is expecting to be severely criticised personally and wonders whether it is going to affect his ability to take on the chairmanship of Lloyds Bank, of which he is currently Deputy. I told Ronnie that, in circumstances where personal friendships might be involved in the publication of a report, it was absolutely essential that I should decide everything myself and nothing was to be shown to anybody else without my consent. I don't want to get into any further trouble and anyway this is a very big issue involving influential people and important questions: it has got to be handled properly.

This evening at 8 I went to the Hampstead Labour Party meeting. I have never spoken from a text at a Labour Party meeting before, and I didn't like doing it. There were very few real working people there and it was mainly young students shouting about Vietnam and Rhodesia and prescription charges. They didn't want me to have the opportunity of answering.

Thursday 25 January

At Cabinet we discussed the *Pueblo*, the American electronic eavesdropping ship which has been picked up by the North Koreans inside Korean territorial waters. One or two people wanted to know why we had come out in favour of the American line and Denis said that we were immensely dependent upon information from the American electronic eavesdropping ships. That more or less settled it but it is the first time I remember a Government commenting favourably upon spying activities, even of an ally. I thought spies were repudiated as soon as they were discovered.

Lord Nelson, Chairman of English Electric, and Terence Maxwell, Chairman of ICT, came to see me. What has happened is that Plessey have now offered to buy half of ICT which is unacceptable. English Electric on the other hand has offered ICT equity and equal representation with them, and ICT want to know what is acceptable to me. This raises quite a different question because if you had a merged ICT and English Electric linked to Plessey it wouldn't be an independent computer corporation at all.

I decided that I would go and see Field Marshal Harding of Plessey to head him off, so at 10 I rang up Harding and said, 'Can I come and see you?' He said, 'I'm just going to bed.' So I said, 'Well, I just wanted to catch up.' He said, 'Well, all right.' So after the vote William Knighton and I went along to see him. He was in pyjamas and bare feet and a silk dressing gown. I said I hadn't talked to him for some time and I only wanted to keep in touch. We had an interest in a genuinely independent computer corporation. He told me his board was meeting tomorrow and this visit was therefore quite useful.

Saturday 27 January

In the evening Caroline and I went to dinner with Peter and Liz Shore as co-guests of Bridget and Dick Clements [Editor of *Tribune*]. I like the Clements very much and am devoted to the Shores. Dick is always arguing that he represents the great continuing block of the Party, and he has to be critical of the Government to keep up the confidence of the Party. I argued with him that this was the moment when we really did need support from our friends because the Opposition was determined to get us out if they possibly could.

Monday 29 January
Dragged myself out of bed this morning with a streaming cold and went to London Airport where Harold Winterbourne [Chief Press Officer], Barrie Smith [Assistant Private Secretary] and I caught our little HS125 executive jet and flew to Strasbourg where I was to address the Council of Europe.

We were met at the airport there by Basil Boothby, the permanent British representative at the Council of Europe – an ageing and rather snobbish-looking Foreign Office official. He took me round Strasbourg, which is a beautiful city, all the more beautiful for not having been damaged by the Germans in either the First or Second World War.

We had lunch as the guests of Geoffrey de Freitas, President of the Council of Europe. On one side of me was Signor Montini, the Pope's* brother. When I said to him, 'I wish your brother would visit England', I wondered whether this was perhaps being disrespectful. It was a bit like saying, 'How is the Virgin Mary – do remember me to her when you see her!'

After lunch we went into the Assembly and I was singularly unimpressed. The building had a postwar, prefabricated, international airline terminal look about it, thinly populated with people sitting at desks looking a bit run-down and informal. Anyway, a legislature that isn't in existence to control an executive is a very negative thing. Executives must have Parliaments to watch them and I didn't feel a Parliament without a Government had much of a role. I was half asleep most of the time since I was so tired and feeling so lousy.

I was called to speak on European technological collaboration. I had prepared my speech very carefully and it had been crawled over by the Foreign Office, and Harold Wilson had added one or two phrases. Basically, what I was trying to say was that we still believe in a European technological community. However, there is a veto: we have now got to consider our national interests. We are prepared to cooperate with anybody; we don't want to sabotage the Commission; we welcome the Benelux proposals for cooperation with the Five. But as far as we are concerned, we have got to work with anyone who will work with us and we will maintain collaboration with the Americans, we are going to work with the Russians, and Eastern Europe and so on.

I didn't feel the speech went down well, I found it a rather difficult audience.

* Pope Paul VI, Giovani Battista, Cardinal Montini.

Tuesday 30 January

Frank Schon came into the office this morning at 9.30. He told me rather an interesting thing about the banker, Siegmund Warburg. Warburg had been the man responsible for coordinating the collection of money from rich millionaire Jews to support Israel during the Six Day War last summer and he had managed to raise £50 million during that period, of which about £7 million came from Britain, about £10 million from Germany and the rest from the United States and Canada. Schon also told me that the rich Jews abroad were sick of financing Israel and made it a condition that if they were going to provide money, they should have some scope for suggesting how Israeli industry should be reorganised to make it more profitable. He had been given that job.

At 11.30, I went to Overseas Policy and Defence Committee (OPD) where there was an interesting discussion on the Non-Proliferation Treaty.* Denis Healey launched into a major attack of the NPT and said that, if taken literally, Articles 1 and 2 prohibited transfer of the control of nuclear weapons from a nuclear to a non-nuclear power, and would in fact entirely invalidate NATO. He said there were 7,000 nuclear weapons in Europe – I didn't know that figure before. With the exception of our own strategic weapons – since the V Bomber force is entirely under British control – our tactical nuclear weapons and the German tactical nuclear weapons and everybody else's tactical nuclear weapons are under American custodian groups. At a certain stage in a war which might develop, the American custodian groups would hand them over – bombs or missiles – to the relevant forces, German, British and so on. Although these would then be used by those forces in accordance with guidelines laid down by the American Supreme Commander under the President, this did in fact constitute a transfer of authority to the Europeans and this was incompatible with the Non-Proliferation Treaty.

Denis was obviously trying to get the whole Non-Proliferation Treaty destroyed and this was unthinkable. When Harold said to him, 'Why didn't you raise this before?' he had no answer, because he didn't think the Treaty had been taken seriously. When he was asked about the Americans, he said that he didn't know what their view was but the Russians, once the Treaty was signed, would say that it invalidated NATO strategy, that we were in breach of the NPT, and so on.

Fred Mulley struggled back on behalf of the Foreign Office and it was agreed that we would have to make our position absolutely plain, if necessary making a statement in advance of signing.

Quite frankly, if the discussion could have been reproduced publicly,

*A draft treaty attempting to prevent the spread of nuclear weapons to non-nuclear states. It was adopted by the UN General Assembly in June 1968, and came into force in March 1970 when ninety-seven countries had signed the treaty.

Denis's position with the Party, let alone the public, would have been appalling: he is an odd man, Denis Healey. I think he is nursing a great grudge about losing the F-111.

Otto came in later about honours. He presented me with a very breezy list of people and I resented this for a number of reasons. First of all, I don't like honours. Second, they are always sent to me with a forty-eight-hour deadline, so, in effect, I really don't have any opportunity to change them. Third, my position is that of a constitutional monarch – Otto will come in and explain why I can't do what I want. So when I saw the list, I said, 'Why don't we ever recommend trade unionists?'

'Oh,' he said, 'that's for the Ministry of Labour.'

'Why don't we recommend Dr Curran, the Vice-Chancellor of Strathclyde? He was on our Advisory Committee.'

'Oh, that's the Department of Education and Science.'

'Well then,' I said. 'On knighthoods, you've put down Sutherland, the rather mediocre Chairman and Managing Director of Marconi, who is also the Chairman of the Conference of the Electronics Industry. What about Arnold Weinstock? he's just done the GEC/AEI deal.'

'I assure you, Minister, I couldn't put that forward convincingly.'

'You put forward things that aren't altogether convincing to me,' I replied.

'Oh well, Helsby wouldn't have it.'

Of course it turns out that a group of civil servants crawls over this list and Ministers have no real say at all. John Stonehouse had put forward a private enterprise arms salesman merchant-of-death type who handled the Saudi Arabian arms deal. Apparently the Ambassador in Jeddah thought he really *was* unsuitable! Of course the more Otto tried to justify his list, the worse he made it because I was clearly a very minor element in the decisions. 'I'll ask Helsby whether he would agree to consider Weinstock,' he suggested.

'That's no good,' I said, and he replied, 'If we put it in and it's turned down, we shall lose a knighthood,' as if somehow getting the ration was more important than getting the right person. But I didn't want to pursue it too much. It wasn't worth it.

Dinner with Verdet at the Rumanian Embassy. The son of a miner, he had been a miner himself and had studied economics. We had a lot of jokes and fun and he said that the Rumanian Planning Committee had a saying: that mini-skirts concealed the essentials but raised the hopes. I said that reminded me of a Five-Year Plan which also conceals the essentials and raises expectations.

Wednesday 31 January
At 12.30 to the PLP meeting for the resolution calling for the one-month suspension from the PLP of the twenty-eight people who abstained on

the vote of confidence on the 'cuts package'. This is less than withdrawing the Whip and is a useful disciplinary measure but, I must say, my sympathy was entirely on the side of the rebels. I got there just as John Mendelson was finishing a very fiery attack. He was followed by Emrys Hughes* who made a brilliant speech of the kind that Father would have been delighted to hear.

He began, 'Comrade Chairman and Comrade Members of the Jury. In the course of my life, I have appeared before five court martials, two civil courts and two meetings of the Parliamentary Labour Party designed to expel me. I have lost on every occasion and I don't expect to do any better today.' Then he said, 'This is a matter of conscience and loyalty, both very difficult questions. When I was appearing before a court martial in the First World War, because I declined to fight, they said, "Mr Hughes, you are not a Christian and therefore you have no conscience."

'So I haven't had a conscience for fifty years and I can't claim exemption on those grounds. As to loyalties, it depends whose loyalty you are talking about. If you are talking about your loyalty to your beliefs, to your manifesto, to your local Party, to your electors, to the Parliamentary Labour Party, to the Cabinet, to the Prime Minister, loyalty gets you nowhere. What does it mean? As a matter of fact,' he said, 'if you expel me, it will increase my majority at the next election.'

Then he went on to say that as an old Member he had listened to all the new Members who had come in and had been much encouraged by what they had said but when the Parliamentary Labour Party meeting turned itself into a quasi-judicial body it made itself ridiculous.

It was a most powerful speech and really stirred me. There were a few other speeches and then Michael Foot made a great denunciation of Cabinet and said they had started the trouble. But it was all quite good-humoured and in the end we suspended them all.

Ronnie Melville came to see me again, still worried about the Bristol Siddeley report because Verdon-Smith is due to be made Chairman of Lloyds Bank on 16 February, and the question is whether one ought to show him the report in advance, and what happens if he decides, on reading it, that he can't take on the chairmanship, or Lloyds won't have him? It is a very complicated business. I have given strict instructions that under no circumstances is anything to be done without my knowing. But the report is being sent to the Treasury Solicitor to see whether the Director of Public Prosecutions may find it necessary to take action.

* Labour MP for Ayrshire South, 1946–69.

Thursday 1 February

Cabinet, where the main substantial item was the scheme for the House of Lords reform, a compromise scheme under which the hereditary peers would all lose their voting rights but would remain as speaking peers during their own lifetime. There was quite a discussion about it and the Tories apparently are prepared to accept it.

Jim Callaghan said he wasn't much in favour but on balance he believed it was workable. George Brown said he wasn't very keen and Barbara Castle thought it strengthened the House of Lords.

Then I chipped in and said I would like to go a great deal further but recognised that this scheme had advantages. I said I thought it would have one uncovenanted advantage of cutting away the Tory linkage to the network of feudal privilege and this might, in rural areas, be very useful; and it would reduce the appeal of the Tory Party to the working man in the deferential vote. But I did say I was a little doubtful about patronage, a second chamber built up over twenty years by the patronage of four or five Prime Ministers, however good it was, and I also said that I thought the whole business of nobility was quite ridiculous. Why make a man Lord so-and-so to put him in the House of Lords? Then I made one other point about retirement. I said you really do *not* want to have retirement ages in the House of Lords, because promotion to the Upper House is the way of getting rid of your old MPs. What will happen when Manny Shinwell* gets an artificial heart!

Friday 2 February

After seeing Verdet in the morning, I went to Roy Jenkins's office for a meeting with him, Elwyn Jones, Jack Diamond, John Stonehouse, Ronnie Melville and others, including the Treasury Solicitor, to discuss what should be done about the report dealing with the overcharging by Bristol Siddeley for the overhaul of engines between 1959/60 and 1964.

The report does criticise the Department for incompetence in the early days, but the really important thing about it is that Verdon-Smith is implicated as Chairman of Bristol Siddeley and it makes it clear that the company engaged in intentional deceit. Roy had wanted to send the report to Verdon-Smith who is due to become Chairman of Lloyds Bank in two weeks in order that he got it in time to withdraw. However, when Elwyn Jones indicated that prosecution might emerge from a study of it, it became clear that we could neither publish the report in these circumstances nor let Verdon-Smith see it. So it was agreed that there would be further discussion after the weekend when the Attorney-General would have a working party looking into the report and would

---

*Born 1884, Labour MP for Easington until 1970. Later Lord Shinwell.

consider whether or not it should be referred to the Director of Public Prosecutions.

Back to the office. At 3 Frank Kearton came to see me, and told me one rather interesting thing about Alf Robens, Chairman of the National Coal Board. He said that Alf was going round telling everybody that his decision to leave the House of Commons and go to the Coal Board was the greatest mistake of his life and that if he had stayed, he would have been Prime Minister. He was now evidently playing for the premiership of a theoretical Coalition Government. This is almost incredible but it fits in with Alf's particular type of megalomania.

Monday 5 February

Arnold Weinstock phoned. He said that he had read the Hansard of the Industrial Expansion Bill Second Reading and thought there was scope for a Government that was really determined to modernise industry, and added he would be glad to help in any way he could. So I suggested we should have lunch together. Of course, if I were suspicious, I might say that he wanted to woo me over a row going on today about the closure of the AEI plant at Woolwich under the AEI-GEC merger. He may be genuine and anyway we do get on well.

At 12 I went to the Parliamentary Procedure Committee – a high-powered ministerial committee with Dick Crossman in the chair.

The question at issue was a complaint by Fred Peart that the new Select Committee on Agriculture wanted to have a lot of information from his Department about the basis on which it planned our country's food supplies. Fred thought this was quite intolerable and in the discussion there was a mass of protest from Ministers who said it was scandalous that the Select Committee should be asking all these questions and couldn't we stop them. It was one of those real issues where you found Ministers divided between those who regarded themselves as having joined the 'other side', namely the Government side against the governed, and those like Dick Crossman and myself – very few in number – who regard our job as being to use select committees to open up the secrecy of government. You will never get any agreement on this but I argued as strongly as I could that select committees were in the interests of good government: people just looked at me sceptically and wouldn't believe it.

Then I went back to lunch, where I abandoned sandwiches in favour of diet biscuits.

Just after lunch Peter Shore rang me up to ask if it was going to be possible to raise Vietnam at Cabinet tomorrow because the Prime Minister is going to Washington on Wednesday and Peter thought it would be a good idea to make an issue of it. Overseas affairs is not on the agenda but I think we are bound to discuss the position or we shall lose our chance.

Back to the office and we had Hugh Scanlon with a deputation from the Confederation of Shipbuilding and Engineering Unions, worried about American investment in Britain. We tried to reassure them that we had done our best on the motor industry; that on the computer industry we had really helped; and that on the machine tools we were trying. But Hugh Scanlon just said that we should stop all US investment. I found him ineffective and obscurantist about it all.

Tuesday 6 February
I went to lunch with Cecil King at the *Daily Mirror* headquarters. As we were sitting down over coffee, he said to me, more or less out of the blue, 'I cannot understand why Ministers are so cheerful when the economic situation is so critical. Ministers are the only people who *are* cheerful. Don't they know what's going on?'

When I probed him as to what he meant, he said, didn't I realise that a second devaluation was possible this month, was likely during the next three months, might be postponed until the summer, but was certain this year. He said this was the unanimous view of the City and others with a knowledge of the situation. When I said that I thought devaluation had been successful and that our prospects of a surplus in 1969 were good, he cited Cromer, former Governor of the Bank of England, who he said shared his view, the United States Ambassador who agreed with him that the Government was finished, and others. He even said that Sir William Armstrong at the Treasury was extremely depressed about the outlook.

He was particularly critical of the failure of contingency planning for devaluation, although I explained to him that you simply couldn't have contingency planning without the fact of devaluation getting out. He was also very critical about the slowness of the Government's response and of its inadequacy. He laid great stress on the consumer boom and said he was of the opinion that nothing could now save the situation.

I listened to what he had to say, though I did make one or two points on the other side. But of course, if I had pushed very hard, it would have confirmed his original view that Ministers were so out of touch that they simply didn't know what was going on. When I asked him what he thought should be done about it, he said nothing. So I asked what was his policy? Did he think that a Coalition Government was necessary? Yes, indeed he did.

He said that although new politicians don't like it, the great British public wants a coalition and he pointed to a recent Gallup poll. He said that the Tories believed that there would be a major collapse, a General Election and they would sweep into power; but he thought there would be no time for an Election and that the situation would require immediate action. When I asked him who the new Prime Minister would be, he said he would have to be a member of the present Cabinet.

'Can you visualise Wilson and Heath sitting down in Cabinet together?'

'Certainly not. Wilson would be totally swept away. Nobody believes a word he says and he has no future whatsoever.' Heath was a political fool and King cited Heath's comment yesterday that the British should support the Americans on Vietnam. 'The man has no political sense,' he said. 'After all those pictures of the Vietnam War that have just appeared on television, why on earth did he have to stick his neck out and identify himself with the Americans?'

I asked him whether Maudling* might be more acceptable and he said that Maudling was totally unacceptable to the City because of his Budget of 1963. What about Macleod? He said the trouble with Macleod was that 'because he is effective in Parliament, you think he is effective in public but that hunched-up figure certainly is not. No, it would have to be a member of the Labour Cabinet.'

I asked about Roy Jenkins. Oh no, Roy Jenkins would go down in the crash, and indeed, Roy Jenkins had been a great disappointment to him. Here was a young man who had come in at a critical time with the opportunity to make a real reputation for himself and he was just as bad as anyone else. Suave and debonair but apparently quite unconcerned with the nature of the crisis.

Jim Callaghan, whom he had sharply criticised for his handling of the devaluation announcement, was obviously ruled out. George Brown was a non-starter. Dick Crossman was unacceptable.

'Denis Healey?' I asked.

'Ah,' said Cecil King. 'It could be him.'

'The trouble with Denis Healey,' I replied – then correcting myself – 'the fact about Denis Healey is that he has no following in the Parliamentary Labour Party.'

'Oh, that wouldn't matter at all,' said King. 'In these circumstances it would be of no consequence and anyway, the Tories don't like him either.' He then went on to stress that with the prospect of three million unemployed the situation would be as it was in the 1940s and there is no doubt that a coalition would be established.

I listened and said that what seemed to be interesting and important to me was that he *thought* it. He took this to be my disbelief of his analysis, but I said that I was not in a position to assess what he said. Although I had access to certain papers, I didn't get access to all the papers and it

---

* Reginald Maudling, Conservative MP for Barnet; Chancellor of the Exchequer, 1962–4.

could very well be that he, who is of course a Director of the Bank of England, would know more than I would.

I said that my optimism about the future was based on the fact that we could now look forward to the successful development of industrial policy which would begin to produce results and that I could cite the examples of Leyland and GEC-AEI, shipbuilding, and so on.

Literally as we said goodbye, with an air of authority which I thought was derived from an anticipation of his own projected powers of patronage, he added, 'There may well be a larger part for you to play.'

As I reflected on this conversation, a number of thoughts came to mind. One was that he was slightly unbalanced. Second, if it was true that this was being said in the City and to him, it was almost certain this was getting abroad and therefore the confidence problem was very serious. Third, when this situation developed, he was in a position to help trigger it off. The entire weight of IPC would be thrown against Wilson in favour of a coalition and probably in favour of Denis Healey as well. This is something that simply cannot be ignored.

At 10.30, I rang Peter Shore. We both scrambled our phones and I told him what Cecil King had said. He felt it was sufficiently important for me to tell Harold. I rang Harold at 11.30, and I told him the gist of what I had heard. He was interested and said I should write it down. So in my own hand I wrote a short note of the meeting, just covering the salient points, including King's view that devaluation would be likely to occur again and his preference for Denis Healey as Prime Minister of a Coalition Government. I shall sit back and keep it as a private note of my own.

Harold was rather agitated and excited to hear this story and said Cecil King was mad – a view with which I would not really disagree.

Wednesday 7 February
I had lunch with Geoffrey Goodman of the *Sun* at Beoty's Restaurant. He asked whether I knew what his Chairman, Cecil King, was saying about Harold Wilson and the Government at dinner parties all over the place.

I didn't say I had had lunch with Cecil King but I did pursue the coalition theme fully and said that I thought those of us who were determined to keep the Party independent ought to keep our powder dry and be ready to take action if anything happened. I was pitching it a bit high, but I left an impression in his mind and it wasn't a bad thing.

Thursday 8 February
There was a meeting of newspaper publishers on information retrieval at which I took the chair. The first big news was that IPC and Lord Thomson, Chairman of Thomson Organisation, had decided not to go

in for a consortium and Bob Maxwell, Chairman of Pergamon Press, was thoroughly upset. He saw me beforehand to say that I should put my foot down at the meeting. He was extremely offensive to me and to the others.

Jeremy Bray stayed behind in the office and asked whether I had considered the possibility of becoming General Secretary of the Party when Len Williams goes. I said I couldn't see how I could give up Parliament or the Cabinet but otherwise I was potentially interested in the idea of doing work in that direction. He said if it was thought that I really was a candidate, there would be a great bandwagon – he was clearly offering himself as campaign manager.

My interest in the role of General Secretary of the Labour Party had its origins in the early days of the Labour Party, when it had been a job of major significance. For example, Arthur Henderson was both General Secretary of the Party and Foreign Secretary in the 1929–31 Labour Cabinet. However, the Party came to feel that it needed a voice of its own and that if its General Secretary was also to be a Cabinet Minister that voice would be submerged in collective Cabinet responsibility in the event of a conflict between the Party and a Labour Cabinet when Labour was in power.

Therefore, in the 1930s when Henderson retired as General Secretary, the Conference overturned a recommendation of the National Executive that Members of Parliament should be eligible for this post and insisted that in future, the General Secretary should be outside Parliament. It was on this basis that Jim Middleton and later Morgan Phillips assumed the role. But, not being in Parliament, they were not publicly regarded as significant political figures and indeed General Secretaries tended to become agents for the parliamentary leader, running the Party office in his own interests.

This point came back into focus when Len Williams retired and various feelers were put out to me suggesting that I might seek appointment as his successor. But to give up a seat in Parliament, not to mention a Cabinet position, for the general secretaryship would have effectively moved me from the position of influence which I held, even if (which was by no means certain) the National Executive was prepared to appoint me. I therefore made it clear that I would only be interested in the appointment if the Conference could be persuaded to change the rules back to those that existed at Henderson's time.

When Ron Hayward came to be appointed in 1972, he ensured that his terms of reference would give him the right to speak on behalf of Conference policy even if it involved him in a conflict with a Labour Cabinet. He regularly mentioned these terms of reference and as a result his relations with Harold Wilson were always considerably strained.

I had dinner with Peter Shore and Tommy Balogh at the St Stephen's Restaurant. I put to Tommy the possibility that the City could be planning a coup against the Government. He was sufficiently worried to be quite agitated about it. It was rather a depressing evening which later I discovered had given him nightmares.

Friday 9 February
I phoned John Silkin in the evening and outlined what Cecil King had told me. He agreed that he would come to my home tomorrow night to discuss it.

Jeremy Bray rang me and I told him that, on reflection, I didn't think it would be possible for me to be known to be making a bid for the secretaryship of the Party because this would imply that I was ready to give up the Cabinet, which I certainly wasn't.

Among other things Jeremy said was that he had spoken to Michael Posner, Economic Adviser to the Treasury, who had just come back from the International Monetary Fund meetings in Paris and he told him that the British delegation of civil servants had said some rather ugly things about the state of the economy.

Saturday 10 February
In the evening John and Rosalind Silkin, Peter and Liz Shore and Tommy and Pen Balogh came over at 11 and stayed until 2.15. I put my conspiracy theory to them.

We agreed in general that the press should be alerted to this and that Harold should be told and also that we should prepare some sort of contingency plan.

Sunday 11 February
This morning I dictated the story about the City plot against the Government in roughly the form I would like to see it in the papers. I rang Peter and read it to him. He said he thought it contained too much and might even precipitate the thing we were trying to avoid. I decided to hang on to it and do nothing for the moment.

Peter thought that we had best be guided by Harold. The plain truth is that this plot couldn't succeed but it might produce a new Labour Prime Minister and that, of course, is what the Tories want more than anything. I think Harold is in serious danger.

I rang Dick Crossman and asked him how things were going. He told me he had had dinner with Hugh Cudlipp who said that the whole devaluation exercise had gone wrong, that we would have to devalue in the summer, that we would have a National Government and more or less sounded Dick out to see if he would be interested in leading it. Dick replied that he was Harold's henchman and if Harold went, he would go and therefore it was no good asking him. But he got the impression that Jim Callaghan and Denis Healey had been fishing in these waters, which exactly confirms what I thought myself.

Dick was extremely depressed. He said that Harold never consulted him, never consulted Roy Jenkins, he only saw Roy about every ten days, and that his dreams of the three of them reaching decisions had disappeared. He said people had persuaded Harold that he, Dick, had shifted his loyalty to Roy. He said Harold did no strategic thinking at all and he made it pretty clear that he thought we were coming to the end of Harold's premiership. He was bitterly contemptuous of Gerald Kaufman, Trevor Lloyd-Hughes [Wilson's Press Secretary] and Marcia, a little inner group who, with John Silkin, didn't give Harold good advice.

But there it is. I established my good relations with Dick again and I think in a situation like this, it is better to be friendly to everybody rather than to be just one of Harold's private advisers.

After that, I rang Tony Crosland who has returned from New Delhi. He said devaluation was clearly going to be a great success and that Sir Richard Powell, his Permanent Secretary, had phoned him to tell him this, which was a slightly sinister thing.

I told him I had heard of those who suggested it might go wrong, and he said that this was just the City being silly; that Kenneth Keith had come to him a month ago to say that he thought that there might be another devaluation but this was nonsense; that the City had no political sense and therefore there was nothing really to worry about. I said that I had missed him very much and hoped we could have a talk; he said he would like that.

I rang Peter again. Peter is very worried about the next fortnight. He told me that Roy Jenkins couldn't work as hard as he and I did, and had to have weekends off, didn't work in the evenings and, generally speaking, operated like a pre-1914 Minister. This routine has probably shaken the Treasury but it is the way to survive; frankly the pressure of life at the moment is too much for me.

Tuesday 13 February

I worked in the office until about 9.15, then went back to the Commons and had a long talk to Jeremy Thorpe, who is very amusing and described how much he liked Harold, and mentioned that the possibility of a coalition between the Liberals and the Labour Party had come up informally in talking to Harold in the 1966 Election.

Jeremy said that his conditions had been the dropping of the steel nationalisation and the alternative vote (proportional representation) for a subsequent election. Harold had said it was a high price to pay and Jeremy said, 'If it is necessary, I have a feeling you will pay it.'

Jeremy had recently been to Zambia to see Kenneth Kaunda and when he got back, Harold said to him, 'Does he think there'll be a sell-out over Rhodesia?' Jeremy said 'No' and Harold had asked why.

'Because,' said Jeremy, 'I told him there were no buyers.' Harold had thoroughly enjoyed the joke.

Wednesday 14 February
To Overseas Policy and Defence Committee where we had the second round on the Non-Proliferation Treaty. Denis Healey had tried to kill it at the last meeting on the grounds that it conflicted with NATO strategy, but this time the Law Officers and the Foreign Office had got together and proved that there was nothing whatsoever in Denis's objections. Harold was glad to see Denis embarrassed by this. Denis stuck to his guns, but I must say his guns were spiked.

Back to the office for a meeting with Verdon-Smith who had asked to see John Stonehouse. I had decided that I ought to see Verdon-Smith myself and it was a very tense moment. He said the thing that worried him most was the likely publicity about the report before it was published. He complained that the press already knew about it and the Department was briefing against him.

I stopped him in his tracks and said that only three or four people in the Department knew about it, that I was keeping the matter under my personal control throughout and that I simply did not believe what he had said.

Well, he hummed and hawed and said that the *Daily Express* had been bothering him and I pointed out that this was because they had read his statement in the papers this morning or yesterday, to the effect that he was not taking Lloyds Bank and they knew it was in connection with the Bristol Siddeley affair, but this was very different from saying that the report had got out. I think this threw him slightly and, after a rambling continuation, he went on to say that he thought the enquiry had been conducted most injudicially. Ronnie Melville stopped him to remind him that everybody who had been associated with the inquiry, including the company, had agreed the way in which it should work.

His final point was that the report would do great damage to Government and to the industry to which he had devoted his life; and he said, with obvious and deep emotion, 'It could mean personal disaster and tragedy for all the things for which I have stood.'

I am afraid I was rather cold, though with John and Ronnie Melville and me all facing him. I felt a certain human sympathy. But he is a very slippery customer. He finished up by saying that he hoped it would not affect my respect and regard for him. He said that although I might think he had behaved foolishly and unwisely, that was very different from saying he had behaved dishonestly.

Then I went in the car to Oxford and addressed David Butler's seminar on technology and politics. While I was in Oxford, I had a message from William Knighton to ring George Harriman and Donald

Stokes and my suspicions were right. The BMH-Leyland merger is in peril. I rang Donald Stokes first and he said that, broadly speaking, the explanation was that the figures that had been produced by Harriman at their earliest discussions were completely phoney.

Thursday 15 February
Roared down to Woolwich to speak at the Polytechnic. One young man got up and said, 'What good are you to us? You may be able to speak well, but you've got no qualifications; you're just an amateur. What can you do for us?' He said it unpleasantly and aggressively and I answered very directly. I said I wanted more engineers in politics. I wanted people with expertise but they would have to be elected. This was what the system meant and, anyway, I was a professional having been twenty years in Parliament, concerned with politics, which was highly professional. This got a lot of applause.

After that I was caught by some AEI people from the Woolwich factory which is being closed under the GEC-AEI merger. They were very upset.

Friday 16 February
Mr Reid, the Vice-President of the Radio Corporation of America, came to see me this morning. When we had finished our talks, we discussed Vietnam and he said he couldn't see why there should be so much talk about tactical nuclear weapons. Surely, he thought, the most sensible thing to do was just to use them in Vietnam. It was, I am afraid, a typical episode and I have no doubt that British businessmen would be as bad. God preserve us from businessmen in politics.

Saturday 17 February
Mark Arnold-Forster came to collect Kate after our children's party so I invited him down to my basement office for a short talk and decided on the spot that I would tell him what I knew about the Cecil King business. I did it very carefully, with three objectives in mind. First, not to reveal what had been said to me in confidence by Cecil King; this was mainly in self-defence. Second, not to mention at all the possible economic danger points that lay ahead because these would be extremely serious if they got out – they might trigger off the things we were trying to avoid. Third, hardly to mention Harold at all because I want this presented as an attack upon the Government and not on Harold Wilson personally.

The more he listened to my analysis and the way in which it might work, the more struck he was and he said he would find out what his colleagues thought. He went away and later rang to tell me that they were interested: he also added one or two things, including that he had been to see Jo Grimond who had been on the phone to Macleod. He thought Jo Grimond had decided he would like a coalition under Roy Jenkins with himself and Macleod.

I rang Geoffrey Goodman who told me a bit more. He said Denis Healey was pouring stuff in to the *Daily Mirror*, including the voting figures on critical issues in the Cabinet, to persuade Cecil King that Harold was weak.

After that I contacted Woodrow Wyatt [Labour MP for Bosworth]. He is an old friend of mine and I am rather fond of him. He said, 'Oh, this coalition talk, there is really nothing in it at all. There are a lot of people who would like to try it on but it isn't a starter.' We discussed what Desmond Donnelly said this morning when he called on Cabinet Ministers to strike and destroy the Prime Minister.* It was in all the papers. Desmond was pretty much dismissed by Woodrow Wyatt.

But I have now released my story and I know that the *Guardian* is having a serious meeting tomorrow to decide what to do.

Sunday 18 February
At midnight I went out to the Kensington Air Terminal and picked up Monday's *Guardian* and there it was on the front page, 'Cecil King Takes Soundings', the whole thing written from a political angle by Francis Boyd, identifying what Cecil King had been trying to do. No mention of me and no mention of any economic pitfalls, and ending up with a warning to any Labour or Conservative MP who was tempted by this idea that it would be the end of his political career and of parliamentary democracy.

Wednesday 21 February
Melissa, Joshua, Caroline and I went to the Mermaid Theatre to see a play organised by the Molecule Club about light. In the audience were hundreds of schoolchildren and Spike Milligan and a few bigwigs, including the Duke of Edinburgh. As Caroline and I talked to Spike the Duke came up and said, 'Sorry to interrupt your conversation.' We all went and had a cup of tea and Joshua and Melissa were introduced to the Duke: it was very funny because Melissa was sucking her hair and saying what she thought about education, completely unmoved, while Joshua kept interrupting his conversation to turn round and pick up more sandwiches.

Mark Arnold-Forster rang up to say he had heard that Alf Robens saw the miners' MPs twice in a week and was absolutely certain that,

---

*Donnelly, the Labour MP for Pembroke, had resigned the Whip in protest against Labour's policy on withdrawal East of Suez, and on South African arms. He was expelled from the Labour Party in April 1968.

when the moment came, he would be able to draw them en bloc from supporting the Government. This was one of the factors he thought he could use to bring about the coalition. Incidentally, the coalition story has been going strong and has done exactly what I wanted it to do – vaccinate the political system against it.

Friday 23 February
Up very early and by helicopter to Winfrith with William Knighton for the opening of the Steam Generating Heavy Water Reactor. It was a tremendous affair which has received a lot of adverse press publicity because the whole day was to cost about £15,000 and 700 guests were to get lunch at £7 a head. At lunch I found myself sitting next to the Duke of Edinburgh.

We began by talking about Europe and it was evident that he was not a keen European and thought British opinion would be opposed to our joining now that the opportunity had passed. I said I thought this was perhaps inaccurate and that we would need a larger economic unit because industry was now on a bigger scale than national institutions. I explained that I was really a federalist. This worried him enormously, no doubt because the royal family wouldn't have much of a place in a Federal Europe.

Then we talked about the institution of Government and he said he thought it was a mistake to overcentralise, warmly supporting Welsh and Scottish nationalism; and so do I. But he did say he thought advice ought to be integrated at different levels. I asked him how he thought the monarchy would work over the next twenty-five years. His answers were rather interesting. He thought the first thing to do would be to get rid entirely of the Commonwealth angle by which he meant the Queen being Queen of Canada as well as of Britain. 'They don't want us and they will have to be a republic or something.'

He wanted to connect the monarchy more directly with Ministers and said he thought that Privy Councils were an absolute waste of time; that the Prime Minister's audience with the Queen should be broadened out to include other Ministers who could explain things to her.

I said I didn't think that would help the monarchy at all because when this Government got even less popular, which was possible, it would just identify the monarch more with us. He said, 'You wouldn't want the Queen to meet the *Opposition*, would you?' I said I didn't think that would help the monarchy. He said he wasn't thinking of the monarchy but of the national interest and he thought that if the monarchy didn't meet the national interest, he would opt out altogether. Quite what he meant by that, I don't know.

We went on to discuss the sort of people who were pro-monarchy. He said, 'Well, if you go to the East End they wave their little flags and they are very keen on the monarchy.' I said this sounded to me like a lot of Labour voters. But, he admitted, when people got cars and a bit more middle class, they weren't interested in or they didn't want to show their affection for the monarchy. I didn't disabuse him of this idea.

He then said he thought the Ombudsman should have been put into the Royal Household in order to make the monarchy seem closer to the people and to represent the nation. I said I thought this was nonsense. The Duke said that he acted as a sort of unofficial Ombudsman and I think he does.

We went on to discuss ceremonial and the effect on it of television. He said that television really killed all ceremonial and I explained that was why Bessie Braddock would never appear on television. I don't think he much liked the comparison of Bessie Braddock with the Queen, though I am not sure there isn't something of a parallel.

I tried to point out that the monarchy was linked in many people's minds with a lot of reactionary forces. I said that during my peerage case I had had letters from many people who said that they had left Britain because they felt that the top jobs in industry or politics were reserved for those who had inherited their positions and that whenever I had tried to deal with the reform of the House of Lords I was always told you couldn't do this without threatening the monarchy. This sounded like loyalism, but top people were really leaning on the monarchy to prop themselves up.

He seemed rather shaken by this and he was very critical of our plans to reform the Lords. He said they were based on prejudice rather than on thinking and we ought to have an elected second house. I said, 'Well, yes, I rather agree with you but as you know we haven't got a very radical Government. We are just doing what the British always do – adjusting – but we are getting rid of hereditary peers and I think that's quite right. If you do want a second chamber, I would rather get ERNIE, the Premium Bond machine, to give you one than have the hereditary House of Lords.'

That was how we left it. It was the first time I had had a proper talk with him and I felt as if he were a Tory MP, which is just about what he is. Altogether it was a revealing discussion: he is a thoughtful and intelligent person.

I caught the helicopter home and in the evening we all came down to Stansgate. It was quiet and Melissa and Joshua were excited, and Hilary very obligingly slept downstairs so that they wouldn't be frightened.

Wednesday 28 February

Went to the House of Commons where I made my statement on Bristol Siddeley. I read it out, describing the deceit and the intention to misrepresent, the exorbitant profits, and the fact that it was known at all levels of management. This caused an absolute sensation. There were a lot of questions about prosecutions and I just had to refer them to the Attorney's decision.

Thursday 7 March
Cabinet this morning. The Rhodesia hangings[2] were discussed briefly. Harold was very tough, saying this meant the end of everything and yet you knew that in his heart he was longing to talk to Smith and settle the whole thing.

Apa Pant, the High Commissioner for India, came to see me. Before he came I had a note from the security services saying he was a suspect person, that we were to treat him with circumspection, that he was anti-British, and so on. A very unusual note to get. In fact, all we talked about was theology and he said he would be very sorry if Britain ever ceased to be a Christian country. He said he had sent his own children to public school in India with compulsory religious education. It was an odd talk from which I concluded that he was an ageing aristocratic Indian parlour pink, no doubt with a fellow-travelling background but innocent now.

To Bristol for the Annual General Meeting. There were quite a few people there and after we had got through the regular business I gave my annual report. Then all hell broke loose.

We had Bates from the Stockwood Party, bitterly attacking the Labour Party for having betrayed everything, calling for the nationalisation of 350 companies, and saying that devaluation was a capitalist trick to lower working class standards of living. Herbert Rogers said the situation was like the Social Democrats who paved the way for Hitler.

The whole thing was hysterical and bore no relation to real problems at all. I got rather concerned and did my best to answer. But I did say that living standards would have to fall this year and that this was a necessary part of getting the economy right.

Throughout my tenure at the Ministry of Technology and later at the Department of Energy, the development of nuclear energy, and particularly the implications of the 'Acarus' centrifuge project, concerned me. In 1966, Sir William Penney, then Chairman of the Atomic Energy Authority, had come to tell me that the AEA had achieved a technical breakthrough which would allow uranium to be enriched by the centrifuge process, involving the high-speed rotation of containers, rather than the gas diffusion process which was very expensive and used enormous amounts of electricity.

The centrifuge technique had been used widely for non nuclear purposes but its nuclear application had been thought not to exist until the Americans invented a special fitting, the Endcap, which allowed the centrifuges to rotate at the necessary speed to produce enriched uranium.

The significance was twofold: first, now that we knew we could produce enriched uranium by this process we would not need to proceed with the Capenhurst nuclear energy plant, which was to employ gas diffusion. Second, by discovering a way of enriching uranium very cheaply on a small scale, the risk of nuclear proliferation would become much greater because whereas gas diffusion plants could be picked up because of the heat they released into the atmosphere, centrifuges did not generate heat and could therefore go on undiscovered.

The centrifuge itself had first been invented by a German called Dr Zipper, who had worked on it during the war and had then gone to the Soviet Union, where it was thought he had passed on the technology to them; subsequently he had been to the US where he also had apparently conveyed the technical information to their Atomic Energy Commission.

It was never certain that the centrifuge would work until the US Atomic Energy Commission decided to classify work on the project: previously it had been a theoretical project about which scientists across the world were free to talk to each other. It was the certain discovery that the centrifuge was capable of enriching uranium that led Sir William Penney to propose the 'Acarus' project in Britain. At about the same time in 1966, the Dutch announced that they had produced a centrifuge and the Germans claimed that they too had developed it. It was as a result of this that the proposal for a tripartite agreement between the three countries to produce the centrifuge jointly emerged.

The political issues involved were complex. The centrifuge depended on the American Endcap, which was covered by a patent and which required me, as the relevant British Minister, to get permission from the US to use it. There was also great anxiety that if the Germans developed the centrifuge they would then have an opportunity to produce nuclear weapons undetected; therefore we had an interest in the tripartite arrangement and agreed to compromise on the work done in Britain and set up the first centrifuge project in Holland at Almelo, where the tripartite treaty was subsequently signed. This is the background to a complicated story. It was raised with me by Kosygin when I visited him in the Kremlin in May 1969 because the Russians, like ourselves and the Dutch, feared that the Germans might use their work on the centrifuge as a point of entry into the production of nuclear weapons.

Dr Luns, the Dutch Foreign Minister, who was passionately anti-German, had a very good opportunity to combine these sentiments with the promotion of Dutch interests, by uniting with Britain so that Holland would not be overwhelmed by German technology in the production of the centrifuge. Many of the entries in this part of the diary touch on aspects of these negotiations with European Governments.

Some members of the British Cabinet were very concerned about the centrifuge because they were afraid that by going in with the Dutch and Germans and using an American patent for this purpose we might undermine our nuclear relationship with the US, upon which we depended for the regular supply of nuclear technology, nuclear weapons and, above all, for access to the American international satellite and intelligence systems at the very centre of the so-called Anglo-American special relationship.

It was not until the Foreign Office and the Ministry of Defence were satisfied that there was no risk of a breach with the US that we got the necessary clearance to go ahead with the Dutch and Germans and signed the Treaty of Almelo in December 1969. Our relations with France were involved in these negotiations because the French were developing a gas diffusion plant at Pierrelatte which they hoped would become a commercial operation and would enable them to supply enriched uranium all over the world. But since the centrifuge process was so much cheaper, it was clear that the Almelo project would undercut the French. There was therefore a delicate element to relations with France, whose approval the Cabinet needed to secure entry into the Common Market; Germany, Holland and France were related by their joint partnership in Euratom, the atomic body of the Common Market. This is how it came to be that a simple but important technical development, which was not intrinsically nuclear in character but was purely a development of high technology engineering, entered into so many central questions of inter-governmental relations between the US, Britain, the Common Market and the Russians.

Friday 8 March

Solly Zuckerman came to see me in a tremendous panic. Apparently Harold has received my minute about 'Acarus', that we must decide whether or not we are going in with the Dutch on the centrifuge or whether we are going to let the Dutch go in alone with the Germans; and we had, to some extent, misled the Dutch in the way the Americans had misled us on centrifuge development. Harold had decided to send Solly to see the Dutch Ambassador. Solly seemed to be playing a rather curious role. He said that the Atomic Energy Authority had refused to cooperate with the French on advanced gas-cooled reactors. The plain truth is that the Atomic Energy Authority would like to, but Harold quite rightly laid down that we weren't to do bilateral nuclear work with the French until the question of entry to Europe was settled. Solly evidently hadn't known that or, if he had, he had forgotten.

He told me that the Italians had asked for enriched uranium for a land-based nuclear reactor intended for warships and that this had been turned down; and that the Italians had now got it from the French and were disgusted with our attitude to the supply of enriched uranium. Well, this has never been brought to my attention at all, which is appalling. Solly apparently had sided with the Ministry of Defence who were opposed to supplying it to the Italians. It revealed the most serious lack of communication.

I had a row with Otto Clarke about the Public Expenditure Survey Committee. He had put in figures for the next five years for the Ministry of Technology without telling me. I said this wasn't good enough and I must see them. He said it was impossible. Well, that is nonsense. This is the most important single decision a Minister takes in the course of the year.

Had lunch at Lime Grove with John Grist and a bunch of producers, including Michael Barratt and Peter Pagnamenta from current affairs programmes. I told them that in my view, the BBC absolutely failed in its function because it didn't publish things, it always edited things and it always wanted to squeeze people into their programmes instead of providing facilities for people to say what they wanted to say.

Sunday 10 March
I left for Paris at 3.45 with Gordon Bowen and William Knighton. We drove straight to the Residency in Paris where the Ambassador, Reilly, was waiting. The Ambassador was perfectly prepared to accept the idea that there would be no further cooperation with the French on nuclear energy in present circumstances.

After about half an hour, I indicated to Gordon Bowen and Alan Smith, Scientific Counsellor, that they should leave us and I then told the Ambassador the whole story about 'Acarus'. He was quick to pick up the important points, namely that the cost of enriched uranium would be reduced by about 20 per cent; that this made possible the provision of supplies to almost any country; this would encourage the spread of nuclear weapons; and that among other things, Pierrelatte was just about the most expensive junk heap going. Reilly himself was the founder of the Scientific Relations Department of the Foreign Office and I think he was probably the best Ambassador who could be told.

Monday 11 March
Up this morning and to La Muette to the opening of the Science Ministers' meeting. Stoltenberg, the German Minister for Scientific Research, was elected chairman and we began work on the first paper on the technological gap.

We had lunch in the Bois de Boulogne as Stoltenberg's guests and I sat opposite the Irish Ambassador to the Organisation for Economic Cooperation and Development. He said there was a certain lack of credibility with Britain because economic recovery was so often promised and never quite happened and until we got into regular surplus, we were not taken very seriously – certainly in the context of applying to Europe.

In the afternoon I went back to the session and Patrick Gordon Walker was late. In fact, it is worth mentioning Patrick Gordon Walker's behaviour throughout this conference: he missed a lot of the morning session because he was looking at the tapestries, this afternoon he was viewing the Impressionists, he read the papers most of the time, wore earphones unplugged, did crossword puzzles and generally speaking was the laziest man I have ever known. He is attractive personally, but he ought to be dismissed.

Just before dinner I managed to have a word with the Dutch Economic Affairs Minister, Leo de Block, and repeated what Solly had told the Dutch Ambassador: that we were working on the centrifuge system and would be getting in touch with them. He said that the Dutch were not in such a tremendous hurry to make contact with the Germans and this rather relieved my mind.

After dinner I had a word with Maurice Schumann, the French Minister of Science, who told me how his efforts to promote contact with Britain had been rebuffed. He was dead against any nuclear links with the Germans, at any rate until, as he put it, our Russian friends accept Germany as part of a community of nations. We don't want the Russians to have any suspicions that the Germans are getting access to weapons technology. He didn't really want a joint European enriched uranium plant at the moment so he said we could plan for it later. Meanwhile we would have to buy American.

Wednesday 13 March

Had dinner with Peter Shore, Michael Posner and Tommy Balogh. We discussed the situation, which I should have mentioned earlier, namely the gold rush with the tremendous buying spree which could cause a serious crisis of confidence. It was a rather anxious dinner. We explored all the possibilities but didn't really get anywhere because Tommy kept regarding it as an economic crisis whereas, of course, actually it is a major political crisis.

Thursday 14 March

To the House in the evening and settled down to do my boxes. At about 12.10 am there was a division, and while I was in the Division Lobby, George Brown called me over.

'You're a member of the Cabinet, come here,' he said. Then he told me he had just heard that Harold and Roy had decided to close the gold market in London tomorrow. He said he had not been consulted and it was an absolute scandal and didn't I think so.

I said, 'Are the Americans closing theirs?' He said he didn't know and I said that this would be the thing that would interest me.

George then called over Dick Crossman and said, 'Did you know this?' Dick said yes, and George blew up.

After the division, George gathered Tony Crosland, Dick Marsh, Michael Stewart, George Thomas and others in his room. What had happened was that Harold had been at a meeting all evening and had gone to the Palace for a Privy Council to get this Proclamation out to close the gold market, and George had not been told. While we were all sitting there, George picked up the phone and got through to Harold and exploded. He shouted at Harold and said it was intolerable and there were a lot of discontented Ministers. All we could hear at our end was George saying, 'Will you let me speak, Christ, Christ, will – you – let – me – speak. Now look, look, will you let me speak,' and so on. Then we heard George say, 'Now don't say that: don't say in my condition. That may have been true some other nights, but not tonight. *Don't say in my condition.*' It was obvious Harold was saying he had tried to contact him but that George was drunk. I don't know whether or not he was drunk, because you can't always tell.

George continued to shout at him and Harold must have asked, 'Who's over there?' George told him and Harold said he had no right to call an irregular meeting of Cabinet Ministers, a cabal, and so on.

Finally Michael Stewart took the phone and said, 'Now look, Harold, you must understand we are worried and we have just heard this. We really think we ought to have a meeting.' Harold then apparently said, 'Come to Number 10,' because Michael asked, 'Don't you think it would be wiser if you came over here?' George picked up another phone and said, 'Send my car and my detective to bring the Prime Minister to the House of Commons,' which didn't help.

There was another division and I went on to the Front Bench, told Fred Peart to be available and told Dick Crossman, who said he was busy and anyway he knew all about it. Barbara Castle was tied up in the all-night session on the Transport Bill. Finally, at 1.30 am, I went over to Number 10 with George Thomas. By this time Ray Gunter and all the other Ministers I have mentioned had been gathered, as had Peter Shore, who had been to the Privy Council at the Palace.

George shouted and Harold insisted he had tried to phone him and George said, 'I don't believe it.'

Harold said, 'I tried for an hour and a quarter.'

'I do not believe it.'

Harold got rattled and rather irritated and said, 'I am not going to be called a liar.'

George repeated that he didn't believe it and then demanded that Harold's Private Secretary, Michael Palliser, tell him how long the Prime Minister had tried to contact him. Michael Palliser, of course, wouldn't answer and, frankly, I don't know whether Harold had tried or not. Maybe Harold did think George was drunk; he was certainly behaving as though he were. In the end George stood up and shrieked and bellowed and shouted abuse as he went round the table, then left the room.

Apparently, President Johnson had been closeted with his advisers all day, and in the course of the afternoon there had been a message from the Americans asking us to close the London gold market. We agreed as long as we were able to present the situation as done at the request of the Americans. I think we probably lost £150–£200 million in reserves today and Harold thought if we hadn't closed, we would have lost £400–£500 million. We are on the eve of the other devaluation that Cecil King predicted.

Harold and Roy had been going over this all evening, with meetings starting at 6, until finally at 11 they had all gone off to the Palace for the Privy Council and the order had been made. Tony Crosland and Michael Stewart were very niggled about not having been consulted. I said I didn't think a post-mortem would help and I wanted to know whether there would be a statement or not.

Then Dick Crossman came on the phone and said the news was all round the House and there would have to be a statement. At 2.15, Robert Armstrong, Roy's Private Secretary, began dictating a statement which came at about 2.45 am. We went on arguing and arguing. By this time the press had gathered around Number 10 with flashing cameras.

Harold said that George would have to apologise or go. Peter said, 'Now, calm down. You did very well until you lost your temper with George. Just calm down.' Harold was very overstrained.

Roy's behaviour was very detached and strong and rather impressive. He's got his eye on the main chance and thinks Harold will destroy himself and that he, Roy, will then take over.

Afterwards Peter and I walked back to the House together. I talked to people; Judith Hart and I made a list of Ministers we thought would stick by Harold in a crisis.

George, meanwhile, having stomped out of Number 10, sat ostentatiously on the Back Benches and said he was now a Back Bencher. Of course, everyone left in the Chamber, including the Tories and the lobby, could see this and there he was shouting at everybody that he'd resigned. He behaved so disgracefully that under no circumstances should Harold take him back as Foreign Secretary. But I expect that in the morning Harold will think, 'Oh well, if George goes, there will be trouble on the Back Benches,' and that'll be an end to it.

I talked to Ron Brown* just before leaving; he said George was convinced that Harold had lied to him. George had checked all the switchboards to find out if any messages had been left for him and claimed that there had been none. So he was bitter as hell.

At 6 am I came home. I gave Tony Crosland a lift and he hotly denied that there was any alliance to replace Harold. He and Roy were at daggers drawn and there were great disagreements. But I'm sure Tony, in his heart, thinks that Harold will go. Tony took an optimistic view of our economic situation and didn't take too grim a view even of the gold panic. But with the Bank Holiday, the Cabinet split, gold suspended,

---

* Labour MP for Shoreditch and Finsbury, and brother of George Brown.

and the pound in the front line to the dollar, I should have thought the possibility of the Cecil King-type crisis which we predicted a month ago is very real.

When I got home I began dictating my diary. It's now 8 am on Friday 15, and I'm due back in the office at 9. But I must keep my diary up to date because if the Labour Government falls, as I now think quite possible, then at any rate I shall have documented the circumstances.

Friday 15 March

I went into the office at 9 for a tremendous deputation from the Confederation of Shipbuilding and Engineering Unions about the closure of the Furness shipyard. Danny McGarvey took the chair. They wanted me to take over the yard and run it on the Fairfields basis. I tried to explain the policy we were adopting towards the shipbuilding industry.

But, of course, their real anxiety was that this was set against a background of high and rising chronic unemployment in the old, heavy industries of the North-East of which mining, steel and shipbuilding were classic examples. I listened with a great deal of sympathy.

At 10.30 I went over to Number 10 for a Cabinet meeting. Everyone was there except George Brown and Harold began by explaining the developments of the previous night.

We had a brief talk about the political situation and Dick Marsh said that the events had been quite shattering. He was referring to the way George Brown behaved during the night when he had sat on the Back Benches and at one stage had made comments about the Prime Minister which were audible in the Press Gallery. At another stage he had gone into the Tea Room and spoken very loudly about his resignation. This had been heard by a number of Tory MPs and it was thought that he'd also talked to the lobby correspondents on his way through.

I asked whether the Foreign Secretary was still a member of the Government and Jim Callaghan objected on the grounds that this was entirely a matter between the Minister himself and the Prime Minister and that George was not present. George was, of course, sleeping it off.

Peter and Tommy came to dinner and we talked about Cecil King. Undoubtedly the *Guardian* story about the possibility of a coalition has inoculated the public against it. The important thing is to keep the Parliamentary Labour Party on the right lines because everything depends upon the PLP.

Tommy explained in greater detail what we might and might not do, and it is clear that if things get really bad we shall have to suspend the convertibility of the Sterling Area balances and just make currency convertible for trading purposes. We may also have to deal with the British portfolio investment in the United States, but that would be a pretty drastic step and the Americans would probably rather lend money to us than have a Wall Street collapse as a result of our selling these investments.

Very, very tired after one of the most dramatic twenty-four hours I can ever remember.

Just before I went to bed I heard that George Brown had resigned and that Michael Stewart had been put in his place. So that is the end of George Brown's tenure at the Foreign Office. It began with a threatened resignation because we didn't devalue and ended with a real resignation arising out of the consequences of devaluation. What George will do now is anyone's guess. He is a person of extraordinary intellect, courage and ability, but his instability is such that it is impossible to have him in a Government. I wonder how capable he is of causing trouble from the Back Benches. His resignation now as Foreign Secretary also raises the question of his deputy-leadership of the Party. It is a major political tragedy.

Monday 18 March
To the office this morning and then to the Cabinet to hear the Budget which Roy Jenkins is going to introduce tomorrow. It is a clever Budget from Roy's point of view. It accepts the general Tory thesis that direct taxation cannot increase and imposes an absolutely crushing burden of indirect taxation. But to keep the Left quiet, it closes a lot of loopholes in the tax law and seeks to raise £100 million by a wealth tax.

Then came George Brown's resignation speech. It was not very effective and was heard without much sympathy by Labour Members who witnessed his complete breakdown on Thursday night. But it did include some threatening indications that he might later reveal his objections to the way Harold had been running the Government. We can't be entirely sure that George won't try to bring Harold down in the hope that Roy becomes Prime Minister and then brings him back into the Government.

This evening I had a short talk with Dick Crossman, who is completely disillusioned with Harold. He himself very much wants to be Minister of Defence and is beginning to show some of the signs of George Brown's disease.

I went to the 'Acarus' meeting at Number 10 at 7. I reported on my talks with the Dutch Ministers and asked my colleagues to agree that we should notify the Americans of our intention to cooperate with the Dutch and then consider whether to bring in the Germans. Denis Healey was critical of this, he being 100 per cent pro-American and saying we should not lose the confidence of the United States without being absolutely sure we were getting a good bargain in return.

Michael Stewart was there in his capacity as Foreign Secretary for the first time and was very cautious.

Tuesday 19 March
John Wren-Lewis, the industrialist and writer on theology, came and had a sandwich lunch with me in the office. We had a talk about the ICI survey of the year 2000 which apparently is so explosive in its implications that they have decided not to publish it. It says, in effect, that there is no prospect of the world keeping abreast of the population explosion and therefore we shall not be able to release our own resources to help the under-developed countries because we shall need to use these resources on defence in order to protect ourselves from the attack that will inevitably come from the Southern Hemisphere. It was extremely gloomy.

Thursday 21 March
In the evening Caroline and I went up to Tommy Balogh's party. I had a long talk to Mary Wilson who is very miserable, believing that if anything went right with the Government in the future, Roy would get the credit and Harold would get the blame. I think she may be right as far as the press is concerned. But there's no harm in bolstering her up and I tried to.

Friday 22 March
In the afternoon to Warwick and Leamington for two by-election meetings. The first was in a little primary school and was poorly attended. But the second, at the Courthouse of Warwick, was packed and there were some crusty Tory ladies there with big hats shouting about TSR-2. It was quite like old times and I thoroughly enjoyed it.

I came back on the train with Julian Snow, MP for Lichfield and Tamworth, who said I was neglecting the House of Commons and that I ought to spend more time in the Chamber and in the Palace of Westminster. I think he's right. I am determined to return to politics in a big way, particularly as Roy Jenkins is building up his position and it may be necessary at some stage for a group of us to make a stand. If Roy stands for the deputy-leadership of the Party on the assumption that George Brown resigns, then at the moment he could easily get it and I'm not sure that would be a good thing.

Monday 25 March
This morning the *Guardian* and the *Financial Times* had front-page stories on the attack by senior Ministers on the Department of Economic Affairs. The reports were so similar that it was perfectly evident that there had been a heavy briefing and that this had come very largely from

Roy Jenkins and probably Ray Gunter. Ray enjoys good relations with the industrial correspondents and Roy uses John Harris, his press adviser, quite ruthlessly against anyone who stands in his way.

I had a deputation of civil servants: Gordon Bowen, Michael Michaels, and two of my Under-Secretaries, William Downey and Cliff Baylis, trying to persuade me to do all I could to prevent the House of Commons Select Committee on Nationalised Industries extending its remit to cover firms or organisations receiving Government money. The committee is trying to extend itself to the Bank of England and is also eagerly looking at the National Research Development Corporation, the Industrial Reorganisation Corporation, and Beagle, Shorts and various other companies where we have only a minority interest.

I was tough with them and said I believed in parliamentary accountability and they simply stuck their toes in and said it would make life very difficult for me. I said, 'As a Minister, of course I want Parliament to go away. I don't want it ever to meet again. But as a Member of Parliament, I want Parliament to be there to keep a check on what the executive does: and I shall be a Member of Parliament for much more of my life than I shall be a Minister.' I think this slightly shook them but I said I would consider difficulties arising about particular meetings of the committee in relation to particular organisations and would remit them to Dick Crossman.

Wednesday 27 March
To the NEC and of course there was George Brown, large as life, in his capacity as Deputy-Leader, not having given that up.

There was an argument over whether we should expel Desmond Donnelly. Mikardo said he thought he should be expelled, not for having resigned the Whip, but for what he was saying and doing – attending a lot of Tory meetings. But he thought it would be better for Donnelly's local Party to expel him. Joe Gormley and some of the trade union people said they weren't prepared to accept 'one rule for the rich and one for the rest of them'. If this happened in a local trade union branch, he'd be expelled immediately. Mik's very wise comment got completely overriden. In fact, as it had all leaked out that this expulsion was coming this morning, we couldn't very well not expel him, so we did.

I had lunch at the Commons with Goronwy Roberts, the Minister of State at the Foreign and Commonwealth Office. Goronwy was most interesting. He told me that when George had gone to the Foreign Office in January he had said, 'George, I did not vote for you as Leader and I did not vote for you as Deputy-Leader. I am prepared to serve you absolutely loyally but if you ever shout at me, I shall simply leave the room.' As a result of which, he said, George never had shouted at him.

He said that George, in the last few months at the Foreign Office, had been totally disloyal to Harold, had blackguarded him, had said he was a thug and that he was dishonest. He had said this in the presence of civil servants and indeed had tried to get them to comment on the Prime Minister's veracity. This all confirms my view that George was at the end of his tether when he resigned a couple of weeks ago. It was interesting to get confirmation from Goronwy.

Back to the office and the head of IBM, Eddie Nixon, came with some of his colleagues to see me because I've decided to refer IBM to the Prices and Incomes Board as a result of the 10 per cent increase in their equipment rental charges to British users, which effectively cancels out the benefit of devaluation. He came near to threatening me, saying that if we did this it would affect investment policy by IBM in the future. One of his team said it might affect investment policy by American companies in Britain generally. I said I quite understood this but that, of course, such pressure would only encourage me even more to take action against them.

Just after 5.30, Denning Pearson came to see me, having rung me in great urgency earlier on.

The night of 27 March was a very dramatic one, and I recorded in detail the events which were to result in Rolls Royce clinching the RB-211 engine contract with the US aircraft manufacturers, Lockheed.

The background is as follows: before 1966, the Government had funded aerospace projects virtually on a cost-plus basis, which was how the Olympus 593 engine, also manufactured by Rolls Royce, had been produced for Concorde. In order to try to introduce some financial discipline into the aircraft industry I had insisted that all companies would have to put up money of their own and take a part of the risk, and that our launching aid would be a limited fixed investment so as to give them an incentive to keep costs down. This discipline was not welcomed but was a measure long overdue and it meant that Rolls Royce themselves had to assess the risk before they decided to go ahead with production of new engines.

It had long been clear to me in discussions with Rolls Royce and its Chief Executive, Sir Denning Pearson, that the whole future of the aero-engine company depended on the development of a new high-capacity engine which became known as the RB-211. Pearson said that without this engine, which would be needed for a whole generation of wide-bodied aircraft (including Lockheed TriStar), Rolls would simply fall out of the aero-engine business and would be unable to compete with the two American companies, General Electric and Pratt and Whitney.

I had accepted this argument but insisted that we could not put money into the RB-211 without some evidence that there was an order and it was this task that Pearson and Sir David Huddie, Managing Director of the Aero-Engine Division, had gone to the US to pursue. In the event the required number of orders which would have generated the launching aid from us did not materialise and Pearson came to me on the evening of 27 March to say that the whole future of Rolls Royce was at stake. If they could not launch the RB-211, General Electric or Pratt and Whitney would take his business and the engine would never be produced in Britain. The matter was particularly urgent because the decision was to be made the following day and I had to try to get clearance from colleagues for what was still a speculative order.

In the event the RB-211 turned out to be one of the most profitable engines Rolls Royce produced, although the subsequent collapse of Lockheed did bring Rolls Royce into serious financial difficulties; by this time the Conservatives were in power, and I got the blame for agreeing to fund an engine in an aircraft that was not doing well.

What Pearson said was astonishing. He told me that on his return from America last night, he heard that Lockheed had decided to go ahead with their Airbus on the basis of commitments from only two airlines and had asked Rolls whether they'd be willing to produce the engines on that basis, and make the announcement on Friday. Pearson said this created a very serious problem for him. The Government's launching aid of £456 million had been on the basis that Lockheed would have commitments with three airlines, and this was only two; and if Rolls Royce also went ahead with Douglas, the other American airframe manufacturers, who had a pledge from Pearson, he would have to produce two sets of prototypes which would cost him an extra £20 million. Could we provide him with the money?

I listened very carefully and asked him why it was he couldn't get the money from the City. He said that Rolls were carrying as big a risk as they could; they were carrying the air holding business which was the offset arrangement, and that wasn't anything to do with them.

Anyway, I said I'd talk to Jack Diamond with him and I arranged to see Jack on my own at 7.30.

I had dinner with Caroline, then went and met Jack and told him the story. Jack is a very wise old bird. I like him very much and I think he is probably the best Minister in the Government, as Chief Secretary in charge of public expenditure. He's an accountant and is a very successful businessman.

When I had told him the story he asked, 'What's your advice?'

I said, 'Well, I think we ought to provide the money because if we don't, Denning Pearson won't feel free to accept the Lockheed offer.' And of course, the rest of the Rolls Royce board were meeting at that moment at Denning Pearson's flat and the Lockheed board were due to meet in 50 minutes' time, with a trans-Atlantic call booked tonight to find out the Rolls board's decision.

At 8 we all met in Jack's room. Jack listened attentively and made the same points that I had made. Pearson said, 'Well, I've got my responsibilities to my shareholders; public expenditure is very difficult. I can't take the risk. We'll lose the order.'

Denning Pearson had his Financial Director with him and he's really very broken by this, the poor guy's exhausted.

Jack said, 'I've got to go and see somebody for a minute.' He slipped out with Ian Bancroft, the Under-Secretary at the Treasury, and I went on talking to Denning Pearson. I probed the possibility of getting the money from the City but Denning Pearson stuck out and said it couldn't be done. Then Jack came back and he looked at Denning Pearson and said, 'I'll go half with you. I'll offer you £10 million.'

Denning Pearson replied, 'It's no good. I cannot, on behalf of my shareholders, take the risk.'

Then Jack said, 'Well, that's as far as I can go. I'll guarantee half the sum.'

So I told Denning Pearson, 'Go back and talk to your board and give me a ring when your board have spoken.'

When they had gone I said to him, 'Jack, you're a wise man but I cannot accept this myself without seeing the Prime Minister and the Chancellor.'

Jack said, 'Well, you can't appeal over my head to the Chancellor because I am in charge of public expenditure. You'll have to go to the Prime Minister.'

'It's not a criticism of you,' I replied, 'but I could never sleep again if Rolls lost the order because of this.'

There was a vote on Rhodesia at 10 so I went up to the Division Lobby and took Harold on one side. 'Harold, I think I must talk to you briefly because there's a hiccup on the Rolls Royce Airbus engine order and I must have some money.'

Harold said, 'I thought all was lost.'

I said, 'Not at all, we're nearly there.'

So he said, 'Well, have a word with Roy.'

I went downstairs and discovered Roy was in Birmingham so I went back to see Jack. He was dead tired and said he hadn't had 'more than four and a half hours' sleep since Christmas.' I have never seen anyone looking so pale and drawn.

I appealed to him, 'Look Jack, this really is very serious. Will you allow me to go 70/30 on this extra £20 million in the same way that we have gone 70/30 on the launching aid? Will you allow me to go to £12.6 million?'

He said, 'Look, don't get worried; I've seen a lot of this before. I am a businessman; it'll be all right. They'll accept the ten.'

'Yes, but if they don't will you go to £12.6 million?'

He said, 'Yes.'

I went back and I was absolutely determined, having got Jack's authority to go to £12.6 million, that I would get down below the £10 million that he'd negotiated. Well, the Financial Director rang and said the board had decided to accept. I said, 'Look, we can only accept £18 million as your figure – would half of that do?' So that was nine, a million below what Jack Diamond had proposed. He said he'd put it to his board. He rang back and said they had agreed.

Then I sat down and in my own hand wrote out a letter addressed to Denning Pearson. That letter was worth £9 million. I read it out on the phone and Pearson accepted it and phoned New York. That was how Rolls Royce got the Airbus order.

Now, there are a lot of interesting things about this. One is that when the Tories say, as they regularly do, 'Government should get off the back of industry', they choose to disregard the fact that if industry was on its own, it wouldn't survive in modern, advanced fields such as aircraft, nuclear energy and computers. Two weeks ago I gave £7 million to the computer industry; it couldn't survive without it. I wouldn't mind a man on my back if he had £46 million to stuff in my wallet.

It was a most exciting, dramatic evening, none of which can ever come out. It has to be absolutely secret. But if you ask Rolls Royce, they will tell you the truth – that is that three or four hours of negotiations, which finished just after 11 pm, led to Rolls Royce getting the Airbus engine order.

Came home pretty excited and very tired.

Friday 29 March
Got up early and went to Clifton College in Bristol where there was a conference on world poverty organised by the Christian Education Committee and some fourteen to sixteen year olds were absolutely brilliant talking about birth control and technology and so on. They came from comprehensive schools all over the city and most of them thought Marx was right on the question of the rich getting richer and the poor getting poorer. Half of them were prepared to lower their own living standards, that is to say pay taxation to help developing countries, but none put their hands up when I asked them if they thought their parents would be prepared to do this.

On the 6.30 news, I heard the announcement that Rolls Royce had won the RB-211 contract with Lockheed. A most exciting piece of news and the biggest export order ever, something like £1,000 million in dollars which will accrue to us during the 1970s.

Wednesday 3 April
My forty-third birthday and the children came in with their presents in the morning which was very sweet of them. But it was an awful day for a birthday because I had to go in very early and I was extremely tired, having been to bed so late.

Immediately after lunch Harold came down to my room and we

talked for an hour. I pressed my claim for the leadership of the House if there was a reshuffle but he wanted someone who was a bit more genial and jovial and less worried-looking than me, someone with a trade union background who would drink in the bar all the time and be jolly. This was a requirement. So he's going to appoint Fred Peart.

Then he asked me, 'Were you serious about wanting Education?' (I had told Marcia this when rumours of a reshuffle were rife.)

'Yes, providing I could have an Education Act and make the comprehensive schools thing a really living issue.'

He said he was thinking of Ted Short for it and that Denis Healey had wanted it. He went on to talk about his Inner Cabinet and I said I certainly didn't expect to be excluded for the rest of this Parliament. He had said that this Cabinet would be the first real 'Wilson Cabinet' that would last right through to the next Election. This of course is all bunk. I told him I didn't much fancy being outside the 'real' Cabinet and I raised the question of Peter – he is keen to move Peter from the DEA. I said I thought this would be disastrous; after all the attacks on Peter it would be quite wrong to move him. But Harold replied that Barbara had wanted to take over the DEA and Ray won't move from Labour.

He calmed me down and the Education thing was left as a possibility.

Then I said, 'You know, you have to deal with Roy by building up John Harris.'

'Oh well,' he replied, 'John Junor of the *Daily Express* wanted to come and see me last weekend because they were so keen to keep Roy out. They've been trailing him for six weeks now.'

Thursday 4 April
Got up at 5.45. I was too agitated to sleep.

Bakaiev, the Soviet Minister of Merchant Marine, who is a nice old merchant seaman, came to see me. He plonked a book on my desk on the computerisation of the management of the entire Soviet merchant marine, under which he will know exactly where every ship is, what it's loaded with and where it's going. He will be able to plan its servicing and repair schedule in the various yards around the country. Hearing this rather confirmed my view that Communism is going to score heavily over capitalism with the advent of computers because the Communists got centralised control early but didn't know what to do with it, and had no idea how to manage it, and computers now give them a tool for management. We, on the other hand, had various sophisticated methods of managing things but we didn't have the power, and still don't have the power, and we are going to have to struggle on with something much less adequate.

At 6.15 I went to see Peter at the DEA because there was still a rumour that he was going to be moved. Harold had asked to see Peter at

7.30, me at 8. So we talked for a while and agreed that we must press Harold to get off the back of the DEA, that is to say that Peter should be Secretary of State in his own right.

Peter went off to see Harold and half an hour later I arrived. Harold was all smiles. He had John Silkin outside, and Harold Davies*, Marcia and the usual hangers-on. While I was in there, Roy called from Washington and was obviously pressing for Peter to leave the DEA. Harold was saying on the phone, 'Oh don't worry, he won't be doing the sort of job he's been doing. It will just be regional planning; he won't be doing any of this macro stuff.' I think Harold chose Roy's absence partly so that he could do a reshuffle without being bullied all the time by Roy. No doubt Dick Crossman is being very difficult and Marcia said he was contemptuous of Peter and me.

Anyway, Harold told me that Education was off and that he was going to give it to Ted Short. He was very friendly and said he would have a Chequers meeting to discuss the future policy of the Party. He has no solution at all as to how the relationship between the Government and Transport House is to work.

Friday 5 April

At 11.30 Lord Kings Norton† came to see me with John Hill, Chairman, and Charles Cunningham, Deputy-Chairman, of the AEA. I have asked Kings Norton to be the chairman of a little working party to look at the staffing of Aldermaston, Burghfield and Cardiff. The AEA have said that unless hardening and penetration aids are approved for our atomic weapons, providing work for skilled people at Aldermaston and the two Royal Ordnance factories, it would not be possible to keep even the existing Polaris programme going. When this issue came to Ministers previously, Denis said he was trying to negotiate some exchange with the Americans; and there was an attempt by some Ministers to drive penetration aids and hardening through on the basis that 'you had to keep the skilled teams together'.

Harold was very suspicious of this and so was I, so we agreed to ask Lord Kings Norton to study it. Kings Norton stayed behind afterwards and I explained the real reason why we wanted him there which was to cross-check on what the AEA had said. He quite understood that.

I went up to the Post Office Tower and had lunch with the *Sunday Times* people: Denis Hamilton, the Editor-in-Chief, Harold Evans, the Editor, Keith Richardson, the Technology Correspondent, and Jimmy Margach. We had a very jovial talk.

---

* Labour MP for Leek; PPS to Harold Wilson, 1966–70.
† Formerly Sir Harold Roxbee-Cox, industrialist and Chief Scientist, Ministry of Fuel and Power, 1948–54.

Sunday 7 April
I tried my bicycle out this morning – cycled to my office in twenty-five minutes and back again in about thirty minutes.

Monday 8 April
The National Executive Home Policy Committee gathered to consider a huge wodge of papers. George Brown arrived late and rolling drunk, and Alice Bacon, who had taken the chair, handed it over to George. He behaved outrageously and it was impossible to make any progress. Everybody was very courteous about it but the fact is he's a damned nuisance and I don't see any future in politics for him. I always knew that he would either get a new lease of life after his resignation or break up. I think he's breaking up.

Tuesday 9 April
We had a phone call at 2.15 this morning from Caroline's mother in Cincinnati to say that there was major rioting, shooting and burning there and suggesting that the children should not go. They were very disappointed. But she rang again later in the day to say the rioting was under control so it was agreed they would.

I had lunch with Subramaniam who is the Chairman of the Indian Aeronautics Committee, a distinguished Indian Congress Party member and friend of Mrs Gandhi. They are considering whether they will buy aircraft from us, but their fear is that if they do, and there is another war like the Pakistan-Indian War, we would be neutral and cut off supplies from them. I tried to reassure them on this and they were quite grateful. It was a pleasant lunch. I like the Indians.

Back to see George Harriman to go over the export record of BMC. I am trying very hard to get an aircraft carrier to carry their cars across the Atlantic before the spring selling season disappears. The Ministry of Defence have been predictably difficult but all the manufacturers I have spoken to are very keen about it.

Dinner with Percy Clark, Peter Shore, Terry Pitt, David Kingsley* and some of the Party's publicity team at the Terrazzo Restaurant in Romilly Street to discuss the publicity for the Party over the next few years. It was agreed that I would pursue my index poll idea in Bristol in which I invited people to say whether there should be votes at eighteen or not. They were quite excited by the thought of an MP going to his constituents to get their views instead of going to tell them what he thinks.

*Publicity adviser to the Labour Party, 1962–70, and subsequently to the SDP.

Wednesday 10 April
Miscellaneous Committee on 'Acarus', where the big issue was how we would tell the Americans about our intention to notify the Dutch on centrifuge work. We agreed to send a Foreign Office official to talk to Sir Pat Dean, the US Ambassador. Later in the day, I also decided to send an Atomic Energy Authority member over to talk to the AEA man on Pat Dean's staff. We discussed how we should handle Luns, the Dutch Foreign Minister, when he comes over next week because we promised to talk to him but don't want to give him many details until we know the American reaction.

Denis Healey, predictably, took a totally American view, being absolutely opposed to any of this. He is very anti-European, very pro-American.

Thursday 11 April
Caroline took the children to the airport and they were very excited. They were met in New York and flew on to Cincinnati. Caroline went to the British Museum to work, not being able to bear being at home without them.

Frank Kearton and Charles Villiers, Managing Director of IRC, came in to discuss the nuclear plant industry. I told them there had been a unanimous view that IRC should try for a Single Design Authority but they said that the nuclear plant firms had somewhat lost interest in the AEA and thought the IRC might do better to licence some other systems. One could see all this huge investment in nuclear research absolutely going down the drain. It was a shock to hear it because we had spent about £900 million and the question was whether any of these systems are as good as we thought. Also, it is becoming pretty clear that the Steam Generating Heavy Water Reactor is cheaper than the Advanced Gas-cooled Reactor which means that all the AGR research has effectively been wasted. It is a classic case of what's gone wrong with Britain. Unless you do related industrial research to sell things, you can spend an infinite amount of money and not get a proper return on it. But, on the whole, Frank Kearton was quite attracted by the idea of a Single Design Authority and this is really what I think we will try for first.

Caroline and I arrived home at about the same time and we had a meal out.

Friday 12 April
Good Friday. We had a telegram to say the children had arrived safely. I cleaned up the front and back gardens, fixed the fire, replaced the bulbs, mended Joshua's desk lid and fixed the bath plugs. We had lunch in the garden and in the evening went to an Italian restaurant, then watched *Kind Hearts and Coronets* on the television. A lovely day.

Saturday 13 April
All day doing my constituency letters. Caroline worked in the British Museum. In the evening we went to the new Wimpy Bar at Notting Hill Gate and then watched television.

Monday 15 April
Caroline went to Trafalgar Square for the Aldermaston rally.

Thursday 18 April
Bristol, and I met the local press. I said a word about the Transport Bill and I launched my idea of the index polls, under which people write and tell me what they think about issues. I suggested the first one might be votes at eighteen. The press are a very cynical lot and, of course, as all press men do, reflected the business interests of their proprietors, being more concerned with the level of surtax than with the plight of ordinary people. But that is the British press, and there you are.

Caroline spent the day seeing a couple of headmasters of Bristol comprehensive schools about her draft questionnaire, which she is using for the basis of her book on comprehensive schools.

Saturday 20 April
In the evening Michael and Betsy Zander and Mark Arnold-Forster came in and we went and had a meal at a little French restaurant. Mark had just come from seeing Melina Mercouri, the Greek film star, who had come over for the big Trafalgar Square rally tomorrow, and he had to go away early to write her speech.

Sunday 21 April
Lazy start. It was a lovely day and Caroline sat in the garden. I mowed the grass and scrubbed the basement floor.

The news today is dominated by Enoch Powell's speech in which he raised the racial issue by saying that he thought this country had gone mad to admit so many immigrants and that it was like adding a match to a pile of gunpowder. Enoch is of working class origins; he got a scholarship to a grammar school, did very well academically, became a professor at twenty-four and a brigadier at twenty-nine. But he has never been accepted in the Tory Party. He wasn't offered a job, for example, in the City after he left the Treasury with Peter Thorneycroft[3], and this obviously burned very much into his mind. He has got to have somebody to look down on and this is the way he does it.

Monday 22 April
Enoch Powell was sacked from the Shadow Cabinet this morning by
Heath in a great and rather well publicised effort to reassert his
leadership.

Wednesday 24 April
The press is still full of the repercussions of Enoch Powell's speech just
before the weekend. Yesterday 200 dockers came to the House of
Commons and shouted obscene things at Labour MPs and called Ian
Mikardo a bloody Chinese Jew. He recognised some of the East End
Fascist leaders among these guys. The white trash have picked this
speech up. It has suddenly liberated them and there are strikes all over
the place in support of Enoch Powell. He really has opened Pandora's
Box. I should think Enoch Powell will get an enormous vote in his
constituency, but from the Government's point of view the situation
could be very dangerous and difficult.

I went to the National Executive where most of the time was occupied
with discussion about the arrangements we should make to replace the
General Secretary, Len Williams, who has just been appointed
Governor-General of Mauritius. There was a keen discussion about
whether or not we should attempt to change the rules so as to allow a
Member of Parliament to be General Secretary. I said I thought there
was at least a case for having a member of the Cabinet who could work
with the new General Secretary to try to improve the links between the
Cabinet and the NEC. But Alice Bacon hit out at this and said that the
Inquiry Committee had considered it but felt that nothing should
intervene between the General Secretary and the Prime Minister.
That's perfectly true, but, in fact, the Prime Minister is too busy to
maintain the sort of contact that is necessary. After a long discussion, it
was overwhelmingly agreed that the constitution shouldn't be changed.
Of course an MP could be appointed and would have to resign his seat
on being elected by Conference. I think Jim Callaghan has got Merlyn
Rees in mind and there may be one or two other MPs who, looking at the
future, would think this is a rather more secure job than being an MP in
their present constituencies. The other thing that came up was a
discussion about the salary and we decided to put the salary up to
£4,250, which is reasonable though not anything like large enough
compared with the responsibility involved.

Came home and worked until 6.30, that is to say right plumb through
the night, preparing for the Bristol Siddeley debate – a most distasteful
debate and I am not looking forward to it. It is so complicated that I am
really afraid I can be caught out.

Thursday 25 April

I worked all morning dictating the final text of my Bristol Siddeley speech and the debate began in the afternoon. I opened it and got a reasonably good hearing from the House until I came to the decision to terminate the appointment of Verdon-Smith and Brian Davidson, one of the directors, from the public bodies on which they sat. This produced an absolute outcry from the Tories.

Frederick Corfield, Shadow Aviation spokesman, who spoke after me, said that my integrity and impartiality were an issue in this and David Renton, Conservative MP for Huntingdonshire, who is an old friend of Brian Davidson, launched into the most violent attack and said I would regret this for the rest of my life. And so it went on.

The Labour people cheered, which didn't particularly help because it's really no great pleasure to have done a thing like that. But I am quite sure the Government couldn't have accepted the reports and then let these people go on advising us as if nothing had happened. I know it was right to do this. But I did get a strong impression that I had touched the Old Boy network. Here were all these people who were friends of Verdon-Smith and Davidson and were absolutely furious to think that anyone could punish them for anything that had happened; and they rallied round in a way which really explained the Philby case absolutely perfectly, and in a way, curiously, that the Labour Party would never do to protect one of its own Members.

Friday 26 April

Solly Zuckerman came to see me and we talked about 'Acarus'.

Harold Wilson has decided to set up a committee under Lord Chalfont to discuss European technological collaboration: this, in effect, is the product of Solly complaining to the Prime Minister that things aren't moving fast enough on my front.

Burke Trend also came to tell me that this committee was to be set up under Lord Chalfont. I really blew up and said that if the Prime Minister was dissatisfied with the speed with which things are moving, then he ought to see me. But to set up a committee under the Foreign Office to look at this would be quite wrong because it would get the whole thing off on the wrong foot. I was following a consistent policy and I thought the best thing to do was to leave me to continue. But if there was to be a committee, then I ought to be the chairman of it. Burke Trend was slightly taken aback. He said he would tell the Prime Minister that I was worried about it. I said, 'Don't tell him I am worried about it, tell him I am angry.'

Sunday 28 April

I spent most of the day at Number 10 where we had a joint meeting between the Cabinet and the National Executive. We met in the dining room on the first floor and began with a review of the economic situation. There was some discussion and Mik said that without the four elements – full employment, social equity, fair taxation and fair handling of mergers – an incomes policy would never work.

I got in briefly and said that as far as productivity was concerned we were getting a shift from defence spending to civil spending, from nuclear and aerospace to other expenditure, from intra-mural to extra-mural research, and from research to manufacturing and marketing. Technopolitics were beginning to work and we had developed a number of industrial policies leading to mergers and productivity services.

Roy said that the economy must be made to work in 1968 and then he explained his public strategy.

After a sandwich lunch we had a discussion on social policy introduced by Bill Simpson.

Ted Short said he would like to see more education for society and – this was open to misunderstanding – he didn't believe in a child-orientated education so much as a community-orientated education. He talked about the possibility of having to legislate for comprehensive schools and raised the real risk that there might be teachers unemployed in the next few years as a result of the postponement of the school leaving age.

On race relations Jim Callaghan said we must stand firm but the rate of absorption was a very difficult problem.

We had a quick cup of tea and in the late afternoon George Brown introduced his future policy work. Frank Allaun said the Conference must be supreme on policy matters.

Tony Crosland said we didn't have a communications problem, but our policies were unpopular and we hadn't got growth; nationalism was developing; socialism wasn't and never had been popular with the voters; and we have in fact asked people to pay for the improvements in their own social services, which was the last thing they intended. He said educational reform was very important. I thought it was a very good contribution.

Denis Healey took a very tough line and said there was a risk of fascism, which came appropriately from an ex-Communist. Anyway, he thought the United States elections were the key to the survival of the Government, ie it depended on who became President and what line he took.

Then we had Mikardo on public enterprise and the need to reorganise the limited liability company. He talked about credibility and attacked me for not having introduced enough socialist thought into the changes I was bringing about.

Harold wound up and paid a particular tribute to Mintech and said he was sure the Party would recover. Then we all went home. It was quite useful in the sense that the explosions we expected from the unions didn't occur. But it didn't lead to anything very sensational and I am not sure there was even a real meeting of minds. We did agree however that we would do this on a six-monthly basis.

Tuesday 30 April
Caroline was ill this morning. Her chest infection returned and she had a temperature of over 100 and wasn't well at all.

I am having a great row with Harold at the moment about Alun Chalfont's appointment as chairman of this technical sub-committee on the approach to Europe. This is an attempt to get technological policy out of my hands in relation to Europe. I told Alun Chalfont my doubts and tried to get him to accept our approach to European policy which is industrially-orientated rather than project-orientated. I think he took the point but he's the Minister in charge of our approach to Europe, he has obviously got nothing to do and he's looking in my direction.

In the afternoon I went and had a talk to Harold. I thought he was going to discuss European technology but he didn't. His real concern was leaks and briefings. He told me about the honours list: that John Stonehouse would be a Privy Councillor, that Trevor Huddleston would be Bishop of Birmingham, that he couldn't give the Reverend Elsie Chamberlain a peerage[4] because he wanted it for the Lord Mayor of Liverpool, who was a woman, and he talked about John Harris. I suggested that he appoint John Harris to a big position in Washington or abroad and he was very excited by this; it is indeed the only way of dealing with him.

The trouble is that Harold is very paranoid and I think he is, in a sense, creating the very thing he is afraid of, namely a plot against himself. He just lives in fear of the day when four senior Ministers will come to him and say they won't serve under his leadership and he's planning what he'll do in those circumstances. He had an idea at one time that he would offer himself for reselection with the Parliamentary Party, but I don't know that that would be very wise. It would all be very messy and his authority would be shaken by it. But that is his nature and I think it's probably because he is afraid and isn't quite up to the job. I don't know. Still, he was extremely friendly to me, probably because he believes I am making trouble. But, of course, I am not making half as much trouble as he thinks.

Wednesday 1 May

Airbus is going wrong in a big way. There is a huge escalation of costs and the operating expenses of the plane are not likely to be any better than that of current aircraft. There's also a problem about weight growth and all the rest. It really is pretty grim. If Airbus went wrong, our only option would be to try and get Rolls Royce engines into a Boeing Airbus, exactly comparable, and this might be a better bet. I don't know. It would be the end of our European aircraft policy as such, I think, but we'll just have to see.

Saturday 4 May

In the evening we watched a glorious television programme by Robert Morley called *One Pair of Eyes* in which he was talking about education and which centred round Holland Park School.

Sunday 5 May

To Bristol for the May Day at Transport Hall and who should I meet but Ludmilla Pavlichenko, the Russian war hero – a sniper – who had come to Oxford in 1942 and had delivered an address in Russian at the Town Hall and had been wildly cheered. It wasn't until the interpreter had translated what hideous things she had been describing that the cheers, retrospectively, looked most inappropriate. But the goodwill had been genuine then and it was again today.

Monday 6 May

Frank Kearton came to see me this morning and said that industrialists were very sick of the Government. They were still sore about the Industrial Expansion Bill.* He had been to Swinton College, a Tory educational college, over the weekend with Peter Walker† and Tony Barber and said it looked as if the next Government, by which of course he meant the Tories, would keep the Industrial Reorganisation Corporation going and wouldn't get rid of it, as he had at one time feared.

So I said, 'Well, thanks very much indeed. I have got other things to worry about besides what the next Tory Government is going to do!' But it made me wonder whether we were being hopelessly naïve in trying to work with industry and whether we shouldn't just nationalise them as we always said we would.

This feeling was much reinforced when we came on to talk about the nuclear plant industry. He said that in fact none of the firms involved in

---

* The Bill, passed in February 1968, gave direct powers to the Minister of Technology to provide support for industrial projects which were in the national economic interest.
† Conservative MP for Worcester and senior Opposition Front Bench spokesman.

the manufacture of nuclear plant would agree to a Single Design Authority, that they all objected very strongly to it, that they didn't really need the AEA and what they wanted was to take the profitable parts out of the AEA for their own businesses. It did make me think whether we were being absolutely crazily anti-socialist in doing the sort of things the Ministry of Technology is doing. If I thought that nationalisation was efficient, which, in my heart, I don't believe, I would be in favour of nationalising everything. What I think I must do is to get a public investment and a public shareholding and Government director on the boards of these big companies and just control. But I was rather sick about all this and it depressed me.

Tuesday 7 May
Frank Schon came in in the morning and I told him what Frank Kearton had said, both about the Industrial Expansion Bill and about the Atomic Energy Authority. He blew up and said, 'Those bastards will get you in the end,' which may well be true.

Caroline came in and we were the joint hosts at the International Organisation of Motor Traders at the Banqueting Hall in Whitehall. She dashed home to give dinner for two of her teacher friends, Eric Mottram and Clyde Chitty, and I joined them later. Eric Mottram teaches at LSE and he was in touch with modern thinking by the anarchists and the drop-outs. He talked about their attitude to society: anti-disciplinarian, in favour of a cellular sort of society where people had responsibilities but power was not hierarchical in character. I found it very interesting. It's a long time since I have been part of a general discussion like this. There is a great gap between the people thinking about the future nature of society and those who are trying to run it at the moment.

Wednesday 8 May
After lunch I was very tired and I slept through most of an elaborate sonic bang presentation but managed to persuade the Board of Trade not to ban supersonic flying immediately, before Concorde is even off the ground, which was quite an achievement. In fact, I am trying to get the whole thing postponed as long as I can.

Thursday 9 May
In the middle of the Industrial Policy Committee Harold came in and said that at the Parliamentary Committee [the Inner Cabinet] this morning it had been agreed that the Prices and Incomes Bill should be allowed to expire at the end of next year. He felt that he must get Cabinet authority for a decision of that kind. Ray Gunter was strongly in favour as he hates the Prices and Incomes Policy, as does Dick Marsh,

and they were exchanging significant glances. Peter was in the chair and said he would like to think about it for a while. I was too busy to do anything anyway but it is a sort of climb-down. Roy Jenkins is only interested in the Prices and Incomes Policy to get him through the immediate hump and there are very few disciplinarians of the Peter Shore kind.

To the ITV studios at 11 for the discussion on the local government elections today. As I arrived at the studios one of Harold's staff was waiting for me and found a telephone and put me through to Number 10. Harold told me that Cecil King was coming out tomorrow with a tremendous attack on him in the *Daily Mirror* and he wanted to see me to build up the second stage of the campaign against King. But when I went into the studio the interviewer actually had the text of the article, entitled 'Enough is Enough', saying that Harold was no good and he should go. It said that Britain faced the worst financial crisis in its history and that lies about the reserves would be no answer. Quintin Hogg and Eric Lubbock [Liberal MP for Orpington] and I were on and this was really all we discussed. I said that Cecil King was entitled to whatever view he liked about a leader of a political party, but it was a grave dereliction of duty to throw doubt upon our financial position in that way. Then Eric Lubbock commented that the attack was just because Cecil King hadn't got a job under Wilson, which was a bit cynical. I said that it wasn't surprising, that it was known he had been saying this privately for some time and all that was interesting was that it had come out. Then Quintin got terribly excited in the middle of the discussion and said, 'Get out, get out, get out. Everybody despises your Government; get out, we don't want you any more.'

I just turned to him and said, 'Down, Quintin, down,' as if he were a great dog, which was the best I could do.

Friday 10 May

At about midnight, Harold Wilson rang up and asked if I would go and see him tomorrow morning. Cecil King's attack was the big news in all the papers today and Harold's paranoia is being fed. After he rang, I spoke to Peter and said I was very reluctant to get involved in skulduggery against Cecil King. Peter agreed about this and I managed to talk him out of the idea that Roy Jenkins should be forced to make a declaration of faith. It seemed to me that Harold should make a joke of Cecil King, he should issue a serious message to the Party to steady it in its moment of defeat in the local elections, and that he should probably appoint a Cabinet Minister as Vice-Chairman of the Executive, or to work with the new General Secretary.

Saturday 11 May

I went to see Harold this morning. He was in his sitting room looking, I thought, awfully defeated and quiet. He said, 'I'm not quitting, you know,' as if I might have any doubts about it. I daresay he just suspects everybody, including me, and in the end he may just be left with Gerald Kaufman and Peter. I told him what I thought but he was absolutely opposed to saying anything to the Party. He was going to appear on television and talk to James Margach and release his speech to the PLP Trade Union Group of MPs next Monday. But he was not going to speak to the Party because he said he didn't comment on local government election results. I tried to persuade him that, as Party Leader, people wanted to hear from him. But it was no good; he wouldn't do it and so I decided to do it myself.

Came home and dictated a letter to my Constituency Party. I also dictated a memorandum on the document I think should be published at Conference about the work of the Government and future policy.

Monday 13 May

I opened the Instrumentation Automation and Electronic Exhibition at Olympia. The most fascinating exhibit without any doubt was the Robot Woman on the Honeywell stand. I was completely taken in by this act, which turned out to be a live woman. But it was a most effective and amusing demonstration that really drew the crowds.

Tuesday 14 May

To the House of Lords to see Gerald Gardiner, William Ross and Fred Peart who are now looking into briefing by Ministers against other Ministers. I said it was time we had a lot less secrecy in Government, and I suggested that they might recommend this to Cabinet. For example, I suggested that we ought to publish the composition of all interdepartmental ministerial committees and that we might even go so far as to publish Cabinet papers that were not secret. I cited the example of the Swedes in this respect and said I thought this would encourage the press to talk a lot more about issues and a lot less about personalities. Whether any of this got home or not, I don't know, but I strongly hope it did.

Wednesday 15 May

Flew to Belfast last night and this morning collected Brian Faulkner, the Minister of Commerce in the Northern Ireland Government, and we drove along the motorway to Craigavon to open the new Goodyear factory. Faulkner is a bright guy, very ambitious, they say. He's obviously done a successful job selling Northern Ireland to industrialists abroad and he is a popular figure. We addressed a meeting in the factory and there was a big crowd. I made a speech and said that Goodyear had benefited very greatly from the Government of Northern Ireland in getting the money to help to build this plant, and that the British Government had helped as well. As a matter of fact, my original text had quantified the amount of help the British Government had given but Brian Faulkner had had this removed. As I was more or less his guest, I couldn't fight it but I did realise later that this was part of a political campaign by the Northern Ireland Government to suggest that they were the ones who really were doing all the good things and that the British Government got the blame for everything that went wrong.

Then we went round the plant and it was a really odd experience because the chap who took me round didn't allow me to talk to any of the workers. There were ropes keeping the visitors away from the people actually working at the benches. But I broke through and talked to them.

We had lunch and Faulkner made a speech. Listening to him talking about his world tours to get industry to Northern Ireland gave me an idea of what a tremendous advantage it is to have a separate Government, and I could see why the Scottish Nationalists are enthusiastic about the idea. I asked Faulkner about nationalism and he said that looking at the functions of the Northern Ireland Government and the Parliament, it was a waste of time to have separate legislation, for example for social services, because they always followed the British model exactly. But he did think that in terms of industrial policy, it was a great advantage to be able to spend their money as seemed sensible to them, and I think he is absolutely right.

Leaving the factory, there was a great demonstration of about sixty people who had been waiting to catch me. They were on unofficial strike about the working arrangements agreement reached between the unions and the management. I stopped the car, got out and had a talk to them. They were a muddled lot who complained they weren't getting the same pay as in Wolverhampton and one extremely seedy looking man said he had come out of the RAF after thirty years and was on strike to save the country from the 'wogs'. Of course, there are no immigrants in Northern Ireland at all. I said I couldn't really intervene in a matter between them and their union but I just wanted to have a word with them as they had waited so long and to wish them luck and hoped it all worked out. They cheered me lustily as I left.

Thursday 16 May

Cabinet, and one of the first items that came up was votes at eighteen. Dick Crossman recommended that we should more or less have to accept votes at eighteen in view of our decision to give normal civil rights at eighteen. He made a play of regretting it but he was actually pleased.

Dick Marsh attacked it violently and said he thought we must have

'Give ordinary people more say in decision making'—WEDGWOOD BENN

FRANKLIN

'We're staying on for the debate'

gone absolutely mad if we thought the working class wanted students to be enfranchised. When I was called, I said all that did was to make me wish they had raised the minimum age for entry into the Cabinet to forty-three which would leave Dick out and put me in. But this was important and we had to accept it.

Peter Shore made a very good speech in favour and Gerald Gardiner was in favour. But there was great anxiety on the part of Willie Ross, the Scottish Secretary, and also George Thomas for reasons of nationalism, and it may well be that this will bust us up.

Wednesday 22 May
To the National Executive. Harry Nicholas raised the question of our overwhelming defeats in the local government elections and referred to the mid-term manifesto. Then Barbara Castle took it up. I said the Executive had behaved very stupidly to allow our Party work to disappear and that Ministers really had to be political animals as well. To my surprise, it was agreed that the mid-term manifesto should be prepared for the next Home Policy Committee of the NEC. It was a total success.

Afterwards I had lunch with the French Ambassador, M. de Courcelle, a very civilised man. With him were his counsellor and M. Michel, his scientific attaché. We discussed a number of things including, of course, the situation in France which is in the throes of great disturbances. Michel said he had just come back from Toulouse where he found the students urging the same sort of reforms on the universities that the French Ministry of Education had been urging on them.

To the Cabinet-NEC dinner. George Brown was furious because there had been a story in the evening papers about the mid-term manifesto and he was sure I had given it to the press. In fact, I had neither given the document to the press nor spoken to anybody about the NEC meeting but George was convinced I had. We had quite a useful discussion and Peter Shore and Dick clashed about social policy as Dick Crossman is now in favour of the 'jingle in the pocket' theory, that is to say, less increased expenditure on social welfare and higher wages.

Saturday 25 May
Went to Llandudno to speak at the Welsh Council of Labour Conference. I had prepared a serious speech and the delegates listened intently. I reproduce part of the text here because its examination of the distribution of power and the democratic process excited considerable interest – warmth from the Left and hostility from the media – over the following week.

'We are moving rapidly towards a situation where the pressure for the redistribution of political power will have to be faced as a major political issue. The implications of this for our system of parliamentary democracy, and for the Labour Party which works within it, are far-reaching.

'The redistribution of political power does not mean that it will all be decentralised. Indeed, in some military, industrial and technical areas, centralisation is inevitable. The existence of international organisations, large international corporations, and the acceptance of international standards of measurement and performance all remind us of our interdependence. To dream of living in splendid isolation, grouped together according to historical culture, is to follow a completely romantic illusion.

'The redistribution of power by decentralising it is of great importance. But it is much more complicated than an exercise of geographical fragmentation. It means finding the right level for each decision and seeing that it can be taken at this level. It also means transferring much more power right back to the individual.

'Our parliamentary system has changed radically over the centuries. At first, it was little more than a means by which feudal landowners tamed the power of kings. In the nineteenth century, landowners and industrialists were forced to share their power by the emergence of the middle and working classes. But these people were not content to be represented by anyone other than themselves. That is how the Labour Party came to be formed.

'Looking ahead, we must expect equally radical changes to be made in our system of government to meet the requirements of a new generation. I am not dealing here with the demand for the ownership or control of growing sections of the economy. I am thinking of the demand for more political responsibility and power for the individual than the present system of parliamentary democracy provides.

'I am thinking of a participating democracy under which more and more people will have an opportunity to make their influence felt on decisions that affect them. If that is our objective, which I believe it must be, what special characteristic would a popular democracy have that is now lacking in parliamentary democracy?

'Nothing buttresses the established order so effectively as secrecy. The searchlight of publicity shone on the decision-making process of government would be the best thing that could possibly happen. For centuries, this was the only power that the House of Commons had. The new Ombudsman, the probing of the specialist committees and the partial lifting of the old fifty-year clamp on public records are all moves in the right direction. Opening the Commons Chamber to the television cameras would help too.

'But I would be surprised if the process stopped there. In Sweden, departmental and even Cabinet papers are, unless they involve national security, named individuals or commercial secrets, available for public inspection. In this country, there is already considerable pressure to reveal exactly how the intricate structure of interdepartmental and Cabinet committees actually works.

'The more light we throw on the working of government, the less we shall have of the obsession with personalities. While the public and the press are denied the right to know what is being discussed and how decisions are being arrived at, we are bound to have columns and columns of personal tittle-tattle masquerading as serious political comment.

'Considering the power the mass media now exercise, it is surprising how little thought has been given to the interrelationship between them and democracy.

'A Prime Minister can address the whole nation, if necessary, at an hour's notice. A press tycoon can print his own article on the front page of his own newspaper and have it read by millions. But for ordinary people, or even for extraordinary people with minority views, the only way of answering back is to walk about with a placard and hope the

press or television cameras will take a picture. Compared with the technology available to the mass media, the public is still stuck with a communications system that has hardly changed since the Stone Age.

'Perhaps this is one explanation for the fact that protest is edging ever closer to violence. Those with minority views – strikers, those who dislike immigrants or are immigrants, those who oppose the war in Vietnam, or want self-government for Cornwall – have precious little access to the community through the mass media.

'Minority opinions do find an outlet in books and through relatively small circulation papers and magazines. But access to the microphone or TV camera is very strictly limited – both by the BBC and the commercial TV companies.

'What broadcasting now lacks is any equivalent to the publishing function. At the moment, it is controlled by editors with slots to fill and a few selected minority views get in some of the slots. But three minutes of cross-examination while you're roughed up by a folk hero TV interviewer, or a clip of film showing a protest march on the ten o'clock news, is no substitute for the right to speak.

'The day may well come when independent groups of publishers would be allocated so many hours of broadcasting a month, and told to help those who have something to say, to say it clearly and well, to national audiences. Unless we make a move in that direction, we shall simply be denying ourselves access to a whole range of ideas – good, bad and indifferent – which we ought as responsible citizens to be allowed to know about through the mass media.

'In a world where authoritarianism of the Left or Right is a very real possibility, the question of whether ordinary people can govern themselves by consent is still on trial – as it always has been and always will be. Beyond parliamentary democracy as we know it, we shall have to find a new popular democracy to replace it.'

Wednesday 29 May
I had to go to the PLP meeting at 11 where George Strauss [Labour MP for Vauxhall] made an attack on my Llandudno speech, saying Ministers shouldn't think aloud. I defended myself vigorously. I said a Minister could not be expected to go into a Department but remain silent about the technological problems that were arising, and be accused of 'creating private monopolies'. I didn't know how long people would be prepared to put up with that; and anyway in a few years' time people *would* have a button they could press to indicate their view on television programmes. It was very unlikely we should be able to stop them wanting to use this machine to influence political decisions.

My speech went down very well, particularly the impassioned bit about why Ministers must be free to think aloud.

At about 1 am Harold called me in to discuss Jim Callaghan's speech today in which he had said that the prices and incomes legislation would lapse at the end of next year. Jim had tried to pre-empt our position by announcing it in his speech and Harold was furious and decided to raise it at Cabinet the following morning. He told me that in the process my speech would also have to be criticised.

Thursday 30 May
Cabinet, where Harold raised the question of ministerial speeches and said, in a trenchant defence of the status quo, that my speech had caused a lot of trouble because the Cabinet was responsible for the system of government and if the latter was attacked, it was an attack on the Cabinet. But it was really an excuse to raise Jim's speech on prices and incomes. Jim stood very firm and there was a clash between Michael Stewart, Denis Healey, Dick Crossman and Harold on the one hand, and Jim who simply dug his toes in. John Silkin thinks that Jim is trying to get himself sacked. The only other reference to my speech was from Michael Stewart who said that I had dressed up a lot of old ideas as if they were new, and he wondered whether the role of lecturer in political science was compatible with Cabinet office.

In the Commons later Harold answered questions about my speech. He said, 'My Rt Hon. friend was giving some personal reflections on current political trends.' I think that is the first time a Cabinet Minister's speech has ever admitted to being anything other than the policy of the Government.

Cecil King was sacked today by the board of IPC, which was sensational news.

Sunday 2 June

I phoned Harold today. I said that I had been under a lot of pressure to stand for the General Secretaryship of the Labour Party.

I told him I thought that whoever was General Secretary ought to be an MP and ought to sit in the Cabinet like the Chief Whip. This was with a view to establishing that if I did apply, which today I really was thinking seriously of doing, I would not have to give up a Cabinet position. It's a very difficult decision, this. I am enjoying the Ministry of Technology and on the whole it's going well but I am sure that the reconstruction of the Party is the most important task. I believe it can be done on the basis of stronger trade unions and a PLP with a larger part to play. The student power movement, the Black Power movement and the discontent among trade unionists are very powerful and important new forces in society, and I believe the Labour Party has got to enter into a creative relationship with them.

From 3–8 June I was in Rumania for discussions with the Rumanian Government which were directed towards closer Anglo-Rumanian technological and political links. As Minister of Technology, I made many official visits of this kind and because of my hopes for détente I always seized the opportunities, while I was abroad, of discussing, in an informal way, scientific and industrial policy developments and international affairs.

Apart from a fascinating talk with President Ceausescu, I have not included many details of the formal discussions with Rumanian officials, but rather have emphasised the political developments there and the lighter, informal aspects of the trip.

Monday 3 June

Flew to Bucharest, where we were met by dignitaries led by Alexandru Birladeanu, Chairman of the Science Research Committee, and by the Ambassador, Sir John Chadwick, and Embassy staff.

Dinner with the Ambassador and my staff (Ieuan Maddock, Harry Slater and Barry Smith). The Embassy staff were typical of a British Embassy beleaguered in a Communist country, still fighting the Cold War hard. They made the point that Rumanians had never enjoyed any political freedom at any time in their history, that they had been under the Turks, under the Kings and under Antonescu, and they had not lost a great deal by having a Communist regime, although it was a rigid domestic regime which had not even been told about the position in Czechoslovakia. It was generally thought they were not wildly interested in Britain but did think that they had something to gain by establishing a partnership with us.

Tuesday 4 June

At 9 I was driven to the Council of Ministers for the first meeting with Verdet, the First Deputy Prime Minister. Around him at the table were a range of Government people.

After the exchange of courtesies and inevitable television coverage of the opening session, we sat down and discussed practical issues. Our talks on computers developed into a general discussion about the COCOM embargo and we said that it was in the British national interest to develop as much independence as we could from the United States in the technical field. This was why we had decided to spend a lot more money on micro-electronics, why we were trying to build a strong computer industry; there was nothing the Rumanians could get from the French that they couldn't get from us, and get it quicker, with a higher quality of technology and less dependence on America. This point I had to hammer home again and again.

We finished at about 11.30 and then went to the semi-conductor factory at Baniasa, followed by a visit to the Ministry of Foreign Affairs for a talk with Gheorge Macovescu, the First Deputy Minister for Foreign Affairs. The Ambassador came with me. Macovescu welcomed me and said that my visit marked an important step in the development of closer relations.

I said I didn't regard our different social systems as being static and I hoped that one result of our meeting would be that we would exchange views on the changes that were taking place in both our societies. Macovescu found it a little difficult to accept this concept and said that of course they would sustain their own point of view and history would decide who had been right.

At lunch I heard the news of Senator Robert Kennedy's shooting and it is depressing to think of the violence which makes democratic politics increasingly difficult. Not that the Americans are any different from the Europeans or indeed any other country, but it is more of a shock to discover that this can happen there in such a repetitive way.

At 4.30 I went back to the Council of Ministers for the first proper talk with Birladeanu who was accompanied by a number of others on the science side. When I commented that science was defined in Russia as 'satisfying your curiosity at the expense of the state', Birladeanu said that in Rumania it was said that if you want to spend money you could gamble, if you want to spend it enjoyably, you could spend it on women, but if you want to waste money, you have to go for science.

The Rumanians are pretty tough negotiators and this, I think, is one of their strengths. They are using their customer power in a way that we don't always do in Britain.

At 8 we went and had dinner at the Pascaras Restaurant overlooking a lake. It was a beautiful wooden structure with an orchestra playing on the ground floor and a tremendous gathering of people. Dragos, my interpreter, was there; he had guided me through all these discussions. We had a most enjoyable time.

Birladeanu had been in Russia in 1940. He knew Stalin who he said was a highly intelligent man but had ruled Russia with oriental tyranny. He said Stalinism had paralysed economic science for thirty years and had prevented new thinking from developing. Birladeanu himself had been criticised in 1940 for saying that the factors of production were themselves a commodity.

He said he expected to see a two-party state developing in Rumania later and that no one had yet solved the problem of democratic political freedom in a socialist state. These were the things that interested him.

We sat down with everyone telling jokes and the dinner was just one long laugh. The first joke was about Khrushchev, who won the Nobel Prize for Science because he planted seed in Russia and got the wheat from Canada.

There was another story about Khrushchev coming to Rumania. Sitting down in the Council of Ministers' Room, the first thing he raised with the Rumanian Communist Party was, 'Why do you kill your pigs at only twenty kilograms' weight?' The Rumanians said, 'But we don't, except the little ones which we eat as suckling pigs.' Khrushchev said, 'But you kill them at fifty kilograms instead of 150 kilograms. What do you Rumanians think you are doing?' It was just this degree of authoritarianism that annoyed them.

Khrushchev asked them, 'Why do you Rumanians plant your maize in lines, instead of squares which give you much better production?' Indeed, he referred to this at a major mass public meeting and the Rumanians very modestly did experiments in planting and found that you got better productivity from the rows. This just indicated Khrushchev's belief that he should be running Rumanian agriculture in the same way as he was trying to run it in the Ukraine and everywhere else.

This led them to ask me, 'Can an elephant get a hernia? Yes, if he's trying to lift the productivity of Soviet agriculture.'

They were also very funny about Mao. In China, they said, every television programme begins: 'Good evening, Comrade Mao. This is our television and we welcome you,' and ends: 'Goodnight, Comrade Mao.' Somebody asked, 'Why is that?' And the Chinese said, 'Ah well, you see, Chairman Mao is the only one who has a television set.'

They couldn't explain the Cultural Revolution and I was surprised they didn't have an analysis of it, because it is such an important development. I should think that, as Marxists, they would have, but if they did, they didn't want to tell us.

When de Gaulle came to Rumania, he went to visit a factory and asked one of the workers, 'How much do you earn?' The worker replied, 'I earn eighty lei a day.' De Gaulle said, 'How much does that buy?' So the worker replied, 'It buys you a cow.' So de Gaulle pulled out eighty lei, gave it to the man and said, 'Go and buy me a cow.' The man was absolutely paralysed and didn't know what to do, so he consulted the officials who said, 'You got yourself into this, you had better get out of it.' So he came back and said, 'Mr President, a cow would not be easy for you to take back on your aeroplane. Give me another twenty lei and I'll bring you a hen.'

I told a few jokes. They had a great sense of humour and it was altogether a superb evening. Afterwards, Birladeanu and I walked along the lakeside, over a little bridge and into a rose garden. It was a beautiful evening and the lake was quiet except for the sound of orchestras from the different restaurants around the lake. I hadn't realised what a beautiful city Bucharest is.

Wednesday 5 June
At 5, went to the university where I gave my lecture on technology and politics. Then back to the hotel where I had a drink with Laurence Harvey and Pauline Stone who were here making a film called *The Struggle for Rome*, one of these big international spectaculars being made by a German producer with an international cast.

Then at 8.30 I went to the Ambassador's dinner and there were Deputy-Premier Radulescu, Birladeanu, Moldovan [the Chairman of the State Committee for Price Fixing] and Draganescu, the Minister of Electricity who is also a great computer king, a tall angular intellectual man. I took him round the garden and I told him simply, in the hope that it would feed through to the Rumanian Government, that we were making the most enormous efforts to try to break this COCOM problem. I think he understood.

Afterwards, we sat on the terrace and talked to the Ambassador and his staff. They really gave such a Tory view of Britain. They were wildly anti-Communist and defended the Empire, and were just unspeakable. I said that you had to take a dynamic view of society, that the Rumanians were evolving in a new way and this was very important. I do dislike the British Tory Establishment.

Thursday 6 June
I went to a last meeting with Verdet and we agreed on the communiqué very quickly. While we were waiting for the aide-mémoire associated

with it, we settled down and had about an hour and a half of philosophical discussion. 'If I came back to Rumania in twenty years what difference would I find?' I asked.

Verdet was reluctant to forecast, certainly in that sort of circle – he probably felt I was trying to get at him. He thought the role of the Party would still be a very important one. I said 'Yes, I accept this, but as I get older I become more and more socialist and more and more convinced that public ownership itself doesn't solve the problems of society, and that Marx was quite wrong in supposing it did.' I said that you can develop a socialist as distinct from a feudal society and this was an advance, but you found it didn't do what was claimed for it.

Then we got on to the question of how long it would take to establish socialism in Britain and they made a lot of fun of this and said it would take a very long time. I said, 'Well it may, but we don't want our road to socialism to go via the Lubianka prison and Siberia.' They exactly took that point because although I was talking in terms of the Russian experience rather than Rumanian experience, they have had their own Stalinism.

So then we went on to discuss the different social systems and I said that without wishing to blur the issues, I thought that our two systems were like a piece of cheese and a piece of butter both going round in a soup which technology was making hotter and hotter; that in this technological soup, what would come out would not be butter or cheese but something perhaps between the two. They laughed a lot about this and it became quite a joke – our technological soup.

We drove to the village museum where they are gathering houses from all over Rumania and putting them on display. It really was beautiful. On the way there, I heard that Senator Kennedy, who had been shot a couple of days ago, had now died. It was depressing news.

We flew to Constanza and had dinner with the Mayor in the Casino Restaurant – a huge barn of a place, like an old customs shed on the front at Constanza. We sat at a table with a few people eating in different parts of the room, but we were more or less in the middle of a ballroom and there was a very indifferent orchestra and some rather poor singers. One of them, a woman, was induced by the Head of Protocol to come and stroke my head, which was clearly designed to embarrass me.

I had a long discussion about systems and politics and how cybernetics and perhaps molecular biology could teach us something about the way in which to run systems. This was thought very reactionary. The security man who was officially a protocol man, a big square short guy with grey hair and goggle spectacles, got very angry. I think he was drunk. He didn't understand what I had said but took it to be something disrespectful about the Rumanian system and that, to some extent, ruined the evening.

We went back to the hotel and walked up and down the beach and Dragos, the interpreter, explained to me that it was reactionary in Marxist terms to talk about modelling ourselves on biological species because it ruled out the idea of free will.

Friday 7 June
Went to the Archaeological Museum which was fascinating. We looked at the Roman port where we saw old anchors and equipment just exactly as the Romans had left them. Visited the Mayor in his room, and had a short swim in the Black Sea.

Flew back to Bucharest and in the plane Dragos said he thought there would be two political parties in Rumania. He greatly admired the English. He was the son of a peasant and thought that collectivisation had gone too fast.

I went to the Party offices for my meeting with Nicolae Ceausescu, President and General Secretary of the Party, and Maurer, the Prime Minister, and Birladeanu. The Ambassador accompanied me. I thought it would be a twenty-minute courtesy call but I was there for two and a quarter hours. Ceausescu is about forty-eight, grey-haired, modest mannered, very penetrating in his ability, and I liked him. Maurer is a big old-fashioned Labour stalwart, rather like a well-scrubbed railway guard who had become a Minister in Attlee's Government, or even Ramsay MacDonald's in 1929–31, and Birladeanu, chain smoking. The Ambassador was on my side of the table.

Ceausescu greeted me, and told me he had had a talk with Jennie Lee which he had enjoyed. Then he said he wanted concrete results, and raised the whole question of computers and the need for a third generation. I explained the whole problem all over again, that this was of fundamental interest in the United Kingdom, that Rumanian independence and ours were not so very different, that we did not intend to be let down or scooped by others. I said we were frank, we told them the truth, that the French hadn't anything to offer that touched us. I hoped he hadn't been persuaded by the French that COCOM was some Anglo-Saxon arrangement that didn't apply to deals with France.

He said, 'Well, frankly the French do promise integrated circuits and the dates and deliveries are laid down.'

So I answered, 'Well, anything they can offer we can offer too, and I can offer it now subject to the same conditions.'

We got a bit further into this and Ceausescu told me that de Gaulle had said that embargos were made to be broken. Ceausescu indicated that the French believed that the embargo was simply to preserve American economic interests until the Americans themselves could trade with Eastern Europe. I think the French are just about right.

We had a philosophical discussion which took up most of the time, about two roads to socialism. I cross-examined him about central planning. I said that when you do move towards a market-oriented economy, even under socialism, you are in effect leaving the decision about production to be made by those who are producing for the market and, therefore, it wasn't possible to have as much central planning as you thought. He wasn't able to answer this but he thought that central planning would still have a key role – and of course in some sectors it would, for example in the decision to buy and introduce computers.

We got on to the possibility of a dialogue between the Labour and Communist Parties. I said that during the Cold War, we hadn't had the opportunities for talks like this and I suggested that he might apply for the general secretaryship of the Labour Party, at which he laughed. They were saying that we had more or less sold out to private ownership, but the Ambassador chipped in and said that the Industrial Expansion Bill was an opportunity by which the Government could take shares in private ownership as a condition of making money available. I was a little surprised that he had realised the political and economic significance of what we were doing.

I raised the possibility that decision-making would break down in advanced societies, and talked about the way in which the institutions needed to be rebuilt to reflect modern power. I asked about the possible redundancy of the state, and when the 'withering away of the state' might come.

Ceausescu contributed vigorously. He was strongly in favour of the acceptance of free will, he thought the withering away of the state would be very welcome though he didn't quite see the withering away of the Party. I discussed with him the possibility of us all becoming redundant. Finally, at 4.20 I left.

To the Ambassador's party, the British guests arriving early, at 6 o'clock, so that we could have a little ceremony of holding our glasses while the Ambassador toasted the Queen. The chap on the balcony played the National Anthem from an old gramophone record, and we all stood there. It was a most ludicrous, public school, boy-scout event.

I talked to an enormous number of people. The staff of the Embassy said it had been very exciting for them having us there and we'd inspired them, and so on. But the real point about the evening was that Verdet, Radulescu, Birladeanu, and the Minister of Machine Building, the Minister of Justice, and the Minister of Mines – six Ministers – actually came to the party. It was the first time they had ever been to the Embassy and we sat at a special table and just told jokes about the Russians, the Americans and ourselves.

Radulescu said that mining mechanisation meant you had a lot of machinery and no coal. Birladeanu said the Ukranians were very lazy and he recalled a time when there had been a German bombing raid in the Ukraine. A horse had fallen into a pit and when the smoke cleared there was one Ukranian trying to help the horse out, and fifteen others advising. Radulescu said he had asked Castro about his beard and Castro said he was going to keep his beard until American imperialism ended.

Saturday 8 June
Got up at an ungodly hour. Left the hotel and met Birladeanu and Moldovan who had come to see us off at the airport. Talked a bit about Stalin and they stressed again that he was very intelligent and decisive and had advised Rumania to slow down its collectivisation programme on the grounds that the Russians had no alternative as the Soviet Union was a pioneer; but that Rumania could do it in its own time in a more leisurely way.

Well, that was about it. They all waved and we got in our plane and we talked all the way back to London.

Sunday 9 June
I went to the office and heard that John Stonehouse had attacked me this weekend for my Llandudno speech. I talked to him about it and I think he was a bit embarrassed. The truth is he didn't agree with the speech. He had made some reference that he realised would be hostile and I think the press had picked it up and said, not unreasonably, that it was an attack. But I explained my view that the future ought to be open to discussion and there was no reason why there should be collective Cabinet or even collective ministerial responsibility about the future.

Worked until midnight and decided I would try for the general secretaryship of the Party by making a case for a change in the rules.

Thursday 13 June
Watched the World Revolutionary Students on television. There was the man they called Danny the Red, Daniel Cohn Bendit, a Crippendorf from Germany who looked as if he were a retired Jesuit; Tariq Ali who was President of the Oxford Union; a beautiful Yugoslav woman who said Tito was wonderful; and a variety of others from different countries. In a way, they are saying many of the things I am about the need for participation and the obsolescence of our institutions.

On to the BBC to do a discussion with Bob McKenzie, the LSE sociology professor, Edward Boyle [Conservative MP for Handsworth], Eric Lubbock and Ian Trethowan of *The Times*, about the two by-elections today.* Bob was saying it was high-level balderdash to say that

* Sheffield Brightside, caused by the death of Richard Winterbottom (Labour), was held by Edward Griffiths; Oldham West, previously Labour, was won by Bruce Campbell (Conservative).

institutions were what mattered. So I attacked low-level balderdash which was the continual gossip of the sort he encouraged about political personalities, creeping over Gallup polls and all that.

Friday 14 June

I went to Bristol University at about 3 and attended, incognito, the 'Free University' which has been set up. The first session was on the subject of Revolution, the second was on Black Power, and the third on Vietnam.

I realised all of a sudden that for three and a half or four years I have done absolutely no basic thinking about politics. I have just been a departmental Minister and this is the great gap – this is how parties get ossified and out of touch. It isn't that we are so busy we can't talk to our constituents. That isn't true. It is that we haven't found time to think. I thought they asked a lot of important questions and I enjoyed it. I wasn't recognised. I opened my shirt collar and put on my specs and took off my jacket and nobody took the slightest notice of me.

Saturday 15 June

Ken Tynan, the film critic, brought a colour film unit to do a TV interview with me on his contemporaries at Oxford. I used the opportunity to attack Oxbridge. I said I thought it was out of touch, that it represented a tiny minority of people and that education had not really prepared me for life at all. I'm afraid it may be the most critical contribution in the programme.

Caroline's friend, Shirley Fisher, came to dinner and Eric Mottram brought nine of his graduates in, mostly school teachers and mature students, who had been doing courses with him on Self and Community in America. One of them was an American journalist and a Black Power advocate. The others were anarchists, syndicalists, and Trotskyites. It was a stimulating evening. We talked until about 2.45 am. I think they found me very reactionary but then I suppose I am now. Stephen and Hilary stayed up until very late.

Monday 17 June

Our nineteenth wedding anniversary.

At the Strategic Exports meeting, I won a total victory on the COCOM restrictions which prevented us selling computers to the Rumanians and the Eastern Europeans, by which I mean that the companies were authorised to start negotiating for the supply of advanced equipment. In a week's time, we shall meet again and notify the Americans and our COCOM partners. We shall have a battle on our hands but we shan't be scooped by the French.

Caroline came in and we had our anniversary dinner at the House of Commons which was great fun. A very happy nineteen years of married life. Now that the children are all at school, Caroline is developing her own interests to the full. She's very busy at the moment, working on her book on comprehensive education in Britain (with Brian Simon of Leicester University) and preparing the computerised questionnaire to a thousand comprehensive schools: she is also a leading light on the Comprehensive Schools Committee. She has this extraordinary capacity to attract the loyalty and affection of the people who work with her. Quite apart from that, she advises me more directly and effectively than anyone else and I rely upon her enormously. It is a very happy partnership. Her new work, which is combined with her National Extension College teaching and a host of friendships and correspondents all over the world, gives her great satisfaction. I have got four nice children and I am a very lucky man.

Tuesday 18 June
At 8 I had breakfast with Alexandru Birladeanu, Deputy Prime Minister of Rumania and Chairman of their National Science Committee who is over here. He was staying at the Royal Garden Hotel with his delegation on their way to the United States. He was hoping to get most favoured nation treatment from the Americans on trade grounds but Rumanian support for the North Vietnamese had made things difficult.

He told me that he wanted to be frank with me and that he would be having talks with IBM in America about the possibility that they might supply Rumania's needs. He would prefer to deal with ICL because he thought they were cheaper but he had to look for the best equipment he could find. I suggested that he talk to RCA when he was in New York, because the computer technology that ICL would be using was based on RCA's licences and they might well be interested in breaking into Eastern Europe through ICL. He took this on board.

After we had dealt with our business, we talked for a while about the student disturbances. He said his daughter was a student, that the students had no clear policy, they were just negative, and when they got married and had children and responsibilities their attitudes would alter. He told me that in Yugoslavia the students are marching with placards saying, 'Down with the Communist Bourgeoisie', about which we laughed.

Wednesday 19 June
I had a message that Harold wanted to see me and I went across at about 7.45 pm and stayed for an hour. He had Fulton with him. He was tremendously keen to get the Cabinet to agree tomorrow that we would accept, in principle, the three major recommendations of the Fulton Report[5] and he wanted to be sure I was on the right side. Well, this is damned silly because I had made more references to Fulton in every

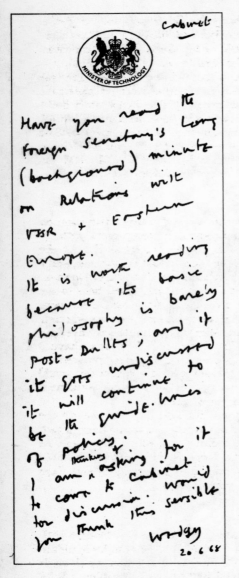

MINISTER OF TECHNOLOGY

Cabinet

Have you read the Foreign Secretary's long (background) minute on Relations with USSR + Eastern Europe.

It is worth reading because its basic philosophy is barely post-Dulles; and if it gets undiscussed it will continue to be the guide-lines of policy.

I am thinking of asking for it to come to Cabinet for discussion. Would you think this sensible

Wedgy
20.6.68

LORD
PRES

PURE COLD
WAR

Note from TB to Richard Crossman in Cabinet, 20 June 1968 and Crossman's reply.

speech since the Election than anybody else. But he said that the 'Junta' led by Roy and Denis and others had been opposed to it and that there would be a big battle and this would be like the African arms deal all over again, and so on. He really has such a conspiratorial mind.

Tom Bradley [Labour MP for Leicester North East] came up to me after the NEC publicity cocktail party and said that I should take on the general secretaryship. I said I would certainly give up my salary and I would give up my Department, though with some reluctance, but if I were cut off from papers by not being a member of Cabinet, it would be impossible and I would not be prepared to accept that. I think that got through so that I am not pleading to be given the job. If I am approached, it has got to be on the right conditions.

Thursday 20 June

I went to Cabinet this morning where we had a futile discussion on Lords reform. Then we went on to the legislative programme with the usual ridiculous bidding as to who should get what Bill in the programme. Ted Short said the whole thing should be planned, and I said it was time we looked again at legislation and it was absurd to go on with first and second and third readings when this dated back to the times when there were no printed Bills. We ought to have a lot more Enabling Bills[6] and Omnibus Law Reform Bills and this would really revolutionise procedure. Then I said, 'Why do we have to have five days on the Queen's Speech?' to which Willy Ross added, 'Why do we have to have the Queen?' and I really felt we were making some progress.

After that we got on to Fulton. Harold opened and said this would take a lot of consideration; that he thought the Government would need to respond quite quickly and he favoured this.

Then Roy, who tended to agree with him, pointed out all the difficulties. It would mean more civil servants, which would be criticised. It would mean extra public expenditure for which there was no accommodation. It would upset the Treasury. He thought we should respond cautiously, perhaps move slowly into it towards the end of the year. This was really his way of trying to finish it.

Friday 21 June

To Bristol, and a Party meeting. Afterwards, I rang Ray Dobson [MP for Bristol North East]. He was just leaving his house with his friends to go to a dance at the Long Ashton Country Club so I went up there. It was the first time in donkey's years I had been to an ordinary RAF officers' mess-type dance. I had a drink with Ray, and then I went back to the hotel at about 3 am and decided to return to London. As I was looking up the trains, the singer Adam Faith, came in and I took his order for breakfast before he realised I wasn't working for the hotel. He was passionately anti the House of Lords, which was interesting.

Saturday 22 June

Really very tired this morning. Went out and did a bit of shopping, then took Melissa and Kate Arnold-Forster to see *A Man For All Seasons* with Paul Scofield. An absolutely brilliant film about the execution of Sir Thomas More.

Tuesday 25 June

To Cabinet, and at the very beginning Harold raised the question of the leaks on the Lords reform which could only have come from two Ministers and which constituted a definite attempt to do damage to him. He said this was not good enough and if anyone were to take over and occupy his chair, they would very soon find themselves with the same difficulties. I thought it was really a rather unwise thing to have said because it looked as if he was badly rattled.

We spent a long time on the Fulton Report and it was agreed that it should be published.

I was wanted by Harold at 12.45 and he raised with me my speech in Llandudno and a follow-up article in *Tribune*. He said they had led to complaints that it was an attack on the Government. I said it certainly wasn't and that I must be free to think aloud. In the end he just yielded completely. The truth is, if you do stand up to Harold, he does capitulate.

He also raised the BBC television broadcast I am due to do tomorrow night in Bristol on the students' revolt. He said I shouldn't do it because it was below my ministerial level. He said, 'You're a Cabinet Minister, not a Member for Bristol.' I said, 'Yes, but I am a member of the NEC,' and I added that the trouble with the Party was that we were decapitated, we weren't articulating the anxieties of ordinary people, and so on.

After that I told him that I wanted to do the Balfour Lecture in Israel, and he gave way on that immediately so it was well worthwhile seeing him.

Wednesday 26 June

I went to the National Executive this morning and the main business was the question of the general secretaryship. Thirty-six people had applied, including about three MPs who had indicated their readiness to give up their seats. It was agreed that none of them was suitable. After a lot of hoo-ing and haw-ing, it became perfectly clear that they didn't intend having anybody who was in Parliament and the successful candidate would have to resign his seat. So that was the end of that as far as I was concerned.

Rushed to the station and caught the 7.45 with Norman St John Stevas [Tory MP for Chelmsford] and we went down to Bristol together to do the BBC television student revolt broadcast. The BBC had laid it on very badly; the whole thing was made into an aggressive gathering and they had asked a lot of silly people on to the panel.

The students attacked me because I was the representative of the Labour Government and a Minister and all the rest. They asked me about Biafra and a lot of things about which I know absolutely nothing. I did the best I could but I monopolised the programme in a way because they were going for me over unemployment and education. I was rather on their side over this. They were quite a nice crowd and I said, 'Let's have a sit-in one night, starting at about 10 and going on until about 3.' They agreed to fix this up in the autumn.

Thursday 27 June
This evening Caroline and I went to the Royal Society for their 'Conversazione' at Carlton House Terrace, their beautiful new premises in the old German Embassy. Pat Blackett showed us the pictures. Then we talked to another Fellow, Professor Av Mitchison, and I asked him whether molecular biology had anything to offer political scientists. He said this reminded him of Hobbes' and other reactionary views. This, of course, explains why the Communists in Rumania were so opposed to it. They thought it was a very retrogressive idea because it suggests that free will doesn't exist and also that a hierarchical structure would be necessary. Indeed Av told me that the Russians had been very anti-DNA at one stage (the theory worked out at Cavendish), because they thought the idea that one cell could dominate others was basically reactionary.

After that we went to the Royal Academy at Burlington House where Jeremy Thorpe and Caroline Alpass, his new wife, were giving a huge party to celebrate their wedding. Spoke to Christopher Mayhew and Cicely. Chris was saying how ill-behaved and ill-mannered all the students in revolt were and how Tariq Ali was living on his father's money. Of course, Chris himself, who was a socialist years ago, if that's not too unkind, lived on his father's money. Chris is very reactionary. There is really no difference between him and a Tory; but Chris simply dislikes the Tories for public school type reasons.

Sunday 30 June
It was a lovely day, hot and sunny, and Caroline worked upstairs. She has had a tremendous success with her questionnaire on the comprehensive schools, about 50 per cent replies within a week, which is

almost unheard of. I worked on my boxes, on my constituency correspondence and paid my bills.

Ray Gunter has resigned and Harold rang up to say he wanted to move Roy Mason to the Ministry of Power because he is a miner and the Ministry of Power is the front-line Department for the conflict between nuclear fuel and the mining industry. He wanted John Stonehouse to go to the Post Office because he felt it was time he had a Department of his own and wanted to send Bill Rodgers to me. I said I thought that wouldn't be a good idea. Bill Rodgers dislikes me very much and I didn't think it would work. In the end I got Curly Mallalieu, which was probably as good an outcome as I could expect.

Peter Shore and Wayland Young* came over to have a drink in the garden on their way to dinner at Wayland's house. Wayland said he thought that the next big disarmament struggle would be against biological and chemical warfare and the Party ought to be quite clear on that.

Peter stayed afterwards and told me that the economic situation was very serious indeed and the possibility of another collapse couldn't be ruled out between now and the end of the year, possibly even this month. It was this that was putting all the pressure on Roy Jenkins and explains why we have got to look at public expenditure with a view to cutting down again.

If that does go wrong, we shall either have import controls or let the pound float. Peter is quite right in what he said years ago, that a bankrupt society has got enormous power vis-à-vis the world community because the world doesn't want to see that country collapse.

Monday 1 July

I went to the House of Lords for the first meeting of the new working group on House of Lords reform. The White Paper which had been prepared really was setting out all the advantages of the House of Lords, saying how a second chamber preserved individual freedom, and containing the most unacceptable rubbish. I said that I was in favour of cutting the powers of the Lords still more sharply. I advocated the appointment of people to the House of Lords as Privy Councillors and members having salaries on a daily consultancy basis rather than annually. The Prime Minister could give a man a job for life at a salary for life and the effect of this enormous patronage, before he was appointed a Peer, would be quite undesirable. Of course, once in the Lords he would be completely free, but it's the anticipation of patronage that is the problem.

---

* Lord Kennet, Parliamentary Secretary at the Ministry of Housing and Local Government, 1966–70.

Dick Crossman is absolutely committed to the scheme, and naturally Frank Beswick, Eddie Shackleton and the Lord Chancellor opposed me, as did Michael Stewart. But I stuck to my guns and it was agreed that we should go back to Cabinet and ask them whether they wanted this to go ahead or whether they were in favour of a more radical scheme. The boys had been completely won over by the Tory half-promise to support it. They believe that even though the talks have broken down, the Tories still would support a scheme of this kind. But I am not sure they would.

Tuesday 2 July

To the House for the Strategic Exports Committee with Tony Crosland in the chair. There were Curly Mallalieu, Wilfred Brown from the Board of Trade, Goronwy Roberts representing the Foreign Office and John Morris, Minister of Defence for Equipment. We more or less carried the day on making an approach to the Americans about computers, although the Foreign Office were against this because they thought we would be considered unreliable by the US Government. The Defence people were doubtful because we have got some secret links with the Americans in the exchange of Intelligence and the supply of enriched uranium, and know-how for the Polaris submarines. We are much more closely tied up to the Americans than anyone has ever made public. But subject to the reservation of the Foreign Secretary, it was agreed that a high-level approach should be made to the Americans and it was left to the Foreign Secretary to decide whether he wanted to reserve his position and take it to the Overseas Policy and Defence Committee.

After that I had to go to the Banqueting Hall to host the Machine Tools Trade Association Reception and I found everyone was in black tie and nobody had told me. Afterwards, the Brigade of Guards band came and marched up and down. This was just laid on for foreign tourists and all of a sudden one could see that great ceremonial and the things that represented the Empire were now just gimmicks designed to sell goods abroad.

There's a blazing row about Ray Gunter's resignation broadcast last night in which he indicated that Harold Wilson should go, although he put it in a very phoney way. He said he was going back to the people 'from whence he came' and broadened his attack to include the intellectuals in the Party. But it hasn't done him a lot of good, and it has annoyed the 'Junta', rather weakening their position and hence strengthening Harold's.

Wednesday 3 July

Had dinner with Jim Callaghan tonight. Jim is a nice chap but he is bitterly hostile to Harold. This, I think, arises in part from Harold's suspicions of the plot of two years ago, the plot that never existed.

I learned that Ray Gunter had really done a great deal of damage to the cause of the Right and has written himself off. Nobody likes Ray Gunter; he was always referred to as the ticket collector by the Trade Union Group which he never attended, and apparently he didn't stand for the Executive last year because his union [Transport Salaried Staffs Association] simply wouldn't renominate him. But he has always been popular with the industrial correspondents and leaked what was happening. That's how he got his reputation.

Friday 12 July
Tommy Balogh came to lunch. He is really miserable even though he has got a peerage and Dick Crossman has taken him on as his general adviser.

I dashed home and went to Fox Primary School for the open day. I saw Melissa's and Joshua's work. They are so happy in their school.

Tuesday 16 July
Sir Arnold Hall came to see me at my request to discuss Airbus. He says he is putting £3–£4 million at risk in terms of the capital equipment for the work he is doing and is prepared to put another £5 million in. But he wants us to cover £30 million education costs for the aircraft and I am not prepared to do that, while he is not prepared to reduce his profits in order to allow us to reduce our levy if it is necessary to sell the aircraft. That more or less kills Airbus.

In the evening Caroline and I went to dinner at Number 10, where Kenneth Kaunda, President of Zambia, was guest of honour. He remembered that we had met in Delhi in 1961 for the conference on Goa organised by the Indian Council for Africa.

Harold made a good little speech welcoming him there. Then Kenneth got up and said he had been very critical of Harold but it hadn't been personal. He kept punctuating the speech with 'Harold this' and 'Harold that' in a very intimate and friendly way. But the Africans are extremely critical of us as they think we have sold out on South Africa. Kenneth has so many friends within the Labour Party, he must sense the goodwill there is.

I sat next to a member of the Zambian delegation and he said that the Zambian analysis was that South Africa would maintain itself for another twenty-five years. He thought that when the day of reckoning came and the guerrillas really became active with Chinese and Russian support, then the Americans and the British would support South Africa. I must admit this seemed to me a perfectly tenable analysis. It is a terrible thought but in fact what will happen in South Africa is that it will be a nationalist rising which the Communists will support; and in pursuit of our own interests, our investments, and so on, we shall simply go to the help of the regime. It is no more attractive than the South Korean regime, for example, or the South Vietnam regime, but it gives one an idea of what a tremendous division there is going to be in the world when this really does blow up.

Caroline and I talked to a lot of people afterwards, including Dora Bryan, and I had a chat to Marcia. It was a very friendly evening.

Thursday 18 July
Solly Zuckerman called in to see me; his main complaint at the moment is against Denis Healey, whom he hates because Denis is just obstructing disarmament and the attack on both chemical and biological warfare which Solly is very keen on.

I went over to Number 10 for a meeting with Kaunda. He gave his analysis and it was rather like what I had heard on Tuesday night. He said he thought there would be a great conflagration in South Africa, that the freedom fighters were trained in Eastern Europe and ideological cadres were being built up, which he didn't believe would help the freedom fighters. He had no resources, it wasn't that he was not sympathetic to the freedom fighters, Zambia was geographically involved and was subject to attacks from Portugal and also from Southern Rhodesia.

Cabinet followed immediately afterwards. We discussed the question of Lords reform and it was agreed that the compromise plan which had been arrived at with the Tories should be brought forward as our unilateral plan in the autumn. I said I didn't like it very much but I was in a minority of one.

The Public Schools Commission Report was before us. Caroline had done a great deal of work on this and given me a big brief but Harold didn't want to discuss it. It was agreed that it would be published without any Government comment. It was a terrible report suggesting that 50 per cent of public schools should be opened to ordinary boys, but that would in fact limit intake to those of reasonably high ability – a ghastly document.

Went back to a huge Private Office party to celebrate a variety of things, William Knighton's promotion, John Stonehouse's Privy Councillorship, Edmund Dell's promotion to Minister of State, the Industrial Expansion Bill and the computer merger and anything else we could think of.

Saturday 20 July
Hilary and I arrived at Durham at 5.30 for the Miners' Gala. We went to the hotel and I worked on my speech for a bit, then we went on the balcony and saw the bands come by. It was pouring with rain as it had been in the past and it was a gloomy sight.

George was there showing off and waving to the crowds but he was, at any rate, courteous to Hilary, which was something I didn't expect. Harold and Mary were there, and Barbara Castle and Dick Marsh. We were both extremely tired after our short night on the sleeper. It was still pelting with rain and there was a much bigger crowd watching the first platform than there was ours, about thirty people, I should think, with umbrellas. I spoke for ten minutes.

We walked back and, just before lunch, I saw the Czech Ambassador who had come up for the Gala. He wasn't particularly worried about the situation in Czechoslovakia. He was talking animatedly to Vassev who had come up too. The Yugoslav Ambassador similarly thought that nothing much would happen, which was a comfort.

Then we stood on the balcony again and caught the autograph books and signed them and threw them back. Hilary adored that.

Tuesday 23 July

I had a talk to Frank Allaun at the House of Commons. He told me there had been a most terrible row at the Drafting Committee for the general secretaryship. It was agreed at the very beginning that we would advertise, and of course none of the people who applied were accepted. So after that, a Drafting Committee was set up: Harold Wilson, Jim Callaghan, Jennie Lee, Eirene White, Frank Allaun, Joe Gormley, Harry Nicholas, George Brown and one other. At the first meeting, attended by everyone except George, they agreed that they would recommend a single name unanimously to the Executive. First they would approach Alf Allen of USDAW, and if he refused, Tony Greenwood would be approached. Alf Allen did refuse, so Tony Greenwood was told that it was the unanimous wish of the committee that he should go forward.

But there was a meeting yesterday at which George and Jim broke away from the original proposal and put forward Harry Nicholas, who agreed to let his name go forward and then left the meeting. There followed a tremendous row. Frank told me that three or four members of the committee got up and stamped out in the middle, and it was ghastly. In the end, Jennie, Eirene, Harold and Frank voted for Tony Greenwood. Jim and George were against, and Harry Nicholas didn't vote, having left the room when he was being discussed.

I was told by Frank that all this would come up tomorrow.

Wednesday 24 July

To the Executive at 10. Jennie Lee reported what had happened and said she greatly regretted the leaks which had occurred. Then Tony Greenwood left the room.

After that, George moved that Harry Nicholas be selected as General

Secretary. He said the age problem wasn't too difficult, Harry having retired from the TGWU, and in fact there was something to be said for having a short-term General Secretary who came to reorganise the Secretaryship without being responsible for carrying on.

Tom Driberg said there was no ideological difference between the two. He was rather in favour of Tony Greenwood. Joe Gormley thought it was simply filthy to introduce a new candidate at a late stage. He was for Tony Greenwood. In Frank Allaun's view, the image of the Party required a younger man, ie Tony Greenwood, and Ian Mikardo, agreeing that age was a big factor, went for Greenwood.

Harold Wilson then gave a long speech mainly justifying himself and saying how he had stayed out of it all and denounced the manoeuvring that had been done by an enemy. He acquitted himself completely of any improper action and talked about the Tory press and said this was intended to impose a humiliation on him. Generally speaking, he gave a long and rather unsatisfactory account. But that is Harold: he sees everything personally.

Frank Chapple came out for Tony Greenwood, saying he didn't favour either of them but he thought it would be a smack in the eye for Harold if Tony Greenwood was defeated, a remark which George said was actionable; 'manoeuvring' could only refer to him, and so on.

Eventually there was a vote and it was fourteen to twelve in favour of Harry Nicholas.

Harold's face was like thunder, and Tony and Harry were brought in after they had been told the result. Tony made a very courteous speech and said that an extremely good man had been picked, and he wished him all the best. Harry said he had to leave as he had a meeting in Germany and if he stayed it would be very awkward; he didn't want to say anything to the press anyway. I think this will be the general Harry Nicholas attitude to the press.

We got through some more business, then we all went to Len Williams's farewell lunch at St Ermine's Hotel. There were Len and his wife whom I have always liked. I sat between Tom Bradley and Joan Lestor. Tom Bradley told me that if I had put my name forward I would certainly have beaten Harry Nicholas and Tony Greenwood, which I strongly doubt, but it was interesting that he thought that.

Jennie made a speech in which she said, 'Your Excellency Sir Leonard Williams', Len having been knighted yesterday and appointed Governor-General of Mauritius, 'How nice to see you here . . . the Queen has graciously appointed you . . .' and so on.

Then Len made a speech in which he said that he couldn't say anything controversial as he was now the Queen's Governor-General, but he wanted to wish those who were here success with the work they had undertaken. It was quite incredible that here was a guy whose heart had been in the Labour Party for years and he just absolutely chickened out at the end.

Then Harold made a speech and God, it was awful, but one thing was very funny. Harold went on about the Queen having picked him and how he had been made a Knight Grand Cross of St Michael and St George. George interrupted and said, 'St George is the only one who matters.' So Harold retorted, 'If you remember Gibbon, St Michael was an archangel and St George was a crook.' George took this very personally. But it provided just the sort of diversion we wanted.

Jennie said that we were giving Williams a cheque to buy anything he wanted, anything to remind him of the Labour Party, and I said 'knives', which was picked up and reported in the press later.

It was a pretty unpleasant lunch.

At the House of Commons there was a debate on Tam Dalyell who had released information given to him as a member of the Science and Technology Committee on the Porton Chemical Warfare Establishment. I went into the Lobby because I understood it was a three-line whip. But I just couldn't face voting with all those Tories against Tam so I saw the Chief Whip and said 'I can't,' and he said, 'Well, don't bother,' so I went into the lavatory and I didn't vote.

Thursday 25 July

This morning Prince Charles came to visit Mintech. I greeted him at the lift, then he came along to my room with Otto and William Knighton. I explained what Mintech was about and said we had lived in an Empire for a hundred years and our industry was too small scale and reminded him that imperialism at the time of Joe Chamberlain was the means by which this country earned its living.

I told him that I had kept newspapers from his grandfather's coronation, and explained how the Empire had been everything then. But this had all gone now and we were engaged in industrial restructuring, gearing our research more closely to the needs of industry and productivity services. My usual little talk.

He asked about relations with other Departments and I told him about the Ministry of Power and the Department of Education and Science.

Then we got on to Concorde and he asked, 'Are you responsible for that?'

'Yes, it is a bit of a nightmare,' I replied.

He said, 'Well, you couldn't cancel it now.' Then the photographers came in and took some pictures of us talking and I asked, 'What is your real interest?'

'Archaeology,' he replied.

So I said, 'It's very odd we never did any proper archaeological study otherwise we might have learned something about Roman technology.'

I took him through the Private Office and he shook hands with a few people. He is going to be here for a couple of days.

Tuesday 30 July
Economic Policy Committee [SEP] where we discussed the British Leyland bus factory in Cumberland. The amount of money required to get this factory there is absolutely astronomical. But we were faced with the position that if we didn't make an offer to Donald Stokes, West Cumberland would simply be written off as an area. So, against the resistance of Denis Healey and Roy Jenkins, it was agreed to offer Donald Stokes something like £2.5 million, whereas I think he really wants £4.8 million to do it.

Thursday 1 August
I went to the office early and Ieuan Maddock came in to report on his mission to Washington. I had sent him over there last week to inform the Americans of our desire to sell advanced computers to Rumania and the Soviet Union. The Rumanians and the Russians were in a tremendous hurry to get the matter cleared up. Apparently, the Americans were icy cold. The Defense Department and the CIA were represented at the meeting, as well as the Presidential Office on Science and Technology. They were simply horrified at the thought of our making available integrated circuit know-how to the Russians because, they said, this computer-backed defence planning was an area in which the Russians were very defective and it was crazy for us to supply American technology to the Russians.

Of course, they can stop it; that was why we went to ask them. It was a slightly shaking experience for the Americans, and I think it rather shook our people too. In fairness to Michael Stewart, he had warned us that this would cause a great deal of trouble and our Ambassador was very upset about it. The Defence Attaché in the Washington Embassy had written to the Chief of Defense Staff to warn him that the US Defense Department was very hostile to Eastern European technological agreements. This has become quite an issue with Denis Healey and Michael Stewart, opposed by Tony Crosland and myself, with Harold very sympathetic to us though aware of the defence considerations.

Anyway, we got a black eye from the Americans but this is the beginning of our establishment of independence. Now that we are no longer close allies of the Americans in the Vietnam War, they have been closing down on information to us over a prolonged period and I am not sure there is much of the special relationship left anyway. There's another consideration: within a few months, the Americans will be into

Eastern Europe themselves and this has helped to break down the psychological barrier to trade with the Russians.

I went over to Number 10 for an Overseas Policy and Defence meeting. Apparently the Foreign Office, without any authority from anybody, had told Vosper Thorneycroft that it was all right to sell warships to the Greek Government and they were going ahead. The contracts were due to be signed and the question was, should we agree.

Denis Healey was very strongly in favour – of course – so was Michael Stewart on the grounds that we must keep our NATO partners well armed. I didn't say anything and was torn between detesting the Greek Government and feeling that, if we did apply this strict political test to our arms expenditure, we should lose a lot of other civil contracts which would ultimately undermine our economy. Harold wavered about it. In the end we agreed that the Export Credit Guarantee Department should slow down the granting of the credits until after the Referendum in Greece and prospects of a slow return to constitutional government have become apparent, which at any rate postpones it beyond the Labour Party Conference. But there will be a hell of a row if it comes out, as it will.

Then Cabinet. Concorde came first. I presented the case for it and said I thought the right thing to do was to get the French to agree to criteria by which we would judge the project when it had flown and we had an opportunity to see whether it was going to succeed or not. There was a surprising amount of sympathy in Cabinet. It wasn't as difficult as I thought.

I did lose on the point that if the French were not prepared even to discuss criteria, we should cancel there and then. Legally, we would be in a very strong position if this did happen but it would mean we wouldn't have seen the aircraft fly. So I put in a reservation and at the end of the minute I got a special provision inserted that I dissented from that view and that meanwhile I had the right to try to make Concorde succeed. I really must be allowed to do this because I can't have a situation in which I am secretly trying to cancel and hence to wreck the project.

I said goodbye to William Knighton who had been with me for two years and was moving on to take over the Finance and General Purposes Branch of the office. He had been an excellent Private Secretary politically. He has a good analytical mind and is very cheerful and imperturbable and he runs the Whitehall machine efficiently. I am sorry to see him go.

Saturday 3 August
Absolutely exhausted this morning. Barry Smith came with some 'Top Secret UK Eyes Only Atomic' papers relating to the Kings Norton

inquiry and the Rothschild minority report on Aldermaston, which recommended against further development of our nuclear weapons programme. This raised a major political issue and I have asked for advice in my own office and for John Hill's. I am letting Denis Healey and Number 10 see it.

After lunch, I drove to Stansgate with the roof rack crammed with suitcases, the boot packed and the whole family in the car. The holiday had really begun and not a day too soon.

Wednesday 21 August

A day that will not be forgotten. It was Stephen's birthday. That was the first thought in our minds when we woke up and then we heard the news that the Russians and the Warsaw Pact countries had invaded Czechoslovakia. My spirits sank, because, although we had half expected this might happen in the summer we thought it had all been patched up: this really takes you right back to Hungary in 1956.

I phoned Lord Harding who had moved against English Electric today. He told me he was going to see Lord Nelson to put the proposal for a merger but if a merger wasn't agreed, then they would put in a take-over bid.

Later in the day I had a conversation with Nelson who is thoroughly upset.

The rest of the day was devoted to Stephen's birthday and, it being his seventeenth, he was able to drive on the highway. We went to Maldon together in the car, did some hill starts and then came back and had a lovely birthday party.

Cabinet has been called tomorrow on the Czechoslovakian situation.

Thursday 22 August

Up at 5.30 and to London for the Cabinet.

It was generally agreed that we didn't want to interfere with trade with the Soviet Union because, even in the height of the Berlin Air Lift or the Hungarian situation, we had still traded with the Russians. But there was a very strong feeling that ministerial visits and exchanges would have to be checked.

From my immediate point of view, of course, it has absolutely knocked every prospect of the computer deal completely out of the window because the Americans, who were bitterly opposed to my suggestion that we should supply computer technology to Russia and Rumania, will be adamant and Ministers opposed to it will have their hand greatly strengthened. So that is very disappointing. It also means my Russian visit is affected.

Dick Crossman thought we could do more, eg propaganda from the BBC. He is still the psychological warrior in moments of crisis.

Eddie Shackleton took a very strict defence view, saying that surely the important thing for stability in Europe was that each superpower should have its own sphere of influence and better that the Russians control Czechoslovakia than that there be any disturbance to the Western European status quo which might create a dangerous situation.

I did ask whether the hot line was being used and whether we had really taken into account the tremendous damage the Russians had done to the world Communist movement which is completely split on this, with the British, French and Italian Communist Parties, and the Chinese, denouncing it.

But it was an unsatisfactory position. We agreed that Parliament would be recalled on Monday. There wasn't much we could do but we felt we owed it to the Czechs to show that we did care.

Back to Stansgate.

Friday 23 August

Joan and Brian Simon arrived early this morning. Brian is Professor of Education at Leicester, the son of old Lord Simon of Wythenshawe, a former Liberal who became Labour. Brian is writing the book on comprehensive education with Caroline and is also a member of the Central Committee of the Communist Party. He had in fact just come back from a visit to Czechoslovakia in the course of the summer. They have many friends there and they were very upset indeed about what had happened.

Saturday 24 August

The Simons left at 6.30 this morning and they were due back tonight but phoned to say they couldn't return and we quite understood. I think he got deeply involved in the various meetings that happened, and we noticed that the statement the Communist Party issued was highly critical, so he apparently had won the day.

Sunday 25 August

Slightly better news from Czechoslovakia. The disappearance of Dubcek, First Secretary of the Party, has caused a great deal of anxiety but there are now rumours that he is in Moscow with General Svoboda, the President, and maybe something will emerge from it.

Monday 26 August

To the House of Commons for lunch and talked to one or two people. The Czech debate was, in a curious way, unsatisfactory. Universal condemnation by both sides didn't help much but that is all we could do.

Had dinner with Peter Shore at the Festival Hall and he told me that the economic prospects were grim. The National Economic Survey suggesting there would be a deficit of £600 million this year, when we had expected a surplus by the end of the year, was probably not far off beam. I imagine import controls will now have to be re-examined and that was certainly Peter's view.

Thursday 29 August
Stansgate. I think it has been the worst August for years.

Stephen goes around with a camera and takes lots of sunset movies and Mother goes in every night and tells the 'babies' [Melissa and Joshua] Bible stories. Melissa is busy writing another 'novel'. She is always doing that.

Tuesday 3 September
We spent the whole day clearing, washing and cleaning.

Finally left about 3 o'clock in two cars and Stephen drove into London with me beside him, and did terribly well considering we arrived in the thick of the rush-hour traffic. Melissa went off to stay with a friend and we got unpacked and heard that Stephen had got a C in Higher Maths and thus has ten O levels.

Thursday 5 September
To the office and I saw James Webb of NASA who told me that they were going to have a man on the moon by the end of next year or early 1970. He said NASA now had a tremendous lift-off capacity. They spent between $36 and $40 million a year, and altogether $1 billion on space in the last seven or eight years since they began development.

Then there was a combined meeting of the Committees on Strategic Exports and Commercial Policy, to discuss Eastern European trade and the position after the Czech crisis. Broadly speaking, we agreed not to interfere with trade or working parties on technology or any of the things that had been got underway recently, but that ministerial visits would be out. On the strategic side, we found ourselves in real difficulties because, together with the Board of Trade, with a great deal of effort we had managed to mount a campaign for restricting the operation of COCOM by reducing the number of items on the embargo list, and it is going to be almost impossible to hold that position. We agreed to try to get the whole review postponed until the atmosphere was better.

On the supply of equipment such as computers to Eastern Europe, it was reported that we had got a flea in the ear from Washington in the summer. Harold Lever, who had been over there, said it had almost cost him a very pleasant dinner with the Americans and so, although we have left our application to trade in computers with Eastern Europe on the table, we don't expect a favourable reply, and we are not going to press it. This is the price the Russians pay and I am afraid it is a price we will also pay in terms of orders.

Also, the Spey Engine which Rolls Royce were asked to supply to Rumania has fallen by the board as Rumania is now looked on not as an independent country which might usefully receive help from us but as a member of the Warsaw Pact – despite the fact that Ceausescu made a courageous speech attacking the invasion of Czechoslovakia. But my aims to encourage further trade with Russia and to break through this whole strategic nonsense, have come unstuck.

In the afternoon, I had a deputation from Arnold Weinstock, George Nelson and Toby Aldington [Chairman of GEC] to tell me that GEC and English Electric had decided to merge and they wanted my support. They had just come from the Board of Trade and I went over the ground with them very carefully. There are areas of natural fit between the two companies which will amount to £1,000 million turnover: about the same size as Philips and Siemens.

I found them agreeable and they promised that they would cooperate on discussions on redundancy. But the creation of these new mammoth private companies with Government support and encouragement is a very big political issue which has to be tackled.

Wednesday 11 September
Up at 6 and Ron Vaughan drove me to the Rocket Propulsion Establishment, a typical Ministry of Aviation place with a rural atmosphere and an impression that all the guys had gone native, were members of the Rotary Club, had the farmers in for dinner and played a lot of golf and lived in nice country houses. There was none of the industrial pressure you get elsewhere; no doubt they have high technical standards but I am slightly confirmed in my view that research ought to be connected to industry rather than done by Government.

Friday 13 September
In the afternoon, Fred Mulley came along absolutely wild with rage at the delay he said we had been imposing on the ratification of the Non-Proliferation Treaty.

This is a highly difficult technical issue, and the people in my Department are, on the whole, hostile to the NPT and always have been. Michael Michaels, head of the Atomic Energy Division, has not been completely frank in telling me what is going on. But his argument is that unless we get the safeguards – which currently ensure that non-nuclear powers cannot divert material from civil nuclear programmes to nuclear weapons – amended to meet the anxieties of the near-nuclear powers, the whole Treaty will go wrong. But the Foreign Office, and particularly Fred Mulley, feel that this is just a way of postponing the ratification. He told me if I didn't clear this up, he would report to Michael Stewart, who would get the Prime Minister on to me.

Michael Michaels probably knows more about nuclear safeguards than anyone; he has been working on them for twelve years, and is absolutely convinced that the line we are taking is doing us a lot of damage with our European partners. It will affect our atomic product exports, and could lead to a delay, or indeed the collapse, of the NPT.

He is quite right to put these points to me but what he is not right to do is to act entirely off his own bat and go ahead without consulting me, as he has done.

I minuted Michael Stewart anyway, telling him that officials had recommended a delay in ratification for the reasons I had given and also that they were of the opinion that, although we shouldn't initiate them ourselves, if proposals came for amending the safeguards, we should play a creative part.

Monday 16 September
Into the office early and we considered the Chancellor's latest proposals on Shorts. In effect he will find £2 million for the current year, try to get the remaining £2 million from the Northern Ireland Government but will not allow capital reconstruction. And he wants the ban on complete aircraft imposed on Shorts. In the end, this was the only thing we could do because the Treasury simply won't fork out money for Shorts. There is also an awful lot of feeling against Northern Ireland and the amount of public money we are providing for Northern Ireland industry compared with our own in this country.

Tuesday 17 September
This morning I went by helicopter to the Farnborough Air Show. It was cold and wet and I had to squish around on the runways with Green, the President of the Society of British Aircraft Constructors.

Because the weather was bad a large number of manufacturers had not made arrangements to greet visitors. Not that it mattered, a Minister not being greeted, but I might have been a customer and there were some aircraft totally locked up while others had fitters inside who didn't know the price of the aircraft or what it did, or anything. This all reflected not only on the sales ability of the firm in question but also on the total incapacity of the firm to convey to the people attending the air show the importance of selling aircraft. Otherwise it was pretty good, and I was impressed by Beagle, mainly because its Chairman, Peter Masefield, was resolutely standing under an umbrella selling his aircraft.

At lunch I sat next but one to General Lemnitzer, the Supreme Commander of SHAPE, [Supreme Headquarters Allied Powers in

Europe]. He told me an interesting and amusing story, although he didn't realise it. I had asked him about the Russian invasion of Czechoslovakia and he had said what an incredibly competent military operation it had been, how the Russians had maintained signal security and the Americans had known nothing about it in advance. Indeed, I learned later that Lemnitzer himself had been to Salonika the night before the invasion and clearly wouldn't have gone if he had had any forewarning. But he did tell me how the Russians had captured Prague with an airborne division without any bloodshed. Apparently at about midnight, an Aeroflot airliner flying over Prague radioed through to the control tower saying it had a malfunctioning engine and asked if it could land.

The Czechs helped them in and on the plane were seventy security police and air traffic controllers who knew the layout of Prague airport absolutely perfectly. They simply overpowered the Czech air traffic controllers and took control with hardly any casualties and allowed the airborne division to land by dawn.

I was very impressed by his account and asked how he got hold of this story. He said Shirley Temple Black had told him. 'She is a very capable woman,' he said, which also gave away his political views as she is an extreme right-wing McCarthyite Republican. It fascinated and amused me that a five-star general, and the Pentagon and the White House, should have got the only information of any value about the invasion from a film star, a former child actress. But he didn't see the joke.

Wednesday 18 September

I flew to Aberdeen, arriving there at about 1, and went to the Torrey Fish Station, an impressive little place fighting an uphill battle against the conservatism of the fishing industry. While I was there I heard a nice story about fish gutting machines, in which the Germans have a complete monopoly with all the patents, and a little Shetland farmer called Mr Smith who invented a circular saw with brushes and water jets which avoided all these patents and did the job much more cheaply. It is a tribute really to the inventive genius of the individual and the farsightedness of the Torrey people, who realised its significance.

Got home and went to the Society of British Aircraft Constructors dinner where Prince Bernhard of the Netherlands was the guest speaker. He made a *Daily Express*-type speech saying that the industry was farsighted and all Governments were myopic in respect of space. It went down like a bomb of course. I find it offensive meeting these big industrialists who live on Government work, who are financed by Government, and who are violently, bitterly anti-Government from beginning to end.

Tuesday 24 September

All day from 11 to 7 on talks with Jean Chamant, French Minister of Transport, on Concorde, both of us backed by a huge delegation. We sat down after a cup of coffee and began the discussions, exchanging words about our confidence in the project and all that. Then I came forward and said we really needed criteria to judge how it should work. Chamant produced a paper which said that there would be criteria and that if there were not a lot of airline orders by the end of 1969 the whole thing would have to be called off.

We heard that the French were a little afraid in case their Treasury discovered that we were even contemplating going up to a figure as high as £560 million. I also learned that Concorde had some enemies – including, I think, Couve de Murville, now Prime Minister, who was extremely hostile to it.

I thought we were almost there but for two points of difference. One was that the French didn't want the criteria to be activated until the end of 1969; and second, although they were ready to *recommend* to their Government that the other side be discharged from the obligation to continue, there was no *commitment* that this action would be accepted by the French Government or by our Government and on this I called in the Attorney who came over and joined us for a moment. It was really quite a successful and rather an enjoyable negotiation.

Friday 27 September

Blackpool, and at the NEC all morning for the pre-Conference sessions. We got on to the mid-term manifesto and this was agreed. George Brown, Frank Chapple, Jim Callaghan and I were allocated to have a look at it again in the course of the evening.

This afternoon Nora Beloff of the *Observer* came in. She was miserable because Dick Crossman wasn't there to brief her so I told her what the Conference would be like, namely we would be massacred on prices and incomes on Monday but that it would be a good Conference. So she was all set to write a crisis piece.

At 6 I went to Jim Callaghan's room for the redrafting of the manifesto and we had a huge argument about whether the wealth tax should be included in it or not. Finally, very late, we read the final draft of the manifesto which really looks rather good. George has completely altered his view. Having been bitterly opposed to it all along, he is now quite keen on it.

Sunday 29 September

I did a *World at One* interview about the mid-term manifesto. There has been an awful lot of confusion about it. *The Times* had a leading article denouncing me for having proposed the wealth tax.

NEC this afternoon and the problem arose of what attitude we should adopt towards the resolution from the Transport and General Workers' Union calling for the repeal of the prices and incomes legislation. It was a very tense discussion with a denunciation of the Government and Jim Callaghan wobbling and George Brown being on the side of the Government.

I brought forward another resolution saying that we had to recognise the fact that the Government was elected on a policy including prices and incomes approved by Conference. This was one of the central planks in the programme which appeared to many people to strike at the basis of free collective bargaining and aroused deep and widespread objections at each and every level of the Labour and Trade Union Movements. The Labour Government itself was committed to the policy, believing it to be essential, and the outright repudiation by Conference of the policy might weaken the Government and replace it with a Tory one. The Labour Government was entitled to ask the Conference for sufficient time to allow its policy to be assessed in all its aspects and to be developed in the light of experience, with further discussions with the Government and leaders of both sides of industry. My resolution called upon the Executive to set up a joint working party to review existing policy, to seek a reconciliation between the new and more demanding requirements of economic planning in a socialist society and the fundamental rights of free trade unionism, and finally to report on the results of these discussions in a document to be presented to Conference as soon as possible so that the policy could be debated before the next Election manifesto.

I checked this with Barbara Castle in the morning and she was quite happy about it and I very nearly got it accepted but in the end the NEC resolution asking Conference to reject the TGWU motion was carried by one vote and so that settled it.

Frank Allaun suggested that the Czech invasion should be denounced, but that the points in various resolutions dealing with the role of NATO should be dealt with separately.

Monday 30 September
Caroline went off to visit two schools in Preston and I went to the opening of the Conference. Jennie Lee made a good speech as Chairman and was interrupted by a miners' demonstration which she applauded herself and then said, 'I am sure that being miners you wouldn't want to interfere with the right of us to speak to each other. You have made your point and now will you let us continue.' They put down their banners and went away. It was very moving.

We had huge debates on economic policy with Roy and Barbara speaking. Roy was very tough, 'laying it on the line' as the *Evening*

Standard said. Barbara, not at her very best, was defeated five to one.

In the evening Caroline and I went to the BBC party and I raised with Oliver Whitley [Chief Assistant to the Director-General] and Frank Gillard [Director of Sound] and others my general feeling about the BBC's trivialising of important issues. Harold won't broadcast with them and they think this feud is continuing.

Tuesday 1 October
Harold Wilson made a successful speech, pedestrian in character, but full of achievements, having begun with an opening tilt at the BBC. They cheered him wildly and he said that this was what the BBC would no doubt call a hostile reception – the Conference laughed but the BBC were terribly upset.

Wednesday 2 October
George Brown introduced the mid-term manifesto in an unscripted speech that lasted fifty minutes and was very jolly. It was good: he took most of my points and I wound up and got quite a reasonable reception for a speech which had had to be greatly compressed.

Had dinner with Dick Marsh and Kenneth Harris of the *Observer*. Dick said he was thinking of giving up politics and going back into the Trade Union Movement. Kenneth Harris said, in his usual odious flattering way, that either Dick or I would be Prime Minister. Dick said it wouldn't be him and I said it wouldn't be me, so that left Kenneth Harris rather in the soup.

Thursday 3 October
Foreign affairs debate at Conference. Although the platform was defeated on some issues, Michael made a good speech.

Dinner with Elwyn Jones and Arthur Irvine [Labour MP for Liverpool Edge Hill] who is funny. Elwyn told a story about a judge who had the Counsel, Sir Norman Birkett, in court with him once. Norman Birkett was apparently very pompous and unpopular with the bench. It was a gambling case and Birkett began by saying, 'Gentlemen of the jury, this case concerns a gambling game known as roulette which, as you know, is played with cards.' The judge leaned forward, tapped his fingers on the bench and said, 'Gentlemen of the jury, I have wanted to say this for thirty years, "Balls, Sir Norman, balls." ' A splendid schoolboy lawyers' joke.

Monday 7 October
In the evening I went to a North Kensington Labour Party meeting, the first one held there, I think, since the '66 Election, and some Black Power people were there. They just laughed at the speaker before me. When I

got up they began shouting. So I said, 'Look, I don't want to make a speech. I make about three a week and I would much rather listen to you.' So they came forward and sat in the front, a Black Power man abused me and said I was a lord and the British working movement was bourgeois and so on, and it became interesting after that.

Tuesday 8 October
I went to Cabinet, having heard on the news this morning that a plan had been developed for Harold to go and visit Smith on the *Fearless* in Gibraltar. Everybody except Barbara said he should go. I made a little speech and said it would be taken as a sense of betrayal and it was important to know why. It was because the Labour Party had kidded itself that it had always given freedom to other countries, whereas it had always surrendered to the local power centre which in most cases had been native, but in this case was white. I said it was very important not to present this as a great success but as a defeat and we had to accept that it was.

Then I also raised the question of disassociating ourselves from the Vietnam War, because the rumours are that the Americans are going to stop the bombing in North Vietnam and I was afraid we would be the last Government in the world to come out against the war. It was agreed we would discuss this when the Foreign Secretary got back.

Wednesday 9 October
In the evening Caroline and I went to the French Embassy, a typical unbearable French Embassy affair. I do hate their parties; they are so full of snotty women and the international set. But I had a lovely talk to Pungam, the Rumanian Ambassador, and to John Stonehouse and to the Yugoslav Ambassador whom I like very much. He told me that my Llandudno speech had been discussed by the Yugoslav Cabinet and I told him I was going to make another one which would include a reference to the need for Marx to be studied in the Social Democratic Movement.

I found a letter awaiting for me from the University of Bradford, offering me an Honorary Doctorate of Technology, which is a great honour.

Monday 14 October
Had lunch with Klaus von Dohnanyi [the German Secretary of State for Economic Affairs] at Admiralty House. The security services had given me a secret note on what he had said, namely that he thought the Germans would assign leadership to us on the multi-role combat aircraft so long as we went in on Airbus. It shows the security people are always at work, even on our alleged allies.

Dohnanyi again in the afternoon and we went over the aircraft issue. We told him how experienced we were and we really couldn't give the whole thing up.

Wednesday 16 October
An Overseas Policy and Defence Committee meeting on European policy where Michael Stewart wanted to bring forward a new initiative through the Western European Union for political and defence collaboration and Denis Healey made the point that we mustn't exclude the Americans and thus precipitate their withdrawal from Europe.

Thursday 17 October
My speech on broadcasting policy to be made tomorrow came back from Transport House and I saw to it that it went round to Fred Peart, as Leader of the House, John Silkin, the Chief Whip, John Stonehouse, the Postmaster General, Gerald Kaufman at Number 10, and Charles Hill, Chairman of the BBC, with a little note.

Friday 18 October
To Bristol and Hanham for the meeting on the role of broadcasting. The local Party had got together a few more people than would otherwise have been there. The place was chock-a-block with journalists and television people. I had been on the phone during the day and discovered that Number 10 didn't want me to comment on it on any television or radio broadcasts afterwards. Harold is obviously rather angry.

This speech was bitterly attacked by the press and deeply offended the BBC who objected to the possibility of interference with their independence. The critique developed in this speech, the first of its kind, anticipated and precipitated subsequent debate about greater democratic control in mass communications.

'The mass media, and especially broadcasting, now play a large part in shaping our attitudes, our outlook, our values and indeed the whole nature of our society. Those engaged in active politics who speak or write about these matters are suspect on two grounds: first, because the complete independence of the mass media from Government control is an essential ingredient of our special brand of personal freedom; second, because of the notorious love-hate relationship between politicians and broadcasters which is so permanent and intense that a politician's criticisms are almost automatically dismissed as being motivated by Party feeling.

'To focus the argument more clearly, I want to talk about the role of the BBC as the prime national instrument in broadcasting. I am *not* proposing direct Government control of the mass media, to which I would be wholly opposed. Nor am I making, for the purpose of this argument, any complaint of political bias. Arguments about political balance are quite separate and ought to be conducted quite separately from any debate on the future of mass communications.

'Broadcasting should be used, to the full, to help individual men and women to live useful and full lives. That is to say that, in its broadest sense, communications should serve the people and not become their master. But if it is to do this, it has to make available the sort of information and programmes which are really relevant to human needs. These needs include the need to be entertained, the need to be informed and the need to be educated. The original BBC charter recognised this.

'Now, a new dimension has to be added to this basic requirement. This is the need for helping us to adjust to the enormous changes which are occurring in society, and which are far greater for this generation than for any generation that has ever gone before it. We therefore have to add a new criterion relating to the method. If the broadcasting organisations are to perform their task, they must allow us to meet our objectives by talking to each other. Availability of access to the mass media becomes an integral part of the operational requirement.

'Looking back over the history of the BBC, the general level of information, education and culture has risen sharply. It has also given pleasure to millions of people by bringing them entertainment, sporting events, drama and music. Criticisms must be set in the balance against these formidable achievements and a record of service to the public which is widely recognised and appreciated.

'However, in recent years, this objectivity has been replaced by a growing tendency to personalise news presentation. The news reader has almost become a commentator; the gap between news and comment has greatly narrowed. This tendency to personalisation, carrying with it editorial powers exercised by individual commentators, has even more serious implications for other types of programmes.

'The BBC retains, either on the staff or on contract, a whole host of commentators who, being quite free to comment, carry with them some inevitable suggestion of BBC authority. True, the BBC, through its Board of Governors, has no collective view on public matters and very rarely issues a statement of any kind. But listeners and viewers have come to expect from certain well-known broadcasters a particular line of thought which is peculiar to them, but which, through the power of the medium, inevitably shapes public thinking.

'Nobody wants to go back to the earlier tradition. Quite the reverse. What is wrong is that availability of access is still too restricted in that it is almost limited to a few hundred broadcasters, chosen by the BBC.

'First, in respect of the choice of subjects: Britain has thousands of problems which would merit the attention of the broadcasting authorities. Certain ones are regularly picked out for treatment. They include the most important, but do not by any means cover all those that are important. The choice is supposedly influenced by the interests of the mass audience and it is here that the influence of the programme ratings begins to be felt. It would be surprising if the sort of subjects that are guaranteed to get a large audience in the popular newspapers were not equally effective on the radio or TV. This is exactly what is happening.

'Second, in respect of the presentation of the subject. Here too, the influence of the ratings is very strong and so is the pressure of time. Important subjects are skimped, important discussions are telescoped and conflicts are artificially sharpened. The result is inevitably to make for triviality and superficiality, over-simplifying what is immensely complicated and sensationalising almost everything that is touched on.

'Third, by choice of people. Any BBC producer soon learns that a certain sort of person will give him just what he wants, in the time allowed, in colourful language and with an agreeable manner, so these people are used again and again. They may well not be the best qualified people in their field. They are not chosen because they are. They are chosen because they fit neatly into an editorial slot.

'If these criticisms are put to the BBC you will get a variety of answers. While professing a general sympathy with the desire to deal with matters more deeply, they point out that the public won't have any patience with longer expositions which they find boring.

'The BBC ultimately rests its case upon its own profound belief in its editorial duty. What began as a Reithian concept that was openly paternalistic, has broadened into a view that runs something like this: the BBC has a positive duty, acting for the public, to probe and challenge and question all the centres of power that are growing up in the modern society – political, industrial and social. Seen like this, the idea of balance has now become for them a balance between the BBC and the people they are investigating so that half of every argument belongs, as of right, to the BBC as it performs its painful, relentless but necessary duty to the British public.

'Under this banner, it has appointed itself investigator-in-chief into the alleged inefficiencies of British management, the alleged obstructionism of British trade unions and, of course, the wilful way of foreigners. When British interests are threatened, the Government no longer sends a gun-boat. The BBC sends a *Panorama* team with instructions to bring back the head of the offender, to be shown on the box.

'All this amounts to enormous accumulation of power. With the exception of Government itself, there is scarcely any other body in Britain enjoying as much power as the BBC. And since the Government, quite properly, keeps at arm's length from the BBC and makes no effort whatsoever to make it account for what it does, it stands in a position of almost unique and unchallenged influence.

'Of course, the Board of Governors are appointed to supervise the Corporation in the public interest. They are men and women of distinction and have a fine awareness of human values. But unlike the Governors of the ITA, they actually employ the people whom it is their duty to supervise, and they would not be human if they did not have a protective interest in their own employees which expresses itself in an understandable preference for issuing their directives in private, thus depriving the public of any knowledge of the operation of such public accountability as does exist.

'Virtually the entire output of the BBC is produced under editorial conditions. The subjects, handling and people are chosen by the staff to fit in programme slots which have been predetermined quarter by quarter. Occasionally the framework is adapted, as for example at Party conferences or major sporting events. But even there, the presentation is by and through the BBC.

'It is as if the only printed material available for us were newspapers. There is no publishing done by the BBC on radio or television. Nobody (except in party political or election broadcasts) is ever allowed to develop an argument in his own way, and at sufficient length, to confront the public with what would be the broadcasting equivalent of a book.

'We have lived with this publishing gap since the BBC was established, and we may be so used to it that many of us do not realise what we are missing. What we are missing is the opportunity to hear directly, from those who have something to say to us all, what it is they want to say to us.

'Perhaps, the most immediate example of this at this moment comes from the expected demonstrations by students and others in London and other major cities. We all know that if these demonstrations follow the pattern of some earlier ones they will get extensive television coverage on the day. If there are tussles, we shall see them in vivid pictures in the news bulletins, and they will trigger off a whole series of discussions among the usual panel of pundits who will talk absolutely predictably about their significance and the problems of law and order. But the one thing we shan't get, whether before, during or after, is any opportunity to hear, first-hand, at length and in peace, the views of those who are organising these demonstrations.

'If they were invited to speak, what they might say would be very unacceptable to millions of people and probably the overwhelming majority. In part they are protesting against the very denial to them and others of any real access for their views on the mass media. All they can be certain of is that their demonstrations will be fully covered in the mass media and undoubtedly that knowledge itself stimulates the demonstrations. If law and order were ever to break down, in part or in whole, in Britain, the policy of restricted access and unrestricted coverage would have to bear a very considerable part of the responsibility.

'But of course, it is not only the demonstrators who ought to be heard. According to the motor manufacturers, this country has lost £48 million of exports this year due to industrial disputes. There have been countless snippets about this on news bulletins and comments in current affairs programmes. But to the best of my knowledge, neither the motor manufacturers nor the trade unions have been offered even an hour apiece to tell the public how they see it, or even to address their own management or members.

'Almost all we see of trade union or business leaders are hurried little street interviews when they are pinned against a wall by a battery of accusing microphones, wielded by interrogators who have just come from covering an air crash and are on their way to a hospital where quins have been born. Is it any wonder that so few of us really understand the complexity of some current problems in industrial relations which are really going to condition our prospects of economic success or failure?

'It is here that the BBC's greatest weakness in the handling of public affairs becomes most apparent. It is not a question of balance between Labour and Conservative that matters. It is the BBC's failure to provide the means by which the true complexity of affairs can be explained, without which the gap between political leaders and people will inevitably tend to widen and widen. If politics are dealt with superficially and politicians are presented in a context designed to extract the maximum entertainment value from them, it is not surprising that the public should learn from the BBC a contempt for all those in public life.

'I am certainly not arguing that it is the duty of the BBC to put on politicians in a way that makes them appear attractive or to create a favourable impression. Indeed, it may well be that if the full depth of thinking that lies behind certain political arguments was fully deployed on the air, it would stimulate far more fundamental criticisms. What is wrong now is that most politicians are being criticised for the wrong reasons.

'But it would be a great mistake to think that the need for a publishing function is confined to public affairs and politics. There are thousands of organisations – from the British Medical Association through to the engineering institutions, or the consumer or women's organisations – who have a great deal to say and are denied access. If broadcasting is not reorganised to enable us to hear, in our own time, what those who are working on contemporary problems want to tell us, then the task of adapting ourselves will become almost impossible.

'All this involves a complete redefinition of the meaning of "topicality". The common definition of topicality is that which is happening today. But as the timescale of development lengthens, the meaning of topicality must change too. What is actually topical today is what is being decided today, even though the consequences of that decision may not be apparent for five or ten years.

'The BBC has assumed part of the role of Parliament. It is the current talking shop, the national town meeting of the air, the village council. But access to it is strictly limited. Admission is by ticket only. It is just not enough. We have got to find a better way and give access to far more people than now are allowed to broadcast.

'The trouble is that we have extended the overwhelming technical case for having a monolithic broadcasting organisation into a case for unifying programme output control under a single Board of Governors. Broadcasting is really too important to be left to the broadcasters, and somehow we must find some new way of using radio and television to allow us to talk to each other.

'We've got to fight all over again the same battles that were fought centuries ago to get rid of the licence to print and the same battles to establish representative broadcasting in place of the benevolent paternalism by the constitutional monarchs who reside in the palatial Broadcasting House.

'It is now a prime national task to find some way of doing this. It must be based on, and built around, the firm framework of public service control and operation, and not dismembered and handed over to the commercial forces which already control every other one of the mass media except the BBC. For in the BBC we have an instrument of responsible communication which is quite capable of being re-fashioned to meet our needs in the Seventies and Eighties as it did so brilliantly in the Twenties, Thirties, and Forties.'

Monday 21 October
There is a major row raging over my BBC speech. *The Times* led this morning with a heading saying that Gunter asked the Prime Minister to repudiate me so I am not out of the wood yet, but with all the other papers 'up against' me, I must expect a certain amount of trouble.

By and large, I am getting a very friendly reception from the Party, although some Labour Members have tabled a motion of support for the independence of the BBC: but then I don't disagree with that myself.

Crossman is furious because I apparently scooped his Granada lecture which he has been working on and was delivering tonight. I didn't watch it but I went and bought the papers at the West London

Air Terminal before midnight and they were full of what he had said. It was, in effect, quite a different speech from mine, arguing that politics should be treated more seriously on television, and it was not at all an argument for greater access.

Tuesday 22 October
To the first of the little dinners that the ageing Left are giving. This time it was in Barbara Castle's flat with Judith Hart, Tommy Balogh, Gerald Gardiner and Dick Crossman. We had a tremendous row. Dick attacked me for having scooped his speech. That is the only way he regards it – purely personally – and I said I had gathered he had been angry when I had read about it in the papers. He said, 'When I am angry I tell everyone.' I didn't make much of it except to say that I hadn't thought an awful lot about his speech; but relations with Dick are going to be very difficult for some time. Frankly, I don't give a damn.

Afterwards Caroline and I went to the American Ambassador's party. I don't know why he was giving it, but the US administration had come to an end and he probably thinks his time as Ambassador is limited. Robin Day was there and he too was very angry about my speech although his complaints against the BBC were rather similar to my own.

Wednesday 23 October
I went to the office and I had a brief word with Derek Moon. Poor Derek is having a terrible time over the broadcast speech. I showed him the memorandum that Harold had put out to all Ministers. It said that Ministers must remember that they are Ministers and they can't be schizophrenic; philosophic innovators had better be careful; and 'gurus should be confined to the Wolverhampton circuit'. Really a most insulting document. Harold can't resist being funny and he must have enjoyed dictating it. But as it was sent to all Ministers, it is almost bound to get out to the press and if it does, it will do him a hell of a lot of harm because Judith Hart*, who is supposed to be responsible for greater public participation in Government, will find that her job is the 'Minister for Vetting Other Ministers' Speeches'. Of course, most people simply won't put up with it.

David Kingsley came to the office for a sandwich lunch. I like him. He is certainly the brightest advertising man in the business. He said the mistake I had made was to launch the BBC speech in Hanham instead of

---

* In the Government reorganisation of October 1968, Judith Hart joined the Cabinet as Paymaster General; Michael Stewart assumed responsibility for a combined Foreign and Commonwealth Affairs Office; and Richard Crossman took over a merged Department of Health and Social Security. Fred Peart became Lord President of the Council and Jack Diamond, Chief Secretary to the Treasury, entered Cabinet.

before a responsible group of communicators, which was probably true. But it's a bit humiliating that you can't talk honestly to your constituents until you have bought the Establishment.

Thursday 24 October

Harold's 'guru' minute was reported in the press today and, as I expected, triggered off a lot of cartoons showing Judith Hart censoring Ministers' speeches. I think Harold has been punished enough for that.

Cabinet this morning. Dick Crossman apologised to me beforehand for his behaviour on Tuesday. We had a Cabinet photograph taken, the first one I have been in. John Silkin told me he had enquired whether, as Chief Whip, he would be in it and Harold had consulted Burke Trend, who told him that it had never been the case before. I raised it directly with Burke Trend, and he said that Harold would not agree to it on the grounds that it hadn't been done before. Burke Trend himself, I might add, as Secretary to the Cabinet, is in it even though *he* is not a member.

After lunch I had Purnell in about a chap at RAE Farnborough who is suspected of being a Soviet spy and apparently has been posting photocopies of secret documents to the Russian Embassy – posting them, would you believe! They are hoping to pick him up tomorrow.

I dashed into the House to hear Harold answer Parliamentary Questions about my speech and he did reasonably well. He did get on the record the fact that I had never said I was in favour of any Government control.

Friday 25 October

Had a talk to Derek Moon and we discussed the tactics about Number 10. The fact is that Trevor Lloyd-Hughes is the cause of most of the trouble. He's the one who gets on to Derek and is trying to prevent me from making these speeches, and I am just not going to be bullied by Trevor Lloyd-Hughes. I work through Judith Hart and John Silkin and so poor Derek does actually get the backlash.

Tonight was the *Frost Programme* about broadcasting which I had cleared yesterday with Number 10, though they were very reluctant to do so. What had begun as a forty-five-minute interview with David Frost had been shrunk to a shorter programme including Paul Bryan, Conservative MP for Howden, whom, David Frost said, the ITA had insisted on having on. I don't know if that is true or not. But when I heard this earlier, I said, 'Look, don't let's have a Party political bickering argument; let's turn it over to the audience and let them ask questions.' David Frost agreed to that although Caroline was very doubtful and so was Derek Moon, when I consulted them.

Went to the show. They had, in fact, invited some young Conservatives and special people to participate although David Frost assured me that it was a perfectly ordinary audience. I felt the whole thing was absolutely phoney and afterwards when I talked to the people who produced the programme, they knew nothing about what was going on in the world. They were just with-it arts graduates who had left Sussex University or Oxbridge, and it frightened me to think that mass communications were entirely in the hands of these people.

Sunday 27 October

At Stansgate. Up early and went to buy the papers which had still got a bit about the broadcast controversy. Gave Caroline breakfast in bed and I looked around the garden, but I worked most of the day on letters and boxes.

Caroline just loves the place and the great benefits of being away from access via the telephone. We waited up for Stephen to phone because he went to the vast anti-Vietnam demonstration today in Grosvenor Square, which everybody thought would lead to violence but which, in fact, didn't.

Tuesday 29 October

To Number 10 where the Queen's speech was read, and for the traditional party before Parliament opens. It was awfully dull.

I heard that Trevor Lloyd-Hughes was violently opposed to my speech and Judith Hart told me that this evening, while she was upstairs at the party, she left my latest speech in her coat pocket and when she came back, found it had disappeared. She spoke to the messenger who said that Lloyd-Hughes had taken it back to his office: so he is really the enemy in this.

Thursday 31 October

Cabinet, where we had a discussion on Rhodesia and it was agreed to send George Thomson out to Salisbury. Harold is absolutely determined to settle with Ian Smith and nothing one can say can stop him, so I didn't participate.

Then I went to see Denis Healey about the Kings Norton Report on Aldermaston. In December last year we had a meeting to consider whether or not to go ahead with the nuclear weapons programme and whether we should accept Denis Healey's proposal to harden the Polaris missiles. I saw Kings Norton in the spring, he reported in July and, in fact, he really covered up for Aldermaston, which is heavily overstaffed. But Rothschild put in a minority report, which was outside the terms of reference, not only disagreeing with a lot of what was said in the report, but also saying that, in his opinion, it wasn't worth keeping nuclear weapons. I was told by Number 10 afterwards that I was not to talk to Kings Norton or to Rothschild about this until Ministers had met.

Then Otto Clarke, John Hill and Sir James Dunnett, Permanent Under-Secretary at the Ministry of Defence, cooked up a minute for me to put in to Ministers, brushing aside Rothschild and simply saying we ought to run Aldermaston down a bit.

Saturday 2 November
In the evening I went with Caroline to Fenner Brockway's eightieth birthday party at the House of Commons. Barbara Castle and Gerald Gardiner spoke, and I sat next to Lady Gifford, Caroline next to Lord Gifford, a left-wing lawyer. Barbara made a very moving speech, saying that her father had said to her years ago, 'That man frightens me. He is too like Jesus Christ.' Then she went through his career and described the difference between Fenner's approach to problems and hers: hers had been shallow and narrow and his had been deep, on the basis of personal relationships working with other people. It was a very good speech.

Gerald Gardiner followed and then Fenner got up and spoke for an hour on ethics. He attacked the Labour Government for having betrayed its socialism and for its materialism; for having supported the wars in Vietnam and Biafra; and for its prices and incomes policy, freezing the existing distribution of incomes. He really made us feel very uncomfortable, the way prophets must have made the Kings of Israel feel uncomfortable. But it was the best political evening I have been to for a long time.

Monday 4 November
To the Economic Policy Committee, where Harold Wilson presided and most of the discussion was on Peter's planning document. This is an enormously long document, stuffed with figures designed to replace the National Plan, not with a particular target of 4 per cent but with a new two-tier system which would give us alternative targets for growth. It had been produced at the last minute; we were told we had to publish it almost immediately, and it got an appalling reception.

Roy was hostile; so was Tony Crosland. Barbara was opposed because it revealed the fact that we should be accepting a higher level of unemployment than she was prepared to accept. Dick was against it because it revealed the figures for social service spending. I was about the only person who had a good word for it and said we needed to have some industrial figures as a basis for talking to the various industries. But I wanted to see us move towards a firm's eye-view of the problem rather than an industry view. It was agreed that the document should be completely rewritten and come back to us in a fortnight to have a look at. My fear, frankly, is that Peter is such a theoretical person that he doesn't see the practical difficulties of his proposals.

When he was at the DEA in charge of prices and incomes, he brought forward a prices and incomes policy under which the Secretary of State would have the power to veto wage and price increases personally, even without them going to the Prices and Incomes Board. This might have been accepted in wartime but was quite impossible in peacetime. And although the Cabinet discussed it for some time – without enthusiasm – it was obviously impracticable and, for this reason, he lost responsibility for prices and incomes policy, which has gone to Barbara Castle in her new Department. I want to help him as much as I can, but this new plan is going to run into terrible difficulties and I am afraid if this fails, Peter's position at DEA will become impossible.

Wednesday 6 November

I left for Israel this morning with Barry Smith. The Ambassador, Aharon Remez, came to see me off at the airport and I had a talk with him in the VIP suite. He told me that Ben-Gurion, who is living in his kibbutz, is in the present circumstances politically a dove, because Ben-Gurion is now afraid that if Israel grows to the point where it contains many more Arabs, it will change the character of the Zionist State, and he was therefore against further expansion. He is writing his history of the Jews, is extremely interested in the role of China and feels that nobody takes China seriously enough. He also believes that Britain has a very big role to play, probably out of sentiment, but his great fear is that we might go 'Scandinavian', which would be very unattractive.

We arrived at Lod a bit early because, owing to engine trouble, we had not been able to land at Athens. We were met by Michael Hadow, the British Ambassador, Max Varon, a former Israeli Ambassador to Burma who is now in the Israeli Foreign Office division which covers Britain, and General Chaim Herzog, the son of the former Chief Rabbi in Israel.

I was afraid the Israelis would want to take me to the Old City of Jerusalem and into the occupied territories, and I could not go under their auspices in case I was photographed which would create embarrassment. So we agreed that I would go on my own with the British Consul-General in Jerusalem, tomorrow. We went in the car to Jerusalem with Max Varon who told me of Moshe Dayan's great success as the leader of the occupied territories; a sort of colonial administrator operating by indirect rule in the way the British colonial officials did through the Arabs. Of course Dayan, the Defence Minister, the man with the eyepatch, the brilliant general, is regarded as the great activist who wants to consolidate the Israeli frontiers on the new basis and he is a very powerful figure in the Cabinet against others – of whom Prime Minister Eshkol and Foreign Minister Abba Eban are the most notable –

who believe that they have got to get on with the Jarring Mission[7] and the UN.

We arrived at the King David Hotel. There was a full moon and my room was facing the Old City with the walls illuminated. It was a beautiful evening. Last time I had been here in 1963, I could see the Arab Legionnaires looking over the parapet, as it were, towards the Israeli-held part of the city.

The American election results had me on tenterhooks all day and I had brought my radio and listened until I found a station I could understand. It was obvious from the number of times that 'Nixon, Nixon, Nixon' was mentioned that he had won the election with a fairly substantial majority.

Thursday 7 November

I got up just after 6 and watched the sun rise over the Old City. Then I had breakfast and took my movie camera and walked down the hill, across the old no-man's-land, through the Jaffa Gate and into the Old City, taking a lot of film. Came to the Wailing Wall and there was Barry Smith, who had set off ahead of me, so we walked round the Old City together. They have cleaned it up quite a lot and there is a permanent water supply which was not there when the Arabs held the City. There is much less smell and dust. We walked round, went into the Holy Sepulchre where the guide thought Barry was my son, which was rather amusing since Barry is thirty-six.

I had been to the Holy Sepulchre in 1945 and I must say, looking at it all now and seeing the Jewish Orthodox rabbis and the Greek Orthodox priests and the Armenians and the Arabs and so on, the origins of Christianity interest me less and less. I think one just does have to look on Jesus Christ as a teacher whose teachings survive because they contain permanent truths. He had a lot to say that is relevant to man today. But all the mystery and mythology is complete nonsense: it has got no bearing on the value of his teaching, and the idea of his resurrection and ascension and so on are really magic myths like the myths of the Old Testament. I do not think there is anything in them at all. Having reached this conclusion after a great deal of thought and having visited the Anti-Religious Museum in Leningrad eight years ago, my mind is clearer. This way of looking at it would help us to rehabilitate Christ as a teacher when there is some big moral choice to be made.

At 10.30 John Lewen, the British Consul-General, met us in his car and we went round the Mount of Olives and Gethsemane and Mount Scopus.

Then I was taken to the Foreign Office where I saw Mr Varon. I had given him a copy of my speech last night which included this rather delicate bit about the Israelis making the Jarring Mission succeed. He said he thought the difficult points were 'well-upholstered', which was an amusing diplomatic phrase.

I went to see Gideon Rafael, the Permanent Secretary at the Foreign Ministry, and he took a world view. He pointed to the Middle East and showed how central it was to the world. He drew attention to the Russians who were building up their naval forces there. There is quite a big Russian fleet in the Eastern Mediterranean. He thought they wanted to control Egypt as Britain had in the past. They wanted to get rid of the American fleet and they needed the Suez Canal* in order to move a fleet through to Asia in the event of trouble with China. From this he drew the conclusion that the Russians would be happy to come to terms with the Israelis because they had great respect for Israeli military power. Indeed, he said, the Russians had made some approaches to him about it.

He also said the Maltese had been in touch with him because they very much want the Canal reopened so that they can do their ship repair work for large tankers in the Mediterranean.

I said I thought that was interesting, but if the Russians wanted the Canal so much, did he really think they would depend upon Israeli goodwill? And was it not possible that they would support the Egyptians, give them air cover perhaps, rather as the French had done at the time of the Sinai campaign, to enable the Egyptians to get control of both sides of the Canal so that they could reopen it?

'Well, if that happens, it would mean all-out war,' he said, implying that Israel would be ready to take on the Russians as well. But the Russians have let it be known in Israel that there will be no more Arab defeats and I think this is a very dangerous doctrine. But I listened to it. He thought the Americans would be bound to come in and support Israel militarily because they would not be prepared to see the Russians consolidate themselves in the Middle East at American expense.

I thought this philosophy was just a little bit too grand for a country of Israel's size, despite its tremendous military achievements and the high degree of motivation of its people.

He was not too worried if the Jarring Mission failed because he thought Nasser would be overthrown within the next year or eighteen months, partly because he has not succeeded politically in solving Egypt's domestic problems and partly because his health is not very good. He thought he would be replaced by a military coup, and the Generals would be in favour of peace in Israel. He drew a sort of parallel with the end of confrontation. But the danger of this is that the Israelis think time is on their side, and I am not so sure it is.

* The Suez Canal was closed on 6 June 1967 during the Six-Day War, and reopened in 1975.

After a bit of muddle about where we were to go, we went next to the Knesset and Yigal Allon, the Deputy Prime Minister, gave me lunch. Amongst the guests was Lord Sieff.*

Allon himself, who pretended to know me although we had never met, said that the Israelis found the attitude of Julian Amery and Duncan Sandys† much more attractive than that of the Labour Party and they sometimes wondered why they retained special links with the Labour Party. This is the real dilemma in which Israel finds herself. She is bound to support the most reactionary regimes in the Middle East because these are the ones that are least active in their attacks upon her.

As far as Britain's position was concerned, Hadow took the view that we should stop lecturing the world and let it be known that we are going to approach problems much more commercially. I think there is some merit in this; the last remnant of the British imperial myth is that having given up our military power, we are now in a position to exert moral power in international affairs.

Friday 8 November

Up early and Barry Smith, Max Varon and I picked up an Allouette helicopter with an Israeli major and lieutenant and flew round the Old City, then to Bethlehem past the Massada Monastery where my camera broke. Massada was a most remarkable sight. I had heard about it but had not really got the full flavour of it. You have to see it to realise what an incredible achievement it was: for Herod to have built that great palace on top of this bare mountain in the desert, for the Zealots to have captured it, then for the Romans to have built a wall and four camps round it and finally to have captured it, only to find the Zealots had killed themselves.

We came back by helicopter, crossing over various Bedouin tents in the desert, and landed at the Weizmann Institute at Rehovoth on a tiny bit of green grass and were met by Michael Feldman, a biologist.

We went and looked at some of the exhibits of Weizmann's life and had a talk with Feldman about his work, particularly in the field of DNA and proteins. He restated the chicken and egg problem in terms of DNA and protein, and talked about cell growth and the possibility of stimulating cells to replace organs that have died; he said the time would soon come when you could take a single cell of a human being and say, 'This man prefers Bach to Mozart.'

He talked about genetic decline and how natural selection was not operating to kill off the less satisfactory strains; he referred to the

* Israel Sieff, President of Marks & Spencer, 1967–72, and Honorary President of the Zionist Federation of Great Britain.

† Julian Amery, Conservative Minister of Aviation, 1962–4; Duncan Sandys, a former Conservative Minister of Defence and Secretary of State for Commonwealth Relations.

building up of sperm banks which would enable the level to be lifted again and the political problems these would raise.

Saturday 16 November

I went by car to Chequers, the first time I had been to a Chequers meeting for over a year, on which occasion Peter had been made Secretary of State for Economic Affairs. We had a preliminary talk before dinner and each of us was asked to give our assessment of how things stood.

After dinner we began in earnest in the long gallery. Harold sat in a big easy chair on the right of a blazing wood fire. Next to him was Judith Hart, next to Judith was John Silkin, next to John was Harold Davies, then me, on my left Peter Shore and on the sofa facing Harold, Gerald Kaufman, Marcia Williams and Thomas Balogh.

It was decided to go round the room and collect views and Judith spoke first. She thought the basic problems of poverty had been solved, that people required rather different interests, and she came out with the 'participation' argument. John Silkin said people weren't interested in participation, he thought that Harold was the key figure and we had to think a great deal about his position.

Harold Davies made two points. First, that we shouldn't concern ourselves with the question of higher education, but there was a great deal of interest among people in primary schools, ordinary secondary schools and further education. Later, when we came to talk about industry, he said he thought it was essential we should take more interest in technicians, foremen, lower level management, who felt they had been left out by the Labour Party. I agreed with both those views.

When it came to my turn, I said that in terms of an Election, there was a problem of getting the electorate to see us as a Government giving leadership. One of the functions of leadership was to explain things. And if we had been criticised it was for this lack of leadership. We had to take the public into our confidence more. I thought the key to all this was an Election theme based on the idea of the responsible society.

Responsibility involves a lot of things. First of all, you must tell people the truth, and the truth is that Britain is alone. We have been thrown out of the Empire, the Commonwealth idea has gone, in most senses the special relationship with America has been eroded. We are not in the Common Market. We are alone, we are responsible for our own fate. Second, we must interpret responsibility to mean that we are sharing power. This is where participation comes in. Third, social responsibility: we must accept that we need a strong community structure, international responsibility in aid to overseas countries, and the responsibility to educate. Finally, we had to get people to believe in Britain again: we had had terrible knocks, but it was time people saw that we, as compared to France, America, Germany or Greece, had a fair society, and they should welcome it and see that the responsible society in Britain was something worth preserving.

I went on to talk about the mixed economy. It was time we got rid of the shibboleths of laissez faire capitalism versus centralised Communism. Here we had a mixed economy, mixed enterprise, and this was something we wanted to develop; we ought to explain it and give it some life and vitality. This was warmly welcomed by Peter who spoke next and he argued that we had to look ahead and see what was going to happen.

Marcia said we had all underestimated Harold, we had to give more importance to Harold's role. Tommy Balogh said that as far as he was concerned, if the economy wasn't right all would come to an end, and that the unions were an irresponsible group who had to be dealt with.

Harold summed up and said he was attracted by my idea. Judith thought it sounded too safe and dull. I said, 'Not at all, because what we are talking about is the responsibility for changing Britain. This is the idea that "Britain belongs to you".'

John Silkin said again that he thought people didn't want to participate and I said, 'Maybe not everybody, but responsible people want to participate. We ought to be in contact with responsible people, and anyway there was something about the idea of a responsible society which differentiated us from the Tories, who were by definition irresponsible.'

Harold made a great point of this. 'Yes, we must have our demonology and the demons are those who are irresponsible.' I added that as far as Harold's own role was concerned, he ought not to be Dr Wilson who looked after everything for you but cultivate his image as a teacher, a 'guru' (which was a reference to his minute about my speech on broadcasting). He laughed and said he couldn't see himself as a guru, and I said, 'Well, I can see you as a teacher, very experienced; you've been Prime Minister now for years, people turn to you.' John Silkin thought Harold's great strength was that he was a tough guy who couldn't be pushed down, had the courage to do unpopular things.

Then we had another round about trade unions. Harold opened it, referred to the problem of the irresponsible unions; the prices and incomes policy was more or less dead; we couldn't legislate again because we wouldn't get it through. Judith said that, whatever its merits, we had to accept that politically we wouldn't get trade union legislation through, and it stirred up the trade unions and the PLP against us.

I told Harold I had sent a memorandum to Barbara Castle about my proposal for an IRC (Industrial Reorganisation Corporation) for the unions, and he said his mind had been working on the same lines. We agreed that instead of the prices and incomes legislation, we should have strike ballots and a cooling-off period, and in this way we would say we were going to control the trade unions by democratising them.

We broke up at 11.30 and Ron Vaughan brought us back. I told John Silkin that I didn't intend, now that I had been readmitted to the Kitchen Cabinet, to stop making speeches because I thought speeches and the teaching role were useful. He had rebuked me a year ago for being a departmental Minister and not thinking about politics; in the last six months I have been much more than a departmental Minister, which is what has been getting me into trouble with Harold. But now I have got my freedom, I am not going to give it up in return for the right to give him advice.

We had a brief discussion about Enoch Powell. John Silkin, thinking of fascism and anti-semitism, was extremely worried by him, and the others thought he was a very evil man. I said I knew him, and I thought I knew why he was doing it; he really represented the rejected working class membership of the Tory Party. I thought he was defusing the issue before the next Election, and that anyway he was more of a threat to the Tory Party than he was to us.

Monday 18 November
I went to the Parliamentary Procedure Committee at 11.30 to consider a single, simple point on whether the Select Committee on Nationalised Industries should be allowed to investigate those concerns in which the Government had either total ownership or a majority control, including the Bank of England, which is what this committee really wanted to look at. Harold Lever presented his paper in which he recommended that the committee should not be allowed to do this. I didn't accept that view.

I said that I recognised that a commercial concern which the Government owned should not be subjected to unfair scrutiny to which its competitors would not be exposed, but that if the committee really thought that the pressure for accountability which was now mounting both in respect of private as well as public enterprise could be pushed aside in this way, they were quite wrong.

Peter Shore and Frank Beswick supported me but Dick Marsh and most other Ministers, including Fred Peart, the Chairman, were bitterly opposed to it. As this was an interesting point, it was held to be quite separate from the item on the agenda, and so we had to abandon it. It is typical of the way the Government works. Nothing of any real interest or principle is ever allowed to arise on committees. But still we started it.

At 3.30 I had Solly Zuckerman in to discuss the Non-Proliferation Treaty. I had been rather opposed to an early ratification because I was afraid it would interfere with my freedom of action in selling British nuclear products commercially abroad, but the Foreign Office have climbed down a bit on this and Solly Zuckerman and I discussed much more fully the effect of the centrifuge on non-proliferation. For example, Britain will be making available to the Germans a more convenient and cheaper supply of enriched uranium by this new method than the French have, who will be very upset about it. We have to face all sorts of difficulties and I decided to minute the PM again.

Tuesday 19 November

The world money crisis is now building up; the franc is under very heavy pressure and everyone is trying to get the mark to be revalued and this is having a serious effect on sterling, though, as I am not a member of the little inner ministerial committee that looks at the economy, I don't know anything except what I read in the papers (which indicates considerable leaking by the Treasury).

I went to the annual dinner of the British National Export Council at which Harold made an amusing speech. Almost every Minister was there except for Roy Jenkins who has had to fly to Bonn because of the growing seriousness of the economic crisis and the rumours of franc devaluation.

I was sitting between Lord Mancroft and Lord Clydesmuir, both of whom are Tory hereditary peers in business, and as I looked round it made me wonder whether there was any prospect at all of getting our exports up if there were such a lot of amateurs about. But still, we are fundamentally changing the whole character of our economy, and that is the main thing.

Wednesday 20 November

I had a bad cold and chest. Went in to the office in the morning and then went to the Nuclear Policy Committee where I was called in on item No. 2, the NPT and the centrifuge.

I explained the background and warned them that the Americans might be worried on security or commercial grounds, the Russians might think we were trying to help the Germans build the bomb, the PLP might be worried about the political dangers, and that we should do a proper briefing arrangement. I am afraid the effect of saying this was to alarm some of my colleagues, and it was left over till the following day's meeting of the Parliamentary Committee [Inner Cabinet].

Saw Gilbert Hunt, Managing Director of Rootes [Chrysler], and he told me about Chrysler's international planning, which confirmed what I had known for a long time, that these big industrial companies plan on an international basis and regard Governments as being mere parish councils.

I went to the House of Commons and voted on Lords reform and got home about 11 feeling awful.

Thursday 21 November

Parliamentary Committee at 10.15 for the item on the Non-Proliferation Treaty which I am now in favour of ratifying, and also to say a word about centrifuges. But this thoroughly alarmed Dick Crossman, Jack Diamond and George Thomas who thought we were going to be giving the bomb to the Germans. The committee was not keen to go on with the meeting while Roy Jenkins was in Bonn, at the big international monetary conference* of Financial Ministers, the 'Group of Ten', called by the Germans; indeed Harold Lever had returned this morning from Bonn.

What he had to say was that the Germans had firmly declined to revalue the mark despite considerable pressure from Britain. The French were threatening to devalue the franc to such an extent that it would bring down the pound and the dollar, and we were being asked to contribute a package which he described. It consists of import deposits, which I welcome.

Well, at 7 I went back to the Parliamentary Committee which met in Harold's room at the House of Commons. Roy had sent a message to say that, in his view, the package was essential. It was a contribution the deficit countries had to make. And so the question arose then of Purchase Tax, and I said I would be prepared to accept the increase in Purchase Tax if I could raise the question of Hire Purchase terms later, which was acceptable to Roy.

Most of the ensuing argument was when we should make our statement. Would Roy be back in time tomorrow? Would the Bonn conference end tonight? Apparently the prospects of this happening were very much reduced by the fact that Schiller, the German Finance Minister, is a very bad chairman. And of course the Germans are showing their economic and industrial strength and just defying everybody. I don't blame them in a way because they've been looked down on for years and now at last they feel they're coming into their own again. It's the first time they've shown their muscle since the War. But I urged that we should be very careful to bring it all together, to try to get the French devaluation of the franc, which is now likely to be 11 per cent, brought forward at the same time as our package, in case people thought our package didn't contemplate, or didn't include, the devaluation which the French were going to make. This view commanded a lot of support. I felt for the first time that on an economic matter the Cabinet or rather the Parliamentary Committee was listening carefully to me.

---

* It was after this meeting that Roy Jenkins stated that money supply figures would have to be monitored as a condition of support for the pound. This was the beginning of monetarism, ten years before Mrs Thatcher became Prime Minister.

What really impressed me was the extent to which power had slipped through our fingers. In defence matters we are wholly tied to the Americans. Denis Healey is always making out that we are completely dependent upon the Americans for the supply of our nuclear fuel for the Polaris submarines and indeed for the know-how for the Polaris missiles, which is true. On financial matters, because we're in deficit, we're in the hands of the bankers. And on monetary matters we're in the hands of the world community.

Then yesterday, when I saw Hunt of Rootes, it was clear that on industrial matters things were decided in Detroit and not in London. It was interesting – I won't say sad because you've got to be realistic – to think that the British Parliament, the House of Commons, meant nothing. The Cabinet meant nothing. The Prime Minister was just at the other end of a phone, receiving dictation from the Chancellor of the Exchequer, who was himself being dictated to by the world monetary conference. This is the reality of life.

National sovereignty in the civil sense has completely disappeared. And as if that wasn't bad enough, the Government in Whitehall has also got to share its remaining powers with the Scots and the Welsh, and this redistribution of political power is becoming a major issue.

Friday 22 November

This morning there was a Parliamentary Committee at 9, where we heard the latest news from Bonn, followed by Cabinet. The question was would the Chancellor be able to get back in time to make a statement in the Commons?

I passed a note to Jim Callaghan which he appreciated enormously saying, 'The real issue is whether John Harris (Roy Jenkins's press adviser) can persuade the Germans to revalue, the French to devalue, and the Americans to deflate, and we shall have to wait till tomorrow's Miscellany column in the *Guardian* to find out.' Jim killed himself with laughter when he saw that and passed it round. I also sent a note to Barbara, after I'd been complaining that the Treasury was briefing and therefore putting us in a position whereby we had to accept what had been done, saying: 'Our problem isn't leaks but the fact that we're all being soaked by a water cannon wielded by the Treasury press officers.' Jim replied to my note saying: 'Barbara's "touch on the tiller" will rank with my "steady-as-she-goes"' – Jim having used in his Budget speech eighteen months ago the phrase 'steady-as-she-goes' to suggest the ship was on course, and Barbara having said at the Bassetlaw by-election recently that changes to hire purchase were a 'touch on the tiller'.

But we are all caught out. The fact is that all our estimates have been wrong. We have allowed consumption to go on at too great a rate and it is now catching up with us. I found Harold rather endearing today when he said he wasn't really sure what he ought to do himself; not panicking, but just admitting that he doesn't quite know what to do.

Well, that went on till 11.20 and then I raised the centrifuge. Denis Healey launched in exactly as he'd done yesterday and the day before and said that the Cabinet was being 'bounced'. It was quite untrue because he knew quite well why it had to be secret. But he made out that the Americans were going to be very difficult about this, which I don't think is the case, and he carried a lot of weight. There were members of the Cabinet who were suddenly faced with a move from Top Secret at one minute to a press briefing, which I'd laid on tentatively for this afternoon, the next. It was just too much for them to take, so it was agreed I could put out my written statement following Stoltenberg's message to his Euratom partners, but I couldn't give a press briefing.

I came out with Dick, and he said at the top of his voice: 'Of course this is going to be inadequate, of course it's going to be inadequate, and everybody knows we ourselves shall have to devalue again soon.' His voice boomed up and down the corridors and somebody heard it on the stairs above. This is Dick, the great leaker, an incredibly inadequate man, like Hugh Dalton. He just can't keep his mouth shut.

Then I had a tremendous briefing meeting with Fred Mulley, Solly Zuckerman, John Hill and AEA officials, Michael Michaels, and a Defence official, to discuss the brief for the Anglo–German–Dutch talks at The Hague on Monday. What came out of the meeting, which I had suspected but had never been properly told, was that we have an arrangement with the Americans under which we are absolutely tied hand and foot to them, and we can't pass any of our nuclear technology over to anybody else without their permission. Naturally, they don't want to see us taking advantage of our nuclear knowledge, which would make money for ourselves; the harsh reality is that de Gaulle is right, that although the special relationship doesn't give us political advantages any more, it certainly ties us, and this is what upsets Solly so much. This is another aspect of our complete dependence on the Americans, and one day we'll have to sort it out. I don't know how, but we shall have to.

Sunday 24 November

The papers this morning are full of the news that de Gaulle has refused to devalue the franc. I must say I laughed myself sick all day. From all accounts at the Bonn conference last week the French threatened to devalue by 25 per cent and said they could not accept a devaluation of less than 11.11 per cent. And then in the event de Gaulle has refused to do it.

This afternoon Caroline and I went for an hour and a half's walk in Kensington Gardens. It was a very nice quiet day. I was picked up about

7 and flew to The Hague for the talks on the centrifuge, with Michael Michaels, Fred Mulley and Christopher Audland from the Foreign Office. We went straight to the British Embassy.

Looking at the minutes for last Friday's Cabinet it became evident that the Prime Minister in his summing up had said that I couldn't commit the British Government to exchange technical information at this meeting. I hadn't recalled the wording exactly in this form; but it looked as if I were going to be put in the position of being unable to go ahead with this very meeting on the centrifuge which the British had brought about with a great deal of effort over the last few months. So we sat down and I drafted a telegram to the Prime Minister, referring to the minutes, saying that the meeting had been carefully prepared and that we were not intending to exchange technical details at the moment, but that if I found that I couldn't go as far as the Dutch and the Germans my position really would be completely undermined.

Solly backed this up by phoning Burke Trend from the Embassy but Burke was a bit unsympathetic because he said the Cabinet minutes had been in my hands since Friday. Well, of course this was true but I hadn't tackled my box until Saturday night and it was Sunday morning, this morning, before I went to bed. But we worked out the strategy again and then I went back to the hotel.

Monday 25 November
Breakfast in my room. Worked on the final preparation of my speaking notes for the various items we were going to discuss, and then to the hall where the meeting was held, a beautiful one overlooking a lake, and it was the room in which the Spaniards and the Dutch signed the twelve-year truce at the beginning of the seventeenth century. It's where the Dutch Cabinet meets, surrounded by the most beautiful paintings and carved plaster figures.

During the course of the morning I had a telegram from Harold saying that the Cabinet minutes had been correctly worded, but that as he understood it the strategy I intended to pursue was within those limits and I could go ahead on that basis.

At this one-day meeting we discussed the scope of an agreement, the siting of factories, safeguards and supervision, and the commitment of individual countries to enriched uranium. It was finally agreed that there would be another official meeting in December, and Ministers would meet again in Bonn in February 1969.

At 5.10 we went into a televised press conference. I must say continental Ministers treat the press with a lot more arrogance than we do. The Dutch and Germans were asked a few questions and brushed them off. We dashed in the car to the airport in Amsterdam in time to fly back for the economics debate.

Tuesday 26 November

Hilary's birthday and he had his presents early in the morning. I had a discussion in the office first of all about Ford. We know from papers that had been smuggled out to Stan Newens, MP for Epping, by friends of his who work for Ford, that they are planning, under their Ford of Europe proposals, to sell the Escort from Germany and not from Britain, and this is the first big test of the conflict of interests between an international company with a plant in Britain and a nation state.

Economic Policy Committee at 11. Peter Shore's planning document in a much abbreviated form came forward. Peter glossed over the difficulties, it was too intellectually presented and it didn't relate directly to the needs of the economy. Roy Jenkins waded in and said, 'Quite frankly I am against this document. I think the whole thing should be postponed and I can't undertake that even if it is postponed it will ever be publishable.'

Tony Crosland agreed. We went round the table, and I was the only one there who attacked the critics of the document, and said this was much more serious, it was an attack on the idea of planning and not just on this document. Dick Marsh said it was silly to publish something when we weren't in control of the economy, and I replied, 'Of course, we have never been in control of the economy, but it's not just the DEA's planning forecasts which are a hostage to fortune, I can recall a lot of Chancellors who made wildly optimistic forecasts; we must get out to the industrial end and listen to what they have to say.' I got a note from George Thomas, which was very obliging of him, saying that my speech was one of the very best speeches he had heard since he joined the Cabinet.

I am beginning to see now what has gone wrong with our economic policy. We have sat and pored over figures week after week and haven't listened to industry: there is no voice of industry in the Government, and there must be a Ministry of Industry which will bring in the voice and make it audible. The DEA is just like the Treasury, it proceeds by revealed truth. Anyway Peter was pleased I supported him and he just scraped home, so the document goes out as a working document without committing Ministers.

Then we went over to the House of Commons for Cabinet at 12.15 because there was likely to be a vote, and Roy reported on the Bonn conference, not that he added very much to what had been said in the papers. Denis raised the question of the occasion last week when the German Ambassador had been summoned after midnight to Number 10 and Harold and Roy had apparently attacked him on revaluation; according to press reports – I don't know if they are true – they had threatened to withdraw British troops from Germany. Most unlikely that it was true but they probably did hint that there were wider issues at stake.

Harold had to leave to go to the Palace and Roy took the chair. Jim suggested there should be regular meetings of the 'Group of Ten' and I supported this. I said I felt last week that power had drained from the Cabinet to Bonn and the best thing to do was to set up new institutions which allowed us to operate at that level, if that was the level at which we could make progress; that is to say Finance Ministers and bankers sitting side by side.

Wednesday 27 November
Went to see Roy Jenkins. He wanted to talk about a number of things but he was really probing for economies in public expenditure. He was very unhappy about the Kings Norton secret report on Aldermaston, which he thought was a whitewashing document, and said there were more savings to be made there, which I fully accept.

Thursday 28 November
Short lunch in the office with Clive Jenkins, General Secretary of ASTMS. He's a bright, brash Welshman, one of the very few people who is really thinking about the future problems of industry.

ASSET [Association of Supervisory Staffs, Executives and Technicians], which has now merged to become ASTMS, has grown from an income of £60,000 a year in 1961 to £0.5 million today. It's got a roaring membership drive, it's now going straight out for managers, doctors, university people. It's coming in on the great frustration of the technician/manager types who feel squeezed between the worker on the one hand and the rich owner-manager guys, like Lord Nelson and Arnold Weinstock, on the other.

Clive said, and I agree with him, that there is a very poor quality of management in most British firms, comprising people for whom he had no intellectual respect.

John Adams came to see me briefly and told me he had been offered the Director-Generalship of CERN [the Centre Européen pour la Recherche Nucléaire] and asked if I would agree. It means he leaves the AEA but I said Yes. He told me that the reason why Solly Zuckerman hated the AEA was that, during the 1940s and 1950s, the AEA was riding high and these very powerful atomic energy knights – Cockcroft, Bill Penney, Plowden and Hinton* – just sat on the civil scientists and crushed them, and Solly had never forgiven them for it. An interesting psychological comment.

---

* Sir John Cockcroft, Director of the Atomic Energy Research Establishment, Harwell, 1946–58; Lord Penney, Director of the Atomic Weapons Research Establishment, Aldermaston, 1953–9; Lord Plowden, Chairman of the Atomic Energy Authority, 1954–9; Lord Hinton, Chairman of the Central Electricity Generating Board, 1957–64.

Saturday 30 November

Among my letters today was one from a man in Bristol who told me to keep away from the House of Commons for the next fortnight because he had sold some grenades at £3 each to somebody who intended to blow up the Houses of Parliament. Normally one would dismiss a bomb scare letter like that as a hoax but there were certain features of the letter which made it more interesting.

First of all he specified the amount of money he had been paid for each grenade in brackets; he was also concerned that I might be hurt and said that I had helped him once in Bristol, which made the thing rather authentic. He then went on to say that he had heard it was something to do with the Welsh nationalists, and the BBC in Monmouthshire. It so happened that the day after he had posted the letter the Welsh nationalists did stage a sit-in at the BBC studios in Cardiff, so there was enough to make it look quite serious.

I rang the House of Commons Police and got a phone call back, suggesting I take the letter to the local police station, so I sent Stephen round to Ladbroke Grove and he stood in line with a woman who had lost a handbag and a boy whose bike had been pinched. When the policeman asked what he wanted, Stephen said, 'It's about a bomb.' So they whipped him into a private room and he gave them the letter and told them the background. A few minutes later I had a phone call from Inspector Watts of Special Branch, who asked if I would let him have a note of the people I had helped in Bristol. I said that in eighteen years as an MP, I must have helped about 40,000 people, and he asked if I had any correspondence.

It so happened that I had been sorting out my papers this morning and I found all my constituency correspondence going back to 1962, so he sent a Sergeant Easterbrook, a Welshman, and a Detective Stuart and they began going through every letter from 1962 onwards. There was another feature of the warning letter, namely that the writer couldn't come forward as he had done time in Horfield, the Bristol prison, so the police began looking for somebody who might have been a prisoner and whose handwriting resembled that in the letter.

We went to Robin Day's party and when we got back, the police had discovered a man called Scofield who had been in prison in Bristol, and whose children lived in Barbara Castle's constituency. In 1964 I had written to her and managed to get the family reunited, and he had been very grateful. The police found similarities in handwriting between it and the anonymous letter. They asked me if they could take it away.

I began to get a bit worried at this stage because I thought first of all of parliamentary privilege; was he going to be prosecuted if he was found? Secondly I didn't want it known that I had let Special Branch go through my constituency correspondence. So I rang Jim Callaghan and had a word with him and told him what I had done and I got the police to promise that they would neither approach Scofield nor would they prosecute him without telling me. It added to the excitement of the day.

Sunday 1 December

In the morning I was in my office writing speeches and articles, and in the afternoon a Sergeant Montague and Detective Stuart came back to look at more letters because they had discovered that Scofield died about eighteen months ago, so it couldn't be him. I was somewhat relieved. They went through the rest of my letters, found no links and went away.

Monday 2 December

A bomb blew up the Welsh waterpipe to Birmingham and this explains why the police took all these bomb scares seriously. It may well have been the grenades supplied by the man who wrote to me but I didn't hear any more about it after that.

Wednesday 4 December

I had a sandwich, then a meeting with Reg Prentice to see if I could interest him in technological agreements with developing countries. His Department have been fighting a long battle with other Departments who would like to use overseas aid to improve Britain's economic advantage in these countries. I tried to persuade him that I wasn't proposing that, but we should build up agreements in parallel, which would be designed to improve our commercial prospects and would be proposed on this basis. India was a case in point. He was pretty reluctant because the Overseas Development Ministry has got in its mind the idea that it must be the main agency for all government-to-government economic relations with developing countries.

Thursday 5 December

At Cabinet we discussed House of Lords reform which we had to think about again. Jim Callaghan tried as hard as he possibly could to kill it and so did Tony Crosland and Denis Healey but it was agreed we would do it in the New Year.

Stephen passed his driving test – an important family event!

Sunday 8 December

Poor old Tony Crosland slipped on some leaves today and broke his elbow in seven places.

Shirley Williams told us last night that Harold and Roy were going to resign today, according to City rumours, and this had led to a tremendous flight of sterling. Quite untrue but a damaging story and

Dick had blamed the City for it on the 1 o'clock News today: 'Crossman denounces gnomes of Europe'.

It is really as Harold feared earlier in the year when Cecil King began firing off his shots.

Monday 9 December

Economic Policy Committee on public expenditure. Roy had presented a paper suggesting five areas in which we might make major cuts to give us a bit of freedom of manoeuvre: defence, industrial support, agriculture, family allowances and housing. Denis said that if major defence cuts were required he would, unlike on previous occasions, be quite unable to carry them with any confidence and wouldn't have the slightest hesitation in resigning.

So Harold said, 'Well, there are plenty more in the Second Eleven,' which more or less disposed of Denis. This morning *The Times*, in one of its three-column leaders, called for a coalition. This was the Editor, William Rees-Mogg, speaking, on whom a beam of light has descended.

To the Home Policy Committee of the NEC, where there is a row about whether the Home Policy Committee could summon Ministers to explain when their policy differed from Conference resolutions. Harold is hysterical about this, following the Attlee-Churchill correspondence in 1945 about Harold Laski,[8] and Jim Callaghan was looking very sinister.

Tuesday 10 December

I went to Cabinet where Harold began by 'Warning the Plotters'. He said that four senior Ministers had told him that one member of the Cabinet had been going round stirring things up, indicating conspiracy against Harold's own leadership, and that if this went on, without further ado he would simply reconstruct his Government.

Denis Healey and Jim Callaghan are the obvious suspects, and they probably are doing it a little bit, but not as much as Harold thinks. I knew nothing about it one way or the other but I'm sure if there are conspirators that is about the worst possible way of dealing with them.

To the Lobby lunch as a guest of Peter Carver of the *Evening Post*, and Michael Foot made an extremely funny speech. 'Some of my oldest and best friends are in the Cabinet and some of my oldest and bitterest political enemies are in the Cabinet, but such is the alchemy of collective Cabinet responsibility that I can't tell one from the other.' He attacked the idea of a coalition, and the idea held by some MPs that there was a conspiracy in the press.

Wednesday 11 December

I went to Cabinet and the Falkland Islands was the only item; a long discussion. The general view was that the scheme that had been worked out and presented by Michael Stewart, ie signing a memorandum with Argentina saying that we would hand over sovereignty as soon as possible on a date to be fixed, but having a simultaneous document saying we wouldn't do it without the Falkland Islanders' agreement, gave an impression of deviousness.

Michael Stewart was very upset, understandably, but he had gone rather further than his brief and his paper was rejected. I think Harold was a bit embarrassed because he was pretty heavily tied up in this as well.

In the evening I went to dinner at Lime Grove with BBC heads David Attenborough, John Grist, Aubrey Singer, David Webster and Tony Whitby. It was organised to discuss my recent broadcasting speech. They agreed with what I was trying to say but claimed they were doing this anyway. They were hopelessly complacent. But they caught me out because, of course, when I suggested, 'Well, what about a programme on . . . ?' they said, 'Oh, we did one on that last February.' It was like arguing with Harold Wilson who had always made a speech on everything and could refer you to what he said in Swansea in 1963.

We talked for three and a half hours. Aubrey Singer, who made the science programmes, said that when he read my speech he felt he had been defiled, which was very strong language. I held my own, and when they said that there was 'no talent' outside, I said, 'I take that as an invitation to find some.'

Friday 13 December
I went to Bristol and spoke at the Bristol Graduate Club about technology and politics. Just before my lecture there was a message from students at the sit-in in Senate House inviting me to go.

Yesterday I had made enquiries to Shirley Williams about what I should do and she told me the Vice-Chancellor was very worried and not prepared to negotiate with the students. She said I shouldn't go into Senate House and my office were so worried they arranged for a police escort to meet me at the station and at the university, which didn't please me very much because I don't need police to protect me in Bristol or among students. But I felt I couldn't visit the sit-in, so I wrote a little note saying, 'My meeting has just finished, I am going to have some food and I will be in the Grand Hotel later.'

I got back to the hotel just after midnight and three students were waiting for me, having been sent from Senate House. We talked for about two hours. I tried to be as sympathetic as I could. They said the writs against the six people the Vice-Chancellor had had to name were victimisation. I said the Vice-Chancellor is not going to abandon the writs and give up the fight against people who have taken over the building.

In a way, they sympathised with the Vice-Chancellor, Professor Collar – he is an aeronautical engineer – who found this problem on his shoulders and doesn't know what to do, while all the other Vice-Chancellors are breathing down his neck. The pressure has built up, led by the *Western Daily Press* and the Right in Bristol, to use tear-gas, smoke bombs and water cannon to get the students out of Senate House.

Actually the students are being very careful. They let the police in to inspect and have locked up documents; I don't think the Maoists are in control at all, but there are students there from other parts of the country.

Saturday 14 December
The students rang me at about 4 am and said they were meeting in Senate House and agreed that it would be better not to have external interventions. So I said I'd catch my train. I slept a bit on the way and in London I rang the Vice-Chancellor and told him what had happened and he said that he couldn't give up the writs but he might consider abandoning the action for damages. I didn't hear any more from the students, so I rang Shirley and told her what the Vice-Chancellor had said. She will ring the Vice-Chancellor tomorrow and see if we can solve it.

Life is really very crowded. But, looking back, this has been without question my most happy, enjoyable and I think fruitful year as a Minister. These weekend speeches, lectures and letters to constituents are gradually beginning to establish an alternative position to that occupied by Enoch Powell and this is going to be necessary if we are to fight the effective right-wing Fascist-type Government that we could be landed with if we are not careful.

Sunday 15 December
Got up early this morning and went to Chequers for the whole-day meeting of NEDC. This had been called to consider Peter's new planning document but Peter himself has been in hospital all week, and couldn't attend.

Roy Jenkins reviewed the position, the amount we've borrowed from abroad, which was something in the region of £2,000 million since 1959, and said that in effect we were living off the rest of the world. This couldn't go on, it wasn't natural justice that the tenth richest country in the world should expect to be subsidised by the rest; our debts were now £3,000 million and we must aim to get a substantial surplus of £500 million a year. He said that we would find debt management a lot easier if the surplus was being earned. Without the surplus, we couldn't expect to have the debt obligations re-phased. It was a very good speech by

Roy, quiet and steady, and he summed up saying that we had no choice between balance of payments and growth.

George Woodcock didn't challenge the need for a surplus but he thought that if the expansion target was below productive capacity, we would weaken efficiency; and three-quarters of a million unemployed by 1972 was unacceptable to the TUC.

Kenneth Keith agreed with Roy Jenkins; of course the City always does agree with Roy.

At lunch I had a word with Bill Nield, Peter Shore's Permanent Secretary, and he said he was fully convinced of the need for a Ministry of Industry and he had discussed this with Harold but the problem was really a personal one. It would involve taking away chunks of the Board of Trade and Harold wasn't ready to do this.

After lunch, we had a big session on private investment and the engineering industries which I was called upon to introduce. I began to get across the idea, which I had been working on very hard, that Government should be in direct contact with the big companies, and that we had to have a two-tiered relationship with industry. John Davies, Director-General of the CBI, was very suspicious about this and was afraid that it would, in some way, reduce his authority.

Monday 16 December
I went back to Chequers for the second day of talks. This time it was the TUC discussing their economic document, which they wanted to talk to us about before they published it. Sid Greene* introduced it, saying there was a lot of concern about unemployment, and the present rate was politically difficult. He doubted whether the £500 million balance of payments surplus was right. Roy went through much of the same argument as before.

I had to leave at lunchtime to fly to Hamburg with Derek Moon and Barry Smith to talk to the Overseas Club. When I got there, I was met by the Consul-General who told me that there was a big student demonstration on Biafra. I asked that some of the students should come and listen to the lecture, and said that I would meet them afterwards. They had been on hunger strike for three days and they looked very pale. They were accusing us of being murderers for selling arms to Nigeria and the old Nazis who were the head of the Overseas Club rather enjoyed seeing a British socialist Minister being attacked by young Germans on the grounds that we were repeating what happened at Dachau and Belsen. I was presented with a picture of a starving Biafran child, and a

* Sidney Greene, later Lord Greene of Harrow Weald. General Secretary of the National Union of Railwaymen, 1957–74.

very pale girl put a wreath of flowers on my seat. I listened and argued as best I could.

Tuesday 17 December
Up at 6.30 and flew to London. We had a Cabinet meeting and wasted a lot of time discussing whether or not Ministers should send Christmas cards to the Russians.

Wednesday 18 December
Caroline and I gave a Mintech office party, then we looked into John Stonehouse's fabulous party, held in a tent in Queen Anne's Gate with lots of pop stars and a few politicians. It was a real glamour party about which Caroline was very doubtful.

Saturday 21 December
We watched the blast-off of the Apollo 8 spacecraft – the first attempt by man to reach the moon, with Colonel Frank Borman in charge.

Sunday 22 December
Lazy morning. The Mayhews came to lunch. They have the most hideously reactionary view on education and students, élitist to a degree and violently opposed to the revolutionary students. I'm not pro the students but I have a little more sympathy than the Mayhews.

Tuesday 31 December
The last day of the year. Family at Stansgate. I moved the tools into the scullery where it was drier. Stephen went to London for a party and we saw the New Year in.

It has been quite a good year for me. I have got into the Ministry of Technology and I don't have to work quite so hard, though there are a lot of difficult problems. I am enjoying life enormously, after three or four years of worrying a lot. I think I am past that now. I see the next two years before the Election as being very satisfying ones, even if we are thrown out, which is quite possible.

My relations with Harold are good; he has had a very tough two and a half years and come through it and there is no further challenge to his leadership. The Party, despite the great unpopularity of the Government in the country, is surviving, although Party organisation is in a terrible state and it will take all Harry Nicholas's talent to get us back into contact with the public as a whole.

In 1969 I intend to spend a lot more time in Bristol, to begin building my position up locally for the next Election, and to be more political as Minister of Technology, and not just confined to technical problems.

NOTES
Chapter One

1. (p. 21) The Bristol Siddeley affair concerned allegations that Bristol Siddeley Engines Ltd, a subsidiary of Rolls Royce, had for some years been overcharging the Government of the day for work overhauling aero-engines and repairing spare parts. In February 1968 a committee chaired by Sir Roy Wilson to investigate the matter reported that 'the Company budgeted for and achieved exorbitant profits on their overhaul contracts with the Department', achieving 105 per cent profits on certain engines and 40 per cent profits on spare parts between 1959 and 1965. Sir Reginald Verdon-Smith, the Chairman of Bristol Siddeley Engines, and Brian Davidson, a director, were indicted by the report and both were removed from the public bodies to which they had been appointed by the Government.

2. (p. 40) On 6 March 1968 three Africans were executed in Rhodesia after being sentenced to death in 1964 and 1965 in circumstances arousing condemnation in Britain, the United Nations and the Commonwealth. Petitions to the Queen for the exercise of the Royal Prerogative of Mercy were granted on 2 March, but the sentences were carried out on grounds that the 1961 Constitution, in granting internal sovereignty to Rhodesia had 'divested the Crown in the UK of the power to exercise the Royal Prerogative of Mercy'.

3. (p. 59) In January 1958, Peter Thorneycroft (the Chancellor of the Exchequer), Enoch Powell (Financial Secretary to the Treasury) and Nigel Birch (Economic Secretary to the Treasury) resigned from the Conservative Government when Harold Macmillan insisted on higher public expenditure than Thorneycroft and his team were prepared to accept.

4. (p. 63) Trevor Huddleston, Bishop of Masai 1960–68, was not appointed to Birmingham, as Harold Wilson had implied, but became Suffragan Bishop of Stepney, and held that post until 1978. Elsie Chamberlain was the first woman chaplain in the Forces, appointed by my father in 1946 when he was Secretary of State for Air. She was subsequently President of the Congregational Federation.

5. (p. 83) Lord Fulton, a Vice-Chairman of the BBC, was appointed in 1966 to report on the organisation of the Civil Service. The Fulton Report was seen in 1968 as a major reforming report and was bitterly controversial within the Civil Service because it had amongst its recommendations proposals that would have broken down the hierarchy on which the Civil Service rested. It was also opposed by those Ministers who were in the pockets of their senior civil servants. Many of the reforms were subsequently implemented and undoubtedly did improve the structures of the Civil Service.

6. (p. 85) An Enabling Bill is a measure passed by Parliament which confers greater powers on a Minister to make orders which may or may not require specific parliamentary endorsement but which, even if they do, only call for one vote instead of the full and cumbersome legislative procedure required for normal Bills. This practice, which used to be denounced as a socialist plot to

destroy democracy, has in fact become much more common under all Governments, particularly under recent Conservative administrations.

The classic example of an Enabling Act is the European Communities Act of 1972, which actually conveyed full power to the Common Market Commissioners to make laws for Britain which come into force without any requirement for approval by the British Parliament.

7. (p. 118) Following a UN Security Council resolution in November 1967 on the critical Arab-Israeli situation, Dr Gunner Jarring, Swedish Ambassador in Moscow, was appointed to conduct talks with Egypt, Jordan and Israel. The Jarring Mission continued its attempts to mediate from 1968–70, with very little success.

8. (p. 133) During the General Election campaign of 1945, the Chairman of the Labour Party, Harold Laski, stated that Mr Attlee would not be bound by any foreign agreements reached by Winston Churchill (then Prime Minister), and called for a socialist foreign policy. Churchill's response, that the NEC would control an incoming Labour Government, was strongly repudiated by Clem Attlee. The exchange formed an important part of the Election campaign, and Clem Attlee's response has since been taken as an authoritative statement of the independence of the Parliamentary Labour Party from the NEC and Conference.

2
In Place of Strife
January–October 1969

One of the most controversial issues of the 1964–70 Labour Government was the White Paper 'In Place of Strife' brought forward in January 1969 by Barbara Castle, the Secretary of State for Employment and Productivity.

The origins of this White Paper lay in the rising incidence of industrial action in British industry, which Harold Wilson and Barbara Castle believed to be a major obstacle to production, economic growth and investment. The legislation which they sought, as set out in the White Paper, would limit the powers of the trade unions in the field of disputes in a number of ways. The clauses provoking the greatest hostility from trade union leaders and the Parliamentary Labour Party were those conferring powers on the Secretary of State to order a twenty-eight-day 'conciliation pause' before strikes, with financial penalties for contraventions, and to insist on a ballot of members before official strike action.

This policy, the forerunner of Edward Heath's Industrial Relations Act of 1971, was replaced by alternative proposals agreed at a special meeting of the TUC in June 1969. This division between the Government, and its supporters in the PLP and the country was probably one of the most significant episodes of the Labour Government, and was seen as a great defeat for Harold Wilson.

In the first instance, I supported these proposals for reasons which my diary records, but as the argument developed it was clear that such legislation would involve a major clash between the Labour Government and the trade unions, and would undermine trade unionism, so I concluded that the proposals should be abandoned.

My diary for the first six weeks of 1969 was not dictated until mid-February and is therefore something of a precis of events.

Friday 3 January 1969

Up at 6 am to London where we had a Cabinet on Barbara's trade union White Paper. Barbara had rung me on Thursday night to discuss this because she'd decided to talk to the TUC before bringing it to Cabinet. This created a tremendous row. A lot of Cabinet Ministers bitterly resented having read in the press what the proposals were before any papers had been put to us. Dick Crossman was extremely angry, partly because he thought Barbara's White Paper was going to scoop his pensions White Paper, which he had been working on for eleven years, and partly because he thought it was sloppy work.

Jim Callaghan and others, Dick Marsh particularly, were entirely opposed to the idea of 'cooling-off' periods or strike ballots. I joined in and said I was in favour. First of all industrial life is more complex now than it ever has been and you simply cannot have a disturbance in the system anywhere without us all suffering, and second, the democratisation of pressure groups, which is the case for strike ballots, seems right to me.

Sunday 5 January
This morning we had six policemen banging on the front door because they had heard that there was an intruder on the roof. In fact there had been police on the roof in the middle of the night and they had looked through the window of Stephen's room, seen the terrible mess and had come to the conclusion that it had been rifled.

Monday 6 January
We had our weekly ministerial meeting and discussed the *QEII*, Concorde and the Airbus, all of which are in a terrible state. The turbines of the *QEII* aren't working properly, which is worrying; Concorde costs are escalating and the whole question of cancellation is bound to arise again quite quickly.

Thursday 9 January
Another early Cabinet on industrial relations – this thing goes on and on and on. Barbara has made a lot of trouble for herself, quite frankly, by not consulting us earlier, but that can't be helped now. I rather sympathise with her. It is extremely difficult to get anything through and once the Cabinet gets at you, you are severely restricted.

Friday 10 January
I got up early and spent the day with the Beagle Aircraft Company. I was flown up to Leicestershire in a 206, a beautiful aircraft, with the Chairman, Peter Masefield. We saw a tatty little company producing these marvellous aircraft in a shed – just like building Spitfires during the War. I talked to the men in the shop and I told them why we had bought the company and how we were going to leave the management to handle it: we believed in them and hoped that they would support us.

Then in the plane down to Shoreham and saw the Beagle production going on, again talked to the workers from a platform they put up for me. It's part of my idea of talking to people directly.

I flew back to Gatwick in a Beagle Pup and Peter Masefield's son, Charles Masefield, who was the chief test pilot, let me loop-the-loop and do a slow roll which I haven't done for twenty-five years. I thoroughly enjoyed it.

Saturday 11 January
Caroline and I went to Chequers for a dinner for the Commonwealth Prime Ministers' Conference.

I went up to Archbishop Makarios and we had a chat. He said, 'Of course, you know that although I am President of Cyprus, I still have to work on a Sunday.' He was very funny. When I asked him what the attitude of the Greek Orthodox Church was to the pill, he said, 'Well, we leave it to the individual.' He said he was afraid that this question would come up when he visited the Pope, who did in fact say, 'Archbishop, what is the population of Cyprus?' Makarios said he braced himself and gave the answer and the Pope replied, 'That's rather more than I imagined,' and moved on to a different subject. He had a great twinkle in his eye, a most amusing man. I imagine Field Marshal Harding must have had a job with Makarios when Harding was Governor of Cyprus.

William Armstrong, who had had a lot of brandies, was very mellow, indeed rather forthcoming. He said he thought the Labour Party would win the next Election, and that he wouldn't have any hesitation in appointing Edward Heath as a Permanent Secretary. He said he thought he'd be jolly good as a Permanent Secretary, implying that he would be no good as Prime Minister, which I think is being a bit unjust to Heath. He said that the great problem in society now was to find a substitute for war, a substitute for God, a substitute for sex and so on.

Monday 13 January
Today I had my first meeting with Pozderac, the Yugoslav Minister of Industry. I said I would like to see cooperation between Yugoslavia and Britain in a wide perspective, and he told me about the possibilities of buying products from Britain: he's interested in nuclear reactors, aircraft and computers.

John Freeman came to see me before he goes to America as Ambassador. I told him that the Ministry of Technology was viewed suspiciously there because of our Anglo-Russian and Eastern European approaches. I said that we probably do more business with America than anyone else on the nuclear and aircraft side. He said that he thought that where a vital national interest was involved it was probably right to stand up to the Americans. Poor John's had a bit of a problem on his hands because when he was Editor of the *New Statesman* he was highly critical of Nixon and they have dug all this up. He's now busy recanting.

After that I had Sir Leonard Drucquer, Chairman of the Council of

Engineering Institutions. It was amusing because the Engineering Institutions are worried that young engineers aren't joining them, but joining Clive Jenkins's Association of Scientific, Technical and Managerial Staffs. I told him I thought it was because Engineering Institutions weren't doing their job.

Wednesday 15 January
I went to the Yugoslav reception briefly and then on to see *Gone With the Wind* with the Gibsons. I hadn't ever seen it before, marvellous movie.

Thursday 16 January
We approved the industrial relations White Paper at Cabinet. I had participated pretty actively in support of it at various stages; so had Peter Shore, and Harold was obviously set on it.

Stanley Gillen [Vice-President, Ford USA] came to see me to complain that Fords had not had a knighthood since the war, except for Sir Patrick Hennessey's in 1947. So I said I would try and get one for Bill Batty, the Managing Director of Ford. It's ridiculous, but there you are.

I gave a reception for Pozderac at Lancaster House and later Ruth and Seretse Khama came to dinner with us, together with Barbara Stonehouse. Seretse looked extremely ill: he was very thin and quiet. We had a lovely evening. He talked about what it was like being President. He's an old family friend and he is, of course, Melissa's godfather.

John Stonehouse looked in at the end. He's terribly bitter that he hasn't been made head of a Department and can't understand why. The fact is nobody trusts him although he's got this extraordinary ability in dealing with the public. He's got a lot of problems on his hands.

Saturday 18 January
Joe Cort[1] came in the afternoon for a very interesting talk. He's entirely involved in the Czech revolution and bitterly anti-Russian. He describes Russia as Stalinist and Asian. The young people of Prague thought that Britain hadn't done enough to help them, that we had been too negative and careful, and contrasted this with what others had done, though actually as far as the Russians are concerned we've gone way out on a limb, and they pick us out for special abuse at the moment.

He thought that the liberals in Moscow would win and that Brezhnev would be pushed out. He also told me there were rumours that the CIA had created the Czech crisis in order to keep NATO alive. They had fed into the Russian Intelligence network masses of reports that the Germans were about to move into Czechoslovakia and win it over to the Western bloc and the Russians had gone almost crazy, and had reacted by occupying Czechoslovakia. In this way, of course, NATO had been revived. It's a very subtle argument, but the more I move among high

Government officials and study Intelligence operations, even at the very limited level of understanding I have of them, the more I am prepared to believe anything.

Joe himself has broken up with his wife and is going to marry his research assistant. He's very highly regarded and still a Communist, there's no doubt about that, but he's now a democratic Communist of the kind that you get in Britain and Western Europe.

Tuesday 21 January

In the afternoon I went to talk to the entire Mintech staff in Church House. Otto had been a bit worried, because senior officials don't like Ministers going over their heads straight to the staff, but there were a lot of questions, some of them highly critical. One guy got up and said, 'I've been working in the mechanical engineering division for three years and I don't think I've done anything at all that's of any use.' It gave a feeling of contact and I think it was appreciated; I enjoyed it.

Later, David Kingsley and his people gave their presentation to the NEC at the House of Commons and it made a very profound impression. I supported them in advocating that we ought to go out and listen to what people had to say. George Brown, who was slightly tight and had come in late, was sitting at the back and made this the occasion for an attack on me. He said, 'This isn't what the Party is about – just bribing people with promises and abandoning their faith and their principles.' Quite odious, old-fashioned stuff but the fact is George Brown hates my guts.

Caroline and I went to dinner with Arnold Weinstock and his wife; Klaus and Marion Moser were also there. Moser is the head of the Government Statistical Office, an old friend of the Weinstocks. They live in a flat which is fantastic – it is like a first-class cabin on the *QEII* with no evidence of human habitation. If they moved out, somebody else would be able to move in without having to move a single thing.

Arnold is a very complex character. I don't know his background except that he did go to university and he married the daughter of Michael Sobell, who ran an electrical company, and got into the company that way. He began doing very well, bought up General Electric and then bought up AEI, and then English Electric. He is now in the same scale of operation as Fritz Philips or Siemens. I pressed Arnold very hard on attending some of his board meetings.

In fact, he doesn't have board meetings – he doesn't believe in that way of working – but said he'd invite me to his budget meeting and this is to be fixed up. I find him agreeable, easy to work with, but incredibly primitive politically. Not so much reactionary, just primitive; he doesn't know what it's all about. He described Brian Abel-Smith at the LSE as a troublemaker when he is a middle-aged, respectable Fabian social engineer. But certainly I have got good relations with him and I want to build on them.

Friday 24 January

This was a day spent in Bristol on Concorde and I didn't get to bed until 2 this morning.

I went to the Gipsy Patch Lane works where there was a ban on overtime because of sub-contracting, and talked to the men from the top of an ITV truck through my loudspeaker. They shouted and jeered at me but I did the best I could and they did listen. I later discovered that the shop stewards had told the men not to come to the meeting. They had the same sort of reluctance to my being allowed a hearing by the workers as Otto Clarke has when I want to speak to Mintech staff.

In the afternoon, I went to meet the shop stewards, fifteen of them, and they were absolutely violent. They said I was supporting the management in an attempt to depress the workers' standard of living; that I had promised to cancel Concorde at the time the RB-211 order had been won in America. I said to them, 'Look, the problem is this: we don't know whether Concorde is going to be sold; we don't know whether anyone is going to buy; this is the problem. You'll just have to believe me.' I think I made some impact, but they decided to go on with their overtime ban.

Monday 3 February

I took Melissa and Joshua with me this morning to meet Colonel Frank Borman, the American spaceman, who's come to Britain on the first stop of a European goodwill tour. I met him at the front of Millbank Tower and he presented me with a miniature of the module which is going to land on the moon this summer, and then I took him up. I had the little ones [Joshua and Melissa] waiting in the lift and he was awfully sweet with them. We had a most interesting discussion.

He said as far as spin-offs from the moon programme were concerned, the really valuable spin-off was management. Here was a programme that cost $40,000 million and involved 400,000 people. There were four million moving parts in the rocket spacecraft and they had got round the moon and splashed down within a few seconds of the computer predictions. This is undoubtedly a most important feature.

He told me one or two other amazing facts. For example, one thousand million people had heard him read from the Book of Genesis on the other side of the moon on Christmas Eve: 500 million on television and 500 million on sound – about one in four of the world's population. Borman himself said he thought the whole space programme had helped to unite humanity and to unite past and present and he gave a very interesting example. He said that during the flight the children of one of the other astronauts had sent a message through the space centre in Houston asking, 'Who's flying now?', and the answer was Sir Isaac Newton, because at that particular time they were operating without controls, just being carried towards the moon by the force of gravity. 'It united us with Galileo and we felt a part of history,' he said.

Tuesday 4 February

Ray Macdonald, the President of Burroughs, the American computer company, came to see me. I got him to agree to talks between the Department and Burroughs about the nature of their operations in Britain. He said, quite sensibly, that he thought the big international corporations were the equivalent of the chartered companies of earlier centuries who carried technology to new lands, describing how, years ago, the Virginia Company would not allow the native Red Indians to have access to crossbows. I drew a parallel and said, 'I suppose that's why you won't let us make central processors here.' He took it well. He likes to keep in touch with the Ministers in the countries in which he operates and it opened my eyes to other aspects of international company business.

Monday 10 February

The papers are absolutely full of the Cunard row with John Brown Engineering, the builders of *QEII*. Sir Basil Smallpeice of Cunard had issued a statement saying that he won't accept the ship unless there's a totally independent examination of the turbines. He wants to bring in AEI, who are, of course, rivals of John Brown and they won't have it. I decided to put Sir Arnold Lindley, the President of the Institute of Mechanical Engineers, on to it.

Harold Wilson phoned up. He's very angry with Smallpeice and wanted me to tick him off. I spoke to Smallpeice and got him to agree to have Lindley do the examination.

Tuesday 11 February

Two-day trip to Scotland. Derek Moon, Ivor Manley and I flew up in the HS125 and were met by a battery of photographers; we went to John Brown Engineering to look at the turbines. I was amazed at how small they were and rather staggered by the muddled way in which they appear to be repairing them. But there's not much one can do at the moment except hope for the best. I thought the people at John Brown were very self-confident and didn't want to be interfered with.

Then I went by car to the National Engineering Laboratory. There was a dispute going on at the time because the exhibits that had been laid on for my visit had to be completed overnight. But there was no reference made to it. I looked at the work on hydrostatic transmission.

Alex Issigonis, the inventor of the Mini, was there, and he was as excited as anything at the work being done.

Wednesday 12 February
Up at 6.30 to go to the Babcock and Wilcox factory which is threatened with closure. Dick Mabon [Labour MP for Greenock] had come and together with the head of Babcock and Wilcox we went into the canteen to address the workforce. It was just like a prewar scene of thirty years before, with the men in their raincoats and caps, all dirty and brown and no colour at all except for the bright lights of the television cameras covering the meeting. I said I had nothing to promise them but I would do my best. They listened very patiently and asked questions, and there was a cheer as we left.

We travelled to Scott Lithgow's along the Clyde in the ferry, saw them building their big bulk carriers, then to Upper Clyde Shipbuilders and as I went in I saw a tremendous crowd of people shouting and waving placards, 'Wedge Don't Hedge', and 'Let's Go With Labour But Not The Labour Exchange', and all that.

The Upper Clyde Shipbuilders crisis was part of a long saga both of the decline of the British shipbuilding industry and of the particular problems that confronted shipbuilding on the Clyde. In 1948 Britain launched 48 per cent of the world's ships and shipbuilding, one of the oldest industries in Britain, was seen as essential to our industrial role and our role as a great maritime and imperial power.

But the failure of the shipbuilders to invest in new equipment, the fact that the yards were on narrow rivers, ill-suited to deal with the huge tankers and bulk carriers that came to be the mainstay of the maritime fleets of the postwar world, and the British shipping companies' reluctance to buy British ships, all contributed to a steady decline. The problems were exacerbated by the feudal attitude of the shipbuilders who employed a very harsh yard management, locked in combat with a trade union movement heavily entrenched in the old craft structures of the industry.

Soon after the Labour Government came to power in 1964, there was a threat of a closure at the Fairfields Yard at Govan on the Clyde: George Brown, in his capacity as First Secretary and Secretary of State for Economic Affairs, made this a crusade of his own, and trade union money was put into the company, which was to be run on a model basis, and was placed under the chairmanship of Sir Ian Stewart.

However, because of the inherent economic pressures and the hostility of the old shipbuilders who resented the emphasis and advantages apparently conferred upon Fairfields, the new company ran into difficulties. In 1965 Sir Reay Geddes had been appointed to examine the future of the shipbuilding industry and the Geddes Report in the spring of 1966 urged that the shipyards be merged into estuarial units that would allow them to be managed on a larger scale and to attract and sustain a more professional form of management.

It fell to me, as newly appointed Minister of Technology in July 1966, to implement these policies with the help of a newly established Shipbuilding Industry Board (SIB). The board included Sir William Swallow, former Chairman of General Motors in Britain, and Joe Gormley, President of the National Union of Mineworkers.

One of the first functions of the SIB was to group together the Upper Clyde yards, that is to say John Brown, Yarrow, Fairfields and Connell's into the Upper Clyde Shipbuilders group. Anthony Hepper, a young manager who had previously been the Managing Director of Pretty Polly Stockings, and one of George Brown's advisers at the DEA, was put on the Board of the SIB and was persuaded in August 1967 to take over Chairmanship of the UCS group.

By early 1969, the new group had already run into financial difficulties and Hepper was talking about major lay-offs. My diary for 1969 records various missions to Glasgow to talk to the workers and the board of UCS and explain to them that the amount of Government aid was necessarily limited.

By March 1971, UCS ran into another serious crisis and in June UCS was allowed to go bankrupt. It was then that I returned to Glasgow, working closely with UCS shop stewards, notably Jimmy Reid and Jimmy Airlie who were both leading members of the Communist Party and supporting the occupation of the yards.

The shipyards were empty as I walked round with Tony Hepper. I slipped through the gates and walked to a football field where 15,000 people had gathered.

It was a terribly cold day; my face was almost frozen with the cold. I could hardly smile, but I still jumped up on the truck and they listened to me. That was the main thing. I told them that it was difficult to get a match so that jobs were available in exactly the right quantities at exactly the right time. They were cheering and jeering and they didn't know quite what to make of it. They were clearly pleased I had come up to the Clyde to encourage them and I told them to keep their spirits up.

When I had finished my short speech, I jumped off the truck and talked to a few people. A woman came up and gave me a kiss and said, 'He's lovely': there was deep anxiety and criticism but also human warmth.

I went to lunch at Strathclyde University where Mother had arrived. I sat between Lord Todd, the man who discovered Vitamin B1, a most intolerably conceited Scots scientist, and Sam Curran, the Vice-Chancellor, whom I like very much, and Mother sat on the other side of the table. Then we went to the ceremony in the Assembly Hall. Everyone was in bright robes, the organ was playing and I was given the Doctorate of Law, wearing my reindeer cloak and red gown. I felt I had joined the Establishment in a way I had never quite experienced before; quite awe-inspiring.

Saturday 15 February
I had foolishly decided to get home from Bristol tonight so I hired a car and drove through the night. I slept most of the way on the road I think – I kept finding myself drifting off – it was very dangerous. I am sorry I did it but I got home at about 1.15 am, and had twelve hours in bed, which was heavenly.

Tuesday 18 February
At lunch I had William Armstrong over from the Treasury. He is an extremely nice man and we had a talk about the Fulton Report and the problems of organising the Civil Service Department. I told him about my think tank. My idea at the moment about it is that you leave the departmental pyramid under the Permanent Secretary unaltered. But you must put bore holes down into different parts of the pyramid to bring up talent on an entirely non-ranking basis. He told me he was contemplating a comparable sort of organisation. I can see a network of these developing in Whitehall.

Wednesday 19 February
This afternoon Stephen Swingler and Lady Bonham Carter died, and I began to feel very unwell as I always do when anyone dies of a heart attack.

Thursday 20 February
Melissa was twelve today and we had family celebrations.

Lord Kings Norton came to the office and we discussed the Aldermaston Report that he had produced for me last summer. We talked briefly about Lord Rothschild's minority report which recommended the end of nuclear weapons but was outside the terms of reference of the enquiry.

Cabinet, where we had a short discussion on hanging and Jim Callaghan described how he was going to deal with Heath's recent attempt to make political capital out of the crime wave.

We had a long discussion on Europe. A fortnight ago de Gaulle summoned Christopher Soames, our Ambassador in Paris, and suggested direct talks between Britain and France, based on the idea that ultimately Europe would be independent of NATO and the Common Market would break up or change out of all recognition. It seemed that de Gaulle had put a hostage to fortune in our hands, and Michael Stewart immediately told the Americans and the other Common Market countries so that a tremendous row is blowing up. At the same time we are using the Western European Union for political consultations with other members of the Community and the French have decided not to cooperate.

So Anglo-French relations are at about the worst they have been, I should think, since the beginning of this century. I said I thought we ought to be relaxed about it. Things were going our way, we were developing well, we had NATO and technological agreements with the European countries, good relations with EFTA, developing trade and industrial links with the Six, and we shouldn't be too frantic. It slightly upset Michael Stewart but I was just putting my Mintech view of foreign policy.

Fritz Philips, Chairman of Philips NV, came to see me for an urgent talk. The Industrial Reorganisation Corporation have found that Philips' subsidiary in Britain was running a balance of payments deficit by paying over the odds for components and in this way transferring its profits to Holland where taxation was lower. So Charles Villiers, representing the Industrial Reorganisation Corporation, went over to Eindhoven without any Government authority and began to bully the company, and Fritz Philips agreed to come over here.

He is a curious man. He is sixty-four and reminds me of a rabbit – he has long rabbity teeth and keeps sticking his tongue out between his lips, and his eyes dart about. He is a fervent Moral Rearmament man. It was most interesting talking to him: I said I would like to attend a board meeting in Eindhoven to explore the frontier of common interest between the international company and a national government. He invited me and he told me that Philips had amended their articles of association to allow them to serve the whole community and contribute towards prosperity, which I thought was useful.

Tuesday 25 February
My trip to Dagenham was cancelled this morning at Barbara Castle's request because the Ford strike is getting so terribly complicated. It is very difficult to know what to do. Various emergency meetings were called to consider what to do about Upper Clyde. They have very nearly gone into liquidation and we agreed to give them three months' notice and expect some results.

I had a meal at the House, changed into a black tie and went to Number 10 to meet President Nixon who had expressed a desire to meet Cabinet members other than those who were going to dine with him. The whole Cabinet was there, and so were John Freeman and the US Ambassador. John Freeman has apparently made a statement to the effect that he has ceased to be a socialist and to this extent has repudiated his past, but then again Nixon is supposed to have had psychoanalysis and repudiated his, so I suppose it is evens.

After introducing Nixon, Harold brought him round and described everyone's responsibilities. When I told him I was married to a Cincinnati girl, he said, 'Aha, Hamilton County,' which showed what a good politician he was, knowing the county pattern in a particular state. I told him about the Harriers we hoped to sell him and that I did a lot of business with America on aviation and nuclear energy.

Then we went and sat round the Cabinet table and Harold welcomed him formally. It was a rather agreeable atmosphere. Nixon said a word: how he was anxious that cooperation with Britain shouldn't only be about foreign policy but should cover the whole range of domestic matters. He laid great emphasis on the current problems of youth and protest and said that young people had nothing to strive for, and that there was no idealism left – or rather there was, but no scope for it.

Harold was quite contemptuous of the young and said they didn't know what to do, and all that. Judith corrected him and said the young needed to be inspired. One or two other people were asked to speak, then I said, 'Mr President, I spend five days a week trying to introduce technology and the other two thinking about the effect this has on society. Young people today are aware of this and they take it for granted; they have nothing to forget, as older people have, and they think we are suffering from acute institutional obsolescence – and I suspect they are right. It is all very well to mock them for not knowing what to do but I am not sure that *we* know what to do. They are international. Mr Borman spoke to one thousand million people when he read from the Book of Genesis orbiting round the moon: international technology has created a world youth movement.' I said I had a son of seventeen and had learned more from him than he had from me.

Then Denis Healey said something about young people not being interested in technology at all, but that wasn't the point I was making.

Dick Marsh said he had a son of eighteen and young people just liked making trouble, that was the important thing. There was really nothing in student protest to think about: it was just intellectual masturbation. It was a very crude and vulgar comment.

Dick Crossman said that all was lost, that De Gaulle was the silliest old man that ever was; that we were heading for an extreme right-wing period; that the Left had simply created a Gaullist victory in France, and had created Nixon's victory in America. It was a really *New Statesman* defeatist speech of the kind that Dick excels at. But there was a lot of laughter and at the end Nixon said, 'Why don't we have Dick Crossman, and we'll send you Marcuse!' That more or less ended the discussion.

Wednesday 26 February
Went to the National Executive. I saw Jeremy Bray about the publication of his extraordinary book, *Decision in Government*, calling for a complete reform of the machinery of government, which has created a great crisis at Number 10.

Thursday 27 February
Cabinet at 10, where we had Dick Marsh's Green Paper on road policy
which led to a great deal of discussion. He'd left out any reference to the
Channel Tunnel, which was slightly odd.

Then we moved on to what are called rather pedantically 'overseas
affairs', and the de Gaulle crisis after Soames's interview last week. This
has blown up into a tremendous thing and the Foreign Office were
convinced that the French were setting a trap to persuade us to agree to
discussions based on the idea of the Common Market and NATO
disappearing. So they played it very cool and told their allies. De Gaulle
claimed that he had been misunderstood – relations are really very bad.

Friday 28 February
I went over to Number 10 for a meeting of the Parliamentary
Committee. Burke Trend brought up the question of Jeremy Bray's
book, which raises the tremendously important principle of whether
Ministers should be allowed to write things while in office. I said I was in
favour and Peter Shore was on the other side. It was interesting because
my view of people escaping from their narrow responsibilities is really
fundamental to my whole broadcasting lecture and it's beginning to spill
over into my thinking about other things.

I went back and had a sandwich lunch with Jim Callaghan who had
suggested this a couple of weeks ago. He wanted to know what the
Ministry of Technology did. We discussed the boundaries position: he
was trying to think of ways of delaying the introduction of the new
parliamentary boundaries. Then, among other things, he said that he
was determined to get rid of Hugh Scanlon. He said it wouldn't cost
more than £40,000 to run a campaign against Scanlon and it would
save exports to an enormous extent. I expressed some shock at this and I
think he noted it but he is the great machine politician and doesn't
hesitate to organise.

Tuesday 4 March
Saw John Hill first thing in the morning to discuss the delay in the
commissioning of Dounreay and the need for economies in the AEA
which I am insisting on and which he is resisting.

Then I went to the Economic Policy Committee and we had a long
discussion on public expenditure. I proposed that all civil servants
should be judged in their annual report on the basis of whether they had
economised on public expenditure – which created something of a stir.
Then UCS came up and I more or less carried the day except that they
insisted that a firm of accountants went in to look at the figures to satisfy
me that the money was really needed.

A reporter from the *Sheffield Telegraph* carried out a long and interesting interview on computers and privacy. It is a bit outside my scope but I hit upon the idea that the best security against the police state is that everybody should be entitled by law to have a printout of all that was available about them on computer files. If there was an inaccuracy they could raise it and, in any case, would never be put in a position of others knowing things about them that they didn't know themselves.

Otto looked in and said that Harold had told Burke Trend that Nixon had been very impressed by my contribution during the Cabinet meeting, and Harold himself wanted to see my charts on the growth of technology and its impact on society.

Thursday 6 March
I went to the Annual General Meeting of the Bristol South East Constituency Party. They were extremely friendly and the feeling was that the Party is not demoralised but what everybody wants to know is where we are going and what we have got to do. This is the great weakness of pragmatism. It isn't that people want ideology, but they want analysis and explanation and at the moment they are simply not getting it.

Friday 7 March
Nuclear Policy Committee, to consider the position on the centrifuge with the talks coming up this week. I had put in two complicated papers written by Michael Michaels. It took me about four hours to master them, let alone present them. I got more or less what I wanted but Denis Healey launched into a violent attack and said that the whole thing had been badly handled and that a non-departmental Minister should be put in charge. I said that I thought the Prime Minister had been in charge of this and I didn't think he had done it badly at all. That shut Denis up but he was doing everything he possibly could to be difficult because of the American links.

This week has just about finished me.

Sunday 9 March
Lazy lie-in this morning. It was a beautiful day, about the fourth consecutive perfect day and while Caroline worked on her education book, I was in the garden making a visual aid lecture stand. Joshua is away on a two-week school camp.

Monday 10 March
At 4 pm, Gerhard Stoltenberg, the German Minister of Science, Fred Mulley and I met for a couple of hours during which we discussed the Non-Proliferation Treaty. I took the opportunity of saying at the

beginning that we were drawing to the close of a long, exclusive and intimate period of nuclear relationship with the United States, and that we recognised that there were common interests between us and the Germans, commercial interests in the peaceful development of atomic energy – I knew this was what was in the back of Stoltenberg's mind.

In the evening I took Stoltenberg to dinner at Simpson's. We discussed the centrifuge and our relations with France and I indicated discreetly that I thought the Soames affair was rather unfortunate. Then he made it perfectly clear that the Germans wouldn't sign the Non-Proliferation Treaty, even at the earliest, until the end of the year after their elections: it has now become an election issue.

Thursday 13 March

Had Mr Rahnema, the Minister of Science and Higher Education in Iran, and his Deputy-Minister to see me. I didn't think I would really like Rahnema because he is a friend of the Shah and I think the whole Iranian set-up is pretty corrupt, but in fact he was an extremely bright man who has radically reorganised higher education in Iran.

In order to get away from the provision of long specialist medical courses for example, they had 'six-month' doctors, 'one-year' doctors, 'two-year' doctors and put them in positions where they could do immediate good – 'six-month' doctors were distributed as First-Aid doctors in the villages. This encouraged me to say to him, 'Why don't we do a deal? You do an analysis on the needs of your villages, I will give some research and development contracts to industries in this country and we shall do joint marketing in Third countries.' He promised me he would look at this. It was the first time I had really made any progress with anybody on my plans for trying to develop intermediate technology as one of our major exports.

Friday 14 March

Up very early this morning with Ivor Manley and Derek Moon, Gerry Fowler [Parliamentary Secretary] having missed the plane, and flew to Glasgow. This is my big visit to Upper Clyde to try to get over to the men that in fact there is no possibility of Upper Clyde being sustained indefinitely by a safety net. I had ten meetings, and I must have spoken to 7,000 or 8,000 men altogether. I began with the UCS board who conveyed their extreme anxiety and said they had been let down. They had all gathered there thinking they would get three or four years to prove the profitablity of the company.

Then I had a general meeting of the shop stewards from the UCS group and I delivered my first talk and answered questions. It was pretty tough and there were a few shouts. One guy called Sam Barr, a

Communist shop steward, said they simply wouldn't accept redundancy.

I remained in the canteen and the staff of John Brown at Clydebank had arrived, so I gave the same talk, and someone said that Hepper was much too remote in Fitzpatrick House and wasn't keeping in touch with the situation, which I am sure is true.

I tried to address 6,000 hourly-paid workers in the fabricating shed but I was a bit late and missed them, so I stood up with my loudspeaker and addressed as many people as I could gather, but it was a few hundred only. I went over, missing my lunch, to Govan, the Fairfields yard and did a prolonged meeting in the fabricating shed there. It was a rough meeting. At Yarrow I spoke to the staff and the hourly-paid workers. Then I came back while Gerry Fowler spoke at Connell's and gave a press conference at Fitzpatrick House. I had a double confidence problem: I had to shake the confidence of the workers by referring to the absenteeism and unofficial strikes but I also had to encourage the outside world because of course the customers and suppliers were thinking that UCS would collapse.

It was a very tough, very tiring day. But I think my trip to the Clyde created an impression that we are genuinely trying to help. And if you go there and see it for yourself, people relax. They know you know the problems and they don't get so intense.

Monday 17 March
Upper Clyde Shipbuilders is still a great anxiety and relations between the Shipbuilding Industry Board and UCS have completely collapsed because SIB are being obstinate rather than tough and UCS are just declining to pull their finger out.

There are so many people who want the whole thing to fail: Sir Charles Connell, the Deputy-Chairman of UCS, who wants to punish Fairfields for their experiment and believes in the old idea of throwing men out of work to discipline them; Yarrow, the other Deputy-Chairman, who is longing for the moment when he can pull out Yarrows from UCS and make a profit and join up with his old friends in Lower Clyde; then there is Barry Barker of the SIB who wants it to fail for rigid reasons; Victor Chapman and Cliff Baylis in my office who think it can't possibly succeed; and Jack Diamond who isn't prepared to provide the money. There are a lot of enemies of Upper Clyde, quite apart from Lower Clyde, and others, so I am going to have a job propping it up. But I am going to go on trying because the industrial consequences of the failure of Upper Clyde would be tragic.

Down to Southampton to spend the night on the *QEII* which is now complete. Caroline missed the train because Ron was late picking her up but she arrived on the next train and we had a luxurious first-class cabin.

We had dinner with Smallpeice and Hepper and afterwards went round with Captain Warwick. It is a beautifully designed ship. Everybody seemed pleased, especially with the repaired turbines.

Tuesday 25 March

I had Janez Stanovnik, the Executive Secretary of the United Nations Economic Commission for Europe, to see me this morning. The ECE was set up after the war by the UN to stimulate economic cooperation between Eastern and Western Europe and had been sidetracked by the Cold War.

I had been advised that Stanovnik, who is a Yugoslav, had some plans and we should give them cautious encouragement but nothing much more. But after he had spoken a little, I could see all of a sudden the role of the ECE; that after twenty years of frustration by the Cold War we now had an opportunity, with bilateral East-West contacts developing, of building up the ECE to do what it was always intended to do. Stanovnik beamed and said I had put it in a way that he wouldn't have dared to believe possible.

I said, 'Well, I've always been a great UN man and this is a tremendously important area. If you don't try to change us, but build on the encouraging signs, you will make progress.' He was thrilled. I must try and meet him on my way back from Hungary and see whether I couldn't lead a delegation to the ECE myself when next it meets.

Went to Cabinet and Michael Stewart was roasted on Anguilla.[2] We have invaded the island and made ourselves look extremely foolish: Ronald Webster *has* got support and our information was wrong; the plain truth is that we've gone in there because the Americans have indicated in no uncertain terms that they expect us to keep the Communists and Mafia and anybody else out of these Caribbean islands.

So we are just their dog's-body and we've got ourselves into terrible trouble all over the world for no good purpose. Roy Jenkins and Denis attacked the Foreign Office: nobody had a good word to say for Michael Stewart.

Wednesday 26 March

The National Executive was a most important meeting. Joe Gormley's resolution, which indicated that the Executive couldn't support the Industrial Relations White Paper, came up and, as there had already been a discussion, we agreed to proceed to the vote. But then Jim Callaghan said he thought a division between the Government and the Party would be disastrous and he proposed a minor amendment which still criticised the White Paper but only parts of it, instead of the whole thing.

Barbara said she couldn't accept Jim's amendment and she proposed an amendment that the Executive welcomed the fact that she intended to discuss the matter further with the trade unions before legislation.

Then we took the vote. Jim voted not only for Joe's critical resolution but *against* Barbara's amendment welcoming the fact that she was going to be talking to the trade unions. An incredible thing. Eirene White, I think, abstained and the critical resolution was carried.

Saturday 29 March

Went by bike to lunch with the Soviet Ambassador and Gvishiani, Deputy-Chairman of the State Committee for Science and Technology.

We talked about the Economic Commission for Europe because I had had its new Yugoslav chief come to see me recently. He and I agreed we ought to try to get ECE matters dealt with by technological Ministers and not leave it entirely to the Ambassadors.

We then discussed my lecture in Moscow, or rather in Leningrad, and Gvishiani said that he thought it would be a pity simply to give it to students and he would like to get academicians and industrialists, people from the industrial Ministries to come along. He told me he was going to the USA to a United Nations conference. I hoped that he might make contact with the new American Administration, since we attached a great deal of importance to improved relations between the Soviet Union and the USA and this was well received.

Then I cycled off. I think I gave him an impression of a degree of informality in British politics which is absent in the Soviet Union.

Monday 31 March

I had lunch at the House with Eric Heffer, who is suffering from a total collapse of morale. He said that Harold would have to go and he thought that Dick Crossman should become Prime Minister. When an intelligent guy like Eric Heffer thinks that, then things must be pretty bad.

In the afternoon I went to the Ministerial Committee on Security, the supreme body on security matters. Jim Callaghan was in the chair. We had two questions: should we make known negative vetting, and what should we do about Government employees who had been prisoners-of-war of the Communists. On negative vetting we agreed that it wasn't really necessary to make it known to individuals, though we could put to a person who was being vetted a particular query in connection with his own security classification as a matter of management. On employment in security posts of ex-POWs we agreed to be a bit more flexible.

Wednesday 2 April

Bill Swallow and Barry Barker of the Shipbuilding Industry Board came to a sandwich lunch with me. Barker is still hoping and believing that UCS will collapse, Swallow having been won round to the point where he says it is now a social problem and not an economic question at all. But he hasn't even been to visit the UCS board and hasn't therefore got any personal assessment of the situation; I am not going to let it collapse and I think he has got to provide another £3 million.

Went to the Commons and after the 10 o'clock vote I talked in the Tea Room till 11. The boys are very demoralised at the manifest split over the 'In Place of Strife' White Paper. Things are pretty bad, quite frankly.

Thursday 3 April – Friday 4 April

My forty-fourth birthday. I had all my presents from the family and then at 10 I went to the Cabinet, Harold having got back late last night.

The main item was of course the row over Jim Callaghan's behaviour at NEC over Barbara's White Paper. Harold was much more moderate with Jim than I had expected and allowed Jim to get away with an explanation which was simply not true. I am afraid I was rather sharp with him. Barbara was vague and woolly and didn't want any action taken, although if I were her I would have been absolutely furious with Jim. Harold then asked the Cabinet to reaffirm their belief in the White Paper. Jim objected to this and Harold said it was all subject to consultation. We left the meeting without knowing more about where we were than at the beginning. I am afraid Jim is winning.

After the Cabinet Harold leaked the whole thing to the press – about how tough he had been and had warned Ministers they would get fired if they didn't stay in line. It was a perfect example of instant politics. It was so disrespectful of Harold to suggest he had kicked his Ministers into line. The papers the following morning were full of 'Toe the line or get out'. It was his equivalent of the 'dog licence' speech to the PLP and does reveal what a very small man he is.

I went back to the office for a while, where they gave me a pink shirt for my birthday.

Wednesday 9 April

Having heard last night at Stansgate that Concorde 002 was to fly for the first time today I got up at 5, drove to London and caught a plane to Bristol.

We landed at Filton and it was an extraordinary atmosphere. There was this beautiful bird being pulled out on to the tarmac, the most advanced aircraft project anywhere in the world, and it was just like a sort of village cricket match. Juster, the President of Boeing, was there and Ziegler of Sud Aviation, and so on, standing about on the grass because there were no seats; and there was a buffet lunch.

Brian Trubshaw, the test pilot, dressed in his yellow flying suit, kept going backwards and forwards muttering, 'It's the paperwork that's holding us up, it's those chaps doing the paperwork.' As he left to get into his car everyone shouted, 'Good old Trubby, good old Trubby.' I thoroughly enjoyed it as a matter of fact, but I wondered whether the occasion reflected a degree of amateurism in modern technology that wasn't quite right. George Edwards, with his hands plunged into his pockets and his pork pie hat on his head, was walking about like a vicar at a country fete wondering whether everything would go well.

In the end, in the afternoon the plane was pulled out and I stood on the runway and watched the fantastic belching of black smoke, my backbone vibrating with the noise. Then it went along the runway for its final taxi and simply took off. I jumped into a helicopter with Ziegler and Juster and George Edwards and we flew to Fairford where it was to land, but we lost our way and we got there too late to land before the Concorde but we saw it on the ground and I took some movies. There was a fantastic scene of pressmen crowding and fighting all over the place; it was like the landing of Charles Lindbergh in Paris in the 1920s, or one of Amelia Earhart's flights. The crew came down very modestly and they were asked to wave and then there was a press reception.

I flew back in the helicopter to Filton and went to the presentation for the crew. Trubshaw was given a gold cigarette case and George Edwards made a speech in which he congratulated 'those chaps who did the steering. Your gang were very good, Trubby,' he said. 'I remember the days when we brought you in from the RAF; and I would like to say a word about the Minister who in my book is keeping a friendly eye on this in Whitehall,' and all that. The whole thing was just like Biggles or Richmal Crompton's *Just William*; it had an entirely prewar feeling about it.

Monday 14 April

At 10 I went to Cabinet where Roy Jenkins announced his Budget. I was pretty tired and I think dozed through bits of it. I thoroughly dislike knowing something really secret thirty-six hours before it's going to be announced.

I came back to my office and Paul Johnson [Editor of the *New Statesman*] came to lunch. He's a funny man, Paul Johnson. He can't quite make me out, but what I did get across to him was the idea that the whole debate about industrial relations ought now to be taken to the people and that we ought to argue the case much more systematically at factory gates and so on.

At 4 there was a Cabinet meeting after the memorial service for

Eisenhower. The thing that really worried Peter Shore and me was that Roy announced that in his Budget speech he proposed to say that he wanted to drop the existing prices and incomes legislation in November. This was manifestly for political reasons and because of Party opposition. Jim Callaghan, who had been arguing that it should be dropped all along, has won on that, and on the strike ballot. This is what makes Harold's great tough talk to Ministers so totally unsatisfactory because basically it's so phoney.

After Cabinet I worked on my boxes. The position really is that the Government and Harold Wilson himself are in a very shaky position. The morale of the Parliamentary Labour Party is about as low as it's been for a long time.

Tuesday 15 April
I had lunch with the Polish Ambassador and his staff and Arnold Weinstock.

On Anglo-Polish economic relations Arnold Weinstock was hopelessly naïve. He said, 'I've just heard about a new switch we've invented in GEC and it's the best thing ever.'

So the Poles said very courteously, 'Well, we are doing a deal with Ericsson.'

'Oh, you can't buy Ericsson's equipment,' said Weinstock.

'Well,' said the Poles, 'we've been discussing relations with them for about five years and we are just about to sign the agreement.'

'Come and see me,' said Weinstock.

'Well, why don't you come and visit Warsaw,' said the Poles, not without a note of rebuke in their voices.

'Oh, I don't like foreign travel,' said Weinstock. 'Come and see me any time you like.'

Then we went on to the technological agreements and Weinstock couldn't see any case for them at all, although it was obvious that Ericssons had succeeded in getting close to this contract because they've been there for five years and spent a lot of time discussing things. Weinstock somehow assumed that people just buy stuff because it's the best. I was really rather disappointed with Weinstock, and it confirmed my suspicion that his export effort wasn't terribly serious or good.

I came home early. I didn't sit in to hear any of the Budget. I haven't done that for years because it is such a boring experience. Betty Harvie Anderson, one of the Tory women [MP for Renfrewshire East], came to tell me that Swallow's name stunk in the nostrils of the Upper Clyde Shipbuilders.

Wednesday 16 April
I went to Cabinet and here it was proposed by Harold that we drop the

Lords Reform Bill. There was a tremendous argument about it.

Dick Marsh made it clear that he thought the Bill should be totally dropped and not shunted into a siding, as Harold suggested, which had no credibility at all. John Silkin said we couldn't get a guillotine for the Bill.

Gerald Gardiner was for going on and so was Shackleton. Tony Greenwood was worried about it; he is always worried about everything, which doesn't much help.

Michael Stewart and I spoke for continuing the Bill. I said the Government was deeply committed and this really did reflect lack of will. The Bill had substantial merits. It was vital at this stage in Parliament that we shouldn't be frustrated in the last two years. This was a key part of our modernisation of institutions and it had been defeated by the Conservatives of Left and Right, that is to say Michael Foot and Enoch Powell, and this was the combination that was going to defeat us on the Industrial Relations Bill. If we did drop the Bill the Labour Party could never again say anything credible about the House of Lords.

Ronald Higgins came to have lunch. He used to be in the Foreign Office and indeed was Ted Heath's Private Secretary for two and a half years during the entire negotiations on entry into the Common Market under Macmillan.

He has left the FO now and gone to work for the *Observer* as David Astor's aide-de-camp, bridging the management and the editorial sides. He told me he had known Ted Heath as well as anyone could and that Ted Heath's real nature and character had been so suppressed that there was nothing real underneath any more. He had just got a concrete shell round his real self and this is why he never appeared to be sincere. It was a shrewd observation.

Thursday 17 April

I went to the office and had a brief meeting about the computers for the Royal Army Pay Corps and insisted that we had a fight with the Ministry of Defence who, predictably, want American IBM computers.

To the Parliamentary Labour Party meeting on 'In Place of Strife', where Harold was making one of his great speeches. Member after Member warned the Government that you couldn't intervene, and the meeting was almost unanimously against.

Monday 21 April

Economic Policy Committee meeting this morning, where we discussed regional policy and descheduling of Development Areas. It was rather scandalous because Harold has managed to get Merseyside reprieved from descheduling. Barbara was fighting very hard for Blackburn as an

Intermediate Area, although unemployment there is only 1.7 per cent. Tony Crosland was fighting for Grimsby though rather half heartedly, and Tony Greenwood for Rossendale and the Calder Valley and a new road. We also found ourselves tied by a pledge Barbara had given on the Humber Bridge for the Hull by-election. The whole thing was quite revolting, although Peter tells me that the policy he is recommending is perfectly defensible intellectually. I argued that we ought to try to devolve responsibility on to the regional economic planning councils and give them the money, but I lost out and retired.

In the evening I went to the London Chamber of Commerce banquet at the Mansion House for the International Chemical and Petroleum Exhibition. The first man I spoke to, who was from IPC, was criticising unofficial strikers and praising Barbara.

When I said to him, 'You look very brown, have you been away?' he said, 'I have just been to Majorca for two weeks but it was absolutely spoilt for me by all the Jews there.'

So that finished me. The sight of all these businessmen with their medals, sitting in that extraordinary Mansion House Banqueting Hall, just made me think that nothing at all had changed in one hundred years. Fortunately my speech was a summary of all that was wrong with British industry from 1850 onwards. It didn't go down very well but it was exactly what needed to be said.

Wednesday 23 April

To Farnborough this morning with President Saragat of Italy and Pietro Nenni, the Foreign Minister, on part of their state visit. The Earl of Westmoreland was there; he is a very charming man but having him there, as the Lord Lieutenant, and seeing all the flunkies from the Palace, was rather absurd.

Farnborough had organised an exhibition showing their work on aerodynamic design, on carbon fibres with some applications, and on sonic bang and engine noise research, including some very amusing demonstrations of organ music, showing that aeroplane engine noise caused less vibration on church windows than an organ. We watched a Harrier demonstration.

At lunch I talked to Nenni who said that he thought de Gaulle would win the Referendum,[3] though he hoped he wouldn't.

Saturday 26 April

This morning Caroline and I went off in the little HS125 jet to Bradford with Derek Moon for the conferment of my honorary Doctorate of Technology and the opening of the chemical engineering laboratory. We were met at the airport and taken in to see the Vice-Chancellor, E.G. Edwards, who is a supporter of the comprehensive school movement and backed them at the time that all the other Vice-Chancellors were attacking the idea of comprehensive education.

The degree ceremony was done with all the panache of a new university, then lunch, and I opened the new laboratory and made a speech.

Then Professor Page made a very interesting speech and said that he was trying to eliminate the idea of failure from education, which I found most exciting.

Sunday 27 April

I felt pretty ill, with aches and pains and a cough and an upset stomach.

Today de Gaulle was defeated in the French Referendum, contrary to what most experts had anticipated, and he announced just after midnight that he is giving up. That is the end of the latest chapter in de Gaulle's story, beginning eleven years ago in May, when he came to power as a result of the coup in Algiers and the threat by the leaders to land paratroops in Paris.

Monday 28 April

I went to the Economic Policy Committee where we had a discussion on industrial policy in which I tried to contribute. But I found Harold Wilson unusually frosty, more or less cutting me off short and ignoring what I said, concentrating all his attention on Tony Crosland and paying quite inordinate attention to his most inconsequential points.

Lunch with Nenni and Saragat at Number 10 and Nenni was much more forthcoming than previously. When we had the loyal toast, I said to Nenni, 'It makes for a real difficulty for me as a socialist republican to drink the loyal toast.' He said, 'Ah, I feel just the same. When I was a young man we used to sing a song which ran "With the guts of the last priest we shall strangle the last monarch", but as you get older you realise that you don't want to strangle anybody.'

In the evening, I had a depressing dinner with Peter Shore and Douglas Houghton. Peter is convinced that Harold is shifting his power base to the Right. Peter feels threatened by what's happening and also noticed the recent frosty reception that I was getting from Harold. I couldn't think of anything to cheer him up.

Douglas Houghton was exploding with rage at the way in which the Parliamentary Party was being treated, particularly at the Industrial Relations Bill being forced through. He gave me a sort of preview of what his own resignation speech would be.

Wednesday 30 April

There was a tremendous meeting of the PLP at the House. Bob Mellish more or less threatened and bullied us and told us that if we didn't pass the Industrial Relations Bill Parliament would have to be dissolved. Towards the end of the meeting Douglas Houghton banged his hammer and said, 'That's that.'

Then Michael Foot got up to speak and Douglas Houghton went on like a maniac, banging his hammer. The whole thing ended with the same sort of awful ill will that I remember from the 1951–7 period. It made me very gloomy.

Thursday 1 May

There were no daily papers because there was a May Day strike and the printers, among others, were protesting at Barbara Castle's 'In Place of Strife'.

I went to the Overseas Policy and Defence Committee, where we discussed selling Chieftain tanks to Israel and, as always, Dick Crossman made a passionate and extreme speech in favour of Israel, saying we were destined always to let them down and we were hypocritical in our relations with them. He was really quite unhinged.

Michael Stewart was not in favour of selling the tanks, but opinion veered in favour of it and it was agreed that we could let the Israelis know that we would make them available later, although we couldn't sign a contract at the moment. Michael Stewart therefore to some extent got his way, that he didn't want to supply this new and extremely sophisticated equipment before the Four-Power Talks* were complete.

We discussed Rhodesia, where Michael Stewart wanted to send a letter to the Smith regime withdrawing our insistence on the Privy Council as an external guarantee of their Constitution. Barbara Castle and Judith Hart put up a big fight against Stewart and so it was agreed that it would come back to Cabinet.

In the evening Sir Denning Pearson of Rolls Royce was interviewed on television and, after a brilliant first half, said that civil servants were not interested in long-term developments and that when you talked to them or politicians about these things a glazed look came into their faces, as if they were thinking of what they were going to have for lunch. This was so unjust and, in the light of all the help we had given Rolls Royce, so unfair that I wrote him a stinking letter to send once the office had seen it.

Saturday 3 May

Melissa was on the *Braden Show* and was asked about families she saw in television programmes. She said that they were very untypical because, 'we are just indifferent about our parents, we don't get excited about

---

* Throughout 1969 the US, Great Britain, France and the USSR held talks on the Arab-Israeli conflict; Israel opposed any 'Four-Power solution'.

them because we know we have to accept them', and 'you never see people going to the lavatory on television'. All in all it was hilarious.

Monday 5 May

Greeted this morning with a statement by Hepper in the papers that UCS were going into liquidation unless they got £12 million. I called a meeting to discuss this and agreed that I would have to go back to Glasgow.

I had to go to the House this afternoon to answer a Private Notice Question on UCS and said that Hepper's weekend statement had been irresponsible.

Then I had a talk to Sir Eric Yarrow, the Deputy-Chairman of UCS with Sir William Swallow, and tried to persuade him to take on the task of Chairman but he declined. I have great suspicion of Yarrow as he never wanted to come into the UCS venture and now would like to see the group collapse, though the consequences would be terribly serious, knowing that if it did collapse Yarrows could buy themselves out.

In the evening I was at the Commons where people are furious that Dick Crossman should have made his statement about increased charges for teeth and spectacles on the eve of the local government elections. Dick then said that he forgot the local elections were being held and by doing so removes from us the credit we might otherwise have got for being honest with the electorate, despite the political disadvantage entailed!

Wednesday 7 May

Up at 5.30 and Gerry Fowler, members of my office, William Swallow and I went by RAF plane to Glasgow for the UCS crisis. At 9 began a series of talks which went right through to 8 at night.

First of all we talked to the UCS board. Hepper raised with me my reference to his weekend statement as being irresponsible. I told him that in effect he had killed the company stone dead by what he had said, and that he had promised me that he wouldn't say anything over the weekend.

After that, I explained why we couldn't support the Upper Clyde Shipbuilders' Corporate Plan and said they had better go away and think about it.

The Confederation of Shipbuilding and Engineering Unions came into the same room and I went through the same thing with them, trying to get them to take some responsibility.

I had a brief talk to Malcolm Turner, the former Provost of Clydebank, and then I saw the board of UCS for a second time. They produced their plans for a major cut-back. I saw the STUC and got a sympathetic response from the other unions there.

I went out for a bit and came back and met the board alone for the last time. This time they said they would like to think further about alternative proposals.

It had been a whole-day teach-in on the distribution of responsibility back to the people who should exercise it and it showed the terrible dangers of defeatism.

Thursday 8 May

A remarkable Cabinet. Jim got in again on the Industrial Relations Bill and more or less made an open challenge to Harold's leadership. Harold had been fiddling around with the constitutional issues raised by Douglas Houghton's speech yesterday in which Douglas Houghton warned the Government not to go on with the legislation, or else face the possibility of a parliamentary defeat.

Harold is a very small-minded man, he always gets to the least important part of the issue, suggesting ways of downing the Tories or embarrassing Heath or putting Harry Nicholas in his place, when events call for a higher degree of statesmanship. But the really significant thing was that Jim said that he thought that we had no chance of sinking or swimming and it was now a case of 'sink or sink'.

In the course of this discussion I absolutely went for Harold and said that what depressed me most was this view that we were utterly defeated. This was half our trouble. The Cabinet never discussed anything seriously, we were still tied up as if we were civil servants, calling each other by our official names, and I knocked Harold for six. He said we would have to discuss it later and it would come up again under the question of tomorrow's joint meeting with the National Executive.

Then we came on to Rhodesia and we killed the letter that was to be sent to Smith who had overnight made a speech saying the whites would be in charge for a hundred years. So Barbara carried the day on that.

I went to see Michael Stewart about my Russian trip, the first time I had ever been to the Foreign Secretary's office. It was a huge mausoleum of a room, very depressing, I thought. I said to Michael, 'How can you get any new thoughts in here?' and he said, 'Ah, the new thoughts come from the papers,' to which I nearly responded, 'Like our policy on Anguilla, I suppose?'

He took an entirely neutral view of my trip; we discussed what I should do about Gerald Brooke* and he said Brooke was to face fresh charges but that I was to keep it quiet, so that if the Russians did decide to change their minds they wouldn't lose face.

---

*British college lecturer in Russian, imprisoned by the Soviet authorities for five years in 1965 for alleged espionage.

I told him that there was a possibility I might be seeing Kosygin. He said that was all right as long as I *didn't* discuss foreign policy at all. It was a most insulting thing for one Cabinet Minister to say to another but I presume he says it to every Cabinet Minister and I shan't take the slightest notice.

In the evening Caroline and I went to have dinner with the Russian Ambassador, Smirnovsky and his wife and a couple of thuggish new Counsellors at the Embassy, presumably security people. The Ambassador was tight and hurried us out of dinner so quickly that he clearly didn't want to discuss politics.

Friday 9 May
Joshua is eleven today.

We had the all-day joint meeting of the Cabinet and NEC, held in the state dining room at Number 10 with Eirene White in the chair.

Roy Jenkins opened with his usual speech about the economic situation and after a few other speeches, Joe Gormley said that because of our attitudes on prices and incomes and on the Industrial Relations Bill we had given the impression that we didn't trust the Trade Union Movement. John Chalmers of the Boilermakers said the unions were leading the fight for industrial efficiency. Frank Chapple said, 'Expel the Left'.

When it came to me I made a long contribution in which I said that what was wrong was that we had to correct one hundred years of neglect, that we were putting it right slowly, that our relations with industry were very difficult because only our failures came across and not our successes and we needed to consult the Trade Union Movement much more about industrial policy and not just about industrial relations. I explained what Mintech was doing and I said that we were afflicted by the most appalling defeatism, that this was what would really finish us and that we must get things across.

Bill Simpson said that the Cabinet would be defeated at Conference on three major issues – economic policy, prices and incomes and industrial relations – and we had to face this fact.

Then Mikardo said we had done a lot but there was a widening gap between rich and poor – we had failed on growth, on the extension of public enterprise and on the begging bowl.

We had a tremendous sort of Leader-of-the-Party election speech by Denis. He said he was an old Transport House man and all we needed was a switch of 1 per cent of our resources and defence had given that, and there was a risk that we would get into Opposition and destroy ourselves.

Jim talked about the relations between the NEC and the Cabinet. He said the NEC shouldn't niggle on some things the Government did but the Cabinet must prove the overwhelming need for the measures it brought forward, and it hadn't succeeded in some of its measures, which was an obvious reference to the Industrial Relations Bill. The Party existed to increase the popularity of the Trade Union Movement.

Then we had Reg Prentice who said that Ministers were too dependent on their upper-middle-class advisers and that the role of the trade unions needed to be extended.

We ended the morning with Barbara, who described what the Bill had done for the Trade Union Movement and attacked Jim for assuming that the trade unions were antediluvian. It was a passionate and brilliant speech; Barbara really pulls it out of the hat.

After lunch we resumed and Joan Lestor said we had too much blind faith in economists and we had submerged the good we had done. She warned us that support in the country for a trade union bill came from people who wanted to get rid of the trade unions altogether.

Then we had Ted Short, who made an extremely good speech saying we were much too concerned with arithmetic, and he wanted to make education a major Government theme. He talked about his White Paper which would plan the educational system for the next twenty-five years.

He said there couldn't be a major Education Act this Parliament but he wanted to set out in his White Paper the new aim for education, which was to make the most of talent and see that nobody was a failure at any age. He was intending to include the universal provision of pre-school education for children, to repair the neglect of primary schools, to give a reality of secondary school education to all, to raise the school leaving age, and to extend the curriculum. There would be a Bill in the next session to compel local education authorities to submit comprehensive school plans.

He wanted to end the binary system by bringing further and higher education together; and he wanted more adult education as in the Open University, which would get its charter in June, and some modifications for teachers. He wanted to make education a live political issue and he certainly succeeded.

Finally, towards the end, George Brown said, 'Don't be deceived by the cosiness of today into thinking that all is well. Ministers must really hammer home their policies and we have got to recapture industrial goodwill. If you clap Barbara,' he concluded, 'you might also back her.'

Harold wound up and I have no recollection of what he said at all.

Monday 12 May
To the National Executive Home Policy Committee. Work was quite impossible because George Brown was totally drunk and Frank Allaun rebuked him for attacking Terry Pitt. The whole thing was a waste of time.

In the evening I went to see the preview of my BBC *Horizon* programme.* It is not brilliant but I am glad I put so much effort into it.

I rang Harold about my trip to Russia tomorrow. I told him that Michael Stewart had given me a very frosty interview, telling me to keep off politics, and I hoped I would do better than that, and did he have a message for Kosygin? He said yes, and then before giving me the message he asked, 'Is there anyone on the line?' and one of his Private Secretaries answered, so I knew the discussion was monitored, which was a comfort to me because, of course, what he said was totally contrary to what Michael Stewart had told me.

Harold wanted me to send his warmest greetings to Kosygin and to tell him that 'although we had had a difficult year, for reasons which we all understood' (referring to the invasion of Czechoslovakia), he now wanted the best possible relations. He told me to welcome the Soviet initiative in the Middle East and hoped we could make progress on it, and also hoped that in the new situation in Europe following the resignation of de Gaulle, the Russians would see the value of their links with Britain.

He asked me to remind Kosygin that when he had been at Chequers, Harold had told him that our membership of the EEC had as one of its objectives the containment of Germany within a wider community. This was all the more necessary now. I was also to tell Kosygin how much he still regretted the fact that the work they had done together on the Vietnam peace initiative in Chequers in 1967 had not come off.

Being in a position to pass on this message has put a completely new complexion on my desire to see Kosygin, which Michael Stewart was so much against. Harold said I should give this message to the Russians as soon as I arrived and ask for fifteen minutes with Kosygin and that I would probably get an hour.

From 13–20 May 1969 I visited the Soviet Union as part of a series of exchanges, arranged following Premier Kosygin's visit to Britain in 1967, between me as the appropriate British Minister and Academician Vladimir Kirillin, Chairman of the State Committee for Science and Technology.

On our side we were engaged in trying to build up trade, while the Soviet authorities were trying to acquire access to technological developments taking place in Britain. But whereas the highly centralised organisation of the Soviet economy meant that the Russians were able to commit their industry to cooperation, all I could do was to stimulate a greater interest in Soviet trade among British industrialists and for that reason I worked closely with the CBI. Thus the concept of 'Captains of

* This programme subsequently formed the basis of the Roscoe Lecture at the University of Manchester, 25 April 1970. See Appendix IV.

Industry' was invented to bring together the different roles of Soviet industrial Ministers and British industrialists.

I have cut details of lengthy technical discussions from my account, but during my many meetings I was also able to ask frankly about the Soviet economy, and indeed political developments in the USSR, which gave an early indication of the ideas which later emerged with Mikhail Gorbachev as perestroika.

Tuesday 13 May

To London Airport where we boarded the HS125. Solly Zuckerman was already there and on the plane were Ieuan Maddock, Derek Moon and Ivor Manley.

At Copenhagen we were met by the Ambassador Oliver Wright. We were delayed there for two and a half hours with engine trouble so the Ambassador took us for lunch at the Embassy.

Wright is a very intelligent man, very much of the muscular Christian, public school, centre-of-the-road variety. He said he thought that Britain was ungovernable and that it just wasn't possible in modern circumstances to tell people the truth; that there was effectively no choice open to them and that the Labour Government had made all the big mistakes – by which he meant banning arms for Spain and South Africa during its first two weeks – before they really had a grip of the total situation. He saw the function of civil servants as bringing the realities home to new Ministers. He really implied by this that there was no scope for alternative policies. I don't accept this at all but it was interesting that an intelligent and able man should put it forward so crudely.

A brief stop at Helsinki, and we picked up a Russian navigating guide and we got to Moscow at 10.15 pm (Moscow time), where we were met by Gvishiani and Kirillin himself, our interpreter Madame Santalova, the Ambassador, Sir Duncan Wilson, other Embassy staff and by Harry Slater and Cecil Timms, the head of Machine Tools who had gone on ahead of us.

Kirillin was very friendly and there was no mention made at all of the fact that the visit had been postponed. I asked Kirillin about the effect of de Gaulle's disappearance on the European situation. He said he didn't see what difference it would make, which indicated that he is not at all interested in politics. He is first and foremost an engineer doing a very complicated job.

After a brief press conference and a Moscow Radio interview in English, I drove with Kirillin, Gvishiani and Madame Santalova to the Sovietskaya Hotel, and during the car trip I reported Harold Wilson's message for Kosygin and said I very much hoped it would be possible for me to deliver it personally. They said that they would fix it. They were really very warm and friendly and all my anxieties about whether there would be a slightly frosty reception, in view of events, completely evaporated.

We settled in at the hotel, and then went to the Embassy and had a buffet meal with Lady Wilson. Then we disappeared into the 'Cage', the bug-proof room. We discussed the programme, we fixed the press conferences, and I heard that they thought my lecture was a bit weak on the management side.

I described the Prime Minister's message and said I'd dropped a hint to Kirillin and Gvishiani about seeing Kosygin. This created some surprise because Michael Stewart had, of course, sent a message out to the people there telling them that my visit was to be non-political.

This conflict of guidance made them uneasy. The Ambassador stressed the Foreign Secretary's message and said we should just talk about technology and that if they asked about politics to say that it was not our concern. It was an incredibly insulting comment for an Ambassador to make to a Cabinet Minister, but this is the Foreign Office view. Anyway, I had decided that I wouldn't accept it.

Wednesday 14 May
At 10 I went to the State Committee and just before we began our discussion, Kirillin took me aside and said that Kosygin wanted to see me in the Kremlin at 12.

I told the Ambassador and this inevitably curtailed the morning meeting. At Solly Zuckerman's suggestion I also wrote out, on a piece of paper, what Harold Wilson had said to me and gave it to the Ambassador so that he would have something before him to set against Michael Stewart's guidance that I shouldn't talk to anybody about anything interesting.

At 11.45 we left the State Committee office and went to the Kremlin. There was a very modest entrance and a little lift. We went up two floors into a sort of waiting hall and then along a long corridor and turned left along another corridor, all on the inside of a quadrangle. There was a door marked 'Kosygin' in gold lettering on black glass, characteristically Russian. Inside were the Private Secretaries and press and television.

I had taken Duncan Wilson, Solly and Ivor Manley with me and the inner door opened and there was Kosygin at the end of a long table. He walked towards me and we shook hands warmly. Then we sat down at the far end of this long table, with him facing me and the interpreter in the middle, next to me the Ambassador and then Solly Zuckerman and Ivor Manley. On Kosygin's side were Kirillin and Makiev from the Soviet Foreign Ministry and his Private Secretary.

Kosygin greeted me again while we were filmed for television. Then he started. He said that the technological agreement was going very well and that he was satisfied with it, as was Kirillin. Kosygin then reminded me that the Five-Year Plan was being approved next year, and that there was a lot of argument going on about what should and shouldn't be bought and he rather indicated that this was a factor we ought to keep in mind if we expected to boost our sales in the USSR.

Then he expressed considerable interest in atomic energy matters, saying that he had sent somebody to America who had come back and reported that the Americans were making good progress on this. He said he thought there might be scope for cooperation in this field in return for which we would get nuclear fuel.

I later discovered that this included enriched uranium as an offer, as well as natural uranium. So this was an indication that they might be interested in trying to provide an alternative source, other than the Americans or the new centrifuge plan, of enriched uranium for us.

After he had talked about the pollution of rivers in Russia I got in and conveyed Harold Wilson's greetings. I reminded Kosygin of the visit that he and I had paid together to Elliot-Automation in 1967 and I stressed our link with long-term trade and planning, referring to a speech which he had made on this subject when he was in London.

I moved on to fast reactors. I told him how very advanced we were in this field and how we had generated more nuclear power than the rest of the world put together, including the USA: our fast reactor would be on stream in 1970/71. He was evidently impressed.

Then we came on to the monetary situation and the behaviour of Germany. I said that the EEC provided an opportunity for us to supervise the Germans and I drew a parallel between this and the centrifuge arrangement with the Germans, where we were also supervising their work.

Kosygin didn't take up the question of the centrifuge although no doubt it registered in his mind. He did say that it wasn't just a matter of supervising the Germans, it was a matter of *controlling* the Germans and he greatly wished that we had cooperated on that many years ago.

I then congratulated Kosygin, in accordance with Harold's suggestion, on the initiative taken by the Soviet Government in the Middle East. Kosygin nodded his acknowledgement and replied that he wished that Britain was not so dependent on other parties who exercised a negative attitude, which I took to be a reference to the Americans.

He then went on to say that he would like to see the Prime Minister in Moscow in June or July for a day or two for talks 'on matters of common interest'. This proposal immediately gave a certain hardness to the talk with Kosygin and enabled me to bring something back to London. Indeed it involved an immediate cable to London.

I said I would convey this invitation and said that the Prime Minister had made it clear that he knew that we, that is the British and Russians, had had a difficult year 'for reasons you will understand', but that he hoped for the best possible relations. To which Kosygin answered, 'We do not understand the reasons why we have had a difficult year but we would greatly welcome the Prime Minister in Moscow', and he repeated the invitation to Harold again when I said goodbye to him.

It was a very friendly meeting lasting for forty minutes and I had got across all the things that Harold had asked me to say. I was also reminded of what a very competent manager Kosygin is.

I went straight back in the car to the Embassy, drafted a telegram to the Prime Minister to be sent FLASH PERSONAL. Just as I left the Embassy a message came from Makiev, specially asking that 'I shouldn't make known one particular part' of Kosygin's proposals. This was obviously a reference to the invitation to Wilson and as I had no intention of making it public myself, because it would tie Harold's hands, there was no problem.

At 1.15 I went to lunch in the Kremlin and sat next but one to Miznick from Gosplan. He asked after Melissa, which warmed my heart to him. Elyutin, the Minister of Higher Education, was next to me.

I took the opportunity, since I was near Elyutin, of asking about their special schools. He said that about 1 per cent of the children in the Soviet Union went to the special schools and they were reserved for the most gifted children. 'However,' said Elyutin, repeating his observation of two years ago, 'I am very sceptical about special schools for gifted children, because I think they are really for the children of gifted parents.'

He said that they had been doing some tests on the amount of knowledge that was retained and after one year's gap 50 to 80 per cent of what had been taught at school had been forgotten, which was very worrying. On specialisation he said that there was absolutely no specialisation at schools, except in the special schools, right up to university level.

Miznick told me that Kosygin had laid on a computer course for the top 200 people in the Soviet Government, including Ministers, Deputy-Ministers, the chairman of the State Committees and that, on a Tuesday and Friday in April, for three consecutive weeks, there had been ten lectures on the academic, hardware and application aspects of computers. I was impressed at this example of the professionalism of the Soviet Government. One of the most interesting things was that Kosygin had attended most of these lectures himself.

Thursday 15 May
Overslept a bit. Went to the Automation Exhibition to see the Soviet work on process control of large plant. There was an animated model showing the control of an entire industry by a computer system, all

flashing lights, but it was completely theoretical – there was no reference whatsoever to the market, or feedback of market demand.

I went to the British Pavilion and saw a large number of exhibits and some keen young sales representatives. They complained that it was difficult for the manufacturer to follow right through to the user or consumer, which was a point that had also been made the previous day, when the Russians said they had bought some British equipment and the manufacturers had never been in touch with them about it.

Inside one of the tents was Konstantin Rudnev, Minister for Automation. He asked me what I thought of the exhibition and I told him that I had noticed the closed loop in his system with no provision for the market or the customer input. He said that he agreed with me that this was a problem but he had been overruled when it was discussed.

He was very amusing. He told me he had been to Highgate Cemetery and seen the grave of Marx and also the grave of Spencer and later in the middle of town he had seen that Marks and Spencer were still together. We talked a little bit about common problems and I suggested that we ought really to have a joint seminar for our Ministers. Then I had to go and he said, 'Well, you go: I'm too old for anyone to want to see me.' I liked him.

After lunch with Solly Zuckerman, Duncan Wilson, Gvishiani and some other Russians in an extremely good Georgian restaurant, I walked up and down in the street with Gvishiani for about half an hour, talking about computers. I stressed that the restrictions on the computer sales had nothing to do with Anglo-Russian relations but were part of COCOM, which applied to everyone. He understood that.

He said that there was a plan for building computers in COMECON, in the Eastern European countries, and that US General Electric were putting on pressure in the Soviet Union in order to use the Eastern European market to build themselves up against IBM. They were doing this through their French and Italian subsidiaries. He said he was not interested in French computers, which are not good enough, but Siemens were pressing quite hard.

I told him it would be useful to have examples of other firms pushing their products on him. He promised to give me details so long as I didn't then use this information to see that he couldn't get the equipment, which might have been promised despite the restrictions in COCOM.

He assured me that the Soviet defence computers were using the most advanced integrated circuits and that there was really no defence point involved. He said that if ICL couldn't make any progress they had better tell him so and the Soviet Union might cooperate on software.

That was about as far as we got, but it was a completely frank conversation à deux, of a kind one couldn't have had if there had been one of our party or another Russian present.

At 3 pm I went to the State Committee and gave my lecture with great difficulty. I don't think Schwartz did a good job of interpretation. But Kirillin asked about technological forecasting and the balance between pure and applied research and I got questions about information retrieval, about how planning worked in Britain, about manpower planning, about pollution and about deep boring.

At 5 I went back to the Embassy and talked to the Ambassador about Brooke – the *Daily Telegraph* had criticised me for not raising the Brooke question and said that the technological agreement should be terminated if Brooke wasn't released.

Duncan Wilson said that he really regretted having to emphasise this case, because the Soviets then began to conclude that perhaps Brooke *was* a British agent, which he is not. Indeed there's a suspicion that the KGB had laid the whole thing on in order to have a British person held, to balance the Krogers.* I think he was saying that it was possible that the KGB had approached Brooke, representing themselves to be anti-Communist Russians, and had got him interested and he thought he was working for the West, whereas actually he wasn't. Wilson said he had had to speak to Kosygin about it and greatly regretted it. But Smirnovsky's visit to Michael Stewart last Friday did open up the possibility that if Brooke is released next April when the sentence expires, the Krogers may be let out earlier than 1974. But no action was expected for some time and although charges have been brought against Brooke, we want to keep this secret because we are afraid that, once it becomes known, the Russians will feel it is impossible to get off the hook.

Dinner at the Embassy. I tried to talk to Kozyrev, the Deputy-Minister for Foreign Affairs, about the centrifuge. They were reasonably relaxed about it, although they clearly thought it was part of the British tactic to bribe the West Germans to let us into the Common Market. They raised the Non-Proliferation Treaty issue and German power.

I just slogged it out by arguing our case. I stressed the importance of Anglo-Soviet links in the post-de Gaulle situation when the new Germany was getting very powerful, while France was rather weak and I thought that the Russians and ourselves ought to keep fairly close.

After the guests left, we went into the 'Cage' at 10.30, and sent off a number of telegrams about the Nuclear Policy Committee and the centrifuge. The Defence Department are being very difficult about the 'special relationship' and feel that our readiness to make our nuclear technology available to the Dutch and the Germans is likely to cause

---

*Peter and Helen Kroger were Americans living in Britain under New Zealand passports, convicted in June 1961 for twenty years each for espionage offences against Britain. In October 1969 the Krogers were released from prison, in exchange for the return of Gerald Brooke.

trouble with the Americans. A special memorandum is being written containing the whole nature of the Anglo-American nuclear relationship, and this is going to be submitted by the Foreign Secretary, who is also submitting my paper in my absence. It really is a very important meeting.

At 11.30 we went to the station to catch the Red Arrow, one of the marvellous trains still left in the world, to Leningrad.

Friday 16 May

Arrived in Leningrad early with the Ambassador and Lady Wilson and we were greeted by the city officials.

After breakfast we went to the Karl Marx Plant, which makes equipment for chemical fibres, textiles and shoe manufacturing. It's a very old plant, employing about 8,000 people in three factories – to an outsider, it gave the impression of being an old-fashioned plant, the kind you might see in the North of England. Big but very run down, and nobody seemed to be working very hard. I got the feeling that the 'English disease' had set in pretty badly.

Then we had a very jolly lunch with lots of speeches, in which I made I think three and Solly made two. While we were there we heard that the Soviet Venus Probe had landed on Venus and that led to jokes and more speeches.

We went to visit the Deputy-Mayor of Leningrad in the City Hall, a beautiful place, and I presented him with the films made by Sidney Bernstein, Chairman of Granada, on the history of Leningrad.

To the theatre in the evening to see *Aleko*, a one-act opera by Pushkin and Rachmaninoff and then *Schéhérezade* which was exquisite. During the interval I looked at the young Russians who were there, and there were one or two in mini-skirts with long hair and those turtle-neck shirts which are very fashionable in London, or were a year or two ago.

Then we went back to the hotel and had dinner. Madame Santalova asked me why Gvishiani was so popular abroad. I said he was internationally minded, he was interested in management, and he was easy to talk to. She spoke as if a lot of people in Russia were jealous of him because he had married Kosygin's daughter. She asked me if that influenced his standing abroad. I said that it probably did influence it and she said he was careful not to take advantage of it; but there were many people who thought he could help to advance their careers and he was very scrupulous about not doing so.

Saturday 17 May

From 6.30 to 7.45, we went on a car tour of Leningrad in the rain, and I took a lot of movies.

In the evening we had dinner at the hotel with the Ambassador. I had a talk to Lady Wilson, who is an intelligent woman, about security and she said there was someone in the British Embassy who reports on them to the Russians and it was very unpleasant.

She said that anyone who has an affair, whether it's with a Russian or anyone else, is sent home at once, and that when she and the Ambassador had arrived, a couple of typists had been having affairs with diplomats from other Embassies and had been sent back. It was known of course that people rather higher up also had affairs, and there was a feeling of discontent that the junior people should be picked on to return to London.

Sunday 18 May
I had breakfast at 8.30, and then went with our party to the Petrodvorets, Peter the Great's palace which was built to rival Versailles. We looked through the palace and saw the rooms that had been fully restored which were just being opened today. We saw the ceremony of switching on the fountains. It was pouring with rain, icy cold, and generally rather chilling.

After lunch we went to the Leningrad Museum, which is largely dedicated to exhibits of the German attack on Leningrad. One forgets that for 900 days it was under siege. I think about one million people died only twenty-five years ago. We saw a film about the siege, built around the diary of a little girl of about seven called Tanya Soreovitch, who was the Anne Frank of Leningrad.

At 3.30, I went to the Anti-Religious Museum at the Cathedral with Illya Schwartz and Derek Moon, Ivor Manley and a TASS man. I got the same answers that I did on a previous visit, nine years ago, that Christ was not an historical figure but a legend, that the reports of the persecution of Christians in Rome were much exaggerated, and so on. The ecumenical movement was described as being inspired by anti-Communist motives to hold down revolutions everywhere. I heard about the Russian Group who didn't believe in priests, who were in effect Congregationalists.

The museum was crowded – whether that was because it was a Sunday or because it was pouring with rain I don't know – and there was a tendency for people to gather round and listen and for the guide to push them aside, because obviously she didn't want them to hear the questions I was asking.

Then I went back to the hotel and had dinner. I sat next to Schwartz and we discussed the Anti-Religious Museum. He said that he was of course anti-religious but he accepted the case for the spiritual life. Betty Wilson engaged him on the mysteries of creation and the human soul and the need for reverence. Schwartz accepted the need for ritual and explained why the Palace of Weddings had been set up. Duncan Wilson said he was an honest doubter, which seemed to be a very good position to occupy. I argued for the historical validity of Christ as a person. I asked him about anti-semitism and Schwartz said it was illegal but, of course, 'it was inbred'.

Schwartz agreed that the Russians were frightened of the Germans. He explained the Czech invasion in terms of fears about the Germans and said that there was a great deal of popular support for the invasion of Czechoslovakia but he hoped the troops would leave, and never under any circumstances would the Czechs go back to a Novotny situation, a reference to the Stalinism of the early Sixties. He also said how evil Stalin was, which confirmed the view my guide in 1961, Nicky Kutchinsky, had given when I had talked with him about Stalin.

Monday 19 May
We arrived in Moscow, and at 10.15 I went to the Embassy where there was a telegram saying the Americans were toughening up, and the prospects of us providing the advanced computers had diminished. There were problems about software cooperation as well, which was discouraging. I also learned that my reference to British imperialism in my lecture to the State Committee had annoyed the Embassy staff who were trying to say all the time that we never were imperialist. This had been reported in *The Times* in London, came back to Moscow and had created a flurry.

Well, then I went back at 11 o'clock to the State Committee for the final talks and Kirillin described the joint Government commission that he had with France, which incorporated the Ministry of Foreign Trade, Gosplan, the Academy of Sciences and the industrial ministries. He described how this commission covered the whole range of Soviet-French relations, outside diplomacy and trade agreements, and this gave me an impression of the tremendous power of the State Committee in Russia which really is, second only to the Foreign Ministry, the most powerful agent in Soviet relations with the outside world.

At 12.45 we had the press conference. *Moscow News*, Moscow Radio and Moscow Television were all there. I signed the protocol and it was very cordial. There were no questions about Brooke which pleased me.

Then at 6, there was a reception by the State Committee at a restaurant and everybody was there, including Vassev who works in the British Section of the Soviet Foreign Ministry. He told me that he had been Molotov's private secretary, which I had not known. He said the Soviet Government had a weakness for Britain and for the Labour Government, which was intended to be friendly, I suppose.

At 8 I went back to the Embassy and we went to the 'Cage' for a talk. Then we had drinks together. I have got to like the Ambassador very

Denis Healey with wartime Bomber Command Chiefs, Viscount Portal and Sir Arthur Harris, April 1968. Centre background is Barnes Wallis.

George Brown, with wife Sophie, announcing his resignation as Foreign Secretary after his clash with Wilson, March 1968.

Mintech's informal 'foreign policy' initiative: signing a technological agreement with Academician Kirillin, January 1968.

Anthony and Susan Crosland in Smolny, USSR, June 1968.

Facing the President. Nicolae Ceausescu of Rumania, and on Ceausescu's left, Prime Minister Maurer and Vice President Birladeanu, Bucharest, June 1968.

Denis Healey and
John Stonehouse
strike a deal for
Anglo-French
supersonic
fighters, January
1968.

Roy Jenkins during the Common
Market controversy of November 1971.
Five months later he resigned from the
Shadow Cabinet and as Deputy-Leader
of the Labour Party over the issue.

Trade Union Giants
Incoming and outgoing TUC General Secretaries Vic Feather (left) and George Woodcock, September 1968.

Below right: Jack Jones, General Secretary of the TGWU, in a light-hearted moment during the July 1970 dockers' strike.

Above: Hugh Scanlon, President of the AUEW, addressing the Labour Party Conference in October 1968.

The calm before the storm: Hugh Scanlon with Employment Secretary Barbara Castle, April 1968.

Upper Clyde Shipbuilders crisis

Right: Workers' delegation marching to the House of Commons, led by (from left) Frank McElhone, Dennis Skinner, TB and Eric Heffer, June 1971.

Below: Comrades in arms. With UCS shop stewards, including Jimmy Reid and Jimmy Airlie, on Scotland's biggest post-war political demonstration, Glasgow, 23 June 1971.

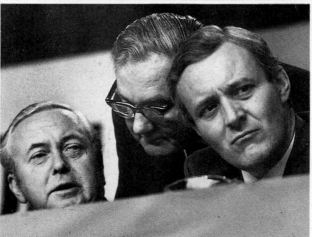

Vic Feather and Hugh Scanlon at the TUC Conference in Blackpool in 1971.

Two Lords and a Commoner: pictured with future peers Wilson and Callaghan at the Labour Party Conference in 1971.

Caroline Benn addressing an Education Conference in London, January 1970.

At the Podium
Emergency meeting to save the RB-211 during the Rolls Royce crisis, February 1971.

The Benn family, October 1969. Clockwise: Joshua, Stephen, Hilary, Caroline, TB and Melissa.

Nixon, flanked by security men, does a walkabout leaving Buckingham Palace, February 1969.

Asserting the special relationship: President Nixon with Harold Wilson on his British tour, February 1969.

Below: Wilson shaking hands with the Italian President Giuseppe Saragat, as veteran Italian Socialist Pietro Nenni, Foreign Minister, looks on, April 1969.

much. He's been with me all the time this week and he thought there was a political gain for Britain in having done the trip.

We had a bite to eat in the Embassy, which Lady Wilson had provided, just cheese and apples and coffee, and at 10.30, Derek Moon, Ivor Manley, Ieuan Maddock and I walked in Red Square, then went back to the hotel where I found a radio, a gift from Kosygin and Gvishiani. I played it a bit, packed and went to bed.

Tuesday 20 May

Ivor didn't wake me as expected as he had made a mistake in the room number and had actually woken Robert Galley, the French Minister of Science. I had a mug of tea made with my little boiler, which I plugged in to the shaver socket. This has made life tolerable this week.

At the airport I bought a few presents and had my last talk with Gvishiani, who had come to see me off, along with Kirillin, Madame Santalova, and the Ambassador.

Gvishiani did say to me how much he had appreciated the tone of my letter last September, postponing my visit after the Czech invasion. As I had drafted this myself, with great care so as not to give more offence than was necessary, I was glad he'd noticed it. He told me how very upset the Russians had been about the cancellation of the Anglo-Soviet historical exhibition, particularly as his wife, Kosygin's daughter, had been responsible for it.

I said, 'Well, there had been a lot of upset about Czechoslovakia in Britain, more so on the Left even than the Right.'

Then I thanked him for the radio and he said, 'We know you listen to the radio a lot,' and with this inadvertent admission that my room was bugged, he added rather hurriedly, 'We remembered that you told us that you listen to the radio a great deal.'

The only other example of bugging that occurred while I was there was that the Ambassador had complained to his wife about the room which they had been given in the Astoria in Leningrad, and they received an apology the following morning.

Kirillin and Gvishiani examined the aircraft and we waved goodbye at 9.15 am.

There was a late night sitting and the Chief Whip wouldn't let me off, so I didn't get home until after midnight. I saw Caroline and the children and gave them their presents, including a balalaika for Stephen.

Thursday 22 May

Nuclear Policy Committee on the centrifuge, where there were two papers, one on guidelines for officials, which went through without any difficulty, and the other on the Anglo-American relationship.

A letter had come in from Sir John Hill suggesting that we may have learned more from the Americans about centrifuge and Endcap than we had recognised or admitted up to now, and this created an absolute explosion.

Denis Healey, as usual, made as much trouble as he possibly could. We did our best to stave it off, but it was agreed that we would get Sir Alfred Pugsley and Bill Penney to report, as quickly as possible, on the extent to which we did owe the Americans for the design of the Endcap.

What was interesting was that the whole Anglo-American special relationship had boiled down to this Endcap. It wasn't that it was very significant because, from the point of view of mechanical engineering, anybody could have guessed it. But it embraces the whole question of trust in Anglo-American relationships and commercial rivalry versus the old nuclear partnership.

I left immediately after the Nuclear Policy meeting and called Michael Michaels over to see me, and then Sir John Hill and Norman Franklin of the AEA.

John Hill was embarrassed; I don't think he had been told everything. I don't think Franklin had been told everything either. This is the trouble with scientists, they regard something as being of minor technical importance; whereas actually it contains a big political point they may not appreciate themselves.

Caroline's draft Education Bill was published today in *Forum* and she was on *The World at One*.

Thursday 29 May

This afternoon Mr Purnell, the Mintech security officer, came to see me. The reason was that the security services have picked up a man who came here twenty-five years ago from Eastern Europe and has now admitted to the security services that he has been working for Soviet Intelligence. He had a job with Marconi and some classified papers were found in his apartment, but the Director of Public Prosecutions does not think there is enough evidence on which to prosecute. During the course of my talk with Mr Purnell he again stressed the appalling dangers presented to commercial security by the Soviet threat.

He told me that he had recently come back from America with the chief security officer of the Pentagon and, when they were having dinner together very late one night, this man said to him, 'I don't know how you can accept the fact that your Minister is chasing around the Soviet Union.' Apparently the resistance to the Anglo-Soviet technological agreement is extremely strong among American defence security people.

One of their anxieties is that military security might leak through from the military side of the Department to the civil side. Purnell told me that there was no reason for this anxiety as the security between the two sides of the Department was very carefully managed, and he said that the Americans had inspected our security system and were satisfied by it. It was an interesting and extraordinary revelation. Here was I, Minister of a British Department, hearing from one of my own officials that another country had inspected our security arrangements and I had never been told about it. It just indicates the extent to which the nuclear and defence cooperation with America over the years has eroded our freedom of action.

On 30 May 1969 I made a one-day trip to Holland to talk to Fritz Philips, Chairman of Philips.

From enquiries made by the Industrial Reorganisation Corporation [IRC], it had become clear in February 1969 that the multinational electrical and electronic company was, for its own purposes, adjusting its price structure so that it was running a balance of payments deficit in Britain. It was quite unacceptable that the company should use transfer prices to make it appear that its subsidiaries in Britain were importing more than they were exporting when in fact the opposite was the case, and it was to discuss this situation that I visited Philips.

A year later the Department received notification that Philips was enjoying a balance of payments surplus in Britain – undoubtedly an effect of my indication to Philips himself that the British Government, particularly the Defence Ministry, would not be prepared to buy their components while they continued this damaging practice to our economy.

Friday 30 May

I got home from a meeting in Eindhoven to find a red box waiting for me. It contained the Penney-Pugsley report on the centrifuge, confirming that the Endcap is in fact of American design, having been transmitted to us in the 1960 agreement on centrifuge exchange.

This evening Harold rang me and I thought it was going to be about this, but in fact he wanted me to attack Ted Heath for having made a speech in America critical of the Government. Well, I was damned if I was going to do that, but I did raise the centrifuge point with him.

Saturday 31 May

Tony Crosland came over for lunch. He is a very curious person. With the radio incident in mind, I asked his advice on what to do about receiving presents from delegations and on visits, and he said, 'Well, of course, if they're good you keep them but if they're not you give them to your office.' A somewhat different view from the one I had taken!

Also he described how he always bet on elections and how he sent Susan to see his stockbroker and his bank manager; and to Pat Hennessy

of Fords when they bought a car so that she could discuss any problems
with him.

Tuesday 3 June

To the Nuclear Policy Committee meeting where we were going to
decide what line should be taken by Solly Zuckerman, who is leaving for
America tonight, and at the centrifuge meeting in Bonn next week.
Denis Healey was completely destructive and he lashed out and
attacked our handling of the whole thing. I argued that we should be
absolutely frank with the Europeans but Michael Stewart was dead
against this. I warned the Committee very seriously that it was one thing
to come to an end of an association by being rather less than frank but it
was another thing to enter into a new partnership on that basis. Indeed,
after the Committee I reiterated my doubts to Burke Trend and said
that I was really being asked to lie. Burke Trend said, with superb and
characteristic Civil Service cynicism, 'Oh, you're not being asked to lie
yet, Minister.' But Harold had been briefed by Solly Zuckerman to the
effect that we must go on with the meeting next Monday in Bonn and it
was fairly clear that we were not to sign anything but were going to go on
with the discussions.

Meanwhile Solly will talk to the US Atomic Energy Commission;
John Freeman will be sent to see William Rogers, the American
Secretary of State, to point out that this is very much in line with
American European Policy for Britain and that was how it was left. But
it was a very unpleasant meeting and Denis Healey was at his most
bloody awful – rude and offensive, difficult and obstructive – and I was
in a rather weak position because the Penney-Pugsley Report had
suggested that the AEA had not been altogether open.

Friday 6 June

I got up at 5.30 and with Steve Spain [official from the Shipbuilding
Division of Mintech] and Derek Moon, Ivor Manley and Eunice Gofton
we flew off for Glasgow. This was my fourth visit to Glasgow this year
and we have got the organisation of it pretty well set now. We took a
portable photocopier with us and had arranged for secretarial and
transport facilities to be available. It was a most exciting and interesting
day.

There was a mass of press at the airport and I gave my comments in
general terms but kept what I was going to tell UCS a guarded secret. I
had told nobody the night before so it couldn't leak and Bill Swallow
had only been notified in general terms that his recommendations had
been accepted.

I went in the car to the Lord Provost's City Chambers where there
were leaders of the Labour, Scottish Nationalist and Conservative

Groups and I told them what I was going to propose and I asked them if they would be so kind as to keep it to themselves till I had told it to the UCS board and unions.

We took over our suite at St Enoch's Hotel and just after 10.45 I met the UCS board. I made a statement announcing that we would be in a position to give £5 million, with £4 million to come later. I stressed that the SIB thought this would be sufficient and so did I. Yarrow made a point about inherited losses but there was no discussion of substance because I wanted them to think about it.

At 11.10 I went to see the unions. Willie Hutchison was chairing the joint union meeting and I described the decision again. Joe Black of the CSEU said that they were between the hammer of the Government and the anvil of the board, which was liquidation. Alex Ferry said that the plan worked out by UCS didn't include closures but would involve painful redundancies.

I didn't ask them to reach a decision but I said I would require their help and at 11.30 I gave a press conference. I said at the end that this was a symptom of the whole problem of Britain at the moment and that nobody should laugh at it or mock it because everybody in Britain is suffering from poor industrial management and bad industrial relations.

It had been a very crowded meeting and it looked as if the point had got across. After that there was nothing to do while waiting for the UCS board, so we had a pleasant lunch and then I had a brief word with local Labour MPs who had attended the press conference.

I went to another meeting with the UCS board at 2 and Hepper said they'd been in continuous session and had taken legal advice and that they had concluded that the right thing to do was to liquidate unless there was another board of management that was prepared to take on the responsibility. I asked them if it was unanimous and there was no response.

I saw the Scottish TUC at 2.30 and I told them things were pretty gloomy. I said that it really was up to the unions to give leadership, since the company might abdicate their responsibilities and I told them in confidence that under the proposals brought forward from SIB there would in fact be an SIB plus Government plus trade union majority of shareholders, which would be satisfactory.

At 5.30 back to the UCS board again and we had some very tough talking. I said that if they liquidated I would regard it as an abdication of their responsibility and a betrayal, and I told them roughly what I would say if the liquidation occurred. I said it wasn't an arithmetical problem, it was a problem of motivation and that Rolls Royce couldn't have survived if there had been as much public discussion of their economic problems as there had been in this case because it would have created a crisis of confidence. I said that radical measures, if they had been taken earlier, would have altered the psychological position quite considerably.

Then Hepper said that if the SIB thought they could manage on this money he'd come to London and ask them to tell him how. I said, 'Mr Hepper. That is the cause of all the trouble. It sometimes seems to the board and to me as if you are regarding yourselves as being up here doing good works in Glasgow instead of accepting management responsibility for the group.' Hepper said that he very much resented the charge of lack of leadership, the discussion took considerable strides and we had an intelligent talk.

At 6.10 I had a brief talk with the UCS unions and told them that it looked as if the situation had collapsed and stressed the need for the unions to take the initiative. Hutchison said that if the company had abdicated he would take the bull by the horns. I said that it looked as though they might abdicate and I was gloomier than I had ever been and described to the UCS unions the possibility of an SIB–trade union– Government majority. The unions said they would see the UCS board.

I walked to the City Hall, accompanied by detectives all the way and had another word with the Lord Provost. I came down in the lift and met the Moderator of the Church of Scotland who was coming to the City Chambers for the Moderator's dinner. It was about that time that things began improving! While I was at the City Chambers the unions and the board were meeting and I discovered later that the unions had really put some stuffing into the board.

At 7.15, roughly, I saw Alex Kitson and Jimmy Milne of the Scottish TUC. I said to them that if the board did liquidate I wanted them to give a united condemnation of it. But I heard at the same time that the unions were more optimistic. At 9 I started dinner and at 9.15 I was called to a joint meeting with the UCS board and the unions and they had produced their 'action plan' which involved 3,000 redundancies among the finishing trades and union cooperation in a most radical action plan, which included a wage stop for eighteen months. I thanked them very much, said that this was a package that hung together and that they would have to assemble it with bank support by next Thursday. Hepper then asked if I would meet the press with them and I said No, since I thought it would be better if I faded out at this stage, but I said I would be very happy to come in later.

At about 9.30 the UCS board and the unions gave a press conference and it sounded encouraging.

The Lord Provost looked in again at about 11.15 and I reported it all to him. Back at St Enoch's, went to bed absolutely exhausted.

Wednesday 11 June
To the NRDC lunch. Harold read from a prepared text. He is quite incapable of speaking without a text – it is an extraordinary characteristic because he remembers everything he has said in the past twenty-five years but he can't deliver a speech impromptu. I was asked to speak and I said that I couldn't rival the Prime Minister in his recollection of history and that one would have a difficult job arguing with a Prime Minister who could remember the Hansard reference and the qualification that he had made in every case.

Thursday 12 June
I went to the Dorchester this morning to see Golda Meir, the Prime Minister of Israel. There were pretty elaborate security precautions all round. She is a tough, articulate and courteous but extremely direct woman with an American accent which makes her look and sound like the Mayor of some mid-Western town.

She gave the usual Israeli spiel – we just want peace, our grandchildren want peace, my grandchildren want peace, Nasser won't face the fact, he is sitting pretty, protected by the Four Powers and you are really keeping him going. I said, 'Yes, but this is of course the Arab strength. Yours is in weapons, in education, dedication, their strength is that they won't accept defeat. This surely does suggest a case for some greater flexibility in Israeli diplomacy. You say, as it were, to the Arabs, all right, if you fight, we'll fight and defeat you; if you make absolute peace with us then we will do this and that.'

She went on to say that since the Americans are now talking to the Russians, the situation could hardly improve. I told her I thought the Americans wouldn't let them down and I asked her how she saw the French position now de Gaulle had gone. Mrs Meir said it could hardly be worse than it was under de Gaulle. I said I thought he was struck down in France partly because of his stand on arms, to which Mrs Meir replied, 'I don't take an evangelistic view!' meaning that she didn't think that God had intervened on the side of the Israelis.

'Well, we all live under the aegis of the Soviet-American alliance,' I said, 'which may protect us from the anti-ballistic missiles and is probably a very good thing. Look at the way in which it prevented the Czech thing from developing out of control.' Mrs Meir replied, 'Yes, but look what happened to the Czechs.'

She asked about arms and I said we had reached a decision which didn't affect the timetable for the supply of the Chieftain tanks. She said, 'All we ask is to be put in the same position as Libya,' referring to our sale of Chieftain tanks to them.

I told her that I accepted their need for ultimate self-reliance and she repeated that Israel couldn't rely on guarantees and she pointed out what had happened in 1956 and 1967. She said she had spoken to Kennedy, who was a friend, but when she had asked him, 'Will you give the Sixth Fleet orders to come in when we need you?' Kennedy had said, 'No.'

Cabinet at 11 and we came on to the burning issue of industrial affairs. For months Harold has been embattled with the TUC and with Barbara Castle, and this was the first opportunity we had had to discuss it for some time. There is growing anxiety in the Cabinet, and I am now joining this anxious group, fearing that an Industrial Relations Bill just can't work. Harold reported on the position and some sort of compromise began to emerge which we hoped would work. When I say we I mean the growing number in the Cabinet who feel that legislation is not on.

Tuesday 17 June
Our twentieth wedding anniversary, a day altogether spoiled for Caroline by the fact that she heard this morning that her mother had got cancer and was shortly going into hospital for treatment. She didn't tell me this all day and even tonight when we had dinner together in the Post Office Tower she didn't want me to know it and only told me very much later, when we got home.

To the Cabinet at Number 10 for a run-round on industrial relations. We went round the table and it became pretty clear that there was an overwhelming majority against the penal clauses. Peter spoke up strongly, as did Judith and it was a very tense discussion. It was agreed we would come back to it this afternoon. But Harold and Barbara were up against it.

I went back to the office and had a meeting with UCS: Hepper and his people from Scotland told me that they were, after all, going to liquidate the following morning and I had at this stage absolutely no authority to prevent them from doing so. So I just listened very carefully and asked them to keep in touch with me.

There was a further Cabinet on industrial relations, which went on and on. I spoke this time and said, 'Harold, we owe you our judgment. This was a discussion that should have taken place a year ago.' I said I was a strong supporter of the White Paper's approach because I thought the damage due to bad industrial relations and strikes was very serious, that interdependence made the industrial system get dislocated by strikes and that there was broad public support for what we had done. I also said that I accepted the necessity for brinkmanship, and I very much regretted the behaviour of some members of the Cabinet.

I was critical of Jim Callaghan, not for thinking what he thought about it, which he was entitled to do, but for saying it publicly in such a way as to undermine our position. But it seemed to me that it was the argument that really mattered and that what we had done was to achieve a great deal and that Harold had brought the TUC a long way. We had a common analysis. It was a difficult matter of judgment but the concept of a 'crunch' and 'credibility' was quite unhelpful, because statutory authoritarianism had its limits.

The problem was a problem of face. The Labour Party had never dealt with industrial disputes; Parliament had never been allowed to debate them because they were always so sensitive and Ministers had been told to keep quiet. Therefore there was no public comment at all, nobody took notice of what the press said, management were distrusted, the national trade union leaders were disinclined to discuss the problem and we had therefore abandoned the whole industrial constituency.

To move from absolute silence about industrial disputes to statutory penalties was too big a jump. We wouldn't win assent for it and it was contrary to the idea of self-regulation. It underestimated the power of public pressure and therefore we should challenge the TUC, open the industrial debate, continue the talks and get them to strengthen their Letter of Guidance on disputes.

Harold and Barbara then became extremely bitter. Harold threatened to resign several times and said he wouldn't do what the Cabinet wanted him to do and they would have to look for a new Leader, and so on; people were completely unmoved by it. His bluff was called and he just looked weak and petty, he spoke too much, he interrupted, he was angry. Barbara was frantic in the usual Barbara sort of way. In the end he said he would meet with the TUC tomorrow and he would tell them what he thought, do what he thought necessary, and the Cabinet would either have to uphold him or repudiate him. That was how it was left.

It was a very, very tense meeting and Harold and Barbara had evidently taken the future into their own hands, relying on the fact that we couldn't get rid of them. But I'm not sure that if it had come to a choice between Harold and Barbara and the survival of the Labour Movement and Government, people would not let them go; and I think Harold knew that and that was why he was so angry. But he did emerge as a small man with no sense of history and as somebody really without leadership qualities. My opinion of Harold Wilson, if I haven't set it down in my diary recently, is very low indeed.

Wednesday 18 June

Cabinet was postponed and postponed and postponed, awaiting the outcome of Harold's negotiations with the TUC. We finally met at 5.50 pm. I went to see Peter beforehand, having told him that I knew Harold would climb down: and Harold and Barbara climbed off the hook and announced that they had found a settlement. Harold said that he told the TUC he had rejected their Letter and that if his demands weren't accepted, a Bill on penal sanctions would be introduced. He proposed that a solemn and binding agreement requiring unions to carry out this new arrangement should be taken by them and would have the same force as the 'Bridlington' Agreement of 1939 which regulated inter-union relationships.

He then went on to describe what a triumph he'd had, that it was a tremendous success. Judith Hart very foolishly suggested that there should be a dinner in honour of Harold and Barbara which didn't go down very well because Harold was furious with Judith for not supporting him, and the rest of the Cabinet saw it as a complete climb-down. Harold was truculent; he had pulled it off again and this was his great achievement and nobody really felt disposed to disagree with him at that particular moment. He went and announced the settlement with the TUC at the Party meeting which of course was popular because it meant the end of the penal sanctions.

Monday 23 June

I had a free morning and I went and had lunch at the Royal Society. Pat Blackett was there and I launched into the Society's educational snobbery because it is an absolute disgrace that the Royal Society should know nothing about the technical colleges, and just deal with the super élite. I suggested that they should also turn their minds towards the links between the technological universities and industry and that they might consider giving some kind of an award.

In the evening I had a talk with John Silkin, Peter and Gerald Kaufman, who was quite awful. I haven't talked to him for a very long time; he is completely cynical now, blown up with his own importance and feeding into Harold the most unsatisfactory ideas which make Harold think that he is God Almighty and everybody else has got to fall into line. It was clear that John Silkin is in the dog-house and Peter is now hated by Harold for what he did on the industrial relations thing. Indeed last Sunday's papers were full of briefings by Harold on how certain Ministers had let him down.

Wednesday 25 June

I went to see Vic Feather at Congress House. Vic kept me waiting for a long time which was an indication of how powerful he felt: he didn't have to bother very much about Cabinet Ministers. He was very pleased with the way things had gone last week and since I believe the trade unions must tackle this problem themselves I was quite pleased too. He agreed to my going to see individual trade unions about the problems of industry and I asked him what he would think about my visiting sites where strikes were in progress. He was very much against that and so I won't be able to do that for a while.

Thursday 26 June
There was another great UCS crisis and the position is that Swallow and Hepper are not on speaking terms. Swallow is now trying to get rid of Hepper and Hepper is being difficult and saying that he won't go without compensation.

Monday 30 June
I went to Gerry Reynolds's memorial service. He died of cancer a few days ago, leaving a wife and several children, and I stood in St Margaret's with tears running down my cheeks. It was immensely sad.

Tuesday 1 July
I was at home all this morning and then had a sandwich lunch with Bill Swallow, Barry Barker and Joe Gormley. It is quite clear UCS would have to pay £50,000 compensation to Hepper to get rid of him and so they agreed he would remain and have somebody underneath him. But Swallow is so terribly tactless and he hates Hepper and Hepper hates Swallow, and they are both extremely stupid, so that we are in serious difficulties still.

Wednesday 2 July
We had an inner office meeting, that is with Ivor Manley, Eunice and Larry Whitty – sort of self-criticism – to see how we could really plan the work to meet our priorities and not just to respond to the pressure of events.

Thursday 3 July
To the Bristol GMC. There was opposition led by Cyril Langham, the Chairman, to my being nominated to the National Executive and Herbert Rogers tried to get me to say that if I was nominated for the Executive, I would always agree with Conference decisions. But the nomination was, in fact, unanimous with the exception of Cyril.

Tuesday 8 July
I came back to the office and McGeorge Bundy [President Kennedy's Special Assistant on National Security] and Solly Zuckerman came to see me about their plan for a centre to study the management of large organisations. It was the first time I had met Bundy and he was much too slick and international jet-set intellectual for my liking. They were off to Russia to discuss it with Gvishiani.

Wednesday 9 July

After Questions I met the National Electronics Council under Lord Mountbatten's chairmanship, and he is a quite intolerable man, I don't know how anybody puts up with him. He dominates it, he bullies people, he puts his own items on the agenda.

Derek Moon came with me to the Free Communications Group, in the Mahatma Gandhi Hall. I discovered that the group had been formed partly in response to speeches I had made on broadcasting last October by journalists including Alexander Cockburn, Gus Mac-Donald, Bruce Page and Neal Ascherson. It was highly revolutionary – a sort of Maoist group. I presented my lecture and then got absolutely hammered by these guys who, like all left-wingers, were totally pessimistic and said nothing could or would be done and they went for me. I fought back as hard as I could, and I greatly enjoyed it.

Friday 11 July

This morning I went with Ivor Manley by helicopter to the Steam Generating Heavy Water Reactor at Winfrith for the Queen's visit. It was a most beautiful day and we had a lovely flight down. When I got there I had a talk to John Hill about the centrifuge and the reorganisation of the AEA and he wants to come and have a talk with me.

The Queen arrived and looked extremely angry. I think the truth is that she is bored but feels she has to look interested or something; anyway she walked round and I followed behind with the Duke of Edinburgh. Of course a Minister during a royal visit is just an office boy.

At lunch the Queen was really rather different, indeed she was very pleasant. First of all we talked about the television programme made about the royal family. She said it might have to be cut for showing in the United States; the American Ambassador had used very long words and made himself look rather ridiculous.

I asked her if royalty had to be so formal. The Queen said that it is just that you have to dress up and be told what to do for Privy Council. Obviously she did not much like the suggestion that the thing was more formal than was necessary.

We talked about the Commonwealth Prime Ministers' meeting and I asked her what impression she had formed of Trudeau. She said that he had been rather disappointing. I gave my view in support of disposable politicians – that, in fact, you could not do more than a certain amount of work before you had to go and refurbish yourself.

Then we moved on to the subject of the Royal Prerogative. I asked her whether, when there was a dissolution contemplated, she ever consulted the Speaker, because he was impartial. She said, 'I am supposed to be impartial but, of course, I can call in whom I like.'

So I asked her, 'Well, suppose, for example, there had been a row on the industrial relations legislation and the Prime Minister had come and asked for a dissolution. It was at least arguable that another Prime Minister would have held together a Government without a dissolution.' She said, 'Well, we had to look up all the precedents on the dissolution,' and I pointed out that it might well have become real if the Parliamentary Labour Party had rejected an Industrial Relations Bill.

We got on to talking about the Lords and the Commons and she raised the redistribution of parliamentary boundaries. I think she wanted to provoke me into saying something but I didn't comment on it.

She told me that the royal train was bulletproof and had two diesels, which had its origins in 1937 when one diesel had broken down and the train had got stuck. That led to Concorde and she said how she wished Trubshaw had seen people applaud when Concorde went over on her birthday and I told her what I had told George Thomas, that if Concorde had crashed into the Palace that day, the occasion would have turned into a coronation.

She said, 'You *can't* cancel Concorde' I pointed out the question was whether we could sell it: that was the real test.

We talked about the Civil Service machine and I remarked that a new Minister coming into a Ministry really was in a position to put the brakes on. 'Presumably,' I said, 'the machine thwarts you too?' I do not think that had quite occurred to her. I went on and talked about the desirability of having a longer Government with Ministers who retired at a certain stage in order to cope with the rate of change.

She is not clever, but she is reasonably intelligent and she is experienced: she has been involved in Government now for eighteen years. She knew about the test routes for Concorde and that they would be going up the West of Scotland. So either she had been reading Cabinet papers or her Private Secretary had briefed her on this particular matter.

I proposed her health, having got my Private Secretary, Ivor Manley, to speak to Sir Martin Charteris, her Assistant Private Secretary, a typical pyramid operation, rather than asking her directly 'Should I propose a toast?'

On the way out I had a brief word with the Duke who, as usual, was talking about high taxation as a major disincentive.

Monday 14 July
We had a briefing meeting for the Tory, Liberal and Labour Science and Technology Groups at the Ministry of Technology. I had laid this on because I was very keen that the Tories should not come out firmly against the Ministry of Technology as it would have such a damaging effect on the morale of the Department. So David Price, Harry Legge-

Bourke, Ian Orr-Ewing, Eric Moonman* and Eric Lubbock and one or two others came for the day.

It had the double effect of convincing the Tories we were doing a useful job and at the same time convincing our people (I mean our officials) that it would be absolute hell if the Tories won the Election!

I had a long talk to Jeremy Bray who is very upset that Harold and Peter Shore have objected to publication of his book and is seriously thinking of resigning. I tried to cheer him up as best I could.

It was a very late-night sitting. I got to bed at about 4 o'clock.

Tuesday 15 July

I took Melissa to the Speaker's party and she was absolutely sweet. She met Denis Healey and Barbara Castle and Peter Shore, but she wouldn't speak to Gerald Nabarro! She was so good and self-possessed. It was the first public engagement she had attended.

Saturday 19 July

Tonight the great news is that the Apollo moon landing takes place tomorrow. We are all getting very excited about it.

Also there is news from America that Senator Edward Kennedy took a girl from a party in New England and crashed over a bridge and the girl drowned. It is a sensational story.

Monday 21 July

I woke at about 2 am and dozed off until about 3.30 or 4. Joshua woke me up and we watched Neil Armstrong descending from the Apollo capsule, saw him put his foot on the surface of the moon and then he and Buz Aldrin walked around. It was a most fantastic day.

Tuesday 22 July

We had Cabinet and we discussed the Lords and boundaries and agreed to postpone them. We also discussed entry into the EEC and there was the beginning of a revolt by Peter Shore. Denis Healey said it was better to wait in the hope that Enoch Powell would make an issue of it with Heath and split the Tory Party rather than us.

We heard that Gerald Brooke was being exchanged for the Krogers.

---

* David Price, Conservative MP for Eastleigh and Opposition spokesman on Science and Technology; Sir Harry Legge-Bourke, Conservative MP for the Isle of Ely; Sir Ian Orr-Ewing, Conservative MP for Hendon; Eric Moonman, Labour MP for Billericay.

Thursday 24 July

After Cabinet I asked whether Harold was going to see me today. He said, 'Come in straight away,' so I went in.

I said I wanted to talk to him about the machinery of government and he then told me what changes he had in mind. He was going to give me the chemical industry from the Board of Trade and the NEDC responsibilities including the National Plan from the DEA. I said, 'Would that be a Secretary of State's job?' He said, 'No, I need that for my major restructuring.'

He went on to attack Peter Shore who, he said, was very bureaucratic and had been a great disappointment and that he, Harold, should never have given up the overlordship of DEA. I said he should never have taken it on, because it had put Peter in a very difficult position.

Then he attacked Judith and said she was just a prattling woman who had done absolutely nothing and if she wanted to be a PPS to a junior Minister she had better go and do that instead of trying to be in the Cabinet. He was very scornful.

He accused Dick Marsh of always leaking, Tony Crosland of always leaking to the journalist Alan Watkins, and complained of Jim Callaghan. He said that he was going to do major restructuring and heads would have to roll. He asked if I would keep an eye out for plots and said that Ministers were meeting in secret and the Campaign for Democratic Socialism was still active.

Generally speaking the whole thing was just paranoid and he talked about his magic and said, 'Isn't there always magic in my reshuffle, just as there's magic in my honours list – like giving D'Oliviera* an OBE.' You just couldn't communicate with him.

It was perfectly evident that he had not forgotten what Peter had done. He said, 'Barbara and I will never forget Peter's speech on industrial relations.' It was clear he intended to get rid of Peter and I think of Judith, and to have a smaller Cabinet.

I went out shaken by this, having concluded that the man had gone mad, ought to be removed, that the great case for the parliamentary system was that it did remove people. I just felt contempt for him. Maybe I will get slightly promoted in the reshuffle, if ever it comes in this form in the autumn. But I just feel that Harold is finished.

---

* Basil D'Oliviera, a 'Cape Coloured' South African, who moved to Britain and played Test cricket for England. In 1969 an MCC tour of South Africa was cancelled because D'Oliviera was in the MCC team.

Monday 28 July
I had a word with Otto and we had a bit of a talk about Europe. Two years ago when we were discussing entry into Europe, Otto was passionately in favour of it. He urged me and pressed me, telling me entry was essential for investment and that Whitehall would dominate the Common Market because it was so full of experienced people. But now, to my surprise and interest, he was rather hostile to the EEC and thought it wouldn't come off.

He thought that the balance of payments disadvantages due to the agricultural policy were very great and that the natural link was between us and the United States; indeed he even denied that he had been in favour of it two years ago, which was nonsense.

But it is a straw in the wind and my own guess would be that our entry into Europe would not be easy and that public opinion is not so sympathetic. I found it a useful discussion.

Tuesday 5 August
At Stansgate, and a perfect day, completely windless with a hot sun. The whole family went swimming. We are enjoying the holiday enormously.

I have begun some yoga exercises. Caroline is working on an article on women's education for the *Sunday Times*.

Monday 11 August
Caroline and I drove to London and I went to the Campaign Committee at Transport House. In fact, I was the only member of the Government there because Harold was in the Scilly Isles, Denis Healey is convalescing and Bob Mellish is presumably on holiday. Eirene White was in the chair.

David Kingsley presented his campaign for a future Election, to begin with a big bang on the Bank Holiday Monday at the very end of the month. The major slogan is 'Labour has got Life and Soul' and the sub-slogan is 'When it comes down to it, aren't Labour's ideals yours as well?'

David presented this very skilfully. He said, 'You've got something here which reflects the truth, and everybody knows that this is the case with the Labour Party. It has got a great deal of life and vitality; hence its splits and arguments. It also has soul, that is to say it reflects people's aspirations and, of course, the phrase "life and soul of the party" is a well-known one which also helps.'

He showed us a number of posters, including one of Harold in the middle of a large number of people, which is the way he should be shown. He proposed we might consider putting up a poster of Heath saying, 'This poster is paid for by the Labour Party', or, more seriously, putting Heath and Wilson side by side and under Wilson saying,

'Labour has got life and soul'. We were not very keen on this on the grounds that you shouldn't attack your opponents personally.

Friday 15 August
Pelting with rain all day. Caroline worked on her article on women's education and Stephen got his A level results envelope. He said nothing all day.

Today we heard on the news that UK troops had been committed to maintain law and order in Derry during the troubles that arose out of the Apprentice Boys' annual march.

We had discussed this in Cabinet before the end of July and agreed that troops could be used, so long as the Prime Minister, the Home Secretary, the Defence Secretary and the Foreign Secretary kept in touch with each other. So it looks as though civil war in Ulster has almost begun.

Saturday 16 August
Stephen woke us at 2.45, having finally opened his results, and told us he had got an A in History, a B in Music, and a C in Pure Maths.

Hilary went off to Scotland with his friend Alan Burton.

Sunday 17 August
I had a message last night from Ivor Manley saying there would be an emergency Cabinet on Tuesday to consider the situation in Ulster.

The crisis in Northern Ireland had been slowly building up with riots in July and August. On 12 August in Londonderry fighting broke out between Protestants and Catholics during the Apprentice Boys' march, and in the ensuing violence Catholics' homes were burned. Troops were moved into Londonderry, and then into Belfast, where the trouble had spread, after appeals to Roy Hattersley, the Minister of Defence for Administration, who was deputising for Denis Healey, from the Royal Ulster Constabulary and from Bernadette Devlin, Independent Unity MP for Mid-Ulster.

Tuesday 19 August
Ron Vaughan took me to London and Caroline came with me. We arrived home at 11 and found the Comprehensive Schools Committee, which uses my office in the basement, in action. I went off to the Cabinet.

I had underestimated the immense excitement over the Ulster thing. Downing Street was cordoned off and there was a mass of photographers and television cameras outside Number 10.

There were jokes in Cabinet about my new beard and Michael Stewart reminded me of what Attlee had said when Sydney Silverman, MP for Nelson and Colne, grew a beard. He had said, 'I move previous face' and indeed Harold began by saying, 'Motions to move previous face are out of order.'

We then settled down to discuss the Ulster situation. A paper by Jim Callaghan was passed around which made five recommendations.

First, that the 12,000 B Specials [the Protestant Ulster Special Constabulary] should be disarmed; second, that we consider a Bill transferring some authority to Westminster; third, that there should be advisers attached to the Northern Ireland Government; fourth, that we might consider a coalition or, at any rate, more elements brought into the Northern Ireland Government; and fifth, that a Community Relations Organisation might be set up, possibly with a Minister on the spot, to examine complaints of discrimination.

Jim opened quietly and extremely well. He said he had been prescient in July in warning us that there was a very poor Intelligence Service in Ulster; he had seen Chichester-Clark* and asked him about the demonstrations before they occurred and had not wanted them banned. He said Hattersley had done an extremely good job at the Ministry of Defence in Denis's absence, the troops had been welcomed by the people and indeed there had been many appeals for help at different stages.

The Stormont Government say it is the IRA who are the cause of the trouble but this does not conform to British Intelligence. The Catholics were defending themselves with ferocity, as Jim put it, and it was really because of that fear that the situation had got out of control. Jim said we must remove the cause of the fear, ie get rid of the B Specials, and he would like to see Peacocke, the Inspector-General of the Royal Ulster Constabulary, replaced by a British Chief Constable. The Northern Ireland Labour Party agreed the recommendations in his paper but they fear that if the B Specials are disarmed, there will be secret arms caches kept and used. Jim pointed out that the B Specials got no police training, only shooting practice.

Denis Healey said there had been a welcome for the troops but he agreed that they had reached the peak of the honeymoon period and we must defuse the situation today. He said that the military were the only people who knew Ulster, since there was no Intelligence at all coming from the Protestant side. There were enough troops unless there was real trouble and, although he had sympathy with the Catholics, he had to point out that if we put the majority of the population against us, we should be once again in the 1911–14 situation (when Carson headed Ulster Protestant opposition to the Home Rule proposals of the Liberal Government).

*James Chichester-Clark, Prime Minister of Northern Ireland, 1969–71; Unionist MP for South Derry, Northern Ireland Parliament, 1960–72.

He was, therefore, somewhat doubtful about Jim Callaghan's proposals. He himself wanted the B Specials limited to guarding key points and frontier work and the defence of police stations. He wanted them to give up their arms, which they currently keep at home. But the Royal Ulster Constabulary would then have to store the weapons and there was a danger that the IRA would attack the police stations to steal them.

Denis thought it was better to get Chichester-Clark, or another Ulsterman, to carry the can and he raised the question of whether the army should be allowed to crater, that is to say blow up, the minor roads into Eire. He said there were about 1,000 IRA people who were a mixture of old Marxists and old patriots; the RUC was inefficient and its Intelligence was terrible; Dublin was not very effective; and the IRA itself was not effectively penetrated by Intelligence.

Dick Crossman intervened and said that Chichester-Clark had told him that the B Specials would not be used in Catholic areas. The Inspector-General who controlled the RUC and the B Specials apparently treated Ministers like office boys and it had shocked Dick very much.

Harold said that all the objectives were agreed, that he had warned Chichester-Clark that we cannot be his hatchet men and if British troops are used, we cannot avoid responsibility. The RUC would never control Bogside in Derry. We must tackle the first task first, namely restore law and order, and we must be neutral between the factions. We want to be firm and cool and fair, but avoid a political row in the UK because he did not want to recall Parliament or take over the Government from Northern Ireland.

Then, after that, he said we should take a look at the long-term situation. He thought the communiqué tonight might include a declaration of principles: that the border was not at issue, that this was a domestic matter for the UK, that we must find out where the responsibility lies, that Ulster had the continuing responsibility, and that the use of troops was temporary. The communiqué should also contain some message about reform, housing and local government and make some reference to human rights to indicate that we believe that everyone in the United Kingdom is entitled to full rights.

Jim warned, 'Don't underestimate the capacity of the Ulster Unionists for creating mischief in the Tory Party. You can never be sure they won't, and we should be very reluctant to take over.' He said he thought Chichester-Clark was anxious to help because he was a very frightened man.

He said we must hold the arms of the B Specials and try to get an amnesty on other arms. Peacocke and his colleagues really ought to go and perhaps they would resign. Fortunately Peacocke had already refused two inquiries into the role and structure of the RUC proposed by Northern Ireland Ministers so he had put himself in the wrong.

Jim continued that a British head of the RUC should be seconded and the Home Office should inspect it in future, and that a senior civil servant should be lent from London to the Prime Minister's Office and the Ulster Home Office. In fact, there was now liaison between the Ulster Government, the police and the military on the placing of troops.

Therefore, as Dick pointed out, the United Kingdom is *effectively* in control.

Jim denied this, and said that if Chichester-Clark refused we could insist, but you could not take the troops out again because it would leave chaos.

Roy said, 'What would we do if Chichester-Clark rejects? We have got three months to deal with the underlying problem.'

Denis stressed that it would take time. We must keep the Protestants quiet. That was Denis's major concern and therefore he wanted to see a new role for the B Specials, mainly to stop them keeping their arms at home.

Jim went on to say he thought a Minister for Community Relations and a mixed commission might be worthwhile and should we consider suggesting proportional representation in Ulster?

Dick said, 'For heaven's sake be careful because that will be taken up by the Scottish Nationalists and the Welsh Nationalists and we shall be in serious difficulties.' So it was agreed not to pursue that.

Jim then considered the possibility of a broadly-based Government.

Denis stressed again, 'Let's keep Chichester-Clark carrying the can.'

Jim agreed. 'Yes, I too want to avoid responsibility.'

Michael Stewart thought Eire had made a mistake in pushing its case for UN forces. The Security Council would be meeting tomorrow with Spain in the chair – which was unfortunate for us because of the current Gibraltar problems – and it was possible that the item might fail to get on the agenda. The Eire Foreign Minister wanted to speak in support of putting it on the agenda and Britain has decided not to oppose that. Michael Stewart was very relaxed and said that he did not think world aspects should dominate our handling of the matter. Britain cannot walk out of Ulster entirely, although we had considered it as an alternative. This was an interesting thing for him to say because it would never have been admitted publicly. He thought that awful as it would be to take over responsibility, it would be less awful than walking out. There had to be some results tonight and the B Specials were the key.

That more or less got us to the point of giving sufficient authority to Harold, Jim, Denis, Lord Stonham [Minister of State at the Home Office] and Michael Stewart, who were going to meet Chichester-Clark at 5.

I said that I was in full agreement with Jim's paper. We could not afford a crunch with Chichester-Clark which we did not immediately win because we could not have our troops working there after Chichester-Clark had defied our wishes; this would cause political trouble at home. We had two problems: one was, will the troops be necessary for ever and ever and will it prevent us getting out, and the other was, if we make a declaration of principles, will the troops find themselves committed to enforce them?

I said I thought there was a danger that if both power in Ulster and the objectives in Ulster were exercised in London we should find ourselves very deeply involved and, looking into my crystal ball, I wanted to see what was going to happen next. I did not want to find that we had drifted into administering Ulster without really thinking about it.

Judith Hart said the B Specials were the priority. Bob Mellish said that if the worst came to the worst, we could always threaten Chichester-Clark. George Thomas talked about the hooligans who were supporting the Protestants and hoped we could relieve the distress a little bit.

Dick Crossman said, 'Perhaps we should have a Minister sent from London,' and Harold replied that we would look at that later. Dick also thought it was necessary to keep Maudling with us to maintain bipartisanship.

Then Harold gave us another great warning on keeping it secret and avoiding any hint of split. There has not really been a split in today's Cabinet, although there is a difference of emphasis between Jim and Denis.

Cledwyn Hughes said, 'It's a pity that the Catholics and Protestants can't cooperate a bit more at the religious level.'

Tony Greenwood supported Jim and was against cratering. There was a further discussion on cratering and Roy said he would agree to it if it was necessary for the negotiations. Then the question arose as to whether the B Specials should be used on the border and the general agreement was that they should not be.

The meeting was quiet and Jim, I thought, did very well. Harold was all right except that, as usual, he was much too tactical and there was too little thinking about the future. Denis was realistic in seeing that he might find himself in a position of sending in the troops against all the Protestants. I wonder whether people understood how serious the situation was – whether, in fact, this was not the beginning of ten more years of Irish politics at Westminster which would be very unpleasant. None of us had thought it out very carefully.

I went home and waited and waited in case there was another Cabinet meeting but in the end Harold managed to carry Chichester-Clark on the proposals which were published this evening; not to disarm the B Specials but to bring them under the control of General Freeland [GOC, Northern Ireland]. It is a compromise because he will actually collect their arms and keep them in armouries. That is the most effective way of dealing with them.

Caroline and I got back to Stansgate about 1 am, both pretty tired.

Wednesday 3 September

At 12.30 Harold wanted to see me and I wondered if this was the reshuffle. He began in a very relaxed way. He said he wanted to talk to me about the Campaign Committee, how very difficult Harry Nicholas was, and how he, Harold, had been told nothing about the campaign.

Then we discussed how the campaign should be run for a while. He said the Cabinet would be having a general discussion about the forthcoming year, which I think is very sensible, a thing we have never done.

After that, we got on to the paper I had written, to be discussed soon by the Inner Cabinet, which I shall be invited to attend.

Finally we got on to the question of the reshuffle. He said he had been very struck by the proposal I had made for a Ministry of Industry and Technology. He thought he might possibly want me for something else – a brand new job bringing Housing, Local Government, Transport and DEA Regional Policy together, a sort of Secretary of State for England, and was I interested?

My first instincts were suspicious because if my Department is going to be built up, I am not going to be there to do it. Also I wondered if this was one of Harold's gimmicks. So I said I had doubts about it. He was clearly trying to find room for Denis Healey, whom he wants to move from Defence into a new job and he thought this would look good: Denis Healey, the first Minister of Industry.

He wanted Barbara to go into Land and Planning but she does not want to go back to Transport, which she feels would be a demotion and also, Harold said, 'She is nursing a dead baby.' This was a reference to 'In Place of Strife' and of course she wants to stay and make something of Employment. Harold has got personality difficulties but I did not make quite as much fuss as I should have done.

Sunday 7 September

There is a panic developing over my message to the Mintech staff. This is something that goes right back to 1966 when I began to identify objectives for the Department and later, when I worked on my pyramid theory and set up the sabbaticals to which Otto was very much opposed.

When Part Two, which contained the ideas for overcoming problems with the pyramid, reached the office, there was absolute chaos, and all the Under-Secretaries below John Leckie, the Deputy-Secretary, met. I then had a message saying that in no circumstances should I circulate this outside the office until Otto had seen it.

I decided to ring Otto Clarke in order to clarify things and he agreed to come at 11.30.

I dressed up for fun in my best suit, smoked a cigar, wore my old school tie and black shoes. He arrived in a 1930s' open-necked shirt and baggy pants, looking exactly as all Englishmen do at the weekends. He was completely surprised to find me like this, and I disarmed him by saying I had decided to send out the first part of the message, which was the Objectives of the Department, and the second part I'd discuss with the Civil Service Department.

At about 2.30 the phone rang and a mid-European voice said, 'Is that 5503?'

'Yes.'

'Is that the Minister of Technology?'

'Yes.'

'You have twenty-four hours to live,' and the caller rang off.

I didn't know whether to take this seriously or not but I phoned the police and they sent someone round and ultimately got on to the Special Branch. This man may be an émigré from Yugoslavia or Hungary who is angry that I am going there tomorrow and wants to frighten me off doing so.

I had another phone call from the same person who gave a maniacal laugh and rang off.

From 8–17 September I visited Yugoslavia, Hungary and, very briefly, Czechoslovakia as part of my ministerial visits to Eastern European countries, to negotiate and sign technological agreements.

Yugoslavia was, of course, in a special position since the break with Stalin in 1948, and the Yugoslavs were very proud of their work on self-management, which interested me greatly because of the total lack of industrial democracy in both the private and the public sectors in Britain. They were trying to run a socialist society within a one-Party state but combining industrial democracy – or self-management – with a market economy, which was very difficult in a country made up of so many differing components. My relations with the Yugoslavs were close and I found the visit both fascinating and entertaining.

From Yugoslavia I went on to Budapest where I gave a lecture which was very open in character, appealing to the Hungarian initiative in economic matters. It was no surprise to realise that Hungary would be one of the first countries in the COMECON bloc to experiment with economic reforms of a kind later tried in other parts of Eastern Europe, culminating in the Gorbachev reforms of 1987.

Thursday 18 September

To Transport House for the Cabinet photographs. It was pretty evident that those who were there would be in the Government after the reshuffle, otherwise we would not have been asked.

To Bristol for a public meeting at St Bernadette's Catholic School. This was my third public meeting at which the Fascists had been present. I wondered what they would do, whether they would make trouble. I returned a soft answer to them when they put their points about the Common Market, the permissive society, hanging and immigrants, and so far they have not caused trouble. My principle is that if you treat people reasonably, you will get the best out of them. You can turn almost anybody into a raving lunatic by being too abusive.

Friday 19 September

Up at 4.45 and flew to Liverpool with Derek Moon and Larry Whitty to the GEC-English Electric factories where 3,000 redundancies have been announced.

We went straight to the Netherton factory with Eric Heffer and Simon Mahon, the local Labour MPs. I was greeted by the management, and then went round with the shop stewards. They were a very decent crowd and they had a great possessive sense about the place: this was their factory. I told them frankly that there was not much hope of saving jobs but I wanted to talk to them.

I went to see the Lord Mayor and he was very grateful I had come because it was a tremendous problem for him. He was being severely criticised, I think, because of what had happened. After I had seen the Lord Mayor, I had a succession of other meetings. I met the MPs with officials and privately. I met the trade union officials, two of whom were extremely offensive, and made no progress at all.

Then there was a lunch at the City Hall. I met Arnold Weinstock, who had come up with Jack Scamp of AEI and I talked to the management there. At lunch I talked to the leaders of the Labour and Conservative groups, and MPs. Then we had a big meeting and I tried to get everybody to come to agreement as to what we should do next. Eric Heffer and Simon Mahon were difficult and so were the trade union leaders. The shop stewards' 'Action Committee' had turned up to speak to us and the trade union officials would not let them in to the meeting. Weinstock was abused and I had to stand up for him.

Then I found that the Action Committee were waiting to see me so I went to meet them: they said that Weinstock had refused to meet them. At that moment Weinstock turned up and when I left they were all talking. It was really an extremely interesting day. I think all I did was to get people to talk to each other.

Tuesday 23 September
I had a discussion with Jeremy Bray. He is very agitated and determined to leave the Ministry of Technology and it does not look as if there is much I can do to stop him.

I had to go and see Harold again about Jeremy and about the reshuffle. I told Harold I thought he had been very decent in letting Jeremy publish the articles in the *Guardian* but Harold was evidently determined to get rid of him. He made this very clear.

Thursday 25 September
Cabinet. Talked about hanging – where Jim Callaghan is determined to get through his legislation to make the abolition of hanging permanent by the end of this year to avoid it coming up into the Election period – and the Common Market, where everyone is beginning to wobble because the public polls are so hostile to it.

Jeremy Bray resigned today. He wrote an enormously long letter to Harold quoting Milton. There you are, you cannot stop him. He was in a highly emotional mood and the contempt with which Harold speaks of him irritates me enormously, but Jeremy has made a great mistake. I told him I thought the Ministry of Technology would be big enough to allow him to do the sort of work he wanted, which is industrial demand management.

There was an Overseas Policy and Defence Committee meeting where it was agreed not to sell any Wasp helicopters to South Africa. There was some criticism of it but to break the embargo on military helicopters for a few hundred thousand pounds would have been crazy in an Election year.

Sunday 28 September
Conference, and a late lie-in and after lunch we had the NEC. I moved that the press be admitted because everything had been leaked. This was very nearly carried.

I got as near as I could to proposing that there should be a Referendum on our decision to go into the EEC. I had almost got it out when Harold realised what I was going to say, and stopped it: I didn't fight the issue. But I know perfectly well that no Government will agree to go into the EEC if there isn't more enthusiasm than there is at the moment.

Saturday 4 October
To Number 10 where of course Ministers affected by the reshuffle had been coming and going all day. Harold told me he wanted me to remain Minister of Technology and take over the whole Ministry of Power, all the industry divisions from the Board of Trade and their industrial

location work, and the industrial side of the DEA. I called Otto in and he knew exactly what it involved. This evening I had just a bit of time to think it all over. It is an enormous job that I have been given and I must say I was staggered to find the whole Ministry of Power coming over to me but I couldn't ring anybody up to talk about it.

Sunday 5 October
I planned what I was going to do with this new huge department and at 6 the announcement was made on TV. The growth of the Ministry of Technology was *the* news; there was no question this was the main story of the day. Crosland has been given the job of Secretary of State for England, coordinating transport and housing and he is obviously very sick about it because he doesn't think there is anything in the job. I have been given the Ministry of Industry job which is what I really wanted.

NOTES
Chapter Two

1. (p. 143) Dr Joseph Cort was an American physicist whom I helped in 1954, during his persecution in and exile from the US in the McCarthyite years. He went to Czechoslovakia as a political refugee, eventually returning to the US after his passport had been returned to him.

2. (p. 156) The tiny West Indian island of Anguilla, which had a population of 6,000, had declared its independence from the British St Kitts-Nevis group in June 1967; in January 1969 it announced that it was adopting a republican constitution, and Ronald Webster was elected President. The British Government refused to recognise Anguillan independence and on 19 March sent 300 paratroopers on ships from Antigua to occupy the island, withdrawing them in September 1969.

3. (p. 162) In February 1969 President de Gaulle announced that there would be a Referendum in France inviting the French electorate to accept or reject a Government Reform Bill introducing wide constitutional and administrative changes. De Gaulle used the Referendum issue to attack strikes and discontent in France and staked his Presidency, which he had held since 1959, on the outcome, declaring that he would resign if the vote, on 27 April, was *Non*.

3
Yesterday's Men
October 1969–June 1970

The effect of the Government changes made by Harold Wilson was to create two new super-Ministries, headed by me and by Tony Crosland. The Department of Economic Affairs was abolished but Peter Shore remained in the Cabinet. The Ministry of Technology took over the Ministry of Power in its entirety and certain functions of the Department of Economic Affairs, as well as assuming responsibility for regional and industrial policy from the Board of Trade. The expansion of the Ministry brought with it new appointments: Harold Lever, my Number Two, was put in the Cabinet as Paymaster General; Neil Carmichael (MP for Glasgow Woodside) and Ernest Davies (MP for Stretford) replaced Jeremy Bray and Gerry Fowler as Joint Parliamentary Secretaries and Alan Williams (MP for Swansea West) was appointed as a third.

Reg Prentice was initially made Minister of State at my new Department, but resigned after three days, and was replaced by Lord Delacourt-Smith (Charles Smith), and Eric Varley replaced Curly Mallalieu.

I allocated responsibilities between five groups. The Industry group was headed by Harold Lever, who also liaised with the IRC and the CBI. The Regional group was led by Eric Varley, and dealt with the location of industry in the regions and with the Board of Trade. The Aviation group under Charles Smith was responsible for aviation and hovercraft. Ernest Davies and the Research group oversaw research departments generally and the Economic group headed by Alan Williams was concerned with the nationalised industries and mineral development. The enlarged Ministry employed 38,900 people.

Monday 6 October

The photographers had arrived at home at 8 to take pictures and found that I had left an hour earlier.

I looked in at the Ministry of Power and then went with Larry Whitty, my new Assistant Private Secretary, to Telford New Town by air. I should add that Harold had warned me on Saturday that I might have to go to Balmoral to kiss hands with the Queen on appointment, and I said, 'How ridiculous. I can't anyway, I'm going to Telford.' He said, 'Well, the Palace insist.' Later the Privy Council office rang me up and said that I had to go, and that the Prime Minister insisted.

So I rang Harold, who denied this, and in the end I got out of it, but not without a very sharp exchange with the Privy Council office. The relations between Number 10 and the Privy Council office are not warm. But I was damned if I was going to waste a whole day going to Balmoral, particularly as I had committed myself to Telford.

Gerry Fowler met me at Telford, and I went to GKN's and Sankey's factories, and to Automatic Pressings, and talked to the trades council. Then to Gerry Fowler's house, to the Labour Club, and finally to a Rotary dinner. Got home at 12.30, really exhausted.

Tuesday 7 October

I had drinks for all the new top staff, with Reg Prentice among others. Reg is very uneasy. He obviously regrets having taken on the job and he spoke to me anxiously today about his room and facilities.

I had to go to see Harold in the evening. He told me he was going to put me in the Inner Cabinet.

Wednesday 8 October

Reg Prentice came to see me and told me that he was going to go. I think he was annoyed to find he was Number Three in my Department, and not Number Two, and that it hadn't been made clear to him. I think he has also had second thoughts about technology and was a bit upset to have given up his own Department. Generally speaking, he was sort of half-tricked into taking it on.

Stephen went to Keele today, the first one of our children off to university.

Saturday 11 October

Caroline held a seminar this morning and I went to Bristol to open an old people's club. Though it was rather an exhausting way to spend a Saturday, I did it deliberately because there is bound to be suspicion that, with my new job, I will neglect the constituency.

Tuesday 14 October

I saw the Confederation of Shipbuilding and Engineering Unions for the first of my meetings on the links between the new Department and the trade unions. Hugh Scanlon was in the chair.

In the evening Caroline and I went to Number 10 for a dinner for the American astronauts, the first three men to have been on the moon. Neil Armstrong and Buz Aldrin and their wives were there and we were scheduled to look after Colonel Mike Collins and his wife Pat. Harold had laid on the evening in grand style with lots of television coverage.

We took our pair round and introduced them to everybody. I sat next to Pat Collins who is a very intelligent and delightful woman. I felt sorry that she had George Brown, who was completely pickled, on the other side of her.

Harold made a most stilted speech which he read entirely from a text and Neil Armstrong shamed him by getting up without a single note and making a much better one. Then George Brown got up and gave an unofficial toast to another Collins, Michael Collins, the Irish leader. William Armstrong, the head of the Civil Service, said a word about the Armstrongs. I dashed back to the House to vote, leaving Caroline there and when I came back hundreds were there – stage celebrities, spastic children, schoolboys: it was a memorable evening.

Wednesday 15 October
Lunch with Tom Paine, Administrator of NASA. He is a highly civilised, very whimsical man, and I liked him very much. He has been in a think tank and he described people who make good members of think tanks as 'T-shaped' men, that is to say with a very deep interest in their own subject but also with a very broad and general knowledge on top. He made a little speech describing space as the seventh continent, which was only ninety or one hundred miles away and simply required acceleration of 17,000 miles faster than the speed of the movement of the earth in order to get to it. This seventh continent, which at the moment simply reflected things from earth, would one day be able to hold computer banks with information. Then he talked about the moon as the eighth continent and Mars as the ninth, and so on. The reference to space as being a usable area around the world was a very stimulating idea.

Sunday 19 October
The papers this week, commenting on Harold Lever's appointment, suggest that Harold Wilson put him there to keep an eye on me, that he was really going to run the Department, and that there was going to be a split. Harold rang me up to apologise.

Wednesday 22 October
I went to Buckingham Palace at lunchtime to be sworn in as Minister of Power. I was greeted by Godfrey Agnew, who is the Clerk of the Privy Council, and I said how much I appreciated being able to fulfil my engagements and not have to go to Balmoral to be sworn in.

He said how very upset the Queen had been at the newspaper story that other Ministers who had gone up there had not enjoyed it and had thought it a waste of time. I said, 'Everybody nowadays has got to get used to criticism, you can't avoid it.' He said, 'Not by a Minister. By a politician perhaps, but comments by a Minister undermine the respect for authority.'

You felt that here was a man trying to preserve the monarchy on the basis that you couldn't conceivably discuss it, because if you did its authority might be undermined. It was so interesting.

Anyway, I went in and I affirmed as Minister of Power. Then, forty-four seconds later, I heard the Transfer of Functions Order being approved, so I was Minister of Power for forty-four seconds and then that Department was dissolved.

In the evening, Caroline and I went to dinner with the Yugoslav Ambassador. After dinner, Sir Thomas Brimelow* was expounding the brake theory of the Civil Service, that it was the civil servants' function to see that nothing much happened. Ministers were there to provide a little bit of impetus but the Civil Service would keep the brakes on. I think the Ambassador was staggered to hear all this being said.

Friday 24 October
Slept for eleven hours. Worked at home this morning. Had to change the phone number again because the *Evening Standard* have got hold of the story of the death threat and I was afraid they would publish my new number.

Sunday 26 October
Another glorious day. This October has been the driest for 200 years and the warmest for 100 years. An absolutely perfect month.

I cycled over to have a talk to Tony Crosland. I should add that Tony is furious about the re-allocation of duties. He is upset to have lost the Board of Trade. He does not think it should have been cut up, and he is angry at the way in which he himself has been treated: he thinks his new Department is a non-department, which it is.

Thursday 30 October
At Cabinet, Harold said he wanted everyone to start kicking Heath in the groin. People were nodding wisely and we were going on to the next item so I decided to speak up. I said, 'Look, I don't agree with this. You've been attacked for three years, Harold, and your standing is very high. Heath has been ignored for three years, and his standing is very low; I don't think you're right.'

Everybody else chipped in and concurred. Denis Healey, Tony Crosland and Roy agreed, and Harold Lever came up afterwards and

* Deputy Under-Secretary of State, Foreign and Commonwealth Office; Ambassador to Poland, 1966–9.

said he did too, so I was quite encouraged. If Harold wants to do it, that's up to him, but I am damned if I will.

In the evening Caroline and I gave a farewell party for Bill Mallalieu and his wife, Gerry Fowler and his wife and Jeremy Bray in the office. At 10.30 I was driven to the ITN studios to take part in the by-election* programme with Quintin Hogg and Jo Grimond. I did my best but Alastair Burnet [Editor of the *Economist*] made a lot of very contemptuous comments about politics.

He said some constituencies were up for grabs and he gave the latest betting figures. He said of one count, 'No wonder the candidates look worried, they've no doubt got money on the result.' I just went for him and said this cheapened, vulgarised and denigrated politics and there were two sorts of politics: the real politics of people facing problems, and this artificial gladiatorial business. Burnet crumpled. Nobody stuck up for him and I am glad I said it.

Friday 31 October

Flew to Cardiff and visited a colliery. It was the first time I had ever been down a mine in Britain, and I crawled about 150 yards on my knees. It was pretty grim.

Monday 3 November

Dr Eklund, Secretary-General of the International Atomic Energy Authority, who is here on a visit as my guest, came in. He thought the Non-Proliferation Treaty had now run out of steam and that if the underground tests done by the Americans were to go on, this would really completely defeat the treaty.

Wednesday 5 November

To NEDC where Roy began by dealing with the money supply policy he is pursuing, which is domestic credit expansion policy.

Came home for fireworks and worked late. Gradually emerging from a couple of weeks of real exhaustion.

I only had one bit of business at home tonight. I have been trying to put my oar in to be sure that the British don't join in the American underground tests of nuclear weapons without, at least, a meeting of Ministers to discuss it. Denis Healey has been determined to get British nuclear weapons tested underground in the US, and since I put my foot

---

*Five by-elections were held on 30 October 1969. Labour held on to four seats, with greatly reduced majorities: Islington North (Michael O'Halloran), Paddington North (Arthur Latham), Glasgow Gorbals (Frank McElhone) and Newcastle-Under-Lyme (John Golding). At Swindon the Conservative, Christopher Ward, won the seat from Labour with a 12.8 per cent swing.

down, he has been trying to get at me. In the end I decided to ring Number 10, and I put the points to a Private Secretary to pass on to the Prime Minister; I said I would abide by his decision, but I don't know whether Harold cares one way or the other.

Thursday 6 November

To Cabinet this morning where we spent most of our time discussing Jim Callaghan's paper on the replacement of the B Specials in Ulster by the new Royal Ulster Regiment.

Had lunch with Peter Zinkin of the *Morning Star*. He was friendly and as the Right is now beginning to emerge quite powerfully in Britain, the Left is obviously going to be more enthusiastic about the re-election of a Labour Government. This is useful to remember. It means that the party workers in the constituencies will be driven to work for us by the thought that Enoch Powell might be the leading light in the next Tory Government.

Wednesday 12 November

To Overseas Policy and Defence Committee where we talked about the Duncan Committee's Report on British political representation over-seas, and had a long philosophical discussion about whether the Chairman, Sir Val Duncan* and his colleagues had been right to talk about 'areas of concentration' and 'outer areas'. I produced an analysis of a rather different kind. I said there were three functions which were quite separate in foreign affairs. One was what one might call world affairs or problems in which the Government may or may not have a role in finding a solution, such as overseas aid or UN business. Second, Britain's external policy in relation to, for example, NATO or the Monetary Fund. And third, bilateral relations between Britain and individual countries which would be very much wider than diplomatic activity and would include trade, technology and culture.

I thought that we should look at each post in the light of these three criteria, and would find that many of them hardly needed political representation at all. This theme was taken up by Harold who liked it. In the end we drove Michael Stewart a little way towards what we wanted. Roy Jenkins was of course mainly interested in cutting down the cost of our diplomatic posts.

I went to the NEC Youth Committee where we planned an approach to Jack Straw, the President of the NUS, and Hugh Anderson, the President of the Cambridge Labour Club, who are first-rate students and who want to establish links with the Labour Party.

Then at 7 I went to UPW House in Clapham for a party for Joe Slater,

---

* Chairman of Rio Tinto-Zinc Corporation.

laid on by the Union of Post Office Workers, to thank him for five years as Assistant Postmaster General. It was a marvellous family evening. The President of the UPW spoke first. Then Tom Jackson, the General Secretary, who made a very impressive speech saying they had brought Joe home to thank him for all he had done.

Joe Slater made an extremely moving speech, he almost broke down. I was asked to speak for a moment, and we recollected together the time we had had at the Post Office.

Friday 14 November
At lunchtime to the Dorchester for a surprise lunch for Joe Lockwood, the Chairman of EMI. There were a lot of distinguished industrialists there including Jules Thorn, Sir Edward Lewis, Chairman of Decca, and Charles Villiers of IRC.

We had a fascinating discussion about what it was in British society that made us less efficient than the Americans, the Japanese or the Germans. They were concentrating upon the lack of motivation of the workforce and various other things but they really left out of account the whole social fabric of society, namely the poor educational system, and so on.

Saturday 15 November
Jonathan Cape have expressed an interest in publishing some of my speeches so I looked out forty-seven of the 500 or so that I have delivered over the last five years, only one of which had been delivered in the House of Commons, and put them together. It was an indication of the extent to which Parliament limits its discussion to matters that concern my Department, as compared with the range of speeches that are made at dinners, universities and elsewhere.

Monday 17 November
At 11, I went to the Campaign Committee where David Kingsley presented a report on the first round of the advertising campaign, 'Labour has Life and Soul' and 'When it Comes Down to it Aren't Their Ideals Yours as Well?'

Denis Healey said we must present ourselves as a Government that could govern. Jim Callaghan warned that people might not like change and might want a quieter life which I thought was a bit of a dig at the dynamic Ministry of Technology! Generally there was a consensus and it was agreed we would do a television programme before Christmas and a party political broadcast at the end of the year, in which I would be the party spokesman.

Incidentally, *The Times* had an amusing two-column article by David Wood called 'Sandwiches with Benn'. It began by mocking me about my sandwich lunches, then said how industrialists were working happily with me and that the Tories were worried about it.

We had the Mintech board lunch. Harold Lever responded to *The Times* by producing some smoked salmon, freshly baked bread and cheese and some other things. It has become a bit of a joke. Next week I am going to take my sandwiches in a red handkerchief and see whether I can't lower our standards still further.

We discussed the need to ensure that there was adequate supply of stocks of fuel for the winter: corrosion in the bolts in the Magnox power stations has led to a 25 per cent cutback in their utilisation, and it is potentially a great tragedy if corrosion prevents these nuclear power stations from being used at all.

Tuesday 18 November

All-day Neddy [NEDC] conference at Lancaster House. This was a very big affair involving the whole of the National Economic Development Council with the Prime Minister in the chair and the chairmen of the various little Neddies [EDCs] whose job it was to present their reports.

I had stayed up very late preparing my comments on each industry and I said a word at the beginning to explain how we looked on the exercise. We went right through my points, beginning with the motor industry, presented by Lord Rootes of Chrysler, on to electrical engineering, mechanical engineering, machine tools, and in the afternoon we had the chemical, paper and board industries.

Harold had to leave about 12.30 so I took the chair for the end of the morning session and after he had gone I said it was quite untrue that he had another engagement but had heard there were going to be sandwiches for lunch and had gone to look for a good meal. Everyone laughed, and it was a useful friendly meeting.

It is quite clear to me now that we have to make these reviews with the EDCs the basis of annual planning, bringing together industry and Government, until we can weave in the plans of industry – particularly the corporate strategies of the big firms – with national planning.

I was pretty tired by the time I got back to the office and I had an oral report on Concorde which suggested the cost had risen again, there were technical problems on noise, and a new nozzle might cost between £20 million and £40 million. It all looks pretty grim.

Then I worked on. Had fish and chips in the office and went to the House of Commons to vote.

Wednesday 19 November

The Apollo 12 landed this morning and there was a moon walk, which, unfortunately, we weren't able to see because the television set had broken down.

I went to the Nuclear Policy Committee on the centrifuge. All was well. Denis Healey had withdrawn his objection and the Americans have agreed to our transfer of the Endcap technology which we acquired from them, and except for various tiny questions about how we handled the weapons issue, and so on, it was all agreed, and I was very pleased.

With Caroline to the Press Gallery lunch. George Clark of *The Times*, who is very agreeable, was in the chair. Fred Peart had told me that he was once in CND.

Denning Pearson came along to talk about Rolls Royce and he said that owing to lack of turnover in the airlines and a falling off in ordering, the profitability of Rolls has been affected; he now has to tighten his machine, lay some people off and close some minor factories. He wanted to know how to handle it. As Charles Smith is in charge of aviation and also of relations with the trade unions, it was a good test case as to how this sort of thing should be tackled. I found it useful and I did have a chance of mentioning to Pearson that he wasn't to let Dan Haughton of Lockheed go ahead with the long range Tri-jet without him, and consequently us, being consulted.

Thursday 20 November
The main item at Cabinet was the prices and incomes norms. Barbara wanted from 2.5 to 4.5 per cent but the current rate of settlements is going at about 8.5 per cent and so there is no reality in the figure. Roy Jenkins was very keen that we shouldn't appear to confirm publicly a figure above what was economically sensible, namely 3.5 per cent.

I strongly supported him on the grounds that prices and incomes were moving out of the enforcement and into the educational era, and we would have to say to people that 3.5 per cent is what the country can pay itself on the basis of its production. If anyone goes above that then somebody else has less, or we take it away in taxation, or it weakens our export competitiveness and we lose jobs, or we run into crisis and we have another freeze. It's just not possible to have more than 3.5 per cent overall without grave damage. Price increases would follow. Barbara's range was accepted.

Monday 24 November
I had lunch at *The Times* and sat between Ken Thomson, Lord Thomson's son, and William Rees-Mogg who is a completely Edwardian figure. He's got two daughters whom he's educating with the help of a governess: he has absolutely no sense of modernity about him at all and yet somehow you're not afraid of those sort of people any more because you don't feel that they command much power.

To Wellingborough in the evening to speak at a by-election meeting.*

Tuesday 25 November
Went early to the office and had Cabinet, with another public expenditure discussion. At one point in the debate, Peter chipped in and said that he was in favour of higher public expenditure as part of the principle of the Labour Party, and Tony Crosland said that he was in favour of higher expenditure but that he didn't intend to mention it until after the Election. I said that I was in favour of it but I regarded the Election as the period when one educated the public in the implications of higher expenditure. I said I was making a lot of speeches about taxation, indicating how necessary it was. The discussion was a very good example of the extent to which the Cabinet divides itself into those who think that you should be a socialist by stealth and then act decisively and with crunches and confrontations and those who believe, as I do, that politics is all a matter of winning the argument.

To Peter Shore's office for a meeting of the NEC Policy Coordinating Committee which I have just joined, with Roy, Peter, Harry Nicholas, Terry Pitt, George Brown and Michael Stewart. George was sloshed and attacked Roy on the housing figures, saying we had to do better than we had done. Then George turned on Peter and was pretty rude to him and finally he turned on me and said, 'Do you ever go to any by-elections?'

I said, 'I go to speak all over the place.'

He said, 'I bet you haven't been to Wellingborough.'

I said, 'I was there last night.'

'Did you have a crowded meeting?'

'It was absolutely packed,' I replied, 'and I spent most of my time answering questions about your Vietnam speech.' (Last week George had said on the radio, in relation to the Pinkville massacre,† that the Americans should stop weeping about it and get on with the job.)

Caroline and I went to the Annenbergs' Embassy party. Walter Annenberg is the new American Ambassador, and has spent a million dollars on the house in Regent's Park. It was sickening and the whole Tory Establishment was there: Lord Snowdon, Princess Margaret, Heath, and the top business chaps – Weinstock, and so on. We did have

---

* A by-election was held at Wellingborough on 4 December, 1969 due to the death of Labour MP Harry Howarth. The Conservative candidate, Peter Fry, won the seat. On the same day, a Conservative candidate, Jeffrey Archer, held Louth where a by-election was caused by the death of Sir Cyril Osborne.

† In March 1968, a platoon of American soldiers had murdered between 200 and 500 villagers in My Lai, South Vietnam, in an area dubbed 'Pinkville'. The atrocity was covered up and its true extent revealed only in late 1969.

a little talk to Harry Evans of the *Sunday Times* and Caroline had a long argument with Arnold Weinstock about Clive Jenkins.

Wednesday 26 November

Hilary was sixteen today; he got money for clothes. Stephen phoned from Keele – he had been to Manchester to demonstrate against the Springboks, the South African rugby team which is touring Britain.

To the Economic Policy Committee, where the Upper Clyde Shipbuilders problem came up. They have got into serious difficulty and want a substantial sum of money, and Jack Diamond was in favour of liquidating. In my paper I said we couldn't justify any more money on industrial grounds, but Harold chipped in and said that on political grounds, we couldn't have 8.5 per cent male unemployment on the Clyde – which I agree with absolutely. So we decided to set up a committee to see what was the minimum we could give to keep them going.

Thursday 27 November

At Cabinet we had a discussion about hanging. The problem as Harold sees it is how to prevent the hanging issue becoming public during the current by-election campaigning and, at the same time, win the vote which will get the five-year experiment[1] carried through before Christmas. This is news management of a very high order. But most of the things that Harold thinks about are really news management, and I am not sure I really very much approve of this, though I am in favour of being sensible and not announcing difficult things at a time of great importance. But having said that I do think we go too far.

Then we had a discussion paper from Michael Stewart on the civil war in which Biafra wants to secede from Nigeria. The paper was rigid in support of Nigeria and Barbara made an impassioned speech against the policy. I agreed with Roy Jenkins who said that he always began by being unsympathetic to the FO view and then found in the end that they had made their case. I think it is very difficult to see how we could support Biafra. Biafra refuses to have mercy flights in the daytime because that would interfere with their night flights carrying arms, so Colonel Ojukwu, the Biafran leader, is in effect starving the Biafrans as a political weapon.

Dick Crossman gave a great speech about the birth of a nation and how this was similiar to the situation in Palestine in 1947. But others thought it was more like the American Civil War where a new nation did not emerge.

Monday 1 December

I had a very sad and painful meeting with Peter Masefield and the board of Beagle to tell them that the Government was not prepared to continue to support them and there was no alternative but to ask the bank to set up a receiver and manager.

At the House of Commons for an all-night sitting.

Tuesday 2 December

I made a statement on Beagle in the House of Commons which went down well although I was nervous, having supported them up to this point.

I had a long meeting on Magnox reactors with the Chief Nuclear Inspector, and the Chief Scientist at the Ministry of Power and a lot of other people. I delved into the question of safety and discovered that the corrosion of the bolts could lead to a failure to control the reactors; in which case the fuel would melt and get into the heat exchangers, and there could be a release of nuclear activity – radioactive material – which could cause a major tragedy. So I gave strict instructions for an early warning system. The AEA and the CEGB are to be informed immediately, and I shall put a paper in to the Prime Minister. I am statutorily responsible for nuclear safety and this is a matter I take very seriously.

Thursday 4 December

Cabinet, and I spoke up very strongly against the posture Michael Stewart continues to adopt on Vietnam. I said that I bitterly resisted the idea that this argument was anti-American, because the Labour Party was traditionally against Britain's imperial posture and that was not anti-British. There were many people in America who took the same line as we did. This was an American tragedy but there was no reason why we should come out in support of American policy, particularly since we didn't know what American policy was.

Roy Jenkins agreed with me, though he felt that what I had said about Michael Stewart wasn't fair as he wasn't there, and George Thomson said the same. So I withdrew my reference to Michael Stewart but I did press the point. As a matter of fact George Thomson later said he agreed with me on the merits of it.

I made an oral report on the problem in the Magnox station. Harold didn't want it known that Ministers had discussed it, but I can't keep it quiet because I have got to safeguard the stations and the people around them.

Monday 8 December

Cabinet this morning, and we discussed prices and incomes, the last opportunity to consider Part Two of Barbara Castle's policy. We also went right through and considered the norm, which is to be 2.5 to 4.5 per cent.

Then we went on to discuss how we could handle hanging in the light of the Tory decision to vote against us, with a vote of censure thrown in for good measure. In fact today's meeting of the Cabinet was specially organised to allow us to claim last week that we wouldn't make up our minds on hanging until today, lest anyone should charge us with having made the decision before last Thursday's by-election, and having failed to announce it.

It is news management carried to the final extreme, and indeed about half of our time is spent on how to present things, how to time things, how to adjust things. This is the way that Government is now reacting to the need to win support: it isn't enough simply to reach a decision and carry it out. I find it unattractive because it is a form of deception; on the other hand, it is a recognition by the Cabinet that this really matters. To this extent it is a new stream of reality entering into our thinking which previously wasn't there.

After that I went to hear the PM in the foreign affairs debate on Nigeria, Greece and Vietnam. Harold was presenting himself in a new light, explaining what it was all about, the moral difficulties, and so on. I didn't find it very convincing but it was rather better than the idea that Britain is a world power, which Harold, alone among his colleagues, still believes.

I went to Number 10 to see Harold on the ICL position. He poured himself another whisky as I arrived and I think he found the strain of the foreign affairs debate rather great. I found him a bit squiffy, not out of control in any way but he looked a bit like George Brown.

Had dinner with Harold Lever, Barbara Castle, Tommy Balogh and Peter Shore in Harold Lever's fabulous flat in Eaton Square. Tommy talked most of the time, and was arguing that if only Harold did this, and if only Harold did that, and that all my economic advisers were no good, that I may be laughing now but that I'll be crying later, and so on.

So I said, 'Tommy, one of the reasons that you are not influential is that you hop around on the outside attributing all our problems to the personality or character or view of individuals on the inside, and you have to work with the people you have got – that is the only way you can get on.'

I think this hurt him, although the others were pleased I had said it. Apparently he has separated from his wife Pen and is pretty miserable at the moment. Barbara was very depressed because she sees her whole prices and incomes policy crumbling and we did agree that if the wage increases went on at the present rate of settlement, there would be no room for manoeuvre, Roy would not have much opportunity for flexibility in his Budget, nor would we have much room for getting a higher rate of growth.

Tuesday 9 December

I went to the Inner Cabinet, where Fred Peart asked why the Education Bill had not come forward and Harold said there was 'some technical problem'.

'I don't like the way it's worded,' he said. 'It says we shouldn't select people by aptitude or ability and surely that is not what it is about. It is about getting comprehensive schools, not an attack on the grammar schools.' Thus he revealed with staggering simplicity that he doesn't understand the Party's education policy at all.

Thursday 11 December

To Cabinet where we discussed the Commission on Industry and Manpower.* Tony Crosland led a great attack on the concept, but I supported Barbara and said it was a great mistake to present this as being more significant than it really was. I was also critical of the negative view that Michael Stewart had taken on the prospect of a conference proposed by the Warsaw Pact powers on security in Europe. I thought that with the Americans now talking to the Russians, with the Strategic Arms Limitation issue, and with the Germans talking to the Poles and the Russians about relations between West Germany and her Eastern neighbours, Britain looked pretty negative.

I felt that with an Election coming up, a really good European security policy might well turn out to be highly significant. Harold said he agreed with my instinct but thought we had not been negative and Michael Stewart rebutted the charge: he is frankly a very bad Foreign Secretary, simply reflecting the wisdom of his Department and he never carries the day at all.

I met a deputation from Nottinghamshire and Derbyshire led by Tom Swain [Labour MP for NE Derbyshire] who asked for an extension of the intermediate area. This was the first regional deputation I had received under the terms of my new responsibilities.

Tuesday 16 December

To the House of Commons to vote to abolish the death penalty and got home late very tired.

Wednesday 17 December

Went to the National Executive this morning and since Joe Gormley withdrew his motion condemning the Government for reintroducing Part Two of the prices and incomes policy, there was really no business of any consequence.

*The organisation which was intended to take over the work of the Monopolies Commission and the Prices and Incomes Board when the prices and incomes policy expired. The proposal was superseded by the General Election of 1970.

Over to the St Ermine's Hotel for a Labour Party lunch for the student leaders. This had been organised by Reg Underhill, Harry Nicholas and Joan Lestor in order to put us in contact with a new generation of student leaders, to organise some activity between now and the Election at the universities, technical colleges, polytechnics and teacher training colleges.

From there to the Central Hall where about 2,000 people from Mintech had been gathered and I sat on a table with a mike round my neck and spoke about the work of the Department for half an hour. Then Harold Lever, Otto Clarke, Neil Carmichael, Pitblado, Ronnie Melville and I had a sort of question-and-answer session. I think the main success was that one embedded in the minds of the people who attended some conception of what the Minister was like and what the policy was all about. No doubt they are cynical and not all that interested; but it certainly is a lot better than working in a Department where you never meet a Minister or know anything about him.

I went and had a talk to Harold, before I came home in the evening, to tell him I was strongly opposed to the line being taken by Denis Healey on the use of gas in war. In 1930 the then Labour Government had subscribed to a protocol opposing the use of gas and the question has arisen again in connection with this new and rather less harmful teargas, CS. The Ministry of Defence want us to be able to use it.

I wouldn't have known anything about it if Bill Epstein of the United Nations Disarmament section, a very old friend of mine, hadn't rung me about two or three weeks ago and told me that the British were wobbling on this point.

As he said, it is one thing to use gas in peacetime when you are trying to control riots, but in war, the only time you want to use gas is to flush out people in bunkers and as they emerge, coughing, you mow them down. I put this to Harold but he said it was quite untrue because we weren't a country that was interested in doing a Pinkville. But the truth is that Denis Healey wants to maintain as much freedom of action as he can for the Forces and the general attitude is that if the Americans want to do something, the British ought not to differ from them. This is the plain truth about our position in the world; we are just number two to the United States on everything. You will never shift that. Even the approach to Europe still means we have to go to the Americans for permission. This is the whole basis on which the British Government has operated, certainly since 1941.

Thursday 18 December
Went into the office this morning and Raymond Mondon, the new French Minister of Transport, arrived about an hour late for talks on Concorde. I had been firmly instructed that under no circumstances was

I to refer to, or to give Mondon, the document produced by the Concorde Economic Prospects Committee, because it was thought that if I did give the French any reason to believe that we had taken a very gloomy view of Concorde's prospects, and had still decided to go on beyond the end of the year, then it might weaken our case at the International Court if we subsequently withdrew unilaterally.

I had argued strongly about this and sent a minute to Harold saying I disagreed with the Attorney-General's view and I had my duties to the House of Commons to consider, as I was answerable for the public money I was spending. I would find it hard to explain how it was that I had failed to give my French partner a report which was very pessimistic in character. But it was all to no avail, because when the Attorney-General says something, everyone falls into line, particularly when there is so much at stake, as in this case. The Treasury supported the Attorney-General.

The first item was the legal position: I had to use a special form of words and we had the whole thing tape-recorded secretly so that we would have on record exactly what Mondon had said. I described the Government's legal view that we were entitled not to go on after 31 December but that we had decided to go on until 30 June; thereafter we believed that both Governments could only go forward to the extent that each agreed with the other. Mondon said he dissented from that view, but he didn't pursue it.

So we then went on to the much more practical problems of the payload and the range, the selling price and the profits and the levy on the aircraft. We finished by lunchtime and had lunch at Lancaster House. M. de Courcelle, the Ambassador, was there, as was Bernard Lathière, who is really the brains behind the French policy group on Concorde. We had a jolly lunch. Mondon is a most agreeable man personally, much preferable to Chamant. I asked him how the French Government worked on Concorde and he said, 'Well, the President will ask for a paper on it and I will send him a draft, then he will ask for some amendments. Then I'll go and discuss it with him and then it will perhaps go before the Council of Ministers and be agreed. Or the Prime Minister may have a working group on it.'

Clearly, in the French Government, Ministers are in effect like officials – they all huddle round a meeting presided over by the Prime Minister or the President who will hear the argument and then decide. There is no question of collecting the voices in the way that we conduct Cabinet committees. It is virtually benevolent paternalism by the President and Prime Minister over their Ministers. I daresay this produces better results – I don't know – but it certainly is very different to our system.

I went back to my office and found that Number 10 had objected to my making a statement in the House about the true position of electricity, fuel and power. I had foolishly sent over to Number 10 the text of a written answer that I wanted to give, and apparently this had been opposed by the PM and by Trevor Lloyd-Hughes. So I rang Trevor Lloyd-Hughes and tried to persuade him I should do it.

Then I got on to the Prime Minister to get it reversed, and he said I should get on to Fred Peart. Fred, like everybody else, both official and ministerial, was opposed to the statement on the grounds that it would create a sense of crisis, whereas what I wanted to do was to have the position truthfully reported to the public and put on the record, so if there was a row there would be something to refer back to. I also think people are entitled to know what the fuel position is. I found that all the people responsible opposed it, and I wasn't able to go ahead with my statement. It made me wonder whether my judgment was right.

Friday 19 December

Went to the House to make a statement on the centrifuge collaboration which has been successfully brought to a conclusion with the Dutch and Germans. In the end the Dutch abandoned their opposition to our using the centrifuge technology for military purposes and also let us have the headquarters in Britain. We made a concession for a rather bigger plant in Holland and the Germans have got the prime contract for construction of the plants and for the technology.

Then I went straight to a meeting at Number 10. I complained strongly to the PM that I had not been allowed to make a statement on the power crisis, and I said that if there was an unofficial strike of power workers on 5 January, as is expected, I intended to go to one of the power stations and talk to the men. I have always been prevented from doing this by Barbara's Department, which doesn't believe that Ministers should intervene in industrial disputes. But I really do think this would be a good case for going along myself and seeing one of the power stations. I believe that West Ham is the best, and that is where George Wake, the Communist union leader, is.

I had Sir John Hill of the AEA and Sir Stanley Brown, Chairman of the CEGB, to see me about the corrosion in the Magnox stations. I was pretty stern and tried to get the truth out of them about the risk to life. They both argued that the stations were as safe as they could be, and that there would be plenty of notice of any possibility of breakdown. I told them I was going to call in an independent engineer to advise me and they didn't seem to disagree with that. But they were both very worried about the Science and Technology Select Committee reporting on the problems in power stations in January. I said I would have a word with its Chairman, Arthur Palmer, about this.

What worried Hill and Brown was the possibility that this might damage our nuclear exports, and they said these problems of corrosion were no more serious than they had faced in the past. They said it was typical of Britain to knock its own achievements. But they were pretty worried about the position. I am not sure I can let this concern for our exports stand in the way of safety, and I said that in the Christmas recess I would be going to Bradwell, where the corrosion is worst, in order to get an idea of developments there and have the problem explained to me more fully.

Thursday 25 December
Melissa and Joshua woke up at 4.30 am and exchanged their presents. We had ours in the bedroom. It was a wonderful Christmas, Caroline having done all the work. After lunch Stephen, Hilary and Melissa played a madrigal, and we had the call from Cincinnati. In the evening Stephen and I went to see Aunt Weena who is nearly eighty-eight and in a nursing home in Ealing after her stroke. Then to see Aunt Rene,* took a bottle of whisky to the Mintech nightguard, finished up with Mother and Buddy and finally got to bed about 1 am.

Wednesday 31 December
Went to Bradwell Power Station today and Sir Stanley Brown, and Mr Weeks, head of the CEGB study group on the Magnox corrosion, were there. I was met by the Station Superintendent and accompanied by people who had come straight down from London – Jack Rampton, who is the Deputy-Secretary in charge, Trevor Griffiths, the Chief Nuclear Inspector, and John Bowder, my Assistant Private Secretary. I spent about an hour and a half with the working model, seeing exactly what the problem was, then went to have a look at the refuelling operation by closed circuit colour TV, and to the control room. I saw a film of the removal of the sample basket which had taken place last year, and had lunch with the group.

I'm very glad I went because it indicated the real nature of the problem, which is seen by the CEGB not so much as a safety problem but as a problem that might affect the economics of the power station. The danger is that the very high temperature CO_2 gas which goes through the fuel elements has had the effect of oxidising or corroding the bolts holding the core restraint, and corroding all the other bolts in the reactor.

If, by any chance, there were any displacement of the graphite blocks in which the fuel elements run or, even more serious, of the channels into which the control rods drop, you might lose control of the reactor and it

---

* Weena was an old family friend, Miss Margaret Buchanan, who worked for many years nursing the mentally disturbed; Aunt Rene was my father's sister, Irene.

is possible that one of the fuel elements might melt. If there was at the same time a rupture in the heat exchanger circuit you could get a tremendously overheated reactor with the fuel elements melting, causing a major nuclear accident that would kill many thousands of people in the area of Bradwell and would create a radio-active cloud that might kill people in London.

The real question is, do the control rods go in and out easily and could this be affected by further corrosion? They currently drop in 100 of them in 1.2 seconds and there's no reason to believe at the moment that this will change. But the position is being watched very carefully.

Mr Griffiths told me that he would keep an eye on the situation in order to lay down the rules about a shutdown for further inspection if he thought that the temperatures being operated were too high. The temperature has risen progressively since the station's inception in the early Sixties, although recently it was reduced from 390 degrees centigrade to 360 degrees. But in view of the problem of the fuel situation this winter, the fear of a power strike and the cold weather, the CEGB has decided to increase the temperature to 380 degrees, with the result that the old rate of corrosion, about twice the rate of corrosion at 360 degrees, has resumed. This is taking a calculated risk, so as not to dislocate industry.

I wrote a brief report on this and I am now trying to get an independent engineer to take on the job of reading all the documents and advising me.

While I was with Stanley Brown we had a brief discussion about the possibility of a power strike: he thought it unlikely that this would lose all that number of megawatts but he was very worried that George Wake from West Ham power station had been asked by the BBC to go on television tonight, and he asked me whether I could try to get the BBC to stop it. Knowing that this would be the worst possible thing to do, I refused.

Stanley Brown also showed me the message he was putting out later this week in *Power News*, threatening the unofficial strikers with dismissal. The position is a bit worrying. I am still in discussion with the Department about whether I should visit one of the power stations where there is a strike.

I returned to Stansgate later than I had intended; this is, of course, the last night of the year and of the decade. Looking back over the ten years, it has been the most remarkable period, politically, of my life. Ten years ago tonight I was out of Parliament, a disqualified peer, Father was dead, my income had stopped, I was just beginning a long and difficult peerage struggle with no certainty that I would ever get back into Parliament again. The Labour Party was at its weakest ebb for years, with the Conservatives just having won a very big Election victory. Now, here I am at the end of the decade, a senior Minister with a very big Department. The Labour Party, though not by any means secure in its parliamentary position, is at least not without hope of being re-elected next year or in 1971.

If I look at the last twelve months, the year has also been quite remarkable, with the Ministry of Technology enormously increased in size, and the Ministry of Power, huge parts of the Board of Trade and part of the Department of Economic Affairs to look after. A member of the Inner Cabinet and of the NEC's Campaign Committee, I am, in some respects, at the peak of my political life. This time next year we could be out again, I could be out of Parliament and the whole cycle could begin again. But it has been a very exciting time to be in office.

The decade began with four children, the oldest nine, the youngest eighteen months; it ends with Stephen at college, and the other three at comprehensive schools. Caroline has emerged from being a mother to being an expert on education with a national reputation, on the eve of launching her book about comprehensive education.

Sunday 4 January 1970
Caroline's article on education for women over the past hundred years appeared in the *Sunday Times* colour supplement. The house was full of people all day.

Monday 5 January
First day back in the office, had a talk with Derek Moon. Denning Pearson came to discuss the prospects of launching the Lockheed long range jet, the TriStar. I had to really damp him down a little bit. I am afraid if we do go ahead with this we might find ourselves repeating on behalf of Rolls Royce the errors of the Fifties and Sixties in support of civil aircraft.

I had the weekly lunch today with Ministers and officials and we discussed the power strike; I put round a paper written for Cabinet about the use of persuasion in industrial disputes, urging the right of Ministers to participate in the argument.

Tuesday 6 January
I went to the Campaign Committee this morning. Mark Abrams, Chairman of Research Services Ltd, reported on the attitude of younger voters. I found one or two things interesting but also discouraging. For example, young people were not interested in education, that is to say they were against the raising of the school leaving age. This made a big impact on the Prime Minister and Jim Callaghan and one or two others who don't want to raise the school leaving age. All of a sudden one could see how very big decisions could be taken by Government on the basis of

the most inadequate evidence which confirms their prejudices. I realise we will have to fight very hard on that.

Harold Lever came in and I found we were absolutely as one on the subject of the ICI-Viyella textile merger, he being very keen on going for a big solution, with a national fibre corporation separated from the textile manufacturers.

In the evening Caroline, Stephen and I went to Peter Townsend's party. Peter teaches at Essex and I was surrounded by three of his young sociology students who just called me a Fascist and called me it so often I got rather angry. A dull German professor linked me with a lot of other Fascists and when I said to him, 'Could you give me the names of any world politicians who disagree with you but are not Fascists?', he said, 'That is a Fascist's sort of question.' He defined fascism as a belief in technology, and technology as a belief in the use of machines to change social values. Altogether I thought he was very poor stuff, of the kind you get among sociologists who don't study technology or industry or what is happening in the world. We very foolishly stayed till about 2, and I had to work on my boxes till 4.

Tuesday 13 January

Had a meeting this morning on the Home Office computer issue. The Home Office put out a tender and though IBM was the cheapest, Burroughs seemed best and ICL came a poor third. Since this contract is of such importance to ICL, partly to keep their 'System Four' in production, partly because of the £50–100 million potential orders in Eastern Europe and partly because of development area interests in Kidsgrove and Winsford, I thought I would make a fight of it. But the Department is not keen.

To Cabinet where we discussed Biafra and it was generally thought that our support for the Nigerian Government would give us a good chance of being able to help on the aid questions.

After lunch Lord Harding looked in for a moment to ask me for a knighthood for John Clark, Managing Director of Plessey.

Wednesday 14 January

We had an Inner Cabinet meeting on political strategy, where I made the point that we really must try to get away from the sense of crisis. The general view was that this was very necessary. Harold talked about an October Election but with the possibility of our having to go earlier.

I went to the National Executive Youth Committee where we agreed to set up Students for Labour and then came back to the office to meet Mary Goldring of the *Economist*, a very bright but extremely conceited and difficult woman.

Thursday 15 January
Cabinet this morning and Barbara Castle produced her report on the Commission on Industry and Manpower, and as usual there were no proper papers. Barbara believes that if you give information to the Cabinet, Ministers won't agree with what you want to do, so she tries to get through a presentation orally, always under tremendous pressure because of a press conference which is just about to take place, for which she has to leave early to get her hair done. But there was such a reaction against this tactic that it was agreed that it would have to come back to Cabinet later.

David Wood of *The Times* came to a lunch of sandwiches and claret. He wrote the 'Sandwiches with Benn' piece and believes the Tories would have to have the same sort of relationship with industry that we have.

Then Stanley Gillen and Bill Batty of Ford came to tell me that the Cortina would be discontinued as an export to the United States later this year because the American Ford Company had decided to build their own model; they also said that, because market research has revealed that Americans prefer German cars to British, the company had decided to import the Capri, made in Germany, rather than the British Capri. This was a very serious statement indeed and I made quite a lot of it. They told me the German Capri would have some British equipment in it, and that American Ford would have engines from Britain so that exports to the US would grow, but the German exports from the German Ford company would grow three times as fast. They stated the Capri could be built in Germany with 20 to 25 per cent less manpower, though price was not the factor that determined this.

When I began being difficult, Stanley Gillen was difficult back so I said that we had better have a proper meeting and thereafter decided that I would write to Henry Ford and get him to come to London to discuss the issue.

Monday 19 January
To Economic Policy Committee. The second item was the Home Office computer issue, and although I lost on buying ICL as I had half expected I did get an agreement that Eddie Shackleton and I should discuss future purchasing between ourselves. There was an item on population – that the population of the UK would rise by 13 million between now and the end of the century – and Solly Zuckerman had asked for a special population group to look at it. This was agreed hurriedly and it was also agreed not to make much of it as it might stimulate further criticism of immigration and give Enoch Powell a chance to make more trouble.

To Number 10 to discuss a report produced by Bill Neild on our entry to Europe, which is to be published as a White Paper soon. It reveals a total cost of anything from £100 million to £8–900 million based on the price of the agricultural programme and the initial impact effect – all adverse – on the industrial side. I proposed that we should play it a bit softly at the moment and not suggest that it was an all or nothing issue, but this was not welcome either to Roy Jenkins or to the PM himself.

Tuesday 20 January

Caroline went to her educational conference at the Festival Hall all day, organised by the Encyclopaedia Britannica, and spoke about educating the full ability range. Edward Boyle attended and made a very pompous and inadequate speech.

I went to the Campaign Committee where we had a long debate on whether we should authorise David Kingsley to reproduce the Tory advertisement, 'Bunglers or Liars', and answer it ourselves. In the end there was general agreement that we shouldn't.

Wednesday 21 January

At the Overseas Policy and Defence Committee Denis Healey presented his annual defence White Paper. I tried to make a few amendments to remove some of the more obviously anti-Russian passages which Denis had inserted, no doubt in order to prove what a tough character he is. I failed, but I am glad I made the effort.

Thursday 22 January

I met Dan Haughton, Chairman of Lockheed, this morning about the prospects for the Lockheed long-range aircraft in Europe. Lufthansa, who were going to decide in February, have now set back their decision by six months and Denning Pearson, who was with me, said that the RB-211-50 series engine must be launched for the European Airbus. I can't commit myself to do that and he knows it, but he is rather worried at the way things have gone. For my part, I am not anxious to rush into anything. The customers – the airlines – are all reluctant to commit themselves to new aircraft at this moment and this is no basis for a commitment of many tens of millions of pounds more of Government money.

To Cabinet where we discussed how to handle Brian Walden's Privacy Bill[2] which comes up tomorrow. It was another example of the Government being caught on the hop without any advance thinking, even though the question of privacy and computers has been a public issue for five or six years. I tried to raise it when I was at the Post Office and the Home Office prevented me because they were afraid it would lead to interest in the way the security services operate. As a Government we are also illiberal and that is the worst combination – shortage of vision and basic illiberality.

Friday 23 January

Lunch at Number 10 with the Prime Minister and the French Foreign Minister, Maurice Schumann, whom I knew as Minister of Science. At the lunch Baron de Courcelle, who has been the French Ambassador in London for nearly eight years, told me about the ups and downs of that period and how de Gaulle felt that Macmillan had tricked him in 1962 when he signed the Nassau Agreement with the Americans for the supply of Polaris. It seems the bitterness in Paris was much greater than we had ever understood. But de Courcelle was quite optimistic now.

On my other side I talked to Burke Trend about the difficulty of getting papers actually written by Ministers themselves discussed at the informal Cabinet Management Committee. Burke, who is a very charming public-school headmaster type with absolutely no experience of real life, said that Ministers must make an effort to devote more time to long-term thinking. But of course we don't because we don't want to, not because there isn't time. There is time for anything you have to do and want to do, and Harold Wilson simply doesn't like forward thinking. We are getting a little bit from him now only because he realises that there must be some sort of an Election strategy.

After lunch Harold welcomed Schumann, who described his plans for the entry of 'England', as he persisted in calling us, into the Common Market. The negotiations would begin in the summer and we all hoped they would be fairly quick and simple, concentrating on the main points. Then he talked a little about the Middle East and explained his air deal with the Libyans, which precluded them from using the Mirage jets against Israel, or so he claimed, and he put it in the same category as our Chieftain tank deal with Libya (which incidentally we haven't yet confirmed). Then on the approach to the Russians, Michael Stewart gave the negative and hostile Foreign Office attitude to direct talks with the Russians at a European security conference, on the grounds that this would give the Russians all they wanted, as if it was some sort of a football game that we were engaged in. Michael Stewart is the most unattractive Cold War warrior, his attitude is a completely transparent plastic bag covering and preserving old Foreign Office policies. There is absolutely no reason why Britain should not be at least as responsive in dealing with the Russians as the German Government now are under Willy Brandt, or the Italians with their tremendous trade activities, or the French. It is only because the Foreign Office are still in the Cold War stage and have always got their eyes turned over their shoulders to the United States. That is the real reason why we adopt these policies. But the Americans themselves are engaged in talks with the Russians and the Chinese so it makes the whole thing even more puzzling. It is as if we are determined to be the least forthcoming in discussions with the East.

After lunch I dashed to Euston, caught the train to Keele by a few seconds and was met at the station by the Keele University Fabians. We collected Stephen, had a meal in the cafeteria, and I spoke in the auditorium to about 350 people, despite the fact that the anarchists had put out a pamphlet against me, describing me as a 'turd', the man who was suppressing technology and just trying to strengthen capitalism. The leaflet appealed to people to boycott the meeting and only one or two of the revolutionary socialists came: I would have preferred a bit more opposition.

Afterwards I went to talk informally to some of the students, who, like most students of that age, were more concerned with who was president of the union than with what was happening outside. At about 1 am I went back to Stephen's room. He told me he would like to take a year off as he felt the university was rather remote, and maybe do a course on computer programming. I think he does find Keele a bit isolated from the community – after living in London he is now on a campus in the countryside, very far away even from Stoke or Newcastle-Under-Lyme.

Monday 26 January
Over the weekend, Keith Joseph had made a tremendous speech in which he denounced the idea that Government and industry could work close together and said that competition was 'magic', and technocracy inefficient. It was a very interesting speech to read because it did throw into relief the distinction between his view and mine, at the same time as underlining certain similarities, in that I was pushing for the efficiency of industry and perhaps underestimating the human factors. I felt that my position must look near enough to his to alienate the students at Keele the way it did. But certainly it made the Ministry of Technology controversial and this is what we need. I shall make a major speech answering him.

I had an hour-long private talk with Barbara Castle about my paper, 'Persuasion in Industrial Disputes', which I had written over Christmas and am going to have discussed at the Management Committee. Barbara for her part showed me the minute from Conrad Heron, her Deputy Under-Secretary, which said in effect that the purpose of my paper was to try to take over her business, that it would be ineffective, that it would annoy the trade unions, and generally speaking pouring cold water on it. But Barbara was quite sympathetic. She wondered why I hadn't brought officials. She said her Private Office had told her that they understood that I didn't want officials. So I think we revealed a little Private Office plot, because later both offices were very embarrassed about it. But when Ministers write their own papers, Departments don't like to be involved. It is very interesting to see how you get elbowed out if you don't accept the conventional wisdom conveyed to you by your officials.

Tuesday 27 January

Holland Park School is on strike and there is a big poster in our window supporting the striking teachers. Hilary has written an article in the school magazine *Focus* and generally speaking we are right in the middle of it all, and *The Times* this morning made a reference to Hilary's article. Then I had a meeting on defence research to see if I could beaver away at a new system for getting down Mintech's commitment.

Roy Bradford, the Minister of Development in Ulster, came to present his difficulties and asked what Mintech could do to help him. He invited me over to Ulster.

Don Ryder, the Chairman of the Reed Paper Company, wanted to meet and talk about IPC, for which Reeds have put in a bid. The truth is that Hugh Cudlipp is incapable of managing a big business like IPC, has run into serious difficulties, and it was on his initiative that the approach to Reed was made. Cudlipp would revert to being a newspaper man, as editorial Vice-Chairman of IPC.

Thursday 29 January

To SEP in the Cabinet Office held, in Harold's absence, under Roy Jenkins's chairmanship.

The first question was whether or not we should take manufacturing powers in the Electricity Bill.* The office was dead against it and had persuaded Harold Lever on regular Tory, plus Civil Service, grounds not to support it. When I discovered this I talked to him and he conceded that if there was trouble at the committee stage we would introduce a clause with these manufacturing powers.

Peter Shore had heard this and was very angry with Harold Lever, whom he had seen with Fred Peart; but Harold, with the support of Jack Diamond, had stuck to his guns against the inclusion of manufacturing powers. So Fred Peart had brought it to SEP, where I supported the clause giving these powers. Roy Jenkins said, 'Now that the Paymaster-General is locked up in a cupboard at the Ministry of Technology there seems to have been a change of view.' So I said, 'If only you would lock up the Chief Secretary of the Treasury, we would never have had any difficulty at all.'

Then I went over to the TGWU for my first big union meeting with Jack Jones and the national officers. It was in fact the first time a Cabinet Minister had ever attended a meeting of the TGWU national officers and the first time that I had attended any union since being Postmaster-General, when I had gone to the executive committee of the UPW and

---

* This would have given the national electricity authority the powers to manufacture equipment it needed for its own purposes. Under the original nationalisation Act manufacturing powers were prohibited.

the POEU. I had Ivor Manley, Charles Smith and some of my officials
with me.

I was welcomed by Jack, then I described the work of Mintech and
there were a number of questions. Bob Davies asked why the TGWU
textile group hadn't been consulted on the ICI-Viyella issue. There
were questions about industrial training and a number of other points.
It was a useful start and I think if we had had a bit more time and done
this a bit earlier, we might have had better relations between the unions
and the Government.

In the evening I went to a dinner in the House of Commons given by
the Editor of the *Scotsman*, Alastair Dunnett, who was accompanied by
Alistair Stewart, the London editor, and the Lobby man. Willie Ross,
Denis Healey and Shirley Williams were also there, with Donald Dewar
[Labour MP for Aberdeen South]. I must say Dunnett and Willie Ross
are both typically conceited Scotsmen: both talking simultaneously,
Willie describing the marvellous speeches he had made on the
Bannockburn celebrations, Dunnett commenting on his own leading
articles and neither listening to the other, nor terribly caring that the
other wasn't listening to him. But Dunnett invited me to meet his team
at the *Scotsman* in Edinburgh and I said I would very much like to do
that. I don't know if Willie Ross will be all that pleased.

Friday 30 January
Jack Diamond came over to Mintech to discuss the nuclear fuel industry
finance scheme. The Beagle crisis has brought into the forefront of
everybody's minds the problem of what governments do with creditors
in the event of a bankruptcy, and Jack Diamond has been scrutinising
each of the projects we have brought forward to see how we could guard
against similar difficulties. His eyes lit upon the Nuclear Fuel Company
and the Radio Chemical Company Bills which are just coming forward;
he blocked their discussion at Legislation Committee last week, which
was awkward for me but guaranteed that we would talk about it.

In fact I persuaded him that the Nuclear Fuel Company couldn't go
bust because it would have twenty-year contracts to produce fuel
elements for nuclear power stations in Britain and abroad. But the
Radio Chemical Company might be more vulnerable and I agreed that
on the notepaper it should be made clear that this was a company under
the Companies Act with limited liability, that the directors should
produce a quarterly statement of accounts, and that we should have an
early warning system indicating when the trade credit reached a certain
limit, so that we would have the time to stop the company before the
problem could arise.

Caroline's 'Education in 1980' pamphlet, to which she and a number of others had contributed, came out today, published by the Fabian Society.

Saturday 31 January
Lazy morning, then went and did a bit of shopping, repaired Caroline's lamp, my early morning tea machine and generally speaking busied myself with chores. Did my constituency correspondence in the evening.

Sunday 1 February
Caroline was working with Brian Simon all day, finishing her book. In the evening we talked about her idea for a play depicting the relationship between Babbage, the inventor of the first mechanical computer, and Lady Lovelace, the mathematician and daughter of Byron. I thought of an idea for a spy thriller about a secretarial agency in London which both the Russians and the Americans were using.

Monday 2 February
Inner Cabinet meeting on the political strategy for the next six months. Not a very satisfactory meeting, in which everybody talked more or less endlessly. I said I thought that the Selsdon Park meeting, which the Tories had over the weekend, had been helpful to us because the Tories were exposing their true intentions and this would rally the faithful, and stir up Labour voters to realise what they would lose if the Tories were elected.

I thought that what we needed was a selective counter-attack and I said that I intended to reply to Sir Keith Joseph's speech which had been a pure and unadulterated nineteenth-century Powellite speech. Looking ahead, I said I thought one of our difficulties was that the Tories seemed to be thinking of the Seventies whereas the Labour Party looked as if it was just at the end of its period of office and didn't have much to say beyond that. I thought what was needed was some analysis of the situation and that each Minister should be asked to think what he would do in his Department if he were left there for another five years.

Tuesday 3 February
The unemployment debate was opened by Robert Carr, the Tory employment spokesman, with a series of quotations made by the Prime Minister saying he'd never squeeze the economy, then showing that he had and that unemployment was higher.

Barbara was much embarrassed because Robert Carr attacked her for not having participated. I wound up and I didn't do very well: I was too aggressive and the Tories interrupted me a great deal of the time. It was a slightly unsatisfactory debate.

Jeremy Bray came in for a talk to me and asked me plainly if I thought there was any chance of his being given a job again in the Government. I said no, quite frankly, although I thought after the Elections there might be. Surely, he said, Harold realised that his book had been taken seriously and had not been an attack on the Government. I said, 'Look, the better your book goes down the more angry Harold will be that his judgment had been called into question, and the less likely he is to give you a job.' I think he realised he had made a mistake. Indeed Kate Chaplin, his private secretary in Mintech, thought he knew this in the end, but that his wife Elizabeth had pushed him into it, which is interesting. Although Jeremy has got many talents he has not much idea of what is politically advisable.

Wednesday 4 February
The Education Bill was published today and I got copies over to Caroline as quickly as I could; it contains one provision that comprehensive schools will be allowed to maintain selectivity for children entering the sixth form, which is quite unacceptable, and so this is an issue on which she is now going to campaign.

Thursday 5 February
Up early. Went to Cabinet where we discussed our attitude to the Abortion Act Amendment Bill.* Dick said he was very strongly against amendment on the grounds that it would be impossible to administer the Health Service if Parliament could change the law all the time. A very curious change of front for a man who does genuinely believe in the role of Parliament. But we agreed we couldn't put a whip on against this amendment for political reasons.

I went to the Bank of England for lunch with the Governor, Sir Leslie O'Brien, at his invitation. I have never been to the Bank of England before and one really did have to go through about five great iron gates as if one were entering a prison. We then went up to the most beautiful dining room. He is a nice man, very agreeable but totally out of touch because he has worked for the Bank all his life and doesn't understand the attacks on him from outside.

Fred Catherwood had told me that the City has absolutely rejected the idea of an Economic Development Committee in the City, which the TUC want; and O'Brien is engaged in a fight against Ian Mikardo of the Select Committee on the Nationalised Industries, which wants to know more about the Bank. He said the usual stupid things about trade unions and wished the shareholders would play a larger part in companies. He lives in a dream world. I asked him, 'Why don't you go to the House of

---

* Sponsored by Goodman Irvine, Conservative MP for Rye. The Bill, which attempted to limit the scope of the 1967 Abortion Act, was 'talked out' in debate.

Commons and talk to people? You are a very important person who plays a creative part in maintaining the economy. Why don't you go out and meet people?' And it occurred to me with a great sort of flash of lightning that this is what is wrong with the City: the people in it don't make any effort to broaden their interests.

Friday 6 February
Got up at 6.30, flew to Bristol in one of the Dove aircraft from Farnborough. Attended the symposium on Concorde in the Grand Hotel, organised by *Time* and *Life* and BAC together and spoke briefly on Concorde – a real selling speech. Came out and did a little bit of television and radio.

To the Ministry of Technology Office with the new Regional Director and addressed forty or fifty people there.

I walked to the High Street and sat in a pub for a couple of hours writing letters. Went to an engineers' union meeting in the Boot and Shoe Office in Kingswood and had a most enjoyable discussion with them about economic policy, prices and wages, incomes, and so on.

Back to the hotel and watched Lyndon Johnson on television justifying his Vietnam War policy to Walter Cronkite. What was interesting was that Johnson was still determined to prove he was right and couldn't forgive his opponents like Senator Fulbright; so he displayed none of the reflective qualities of the former leader but was still the combative man engaged in self-justification. But he told only a part of the story, although he did spill the beans about what Dean Rusk and former Defense Secretary Clark Clifford had said at particular times, in marked contrast with our thirty-year rule which prevents anyone from saying anything at all.

Monday 9 February
In the afternoon Tom Paine, the Administrator of NASA, came to see. He was accompanied by Mr Schmidt, a mysterious German of about forty with a club foot, who accompanies him everywhere and who is his personal thinker, but who never says anything.

Tom Paine described NASA's forward planning which has recently suffered a fairly substantial cut in its budget – I think he said they were going to sack 40,000 people this year and concentrate on three areas. One, the development of the probes to other planets; second, the space-shuttle rocket, the reusable shuttle, allowing them to go up and down to satellites in orbit, which would then in effect become laboratory planets; third, to concentrate huge banks of computers in the United States that the world might want to buy. I listened to this and frankly felt like a native being confronted by a man from an advanced society because the gap in technological capability between the United States and Britain, or indeed Europe, is widening so much. Tom wanted me to go along with some of these projects and I said I would have to consider them but I was trying to divert such effort as we had into things that would produce a more obvious return. He took this to be a lack of confidence in our capability which it was not, it was a different priority. But when I mentioned the poor standard of bus service in the US, he reacted positively – no doubt this is a charge he has to face regularly in the United States.

Tuesday 10 February

To SEP where we discussed the takeover bid by the Reed Company for IPC. Barbara had put in a proposal that this be referred to the Monopolies Commission but Harold was very much opposed, the reason being that IPC owns the *Daily Mirror* – a very important political paper for us – and he didn't want a delay to lead to another takeover bid which might result in the *Daily Mirror* being anti-Labour at the next Election. That was the crude simple issue.

I said I thought there were two aspects we had to consider. One was how we should handle the control of big companies when they failed, because you couldn't go on merging for ever; what happened if Reed-IPC went wrong or Rolls-Royce went wrong. We would have to develop new machinery for that. And second, here was an issue of control of the mass media that we ought to face. But there wasn't a great deal of interest.

Finally we discussed UCS where there is a new crisis: Jack Diamond was only prepared to release £2.5 million for the company, whereas Harold Lever had wanted at least £4 million out of the total of £7 million we had been authorised. Jack Diamond became extremely tough and said he was certain that the company had figures that they were not giving us; so it was agreed to send him up to Glasgow tomorrow to have a look.

Wednesday 11 February

To the Management Committee where Harold made a twenty-minute opening speech about the bias of the BBC against him personally; he remembered everything that had ever happened over the years. How badly he'd been treated by *Woman's Hour*, how Heath had been given more time on *Panorama*, etc. I listened, though I was extremely bored by it, as were most other members of the committee.

At the end I said, 'Well, Prime Minister, this is undoubtedly true, but doesn't it raise the question of whether we ought not to appear on programmes ourselves? For example, I have been prevented from appearing on two programmes in the past two months – one was a programme that the BBC wanted to broadcast about where power resided in society and the other was a programme on the mass media which Granada was producing. At official level at Number 10 both of these were stopped.'

I knew quite well that Harold had stopped both of them, and Harold said, 'Oh well, those were outside your subject and it is necessary to protect Ministers.'

I said, 'Surely a senior Minister can cope with questions on Biafra or the mass media. If we make a mistake we just get fired. It is absurd to fight with our hands tied behind our backs, with these ridiculous rules for Ministers.' I didn't get a lot of support from colleagues but I am glad I said it because I think it will stop or check Harold from making these absurd complaints. He is obsessed with the mass media.

I spoke in the motor industry censure debate which had been opened by Keith Joseph, and I had to say that we couldn't ease the restrictions on the motor industry. I came out for a moment to meet a deputation of Tory MPs from Northern Ireland about unemployment there. Compared to the Labour MPs who come on these employment questions, who are dedicated and determined, these chaps just do it as a matter of form and one could see the real difference between being represented by Tory MPs and by Labour MPs.

Thursday 12 February

I went to Cabinet which was largely taken up with the problems of various pay claims: the Forces' claim which had been looked at by the Prices and Incomes Board and involved a substantial increase of about 25 per cent over two years, the nurses' pay, where Dick Crossman wanted to offer them 20 per cent, teachers, where Ted Short is faced with an intransigent union who won't accept arbitration, the Civil Service, who have got a claim in, and some Post Office workers.

Roy Jenkins said a word about it at the beginning. He felt bound to tell the Cabinet that, 'If this rate of settlement goes on, we'll be faced with a serious economic crisis this summer or autumn.'

Jim Callaghan passed me a little note saying, 'Tony, which do you prefer, mutiny or a run on the pound in July? Jim.' I sent a note back saying I didn't think anyone would notice a mutiny because the street would be blocked by farmers with their tractors, television would have been stopped by the engineers, the posts would be on strike and anyway I might be demonstrating myself in July against my impending redundancy.

Each of the Ministers then made his case, Denis Healey warning that there would be trouble if the full increase to the Forces wasn't made available immediately, Dick Crossman saying the nurses were a case on their own, Ted Short explaining what would happen if the teachers' claim wasn't dealt with, and John Stonehouse urging another 1.7 per cent for postal workers. I think I had most sympathy with Ted Short. Dick has managed to get away with it fairly easily. John Stonehouse has been leaking to the press at every stage of the negotiations, which has ruined his case, and Denis Healey just went on and on and really bored the meeting. The fact is there is an overwhelming case for each claim but the overall case against paying them all at the rate requested is unanswerable.

What shocked me most was that Harold said he had a solution: that we should pay interim settlements in the spring, a second stage in the autumn and a third stage next spring. He said this would have the advantage that if there was an Election in the autumn we would only have to absorb the higher sums after the Election. And if the Tories should win the Election, we shall have left a big burden of problems on their plate, and as they would probably only get elected on a small majority it would put them in a very difficult position. He hinted that we might then get back in at an Election that took place soon after that.

It was the crudest political statement I had yet heard, and I felt inclined to say, 'Look, if I have to lose my job, that's bad, if I have to lose my seat that will be very sad, but I am determined to stick to my self-respect.' But I didn't; in fact Roy came in and said he was concerned to hear that view put forward, since we had worked for so long to build up the surplus and he thought that if the Labour Government went out again in an air of economic crisis it would be extremely damaging. My opinion of Harold dropped to about its lowest.

Over to the House of Commons where Bernadette Devlin had come with three trade union representatives to discuss unemployment in Northern Ireland, notably at Shorts and at Harland and Wolff. I had the difficult job of reminding them that under the Constitution this was the responsibility of the Ulster Government. She was trying to push me beyond this and was talking about workers' control of factories, and I found myself in very strong sympathy with her but wasn't able to say anything about it. She wrote down everything I said. As compared with the Tory MPs who had come the previous day I must say it was the most outstanding presentation. She had really done her homework and I was most impressed.

Then I went to dinner at Number 10 with members of the Royal Society. The Prime Minister has been elected a Fellow and this is his way of saying thank you, the first time, I believe, the Royal Society had been to Number 10 for a long time. I sat next to Professor Fred Hoyle, who explained the new developments in astronomy and the effect this will have on the laws of physics, the possibility, for example, that the laws of physics are relative and not absolute, and things of this kind.

After dinner we had to vote on the second reading of the Comprehensive Education Bill, which Ted Short had introduced. I should add that Ted Short was at the dinner and Harold said to him, 'This is non-controversial now, I understand,' and Ted said, 'Well yes, except for Caroline Benn.' I don't think the PM caught what was being said, but of course Caroline has been very critical of one provision of the Education Bill which allows selection to continue in sixth forms and she had circulated all Labour MPs to try to get an amendment moved. She is a great admirer of Ted Short but she is quite convinced that the Department of Education and Science pulled a fast one on him with that one.

We moved to the Cabinet Room and Sir Harold Thompson described the international work of the Royal Society. We discussed education, and Pat Blackett made a speech in which he said that as mass higher education developed it was absolutely necessary to be selective and have an élite – he actually used the word élite – who would be doing the research, and we couldn't have research spreading to all these educational institutions. Sir Harrie Massey, Chairman of the Council for Scientific Policy, said that you couldn't have any nonsense about democracy in higher education.

One could hear re-enacted almost all the arguments that led to the 1944 tripartite system of secondary education. Harold was nodding wisely and Gerry Fowler chipped in and appeared to be assenting. The only person I found even vaguely in line with me was Solly Zuckerman.

I listened for as long as I could, then forced myself into the discussion and said that I found this view absolutely unacceptable. I said that we have had the argument that if you increase the number of people being educated standards will drop, but in Britain this has always proved to be unfounded. There were huge untapped resources among people in Britain which had never been fully used, and our great weakness had been that we had concentrated on the so-called 'best' at the expense of the average.

I compared the University of Cincinnati, which had everything from a world-famous medical school down to teaching policemen how to handle violence and the social origins of violence, with Bristol where there was a university, a technical university, a polytechnic, and colleges of education. I said we must move towards a comprehensive higher system and that status was the enemy of excellence; I wanted centres of relevance which embraced excellence, but I believed that excellence repudiated relevance on the grounds that it corrupted the purity of intellectual work.

This was not very popular. Harold, who was disapproving of the fact that I should have spoiled the nature of the discussion like this, said, 'Well, you are obviously in a minority of one.'

So I said, 'Well, Prime Minister, you and I have just come back from the House of Commons to vote against a selective system in secondary education and I am simply making the case for not repeating this same mistake in higher education.' I don't think he liked it at all. Curiously, his Private Secretary, Michael Halls, came up to me afterwards and congratulated me on my speech. It was quite a memorable evening. I was absolutely sick of the attitude of the Royal Society and inevitably of the views of Harold Wilson, for whom I have in some respects the greatest contempt.

Friday 13 February
Saw the TUC Economic and Production Committees with Sid Greene and Vic Feather about the links between ourselves and unions.

Lunch at Au Savarin with John Torode of the *Guardian*, one of their industrial correspondents. He's a curious man with long hair, looks like a motor racing enthusiast. He had his foot in plaster from a ski-ing accident. Pretty sceptical, I should think. I tried to be friendly, but I don't make much of an impact on a certain type of Fleet Street journalist; usually humanities educated, left-wing in a vaguely permissive sort of way and deeply cynical about everything active that may be going on.

Monday 16 February
Stayed at home this morning, the first time for a year, having asked Eunice to arrange a morning free because it was half term.

In the afternoon I had an hour's talk with Otto Clarke. He had gathered together a group of people who had put in a blast against my paper* saying it was an attack on scientists and engineers. I tried to win them round: I said the main problem was that the public must be allowed to discuss developments in advance.

The more I think about it the more important I think it is to broaden the public understanding and not have a private industrial élite making the decisions. Also, I think it is more a matter of the accountability of big corporations to the public, and much less a matter of science as such.

Tuesday 17 February
Inner Cabinet was brief this morning because Barbara was ill and therefore we couldn't discuss the strategy on prices and incomes. We just went along and had a short discussion on the future of the sixpence. Roy Jenkins wanted another month to think about it. I urged that we should say that we won't take it out of circulation if there is a real demand for it.

There was a very significant development over UCS. In my diary last week, I referred to the fact that Jack Diamond went up to Upper Clyde.

---

*Preview of a Royal Society lecture to the Manchester Technological Association given on 25 February 1970. See Appendix III.

He found himself confronted by six chartered accountants and was very impressed by their figures so he agreed to pay the full £7 million to UCS, as authorised by the Cabinet, Harold Lever having asked for £4 million and Jack previously being prepared to give only £2.5 million. In addition he has decided to dismantle the monitoring system because he is afraid that if you monitor you would have to pay the creditors.

Wednesday 18 February

Had dinner – which was not helpful – at the Crossmans with Barbara, Peter and Tommy. It all began with a discussion of the sort of Budget we wanted. If Roy thought we were going to win the Election he would produce a Budget that would help us, and if he thought we were going to lose he would produce a Budget that would allow him to leave as the Iron Chancellor, with his reputation unaffected, indeed higher in the City. Barbara said that Roy would then go into the City and get a well-paid job and this was his real interest. Tommy said this was quite compatible with being active in the Labour Party in Opposition, which I don't really believe. Dick said he would talk to Roy.

I said I thought Roy very much wanted to be Prime Minister and was reckoning on the one hand that if we were defeated in the next Election he would succeed Harold as Leader of the Party; on the other hand, he would like us to win because he wanted to be Foreign Secretary, and subsequently Prime Minister when Harold was got rid of.

The whole discussion was a complete confirmation of the Fleet Street view of politics and was quite sickening. It wasn't on the merits of the issue at all, ie what sort of Budget we should have. Anyway, we agreed to concentrate on an easement of the construction industry, particularly in the regions, and to push for the reduction of the number of people at the lower end of the tax bracket. I thought there was a case for easing surtax on earned income and raising it on unearned income. Tommy was, as ever, complaining of advisers being no good; Peter thinking seriously about the need for us as Ministers to look at the short-term forecast; Barbara, emotional and excitable, engaged in her long and bitter battle with the unions; Dick thinking now more about writing his book* after the Election is over.

Thursday 19 February

With Hugh Scanlon to lunch. It was quite a coincidence because Barbara had attacked him bitterly in a speech yesterday and I very much wanted to talk to him about the relationship between my Ministry and the trade unions. I felt that our dialogues with the big companies

*This project materialised as *The Crossman Diaries, Volumes I–III*, edited by Janet Morgan, 1974–7.

provided a sort of accountability of their power and I said I would like to see whether, in addition to our talks with the unions, the unions would begin talking directly with the companies. He said this might run counter to the idea of shop-floor democracy which he really believes in. I thought that although talks would take place at a national level between the unions and the big companies, they would have to provide for the delegation of discussions to shop-floor representatives. It was an extremely useful meeting, and I like him.

Friday 20 February
To Bristol for a meeting of local Labour MPs, Party members and the Borough Labour Group on the local elections coming up this year. It was an extremely interesting meeting because the Labour Group has entirely disintegrated: there are only thirty of them left on the Council, they have got no policy whatsoever to put forward for Bristol and their policy statement is simply on rents, cracked pavements and one or two other local irritants.

I urged that we might consider four areas of attack and new policy. One, a total look at the educational needs and provision in Bristol, bringing the university, polytechnic and teacher training college together. Second, that we might consider a communications conference with local editors, the BBC and Harlech TV and the new local radio people to review communications in Bristol. Third, a transport group. Fourth, links between the trade unions and Chamber of Commerce, leading towards industrial democracy in the city. The meeting did reveal the absolute collapse of morale of a political party which was based simply on getting office and holding it.

Monday 23 February
At 10.30 I went to the Inner Cabinet and there was another argument about whether Harold had been badly treated by the BBC.

We had a paper from Barbara hailing the end of the prices and incomes policy and saying we should try to control prices now. But that is itself a dead duck. I stayed for a moment for a brief talk about the Reed-IPC merger and I said I thought there ought to be special provision for appointing people to monitor the editorial independence of IPC. This was turned down flat. The truth is that Harold has done a deal with Hugh Cudlipp to get this through and doesn't want it disturbed. So I was quickly bundled out of that discussion.

Tuesday 24 February
Ivor said to me today, 'You are getting too many "Noes" from Number 10', which had a profound effect on me. I *have* had a lot of noes, so I tried to work out what they had been about; usually broadcasting proposals

that Number 10 had turned down, my paper on government information services and another on persuasion in industrial disputes, and Ivor
made the point that no Minister should have proposals turned down as
often as that. So in the light of this, I didn't, for the time being, pursue
another issue I had in mind.

In the evening Caroline and I had dinner at Number 10 in honour of
the Yugoslav Prime Minister, Mr Ribicic. We had a lively discussion.
Caroline and I had to leave the dinner early because Harold had asked
us to receive the other guests while the speeches went on at dinner. He
had invited a lot of show-business people, which is his new line; it is
attractive in the sense that it makes Number 10 much more interesting
than it used to be when the old Tory businessmen automatically poured
in. But it has annoyed one or two Labour MPs and members of the NEC,
even Harry Nicholas, are angry about it, and think regional organisers
should be invited.

Wednesday 25 February
Meeting with Ribicic at Number 10. He said he was glad to see more and
more people becoming involved in the problems of world peace and he
hoped the interests of the superpowers would not dominate the world.
He had got better relations with the Soviet Union because the Soviet
Union needed Mediterranean friends and access to warm waters, and
there were now closer economic and industrial links with the other
Eastern Europe countries, except for Bulgaria whose claim for Mace-
donia had created a great problem. He also said he had good economic
relations with America, but was critical of their policy in Vietnam, and
their support of Israel.

He was afraid of great power influence disturbing the Balkans, which
was why he had opposed Israeli aggression and the invasion of
Czechoslovakia. Relations with China were normalising because he
thought the Chinese were settling down; he believed that Soviet-Chinese
conflict was not really ideological but more a clash of interests and
China was now actually preparing for a war with the Soviet Union.

Yugoslavia just wanted to be a European country, he added, but was
not getting on very well with, for example, the Germans because of the
problem of reparation and Yugoslavian émigré terrorism in Germany.

Harold then said he was glad relations with Russia were improving
but we couldn't accept the Brezhnev doctrine.* Michael Stewart made
his usual negative speech, saying that we didn't really like the European
conference proposal because our security was bound up with NATO,
and this would have helped East Germany and underwritten the

---

* After the invasion of Czechoslovakia, the Soviet Government justified their action in
the so-called 'Brezhnev doctrine', by insisting on the right to maintain the status quo in
Warsaw Pact countries in order to prevent the overthrow of Communism.

Brezhnev doctrine, though we hadn't rejected the idea outright.

To the Royal Society where I made my speech* to the Manchester Technology Association on technology and the quality of life. I had worked hard on it and it got a very enthusiastic reception.

Thursday 26 February
Yigal Allon, the Deputy Prime Minister of Israel, came to see me with the Ambassador, Aharon Remez. He didn't say very much except that the bomb attacks on international airlines flying to Israel, which have led to many of them refusing to carry freight to Israel, have caused great alarm to the Israeli Cabinet. 'If aircraft aren't going to fly to Israel,' he said, 'they won't fly anywhere else.' This was his real message and I transmitted this to Harold. In general he took the line that it was the four powers that were preventing the Arabs from coming to their senses and that we should withdraw our influence.

It is a world of illusion that the Israelis live in. I am sure they can't be defeated, but I am equally sure they can't consolidate their position and they are losing friends all over the world.

At OPD my paper on uranium from South West Africa came up for discussion and it became clear that the Department had not fully briefed me on this. George Thomson was extremely upset, said this was a breach of the understanding reached two years ago when I had been authorised to let the AEA buy from Rio Algom, subsidiary of Rio Tinto-Zinc, in the expectation that it would come from Canada. So it was clear we had got stuck. There was some suggestion that the AEA had not kept us fully informed, which raised all the memories of last summer and the centrifuge. I simply had to say I would take it back, and I called the office and set up an enquiry about it.

Then Cabinet, where the drugs question came up. Broadly the position is that, under the existing law, the penalty is the same for both trafficking and possessing drugs, hard and soft. We had a paper suggesting that there should be the most heavy penalties for trafficking, particularly in hard drugs, and reduced penalties for possessing cannabis or pot. But Jim had come to the conclusion that, with the strong Tory attacks over law and order and the permissive society, he should not now ease the law. It really was very vulgar stuff because the real argument in favour of easement is of course strong. I said that as a parent I wanted to see trafficking very severely punished but I thought simple possession should be treated more leniently. We just carried it, and the sentence is going to drop from ten to five years, although I had hoped to get it down to three years.

Back to the Commons where we held Auntie Rene's eighty-eighth

* See Appendix III.

birthday party and about fifty Benns of various ages turned up; Stephen came back from Keele and I had arranged for a cake. Margaret Rutherford – very depressed with two broken hips – was there. But Auntie Rene made a marvellous speech about how enjoyable life was as you got older. She had first been inside the House of Commons in 1892 when my grandfather was elected and she was a girl of ten, and Gladstone was Prime Minister – quite remarkable.

I had to go back to my office to meet Henry Ford II who had come over from America at my request, following the announcement that Ford Cortina exports to America were to discontinue and the Capri was to be manufactured and exported from their German factory. Stanley Gillen, Bill Batty and Walter Hayes, Vice-President of Ford of Europe, were present. I put the case as strongly as I could, that this was an extremely important decision. We welcomed the size of the Ford operation in Britain and their investment and export record, but a decision made in Detroit which had led to the blanking out of certain British car exports to America was very serious, with damaging consequences for the British balance of payments and for Britain's reputation for exports.

I questioned him about the survey on which they had based their decision, and Ford said the reasons were much broader than that. British cars had a bad reputation for quality and reliability. I said, 'Doesn't this indicate some defect in quality control?' He rather agreed and said this was being looked at, and did say in the end that he would look again to see whether it was only in the first instance that the cars would be coming from Germany and that exports from Britain might not be ruled out. That was encouraging and it was well worthwhile having the meeting.

Ford went off but Stan Gillen, Bill Batty, Walter Hayes, Otto and others came and had dinner with us at the Café Royal together with Charles Smith and Ieuan Maddock. We had quite a discussion.

I am not very impressed with Batty. He just wanted to bash the workers – a typical British businessman. Walter Hayes is much more sympathetic. He has always been struck by my argument that the BBC and broadcasting is too important to be left to the broadcasters and we considered the whole question of how important issues could be seriously discussed on the air.

Sunday 1 March
In the evening Buckminster Fuller* came to dinner at home with James Mellor who has just edited his work.

---

*American engineer, architect and inventor, who developed the geodesic dome, which combines maximum strength with minimum structure. He wrote *Spaceship Earth* among many other books.

I had read a little bit of Fuller's writing and had found it extremely difficult to understand; it is full of academic technological jargon, but I had been struck by his geodesic domes, by his speech to architects in Mexico City and by one or two other things. He is a short man of seventy-four and is very deaf. I got out my blackboard and he lectured to us from about 6.30 until after midnight, doing drawings, and describing his conception of comprehensive anticipatory design. He talked about the regenerative systems, and the collection and use of waste. He was very optimistic about our capacity to deal with the population problem, saying that mankind had been born to be a success and that it was our job to see that it was. He was very anti-political and thought politics was just corrupt, but I liked him enormously, and found him a very impressive man. Joshua sat there fascinated, and Stephen enjoyed it greatly.

Tuesday 3 March

I had a word with Michael Michaels about the South West African uranium: the truth is that the Atomic Energy Authority two years ago particularly asked officials at the Ministry not to tell Ministers that the uranium came from SW Africa. That is on the record. The minutes say that I insisted it go to Ministers because of its political sensitivity, and I'm afraid there has been a lack of candour by officials in the nuclear field, as there has been in the space field and other aviation matters. Officials just don't tell Ministers in order to avoid trouble.

Then I went over to Number 10 for talks with Chancellor Willy Brandt and I was asked to open on Anglo-German technological collaboration.

I said that on space I would like to consult with German and French Ministers before I went to Washington next month. There was a lot of scope in the defence field, with the multi-role combat aircraft being the most important. I did not say that I understood the Germans were losing interest in the single-seater version (which we had just heard and which is quite serious) because I had been told by *my* officials that Willy Brandt had not been told by *his* officials what was going on.

On to defence, and Denis made an interminable speech in which he said that the Americans would be withdrawing from Germany and it was very important we should sustain American self-confidence. Our job was to try to persuade the Americans to slow down the process a bit. Willy Brandt said, 'Let's be positive about it and talk of a Western European response, rather than a German response to the American withdrawal.'

On Greece Harold said that there was a defence aspect and a human rights aspect, and that he thought that in certain circumstances the Colonels might be replaced by some even more horrible right-wing majors and captains. The question of the German submarines promised to the Greek Government arose, and Harold just said, 'Well, keep it quiet.'

It was a pleasant meeting: Willy Brandt was self-confident and Harold was good. I think Anglo-German relations have probably never been better than they are at the moment.

Wednesday 4 March

We were delayed by snow, but we finally took off at 11 for Almelo, Holland, in an HS125 with Lord Chalfont, Michael Michaels, Derek Moon, Chris Audland and Eunice Gofton. We signed the Treaty,* had a quick drink, a press conference and I gave a couple of television interviews. We had lunch with the burgemeester and I spoke. When we got back into the plane we heard that England was snowed in and we couldn't get back. The question then was what to do. We agreed to extricate ourselves from the British Embassy and we didn't want to stay in Almelo, so we flew to Amsterdam and after hanging about at the airport for a time, we were put in the Amstel Hotel. We had a very nice dinner together with the pilots of the plane.

During the course of the dinner Chalfont was extremely impressive, talking about the need for a more moral foreign policy and saying that we shouldn't give the impression that we would do anything for foreign currency. He hates Denis Healey whom he describes as a thug. He would like to go to the Ministry of Defence as the Minister in charge of administration and he thinks Roy would like to go to the Foreign Office. We reshuffled the Government, putting Denis in the Treasury, Barbara in the Home Office, Jim as Leader of the House. That left the Ministry of Labour for me, which is what I really would like next.

When I was in bed at about 11.30, the phone rang and I was informed that 700 miners had been stranded at the bottom of a pit in Kent because snow had brought power lines down. It sounded serious but I rang Caroline and found that it wasn't a disaster, just an ordinary failure.

Thursday 5 March

I flew back to Northolt, but missed the Cabinet. At 2.30 Keith Joseph came to tell me he had changed his mind and is now opposed to the Green Paper on our research establishments. He is a great admirer of Enoch Powell.

In the afternoon I went to the TGWU Executive Committee with Charles Smith and a couple of others, and it was excellent. They were all

---

*The Treaty of Almelo confirmed the terms of collaboration between the Netherlands, UK and Germany on the development of the centrifuge for uranium enrichment: the plants were to be at Almelo and Capenhurst, the contracting HQ in Germany.

the shop stewards, that is to say the working members of the Committee. I got lots of questions and I felt I had established a real rapport. The question arose, were we becoming neo-Fascist by getting so close to big business? We are not, of course, and I said that this was one of the reasons I wanted to have good contacts with the trade unions by way of a counter-balance. I hoped the trade unions would also have closer contact with industry.

Friday 6 March

Hurried back from Bristol for the Overseas Policy Committee on uranium from South West Africa and it was agreed that the deal would have to go through despite our grave dissatisfaction. There will have to be an enquiry into what actually happened.

Saturday 7 March

I went up to Bradford to address the Yorkshire Regional Labour Conference, working on my red box on the train, and delivered a speech on the waste of talent in life, attacking the idea of examinations, selection and streaming. It wasn't a successful speech – I cannot speak from text and I must remember this in future.

I came back on the train with Harry Nicholas and Ron Hayward, the National Agent, and it was fun talking to them. Harry Nicholas said that he had seen some sex education programmes for children on television and had learned things he hadn't known before. It contrasted sharply with his own experience as a child.

Sunday 8 March

At 9 I left for a meeting of the Inner Cabinet at Chequers with the Prime Minister, Michael Stewart, Roy Jenkins, Dick Crossman, Denis Healey, Barbara Castle, Jim Callaghan, Peter Shore, Bob Mellish, Tony Crosland and Fred Peart; Burke Trend and Michael Halls were present in the morning, although officials didn't come in the afternoon.

We sat in the library on the first floor and the first paper we considered was Jim Callaghan's on law and order, or what he preferred to call the 'war against crime'. This was split into three parts. First, the student question and Harold wanted to know why universities didn't take a stronger line and whether they could withdraw the students' grants. Michael Stewart was attracted to this idea. Dick Crossman said the situation was like the early days of the Weimar Republic, he could see democracy coming to an end, and we should have no hesitation in dealing with people who were destroying free speech.

I chipped in and said that self-discipline was what was required here; that on the merits of the issue students were very often right. I described my meeting with students at the sit-in in Bristol and how they had desperately been seeking a way out of it, and how the thugs – the extremists – had in fact been routed. It was important not to use police in the universities if this could be avoided. Barbara agreed with me, but there was a nasty touch of authoritarianism from other Ministers, which I found depressing. But we did agree that before Ted Short gave his response to the select committee report on student unrest, there should be a meeting for a few Ministers to discuss it.

Then we discussed the extremely difficult problem of the visit by the South African cricket team, and the fear that this would trigger off demonstrations all summer. Jim is going to see all the police chiefs to discuss it. He also said the Commissioner of the Metropolis [Commissioner of the Metropolitan Police] had been invited to meet Ted Heath and that he hadn't objected, but he thought the Commissioner would tell Ted Heath that he didn't want law and order to be mixed up in party politics.

The third element in this discussion was crime and we all agreed that international comparisons would show how much better the situation was in Britain than elsewhere, although there is a rising tide of urban violence. Jim said he would discuss with Charles Hill and Lord Aylestone* the crime and violence on television, on which I very strongly supported him.

Roy began the discussion by saying that he was fed up by the rumours that had appeared in the press that morning to the effect that the Chancellor was at bay and his colleagues were urging a soft Budget. Denis said he thought it was very damaging.

Tony Crosland went on to talk about an employment generation programme, particularly in the regions where the construction industry is badly hit. Another £7 million was proposed for cleaning up our rivers. Harold thought there was a good political point here, since there were many anglers. In the end the choice is a political choice, not an economic one, and this was very evident as we discussed all the alternatives today.

After lunch I went for a walk with Barbara and Peter Shore. Peter is rather an authoritarian on student questions; Barbara is much more sympathetic – this is like the early days of industrial relations strikes in the nineteenth century. The temptation to take fierce measures is strong.

Then we really got on to the hard political stuff. Harold went round the room asking when we thought the Election should be and Denis said he was attracted by the 'long haul' – ie October – but that we should be ready to go earlier if things improved, and Fred said the same. I said, 'Well, if we are ready to go earlier, we had better be ready from June onwards. If it isn't right in June we'll go until October, and if it isn't

*Herbert Bowden, Chairman of IBA, formerly Labour MP for Leicester; Lord President of the Council and Leader of the House of Commons, 1964–6.

right in October we'll go right through to the spring. But don't let's work on a date that is later than we think might be necessary.'

Harold gave his views. He said he had thought about the date for the Election for the last four years or more and the conflict with the World Cup had to be considered, and whether there might be strikes. He was a little afraid of a Tory campaign building up to the autumn and possible attempts to shake confidence in the pound: the weather would be better in the summer, the hours of daylight would be greater. I felt Harold was moving towards an earlier date.

Denis said he thought the expectations of better times to come would be greater than the reality, and so that was a sort of consensus that we should be ready for June.

The next question was what should we fight the Election on? Barbara said that people were bored with the balance of payments; they wanted better benefits and housing was important.

Jim said he thought the environment was too middle class a weapon with which to attack the Tories.

Michael Stewart said that foreign affairs were going rather well, and emphasised the fact that no British soldiers had been killed in action.

Tony Crosland said he thought we ought to cut income tax or release people from the lower ranges of income tax and add it on to SET.

Dick said what he wanted was a working class Budget, a real sloshing working class Budget. People had waited a long time and they were entitled to it. He spoke about relief which would probably cost between £400 million and £600 million.

When I was called, I said I thought that fear of the Tories' right-wing policies would mobilise the faithful, win the middle ground and neutralise the Conservatives. The people would like us because we were a known team but we had to have confidence in ourselves and really believe we would win. It wasn't new policies but the thematic connection of what we had already done that mattered; our job was to explain and interconnect and give leadership involving not promises but visions for the future. Above all, we had to encourage people to have confidence in themselves. I quoted Lao Tzu who said, 'When the best leader's work is done, the people say, We did it ourselves.' This was very important; the issue was the people versus the élite and we had to treat people in an adult way and try to indicate that there was a difference between our mature way of treating people and the hysterical authoritarianism of the Tories. As far as economics was concerned, I was in favour of relaxing as much as we could so that people felt that after two years' hard slog they had earned something. But if there was reflation to be done, let's do it selectively.

Then Fred Peart said that courage, competence, compassion and an egalitarian approach were necessary.

Denis said the public were bored with politics and would like a Government that would relieve them of the responsibility for handling political matters. Then he went on to discuss in detail what he wanted to see in the Budget and at that moment, as Denis was describing in detail how he thought the Budget should be handled, what should happen to SET, income tax and purchase tax, with Dick chipping in, the Wrens came in with tea. Roy was getting agitated at this open discussion of the Budget in front of the women, and so indeed was I. But Denis carried on and the risk of a leak from that, I thought, was enormous.

We discussed whether SET should be increased. There was a general feeling that since it upset the Co-ops so much, it would probably be better not to do it. Then Bob Mellish said to Roy, 'Now look, Roy boy, you're a marvellous chap, you're my favourite Chancellor, but don't do a Cripps on us or we'll never forgive you.' This was exactly what had been suggested in today's papers and Roy didn't like it very much.

Peter said the important thing to go for was a higher rate of growth, perhaps 4 per cent, with selective reflation, particularly in the construction industries in development areas.

Looking back, it was a very pleasant and informal day and much better than formally sitting round a table.

There is no split in the Government at all. Everybody has got confidence in each other although there are differences of emphasis, and I must say that if the Government were run by a little group of that kind, I think it would be quite useful. It is about the same size as my weekly departmental lunch and I should have thought that something similar for the Inner Cabinet would be immensely valuable. That would be the way I would run the top-end Government if I were Prime Minister. I would just have this type of get-together once a week and do it over sandwiches. My guess at the moment is that we have a reasonable chance of winning the Election; I shall have to start electioneering very much harder in Bristol because the Election may come in June or July.

Monday 9 March
At 11 I went to Economic Policy Committee where Barbara produced a paper proposing a new modernised employment service with proper careers advice and placements, and suggesting that responsibility for dole should be given to Health and Social Security. It was a typical Barbara-type consultative document which she wanted us to approve immediately. Here is a very good scheme, nothing has been done about it for five years, it couldn't be implemented for seven years and Barbara wanted an instant decision at the SEP. We said we wouldn't agree to it in principle but that we didn't mind consultations in general terms. We were opposed to a White Paper. Barbara was hopping mad but she does try to railroad stuff through Cabinet and it infuriates everybody.

To the AEU MPs' dinner in the House of Commons. I was asked to speak so I talked about my interest in linking the unions with Mintech and how it was absolutely necessary, to avoid a neo-Fascist state, to have the unions involved from the outset. I went over the problem of the international companies and accountability of their power and how to reconcile this power, which I thought was bound to grow, with the nation state. I ended with the relevance of a wider Europe and the implications for shop-floor democracy.

Thursday 12 March

Cabinet. On Malta, Michael Stewart had produced a paper suggesting that we should yield to the Maltese demand that we pay up to 75 per cent of civil developments to replace our military units there, in place of the 50-50 we had agreed last year, which was itself a concession on the original offer of 25-75 in our favour. Michael put the case that this would help to keep Prime Minister Dr Borg Olivier in power and to keep Dom Mintoff, Leader of the Labour Party, out.* He was supported by Denis Healey. Peter Shore came in and said this was intervening grossly in Maltese politics; Roy thought it would be better to stick by our original position and then we would have something in reserve when the new Government was elected next year. Willie Ross was funny. He said, as he understood it, Dom Mintoff had reached an arrangement with the Catholic Church which had made his election more likely, and that as Prime Minister he might bring the Russians in to use Malta as a naval base. Fortunately, by a narrow majority, the Cabinet decided to stick to its present position of 50-50.

David Purnell, the Mintech security officer, came in, at my request, to talk about the Will Owen case. Will Owen, the Labour MP for Morpeth, has been charged under the Official Secrets Act and I gathered from Purnell that the diplomats who subverted him were Czechs. The Czech Minister of Technology is coming to London in April and I wanted to be absolutely sure it wouldn't correspond with the date of the trial. It is likely to take place in April, but hopefully shortly after the visit of the Czechs: even so, I decided it would not be right to have the Czech Minister to London.

Will Owen had evidently been giving information to the Czechs about secret documents considered by the Select Committee on Estimates since about 1961, indeed most of the documents themselves in 1962-3. Apparently at one stage he wanted to pull himself out of it but was blackmailed into continuing and some thousands of pounds were

* The Foreign Office view was that under Mintoff, Malta would be weakened as a NATO base, and therefore Borg Olivier of the Malta Nationalist Party was to be supported.

unexplained in his bank account. He has in part apologised and it is pretty clear he will get a severe sentence.* The Czech diplomat in question, who is going to be named, is Robert Husak, and apparently he and John Stonehouse used to talk informally and personally while John was at Mintech. Purnell told me he had a record of all these discussions and it appeared that John's name might come out at the trial and the press were going to make a big thing of it. Purnell said he would like to go and see John Stonehouse if I had no objection, and I said I had none. I don't think anything improper will emerge but one can imagine what the press will make of it.

In talking to Purnell one comes up against the real security man. He thoroughly dislikes the technological agreements with Eastern Europe because of the risks that are run, and I had to remind him that as an old-fashioned, radical, non-conformist independent, I wanted to protect something *worth* defending. I thought the development of computerised dossiers would reduce us all to a police state and put people in a position where they recommended to their children not to join anything or do anything which could conceivably get them into trouble.

Later, I picked up Caroline at home and we went to the Austrian Embassy to say goodbye to the Ambassador, then on to Lois and Edward Sieff's for dinner with Lord and Lady Sainsbury, Jeremy Hutchinson,† whom I had known twenty-five years ago when he was the Labour candidate for the City of Westminster, Monsieur Levy, the Permanent Secretary in the French Ministry of Industry, and Natasha Spender, the wife of Stephen Spender. We talked about education and Jeremy Hutchinson was utterly despondent about the younger generation; Teddy Sieff wanted more discipline; Monsieur Levy was extremely pleasant and I got on with him well. Caroline had a talk to Natasha Spender about the way the CIA had financed and used the cultural magazine *Encounter*, through the editor Melvin Lasky, whom I had once met and always distrusted. Natasha said Stephen Spender who was associated with *Encounter* had no idea of where the money was coming from, but he must have been very naïve.

Friday 13 March
I had called a special meeting on oil policy this morning. We had in front of us a major document with twenty-five recommendations, including one that there should be no attempt at state enterprise in oil. This was being slipped through without any discussion and Harold Lever was

---

* Will Owen was found not guilty and acquitted on all charges brought against him under the Official Secrets Act.
† Joseph Edward Sieff was Chairman of Marks & Spencer; Alan Sainsbury was President of J. Sainsbury Ltd, joined the Labour Party in 1945, the SDP in 1981; Jeremy Hutchinson, QC, was formerly married to Peggy Ashcroft.

prepared to let it go forward to officials as the Ministry of Technology view. But I raised a number of issues, including our relations with the international companies; whether in fact there should be any further state enterprise, and questioned the tax point. It shook them, and Otto was extremely cross. It was an interesting study of how the Department worked.

Afterwards Otto came in and I told him that I was proposing to minute the Prime Minister on the bid by the Ministry of Defence to take over the aviation responsibilities. He exploded. He said he had spoken to Ned Dunnett, the Permanent Under-Secretary at Defence, and that Denis Healey and William Armstrong had not needed to be told, and there was no need at all for me to raise it with the Prime Minister. He really was extremely offensive, as he is when he is angry. I said I would have to consider what he had said. Then we went on to discuss appointments and other things and he said again he would be ready to take a nationalised industry appointment if one came up. I shall probably recommend him for the Electricity Council, under the new Bill.

After my talk with Otto, Harold Lever came in in great distress to say that Frank Kearton had just been to see him with a story. Kearton had said, 'I have come to see you because I am very disturbed, and you are the responsible Minister. Courtaulds [of which Kearton was Chairman] had wanted to acquire IPC and I went to see Hugh Cudlipp about it. Hugh Cudlipp said to me that there was no point at all in trying this because the Prime Minister has agreed that it should be taken over by the Reed Paper Group. Well, I didn't believe Hugh Cudlipp so I went to see Don Ryder of Reed's and he said, "Oh this is all fixed with the Prime Minister that we should take over IPC, and indeed the Prime Minister drank a toast to the new company when we went to see him."'

Ryder had told Kearton that Cudlipp would be kept on until after the Election and then that would be the end. 'Then,' said Kearton, 'a very senior civil servant came to speak to my Vice-Chairman, and said, "I just want to warn you off because the Prime Minister has settled this with Don Ryder and Hugh Cudlipp."'

Kearton had been very concerned about all this and Harold Lever said he told him that he was sure there would be no discrimination against Courtaulds, and that indeed Harold and I had agreed two days ago that Courtaulds would have to be treated in exactly the same way.

Harold Lever had then called in the civil servant concerned, in the presence of Sir David Pitblado, the Permanent Secretary on the power side. He admitted that he had been to see the Courtaulds Vice-Chairman and was overcome with shame because he is not responsible in the Department for the merger question. He had done this off his own bat as a service to a friend and had based his opinion simply on Whitehall gossip.

Kearton had argued of course that whereas he had taken no notice of Cudlipp and no notice of Ryder, he had been greatly influenced by what the civil servant had told him.

Harold Lever and I discussed it. He said the PM dices with death and if there were any thought of an inquiry about this, it would be disastrous, particularly as a number of people in the City probably knew about it. There would be a lot of people trying to put Harold Wilson in a spot. Lever wondered whether Kearton was just angry and frustrated that his board had overturned his desire to bid for IPC, or whether he wanted us to know that he had an explosive weapon.

We agreed that we ought to get on to the PM at once. However, the PM was in Cardiff and Michael Halls, his Principal Private Secretary was sick so another PS, Derek Andrews, was brought over from Number 10 and we told him the story: he was very concerned.

Ivor Manley put through a call to Frank Kearton, and Harold Lever took it in my office and I listened on the other line. Harold told him that he had spoken to the civil servant in question who had admitted that it was an extremely foolish thing to have done, and that he had not been authorised to do it. Frank Kearton accepted that. However, Kearton went on to say that in the autumn of last year he had been sitting next to Hugh Cudlipp at dinner and Cudlipp had said to him, 'The Prime Minister and I have been talking about the honours list and we both think that you should have a peerage – I thought you would like to know.' Frank said he thought it scandalous that Hugh Cudlipp should be giving the impression that he, personally, approved the honours list and said that Hugh was a very dangerous friend for Harold to have. Harold Lever did his best in commenting on that and then Frank Kearton rang off.

We agreed that Harold Lever should see the Prime Minister early tomorrow morning. In my view, this is one of the most damaging things that could have happened, although no doubt Harold will get out of it. He'll say he called in Ryder and Cudlipp when he heard about the difficulties of IPC, set up an inquiry in Whitehall to see whether a reference should be made to the Monopolies Commission, and, on his return from Washington, Ministers considered this collectively and decided not to refer it. Of course, if you leave out of account the unauthorised gossip of a civil servant, you could disbelieve what Cudlipp and Ryder said because they both wanted this to go through, and Harold Lever had acted quite properly in reiterating, with my authority, that Courtaulds would be treated in exactly the same way.

However, the plain truth is that Harold *did* see Cudlipp and Ryder secretly without civil servants. He no doubt did drink a toast and did agree to keep to his side of the bargain. When Barbara Castle had actually proposed that it should be referred to the Monopolies

Commission, Harold had ruled against it at the Committee, and although I was briefed to support it, I did not press it. Moreover, when I had come forward with my proposal that there should be some provision for editorial freedom, this was dismissed – undoubtedly Cudlipp and Ryder were reflecting the Prime Minister's view.

Well, that is the story and it is a very unpleasant one but very typical of Harold and the sort of wheeling and dealing and fixing that he likes. But it could get us, and the whole Government, into serious trouble.

Monday 16 March
To NEDC and on the agenda was our application to join the EEC. George Thomson said the negotiations were due to begin in the summer. There was a very desultory discussion with nothing new emerging. Peter Shore, who sat next to me and has always been very anti-EEC, whispered that the whole thing was a complete waste of time.

Thursday 19 March
At Cabinet we had a discussion on whether we should take away the Privy Councillorship from the Chief Justice of Rhodesia, now that Rhodesia has gone against the Crown and is a republic. I find the idea of disloyalty to the Crown as a reason utterly ridiculous, but it certainly puts the Tories in an embarrassing position.

Friday 20 March
Marcia Williams and Gerald Kaufman came for a half-hour sandwich lunch. I must say they are an extraordinary couple. Neither of them has had any contact with reality for ages and they live in the funny closed atmosphere of Number 10. My view that Marcia's instinct was something on which Harold ought to rely has largely collapsed. She is now almost a courtier in a fading court, while Gerald looks sinister and is cynical. Still, it is good to keep in touch with them.

Saturday 21 March
To Blackpool for the North West Conference where I missed the fast train back by five minutes and caught the later one with Ron Hayward. The cable broke and 25,000 watts of electricity flicked outside around the carriage like a whip, with enormous sparks. It was really quite frightening. We were stranded in the middle of the country for two hours before we were pulled out by diesel.

Monday 23 March
With Caroline and Ivor Manley I went on the HS125 from London Airport up to East Midlands Airport, a brand new airport that is not officially open until tomorrow. We were picked up by helicopter and

taken to Sheffield for the Cutlers' Feast. This was provincial Toryism at its peak, everyone wearing decorations. There was a massive representation of the Establishment: the Lord Mayor of London, the Bishop of Ripon in purple, the Master Cutler, and so on.

Wednesday 25 March

To the House of Commons, where I met the Miners' Group of MPs for the second time in a fortnight. I told them I had agreed to the conversion of Hams Hall to dual firing with North Sea Gas but had refused the conversion of Tilbury B station to oil – this pleased them very much.

I had lunch with the American press correspondents. This comes just before my trip to the States and somehow, chatting to them, I felt how much the United States has changed in the last twenty years. Instead of a confident group of journalists, I found, as I expect I will in America in a couple of weeks' time, that the United States has lost confidence in itself, in its world role and in its capacity to maintain domestic peace: I think they are looking to this country a bit more as a civilised and reasonable place in which to live.

Thursday 26 March

Cabinet this morning at the House of Commons. The first problem we discussed was how we could stop Ojukwu from coming to Britain. There have been persistent rumours that he might try to come here from the Ivory Coast where he is based. Michael Stewart would like to stop him coming because it would embarrass our relations with Nigeria, though Jim Callaghan says if he comes through Ireland there is nothing he can do about it.

Then there was a row over Peter Shore's speech last night in which he had thrown some doubt on the Common Market and this has been a major headline. Everybody is discussing it – does this represent the Prime Minister's real thinking about the EEC? Michael Stewart raised it and said it was very embarrassing. It had pleased Fred Peart, of course, very much. Jim Callaghan supported Peter. This is going to be a big bubbling issue, undoubtedly.

The beginning of my Easter Holiday. I really am tired and looking forward to it.

Friday 27 March

Lazy start to the day. I got the family sitting round the table and we completed 2,500 election address envelopes for the Labour candidates in the GLC.

Sunday 29 March
Easter Day. Had a lie-in. Caroline is reading a book called *The Feminine Mystique* about the new Women's Liberation movement which is beginning to develop strongly in the States and even in Britain.

There was a power cut this evening which put us on candles and butane gas for the kettle.

Tuesday 31 March
Another cold day.

I went to the Russian Embassy in Kensington Palace Gardens with Harry Slater where I was greeted by Smirnovsky, the Ambassador, a very charming man. Gvishiani was late as he had been busy all morning. We talked about the Mixed Commission which we have agreed to set up and which will meet in London for the first time this autumn. I suggested November would be a suitable date because the Election will either be over by then or it won't be happening until the spring.

I told him frankly that I would do my best to get this computer problem resolved when I visited America, but that the Americans were difficult. He said he was going over there tonight and asked what he should do in his talks. I said, 'If I were you I should press for a relaxation of COCOM so you have got a choice of the systems you want. Obviously we would like you to buy our system but there's nothing to lose by getting this choice made easier.'

At lunch I said that I greatly regretted that Anglo-Soviet relations were not as good as they might be. I worked very hard at them but we seem to be the villains of the piece in Moscow. Gvishiani, on overhearing this, looked across and said he felt that was the case.

I said, 'Well, I don't know why.' So Solly Zuckerman, who was also present, suggested that it might be the statements that have been made on the nuclear guidelines, outlining situations in which the West would use nuclear weapons first (this being Denis Healey's defence statement). Gvishiani said, 'Everybody has guidelines but you don't have to talk about them.'

Obviously the Soviet Union does regard us as being very hostile. I replied, 'It is a personal view but I think goodwill does matter even in international relations. There is a lot of goodwill for the Soviet Union in Britain, going right back to the support for the Revolution of 1917. Despite the disillusionment during the Stalin period, in the Second World War you were the great heroes, you were our allies before the Americans were, and there is a great deal to build on if only you could find a way of doing it.'

They responded warmly to this and they do regard our operation as intended to be helpful. Solly rang me up later that night and was lyrical in my praise. I think we've been very negative on the East-West conference idea, and we have been hostile to the Russians because of the Cold-War warriors in the Foreign Office.

I got home, did a bit of sorting and shopping, went down to Stansgate and we began to pack up.

Thursday 2 April
Interview with Michael Barrett on the BBC programme *Nationwide* on the motor industry. There has been serious disruption and in particular a strike of 112 inspectors at Vauxhall which has thrown thousands of people out of work.

I was very nervous, curiously, and I didn't do at all well. When I got home Joshua said, 'It was terrible.' Caroline said the lighting was bad and I looked grim and uneasy. I felt grim and uneasy. I do so hate those BBC interviews where instead of talking to you about a problem, they are always aggressive towards you, which makes you defensive and not at your best.

Monday 6 April
Had a word with Peter Shore on the phone tonight. He is very pleased with the reaction to his speech on the Common Market which caused a lot of trouble, because he does believe, very strongly, that the Common Market is an illusion and politically it will be advantageous if it is clear that there are some members of the Government with reservations about entry. My view is different from his. I don't think economics are everything by any manner of means and if we have to have some sort of organisation to control international companies, the Common Market is probably the right one. I think that decision-making is on the move and some decisions have to be taken in Europe, some in London, and an awful lot more at the regional and local level.

Tuesday 7 April
Harry Slater and I had breakfast with Campbell Adamson and the President and Deputy Director-General of the CBI to discuss their talks in Russia. We agreed that it would be useful to build up the Mixed Commission as quickly as we could. We also discussed whether the UN body, the Economic Commission in Europe, might be used. I am very keen on this, and I wanted to sound out the CBI. They weren't enthusiastic.

Then to see Lord Rootes at the office, who reported on his visit to the United States and his discussions with the Anglo-American Chambers of Commerce. It was a rather unnecessary and boring meeting. Rootes is not an exciting person. He has just got to the top by having the right father, as so often happens.

After that I had a briefing with Ronnie Melville before the Ministerial Space Meeting which I had arranged for London today.

Ortoli, the French Minister of Industrial and Scientific Development, and Klaus von Dohnanyi came in and I made a point of being friendly to Ortoli: it was the first time I had met him. Dohnanyi was keen that there should be a German contribution to the NASA post-Apollo programme. I had been told they had put aside £50 million in their budget which is an enormous sum – it's the whole Concorde programme – every year for about ten years. They particularly want to do the nuclear-powered space tug which they could take on with the Americans, and would like to get us lined up for that.

Well, Ortoli was much more cautious than Dohnanyi and so indeed was I. I thought we ought to consider exactly what our objectives were before we went much further. This was the theme throughout – Dohnanyi encouraging us and Ortoli looking at the real objectives and costs.

Over lunch we talked more candidly about international companies, about the work of the three countries, about the problems of technological collaboration, and I put forward the proposal that we might have a little Ministers of Technology club in which we met in each other's capitals every two or three months for lunch, quite informally. I had opened this session by saying that the meeting represented a ministerial revolt against officials, because it takes about three months to write a letter to a French or German Minister, and three months to get a reply – everything has to be looked at so microscopically and this is the sort of situation which leads to the absurdity of Concordes and all that. My lunch proposal was warmly welcomed.

Later, I went to Osterley to speak at an international conference of Jesuits from Britain, Ireland, the United States, Canada, India, Poland, Portugal, and so on. They were all in their middle thirties, just completing their education. I based my talk on the idea that many of the political changes I was describing were also affecting the organisation of the Church.

Wednesday 8 April
I met Kozyrev, the Soviet Deputy Foreign Minister this morning: I had dinner with him at the British Embassy in Moscow last May. He has gold spectacles and looks rather Edwardian, and could be a Bostonian businessman of 1910. He came to impress on me the advantages of the Soviet proposal for an all-European conference. I had absolutely no authority to say anything except by way of making friendly noises.

Kozyrev said, 'Why don't you support the Security Conference?'

I said, 'Let me tell you something about the British character.

Consider the clock, Big Ben. When you look at it, the hands appear to be stationary but inside there is a piece of technology, working away, slowly turning the hands and when you look again in half an hour's time you will find the hands have changed. I am the piece of machinery behind the big clock.'

The analogy appealed to him and he laughed a great deal. Then I said I thought technology had abolished foreign affairs and that you could squeeze the relationships between two countries through a little tunnel called foreign policy. As I left, I whispered to Smirnovsky, 'I hope you realise that this is an initiative of my own and I hope you will see what can be done.'

Caroline and I went to the reception for the Russians at Lancaster House. Lady Clarke told me how much Otto admired politics and my work, and how their son* wanted to be a politician. She is very keen to get on my side at the moment. It must be because Otto is hoping for the Chairmanship of the Electricity Council, to which I would like to appoint him.

Dinner at the Swedish Embassy given by Olaf Palme [Prime Minister of Sweden] who is over here. Caroline sat next to Tony Crosland and on his other side was Lady Greenhill, the wife of Sir Denis Greenhill, the head of the Foreign Office.† Crosland said to her, 'I understand your husband is the head of MI5 or MI6 or MI7 or something.' Lady Greenhill said, 'Well, I've never heard of it.'

In fact Greenhill is alleged to be in charge of MI6 but it was the maddest thing that could possibly be said. Then Crosland didn't have a side plate and made a big fuss about that and pulled the waiter towards him and asked if he could borrow Caroline's side plate. The Ambassador got very agitated, as you can imagine, and asked Caroline, 'Is he always as rude as that?' She said, 'Yes', and he replied, 'Well, I suppose now that George Brown has gone you've got to have somebody like that in the Government.'

I sat next to Dick Mabon's [Labour MP for Greenock] wife who is Jewish and very interested in Buddhism. She was really rather nice. Opposite was George Thomson: I asked him about his talk with Kozyrev and he said he hadn't made much of an impression. I asked George whether he would mind if I tried to get the Economic Commission for Europe escalated up to ministerial level.

I had to vote and missed Olaf's speech but I heard a bit of Harold's, which was odious. I can't quite say why but he is so conceited in his

---

* Charles Clarke became chief adviser to the Leader of the Opposition, Neil Kinnock in 1983.
† Permanent Under-Secretary of State at the Foreign and Commonwealth Office and Head of the Diplomatic Service, 1969–73.

speeches and so ponderous. The only thing that gave me any pleasure was that afterwards Caroline told me that she had been watching Ted Heath's face throughout Harold's speech and it was frozen with envy at the way in which it was assumed that all Governments were Social Democrat.

Afterwards Olaf searched me out. I asked him whether he would be seeing the President on his American trip and he said he hadn't asked to see him. I said I was certain that Nixon would want to. I asked him how he was getting on and he replied it was great fun and he enjoyed it. He is less dramatic and radical than he was a year or two ago when I last met him and presumably confidence is the thing he has got to build up now as Prime Minister.

I talked to Mrs Palme who is a child psychologist and very charming. Caroline said to Gerald Gardiner that the House of Lords was completely out of touch on education: he didn't understand but she made such an impression on him that the following day she got an invitation to go and have dinner with him at the House of Lords.

Thursday 9 April

I had a briefing for the coal debate. Went to the Cabinet where the discussion revolved around a *Daily Mail* story this morning that George Brown and Harold had wanted to go to war in the Middle East in 1967 but the Cabinet had stopped it.

What actually happened in 1967 was that when the UN forces were withdrawn on the insistence of Nasser, and the Egyptians began to take control of the Straits of Tirana again, there had been a move by Harold and George to send an international fleet up through the Straits of Tirana to assert the rights of international passage, and we had been trying to persuade the Norwegians to lead the procession. It was a ludicrous idea. The Americans were very keen to keep out of the row at that particular time, so when Harold went to Washington they made a big fuss of him in the hope, I think, that it would encourage him to go ahead. It looked like 1956 all over again.

In the event it didn't come off and the *Daily Mail's* story that we had thought of intervening by military force between the contestants when the Six Day War broke out is quite untrue. But Harold was determined to issue a statement denying it and this was agreed.

I opened the coal debate with a speech that had been written for me by the office, and I must say it was very dull. The House was almost empty as everyone knew there wasn't going to be a vote. I find the House of Commons very wearisome: I can't smoke, I get very sleepy, I don't listen to what is said. The whole thing is absolutely irrelevant in any but highly controversial debates and then they are usually so extreme in character that they too are unsatisfactory. I don't know what the answer is but maybe we need to have a new look at the House of Commons, even the Chamber itself.

Then I went to have a word with Roy Jenkins at Number 11 and he told me what was in the Budget, saying that he was telling one or two senior Ministers most involved. I thanked him and told him I appreciated it very much. There was no question of my being able to influence him at this stage, so I didn't argue but asked about little things and what the total effect would be. He asked me not to let anyone know that he had consulted me and particularly not to say anything at the Cabinet meeting on the Budget on Monday morning.

Funnily enough, last night at the Swedish Embassy he said to Caroline that I had done something for him a few months ago that he would never forget. I think this must have been at the Chequers meeting when everyone was bashing him and I stood up for him.

Back to the House of Commons where Ronnie Melville had arrived with Chris Hartley [Controller of Aircraft] and Frank Dogget [Deputy-Secretary of Aviation], in a great state of excitement. Denning Pearson wants to make a statement while I am in America on behalf of Rolls Royce that they are discontinuing work on the RB-211-50 series; this would be an absolutely major statement because it would mean the BAC-311 aircraft with a British engine was out, that we had nothing to offer to the European Airbus and that the Lockheed TriStar was also out, as far as Rolls engines were concerned. This would mean that BEA would have to buy a foreign aircraft with a foreign engine and the balance of payments implications of this would be very grave indeed.

I made it clear that Pearson was to be told not to do this, that I would go and see the French and German Ministers as soon as I could before we decided, and we would have a meeting of Ministers to consider this after I got back from America.

Friday 10 April

Sir William Armstrong came in this morning to say that he would like Sir David Pitblado to move to the Civil Service Department, and Sir Ronnie Melville to become Comptroller and Auditor-General, which is very funny. In those circumstances he felt it would be better if Otto Clarke remained for two or three years as my Permanent Secretary, which he was prepared to do. I said that was perfectly agreeable to me.

To Bristol. Mr Jeffries of BAC drove me to Filton where a four-engined Herald was waiting to take me up to Fairford. I got there and was kitted out in flying gear for my flight in Concorde 002. Brian Trubshaw, the chief test pilot, greeted me with the co-pilot and engineer and other members of the crew.

They had a suit all ready for me with W. BENN printed on the front. They gave me a parachute, strapped me into the plane and told me how to escape. It was an extremely uncomfortable seat; the poor navigator was sitting on an upturned bucket or something and trying to do his navigation in such a way as not to disturb me. I took a movie camera on board and they lent me a Sony VTR machine.

Finally we taxied away and began to take off. I was very tightly strapped in, my suit was too small and as we moved away I did wonder whether I wasn't being extremely silly; it would be ludicrous to be killed on a venture of this kind. It was only the fourth time that 002 was going to fly supersonic, so it was a genuine test flight and I had insisted that they treat it as such and take no notice of me. As we took off I was plugged into the intercom and could hear everything that was said. The only thing that went wrong was that the Nacelle doors around the undercarriage didn't close and they had to be put right.

Up we went, over the Isle of Man and Ulster and Stranraer, and then we turned and did a supersonic flight down the Irish Sea, but only at mach 1.05, so I don't think there was a bang. You couldn't feel anything. I took off my wristwatch and I thought I could just hear a faint tick even at supersonic speed. Then they did some tests. They kicked the rudder bar, rotated, turned, cut one engine right back, and so on. Then they came in and I heard a bump and thought they had put the undercarriage down but when I looked I found we had actually landed. I was unloaded, we got out of the plane and we found a mass of photographers. It was great fun. It took me back twenty-five years to the air force.

I changed and went to see the shop stewards from Filton, where there is an unofficial overtime ban over a £4 a week increase. I got my first unofficial and somewhat unusual opportunity to try persuasion in industrial disputes because the management wanted me to do it, and the shop stewards were prepared to talk to me. I made one mistake. I began by saying how serious this was, when I should have let them start and let each of them tell me what the position was. As they talked, I realised that the position was complicated and not entirely their fault. I told them how vital it was that Concorde should succeed and how awful it would be if I arrived in Washington and somebody said, 'What about this unofficial strike at Filton?' They are going to consider what to do at a meeting on Monday.

Tuesday 14 April
The first thing I heard on the news today was that Apollo 13 was in difficulty. Two of its fuel cells and oxygen and power supplies had failed and they had decided not to make a moon landing but to try to get back.

I said goodbye to Caroline, who went off to Cincinnati, and was taken to the airport where I met Bob Marshall, Ivor Manley, Richard Bullock,

Tony Newsome and Derek Moon from the Department. The plane was
late into Washington, with the result that we missed our appointment at
the NASA headquarters at 5. In fact, Dr Tom Paine, the Administrator
of NASA, had flown down to Houston because of the crisis with the
Apollo and so we were greeted by his Number Two, with the Associate
Administrator, the International Director and one or two others.

This first discussion centred upon British and European participation
in the shuttle and post-Apollo programme, and it became clear that
NASA were very keen on our involvement in their future space projects
in order to 'sell' them to the US Treasury. At the end I said I thought
that it was time that we all met together and I suggested that Tom Paine
or the International Director, Arnold Frutkin, or both, might come to
Europe for talks in the summer with the French and the Germans and
myself, quite informally, instead of doing a peripatetic journey around
each. This found general favour.

Wednesday 15 April
Up at 7 and had a bath and read my papers. At 8 John Freeman came
in. It was the first time I had had a long talk to him for eighteen months.
He is still inscrutable, very smart and well groomed and hard to get
through to. He is enjoying being Ambassador in Washington im-
mensely. His wife Catherine told me that he had ready access to
Kissinger in the White House and to William Rogers, the Secretary of
State, and that Nixon called him from time to time for advice.

John feels that his time has gone well. The relationship between his
predecessor, Pat Dean, and Lyndon Johnson was more or less non-
existent in the latter part of LBJ's presidency because Britain was in deep
economic difficulties, our attitude to the Vietnam War had made us
unpopular there, we were pulling out of Eastern Suez and generally
speaking it was the final phase of the burial of the 'special relationship'.
Now with John Freeman, they have got back a little on course, in that
Nixon wants to get advice, wants to talk directly to the men at the top,
and Britain's recovery and America's deeper difficulties have made the
relationship between the two subtly different. Our strong economy now
and the high quality of life in Britain have been features of this
developing relationship. In the pollution field we have a great deal that
we can teach them from our experience, or so they think.

John wanted to stress the need to go carefully on some of the sensitive
issues, particularly the computer issue, and also to be as positive as
possible in responding to the space request.

At 9 we went to the State Department and had a lengthy meeting with
a rotating Chairmanship, starting with Mr Herman Pollack, the
Director of International Scientific and Technological Affairs. We
discussed with him the problems of international technical collaboration

and I began to develop the point that here were great areas of common interest between the United States and Britain which were not reviewed under any existing procedures and that I thought there was a case for having some arrangements which could be as informal as possible. I listed six areas into which all our work naturally dropped, which constitute the beginnings, in effect, of the Ministry of Technology 'foreign policy'.

The first area is, of course, specifically bilateral Anglo-American relations into which the defence issues naturally fell.

The second is Britain and the European Economic Community and what effect our entry would have on relations with the United States and how the new, enlarged Europe would make its mark with the United States. In this category came the NASA space proposal and various aspects which were of concern to the United States and ourselves.

The third area of interest is the relationship between Britain and the Communist countries and I devoted a lot of time to explaining our technological agreements, why we were moving in that direction and the benefits and the problems that would flow from this. The COCOM discussions came into this area.

The fourth is the developing countries, in which area I was hoping to build up a programme: we had sent a mission without any aid content out to India which might be of interest to the US.

Fifth, international industrial issues of enormous significance covering the role of international companies: standards, safety regulations, pollution issues, and so on.

Finally, exchange and experience in handling our problems in our own countries, where we might have a great deal to learn from each other.

Pollack wrote all these down and we discussed the role of international companies. The point that has begun to emerge is that we are opening 'diplomatic relations' with Ford and General Motors and others because they are effectively sovereign states.

A former US Ambassador to Hungary then took over the chair. He looks after the whole of European affairs and he pursued our approach to Western Europe and its effect on our relations with the United States. He said there was some concern in the United States that Britain in the EEC would be more restrictive in trade policy. I tried to reassure them that we were now Europeans who crossed the Atlantic to talk to our American friends, rather than Anglo-Saxons who crossed the Channel to talk to our French and German and Continental friends. I think this subtle change of emphasis did help.

The question of defence procurement came up briefly and Nathaniel Samuels, the Deputy Under-Secretary of State for Economic Affairs, took over. This involved discussions about the 4/70 computer for

Moscow. I drew attention to the fact that President Nixon had been in Bucharest and Henry Ford was now in Moscow and it seemed a very natural area for us to move in, too. It was made pretty clear by Samuels, who is a very bright man, that the issue depended upon the US Defense Department and this was something on which we would have to deal with them directly.

We moved on to the Executive Office of the President where we discussed technology assessment. Immediately after lunch I was asked to open up the discussion. I said that, for many years, it had been thought that the alternative views of society were those propounded by Karl Marx and Henry Ford. But in fact this was no longer true in that the social problems created by Henry Ford's technology drove the community to collective solutions that might appear to owe more to the work of Marx. These thoughts were in my mind while Henry Ford was at this very moment with Kirillin in Moscow.

To the Department of Defense, where Solly Zuckerman, Ronnie Melville and a number of others joined us. They had put a room at our disposal, which was no doubt bugged, so that we could have a preliminary discussion about what we would be raising with them. I realised that this was going to be a very important and difficult meeting.

David Packard and John Foster, the Director of Research and Development, were there. Packard is a big, tough businessman who set up his own business in 1939 in California and has only recently come into the Defense Department in Washington. Foster is an attractive, bright, intellectual, no doubt with a liberal background, who has now become a hardliner. He has a twitch.

I stressed the enormous emphasis that we put on defence work, which was the biggest single block of work in the Ministry of Technology, and that in coming to the Pentagon I felt I was discussing this with them as a Defence Minister and that there were a number of issues that I would like to raise. I thanked them for helping us with aircraft like the Phantom and the C130, expressed pleasure that the Harrier was to be bought, but anxiety about the offset arrangement and how it was being used to keep out some goods that otherwise would have got in. Research and development had not proved successful because the United States was so rigid about the use of information acquired.

Then I talked about our interest in Lockheed. They said they thought Lockheed was going to be in very deep financial trouble for two or three years; they hoped to resolve the defence aspect, but they thought that the market for civil aircraft wouldn't stand up for some time. The airlines were not yet ready to order aircraft. Although they couldn't help us in any way, that was the best judgment they could give. Well, it does suggest that we ought not to do anything to help Rolls Royce to keep ahead with advanced engine work, while the demand is not at all certain.

We had a long discussion about the 4/70s for the Institute of Management Science in Moscow. I gave at length the background and the reason for our technological agreements with Eastern Europe and how we regarded this as a key case under the exceptions procedure in the COCOM agreement. Packard said this created great difficulties for them. They had looked at it very carefully. They knew we wanted to do this, but the sensitivity of the strategic balance was such that they couldn't contemplate doing anything to improve the Soviet capability. I interrupted to say I did not want to use the technological agreements to narrow the strategic gap which was in our favour but that this was really a civil case as far as we could determine it.

Then Packard said that the US Defense Intelligence view was different from ours and they had some evidence that people working at the Soviet Institute were in the defence field. I said our evidence was not of that kind, but that we recognised that you couldn't be 150 per cent certain, if you did supply a computer to Russia, that it wouldn't be used in some way or another for military purposes. But in this case the Russians had offered us an inspection as to 'end-use' – which was remarkable – and went further than anything that had ever been done before. I read out the conditions that ICL had been offered by Gvishiani and I think this slightly shook the Americans. I also pointed out that if the exceptions procedure meant anything at all, it really had to be applied fairly and this had been hanging around for a long time. In any case, there was a 4/70 available in the Gosplan office which had been cleared.

We pursued this matter at length. I said this was a very important interest of ours otherwise I wouldn't have raised it. There were political advantages of knowing about the development of their management systems and as far as I was concerned, if IBM wanted to go into this, it would be a perfectly fair competition and I would have no worries about it at all. The Russians would be in a position to choose. They disavowed any commercial interest here, which I disbelieve in general but about which, in any case, I am sure the Defense Department would not be too concerned.

Then we went on to discuss the point that Foster had made in a recent speech about the amount of Russian research and development in the defence field. This worried Foster very much. I said I thought you had to redefine vulnerability and when you had a society which could be undermined by a single open air concert by the Beatles in Moscow, this was not a society whose hardware need frighten us as much, perhaps, as we appear to think. I said I thought the weakness in Russia was their management problem and that if they had objected to the supply of the computer on the grounds that it raises the level of Russian management, I could have understood it. This surprised them. They said they would look at it again in view of what I had said but I didn't get the feeling that we'd made any impact.

We then came to the post-Apollo question and I asked their view. They said they were very sceptical of the space shuttle which they thought wouldn't come in for many more years, and would be much more expensive than the present systems. I got the feeling that NASA was just trying this on and had been told that it couldn't get any money unless it could find lots of customers. They didn't think it rated very highly with the most efficient rockets that they now had in service. This was really all I needed to know and I didn't press it much further.

I came back to the Embassy and I was pretty tired but I got my notes together.

At 6.30 I went over to the Embassy's Rotunda lecture theatre where about 150 people had been invited. I said I had never felt more unsure about quite what was of interest to them, because there had been a great transformation in Britain that we ourselves hadn't yet fully appreciated and I was sure they couldn't. I began with something cosy and familiar. I showed a picture of the Beefeaters and then the Beatles. Then I went on to show the extraordinary transformation in Britain's position with the disappearance of the Empire, our poor economic performance, and how it was that we had come to set up a Ministry of Technology and what it did. I went through some of our programmes including a mention of Concorde and the nuclear programme; then went on to describe our approach to Europe. I couldn't stop there because the impact of technology on society was so much greater than the impact of government upon technology and I tried to explain exactly how I saw the growth of machine power and its impact on ordinary people. Finally, I showed my redistribution of decision-making chart. There were some good questions and I enjoyed it.

After that, I had dinner with Foster and Packard of the Defense Department and Arnold Frutkin of NASA. Frutkin was much franker after dinner than he had been in the discussions. Clearly NASA just needs money and support in order to sell its programme. I said, 'Why don't you move into other areas like dealing with urban problems?' Quite honestly they are too difficult for NASA. They need skills that NASA hasn't got with its high technology and scientific staff. The current trouble with the Apollo programme which, incidentally, is going rather better now, is all part of the extra difficulty they will face.

Thursday 16 April

Talks all day at the Department of Commerce. Maurice Stans, the Secretary, greeted us. Myron Tribus, the Assistant Secretary, who had heard me last night, was very warm and friendly and Stans gave me an inscribed medallion commemorating my visit. Stans is really an old-time politician who wanted the job of Secretary, having been Director of the Bureau of the Budget under Eisenhower, and I got the feeling that he was licked.

I came back and slept for about half an hour. I was hoping to get a word with Tom Paine on the phone to Houston but this had not been achieved and I had tea with Catherine Freeman, a sort of left-wing socialite who just loves every minute of the Embassy in Washington. She said that John [Freeman] was looking beyond the job here to see what we would be doing if we lost the Election, since he really didn't think he would be asked to stay on by Heath. The question is, at fifty-five, what is the last job a man does? I said I thought the Chairmanship of the BBC would be a marvellous thing if it were available. She thought John hadn't considered it. I said, 'Well it's not a problem confined to him, we may all have it.' But I didn't think we would lose the Election. We walked a little in the beautiful garden: Washington now looks excellent with all the cherry blossom out.

Friday 17 April

Arrived at the Atomic Energy Commission at 9.15 and we were met by Dr Glenn Seaborg the Chairman, and one of the Commissioners, and a very charming man, Dr Clarence Larson of Union Carbide, who had recently been in Australia discussing the supply of enriched uranium to the Australians for their new reactor and a Dr Theos Thompson, who had been over to Capenhurst in connection with the gas centrifuge research and development problems. I had with me Bob Marshall and my team. Seaborg had been at my lecture on Wednesday night and asked for sets of my slides.

We discussed first of all the centrifuge. They expressed anxieties about proliferation and I said that I recognised the dangers but we had taken the view that with this very sensitive technology now becoming much more widely understood, the position was best safeguarded by operating under multilateral arrangements.

On Non-Proliferation Treaty safeguards, they said that there had been some difference of emphasis between the United States and Britain and they hoped we would keep closely together. I explained that this was a matter on which the Foreign Office took the lead: I was the technical adviser. They would understand that politically we were anxious to work within the European framework in order to underline the seriousness of our application to the European Communities which include Euratom. I said I would have to opt out of comment on the exact development of our policy because this was the Foreign Office responsibility, but I didn't really see much difference of view between us.

We went on to the question of the reorganisation of the nuclear industry. They asked me many questions about British Nuclear Fuels Ltd and I explained that it was covered by the Official Secrets Act with limited access and proper police facilities, so that there was no risk here of any weakness on the security side. They were reasonably satisfied, although having worked with the AEA for many years, this is quite a big change.

All in all, it was a very good meeting in that they had their top people and I have now been in the business long enough to know and understand it all on the political level, at any rate. It was well worthwhile and a great investment in goodwill.

From the Atomic Energy Commission, we went to the Department of Transportation where we were greeted by John Volpe, the Secretary of State for Transportation, and the Administrator of the Federal Aviation Agency and a number of other senior officials. This is a new Department and Volpe is the former Governor of Massachussetts, a very shrewd political animal, the man who founded and organised a big company, Volpe Construction, rather the early 'Marples' of the new administration.

I began by saying that we were both members of a very small club of nations that were building supersonic transport, and therefore had common interests in that. We were also both representatives of countries where anxiety about the environment was rising to a very high level of concern and we had to balance these factors.

They had today promulgated a draft rule banning supersonic flights over land but this was to keep it out of the hands of Congress and to forestall any possibility of an attempt to legislate against SST.

Afterwards we went to the National Academy of Sciences for lunch at the request of Samuels of the State Department. While we were there, the splashdown of Apollo 13 took place and we watched it on colour television in the National Academy of Sciences room. It was a very moving occasion with lots of people from the office watching intently as the parachutes opened, the capsule landed in the water and the men were brought onto the ship.

Then I went and packed. Had a word with Catherine Freeman and took some movies on the lawn. David Frost, who now works in America, and Catherine Freeman really fit into the international celebrity set, and I should think John Freeman is very much a creature of the Kennedy-type administration. But I daresay this is what Britain needs. They are certainly better than the stiff old Foreign Office people who have been there before.

Catherine told me yesterday about the visit of the Duke and Duchess of Windsor to the US. They had lunch at the White House and there had been an absolute flurry of telegrams from Buckingham Palace telling the Ambassador that under no circumstances was he to call the Duchess of Windsor 'Her Royal Highness' or bow to her or allow her to be curtsied to. The White House had enquired about this and had to be briefed and Nixon had begun his welcome by saying, 'Your Royal Highness and friends'. John Freeman behaved properly but Catherine said that she curtsied and said 'Your Royal Highness'. This very much pleased the Duke who was still an ageing boy with really a rather pathetic manner about him, Catherine said. He gave again the story of his love affair, how he had been sorry to leave Britain, but he had met a wonderful American girl and had made her very happy. It was the old old love story. Royalty is not exactly the most important aspect of Anglo-American relations but you have to recognise that the royal family are part of the international celebrity scene.

I went with Ivor Manley to the airport and flew off to Cincinnati. Got here at 8.45 and Caroline met me and the spring had really arrived. It was a lovely warm evening and we felt as if the twenty-one years since I first came over had passed unnoticed.

Monday 20 April

Up at 5.45. Took a taxi downtown and flew to Los Angeles where we were met by the Consul-General who had been in China and was a most aggressive talker. In the car he talked all the way along the coast up to Santa Barbara.

We got to the General Electric think tank which Tom Paine of NASA used to run. It is really a multi-disciplinary group of scientists, economists and others tackling a variety of problems: investment, the economics of nuclear ships, development in other countries. They have a contract from the Pentagon to study Chinese technology. They are the kind of people that would be found, if at all in Britain, within Whitehall. They obviously hope to get a contract from me.

Tuesday 21 April

Caroline and I had breakfast in our room. Then Pasadena, for the visit to California College of Technology – Caltech – which has a very close relationship with the Pentagon and other Washington Departments as well as the big aerospace firms. It is really a super-super selective school that began as a technical college. It has nine Nobel prizewinners to its credit and I began to feel a bit uneasy about higher education if this is the way it's going.

At lunch Caroline and I separated. She went with a Lockheed driver to see the Watts district of Los Angeles, which is the black ghetto, and some schools, and I went to Lockheed, where I saw the mock-up of the Lockheed 1011 Tri-Star, the wide-bodied aircraft. Then I sat down with Dan Haughton and Kotchian, the President of Lockheed, and other executives. They are all men in their late fifties, if not early sixties, and they look older than they are. They presented the Lockheed programme and the huge Galaxy transport plane which will hold up to 900 troops. Then they flew us down to Palmdale to see the 1011 production line just beginning and some of the Galaxies.

We flew back and had a final talk with Dan Haughton. They said that Lockheed's finance problems would be solved and the Pentagon would not want the company to fold though the amount of money involved is absolutely enormous. They clearly were worried about how they were going to get it.

Dinner in Beverly Hills and Haughton told stories and I made a speech in which I said how I valued the relations with Lockheed and how they had always been absolutely straight with us, how my interest was not as an engineer but in what engineering was doing for the world.

Wednesday 22 April

To Los Angeles airport and flew to Chicago. We just had time to change for a dinner given by the Consul-General. There were two chaps from Northwestern University, Ralph Burton and Dean Owen. Owen, a Welshman, was part of the brain drain, now the Dean of the Centre of Interdisciplinary Studies. Ralph Burton had been in London with the Office of Naval Research, which is obviously the American technical and scientific espionage centre in Britain. They knew a great deal about Mintech. We talked to the President of the University of Chicago, who had just been to Washington to see Nixon about the problems in the university campuses in America which are now reaching astronomical proportions. Winford Ellis, who was the former President of the British American Chamber of Commerce in Chicago, was much more anxious to attack the university than he was to attack a visiting socialist Minister.

Thursday 23 April

Caroline went to Malcolm X Community College with her close friend, Phyllis, and I went to Northwestern, a private university keen to establish itself firmly as one of the great universities of the United States. They laid on a tremendous press conference (although I had nothing to say) and television interviews. Then I had a brief talk with the people running the interdisciplinary studies group on urban problems, linking economics with sociology, and bio-medical research with engineering, and so on.

But again I got the feeling that here were a lot of highly-paid intellectuals desperately trying to find something to do now that the big defence money was drying up. Caroline meanwhile had been at the Malcolm X Community College where there were no resources, plum in the middle of an area with real problems and that was much more significant in some ways than what Northwestern were working on.

I gave my lecture, basically my *Horizon* talk, on the social control of technology and had to dash from there to New York, where Caroline had dinner in the hotel room while I went to the Consul-General's dinner party. There were $37 billion worth of businessmen there. On my right was an interesting man, Robert Murphy, who had been an Under-Secretary of State under Eisenhower and a representative of the American Government in the Middle East during the Suez crisis. He said that although, of course, he had been opposed to Eden's and Alexander's plans to invade Egypt, he couldn't understand why, having decided to do it, we didn't get on with it, why we stoped when we did: this was 'realpolitik' of a very direct kind and I daresay that's what the French felt. This was why Eden failed.

Opposite me was the head of the consultants McKinsey's, who said he thought that in Britain we had more experience of running a govern-ment and industry, and of the relations between public and private sectors, than any other country in the world. He was really after running a weekend school in the UK at which the McKinsey people could examine what we were doing.

Friday 24 April
Lord Caradon [Hugh Foot], the British representative at the UN, came to breakfast in the hotel. His great desire is to take a British initiative at the UN this year, its twenty-fifth anniversary year. He said he had originally thought there might be a British initiative in checking the arms trade but this had been vetoed by the Foreign Office, no doubt because we are doing so much of it ourselves. Then he had another idea for a Science Committee of the General Assembly and he was working on this.

In the evening I was on the David Frost Show. Noël Coward was the first to be interviewed followed by Dr Reuben who had just written a book called *Everything You Always Wanted to Know About Sex But Were Afraid to Ask*, then Lulu the pop star, then me.

When I was brought in I said that technology was like sex: when you had the desire, you didn't have the opportunity and when you had the opportunity you didn't have the desire; that, like sex, we were all obsessed with technology; and that it all happened in the mind. I tried to demonstrate that if you were determined to control technology you could and I gave some examples – London clean air and the return of fish in the Thames, now that it has been cleaned up.

We caught a BOAC VC10 for London at midnight.

Saturday 25 April
We slept on the way to London, got to the airport at 11.45 and heard that Joshua was in the West London Hospital, where Mother had put him thinking he had appendicitis. We found him bouncing about and brought him home again.

I took Hilary with me in the HS125 to Manchester to give the Roscoe Lecture* which was in fact the same text as I had used in Chicago on the social control of technology.

Monday 27 April
Joshua went back to school today. Caroline wrote hundreds of letters; the typewriter is defective and the drying machine and washing machine are playing up. We are all a bit disenchanted with technology.

There has been a bit of trouble about whether civil servants are allowed to meet Tory Shadow Ministers. Otto has accused Harold of stopping them and Harold denied it but does want to know who is meeting whom. My view is to be very liberal about this but I had to fall into line and said that Otto was to notify Sir Burke Trend of any contacts that he or other civil servants had with the Tory Party.

Tuesday 28 April
We have all been worried about kidnapping attempts because Gerald Nabarro's daughter has been threatened, and so we told the children to be very careful going to and from school.

To SEP where we discussed the flood risk to London. Over the next seven or eight years there is a one in five chance that the river will rise one inch over the walls for one hour, which would cause the most appalling death and destruction. I suggested that there should be an emergency dam, some inflatable structure which would keep the water back while we were waiting for the major barrage to be completed.

Wednesday 29 April
Went to the Management Committee and we devoted a lot of it to the Election timing. The polls are moving heavily in our favour now and a consensus in favour of a June Election seems to be emerging.

Thursday 30 April
Lord Rootes came to tell me that the name of Rootes is being changed to Chrysler in Britain and that Chrysler are putting a lot more money in. It was very obliging of him to come.

I had a political lunch with all my chaps and asked them to give me

* 'Learning to use Power.' See Appendix IV.

their comments on the issues on which Mintech might most successfully fight if there was an early Election.

To the Electricity Council building for the reception for science attachés at the London Embassies. I asked Harry Slater to fix it in our new building overlooking the river. As well as the European attachés I met the Russians and the Chinese. The Chinese thanked me very much for my message congratulating them on the launch of their satellite and I said I would very much like to visit China. They said this might be possible. My guess is that the Chinese are worried about being at odds with both the Russians and the Americans at the same time and are therefore looking for friends. This corresponds with the impression that I got from talking to the Yugoslavs last year. They said that Chinese-Yugoslav relations were improving.

At an appropriate moment I jumped up on a chair and thanked them for having come and, as a year from now there might be an Election coming (at which there was laughter), I thought I would take this opportunity of describing what we were doing. We were really building a new relationship between peoples free of controversy in technology and when the Americans or the Russians or Chinese do well in technological terms we are all pleased. I jumped off the chair and disappeared back to the House.

Sunday 3 May

After lunch I went to Colston Hall, Bristol, where Harold Wilson was speaking. The place was packed and they were cheering and stamping and interrupted numerous times with applause. No doubt Gerald Kaufman kept count. If Harold had dissolved Parliament during his speech they would have torn up the chairs and marched on Westminster. A marvellous meeting.

Then I came back on the train with Harold. He was mainly concerned with his own standing vis-à-vis Heath and his own treatment at the hands of the BBC, which continues to obsess him.

Monday 4 May

I spent the whole morning being cross-examined by the Select Committee on Science and Technology on the Government's computer policy. I have had more than my share of that select committee. It was a long and arduous experience but well worthwhile.

After lunch Otto and Charles Smith and other staff came in to present the problems with Concorde, which are formidable – escalation of cost, delays, refusal by the firms to have any incentive contracts on production or to bear any loss, anxieties with the French, a strike which has delayed flights of 002, and so on. It is very worrying. Ronnie

Melville has been indicating his anxieties in little minutes to me which I have begun to suspect are for the record.

Then he broke in to say, 'Well, Minister, I must tell you that my advice is that we cancel Concorde. I have come to the view we must cancel. It is not an economic aircraft,' (of course it never had been), 'and unless there is some overwhelming national or prestige reason for us to keep it we should cancel.' He said that I was not to believe the figures that were coming from his officials. They always went up, and so on and so on – he really lost control.

So I said, 'Well, this is a very serious thing to state, and you will confirm, I hope, that this is the first time you have said it to me,' and he replied, 'Yes.' Ivor Manley noted that. Then I adjourned the meeting.

Afterwards I had a talk with Otto and told him I was very uneasy about this because it looked as though Ronnie had been building up to a break and this was the most embarrassing moment to do it: I didn't object that he had come to that conclusion, but he could have informed me in a different way.

Otto tried to defend him, saying that Ronnie was very upset and felt it was his duty to give me notice in advance of the report so that I didn't wait for the report to come. But I think Otto himself was pretty worried about what had happened. I said I thought this would make it very difficult for Ronnie to become Comptroller and Auditor-General, which was the job that had been set aside for him, because he would be investigating a project which he had himself masterminded and on which he changed his mind at a late stage.

Tuesday 5 May

A Cabinet on Cambodia and Michael Stewart began by making the most rigid speech. The decision of the Americans to march into Cambodia has triggered off the most tremendous demonstrations in the United States and here we are on the eve of an Election with the possibility of a revolt in the PLP.

There was in fact something of a consensus at Cabinet. I spoke and I said that I thought a formal statement would not be enough, that it wouldn't meet the public mood. We really couldn't support the Americans this time. Dissociation would mean washing our hands. The US policy had really failed. But for Nixon to admit this would be almost impossible because it would be the first US defeat abroad and it would look as though it were a surrender to domestic pressure. It could trigger off a great lack of confidence at home and abroad and therefore we must speak candidly to the US as a friend.

Friday 8 May

While I was in the USA, the polls began to turn in our favour. There are now five polls: Marplan, NOP, Gallup, ORC and the Lou Harris poll in the *Express*, which on average indicate a 3 per cent lead for us. Talked to David Butler at the BBC studios last night. He said that on polling day we should have between a 1 per cent and a 5 per cent lead, which would be a Labour majority of between nine and eighty-nine.

The Tories are obviously pinning a lot of hopes on making some success in the marginals. But certainly at the moment of dictating my diary the position is extremely good – far better than we dreamed possible, and the enormous number of seats we won last night in the municipal elections take us back in popularity to 1966 when we had a Labour majority of 100. So there has been a complete recovery of our fortunes and most people are now talking about a June Election, although there are still a few people who think it would be wrong to take the risk.

Ron Hayward, the National Agent, came to a sandwich lunch. He is a very nice man and he has done extremely well in the less than two years since he has been National Agent. He has thoroughly improved the atmosphere in Transport House and the constituencies, he has made some powerful speeches and won over the Left without upsetting the Right: the old Sara Barker musty image is completely gone. He said to me that I would be Leader of the Party in ten years' time, simply on a statistical basis, which I think is unlikely, but not impossible.

Saturday 9 May

I agreed today that Herbert Rogers would have to be the Election Agent again. Herbert said I ought to give £500 guarantee to the local Party, which I agreed to do, against the expenses.

Monday 11 May

I had a briefing meeting on the situation at Palmers shipbuilding yard in Jarrow, now owned by Vickers. It was famous in the Thirties, because it was the closure of the Palmers yard which brought the Jarrow marchers down to London, and so it has tremendous emotional overtones for us.

Sir Leslie Rowan, Chairman of Vickers, had come last March to tell me they wanted to close it immediately and I had persuaded them to keep it open for a bit. Then they decided to issue the redundancy notices for this coming Friday and I wanted to hold it back, and try and keep it open till we had an opportunity to look at the ship repairing position generally. Of course, with an Election coming, we have an added reason for trying to keep it open.

We agreed on the general line, which was that we would try to persuade Vickers to postpone the closure and get some naval work from the Ministry of Defence for it. There is a Fleet Auxiliary vessel to be ordered in August which is now out to competitive tender. So we are going to hope for the best but that is as much as we can do at the moment.

Tuesday 12 May

Caroline was writing an article for the *Sunday Times*. She is now on the ILEA and is being nominated also for the Chairmanship of the Board of Governors of Holland Park.

I went to the Campaign Committee and the papers this morning described the new little plasticine figures of Tory politicians, called 'Yesterday's Men', which were designed by Alan Aldridge and taken on by David Kingsley and Peter Davies, for use on posters. They really are fantastic publicity people working for us.

In the afternoon I had an impressive deputation of trade union officials and local MPs from Jarrow and Newcastle, pleading with me to try to save the yard. I couldn't promise anything but said I would do my best.

Went to the House in the evening and the NOP today had a 7.5 per cent Labour lead, which has staggered everyone.

Wednesday 13 May

I went to Transport House at 8.30 this morning for a publicity meeting with the advertising people and Percy Clark. They are a very bright crowd and I suggested we might meet every morning at that time. They are putting out a little booklet, based on the German Social Democrat series, 'Why I am voting Labour'. A number of celebrities, among them Sybil Thorndike and Jackie Charlton, are included as well as Barbara, Roy and myself. They are also doing a poster based on members of the Government talking in real situations, so they are sending a photographer this week to take a picture of me while I am in Jarrow.

Went to Euston Road and met the NUM. Lawrence Daly, the General Secretary, was present. They talked very frankly, and criticised the fuel policy: in fact I am doubtful as to whether we have pursued the right line.

Thursday 14 May

We had an Inner Cabinet this morning, and after a long talk it was agreed that the Election would be 18 June. We had a full Cabinet meeting following that, and I was given clearance to use some money for Jarrow, provided I didn't commit the Government to maintain Vickers for ever.

Jack Diamond came over and agreed to let me have £100,000.

I called Yapp of Vickers to tell him this and he was a bit surprised that I had got a decision so quickly. He said he would consider it.

Friday 15 May
Got up at 6 and flew to Newcastle. Had breakfast with Tom Urwin and Ernie Fernyhough [Labour MPs for Houghton-le-Spring and Jarrow] and brought them up to date. Then we went to Palmers yard and first of all had a meeting with the management who were absolutely incompetent. They didn't know how much money they had lost or what their costings were, they knew nothing and it is no wonder the business has got into the state it has. I met the Shipbuilding and Engineering Unions people who were, by contrast, extremely competent, and I told them what I was prepared to offer, then I met the men, who offered to support anything we found necessary to do, and we walked round the yard. We discovered that management were very angry that we had been round the yard, but we went and spoke to them and they still agreed that they would withhold the redundancy notices.

Saturday 16 May
Worked in the morning and then in the evening Melissa came with me to Felixstowe for a rally. There were about 650 people there and they were all very excited: everyone is now expecting the Election.

Sunday 17 May
Meeting of the Cabinet and NEC which had been planned some time ago. It was obvious as soon as we gathered at Number 10 that this was going to be the meeting for launching arrangements for the manifesto, and everyone there expected the Election would come on June 18. Harold opened by saying there would be an announcement soon.

Alice Bacon paid a tribute to Denis Lyons, Peter Davies and David Kingsley and described the 'Life and Soul' theme which began last September, and the 'Yesterday's Men' figures, and this idea is to be followed soon by the posters of 'Labour's winning team'. She said the Election publicity was more or less ready.

Tom Driberg wanted policy depicted on posters and Harry Nicholas said that in law the Election began nineteen working days before polling day and described the legal position. Bill Simpson thought we should try to localise the campaign as much as we could, and Harold said we could use our own advertising in our constituencies, if we pay for it. Percy Clark said the posters on 'the winning team' would be in the form of a leaflet as well, to be used around the country.

Ron Hayward described the trade union liaison, said that all was ready, and although there was a shortage of funds and membership was low, the local government successes had boosted morale. Harry Nicholas said Transport House would give each constituency £200 and Mikardo said Ministers should give Transport House blocks of time for speaking during the Election. Ted Short said, 'Don't forget the Colleges of Education when you go round.'

Then at 11.25 we came on to policy and Harold said we should have to deal with the comparison of our record with the Tory record, with future Labour policy and Tory policy as it had emerged at Selsdon Park. The Tories of course wanted to fight the Election on our record. He said the achievements of the Government would be issued as a guide by Transport House, that we should attack the Tory record and not Tory personalities, that future policy would be laid out in the manifesto and the Government would have to play a large part in writing it. As taxation and public expenditure were going to be key issues, the policies produced must be in line with our public expenditure forecasts.

Mikardo said that it was clear that Tory advertising was going to concentrate on our credibility and this we would have to deal with in our campaign.

We moved on to home policy and Frank Allaun said tax rebates would be paid in July, which should help us, and we must pledge help on housing, supplementary benefits and prescription charges. Tony Crosland took the themes that had been suggested by Transport House in their document and said that equality, participation, the environment, the gap between rich and poor, and particularly a campaign against poverty would be perfectly fair themes.

I was called and I said that I hoped we could introduce some slightly different thinking, in that as a Party we had always concentrated on the management aspects of government, organisation, allocation of resources, but in fact there was a change in the approach and attitude of people as they got better off. We ought to focus our attention much more on people and try to relate all the policies we were bringing forward to the development of the human personality: education, for example, and the undervaluing of experience and the failure built in to our educational system; information – people were not told enough; communications, which were still appalling; the environment; decision-making; bureaucracy. We ought to concentrate more on the average and less on the so-called outstanding. We wanted to get across the idea of partnership and that the future was something people built for themselves, and justice by instalments was the only way democracy could work. If we were going to get away from authoritarianism, which people wouldn't accept any more, whether from bishops or popes, industrialists or Ministers, we had to get some sense of community responsibility. This would be a major political revolution.

Judith Hart talked about the need for participation and grass-roots democracy: the young should be treated as adults, and Britain was a marvellous place to live in (which it is).

Then Ted Short made a very important speech on education. He said he thought it was the major theme and the manifesto should highlight it. The starting point should be that every child was born with a potential and the keynote should be the expansion of opportunity for children, because this was their birthright and was necessary for the community. He said the Green Paper was almost ready, dealing with the comprehensives, higher education and the need to bring parents and teachers more closely into the running of the schools. He talked about the strategy for lengthening the school life, that everyone must get eleven years and that places in higher education would be doubling over the next ten or eleven years.

He referred to the opening of the Open University, the ending of selection, the improvement of the quality of the teaching profession, the need for smaller classes, and said that by September this year for the first time all classes over forty would have gone and we should aim for a limit of thirty. There were certain remaining problems: slum schools and the independent schools, to which he was in favour of making no reference but squeezing them after the Election. He was particularly keen that we shouldn't get bogged down on the independent schools but said that by inspection and control we should be able to deal with them.

Joan Lestor said we had to identify with young people and dictate the issues in the Election – the pre-school years were important, and race relations, not immigration, were now the issue.

That was the end of the morning session and after lunch we went into the garden in euphoric mood and I took some lovely movie pictures of the Cabinet.

Roy Jenkins opened the afternoon session, saying he had had an easier job than he expected because he had been wanting to urge that we shouldn't put specific tax proposals in the manifesto. On the broad public expenditure theme he said the Tories had lost credibility by their proposals. 'Don't let's rival them. Some of the proposals put forward in the course of the morning would cost a great deal of money. If we put in proposals we would have to cost them and that would put us in difficulty.' He said the position had changed because the economic picture had changed; only a year ago, in May 1969, the picture had been very grave.

There was a general assent to this and Frank Allaun said, 'If we don't make reference to a wealth tax, will it be ruled out?' Roy said, 'No, not at all.'

Then we had George Brown, and when he's good he's marvellous. He talked about the manifesto, and said it was a record, it described our aims, attitudes and intentions, and our intentions had to be spelt out. We must have some commitments. The activists must have meat and we had to get the themes right. The themes were social equality, the attack on poverty, quality of life and participation. The manifesto, when written into a record by the next Government, becomes the basis by which we are judged.

Harold agreed with George. He said we mustn't be guided by public opinion polls (I must say that was a bit of a laugh because Harold lives by them), and we didn't have to prove ourselves this time. Prices were the biggest single issue and he thought we might deal with that by referring to the fact that the Tories have opposed us all along the line on our ways of controlling prices, that the Tories' present policies would lead to far higher prices, VAT and the end of council house subsidies. It was very important, he said, that the Tories shouldn't be allowed to forget Selsdon Park. Our manifesto must not be achievements plus promises: what we want is the idea of a developing Government illustrated by what we have done, by what the Tories did, and by what we aim to do.

Mikardo, an excellent chairman, wound up, saying there would be no vote of gratitude, people wanted a sense of urgency and we would have to convey it.

Then we came to foreign policy. Michael Stewart began with a long speech in which he said we had to adjust to the real world; the Tory illusion of a world role for Britain was unrealistic; our approach to Europe was very important; Britain must neither be an aggressor nor a runaway; we wanted to conciliate and relax tension and defence was the key to relaxation of tension. We had played a large part in that relaxation, in disarmament and the NATO conference.

He said that race relations affected our relations with the developing world, and that aid was important. On the United Nations we had a good story to tell. Finally he said, 'If I may turn from foreign policy to the Party generally, our rock is the decent working man and he believes in less for the rich and more for the poor.' Then he produced a phrase which was pure Clem Attlee. He said, 'The decent British working man says to us, "We'll look after the underdog if you'll look after the dirty dog." ' By that he meant the criminals, and we must stand up for Britain and its fundamental decencies of democracy and freedom.

This was greeted with some applause because it was very straight and direct and it was Michael at his very best.

Denis Healey said, very crudely, that the manifesto didn't matter, we couldn't inject new ideas at this stage because it would have to be a book we were writing. We can't tax people for overseas aid. He had saved £3,000 million already on defence and £2,000 million on expenditure. Real cuts had occurred, people cared about security, the army was the most efficient and had the highest morale in the world, and the purpose of defence was to stop war and to stop people killing each other. He believed Britain was a country to be proud of.

This theme of Britain being a country to be proud of emerged from quite a lot of what was said.

After tea, George Thomson said that race and aid were very important and the less said about the Common Market in the Election the better, because we shall negotiate toughly but in good faith and we shall be negotiating from strength. He felt he was walking tall in Europe. Walter Padley said the timing of the Election, if it came early, would keep the EEC out of the arena.

Harold Wilson had a word about the manifesto and laid down who should be on the joint committee to supervise it: Harry Nicholas, Gwyn Morgan, Peter Shore, George Brown, Jim Callaghan, Denis Healey, Douglas Houghton, Mik, myself and a few others. Four people would be drafting the manifesto – Gwyn Morgan, Terry Pitt, Peter Shore and Tom McNally, the International Secretary.

That was the end of the meeting. Afterwards, Ministers went to the Cabinet room and Harold said he just wanted to let us know officially that he was going to see the Queen tomorrow and at 6 o'clock would announce the dissolution of Parliament. He gave us the timetable for the Election, with Parliament meeting the week after next and being dissolved on 29 May, polling day on 18 June. There would be no full Cabinet during the coming week. Jim Callaghan warned us that there was too much euphoria and we would have quite a battle ahead of us and it would start on prices and rents. Jim has this terrible problem of the South African cricket tour, where the Cricket Council have so far absolutely declined to change their attitude.

I went to see Mother after the meeting and came home to begin working on Election plans.

Monday 18 May

Charles Smith looked in this morning for a word about the BAC-311 and the RB-211; I told him the Election was to be on 18 June and we would have to defer all decisions till after the Election.

Then the Chairman of the CEGB, Sir Stanley Brown, came in to see me with the Chief Nuclear Inspector, Trevor Griffiths, for a very serious interview. The Hartlepool power station is to go nuclear and one of the consortia produced designs for an advanced gas-cooled reactor which Mr Griffiths, an engineer, thought were unsatisfactory; he thought the apertures were too great and if there was a serious failure the disaster would be calamitous. The metal doors covering the metal apertures were not sufficiently strong and he was in favour of a concrete pressure-vessel type construction.

He had tried to get the consortium to change the design, but they had declined to do so, as had the CEGB, and he advised me not to authorise and approve the continuation of the work. Stanley Brown is a big, tough, straightforward engineer and I had to say to him, 'Look, you will appreciate that I have got a Chief Nuclear Inspector and I can't possibly disregard his advice.'

Stanley Brown said, 'Will you let us go on with the work and I'll review the problem later?'

'No, I won't,' I replied. 'If you go on now, the pressure to accept less than adequate safety standards will be very strong, because you will have got that much further with the project.'

So he asked, 'Will you get a second opinion?'

I said, 'No, I can't. If my Chief Nuclear Inspector had said he thought something was safe and *I* was uneasy I might get advice to cross check what he says, but if he says it is not safe, I can't conceivably get somebody else in and then override his view.'

He then tried to get Griffiths to say what he would accept and Griffiths said, 'No, I am saying I won't accept this. You will have to put in other plans.'

So he left and then I did a run round with Jack Rampton, my Deputy Secretary, and Griffiths. These are the nuclear problems in a nutshell: first of all, the corrosion problem of the Magnox stations hasn't been solved and it is not impossible that they may have to be closed down early; second, it now appears that there is corrosion in advanced gas-cooled reactors and we haven't got anywhere near a solution for that; third, there is the dissatisfaction with plans for the Hartlepool power station; and fourth, Dungeness B, being built by a consortium made up of Fairey Engineering and International Combustion which has just fallen down on the job, is going to be three years late. All this constitutes a major nuclear policy problem. After the Election we shall have to re-examine the whole thing and see where we stand.

In the afternoon I drove to Bristol with all my Election gear. There was a local Party meeting, at which Herbert was appointed agent, and I was reselected.

Tuesday 19 May

I caught a light plane and flew to Coventry where I was met by Gilbert Hunt and the Rootes people for a presentation of the work of Chrysler, as it is soon to be known in Britain. They have overcome some of their problems and the Avenger is a very successful motor car. Went to Stoke after lunch where the engines are built and I met the trade unions and shop stewards – a very bright and intelligent but critical lot. They said to me, 'You've been conned, you've had the wool pulled over your eyes.' I hit back and said I hadn't, but this breakdown of communication was really appalling. The company should give the shop stewards a presentation, exactly of the kind they have given me; there is no reason why not.

This is the way forward in industry. I have no doubt about it. You have got to recognise that the shop stewards do now represent power in factories and you have to deal with them and give them higher status in your thinking than the customers or the shareholders because they are the guys that build the product.

I caught the helicopter back to London and just got to Peter Shore's office for a long meeting on the manifesto. Everybody was in a bad temper, and there was a flaming row about whether it was right or not. A draft had been submitted and my general theme was that a manifesto ought to be a letter to your constituents, very much more informal and Mik agreed. George said the Party had to commit itself firmly. I think Peter found it a very useless meeting, but I thought it was worthwhile.

Wednesday 20 May

Went to the Publicity Group at Transport House at 8.30, where they are working on leaflets and posters, and I helped with some of the slogans.

A meeting on Mintech 'foreign policy' with Otto and Charles Smith, Bob Marshall, Harry Slater, and the head of the international department, who is an absolute flop. I had asked them to do a run round of the international business that we do and I had dictated a little minute trying to connect it along the lines of my Western European/ Eastern European / American / developing countries / Chinese / international company thinking, linking it with the Economic Commission for Europe and the UN. I got an absolutely negative response. They said it wasn't practicable, it would run counter to the idea of the nation state, it would get us into difficulties promoting British interests, relations between government and industry weren't any closer in Britain than they were in other countries – just no, no, no, all along the line. Well, since I knew I couldn't decide anything before the Election I let it ride and laughed a bit. That was about the last serious policy talk I am going to have before the Election, and clearly they think I will move.

Then we had a meeting of my Private Office Pink Shirt Club with the secretaries, and Kate Chaplin, who is an honorary member, Charlie Graves, Ron Vaughan, Derek Moon, and Sylvia Davies from the press office, and others.

Tuesday 26 May

Hilary was in bed with a cold after a pop concert.

I went at 8.30 to the Publicity Group meeting at Transport House and we talked about the problems of the Wall Street price collapse which we thought might overtake us, and we discussed prices and how to handle them and agreed that one of the best ways of doing it would be to draw attention to the standard of living rather than simply the cost of living.

At 10, to the National Executive to discuss the manifesto in detail. We had a considerable argument about whether or not we ought to put a wealth tax in the programme. We agreed to a form of words that indicated that we believed in greater equality in terms of income but that didn't commit us to any particular method.

At 2, I went back to the office and Mr Yapp of Vickers came to see me. I had a stiff talk with him about Palmers yard. I was trying to persuade him to accept £100,000 and a ship from the MOD for repair to keep the yard open till the autumn. Of course, the Election was a factor in my mind but the thing that had really shaken me about the Palmers yard was the very poor quality of the management, the failure to provide any figures showing how it was going and the feeling that this might be the tip of the iceberg of the ship repairing industry generally.

Thursday 28 May
To Bristol, where the major political problem at the moment is that the envelopes for the Election addresses, which Herbert Rogers ordered a week ago from the regional organiser, have got lost on their way down from Newcastle.

Friday 29 May
The envelope problem is still serious and also there is a great crisis because my Election address is too complicated to be done as quickly as I had wanted and we went around to different printers to get prices for them. It is going to be expensive, and can they be produced in time?

In the afternoon Caroline and Joshua set out from London but the diesel train broke down and so they missed the first part of my adoption meeting in a little school by the corset factory in Redfield. Doug Constable made a most marvellous speech moving my adoption, and I delivered my own speech.

Looking at the campaign at this stage it is pretty evident that public opinion is continuing to swing our way and we are all optimistic.

Sunday 31 May
I worked on my Election preparations. In the evening I drove a very long way up the M1 to Belper to speak for George Brown. George spoke extremely well. I was glad George had asked me to go: my relations with him have not been very good over the years but I have a great admiration for him and his seat is a shaky one. Even so, he has decided to devote most of the Election campaign to going around speaking for other candidates.

Got back at 3 in the morning.

Tuesday 2 June
Went to Transport House at 8 this morning for the first of the meetings with the research group who are preparing notes for candidates.

I went to the Ministry of Technology at 10. Jack Diamond came in to see me about Palmers yard and I wanted to push him up from £100,000 to £200,000. He was extremely understanding, and he did agree I could go up a little bit more.

Wednesday 3 June
Got to Transport House at 7.45 this morning and was there most of the morning for the usual meetings with the research people, the publicity people, Harry Nicholas and the Prime Minister.

In view of Enoch Powell's Election address which had raised the racial issue again, I decided that I would put out a press release on race relations for my speech at Central Hall tonight organised by Hugh Anderson of 'Students for Labour Victory'. So after the PM left for his press conference at 9.50, I went up to Gwyn Morgan's office and dictated a very violent attack upon racialism and I linked it with Heath's silence on Enoch Powell's position. I said that the flag that was being raised in Wolverhampton was getting to look more and more like the flag that fluttered over Belsen. I showed it to Gwyn Morgan and I said, 'This is very strong stuff.' He replied, saying, 'Well, it has to be said.'

In the evening Caroline came with me to the meeting in Central Hall where I was speaking with Jack Jones and others. Hugh Anderson who was expected there didn't turn up until much later. He is a very remarkable man; still only twenty, former President of the Cambridge Union and dying of lung cancer. He has decided to devote the remaining few months of his life to getting the 'Students for Labour' movement going.

I spoke first. I delivered my speech on racialism – copies of it had been made available to the press and BBC television covered it very fully. The audience was quiet and, frankly, it was not a very good meeting. But, at any rate, I delivered my speech. It created tremendous press interest because of the strength of the language used.

Caroline and I came back home and I was immediately summoned to do a BBC television interview in the Election studio with Robin Day, who violently attacked me for my speech. He quoted statements that Heath had made condemning Enoch Powell and I said that if this was the case why did Heath recommend people in Wolverhampton to vote for Powell.

The NOP today showed a 5 per cent lead by Labour.

Thursday 4 June

The Belsen speech has exploded across the Election. There is a tremendous row about it. Every paper is leading on it. Heath demands that Harold repudiates it and indeed demands my dismissal from Government on the same basis that Heath dismissed Enoch Powell.

I left for Bristol very early and phoned Transport House from Marlborough and spoke to Gwyn Morgan. Although Gwyn had seen the text of my speech and approved it beforehand, like many officials he has now got cold feet. Harold is furious about it and has left a message for me to keep off the racial question.

I was interviewed on Harlech Television. I went to Weston-Super-Mare to speak at the Tobacco Workers' Conference and then for a short sleep at the Grand Hotel. I had two meetings in the evening. I rang Caroline, who was a bit worried about the race speech. She thinks I went too far and should have consulted people and got advice before I issued the text. But Peter Shore was very reassuring about it on the phone so I have decided just to hold my ground.

Friday 5 June

I gave a press conference at my headquarters in Bristol for the local press and all they wanted to ask about was the Enoch Powell speech. I said I had nothing to add about it. The papers are beginning to report that Harold is angry, so the press men think I have been disciplined by Harold, which in a sense I have. The truth is that Harold had hoped to keep race out of the Election. But an issue as important as this can't be left out, because an election is a period when the public engages in a great debate about its future and as race is one of the most important questions in the future, it is quite wrong to try to keep it quiet. I am still a bit worried, however, and was encouraged that Doug Constable, whose judgment I very much respect, was in favour of the words I used on the grounds that if you were going to fight evil, you had to use fairly strong weapons. Indeed, he rather reflected on the speech and drew from it the conclusion that the Church was too quiet in its condemnation of evil.

Afterwards I drove to St Albans to take part in *Any Questions* with Norman St John Stevas and Eric Lubbock. The first question was about the Powell speech. Norman St John Stevas who, in all fairness, is not at all a racialist, attacked me violently for it. I defended myself vigorously. Eric Lubbock supported me. I am very glad I did have the opportunity of speaking to a wider audience and giving the reasons why I made the speech.

Then I drove Eric back to London. He is an extremely agreeable man and could easily be in the Labour Party; I wish he were. We talked about his prospects in Orpington, which he is hopeful of retaining.*

Sunday 7 June
I got home from a meeting in Basildon and discovered that Joshua was worried about the tremendous controversy raging round my head over the race speech. One has to remember that children do find arguments involving their parents very upsetting.

Today, Brazil beat England in the World Cup: the political effect of this can't be altogether ignored.

Monday 8 June
I went to Transport House and Percy Clark was angry about my race speech. He felt it represented an undermining of his authority as publicity director to vet speeches put out by Ministers or Party leaders. The stories that appeared in yesterday's papers that my speech would lead to a new vetting procedure for Ministers' speeches by the Prime Minister had derived from Percy.

I saw Harold later this morning and he said nothing about it although he did suggest that I should start raising industrial questions in the Election campaign, and I am happy to do this. The trouble is that the mass media will not report anything you say other than the sensational, or trivial, or personal things. To this extent the media do dictate the nature of the campaign.

Letters began pouring in on the Powell speech: 2:1 against me but some very sympathetic ones saying that my speech was overdue, the first speech that indicated the deep feeling of black people about racism. Some very unpleasant ones stressing the theme of patriotism, how Powell was a Christian gentleman and how the last war against Hitler had been a patriotic war. No sense of course of it having been a moral war against the racialism of the Nazis. An anonymous postcard signed 'Retired army officer' said, 'What was wrong with Belsen? The Jews control everything.' So one had the opportunity on the one hand to assess the depth of hatred which Powell has unleashed and made respectable by his speeches, and on the other hand some comment from people who were worried about what was happening and were glad that it had been brought into the open.

Tuesday 9 June
The *Daily Express* and *Daily Mail* had reports that Caroline had attacked the civil servants in the Department of Education and Science for failing

* Eric Lubbock gained Orpington for the Liberals in a by-election in 1962. He lost the seat to the Conservative Ivor Stanbrook in 1970. He inherited the title of Lord Avebury in 1971 from his cousin.

to support comprehensive education. Actually this was based on a press conference she and Brian Simon gave yesterday to launch the book *Half Way There*, on the comprehensive school movement, published tomorrow by McGraw Hill. It is a major work that has taken them three years to write, and press were trying to introduce some element of controversy without describing the work itself. But it worried her slightly and she wrote letters to the editors about it. Incidentally, the BBC have declined, in reviewing the book, to mention Caroline's name because she is the wife of a Minister; it is so offensive. The newspaper strike started and is going to have the effect of blanking out the Election and press reviews of Caroline's book. But it will be studied all over and it represents an enormous effort by her and Brian Simon.

To Dover in the afternoon where I campaigned for David Ennals who is defending a very small majority there but is fairly optimistic about it. I went to one coalmine and then to the seafront for an open-air meeting and ended up in Dover itself.

Wednesday 10 June
To East Anglia where I spoke at Halesworth, Yarmouth, Lowestoft and Norwich at open-air and indoor meetings. It was a lovely day and I thoroughly enjoyed it.

That is all for today except that Purnell, the security officer, sent me a note alerting me to the fact that Brian Simon was an open Communist and that my wife had been working with him. So I sent a note back to him, which will no doubt go in the file, saying of course I knew about it, I had known it from the beginning and so had she, that he came from a very well known political family. I kept a copy both of the message from the security officer and also my response.

It was an interesting example of an attempt by security people to protect a Minister from a radical wife or from an innocent wife who had got muddled up with radicals. It was also an indication of how slow they were to tumble to the fact that the book was being written and that Brian Simon was associated with it, because he has rung Caroline quite regularly from Communist Party Headquarters and I feel sure that they must have been tapping the telephone at the time.

Thursday 11 June
There was a 7 per cent Labour lead in the Harris opinion poll and the Opinion Research Centre poll this morning. If polls mean anything, these do indicate a substantial Labour victory of 100 seats perhaps. This is creating a new mood in the Party. Harold is going round and doing 'meet the people' tours, based on the Queen in Australia, I suppose. This is the way he is running it and he doesn't want any trouble, and thinks

it's all going to come out all right. Everybody at Transport House is going along with this approach.

At Harold's press conference in the morning, Auberon Waugh, who really is a most unpleasant man, asked the Prime Minister on what date he thought the Conservatives would start opening the concentration camps if they won the Election. I must say, in fairness to Harold, he was very firm. He said that Mr Heath himself had compared racialism, as mouthed by Powell, to what had happened in Germany before the war; although Harold has made it clear all along that he didn't write or vet my speech, and that the language was the choice of the Minister or colleague speaking, he didn't yield an inch on this and for that I am most grateful.

This afternoon I went to Uxbridge and I made my industrial speech. The TV cameras were there but when I made it clear I wasn't going to talk about Enoch Powell but about industrial policy, they just packed up their cameras and left.

On to Slough for Joan Lestor, and it was a stormy meeting, with National Front people. Afterwards, Joan drove me back part of the way. She is worried about the race thing because Nigel Lawson, the Conservative candidate in Slough, has been exploiting it ruthlessly. So she made a serious statement at the meeting today in which she gave her view and it was heard in fair silence.

Friday 12 June

Caroline was tidying up at home after the excitement of the week with the publication of the book. She now has the itch to teach again and I have no doubt that over the next few years she will get back into it somehow or other.

Saturday 13 June

There was a 12.5 per cent lead in the national opinion polls this morning, simply enormous, boosting our confidence no end. I went to Newcastle by train, a long dull journey, and arrived for the Northumberland Miners' Picnic at Bedlington, where there were about 5,000 people. As I arrived, Lawrence Daly was making a tough speech. I spoke and then we had high tea and I went to Sunderland South by car for the MP Gordon Bagier.

Powell's 'enemies within' speech has now come out, in which he says that he suspects that civil servants have been faking the immigration statistics. He draws a comparison with Burgess and Maclean's unpatriotic behaviour, giving the impression that he really has gone entirely round the bend, and this has helped to blank out some of the criticism of me for having attacked him, because this is well beyond the pale as far as the British public is concerned. It is just not acceptable to say that sort of thing about civil servants. Enoch must be under heavy strain: he is calculating the Tories will lose the Election and people will then turn to him.

Sunday 14 June

I had a pretty lazy start this morning. There was only a 2.5 per cent Gallup lead, which was not as good as the previous polls and made one a little anxious. I went to the Hartlepools for a meeting for Ted Leadbitter and then on to Middlesbrough which Arthur Bottomley and Jeremy Bray were fighting.

At this moment I think we are going to win quite comfortably, though there are some anxieties in that the Tories *are* being extremely effective in their approach to women – their Party political to women was a great success. They are hammering and hammering the economic theme and this is beginning to break the credibility of the Government's claim to have solved the economic problems.

Tonight England was finally knocked out of the World Cup which, no doubt, will have another subtle effect on the public.

Monday 15 June

The poor trade figures were hit by Heath and he made a really big issue of them, saying there was an economic crisis and that we had misled the public, that the situation was much more serious than we had admitted and that was why we had called the Election when we had. This was the first real breakthrough by Heath. He has concentrated in effect simply on two things – prices and the economic situation – and although he has been bitterly attacked by the press for his failure and scorned by Harold Wilson and the rest of us, he has stuck, in exactly the way that Home stuck in 1964, to his two themes. In 1964, Home was saying, 'Keep the deterrent' and 'Don't let Labour ruin the economy'. Now Heath is saying, 'The economy is in a terrible state and only we can put it right', and 'We will tackle prices. The housewife should vote for herself.' These twin themes are the ones that are beginning to get through.

Anyway I did loudspeaker work in the evening in the pouring rain advertising meetings. I rang Harold up in Liverpool and said I thought the latest economic scare on the trade figures, and the fact that Heath had now talked openly about another devaluation, really was worth answering, but Harold was relaxed and said Roy was going to make a statement about it and there was nothing to worry about. He sounded as if he was just composing himself for another Election triumph. Having made my point, I left it.

Tuesday 16 June

I did a factory gate meeting at BAC. Caroline arrived this afternoon and we did our evening meetings together. One venue, Avonvale Road

School, was locked so we went and had tea with some people in Mildred Street – a real Coronation Street evening. We had a late meal at the Grand Hotel.

Heath is stressing the devaluation theme quite openly now and Harold Wilson must, at the last minute, defend his record on the one point where we all thought we were strongest.

Wednesday 17 June

The polls averaged a 5 per cent lead this morning, except for ORC. I got up at 5.45 to get flowers for Caroline on our twenty-first wedding anniversary.

I had lunch in Queen Square in the little Berni Inn with Caroline. Did loudspeaker work in the afternoon. Rested in the hotel and then we did our eve of poll meetings at Ruskin Hall, Wick Road, St George Grammar School and High Street, Kingswood. Got back to the hotel very tired. The campaign is now over. My assessment is that we should win by a large majority, certainly with a working majority, and although I have some uneasiness, it is rather less than in previous Elections.

Thursday 18 June

Polling day. Caroline and I went round the polling stations. It is part of a ritual but it has to be done and it is very tiring. A journalist on *Time* magazine from New York looked in to see me for a short talk and wanted to know what our plans were for the future. I talked very confidently. This was for the *Time* cover story, I think. After we had completed the polling stations and committee rooms and loudspeaker work, we were pretty sure of victory by twenty or thirty.

Went back to the Grand Hotel, had a bath, tea and sandwiches and settled down to watch the television before we had to go off to my own count. The first thing that came over the television that was slightly worrying was the result of a poll done by the BBC at Gravesend, in which they had interviewed people as they left the polling station. So this was the first poll, not of voting intentions, but of how people actually voted, and it showed a Conservative majority.

At 11.15 we got the first result and it showed an enormous swing to the Tories and, all of a sudden, there and then, we realised we had lost the Election. There was no question about it. There are regional variations and of course these came out. But the result in this first constituency was so overwhelmingly Tory that it was quite clear that we were out and the Tories were in, possibly with a tremendous majority.

In a fraction of a second, one went from a pretty confident belief in victory to absolute certainty of defeat. It was quite a remarkable experience. By midnight it was clear that they had won and we left in the most appalling fog to find Carlton Park School, where the count was being held.

At 2.30 in the morning my result was declared. My majority had been halved. I was able to keep abreast of what was happening by listening to the results as they came out on my transistor radio.

Harold was not conceding the result but biding his time and I spared a thought for the poor man believing himself due to continue as Prime Minister and discovering he had been defeated. After the declaration I made a short speech and had a short interview with Jonathan Dimbleby, who tried to blame the Election result on my speech against Enoch Powell. At the Walter Baker Hall the Party workers were absolutely desolate. I told them not to worry – that we had been defeated but not routed.

I decided I would go straight back to London and clear right out of the office.

NOTES
Chapter 3

1. (p. 215) The Murder (Abolition of Death Penalty) Act was due to expire on 31 July 1970 unless confirmed by both Houses before then. In December 1969 resolutions were passed in Parliament which continued indefinitely the abolition of the death penalty for murder.

2. (p. 227) Brian Walden, Labour MP for Birmingham All Saints, sponsored the Right of Privacy Bill which in effect sought to protect individual privacy in relation to the use of bugging devices, information from data-processing banks, and so on. The Press Council opposed what they saw as a restriction on press freedom. The second reading was adjourned and the Bill was not pursued in the remaining six months of the Labour Government.

4
The Rift Over Europe
June 1970–December 1971

Friday 19 June
We left Bristol at 5 am with all our junk packed up: I began dozing off a third of the way home so Caroline took over the wheel. We got home at about 7.30, I unpacked the car and drove straight to the office. I just cleared everything out of my room, puting some personal things in my bag to take with me and leaving the rest in the waiting room next door, so that by 8.35 there was no sign that anybody had worked in my office. I thought this was the right thing to do and I couldn't have coped with any of my officials when I had been drained of authority in this way. It was a very emotional experience, a sort of bereavement. It wasn't that I particularly wanted to be a Minister, although the salary is useful, the car is nice and the authority is pleasant: it was this sense of being suddenly and absolutely cut off from work.

I went round and said goodbye to Kate Chaplin and I must say I almost broke down. Jack, one of my messengers, said, 'I have never shaken the hand of a better man,' and that was really more than I could bear. I walked out and left the Millbank Tower never to return. Then straight to the House of Commons and I completely cleared my room there as well. On to Transport House and thanked all the people who had helped. They, too, were very upset and emotional.

When I got home I was told that a meeting of the Inner Cabinet had been called for 4 o'clock. I thought it was a bit much of Harold to have a meeting at Number 10 when we were so obviously defeated. But the Queen was at Ascot or somewhere and was coming back at 6, so Harold planned to resign then. I went in by the Cabinet Office door and we had a brief discussion about the arrangements. Harold said he was going to resign and thanked people. I said we were an ungenerous lot and nobody ever did say thank you in politics and I would like to say what a privilege it was to have served with him in his administration – which was a bit pompous but somebody had to say it. We agreed that we would have to think about the Parliamentary Labour Party and how we organised the Opposition, and that there should be no recriminations or personal attacks – all of which was kind of obvious. There was a shell-shocked feeling to the meeting.

At the end I got my camera out and as Harold left it for the last time, I shot the only movie picture* ever taken in the Cabinet room. To Transport House again where Harold appeared, having just been to the Palace to resign. We stood outside and cheered him – all except for Tom Driberg. He said, 'That man misled us all and picked the wrong date. Why should I cheer for him?' A very sour comment.

Meanwhile Heath had been leaving the Albany and going to Buckingham Palace to become Prime Minister – very exciting – and was seen entering Number 10. At the same time Harold's stuff was going out of the back door and into a furniture van. This was the beginning of Opposition. The thought that the Tories had won was very depressing; not just the thought of Tory Ministers in office but that their whole philosophy had conquered and that this would strengthen all the reactionary forces in society. I shall work very hard in Opposition and concentrate entirely on my political work.

Saturday 20 June

Caroline and I worked all day, she on her editorial for the *Comprehensive Schools Bulletin*. As the new Editor, she has got a lot on her plate, and is now looking for new offices for the Comprehensive Schools Committee who are going to have to move out of 12 Holland Park Avenue. I threw out tons and tons of paper, and began to clear up my office. Joshua hung around and was slightly worried. I played chess with Stephen.

Heath's Cabinet was announced. Geoffrey Rippon† has gone to the Ministry of Technology: he is a very right-wing figure, a member of the Monday Club, and a former Minister of Public Building and Works. I must say that depressed me a bit. I wrote to him but then I tore up the letter because it isn't normally done to write to one's successor.

For the first time in six years, I don't have a series of red boxes; I must admit that it is rather pleasant to be free.

Sunday 21 June

Still throwing out papers. I spoke to George Brown on the phone and he told me that because he had been defeated, he was no longer Deputy-Leader of the Parliamentary Labour Party and couldn't come to the Executive meeting. I said I would be very happy to arrange for him to

---

* When the film, which also contained shots of the Cabinet-NEC meeting in May 1970, was processed, I was told that it was blank – whether this was true or not I never discovered.

† Conservative MP for Hexham, Minister of Public Buildings and Works, 1962–4.

come but he said he didn't want to. I also spoke to Jeremy Bray on the phone, who has lost his seat.

In the evening Tony Crosland asked us over to a talk. Peter Jenkins of the *Guardian* was there. I thoroughly dislike him – he is a real decayed gossip columnist of the Gaitskellite variety. I didn't enjoy it very much.

Monday 22 June

I got up at 4.40 to get Stephen off to Keele.

Lucille was very tearful at the result of the election. When I dictated my goodbye letters, she wept over the typewriter and I must say I was sad myself. People came and collected the various keys that had to be returned to the office.

Caroline went to the ILEA where there was some discussion about the fact that she had voted against the ILEA Labour group on the subject of the middle school at Thamesmead. She has the great advantage that she has got no political ambition and therefore they can't do anything to harm her: they have co-opted her as an expert.

In the afternoon I went to Buckingham Palace for the audience with the Queen and I drove in my own car unlike some ex-Ministers who were still using their official cars, which I thought was slightly odd since we were clearly out. The courtiers could scarcely conceal their delight – Sir Michael Adeane, the equerries, the lady-in-waiting – and were obviously thrilled at what had happened and were being polite to the 'little Labour men'.

I said to the Queen I had enjoyed office and she said, 'You will be seeing more of your family.' I talked about the stamps and thanked her for her help with them. Then she mentioned Concorde, so I said, 'Well, there are a lot of problems and I sometimes wonder whether it shouldn't just be kept to fly up The Mall on the royal birthday.' She laughed at that, and thanked me very much, as if I had somehow done it all for her. It was very courteous of her but I am sure that the idea that the Queen's Ministers are simply advisers, and that she is really the Government, in a position to thank them before they go, is deeply entrenched at the Palace.

Tuesday 23 June

Had dinner with Barbara and Ted Castle at their flat with Dick Crossman, Tommy Balogh, Harold Lever and Peter Shore. Dick has taken on the editorship of the *New Statesman*, which he was going to take over in the autumn anyway even if we had won the Election, once his Pension Bill was through. He was very full of life: a very resilient man.

Tommy Balogh explained that the economic policy hadn't succeeded because the wrong people were in the wrong place. Harold Lever came out with his theory that we had got absolutely obsessed with the exchange rate and that having a deficit is all right, indeed that it is an essential part of growth (which is true), but at the same time if you are inefficient and go on living at a higher standard than you are really earning, then it doesn't work. There is a difference between a deficit associated with real growth and a deficit associated with living beyond your means.

Then we came to the question of who was going to stand for the deputy-leadership. Barbara said she was going to stand, she didn't see why everything should be carved up. 'Why should I go on just accepting the Number Three position, Harold never helped me, this is the moment to stand up and fight,' and so on. The question is whether she would stand against Roy and Jim Callaghan. Dick said, 'Well, we shall support you at the *New Statesman*.' But there was a general feeling that Barbara really shouldn't stand and that it was an explosion of feeling rather than a sensible decision, because after her trouble with 'In Place of Strife' her reputation in the Party had dropped very sharply.

Then I was asked and said that I too would consider standing as Deputy-Leader (I didn't push this) and possibly as Chief Whip.

We all let our hair down, and it was just what we needed.

Wednesday 24 June
A meeting of the former Inner Cabinet at 4: Harold Wilson, Douglas Houghton, Eddie Shackleton, Frank Beswick, Fred Peart, Harry Mitchell, Denis Healey, Roy Jenkins, Michael Stewart, Dick Crossman, Bob Mellish, Barbara Castle, Jim Callaghan, Peter Shore, Tony Crosland, and Secretary of the PLP, Frank Barlow.

Harold Wilson said we would have to consider how to handle the Queen's Speech. He said he would like to see a chairman of the Parliamentary Labour Party elected separately from the leadership of the Party: he obviously hoped Douglas would do it.

Douglas said there would be a meeting of the Party on Monday and gave the dates when the nominations for the deputy-leadership, the Shadow Cabinet and the Chief Whip would open and close. One could already sense the edging of candidates for position, particularly Jim and Roy. Denis said, 'Why don't we *drop* the deputy-leadership?' His soundings of Labour MPs had indicated that there was not much interest in it – this of course was because he knew quite well that he wouldn't be Deputy-Leader and he didn't want anybody else to get into a commanding position.

Harold said he hoped that any candidates for the deputy-leadership would come and see him. He had cleared earlier that the Leader would be elected by acclaim at the first meeting of the Parliamentary Party.

Thursday 25 June
We had the last Pink Shirt Club party at Holland Park Avenue. I
bought blue and white striped tea mugs for everybody and put a pink
handkerchief, pink tie, or a pink rose in each of them. They gave me a
pink tie with the Mintech symbol on it. We had a lovely evening with all
the old gang, and Kate Chaplin, Monty and Derek Moon from the Press
Office were also there. We sat in the garden and played records. They
left me a record of the theme song from *Dr Zhivago* which I had whistled
up and down the Millbank corridors for years. This was effectively the
end of my links with the Private Office after some very happy years.

Saturday 27 June
Slogged away, wrote sixty or seventy cards by hand. After just over a
week I find myself slowly adjusting to the fact that nobody really wants
to know you when you are an ex-Minister. It must be absolute hell if you
retire or are fired and you are out while all your colleagues are still in.
The truth is that it is almost rather comforting that everyone else is out as
well.

Monday 29 June
Today Jeremy Thorpe's wife Caroline was tragically killed in a motor
crash.
    I went to the Commons for the Party meeting where Leo Abse [MP
for Pontypool] got up and made a damaging speech against Harold.
    Leo said that we had fought the Election on the personality of the
Leader, and we had lost. This was therefore a reflection on the cult-of-
leadership policy we had adopted and he thought there was a lot to be
discussed before we chose the Leader. It would be a good thing to let it be
known that the Leader of the Parliamentary Labour Party was licensed
by the PLP rather than the other way round. This was a reference to
Harold's famous dog licence speech in which he had said everybody was
allowed one bite before their licence was taken away. That speech gave
the most tremendous offence at the time.
    But Harold was re-elected by acclamation, with even Leo Abse not
voting against him.

Tuesday 30 June
The real news today is that within a few days of being elected, the Tories
have issued a new circular – 1070 – to replace 1065, which in effect calls a
halt to comprehensive school development. This is going to be a big issue
for the educational movement in this country.

Thursday 2 July
Today was the Debate on the Address with Heath and Wilson speaking.
Harold is incredible, just like an India rubber man, bouncing up again

after his defeat, completely unphased by the fact that he lost, and with the Party just sort of accepting him again. I wouldn't have the strength to accept a defeat of that kind. I think I would be very bad at coming to terms with it.

Monday 6 July

With Caroline to the US Embassy party where we met Otto Clarke who was exceptionally friendly, David Pitblado and William Armstrong. Up until Election day civil servants advise you and can't say a word to your opponents and then afterwards they can say nothing to you and all their help and advice has to be given to your opponents. It is a most artificial relationship.

What I have heard in rumours from the Private Office (because Ivor Manley does tell me a little bit) is that Otto has in fact accepted some of the policies that I put across while I was there, for example, closer links with the trade unions. He is even beginning to accept the international policy. It is no good trying to defeat the Permanent Secretary, you have got to persuade him, which is very much in line with what I believe.

Tuesday 7 July

An economy debate. Roy Jenkins destroyed Macleod on the question of whether or not there had been an economic crisis at the point when the Tories came into power. Macleod had to admit there hadn't. Macleod was extremely ill and made a poor speech. It was rather sad.*

I wound up and didn't make a good speech either. I am not doing very well in the House at the moment.

Wednesday 8 July

We went to the Home Policy Committee meeting of the Executive where Jim Callaghan got himself dug in as Chairman: he is building his power base absolutely everywhere at the moment. Once in the chair he was very reasonable, asking everybody to comment and complimenting us all on what we said. Jim is a skilful politician, there is no question about it; very skilful.

Thursday 9 July

I went to the *New Statesman* board meeting. Dick's idea is to bring new people in once a week and since I have got nothing better to do and it is an opportunity to keep in contact with the *New Statesman*, I agreed:

---

* Macleod died of a heart attack two weeks after this debate. He was succeeded as Chancellor of the Exchequer by Anthony Barber; Geoffrey Rippon moved to the Duchy of Lancaster, in charge of Common Market negotiations; John Davies, a new Back Bench MP, became Minister of Technology (See Principal Persons p. 460).

Tom Baistow, Alan Watkins, Tony Howard and Francis Hope were there: they are thirty- to forty-year-old Oxbridge, right-wing Gaitskellites who are really columnists for the Establishment. Tommy Balogh was also there; he still behaves as if it would be easy to get the economy right if one only took his advice; and Harold Lever, who was brilliant and said that Ministers were just frolicking about on the margins but the real decisions were taken by the Chancellor and the Governor of the Bank of England, who was outside the political arena.

This is interesting because if you don't meet the people whose voice really does count, then of course you can't be effective. All you can do is to bring the Chancellor of the Exchequer, who is the fuse box linking the two systems, to the point of a nervous collapse. I thought Harold identified this very well and it persuaded me that if we did have another Labour Government, the right thing to do would be to invite the Governor of the Bank of England to the economic policy meetings in the same way as the Chiefs of Staff come to Defence meetings.

Frank McElhone, the MP for Glasgow Gorbals, came to see me to say there were about twelve people of whom he was one who thought I should be Leader of the Party and he would like to keep in touch with me on a regular basis.

Monday 20 July
Shadow Cabinet. After we had been through the dull practical business, I asked, 'Are we going to find time in the Shadow Cabinet to discuss the general political situation rather than be just an administrative committee?' Harold said there would be something on the agenda on the current political situation, which isn't exactly what I was saying, but it is better than nothing.

Then I said, 'What about collective Cabinet responsibility?' I asked this with Michael Foot in mind, who has now been elected on to the Shadow Cabinet. Harold said 'Well, ex-members of the Cabinet must stick by the record of the previous Government,' which I accept. As for thinking aloud he thought it would be better if Ministers or rather ex-Ministers were to check their speeches with him. For example, he said, looking at me, he didn't want any speeches on a Referendum on the Common Market.

'Well,' I said, 'I just want it to be known that I do intend to think aloud and I shall do it in an entirely constructive spirit. I shan't criticise anybody because that is not my way of doing it. But I do intend to think aloud. When the boat is sunk you can't exactly rock it' – a phrase that didn't please Harold much. Michael Foot, Crosland and Shirley Williams supported me.

Wednesday 22 July
To Caroline Thorpe's memorial service which was full of the Establishment, but very sad.

Harold appointed me Shadow Spokesman on Industry and Technology – minus fuel and power, which he has given to Michael Foot. So my actual responsibilities are rather less than before.

From 26 July to 30 August we had our annual holiday at Stansgate. I worked on a Fabian pamphlet called The New Politics: A Socialist Reconnaisance,* *which summed up my political conclusions during my period as Minister of Technology.*

Saturday 29 August
Joshua came in at 1.15 in the morning with serious stomach pains. We called a doctor, who diagnosed acute appendicitis so Caroline and I took him to the West London Hospital and he was operated on.

Wednesday 2 September
Lucille came in and I went to the House of Commons to meet the deputation from Palmers yard, led by Ernie Fernyhough. Together we went to the Ministry of Technology, where John Davies, the new Minister, and Nicholas Ridley, his Parliamentary Secretary, received us. It was the first time I had been back to my old Department and it was a curious experience sitting at the back saying nothing, watching the Minister with Ivor Manley and Derek Moon, and all the people who had advised me on shipbuilding, now advising Davies. The general impression given was most unfavourable. He said he could do nothing, that the Government was not prepared to give any money; the all-Party delegation, including Conservatives, got extremely angry. Davies had to go across to the Cabinet and Ridley read the group a lecture on the need for change which, considering he was talking to people from the North-East, which has experienced more change than almost any other part of the country, was a bit unnecessary. He told them that if they were dissatisfied with the management, the company would go bankrupt, another company might buy the assets and they would get a new management – a sort of ABC of nineteenth-century capitalism.

Thursday 3 September
To the *New Statesman*, and found it a bit difficult – partly because everything I say that has any possible entertainment value is retailed to *Private Eye*, partly because Dick Crossman is such a bully, and partly because the *New Statesman* just caters for middle-aged, middle-of-the-road, middle-class Oxbridge arts graduates.

* See Appendix V.

from: NEIL KINNOCK, M.P.

Thanks. Don't be discouraged. Tide is coming in + out of us out of our own ends beyond. Let's discuss. Wrote LC 21/9/70

16th September, 1970

Anthony Wedgewood-Benn, Esq., M.P.,
House of Commons,
LONDON S.W.1.

Dear Tony,

Thank you very much for the advance copy of your Fabian tract:
I must express wholehearted endorsement of your description of
the 'new citizen', the 'new politics' and, although I don't
think you used this particular phrase, the new tyrannies.
Congratulations on a timely and honest piece of work...

You obviously have a more optimistic (and disciplined) approach
and can use the imperatives "got" and "must" in relation to
international corporations, Government and the People with a
great deal more confidence than I have done since I controlled
a Students Union through the Socialist Society. But you are
right.   Now is the time to sweep and not to prod - there are
Inevitabilities about and we must control some and divert others.
I don't think that my failure to reach assertive answers
manifests any lack of courage - it is more probable that, after
that first month in Parliament, my worst fears were over-realised
and I fell victim to the "It's all bloody hopeless and we might
as well be in Disneyland" syndrome.   I think I'll get over that.
I'd better get over it.

I am sorry to have taken so much time to make this confessional
but I felt that I had to finish a letter sometime and, if its
of any interest, you are now acquainted with some of my feelings..

Yours sincerely,

Neil

NEIL KINNOCK

Friday 4 September
To the Fabian Conference, to talk on my pamphlet. Frances Morrell, the press officer from the National Union of Students, was in charge and she had gathered a lot of people there. But this morning the *Guardian* published an extract from the pamphlet, so my talk had less of an impact than I'd hoped.

Sunday 6 September
Caroline was working on her survey of comprehensive schools all day, the survey which she does every year in the absence of any serious research from the DES. I wrote about thirty letters by hand.

Wednesday 9 September
Had lunch with Donald Stokes and the Leyland board. The number of strikes now in the motor industry does indicate a complete breakdown in communication. When we began talking about this, they said that Barbara Castle's speech last year – in which she had said that power was passing to the shop floor – had done more damage than anything else. I said it seemed incredible that if this was true – and none of them denied it – there should be any difficulty about it being openly declared. But they took a very conservative view, and although they were conscious of their own managerial defects, they were still a long way from realising that relations with the workforce required a great deal more time and effort, thought and participation than they were giving.

Thursday 10 September
In the evening I went and had dinner with Peter and Liz Shore and Tommy Balogh, and his new wife-to-be Katherine Storr, who is a distinguished surgeon. Tommy Balogh is leaving his current wife, Pen, to marry her. It is really rather sad. I liked Pen Balogh very much indeed. Katherine Storr is about the same age and looked rather similar.

Caroline loyally went to hear Stan Newens, who lost his seat at Epping, speaking to the North Kensington Labour Party. She is about to be made Chairman of the Holland Park School Governors.

Wednesday 16 September
Went to the Publicity Committee where I had a word with Gwyn Morgan. He told me that Jim Callaghan was in the office twice a week, in close contact with Harry Nicholas. I told him that as Party Vice-Chairman I would like to come to the Heads of Department meetings and he said it would be welcome. Generally speaking, Jim is trying to undermine Harold, I think, and would like to be Leader. It was interesting to get that from Gwyn Morgan, who, it had always been supposed, was Jim's man.

Thursday 17 September
To the Commons. Talked to Peter and Marcia, and to Tommy Balogh. The common view is that the Tories won't try to get us into the Common Market – they will see that the public doesn't want it and won't run any risk. But I wonder if this isn't underestimating Heath's personal passion to get us in and I don't rule out the possibility that it may be a big issue.

Peter Shore is building up for a great attack on the Common Market and I am still building up, slowly and quietly, for my campaign for a Referendum.

In the evening I had an interesting talk with Joshua. He said he had realised that nobody appreciated practical work so he didn't want to be an engineer.

Saturday 19 September
I drove to Buscot for a Fabian seminar with some ex-Ministers and others. The first session was on the machinery of government, with Tommy Balogh in the chair.

Most of the discussion was dominated by Dick Crossman, Barbara Castle and myself all making ministerial confessions, attacking Harold Wilson's style, criticising the lack of strategic discussion in the Government, commenting on relations with civil servants and Members of Parliament, talking about secrecy and considering how to evolve policy in Opposition.

I thoroughly enjoyed it, although it was largely negative, and predictably most of the criticism came from those who had actually been in the Government. Then we had a session on economic policy with Dick Crossman in the chair. The economist, Roger Opie, introduced it and asked how important was economic policy? How relevant was the machinery of government to economic policy? How much could you control – how much was political and how much technical? And should Treasury decisions go into commission with Ministers?

The point that came out was that the decision in 1964 not to devalue did dictate the whole pattern of the Government and yet it was never collectively discussed by Ministers.

Nicky Kaldor asked, 'Do we need to be as precarious as this all the time, right on the edge, couldn't we do better than that?' It was a perfectly fair point but I must say that neither Kaldor nor Balogh, who have been advising the Labour Party on the economy for years, seem to me to have anything real to offer. They fight each other all the time, tell us what to do, and we follow their advice: but I can't say we have done well out of it.

After dinner, which was a fantastic affair, by candlelight with butlers hovering around, and coats-of-arms on the wallpaper, there was a session at which I took the chair, with Dipak Nandy, the Executive

Director of the Runnymede Trust, talking about the urban crisis. He pointed out that the centres of our cities were being surrounded by decaying areas, from which all the rich people moved out, so they became cesspools of poverty watched over by the police and social workers, who came in like colonial administrators. He thought that representative democracy had failed here. Some sort of authoritarianism might be necessary. We had an interesting discussion about how we might handle it: my anarchic arguments came out and were severely tested by the other Fabians.

Monday 21 September

Caroline and I went to lunch with her mother at the Connaught. In the afternoon we went to Hugh Anderson's memorial service. Hugh Anderson is the student who died of cancer at the age of twenty-one; he created a tremendous impression upon everyone who had known him. Harold Wilson was at the service and Bishop Trevor Huddleston preached most movingly about the influence that Hugh had had on his life. Stephen was much impressed; it made me wonder whether he might possibly want to go into the Church.

Sunday 27 September

Executive this afternoon. We considered what attitude we should take towards the TGWU resolution attacking incomes policy, and more or less decided to let it ride. I suggested a special conference on the Common Market which was accepted, so I was rather pleased. Caroline arrived and we went to the TGWU buffet and looked in at the *New Statesman* party, where Peter Paterson of the *Daily Telegraph* said that Harold must go. I attacked him – until it turned out that he was in favour of me replacing him. Then I had a go at John Grist on the BBC's failure to confront the real issues of our time: he said this was due to the fact that Harold Wilson was always attacking the BBC, a ludicrous answer.

Monday 28 September

Conference began. Arthur Skeffington* was there: he is dying of cancer but insisted on coming, and Harry Nicholas read Arthur's Chairman's Address: it was rather touching. We had the debate on education which was full of attacks on the Tories with nothing positive in it, then a trade union debate in which Jack Jones made a tremendous speech which moved Walter Padley to tears. He said that this was what it was all about

---

* Labour MP for Hayes and Harlington. Arthur Skeffington was Chairman of the National Executive, 1969–70, and therefore Chairman of the Conference in 1970. He died in February 1971.

– the class war. In the evening we went to various receptions and I didn't get to bed until 4 am.

The big news was that President Nasser died today.

Wednesday 30 September

In the afternoon went to the National Executive meeting where I was elected Vice-Chairman. Today the platform was defeated and Conference decisions were made binding on the NEC. Harold didn't like that very much.

Conference so far has gone reasonably well – better than most people expected.

Thursday 1 October

We had the economic debate this morning at which Roy Jenkins made a powerful speech, his first as Deputy-Leader and it has entrenched him strongly with the delegates.

In the afternoon I prepared my speech on international companies for a meeting of the International Technology Group but when I got there the slide projector – which Caroline had brought all the way up – stuck and the slides fell out of the box. I felt awfully stupid.

I went over to the meeting on race relations with Joan Lestor and Shirley Williams, and David Pitt* in the chair. It was a marvellous discussion.

Friday 2 October

End of Conference. Mikardo, as new Chairman of the National Executive, made a marvellous winding-up speech. On the train back, I talked to Jim Callaghan about the Party and urged the desirability of having a little inner group of members of the Parliamentary Committee who were also on the Executive to consider the strategy of the Party.

Saturday 3 October

Caroline wrote a biting piece for *Tribune* on the education debate, expressing her great disappointment that nothing more constructive had been said. She has had her book on women's education accepted in principle by Penguin.

The dustmen's strike has begun and the rubbish is beginning to accumulate.

Thursday 8 October

Shadow Cabinet meeting where we had a long session about the Tory

---

* Chairman, Community Relations Commission. First West Indian Chairman of the GLC, 1974–5. Created a life peer (Lord Pitt of Hampstead), 1975.

trade union proposals, with Barbara explaining why they were all different from hers. But there was a general feeling that we didn't want to highlight their proposals because it would put us in a difficulty, we having dropped ours under union pressure.

Then I went to Bristol and met a group from *The Other Paper*, a radical underground newsheet. Got into a bit of a discussion with some Maoists among them, which wasn't very fruitful. We agreed that I will provide them with information about my political ideas and they will keep in touch with me in case there is any value in our contact, but there is a fairly big ideological difference between us.

Friday 9 October

In the evening I saw Terry Walker, the Secretary of South Gloucestershire Labour Party. He suggested I might consider standing for the Kingsfield constituency – which will be made up of Kingswood, Hanham, Mangotsfield, Walmley and Cadbury Heath – which is, in a sense, the old South Gloucestershire seat that Tony Crosland used to represent. It looks as if, with boundary changes, my seat in Bristol is going to be unsafe so if Kingsfield were safer, I might feel I had to take it. On the other hand, it would seem as if I were running away. It is altogether very difficult; but Terry Walker said he would look up the figures and advise.

Tuesday 13 October

Caroline's birthday and the children came in with presents. I gave her an electric typewriter which she needs. She is heavily loaded with her ILEA work, her teaching at the National Extension College, her book on education, her survey of the comprehensives, the editorship of the *CSC Bulletin*, the chairmanship of Holland Park. She has got to be careful.

I went to the Shadow Cabinet this afternoon, where we had a long, boring discussion on the economic situation and everybody hummed and hawed and gave their view. I have no confidence at the moment in Labour economists or the capability of a Labour Government to handle the economy any better than anybody else and I don't believe that this is what politics is about any more. But economic management is so deeply entrenched in the thinking of Harold Wilson and others that it is difficult to get away from it.

In the evening Caroline and I had a lovely dinner at Leith's Restaurant.

Wednesday 14 October

Worked on article for the *Melody Maker* in response to 'Rock – Energy for Revolution', a piece which had struck me as the first article by a young person on the political significance of the rock revolution.

Thursday 15 October

Six years ago today, the Labour Government won the 1964 Election.

This afternoon Heath announced the abolition of the Ministry of Technology. It is being merged with the Department of Trade and Industry,* with Aviation Supply going off separately.

I went up to Manchester and had lunch at the University Business School and on to the Labour Club where I spoke, not very successfully because I was extremely tired. Then I flew back to London to do the BBC *24 Hours* programme on the Government changes.

Friday 16 October

Had a most stimulating breakfast meeting with Buckminster Fuller. He described the necessity throughout history for communities to come to terms with their old timescale. For example in the agricultural timescale everything corresponded to the seasons through one year. Then the early arrival of ships had led people to say, 'when my ship comes in' which was a longer timescale than the one based on 'when the harvest is brought in'. His is a most creative and fertile mind.

Tuesday 20 October

To the Shadow Cabinet where there was a great argument about the award of honours for political services. Heath has written to Harold to say he is resuming political honours and would Harold recommend people, so Harold asked our advice. A number of people were in favour of going back to political honours and were angry that Harold had ever given them up. Jim Callaghan, Fred Peart and Bob Mellish were among those in favour but Ted Short quite rightly said that we can't just go back on this.

I suggested that we write back to Heath and say it is an interesting idea but perhaps the right thing was to have a committee to look at the honours system. This idea was approved although of course Heath won't do it and we shall still have to consider whether we do put in people for honours. But the discussion revealed the Party at its worst, believing that it is entitled to the perquisites which go with being part of the ruling class. With *Sir* Harry Nicholas sitting next to me, I felt pretty disgusted.

In the evening Caroline and I had dinner with the Chinese Chargé d'Affaires, Mr Ma, and his interpreter. It was just like having dinner with a cardinal and his chaplain. We talked about our two languages. They said how Chinese was such a straightforward language and how English was so subtle, which of course is the exact reverse of what we

---

* John Davies became Secretary of State for Trade and Industry and Nicholas Ridley a Parliamentary Under-Secretary. The newly-created Ministry of Aviation Supply had a limited life of eighteen months before merging with the Ministry of Defence.

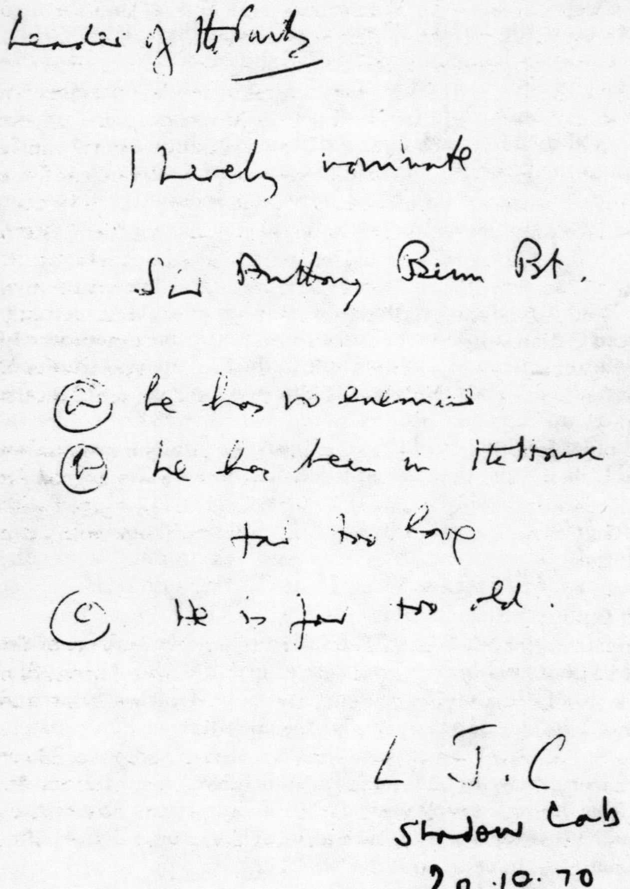

Leader of the Party

I hereby nominate

Sir Anthony Benn Bt.

(a) he has no enemies
(b) he has been in the House
    far too long
(c) He is far too old.

L J. C
Shadow Cab
20 .10. 70

Note from James Callaghan to TB at a Shadow Cabinet meeting, 20 October 1970.

think. They think of the wily Westerners and the straightforward Chinese, while we think of it the other way around.

They were very interested in whether Caroline was an American or not. They asked about her writing, and we discussed the handling of science and technology in education. They explored my view on the possible entry of Britain into the Common Market and were particularly interested in whether Heath would want an Anglo-French nuclear force or not. I said he had stated that he was in favour of it: that was all I knew.

We discussed the arrangements they had now reached with a Western Government – the Canadians – under which China declared its determination to be regarded as the only representative Government of the Chinese. The Canadians had noted that view without actually accepting it and we considered whether the British Government would agree to such an arrangement. I didn't like to ask about the possibility of a visit to China in case I got a 'No', but I did say I hoped we could return their hospitality.

They were most friendly. We did, inevitably, discuss the revisionism in Russia and they said that another violent revolution would be necessary in Russia, in Yugoslavia and in Britain. They disagreed with Marx's view that Britain was a country that might change without a violent revolution.

Wednesday 28 October

Flew up to Edinburgh with Tam Dalyell where David Graham of the Scottish Labour Students met us and drove us to Dundee University. There were a number of hippy students who squeaked balloons and burned incense and shouted, but it wasn't too bad.

Then on to St Andrews, which was a much quieter audience. There were some good questions and we had a meal with them afterwards.

I went to The Binns – the Dalyell family home – and met his two children, Gordon and Moira, and his wife Kathleen, who looked after me most hospitably.

Thursday 29 October

Tam and I went with David Graham to Stirling University, where I had a short discussion with one or two of the leading lights in the Labour Club.

At Glasgow University there was a near riot to begin with. The audience threw paper darts and shouted. I didn't use the microphone and somebody said, 'Why don't you use the microphone?' I replied, 'I'll use the microphone when I get a serious question.' After that it quietened down.

On to Jordan Hill, a huge teachers' training college, which has a tremendously disciplinarian Head and no students' rights at all.

Then Strathclyde University, where I was heckled by Scottish Nationalists.

After that we drove at 100 mph to Edinburgh in Tam's Citroën. In all, I visited eight universities and technical colleges and spoke to about 2,000 students. I am trying to absorb the criticisms that are made, make sense of them and clear my mind. Spent the night at The Binns again.

Friday 30 October
I went with Tam to Grangemouth docks, where we met the dock board, then to BP chemicals. Particularly interesting was the development of edible artificial proteins from the synthesis of bacteria and petrol. The proteins processed from this can be quite tasty.

In the evening I went to the Forth Labour Party buffet and flew back to London with Tam, very late.

Tuesday 3 November
To the House of Commons briefly, then to the Institute of Contemporary Arts to meet some art students to discuss the Coldstream Report: the Report arose from the great trouble at the art colleges two years ago and recommended a new, most unsatisfactory organisation for art education. Frances Morrell had asked me to attend and Jack Straw presided.

Worked at the Commons. I circulated my draft letter to my constituents on the Common Market Referendum idea to Harold, Roy, Jim, Denis, Harold Lever, Gwyn Morgan and Tom McNally. Shirley Williams drove me home and I talked to her about it. I am hoping to get the support of one or two people who are in favour of entry because it would greatly strengthen my case.

Wednesday 4 November
Had lunch with Peter. He is coming out more and more strongly against entry, and has picked up the proposal for the unified monetary system: he rightly points out that this would involve the end of the national sovereignty of this country, but he is making heavy weather of it. I can't get him to agree to the Referendum idea. He thinks I am just interested in the machinery, where he's interested in the substance. In fact I am interested in the substance but I am also interested in the machinery, because that is what politics is about.

Immediately after the General Election of 1970, the Conservative Government began negotiations for British entry into the European Communities – that is to say the Economic Community, the Coal and Steel Community and Euratom. At this time both the Labour and Conservative Governments were committed in their manifestos to a negotiated entry. From September 1970 to June 1971, the Government was engaged in negotiating the terms under which Britain would enter the 'Common Market', and in 1971 produced a White Paper setting out these terms. Meanwhile, opposition to the Common Market had been developing, and found a voice in the all-party Common Market Safeguards Committee, founded by Douglas Jay, former President of the Board of Trade, ex-junior Minister Neil Marten, Conservative MP for Banbury, and Liberal MP Peter Bessell.

Within the Labour Party, dissatisfaction both with the terms of entry and the principle of the Common Market itself was developing. There were growing calls for the issue to be decided in a General Election, and I campaigned both for a special conference of the Labour Party to be held to debate the whole question, and for a Referendum of the British people. My own feeling then was that while I was not opposed in principle to entry into the European Communities, the issue was of such major constitutional significance, because of the loss of sovereignty involved, that it should be put before the British electorate.

For most of 1971 and the following year the Common Market dominated Parliamentary and Party business. A four-day parliamentary debate was held from 21 to 26 July to discuss the Government's White Paper on entry, a debate which ended without a division, and the Government then announced that the principle of entry to the Common Market would be debated from 21 to 28 October 1971, before the Treaty of Accession was signed. The Government motion was: 'That this House approves Her Majesty's Government's decision of principle to join the European Communities on the basis of the arrangements which have been negotiated.' The decision of the Shadow Cabinet to have a three-line whip on this vote, while the Conservatives had a free vote, was defied by sixty nine Labour MPs who thus provided the Conservative Government with a sizeable majority, ensuring that Britain was committed in principle to joining the Common Market.

The Labour Party and the TUC Conferences in 1971 came out against entry into the Market on the terms agreed by Heath's Government and called for a General Election. There were fierce debates in the National Executive, the Parliamentary Labour Party and the Shadow Cabinet, which underlined the difficult relationship between all three. Much of the argument raged around whether Labour Members should, like the Tories, be allowed a free vote in the House of Commons.

On 22 January 1972, the Treaty of Accession was signed and the European Communities Bill was then debated exhaustively (the committee stage was taken unusually in the Chamber of the House of Commons) through 1972. The nature of the Bill denied the House of Commons the opportunity to discuss the individual items in the Treaty of Accession and this denial was further aggravated by a guillotine measure to expedite the Bill's passage, and by the refusal of the Government to consider any amendments. This necessitated voting in a hundred divisions until the Bill finally became law on 17 October 1972.

Thursday 5 November

Harold Wilson came up to me and said, 'I understand you are suggesting a plebiscite on the Common Market. You can't do that.' I said, 'Well, I sent you the draft letter, Harold. Have you seen it yet?' He said, 'No. You had better bring it to the Shadow Cabinet.'

I discovered that it had not been drawn to his attention because he was too busy. I don't blame him for that but this is the moment when I am going to strike out on my own.

Went to the Soviet party this evening to celebrate the Russian Revolution and met Smirnovsky, the Ambassador, and Akimov, from the Science and Technology Committee in Moscow. Sir Denis Green-hill, the Permanent Under-Secretary at the Foreign Office, who is generally thought to be or have been the head of MI6, was also there.

I said, 'I take it, Denis, that we shall have signed the Treaty of Rome by this time next year.' 'Oh, yes, I think so without any doubt. It is absolutely inevitable.' Of course, he didn't know about my Referendum proposal and I was just plugging in to the official view which I got automatically. No doubt he reckoned that at a Russian party everything he said would be recorded, so perhaps he said it for their benefit as well.

Got home late and had a phone call from Patrick Bing, Geoffrey Bing's African godson or adopted son, saying that a number of people had been arrested at Powis Terrace at a firework display. He wanted me to ring up the police station and do something about it. I said, 'Give me the circumstances. Is there anything political about it?' He said, 'No, there is nothing political, it was just a party.' I said, 'I'll ring Bruce Douglas-Mann, the local MP,' and he said, 'We've rung him and there is no reply.' I rang Douglas-Mann's house and his wife said he wasn't back from the House and that they had been ringing her all evening, and somebody had threatened, 'If you don't do something we will burn your house down.' I offered to go to her house and keep an eye on her if she was worried but she said she wasn't. It was all rather mysterious and I couldn't make it out. But clearly there is a lot of anxiety in Kensington about the police. They do pick up kids and search them for drugs, and blacks have a rough time.

Saturday 7 November
Caroline went off to Leicester for a conference and I worked all day on articles.

This evening I took Melissa along to a party given for Mayor John Lindsay of New York and his wife, who was at college with Caroline. John Lindsay is a tall and extremely handsome man but a little too much of a cardboard hero for my liking. Still, he has done a good job in New York and he is the ultimate in responsible WASPs [White Anglo-Saxon Protestants]. He was very sweet to Melissa. As I left I congratulated him on his work in New York and he said, 'Well, I give you five years before these problems hit you in London.' I replied, 'I hope we do as well as you do,' to which he retorted, 'I hope you do a great deal better.'

Sunday 8 November
This afternoon Mick Farren, a woman called Ingrid and a man called John Hopkins came for a talk. Mick is the author of the article 'Rock – Energy for Revolution' in the *Melody Maker*. What I didn't know was that last night these people, who are part of the YIPPIES (the Youth International Party) had been on the David Frost programme and had broken it up.

Farren I didn't care for much. He was a middle class lad of about twenty-six who was in high revolt against the discipline of his parents. John Hopkins, a tortured creature of thirty-three, who looked about forty-eight, is a mathematician and cyberneticist, who had been in jail for six months for smoking pot.

I had quite a dialogue with the underworld or underground – I don't know how you would describe it. Melissa came and talked for a bit. They estimate that there are about half a million people in Britain like themselves and they believe their views are not properly represented in the political system. Second, they want a written constitution, something which brings them in line with some right-wing people. Third, the meeting raised the question of the extent to which there could be a dialogue between a hack bourgeois politician, as they would see me, and Marxist hippies, if that is the way to describe them.

In the evening we watched Jean-Paul Sartre's *Roads to Freedom* on television – a series that has been gripping us all autumn.

Tuesday 10 November
To the Publicity Committee, where I was unanimously elected Chairman.

Came home in the evening with Shirley Williams and watched a profile of Enoch Powell on ATV. The drift to the Right is so evident everywhere now that Enoch Powell can be lauded as a great public hero: I think it is scandalous.

This evening de Gaulle died, the last of the great wartime leaders. I never met him, although I saw him at Churchill's funeral. I think historians will be far more generous to him than the Foreign Office was while he was the President of France 1958–69.

Wednesday 11 November
My letter to my constituents, 'Britain and the Common Market – The Case for a Referendum', was to come before the Shadow Cabinet today. But as Harold was in Paris for de Gaulle's funeral it was just noted and

there was no comment. The only person who understood its real significance was Jim Callaghan who said, 'Tony may be launching a little rubber life-raft which we will all be glad of in a year's time.' That is one way of looking at it. I am in favour of a Referendum on constitutional grounds but even if there isn't going to be much support for those grounds clearly this is one way in which the Labour Party can avoid dividing itself into bits. So that is just about the best result I could have got from the Shadow Cabinet.

Thursday 12 November
This morning I saw Hilary Rubinstein, who has agreed to be my agent, to talk about my idea for a book. He suggested I should write something about change and how change can be achieved. He said that the characteristic of my life that interested him and other people was that I had always tried to change things: this was true of the peerage case, the Post Office and the Ministry of Technology. If I could write a handbook of change geared to a world audience which was a bit more concrete and intelligible than my Fabian pamphlet, he thought it might sell well.

Friday 13 November
Got up at 6 and drove to Wilton Park, the Foreign Office school, where I have been speaking on and off for the last twenty years. I gave my lecture on technology and society to a fairly high-level group of people from all over the world.

Then to Bristol by car to visit Monks Park School. In the evening I went to St George East and West for a ward meeting.

The text of my Referendum paper was released today and this is the beginning of an important phase.

Friday 20 November
Flew in a tiny plane to Newcastle for a meeting with the university students. I got a reasonable hearing though they were very critical, as you would expect.

Then on to Tyne Tees Television to do a discussion on the data bank society with Kenneth Baker – a rather conceited young businessman who has just been elected Tory MP for Marylebone* – and Henry Cooper, the former British heavyweight champion who is an interesting and pleasant man.

---

* The St Marylebone by-election was caused by Quintin Hogg's appointment as Lord Chancellor. Kenneth Baker had been MP for Acton, 1968–70.

Monday 23 November
The Referendum argument is going well and I am winning a bit of support. The anti-Marketeers are pleased, although they had doubts. Douglas Jay I know is happy, Peter Shore is doubtful and thinks it is an irrelevance. I am not making much headway with the pro-Marketeers, but it will take a little time for the idea to sink in.

Tuesday 1 December
The big news this evening is trouble at Holland Park School where a supply teacher engaged on a monthly basis has been advised she can't continue: she told the students she was sacked, and there is trouble. The newspapers have been stirring it all up.

Wednesday 2 December
The press arrived in force at the school. Some photographers gave five or ten bob to some of the kids to break windows and others had given them tomatoes to throw – which were actually thrown back at them! Caroline gave a press conference as best she could. But it is part of the great attack on Holland Park and the comprehensive movement, and upon Caroline and me.

It is a good example of how the mass media operate. Nobody has taken any notice of Holland Park for years because it is a very ordinary comprehensive. But when we send our children there it is immediately described as the fashionable Eton of comprehensives, though it never was. Then there is a change of Government, we are thrown out, you get a bit of trouble like yesterday, the whole thing is built up as being the centre of crime and violence, and the *Daily Sketch* throws its hands up in horror. The police had to be called today – but to get rid of the press.

To the Lobby lunch for John Davies, as the guest of George Clark of *The Times*. John Davies was really lying on a psychiatric couch. He was charming and created a favourable impression, having had a terrible knockabout following his speech about lame ducks in the House of Commons. He compared himself with the Sorcerer's Apprentice – in Disney's *Fantasia* – who started up the music and couldn't stop it. The music was like rushing water and every time he opened the House of Commons door the water poured in. He had to keep the Tory Party sweet, and his constituency Party really wanted a hunting-and-shooting man. The press was difficult and he couldn't control the nationalised industries. One got a glimpse of a man whose life was based on authority, suddenly discovering the problems of running things by consent.

Friday 4 December
To Transport House with Mik, and looked round the office. It is terribly overcrowded and people are not treated properly. You can sense the

frustration. Harry Nicholas is immensely authoritarian, as many trade union leaders are when they are put in a position of power. We had a short and rather difficult meeting with two representatives of the staff council who were very dissatisfied.

Saturday 5 December

In the evening Caroline and I went to David Kingsley's: there were about a hundred people there and a chamber quartet from the London Symphony Orchestra.

I had a talk to Harold, who told me that had we won the Election he would only have continued as Prime Minister for three years. I have often suspected this but he has never said it specifically before. It is an interesting piece of information, because if we win the next Election he wouldn't continue the full term as Prime Minister as he is determined that he will never be defeated again. That means that the next Leader of the Labour Party will be elected within the next few years – that's my view. If I am going to make any sort of bid for the leadership at any stage, I shall have to begin preparing for it soon.

Monday 7 December

There was a power cut at 7.45 this morning because of the go-slow or work-to-rule by the power workers in pursuit of their claim. It lasted for two hours. Went to talk to Harold about the possibility of getting some proper meetings of Party officers every now and again to consider the running of the Party, giving the Party a higher sense of direction, which it entirely lacks. Harry Nicholas is useless and doesn't see Harold often and the Executive is too big to do anything. The officers don't meet, and the Shadow Cabinet is just concerned with parliamentary tactics. And Harold is desperately busy writing his memoirs, or what he insists on calling his record of his administration.

We also discussed the question of the Common Market: he rebuked me again for having launched my Referendum idea and I replied that the Party might need it at some stage, that it might be handy. He said, 'Yes, but why say it now?', although he did add that he was glad that I hadn't come out against the Common Market. I said, 'Well, we have got to discuss it. Anyway I am thinking ahead because I am going to be Chairman of the Party next year.' He responded, 'Do you think I am not thinking ahead?' He always resents any suggestion that he is not farsighted. He made it absolutely clear that he was going to get off the hook by discovering that conditions for entry into Europe were not right.

But what he doesn't understand is that if he does come out against the Common Market it will absolutely wreck his credibility: the Tories will simply put up posters showing what he said about industrial relations when Prime Minister and then what he said when in Opposition under trade union pressure; what he said about the Common Market when Prime Minister and then when in Opposition, again under trade union pressure. And they will put on the bottom of the poster, 'Can you ever trust him again?' It is going to be much more difficult than he thinks.

Wednesday 9 December
Had lunch with Charles Delacourt-Smith and Len Murray, Vic Feather's assistant in the TUC. Like many trade unionists when they get near the top job, Len Murray has become very steady, self-reliant and confident. He made a revealing point. He said that with 9,750,000 members and their families, the trade union movement had always assumed that it represented the British public and the TUC didn't understand why it was necessary to spend money on advertising itself. We urged the case very strongly.

Shadow Cabinet meeting, and I made the case for an early General Election, which was somewhat sniffed at. We discussed the Common Market briefly and then the question of the speakership* came up. We were told that the Tories had offered us the choice between two Tory candidates – Selwyn Lloyd and John Boyd-Carpenter, MP for Kingston-Upon-Thames.

Harold made the most ghastly speech in which he said that we didn't want a strong but a weak Speaker; Selwyn Lloyd would be weak, he was older and his constituency would be shaky. It was such a crude speech and there was no account at all taken of the need for Parliament to have a really strong Speaker at this critical period in its history. Tony Crosland, Michael Foot and I spoke up for a strong Speaker and Harold Lever and Shirley Williams supported us. But in favour of Selwyn Lloyd were Harold Wilson, Fred Peart, Barbara Castle, Ted Short, Roy Jenkins, Bob Mellish, Douglas Houghton and George Thomson. So we agreed we would support Selwyn Lloyd. We should never have agreed to a fix of that kind.

The Party went to the Fabian Executive and had a row with Dick Crossman about whether next year's series of Fabian lectures should be concerned with a lot of detailed social security points or whether they should inject some new ideas into politics – like our attitude towards women, our approach to European questions, and so on. So I was, predictably, put on the committee to consider what the themes should be. I find Dick Crossman absolutely passé. He is interested in

---

* Horace King, the first Labour Speaker, retired in 1970 and his successor was chosen by election because of dissatisfaction with the traditional 'emergence' of a new Speaker. Selwyn Lloyd, MP for the Wirral, was a former Conservative Chancellor and Foreign Secretary.

revelations, in trouble, in sensation, in the detailed Civil Service points but he's awfully slow to pick up the general drift of events.

Thursday 10 December
At Bristol University I moved my motion to set up a joint working party with academic staff and students – bringing together the university, the polytechnic, the technical college and the teachers' training college – to consider relations between those organisations, and between all of them and the industry and community life of the city.

This went down reasonably well at the University Court and was carried, but the ossification of the Court proceedings was evident with the formal atmosphere and all the doctors in their robes.

Tuesday 15 December
I went to the Garden Hotel to speak at a conference organised by the International Organisation of Political Consultants. The president is Hubert Humphrey's PR man, and the main driving force is the American PR expertise in the field of political television. I must admit, I am not attracted by the idea that you can package a candidate just like a product. Still, I accepted the invitation to go because I wanted to hear the Tory Sir Michael Fraser, of Central Office, speaking.

Michael Fraser described the Election campaign of June 1970. He didn't say much of interest except that in retrospect Heath had done well because nobody had expected him to win, but he had stuck to his guns and this had impressed the Tories. Fraser didn't appear to have any historical perspective at all. He said he thought that the Fifties had been marvellous, the Sixties had been 'very difficult', that the Tories had been defeated in 1964 because things were 'difficult', and the Labour Party in 1970 because things were 'difficult'. Then he moved into a cricketing parallel. Just as in a game of cricket, after nobody has scored for a long time, you do get some runs scored, people's faith in the system will return – which is a complete illusion.

Wednesday 16 December
Executive this morning, where there was a frightful row about the Kenyan Asians[1] resolution, which I had carried through the Home Policy and International Committees in support of Joan Lestor and against Jim Callaghan. Jim was livid so I made a few amendments to meet some of Jim's points and this was carried. When Jim realised that he was up against it he simply said, 'We don't want any more blacks in Britain': it really did reveal at bottom what it is all about.

The next item was my resolution advocating a special conference to be held before the Parliamentary Party had voted on the Common Market question. I moved this briefly. Denis said there wouldn't be time to organise a special conference and in any case we couldn't get a hall. Fred Mulley said that if the Tories hurried the legislation, the Labour Party in the House would simply abstain, as if somehow on the greatest issue of the century for Britain, Labour MPs could abstain on the grounds that they hadn't had time to consider it. Roy said something, and then I blew my top. I said this was a grave matter and I was not prepared to explain to my grandchildren that we hadn't voted on the question of British entry into the Common Market because we couldn't get a hall; I was not prepared to abstain and that those who were in favour of entry into Europe had better begin making the case for it instead of hoping to slip it through, which is what they are trying to do.

I carried my resolution on a special conference overwhelmingly, about 14 to 1, I think. Afterwards Roy, with his nostrils distended with rage, said to me, 'There are some of us who will never vote against entry into Europe.' I said, 'I am never going to urge you to do so. If there is a Referendum you can vote for it then, but up till then we will argue that it should be put to the public.' Then Denis said, 'Your "support" for Europe is much distrusted. Why don't you make some speeches in favour?' Well, *he* doesn't make any speeches in favour. So my relations with those two are very poor at the moment. But this is a huge issue and it has got to be dealt with seriously.

Had lunch at the German Embassy with Herr von Hase, the Ambassador. I had heard about a study which had been done on the Federal Chancellor's office in Bonn. He gave me the documents (which have never been published in Germany) and Ray Fletcher [Labour MP for Ilkeston] has agreed to translate them from the German for me. We discussed these arrangements which were intended to make the Chancellor's office more effective. In effect, Willy Brandt is forming his own Government within a Government so that he can crosscheck what every Minister says. His personal advisers will therefore be more powerful than the Ministers. My approach would be to bring Ministers into the inner councils and then let the rest be hived off. It was most interesting and thoroughly enjoyable.

Went to the *New Scientist* Christmas party, then to the Labour Party gathering briefly where Alf Richmond, one of Harold's outer office hangers-on loaned by the *Daily Mirror*, told me that Marcia had not been around for four or five weeks, and kept ringing up and cancelling the Christmas cards and changing arrangements that had been made.

Thursday 17 December
In the *Spectator* today George Gale claimed there was a call-girl ring organised at Holland Park School, so this is another fresh twist in the attack.

Frank McElhone came to see me; he has been on at me for some time.

Broadly speaking, he thinks I should be Leader of the Labour Party and he would like to organise my campaign. I discussed it with him briefly in the summer. He is a decent chap, a Catholic, a fruiterer from Glasgow. We had about half an hour's talk and he gave me lots of advice and said I should organise little groups at home and get some press people on my side.

Friday 18 December
Worked at home and Frances Morrell came to lunch. She wants to get out of the Fabians and would like to get into Transport House. She is an extraordinarily shrewd woman and is very popular.

To the Labour Parliamentary Association dinner, where Harold and I were the only speakers. I paid a warm tribute to Harold for his great role in stirring public interest in 1963/4 and for standing up to attack, and so on. But he rebuked me for having referred to his contribution in the past tense, which I thought was significant.

Then I said something about economics not being the beginning and end of life and we must introduce some new elements into politics, for example attitudes to women and young people. Harold responded blindly with another of his boring balance of payments speeches; we were on different notes.

Wednesday 30 December
Got up early and went to Stansgate, picking up Hilary at Liverpool Street Station on the way. It will be nice to get away from London just for a few days for New Year.

Thursday 31 December
With the defeat of the Government and my disappearance from the Ministry of Technology my whole life has totally altered since the Election. I have spent the last six months engaged in fifty or sixty public meetings, using them to pick up the attitude of people to some new ideas. The first pamphlet I wrote, *The New Politics*, has been a useful focus, and I am committed to writing a book, though in fact I haven't made any progress with it at all. It may be that the right thing to do is to write pamphlets and leave the book for a while.

Although I am the spokesman on trade and industry, I haven't given a great deal of attention to the House of Commons despite there being quite a body of support there for me personally. Bob Mellish said to me the other day he was sure Harold Wilson would not be the Leader of the Labour Party by the end of 1971.

Wednesday 6 January 1971
Hans Janitschek, General Secretary of the Socialist International, came to see me. An Austrian of about thirty-six, and a pupil of Chancellor

Kreisky's, he has travelled extensively, set up a regional office in the Far East, visited Allende in Chile and has established contacts with the African socialists and also with some of the Arab socialist leaders. I put to him my ideas for trying to formulate a policy for the Labour Party when we are members of the European Communities which would bring together not only the Social Democrats in Germany and France but also the Communists, a sort of 'New Deal for Europe' democratic alliance of the Left.

Monday 11 January

Yesterday I worked on my Referendum Bill and today I rang Mark Arnold-Forster and asked if the *Guardian* would like it as a scoop, on the basis that the *Guardian* had asked me how I was getting on with the Referendum and so I had given them my latest working paper. Mark sent someone over to collect it. It is a good way of getting publicity for the provisions of the Bill without the difficulties of actually having to present the Bill myself and getting into trouble with the Shadow Cabinet.

Tuesday 12 January

The *Guardian* ran the article – a big back page story with every clause of the Bill presented. It was excellent.

This afternoon we had the election for the speakership. It was a very amusing occasion. Selwyn Lloyd was nominated. Then Maxwell-Hyslop, Conservative MP for Tiverton, who made a tremendous speech, and Willie Hamilton on our side, both nominated the Labour MP Geoffrey de Freitas, who hadn't been consulted. Geoffrey de Freitas got up in a real panic and begged the House not to elect him. Although I had voted against Selwyn Lloyd in the Shadow Cabinet, I did vote for him in the lobbies: he was elected.

Had a talk to Peter Shore about the Common Market: he is emerging now as the main leader against entry into Europe. I was delighted to get a message from Douglas Jay this evening, asking me if I would speak to the Common Market Safeguards Committee on my Referendum proposal. So I quickly dropped a note to Geoffrey de Freitas asking if he would allow me to come to the Labour Committee for Europe and he agreed. Between the two committees, the Referendum issue is now being taken seriously.

Wednesday 13 January

Shadow Cabinet at 5. Denis Healey raised the question of my Referendum campaign and tried to get the meeting to agree that it should be stopped. I hit back hard and said this was my view, it was just as sincerely held as Roy's view or Fred Peart's view, I wasn't attacking anybody, and I was deadly serious about it. Harold said we would discuss it at next Monday's meeting of the Shadow Cabinet.

Then there was a discussion about Rudi Dutschke, the German student wounded in Berlin in 1968 who has been here as a refugee ever since. The Home Secretary Maudling wants to send him back on the grounds that there is a political security threat in having him here. Jim was a bit embarrassed by the affair and didn't want us to get involved.

At 6 I met Giorgio Fanti of *Paese Sera*, the Italian Communist evening newspaper, and Amendolo, the Italian Communist Party leader, who is in London for a meeting of the Western European Communist Parties. He said he had told the British Communists that they should join Europe, that there was opportunity there and that it was necessary to have some machinery at the Continental level to deal with international companies. I strongly agreed with him, whereas Peter Shore's argument is that it would be disastrous and set back socialism and so on.

The whole discussion rotated round whether socialism was something you had to achieve in one country using the national mechanism or whether you could use bigger and smaller organisations. I sounded out Amendolo on a democratic European alliance of the Left which would provide a focus for the Eastern Europeans, including people like Dubcek, when they gradually return to positions of authority and try to break away from the Stalinist system.

In the evening I had dinner at Kettners restaurant with a Finnish party who are over here. Roy Jenkins, Jim Callaghan, Ron Hayward, Harry Nicholas, Joe Gormley and Gwyn Morgan were also there. We talked about the Referendum and apparently in Finland they do have provision for a Referendum. For the first time I got some contact with Roy Jenkins on the subject. He is looking for a way out of his own difficulties and although he is very much against a Referendum, he is now taking the idea seriously.

Sometime in the course of the last day or two Jim Callaghan said to me that he took a strictly political view of the Common Market. He says he is sitting on the fence but he sees no reason at all why we as a Party shouldn't come out against the Common Market now and if we ever won an Election, apply to join ourselves; indeed this would seem to him perfectly acceptable as a political manoeuvre.

Talking to Roy in the car I invited him back home for a while. I explained the strategy for a Referendum, which he was opposed to. But I think he is anxious to maintain some links with me. I asked him how he saw the future because, I said, I could see a possibility of the Labour Party actually splitting on this, resulting in a broad centre party which was European, flanked by a Powellite Right and a Michael Foot–*Tribune* Left. He said, 'I hope it doesn't come to that,' but he didn't rule it out. It was the first time he had been in our house for six or seven years or maybe longer.

Thursday 14 January

I went on the *24 Hours* programme to discuss the problem of violence with the historian Max Beloff and Robin Blackburn, who had led the LSE revolts. It went well until the end when the presenter, Bob McKenzie said, 'Well now, how do we deal with this. I take it that in the light of the bomb attack on Robert Carr,' which had occurred in the last couple of days, 'we have got to tighten up on security of Ministers, get rid of people like Dutschke, and so on.' I said, 'Wait a minute, you are putting Dutschke in the same sentence as an attempted murderer. That is exactly what you always do. You never treat this issue fairly,' and I launched into an attack on the mass media. Bob was upset and on the defensive, but he was clearly in the wrong.

Monday 18 January

All-day meeting of the Shadow Cabinet. In the afternoon we discussed the Common Market. Denis said he didn't think Heath could promote the EEC unless the Tories carry it through the House without Labour support, but if we were going in the sooner the better because the Government that took us in would lose a General Election. Denis said he had changed his view, having been strongly opposed to it before, he was now in favour of entry. He thought the economic consequences were unpredictable but if we stayed out we would lose more. We had the problem of coping with Japan and if we were outside any bloc we really would suffer. Politically he didn't think it would be significant. There was little prospect of monetary union.

I said that personally I had been opposed but was now in favour. I was a long-term federalist: I didn't think we could decide the main issue before the terms were known but we could discuss how we would approach it. It was a historic decision – it was irreversible and would fundamentally affect our sovereignty. As I understood it, the timetable would be, first, the recommendation at Party Conference (which would probably vote against it) and then the PLP vote. I drew attention to the fact that we simply could not have a free vote in Parliament, with the Shadow Cabinet voting different ways, after the Conference had given its collective view. You couldn't have senior members of the Shadow Cabinet saving Heath on a vote of confidence. I thought it would produce a major crisis in the Party and maybe break the party system. It would create a sense of trickery and do immense damage. We wouldn't be able to claim in future that the Tories were responsible for the impact of the Market because we would have been partly responsible for it.

So I outlined the alternative – that the Conference would come out for a General Election and after the Election we would have a Referendum on entry. This would mean that if you voted Tory you were voting for entry and if you voted Labour you would have the opportunity to choose for yourself. I said if the three Party Leaders couldn't persuade the British public, then it was most unlikely that we should go in; I believed we would win a Referendum and we would be doing ourselves no harm. But they would be totally misjudging the British temperament if they thought it could be slipped through.

Michael Foot said he had always believed we wouldn't get in and he thought that by trying in the past, we had wrecked our relations with the French. There would be a loss of sovereignty and, although he was instinctively against referenda, he thought this was a unique affair and there should be one. That would be the way to defuse it. People did care, he said, and we ought to consider alternative ways of dealing with it – an early meeting was required. If a split in the Party occurred, it would destroy all that we stood for.

George Thomson said that a French veto was unlikely to save us from the decision and it would precipitate a major crisis if we didn't go in. The terms were not very different from what we expected. A Referendum would be difficult, a democratic problem. He thought it would weaken the Labour Party in a General Election campaign, and pointed out the objections of Scottish colleagues, Willie Ross and himself, to a Referendum, commenting, 'We would never have got out of India if we had had a Referendum on that.'

Then Roy Jenkins said it was potentially politically damaging if we stayed out, and he didn't want us to lay down our terms. We should have a serious discussion just after Easter. As for the Referendum it was a unique idea, but not urgent. He thought there were grave disadvantages to a Referendum, because they always helped the right-wing. It was not an irrevocable decision, we *could* get out of the Common Market, he said. Now, if you said that publicly, it would create a scandal in Europe. I was interested he had made the comment.

Jim Callaghan said he was genuinely puzzled and confused and didn't want to wreck the Party. He thought this was more dangerous than the Industrial Relations Bill and we might get a new party splitting away. Harold said he didn't think it would be decided by the summer but he thought the Conference would be against it.

Tuesday 19 January
The postal strike begins tomorrow. I got a death threat letter allegedly from the Empire Loyalists, signed John Bull, this morning. I handed it to the police. It said I was first on the list, then Carr, and then Heath. I was

very flattered by this until I read the envelope and it said Mr Wedgwood Benn, Chancellor of the Exchequer!

Frank McElhone came to talk to me and I appointed him as my PPS. Frank is a relatively new Member, he was the chief magistrate in Glasgow, the only man in Scotland who got telegrams of congratulations from both Celtic and Rangers, and a very active constituency member. He runs a great advice centre in a disused bank, which is staffed every day.

Friday 22 January

I went to Newport and Neil Kinnock picked me up and drove to Bedwelty where I addressed about a hundred people at the annual dinner. It was a marvellous atmosphere. I heard a bit from Neil about his own difficulties as a new young MP in this old mining constituency.

Monday 25 January

Neil Kinnock told me today that he and about thirty others were organising a demonstration tonight against the guillotine on the Industrial Relations Bill and they were planning either to stand up in their places or to stand in front of the Speaker and try to get themselves or the House suspended. I argued with him for a long time, as sympathetically as I could, saying this would be a big step and it would annoy other members of the Party. I thought it worthwhile to go and see Bob Mellish, who was talking to Stan Orme and Callaghan about the same thing, and I did persuade Bob to call a meeting of the Shadow Cabinet in the evening to consider what to do. Michael Foot very sensibly said it would be stupid to make a big thing of this.

But it was agreed that some members of this group should come and meet Roy, Michael Foot, Bob Mellish, Douglas Houghton and Jim Callaghan. So we all dispersed but they failed to persuade the group not to demonstrate. So at about 9.45, they all got up, about thirty of them, including Eric Heffer and Reg Freeson, who are both Front Bench spokesmen, and stood in front of the table and shouted. The Speaker suspended the sitting, having said that this was all extremely boring, as boring as a standing ovation, which was quite a funny remark.

After the first suspension we had agreed to talk to the demonstrators in the Tea Room, but they were determined to go on and when the suspension ended, there they were standing in the middle again. The Tory Chief Whip, Francis Pym, got up and moved that the question be put, and it was put, and there was a vote and the Speaker declined to hear points of order. So that brought it to an end. It was rather surprising and there was a great deal of excitement.

Thursday 28 January

To the Party meeting at 6 which was absolutely packed. Bob lectured those of us who had been absent from votes in a general sense and then Douglas Houghton said we had set up an Action Committee made up of himself, the Leader and Deputy-Leader of the Party, the Chief Whip and Barbara Castle to plan our work for the next week. He produced a code of conduct under which we pledged ourselves not to be away unpaired for the week and not to give any hints to our opposite numbers as to what might be happening – really to declare parliamentary war. He said that at the end of the debate at midnight tonight, when the guillotine falls, there would be something like twenty-one clauses and fourteen amendments that wouldn't have been debated and we could therefore have up to thirty divisions. We could either vote on all those divisions, about seven hours of voting, simply walk out of the House, or vote on certain key divisions. He asked the Party to agree to trust the decision entirely to the Action Committee and that there would be no private enterprise at all. This was accepted. Shirley Summerskill, who is a doctor, got up and commented on the possible health implications of this, but there wasn't much discussion. I talked to a few people in the course of the evening in the Tea Room. Shirley Williams told me she thought Denis Healey would be the Leader of the Party by the end of this Parliament. Her basis of analysis was that Jim was too old, too discredited and right-wing; Roy had boxed himself in totally on Europe and couldn't do anything but vote for entry; while Denis was emerging as a capable, tough, sophisticated political leader.

Anyway it came to midnight, and when the guillotine fell the voting began and we voted twenty-two times. It was a great psychological experience. Here was the Party purging itself of Government in a way because, although it has long since been forgotten because it has happened so often in the past few weeks, it was the final occasion on which we ate our words as a Government and as Ministers on industrial relations, and we went through the lobby time after time after time. We must have spent five hours actually locked in the lobby and it was interesting to see people talking to each other. There was a game of chess going on between Douglas Jay and John Stonehouse. Members began reading the old *Hansards* on the bookshelves. At the end I persuaded a few people to start singing the 'Red Flag'. In the final division as we went through the lobbies, we sang the 'Red Flag', 'Cwm Rhondda' and 'We Shall Overcome' and we filed back into the Chamber and stood and sang. Harold came in and we all threw our order papers in the air. It was ridiculous in a sense and anybody from outside would have thought we were mad but the Tories were very dispirited and we were encouraged. I think it did the Party good.

Monday 1 February
I rang Clive Dunn, one of the television stars of *Dad's Army*, who has just had a tremendous hit record, 'Grandad', and he agreed when he was in Bristol next month to come and meet some old-age pensioners at Memory Hall.

Tuesday 2 February
At the Fabian Executive we discussed the autumn programme. I had put in a paper some time ago suggesting that the Society open its doors to outsiders so that people might come to the Labour Party through Fabian lectures. Dick Crossman had been contemptuous of this at the last Fabian Executive but I was put on the committee to consider the lectures and I had put my paper in and suggested we dealt with young people, with workers' control, with women and with community action generally.

Tonight one or two people attacked this programme but Dick Crossman weighed in and said this was exactly what the Labour Party ought to be doing now – listening to people on the outside. He was making my speech! It was an astonishing transformation. In the end it was agreed we would invite Caroline Coon to speak on behalf of young people and the whole drug culture/alternative society scene, Bill Jones to talk about workers' control, Germaine Greer to talk about the women's movement, and I would do the fourth lecture absorbing all this into the Labour Party, and be chairman of all the lectures.

I went off to the Scottish Group because rumours of the closure of Upper Clyde Shipbuilders had been getting rife during the day. Bruce Millan [MP for Glasgow Craigton] and I were deputed to see John Davies. John in fact was at home so I rang him and he said there wasn't going to be a statement tomorrow and I shouldn't believe all the rumours; he would tell me what was happening. It hadn't gelled yet but he would tell me before it did and, probably, 'there would be some crystallisation' this week, that there were discussions going on about it on an hourly basis. He said more than he should.

Wednesday 3 February
Tonight the House of Commons is buzzing with rumours about something. All we know is that a Tory Whip told somebody that there was going to be a major statement tomorrow which would rock us in our straps. Rumours varied from the possibility that Rolls Royce was going bust to Princess Margaret getting a divorce or the Queen abdicating – that was the spirit in which we went to bed.

Thursday 4 February
This morning it became pretty clear that the Rolls Royce story was the subject of yesterday's rumours.

Went into the House and had a word with Harold Wilson about Rolls Royce and was shown a copy of the statement issued by the board saying they were going into liquidation and that the Government would be making a statement in the afternoon.

At 3.30 the statement was made and it was extremely grave, particularly as it announced that the Government was going to take over Rolls Royce. After that all hell broke loose. I laid on a meeting with the Rolls Royce MPs and we considered a line of action to take. Talked to Frank McElhone who was immensely helpful, and was then approached by BBC and ITV people to do various programmes: I agreed to do the 10 o'clock radio programme and ITN. I worked hard all evening and was continuously on the phone to people.

Saturday 6 February
A series of phone calls to Ivor Manley, Otto Clarke and Derek Moon, just to check what I could of the background to the Rolls Royce story.

On Thursday, Friday and today the press has been full of Rolls Royce and the effect on confidence of losing it, not only on exports but on confidence in the City, and how the ritual slaughter of this company will probably change the course of British politics.

Sunday 7 February
I went down to Bristol and arrived at Transport House, where all the Rolls Royce shop stewards had gathered and Bristol MPs Arthur Palmer and Michael Cocks were there. I reported to the group the background of the Rolls Royce story as far as I had been able to dig it out. They put a lot of questions and raised points of great importance to them. It was useful because there is a great deal of anxiety.

Monday 8 February
Got up early, went to the House of Commons where I met the Rolls Royce shop stewards from Bristol, Derby, Coventry, Northern Ireland and Scotland and talked to them about the debate today. They then met the engineering staff from Derby who had come separately to talk about the RB-211.

In the afternoon we had the Rolls Royce debate which Jeremy Thorpe opened, followed by the Chancellor, Barber, and then me.

Tuesday 9 February
I did *World at One*, following Corfield's statement yesterday at the end of the debate that the RB-211 was no good. I criticised him sharply.

While I was at the radio studio I heard a man called John Tooey, the legislative assistant of New York State Assemblyman Andrew Stein, who is coming here at the end of the week, talking about noise levels in

New York. I would have liked to get in on the act because a Bill proposed by Stein would in fact prevent Concorde operating. It was an interesting new element in the situation.

Wednesday 10 February

This afternoon John Davies made a statement about UCS, giving support to Yarrows, and I welcomed this warmly and, of course, greatly embarrassed Davies with his own Back Benchers, which was the intention. Then we had the all-day debate on the Rolls Royce Nationalisation Bill and Corfield opened, followed by Bill Rodgers. There was no proper legal advice or anything and it was an absolute shambles. I wound up on our side and made a good speech and David Price at the end was confusing and confused.* Hilary came and listened to the debate which dragged on all through the night.

Frances Morrell came and had dinner with me. I put to her the possibility that I might go to America to give evidence to the Stein hearings on Concorde and asked her what she thought of it. She interrogated me very closely and said if this was about the people, not about the aircraft, it might be possible. Her advice was shrewd.

Saturday 13 February

I worked all day on the possibility of this American trip and spoke to Andrew Stein and Tooey themselves about their bill. Frances Morrell was advising me on the phone and I contacted Gordon Farnsworth as editor of Bristol's main paper to get him to come.

Monday 15 February

Went to Transport House with Ian Mikardo to persuade Harry Nicholas that the time was coming when he might retire, and he will in fact go near the end of the year.

Tuesday 16 February

I had a phone call this morning from Willis Martin of the International Air Transport Operators in New York, who said, 'Mr Benn, I represent the airlines, and we don't want you to come to New York – you'll just give publicity to this guy Stein and we know how to fix him. We have people in Albany and we just go straight to the leaders, we don't bother with hearings.' The whole crudity of the American business lobby came out. He said, 'Anyway, who the hell has ever heard of Mr Stein?' So I said, 'Who has ever heard of Ralph Nader? I am sorry but I'm coming and I'm not representing the airlines, I'm not representing the aircraft

---

* Frederick Corfield, Minister of Aviation Supply and Conservative MP for Gloucestershire South; David Price, Parliamentary Secretary, Aviation Supply, and Conservative MP for Eastleigh.

manufacturers, I am representing the workers in Bristol and they would be affected.' Of course, he had forgotten, never having met me, or hadn't cottoned on to the fact, that I was an elected legislator too; but no doubt he will help when I get there.

Had a talk with Corfield at the House of Commons. Corfield does see some merit in my going to New York although he has had the same report from Washington – that Stein's bill is unlikely to get through. The problem is that the enormous expenditure – £40 million – on the new nozzle has not produced the noise reduction expected, and Concorde is going to be a very noisy aircraft. At any rate it is clear that on the Government side I shall get a measure of support.

Wednesday 17 February
Frances Morrell came to breakfast this morning before leaving for New York on an advance mission to try and set up the Concorde trip. I had taken the responsibility of paying her fare and expenses which is going to be heavy for me, I don't know how I am going to pay it back but I shall have to find some way of doing it. She is going to contact the press, set up TV coverage if she can, and try to make contact with Nelson Rockefeller and Lindsay whom we cabled last Sunday.

Saturday 20 February
Up at about 7 and the shop stewards came from Rolls Royce and gave me a letter to pass on to the American trade unions.

We had a tea party for Melissa who is fourteen today. Stephen was home from Keele.

From 22–27 February Gordon Farnsworth, the Editor of the Bristol Evening Post, *Robert Adley (Conservative MP for Bristol North East) and I were in America to give evidence at the hearing of the New York State Assembly, which was part of the general campaign by the anti-Concorde lobby to stop Concorde from being allowed to land. While we were there I had some useful talks with John Volpe, US Secretary of Transportation, visited U Thant at the United Nations and John Lindsay, Mayor of New York.*

Monday 22 February
I have got to leave for New York in about an hour and I haven't packed yet. I think it is going to be a useful trip and I am looking forward to it, although it is going to be very tough and I think the big competition will be to get attention in the US. I hope there are demonstrations of some kind. The hearings will, I think, be televised and I shall go on to Washington. The press handling is the key to the whole thing – the more I think about politics now, the more it is a matter of influencing people through the mass media.

Gordon Farnsworth turned up at 9.30 and we finally left for London Airport where we met Robert Adley on the BOAC VC10 flight to New York. It was a perfect flight over.

When we arrived in New York, at about 1.45 New York time, Frances Morrell was waiting for us with a battery of photographers. We gave a short press conference and TV interviews on the object of our visit.

At 4 the four of us went to the British Consulate-General.

Frances told us that when she had first arrived the Consulate had told her there was no interest in our visit, that a press conference was inadvisable, that it would be impossible to get to see anybody, and that the press release she proposed to put out was much too long. She has been here now since Wednesday, telephoning every single newspaper correspondent, every single television and radio station, local, national and other news desks. She has produced the response she wanted. I think she is remarkable.

We came back to the hotel and when we were there Mayor Lindsay telephoned and spoke to us and we gave him a quick run-down on the problem. He said, 'Why don't you stop in at the City Hall and see us on Wednesday afternoon?'

It is now 11.15 pm and I am sitting in my room at the Gotham Hotel, absolutely exhausted – almost too tired to sleep. There is no doubt that the trip has come at exactly the right moment. Interest in supersonic transport has reached a new peak in the US. Richard Wiggs's book attacking Concorde has been published. Our visit here is one of crucial importance and, as we made clear, we are here to campaign with the American people in favour of the product in Europe which is carrying the livelihood of a quarter of a million people.

Tuesday 23 February

At 9.30 we had the press conference. I made a statement in which we listed the points which were of concern to us – the Bristol interest, the environmental issue, the general problem of the side effects of environmental decisions, the economic and industrial arguments and finally the need for a better decision-making process. The press conference was a tough interrogation by people who were anti-SST, much more like a debate than an ordinary press conference. Then I did a short BBC interview.

At 11 I went over to meet U Thant, Secretary-General of the United Nations, and he said he remembered Father. I briefly presented to him my arguments for the United Nations to take a greater interest in industrial affairs, and I handed him a memorandum I had written, which I had sent to Michael Stewart and discussed with Hugh Foot. He said he might try to introduce these ideas into a speech he was making in the summer.

Afterwards I went back into Brian Urquhart's room and we talked a bit further. Brian has been with the United Nations for many years and knows the international scene very well. He said that U Thant was unpopular in America because the Israeli lobby had mobilised against him. He thought U Thant should go because he was bland and lacked the drive that the United Nations needed.

We talked about Henry Kissinger, the academic who is Nixon's adviser on foreign policy, and he warned against academics who came into politics with no experience of compromise, which is the heart of all politics, and in effect bypassed the whole democratic system. He thought the Germanic method of thinking in the White House was wholly unrelated to reality.

Clive Jenkins turned up, back from Washington where he had been talking to two Senators from California who were anti-SST, anti-Concorde and anti-me because I was here arguing for Concorde.

Wednesday 24 February
At 6 this morning Harlech TV telephoned. I was sound asleep, lying in bed with nothing on, and I picked up the phone in a fuzz. They said, 'We are on the air and we want to interview you straight away, is that all right?' I had no option, so with my head in the pillow and the telephone crammed up against my ear, I was interviewed for about five minutes on the Concorde mission. Later they gave me the tape and it sounded pretty funny. At 9.30 we went over to the BBC building and did a series of interviews for London.

At 10.30 in the Rockefeller Center, we went to see an assistant. Nelson Rockefeller himself was determined not to see us because the environment is a popular issue in America at the moment, and the last thing he wanted was to appear to be sympathetic to some British visitors who were in favour of supersonic aircraft.

Afterwards we went back to the hotel for a quick sandwich in my room, then went downtown in a taxi to see Mayor Lindsay. The taxi was terribly late because the man insisted on taking us through the centre of town, assuming that, as visitors, we wouldn't know there was a faster motorway down the side of Manhattan.

When we got to the City Hall there were huge barricades, police horses and two demonstrations; and inside the City Hall an absolute mass of people milling about, deputations of teachers and Puerto Ricans, and all sorts of people. We got a feeling of the tremendous vitality of American politics. In Bristol the City Hall is treated as if it were Buckingham Palace, the public are kept out, there are no seats, and so on. Lindsay called us in: he is a charming man, but I don't think highly of him – he is too much of a film star, very dapper, very much in the Kennedy mould, the international jet-set type. His wife, Maire, is a much abler and tougher creature. But still it was courteous of him. We began on Concorde, but he said, 'Look, I don't want to discuss that, we agreed this is a purely social call.' So we moved on to his job and how difficult New York was, and so on.

Thursday 25 February

Got up at 6 and Gordon and Robert came in for breakfast. At 11 we went down to the hearing just opposite the City Hall. As we might have expected, it wasn't a real hearing at all, it was just Stein who had booked a room and laid on the mass media. There was a little table and one other guy sitting with him, who was not a member of the Health Committee. So Stein was really left on his own.

A lot of other people came up, including some Republican state Congressmen, who said, 'Look, this guy is really a nit. If you are tough with him he will break down on television.' Obviously they hated his guts. Richard Wiggs of the anti-Concorde Project, John Connell of the Noise Abatement Society and I gave evidence, and Robert Adley and Gordon Farnsworth added something. There was a pilot from one of the airlines and the director of research of another airline. Well, after that I did various interviews with American and Swedish television and then we went back to the BBC. By this time we were pretty tired and we did some more broadcasts for *The World at One*, the *PM* programme and *Today* – we were never sure what time it was in London. It has been a dramatic day. One thing occurred to me – if Stein could have a hearing like that which focused attention on the representative nature of democratic politics, there is no reason why anybody shouldn't have hearings.

Friday 26 February

Up at 5.30 for the Washington Shuttle and from Washington Airport we were driven to the Department of Transportation where Secretary John Volpe, former Governor of Massachusetts and a building contractor, whom I had met a year ago, met us. He was desperately keen to have the Boeing 2707 supersonic plane go ahead, although the pressures against it are immensely strong. They are sure the Russian competition in this field is going to be powerful. The Americans who now sell 80 per cent of the world's aircraft will find that anyone who wants supersonic will have to go to Russia. They are not so worried about Concorde but there is a short period up to the end of March – when the Senate votes on the American supersonic transport – when there is an absolute common interest between us and the Americans. I put all this to Volpe. We then went to the Embassy in the Rolls; I gave a brief press conference, and we saw the Ambassador, Lord Cromer. Cromer had been Governor of the Bank of England when we were elected in 1964 and his speech just before the 1970 Election, saying the incoming Government would face an even more serious economic crisis than Wilson had faced in 1964, had played some part in shaking public confidence in the economic success of the Labour Government.

I dropped in at the Machinists' Union, left a note from the shop stewards in Bristol, then went on to see Senator Proxmire. He has been leading the campaign against Boeing and Concorde and, believe it or not, there was my old friend Howard Shuman working as his assistant. I like Proxmire, a tall rather austere man, of tremendous financial probity, not in an anti-corruption sense but in seeing that public money wasn't wasted. I found myself in a rather silly position because on most issues I would have agreed with him. But I had this particular battle to fight and I said I saw no reason at all why the United States shouldn't cancel their plane, without us cancelling ours. We built the thing and we weren't intending to give it up.

Then I flew back to New York, packed and on to Kennedy airfield to catch our VC10 back to London.

The trip was a dramatic thing to undertake, and the Americans took us very seriously. They treated us courteously but realised that we were part of a domestic controversy, which we were indeed, because the whole supersonic thing was raging at home while we were there.

Frances Morrell was brilliant. Her capacity to beaver away at phone calls, telling people hard news and interesting them, is quite remarkable and she made this issue real in New York against all the expertise of the Madison Avenue people.

Saturday 27 February
Landed at Heathrow where the press and television were out in force. The only way I could get to Bristol was to hire a car to Reading. At Reading I missed the train and had to hire another car all the way to Bristol. I had kept the shop stewards waiting pretty late, but there they were in Central Hall. There was a tremendous welcome and I just sat on the table, extremely tired, and told them everything that had happened as if they had been there themselves. They asked questions, and I said there was no guarantee but I thought we might have killed the Stein Bill.

Monday 1 March
I had dinner with Campbell Adamson of the CBI, Harold, Roy, Harold Lever and several others. Harold laid great emphasis on the fact that all members of the Cabinet at the time at which he was in charge were absolutely committed to the idea of joining the Common Market – although retrospective discipline by an ex-Prime Minister has no significance at all.

One thing that Harold made clear was that he intended to remain

Leader of the Party and to be Prime Minister again. I had a feeling that comment was put in specially for Roy's benefit.

Wednesday 3 March
In the evening I talked to Peter Shore. He is obsessed with the Common Market at the moment. He decided not to sit on the Front Bench with a job from Harold, which is probably wise because he is not prepared to be silent on the EEC. He is fighting terribly hard against the Common Market and is undoubtedly the leader of the anti-Common Market movement simply by dint of all the speeches he is making. I am pushing the Referendum; he thinks this is a bit of a side issue, whereas I think it is going to be the key issue.

Saturday 6 March
Went up by train to Newcastle and talked to the Northumberland Mechanics' Association and then to the dinner at which Vic Feather and Joe Gormley spoke. There were songs and bawdy speeches, and it was an agreeable evening. As a result of the Tories' Industrial Relations Bill, the trade union movement, and the working class even more, have become proud of being the working class. Legislation has succeeded in shutting off the idea that somehow you can escape from your class and come up in a Davis Escape Apparatus, one by one, to join the ruling class, because the ruling class has let you down and is trying to suppress you. There is a tremendous self-confidence in being yourself and what you are. It is 'black is beautiful' applied to the working class, which is marvellous. It oozed out of everything Vic Feather said.

Just sitting and listening I noticed how much everybody made a reference to where they came from – 'He's from this part of Northumberland, or from Durham, of course, I'm from Yorkshire, you're from Lancashire.' I wonder whether we have given anything like enough importance politically to regionalism. I am sure we haven't. We have only looked at it technically and in terms of blueprints.

Wednesday 10 March
Went to Bristol. Clive Dunn was in Bristol at the Old Hippodrome today and at my invitation he came and met the OAPs in Hanham. It was a tremendous success and everyone cheered and clapped.

Tuesday 16 March
In the evening Caroline came and had dinner; we went to the Strangers' Bar with Neil Kinnock, Frank McElhone, Charles Morris, and Norman Buchan. I had to keep going off to vote.

Wednesday 17 March
To the House of Commons Press Gallery lunch which John Davies was addressing. He gave an account of his political philosophy that was quite hair-raising, in the sense that it was much franker than anything we have had in the House of Commons; he attacked me at the end, which was surprising considering I was there. He described an occasion when he alleged I had asked for advice from a number of businessmen about a decision I had to take. One of them had said to John, 'Why doesn't he do nothing for a change!' This was the punch line of his speech, and it went down well with the Lobby to whom he is a bit of a hero. He is interesting to them because he is always getting into trouble.

Thursday 18 March
I went to the Commons for the debate on steel. The news from Washington is that the House of Representatives have voted down the money for the Boeing 2707 supersonic plane.

Tuesday 23 March
We had a special Shadow Cabinet to consider whether, as we approach the end of the Industrial Relations Bill in committee, we are prepared to vote all night, as the Left of the Party and trade union activists want, or whether we should have a series of token votes and go home. Roy Jenkins, Harold Lever, Tony Crosland and that group were against overdoing it, and Bob Mellish was determined we should vote right through, which Fred Peart and Michael Foot supported. I argued for voting all night and having done so, I did stay and voted fifty-three times.

Wednesday 24 March
In the evening Tony Lambert, Vice-President of the Young Liberals, came to see me. The Young Liberals interest me because they have broken away from the traditional politics where the sole function is to put a candidate in to Parliament, and are now deeply engaged in community action. They regard the parliamentary side as a secondary activity.

If the Liberal Party in Parliament is weakened as a result of this then the community action members will have to look for somebody else to support when the Election comes. A revamped Labour Party might be attractive to them. That was my motive in corresponding with them and I will meet them to consider this idea.

Friday 26 March
Jean-Jacques Servan-Schreiber telephoned this morning. As a matter of fact I was still asleep and I wasn't at all sure who he was. But he was back

from America where he had been launching his book, *The Radical Alternative*, and giving evidence in support of Senator Proxmire against the SST. He couldn't understand why I was pro-SST because the fashionable Left is anti, as indeed I would be, frankly, if we were just about to start it. But when I told him it was built in my constituency, being a politician he fully understood and asked if I would like to debate it with him in Paris. I said, 'No, I would not, I can't see any point in it.'

He is a very imaginative person, rich, exceptionally ambitious, and runs a tremendous political office of his own which is influential in France. But he has got poor judgment and his decision to stand against Chaban-Delmas in Bordeaux in the by-election, although he was already a Member of Parliament, did him a great deal of damage.

Wednesday 31 March
Went to the Party meeting this morning on the Budget and had lunch with the Czech Ambassador. We talked about East-West relations and I asked him about Czechoslovakia. I am glad I did because out came the latest official Czech thinking on the 1968 events. A scenario was being developed by Czech leaders in which the manoeuvres by NATO held in August 1968 were in order to provide some sort of a cover for Czechoslovakia to leave the Eastern alliance and join the Western alliance. It all seemed totally incredible to me but, by being courteous and polite and not insulting him, I got it all out although I think he knew I was pretty sceptical. Having been right through the Novotny period, which was Stalinist, and then the Dubcek period, when Dubcek was showing signs of liberalisation, and then having been through the invasion, he has now settled down to the official view of history as put out by the Supreme Soviet and now the new Czech regime.

Friday 2 April
Went to the TGWU in Bristol in the evening for a discussion on the trade unions and the Labour Party – the first of the talks I have set up with Ron Nethercott. I presented my paper on industrial policy as a way of starting the discussion, and as we went round the table, all the boiling, seething discontent with the last Labour Government came out – everything from little insults dealt because Harold wasn't polite when he visited, to the feeling that nobody cared a damn what they thought.

Some of them specifically said that what they needed was a trade union political party of their own to get away from the Labour Party, which of course would be absolutely fatal. I listened to all this and said, 'Let me write a paper about it and I'll put it to you again.' The idea of setting up political action committees which would provide the trade unions themselves with a voice, instead of having to rely entirely on the Labour Party, formed in my mind.

Saturday 3 April
It was my birthday. I got home from Bristol pretty tired for the birthday tea and got a lovely welcome from the family. One of the entertainments was projecting on to the children's bare chests the slides of the heart and lungs from the Medical Dictionary, an amusing and interesting development of educational technology! In the evening we watched James Cagney – or rather Joshua did – on TV.

Sunday 4 April
Mo Mowlam, a friend of Alvin Toffler's, came to see me at his suggestion. She is very bright and has political ambitions.

During the Easter holidays, which the whole family spent in Cincinnati, I took the opportunity of going to Northwestern University to attend a seminar and to give a lecture at the University of Chicago. Professor Milton Friedman's ideas were the centre of our discussions in Chicago and it was the first time I had come across Friedman's influence, which had captured the imagination of American academics and later, of course, came to have a profound impact on British political thinking.

Tuesday 20 April
This evening I did *Late Night Line-Up* on television and I had the chance for the first time to develop my argument that in politics changes come from the bottom. There was an awful discussion with a terrible American broadcaster called Robert MacNeil, who said that the public would only understand things if they were presented by professional communicators, that trade unionists were inarticulate, and so on. He absolutely cooked his own goose by being so crude about it.

Mary Holland from the *Observer* attacked me from the Left and said I was much too optimistic about how things changed and in fact it was a much harder struggle.

Wednesday 21 April
To the Education Sub-Committee of the NEC and got Joan Lestor into the chair. I thought she was preferable to Eirene White or Shirley Williams. While we were sitting there, Joan Lestor was opening her mail and she had a big fat envelope and she tore it open; inside was another envelope which fitted very tightly into the outer one, and as she began pulling the inner envelope out smoke began pouring out of the envelope. So she dropped it on the ground, and I poured water on it, dropped it in a waste-paper basket and called the police who took it away. It was a home-made bomb of some kind and the man who had sent it had fixed some matches on the inner envelope and sandpaper on the outer one. If she had pulled it out quickly it would have burst into flames and blown up, and burned her face.

Caroline was asked to give the annual education lecture at the University of Wales.

Monday 26 April
Went to the Chinese Embassy to see their propaganda ballet film, *Red Detachment of Women*, which was a mixture of a morality play and an early Hollywood musical done in tremendous colour; too long, but interesting.

Wednesday 28 April
To the NEC this morning. My Referendum proposal was defeated, as I was the only person who voted for it. That was very surprising but it encouraged me to go forward to an appeal to the country and the Party.

Sunday 2 May
In Glasgow for May Day. Had breakfast in the hotel and lazed about. Then lunch with the Trades Council and witnessed a tremendous May Day march through the centre of Glasgow – six bands, two choirs and 10,000 people in Queen's Park. I made a speech advocating television programmes made by or for the unions. Afterwards there was a party at Frank and Helen McElhone's house and we came back via the Gorbals and caught the plane home.

Tuesday 4 May
I went this morning to see Ron Evans and one of the chief executives of Harlech Television about their offer of a twenty-five-minute programme to deal with trade union matters in the wake of my May Day speech. My suspicion was that this was just a way of calling my bluff so that I was rather sceptical to begin with but it was a genuine offer and I told them I would give it to the TGWU.

Wednesday 5 May
Had lunch with the Labour Friends of Israel, at the invitation of Ray Fletcher, and Michael Comay, the Israeli Ambassador, gave a talk on the situation in the Middle East. I must say it confirmed all my fears about Israel. He is a South African, has a South African accent, is a big tough military chap and his references to the Arabs were so crude and his philosophy so violently Cold War that it left a very unpleasant flavour in my mouth, and confirmed the wisdom in keeping out of Israeli politics for the moment.

In the evening I went to the *Guardian* 150th anniversary dinner where Willy Brandt and Ted Heath were speaking.

Thursday 6 May

To the House of Commons and met the producer from Harlech Television who is working on the TGWU programme: we agreed it should be done on a 'commune' basis, with all the members of the crew contributing their ideas. They are active trade unionists and this is very much in line with my general philosophy of government by discussion.

Talked to Peter Shore about the EEC. He is as obsessed with this anti-Common Market theme as I am on the Referendum, but we keep in touch.

This evening David Owen [Labour MP for Devonport] approached me and asked me if I would sign a pro-EEC letter in the *Guardian*, and I declined, because it had no provision for consulting people.

Saturday 8 May

Caroline was away all day at her Comprehensive Schools Committee conference on neighbourhood schools. I went to Bristol for a meeting with Transport and General officials and submitted a paper to them suggesting the TGWU should set up a political action committee, and encouraged other unions to follow suit. This was broadly accepted after a discussion about the possibility that it might be seen as a union take-over of the Labour Party. I promised to rewrite the paper to take account of the points that had been made.

In the afternoon I went canvassing in St George. In the evening I went to the Salvation Army Festival in the Citadel, as the guest of Cyril Rickards; I was chairman for the evening and had to introduce each of the band's numbers. Afterwards I hired a car and got home in two and a half hours, pretty tired. But I do like being home on Sunday, particularly as tomorrow is Joshua's birthday.

Monday 10 May

Went to the Shadow Cabinet this morning for the special Common Market meeting and I introduced the discussion. I said I thought there had been a substantial change in the political situation. Although there was some doubt as to whether we should have discussed Europe, it was such an issue we couldn't leave it out. In a matter of weeks we would know what the outcome of the Brussels meeting was, how the Heath-Pompidou meeting had gone, and how the currency crisis that had led the Germans to float against the wishes of the French would affect the situation. There would probably be a White Paper before July and a parliamentary vote before the recess, and we would need our special conference before July.

I said there were tremendous dangers to the Party and some advantage in reserving our position, but we really had to be frank among ourselves: we didn't know what our colleagues thought. The point is, do we want a conference, is it to be a free vote, are we going to have a Shadow Cabinet line, are the public to be consulted? This was an issue that divided us and the method of deciding the issue must be commensurate with its importance. It must be an open position and there was a danger of misjudging the public mood. I suggested we should demand an Election.

I went on to the political situation at home, where Heath had emerged as a strong leader. But the emergence of unemployment as a major issue had changed everything and discussion with the trade unions was our natural point of entry. The Party needed a national campaign on unemployment, the trade union interest had been reawakened and we were recreating the Labour Party. I referred to the political action committees and some of my ideas on industrial policy. Further ahead we ought to study social trends, to develop our themes much more clearly, particularly democratisation, education, the mass media, equality, harmony and diversity and the problem of national identity. We needed to develop an artificial hindsight so that we could leap over the future and try and look back on it.

Harold Lever thought it was hard to estimate the outcome over the EEC, but the Government would like to settle it soon. Denis was very much opposed to a Party conference if the Government was only going to have a 'take note' discussion before the end of July. Harold Lever, like all the pro-Marketeers, hopes the Government will accept a free vote because that way they will be sure of a majority in the House.

Michael Foot made a very powerful speech, and Bob Mellish said he thought there would be a substantial minority either way. Roy Jenkins said some people had strong convictions, meaning himself, then we had Ted Short, who could detect change in public opinion.

Harold Wilson summed up and said there were two issues: unity and the credibility of the Party. He was still pretty pro-Europe but kept his position open.

In the evening Harold was on television talking about the EEC and was awfully shifty. One can sense that there's a big crisis coming because we have heard today that the pro-EEC letter which David Owen asked me to sign was signed by about a hundred members of the PLP, and is appearing in the *Guardian* tomorrow.

Thursday 13 May

Caroline was out all day with the Egyptian Minister of Education and had lunch at Lancaster House with him and Mrs Thatcher, Secretary of State for Education. Dr Rushworth, the new Headmaster of Holland Park School, came home for tea. I voted in the municipal elections and then went to Transport House where we planned the weekend conference between the Shadow Cabinet and the NEC.

Friday 14 May
Presented my Referendum Bill in the House of Commons. I decided not to have anyone else sign it partly because all the people who would have signed it were anti-Europe and this would have been identified, and partly because in the end I thought my best role was to present constructive ideas to the Party around which it could unite, and not be mobilising on one side or the other.

Went to do the ITV *News at Ten* on Davies's statement, and I got back to the hotel exhausted. I listened to some French, which I am learning at the moment.

Monday 17 May
Mother's letter appeared in *The Times* today, arguing in favour of federal unity instead of uniformity in the Congregational Church and said what we want is a mosaic and not a monolith. It was very encouraging.

I went to the final session of a meeting between the Executive and the Shadow Cabinet.

On the question of industrial relations I said that unemployment was a major issue, and it was hard for us to take it on board because we ourselves had not succeeded in curbing it and that the issue had really recreated the Labour Party. I called for a major national campaign. I said it was a natural starting point for our dialogue with the TUC and that what we wanted was not a Labour version of an Industrial Relations Bill or prices and incomes policy but something quite new. I referred to the four points in my paper, which has now been widely discussed: public ownership on a Rolls Royce basis; industrial democracy; a ratio of incomes to get a greater degree of equality; and education, which was the key to the whole thing, particularly raising the general level of education instead of concentrating on the élites.

Denis Healey opened after coffee and talked about economics, how profit was necessary and how incentives for managers were the key. We must have a credible programme for growth and we should do better and have better links with the Trade Union Movement.

Wednesday 19 May
I went to the Executive and scored three victories today. First, I got it agreed that the officers should be in a position to advance the date of the special conference on the EEC if necessary. Second, I upheld the view that, despite an attack by Denis Healey, we should be free to give our money to the liberation movements without any strings attached. And third, I won on the Labour newspaper against a counter-attack by a lot of journalists and Barbara, and Renée Short.

I attended Harry Nicholas's National Executive press briefing, which was unbelievable. He treated the press as if they were a lot of German prisoners of war he was interrogating, or like a magistrate treats people up before him.

Thursday 20 May

Came back on the train from Southampton with Jeremy Thorpe who really is a very nice, agreeable and kind person but has no weight as a party leader – just thinks of the House of Commons as if it were the Oxford Union Debating Society. Absolutely out of touch with modern trends and movements.

Friday 21 May

Dinner in the Harcourt Room at the House of Commons with the graduate and student section of the Institution of Electrical Engineers. They are wildly Tory, have absolutely no idea about the relationship between engineers and society. Lord Nelson of English Electric was there. Why I have anything to do with them I do not know except that I champion their cause and they know it. And to an audience like that, the Concorde trip, which did me a lot of harm with the Left, was popular and seen as a great fight for British freedom and British independence against America.

Monday 24 May

Heath reported to the House on his talks in Paris. During the course of the questions and answers he was asked about a Referendum and he said he adhered to the view of Edmund Burke* who had sat for the constituency of the Right Honourable Gentleman, the member for Bristol South East. This confirmed my belief that I have got to deal with Burke at some stage.

Sunday 30 May

The Party is heading for an extremely difficult summer. There is a small group of highly dedicated Marketeers led by Roy Jenkins, with Bill Rodgers as campaign manager, and including the old Campaign for Democratic Socialism types. They are genuinely pro-Europe (I give them credit for that), but they also see a last opportunity to do to the Labour Party what they failed to do over disarmament and Clause 4, namely to purge it of its trade union wing and of its Left. This group, working with the conservative Europeans, really represents a new political party under the surface in Britain. They think a free vote would

---

* 'Your representative owes you, not his industry only, but his judgement: and he betrays instead of serving you if he sacrifices it to your opinion.' (Burke's Letter to the Electors of Bristol, 3 Nov 1774).

get them off the hook because they would be able to vote with Heath on the grounds that the question was above politics.

Of course the real crunch will come when specific legislation has to go through and any serious European would have to vote with the Government to bring British law into line with Community law. It is inconceivable that such a group, consistently voting with the Government, could do this without severing their links with the Labour Party, and to this extent it is impossible that the Party will do anything other than come out against Europe. But what the pro-Marketeers don't realise yet, though they soon will, is that if this situation becomes impossible for them, much better that they should be coming out against entering Europe without some consultation. This is what my Referendum offers them, but a Referendum is a difficult concept for them to consider and is a relatively novel idea, though Phillip Goodhart, the Tory MP, has written a book on referenda which he sent me and in which he argues that it is a perfectly established constitutional principle.

The anti-Marketeers are annoyed that although I am not anti-Market I do see the possibility of optimising their support by using the General Election/Referendum solution. So I think my role between now and the Conference, at which I become Chairman of the Party, is to present this proposal modestly and on my own. It is of constitutional importance but it also does have the great tactical advantage of keeping the Party united, and I think people will gradually come to see this. And if I am successful in getting constituency Parties to support my resolution (which I have sent round to everybody) and I get an overwhelming majority at Conference on this issue, I think the Parliamentary Party will have to accept it. I have some sympathy with Harold. He knows he can't fight the Conference. On the other hand he wants to preserve his position, and he says he is waiting for the terms to emerge. Actually what he is doing is waiting for the Party to decide and he will then have to give some leadership.

I want to make it clear that I am in favour of Europe. All the arguments against it are short-term arguments, based on what it looks like now, and omit the possibility that we might make changes when the time comes. But I can't get the Party to focus its mind on this and the possibility of a popular front in Western Europe with the Italian and French Communist Parties cooperating with us on areas of policy where a European stance has to be taken. All this will have to come later. Meanwhile I have developed and presented, and am keeping up the campaign for an Election Referendum with passion, sincerity and a little bit of knowledge.

What interests me is that it is beginning to get more and more like my peerage case of ten years ago. I can feel it in my bones that the public are really angry at the way they are being treated. They don't care much about the details of the Common Market or how the Commission in Brussels works and I believe the majority of them think it is inevitable that we will enter. But they are irritated at the way in which it is being done, and just as I mobilised my constituency and public opinion against the Government on the peerage case, I think I might be able to do it again now. Fleet Street is sceptical but it is part of my general campaign on a new philosophy of government.

Friday 4 June
Returned to London today after three most interesting days in Yugoslavia.* The lessons of their self-management applied in the area of our industrial policy and of their decentralisation to the republics for our regional policy are ones that we should study for our own benefit.

Monday 7 June
In the afternoon I went to the Chinese Chargé d'Affaires's office at Portland Place where Mr Pei formally issued an invitation to Caroline and me to visit China in September. For some time during the course of the interview they said nothing about it, to give me a chance to settle down, no doubt, and they asked me what I thought about American policy towards China and the two-China policy. I commented on the very welcome decision by Nixon to lift the ban on trading with China and said I thought the combination of the ping-pong players' visit to China, which had been a great success, and the fact that American opinion was now so strongly against the Vietnam War, had brought the Americans round.

I said I thought that Nixon realised he couldn't be re-elected unless he took a more positive view on the Vietnam War. And I thought that it would be very difficult for the Americans to pursue the two-China policy once Peking was seated in the United Nations.

I asked them about the official British attitude towards the recognition of China and they said they thought the Foreign Office was awaiting the decision of the Americans, which of course is true. Then at last they extended the invitation to visit China. I expressed tremendous gratitude and pleasure, and confirmed what I would like to see while I was there. We are to be the guests of the Chinese Institute of International Affairs.

Tuesday 8 June
In the early afternoon Frank McElhone and I caught the plane to Helsinki for the International Press Institute conference. We went via

---

* At the end of May, I paid a second visit to Yugoslavia for discussions with Yugoslav Ministers and Party officials and gave a lecture at the University of Belgrade.

Copenhagen and arrived very late. We were put up at the Vaakuna Hotel. I had never been so far North as that at this time of the year and although I couldn't see the midnight sun it was light all evening.

Wednesday 9 June
Had breakfast with Roy Fox, who is the Consul-General in the British Embassy in Helsinki, having come back a few months ago from being Deputy High Commissioner in Dacca, East Pakistan. He saw the whole situation deteriorating there and had apparently warned the British Government some time ago that emergency action would have to be taken. He was rather agreeable, middle fifties, strongly Labour, at any rate wanted it to be known he was sympathetic, which I think was genuine.

After coffee with him I went to the conference to take part in the discussion programme called 'The media as seen by world policy makers', the three speakers being Abdou Diouf, the Prime Minister of Senegal, Harry Lee Kuan Yew, Prime Minister of Singapore, and myself, deputising for Harold Wilson. The chairman was Barry Bingham, the editor and proprietor of the *Louisville Journal* – a great American liberal. Diouf made a speech which was so badly translated that I didn't hear a word he said. I spoke and analysed the media in terms of the rival information system they offered to both politics and education and listed ten criteria, which couldn't have been more embarrassing from Harry Lee's point of view because he is under attack for breaking most of them. He gave his account of the attitude of people in Singapore to Western culture.

Friday 11 June
To Bristol to the Jesuits at St Mary on the Quay for a talk called 'How to create a real community'. Afterwards I had supper with Father Norbury and Father Nugent.

Sunday 13 June
Began getting messages that Upper Clyde Shipbuilders was in difficulty. I realised this was going to involve a great deal of work over the next few weeks if anything did go wrong. I began drafting a statement that the Party would be able to put out in the event of UCS going bankrupt. Phone calls to Scotland to Ken Douglas, the new Managing Director of UCS, Jimmy Milne of the Scottish TUC and Frank McElhone and others.

Monday 14 June
Looked through my old files this morning and came across a confidential memorandum written by Nicholas Ridley for Heath in 1969 about

how to cut up UCS. I rang up Mark Arnold-Forster and gave it to him. I received it from Eric Varley – I don't know where he got it from – and I hadn't used it before because I was a bit worried about revealing a document which had been pirated in some way, picked up from a waste-paper basket or whatever. But with the possibility of UCS being knifed today – indeed the near certainty of it – I decided to let it come out.

I drafted a statement on UCS, calling for public ownership and workers' control in the yard itself, and went into the House of Commons. I had a filthy cold and felt terrible. I saw Harold Wilson and he approved the draft.

Davies made his statement in the House that UCS would liquidate, and I attacked him violently, blaming him for it.

Had an urgent meeting with the Scottish Members and then decided to fly up to Clydebank with Hugh McCartney, the local MP. We went to Clydebank Town Hall where all the shop stewards were gathered and I reported what had happened in the House in the afternoon and what a betrayal it was. I was asked what attitude I would adopt to the workers taking control of the yard. I said if they felt this was right I thought their action was fully justified. This of course was encouraging or approving illegal action, but I had thought it all out some time before and I am sure it was the right thing to say. Then I asked them what they wanted me to say in the debate tomorrow. About an hour and a half later I caught the sleeper back to London and prepared for the debate.

Tuesday 15 June
The *Guardian* printed the Ridley story. I worked on my speech all morning and took part in the UCS debate. I really did demolish John Davies because I had kept closely in touch with what everyone was saying, and he made a very poor statement. But the real gift was that he misquoted me yesterday, using something I had said about the Beagle Aircraft Company but attributing it to UCS. Heath listened to it all. It went down very well with the PLP.

Wednesday 16 June
I felt lousy but I got up at 5.30, collected Frank McElhone from his hotel and we went to meet the UCS workers at Euston. They were very orderly and cheerful, about 450 of them led by their shop stewards. I had been trying to get Heath to see them. I rang his office last night but have had no reply yet. They all gathered in Central Hall and I spoke from the platform, and then a message came from Robert Armstrong, Heath's Private Secretary, saying Heath would see them and so I marched with them to Downing Street and the leaders went into Number 10.

Late in the evening I went with Frank McElhone to see the UCS people off. We all shook hands and waved and one of the workers, a young man of about twenty-five with long hair, leaned out of the compartment and gave me a great hug. I must say I felt very moved by their demonstration – they had been tough, determined and dignified.

Thursday 17 June

Our wedding anniversary.

At 2 I went to see Dan McGarvey and Jack Service [General Secretary, Confederation of Shipbuilding and Engineering Unions] at Vic Feather's office. They were going to see Nicholas Ridley at the Department of Trade and Industry today. Vic has absolutely no time for politicians, particularly former members of a Labour Cabinet, and it is hard not to be insulted by him. He treats you rather as the CBI treats you, except that the CBI have rather more respect because they believe in the hierarchy of society in which a Minister is a Minister. But as far as Vic Feather is concerned a Minister, certainly a Labour Minister, is no more than an MP who has got somewhere!

Yesterday's Men was shown on television. This is the programme which was supposed to be a serious look at the Opposition and the makers had brought their cameras into the Shadow Cabinet. In fact it was a complete send-up. It was interesting because they had just taken the insignificant bits and strung them together, which made the whole thing trivial. They knifed Harold as hard as they could.

Friday 18 June

To Scotland by train, this time for a demonstration at Dunbarton, where 5,000 people marched to the park. I called for a General Election, and dubbed it the Declaration of Dumbarton, which Willie Ross and other MPs took up. It was a tremendous meeting over the closure of the Alexandra torpedo factory, which we had got Plessey to take on just over a year ago: Plessey are now closing it down because of the general depression.

In the afternoon we went to the Clydebank yard with Frank to go over with the shop stewards what they wanted to do next. The workforce has theoretically taken over the yard today and, seen from the outside, this looks like a very revolutionary act. But when you get through the barricades and ask, as a friend, 'Well, what are you going to do?', they haven't a strategy, they haven't a plan, they haven't got anything at all. I probed how far they wanted workers' control to go, and they were very uncertain. But it helped me because I found a form of words for a statement that simply said that any management pattern would have to be acceptable to the workers as a whole.

Tuesday 22 June

In the morning John Wall, the Chairman of ICL, and one of his directors, Arthur Humphreys, came to see me about their anxieties that

ICL might be the next big company due for collapse under the Government's disengagement policy, with the tremendous liquidity problems of computer leasing, with the general fall off in business which means that people are not ordering computers, and with the fact that the Government won't finance high technology.

I gave a press conference on my bill to bring UCS into public ownership* which I presented this afternoon, the second of my Private Member's Bills this year, the first being the Referendum Bill.

Wednesday 23 June
This morning Barbara Castle presented her paper to the NEC calling for an early conference on the Common Market in anticipation that there might be a decision by Heath about entry before the summer. Negotiations had been going 'very well' for Heath in the sense that Rippon has found no difficulty in getting an agreement on New Zealand and Commonwealth sugar and various other things – mainly by postponing the problems until after Britain has joined the Community.

Heath was under heavy pressure again from Harold Wilson not to force a decision in Parliament before the end of July, mainly because Harold doesn't want the Labour Conference to have a vote on it. Barbara moved her resolution and I was, of course, in favour. But I said Denis had been quite right in pointing out that if we accepted Barbara's resolution, we would be varying our earlier decision which was to have a special conference only if Parliament had to decide before the recess, and Parliament really isn't going to have to decide now. I thought we ought to look forward to see what would happen. There would be a Government decision announced in a White Paper and to take note of the Government decision would in effect mean we were in favour of going in. Outside Parliament, the Government machine and the Conservative press machine would be working to persuade the people that Britain should join and the Party really must know where it stood. I thought Harold's position was extremely vulnerable. If we didn't have a conference this campaigning would go on and Parliament would in effect assent while the leadership was silent. Then you would have a TUC decision in September which would be a bad thing and Labour's Conference in Brighton would be last of all.

I said I thought Party democracy was very important here and after the history of the last few years we couldn't disregard the opinion of the Party. On this question the decision of the Conference must be decisive. Anyway against the political background of rising unemployment and with the demand for an Election coming up in the autumn you couldn't possibly visualise circumstances under which we would be supporting a

* See Appendix VI.

Tory Government against the Conference. This was a fundamental issue.

Therefore, I supported Barbara and said I would leave what should be done at the conference to the Executive, because I had to leave and go North. I went straight up to Scotland and heard there that the motion to have the conference had been agreed by 13 votes to 11 without my vote.

When we got to Glasgow we were just in time for a tremendous demonstration: 40,000 people marched from St George's Square to Glasgow Green, the biggest political demonstration held in Scotland since before the War. I was pushed to the front and all the shop stewards – every one of them Communists of course – linked arms with me and we walked forward. The meeting was very moving. The Communists, I heard later, have got very worried at the way they think the Labour Party has horned in on the situation and is claiming credit for it, and that is why they had decided to make the meeting 'non-political' and not to allow political banners to be carried. It was an amazing event.

Afterwards I had lunch with Hugh Wyper, the Communist District Secretary of the T & G, whom I like very much: he really ought to be in the Labour Party, but has devoted his life to the Communist Party.

Still had a pretty filthy cold and I must admit I am getting tired.

Tuesday 29 June

I went to see Harold Wilson at 2.30. He is totally obsessed with the leadership question now. He thinks the Referendum issue is the great challenge he has to face and he said to me, 'I know exactly what to do. I am looking ahead to the special conference. I don't want to deal with this conference in isolation, we must have a discussion at the special conference and in September I will present a paper to the Executive which will be the basis of our statement to Conference; then we will have the Conference vote, and then the Parliamentary Party will vote on what to do,' and he was agitated and absolutely preoccupied with his own position. The risk that Jim Callaghan might stand against him is something that worries him very much.

Went over to see Jack Jones at 3.15 to try to win his support. I hadn't been into that office since I had seen Frank Cousins in 1959 when I was appointed Transport spokesman; Jack is a formidable character, very strong and tough. Of course his main concern is simply to campaign all summer on it and get the Market defeated. I said that was a matter for the special conference to decide. What I am anxious to do is have the conference given an opportunity to reach a view on 17 July. He wasn't unsympathetic.

At the end he said that he didn't much fancy the alternative leaders – Jim Callaghan, Roy Jenkins or Denis Healey. I said I didn't fancy a leadership crisis this year, and thought it would be a mistake. But what he was trying to say to me was that he was prepared to give me his support.

Wednesday 30 June
Executive this morning on the special conference again. Harold began by saying that we must see 17 July as just part of our strategy and the NEC should confirm its views at the next ordinary meeting on 28 July and make a statement. Harold would wait to formulate his view when the White Paper was published.

Ian Mikardo said a special conference is just like an Annual Conference. We can't have more than forty-five speeches, perhaps twenty each way, and we must avoid a bitchy procedural wrangle. He attacked Shirley for saying there shouldn't be a firm decision at the conference on entry when she herself had announced her commitment. Why should she be allowed to say what she thought while denying the Party the right to say what it thought?

Friday 2 July
To Bristol. Afterwards to the Transport and General Workers' Union and held a surgery. 250 people attended the meeting in the Transport Hall on the Common Market and I delivered a forty-five-minute speech, my definitive view on the Market. There was a large amount of criticism because the majority of people who had come were just anti-Market. They didn't want to hear the case for the Market, they just wanted to hear the case against. But I argued as fairly as I could, particularly the case for a Referendum. There were a lot of Communists there.

Wednesday 7 July
Got up early, having been asked to take part in a demonstration against the impending closure of the River Don Steelworks in Sheffield. There were about 2,000–3,000 people at the demonstration in Norfolk Park. They had a programme of action and it was a different sort of demonstration from the one in Glasgow. They were practical, hard-headed businesslike people and put great emphasis on the importance of not letting any workers' control ideas slip in. In Scotland they are all revolutionaries, and in the West of England they are all just human beings reflecting human values of a vaguely religious kind. I have become increasingly interested in this question of whether cultural differences haven't been totally underestimated in our political thinking, and whether we shouldn't go about the whole construction of our political philosophy in quite a different way.

Thursday 8 July

To Vienna by train. I was met by Gerfried Buchauer, a former United Nations employee who works as an economist for Ernst Veselsky, the Minister of State, and for Bruno Kreisky, the Chancellor. He told me that Kreisky was a lonely man, no doubt true of all leaders, and that Veselsky never quite knew whether he would be upheld or not.

We went straight to the Parliament, a magnificent place built in the 1880s, about the same time, certainly in the same style, as the British Parliament. It reminded me of the Hungarian Parliament, which was the parallel institution at the time of the Austro-Hungarian Empire.

I met Veselsky, who is about forty, and he took me to see Bruno Pitterman, the former President of the Socialist Party of Austria, now entering retirement.

Pitterman said he would like to see parliamentary links with Rumania, Poland and Yugoslavia, and to study their election process and procedure. He thought we had a lot to learn from that and it would encourage them to think we took them seriously, and indeed that the democratic socialists should act as a magnet for Eastern Europe. I found this highly intelligent. There was much less of the Cold War feeling here than in Britain, partly because the Continentals have suffered so much and are more understanding about the situation than we are with our arrogant insularity.

Friday 9 July

At 12.30 I saw Dr Luchs and a group of trade union economists who said that by law they elected councils of shop stewards, in two groups – white collar and industrial workers – in every company. They had rights concerning work rules and social affairs, and they had to be consulted on hiring and firing of workers. Trade union committees elect to the top of the unions and therefore there is no conflict between the full-time officials and the shop stewards, because in fact the full-time officials are elected by the people elected in the factories.

Minimum wages are negotiated nationally and there are local negotiations on top of that. The employers and employees are consulted on everything; this being so they do support what the Government does and this is the basis of the package deal: the economic partners and the social partners, that is to say industry and the Government (who described each other in these terms), worked closely together and everybody knew everybody else.

At 5.15 I came back to the Chancellery to see Ernst Velesky and he described the policy-making of the Austrian Socialist Party.

Veselsky said that Kreisky was not an economist, and he never spent a sleepless night on economic problems, but he saw that the need for an economic programme was the starting point for a return to power and that the policy had been a model of team work and forward looking.

At 7.45, Peter Jankowitsch, who is Kreisky's private secretary, took me to Kreisky's house. The other guest was Mr Nehru, a cousin of the former Prime Minister of India, whom I had met at one of Walter Lippmann's parties years ago and who is now the Governor of Assam and Nagaland. I met Kreisky's wife and son. They have no guards in the house, and people ring him up direct with problems. He meets all the demonstrators who come to the Chancellery, invites them into a big hall and loudspeakers carry messages out to the public. I find this informality very attractive. Indeed, when I go around the world, I find that there is not one idea that I have that is not already in practice somewhere else. Britain is just a very conservative country.

Anyway, Kreisky took his wife, Jankowitsch, Nehru and myself to the Fischerhaus Restaurant out in the Vienna Woods.

He said that Britain must join the EEC because otherwise we would be isolated – although he clearly understood Wilson's problems. He said that Pompidou was very class-conscious, very conservative and that he had heard via the Rothschilds that if Wilson had still been Prime Minister, Pompidou would never have let us into the Common Market because what he was looking for was a Heath–Pompidou alliance rather than a Wilson–Brandt alliance. Wilson, he said, had a tremendous standing outside Britain even though in Britain he might be under a cloud.

He thought that the Czechs should have fought in 1968 and it was their tragedy that they were incapable of fighting; Kekkonen, the President of Finland, had told him that according to Kosygin there were no strikes in Czechoslovakia since the occupation and this, Kosygin had said, confirmed that the Czechs wanted the Russians in. Kreisky clearly thought that the Soviets would have been very much afraid if they had been confronted with the Czech working class.

With American disorder and the USSR absorbed with China, he thought Europe, which was peaceful and quiet, had a great future, although China was interested in Europe and this was something we ought to begin to take seriously.

Then he spoke of the special relationship which exists between Austria and Hungary – the sort of Hapsburg 'Commonwealth' – and said this was the basis for some real links across the Iron Curtain.

Kreisky talked a great deal. Like all great leaders he is completely egocentric but has the appearance of modesty. It was a lively last evening.

Sunday 11 July
Back from Austria, had a late lie-in this morning. Mowed the lawn, did my laundry, worked in the office, and had half an hour's sunbathing.

The temperature today was 88 degrees Fahrenheit, the hottest day of the year.

Thursday 15 July
Jean-Jacques Servan-Schreiber came to tea with me. He is a curious person, rich, very chic, owns a newspaper, General Secretary of the Radical Party which is not really socialist; but still he has some interesting ideas. He thinks that together with Mitterand, the new President of the Socialist Party who has done a deal with the Communists, he might be able to build up an alliance which will destroy Pompidou in eighteen months' time. He is a useful contact to have but he is not a socialist and is rather anxious to get away from Marxism at a time when I am moving more in that direction. Still, it was nice to see him.

Friday 16 July
I worked at home in the afternoon and in the evening I went to dinner with Hans Janitschek and his wife Elfriede in Hampstead Garden Suburb.

I like Hans; but in his heart he is yearning to be accepted socially and says for him socialism means everybody being allowed to have a Rolls Royce. This is the individual escape from class into prosperity, which is the cancer eating into the Western European Social Democratic parties; it is what Crosland believes. I had quite a clash with Hans when it became clear that he was going to move his children from a state school into a horrible little private school where he believed aristocratic virtues were being taught.

Saturday 17 July
It was a beautiful day. The last two or three weeks have been the best weather I remember in London. Went to the special Labour Party conference to discuss the Common Market at the Central Hall.

There were some brilliant speeches by Peter Shore, John Mackintosh, George Thomson, Michael Foot, Michael Stewart, Eric Heffer, Stan Orme, Jack Jones and Hugh Scanlon. Then Harold spoke and came out clearly against the Market. But it's all over bar the shouting now and he feels he has warded off Jim Callaghan's assault on the leadership, which he almost certainly has.

It was worth having the conference, though there was no decision taken, one way or the other. In fact it was probably better not to have a decision.

The Marketeers had a great celebration in St Ermine's because they have got masses of money. This was for them a defeat in the sense that Harold came down against the Market, but a victory in the sense that they weren't committed by a Party decision.

Afterwards Clive Jenkins and I went over to Mik's room where there was a party of the Left.

Sunday 18 July
This evening I went to Geoffrey Goodman's home in Mill Hill for a gathering of the Left with Michael Foot and Jill Craigie [Michael Foot's wife], Peter and Liz Shore, Dick and Bridget Clements, Alex Jarratt who used to be an official at the Department of Employment and is now Managing Director of IPC, and Leo Abse and his wife.

At dinner Jill Craigie suddenly turned to Peter and me and said, 'I realise that the next Leader of the Party will be one or other of you and you will be getting the knives out for each other; but it's more likely to be Peter.' Peter was flattered but slightly embarrassed by this.

Monday 19 July
PLP meeting at 6.30 and Harold explained the procedure in the House for the Common Market debate on Wednesday. Norman Atkinson came out against Europe on ideological grounds and said that if we were taken in by the Tories, we should pledge ourselves to get out.

Barbara Castle made a speech for forty minutes saying that the Party had been cornered by the Tories on the terms. She said there should be a select committee (which I agree with), devaluation would be necessary for entry, we would surrender our freedom of action, she had always been against entry even in the Cabinet, that when we had reapplied we were not committed to the Common Agricultural Policy and now the French had actually caught us out by entrenching the CAP before we were admitted. She said that the objectives must be to federalise but these were never discussed and if we supported entry we would be accepting a political coalition in this country. It was a powerful ideological case against entry.

Then Roy Jenkins said it had been a good conference on Saturday and there was no great current of anti-Market feeling in the constituency parties. He thought there should be consistency in commitment since the last Labour Cabinet, by a majority, voted to enter and the terms of entry would have been accepted by the Cabinet. If we didn't go in now, he said, it would be worse than if we had never applied. He didn't accept that we must reject entry because the Tories were in power. He attacked the negative insularity of the anti-Marketeers and said that socialism in one country was a slogan and not a policy and socialists in the other EEC countries wanted our help. He said the siege economy was based on the idea of complacency, that we really did depend upon Willy Brandt – the future of Britain depended upon Willy Brandt – and if we rejected Europe we wouldn't have a rugged independence but would be dependent upon America, which would be preoccupied with its own problems. He asked the Party to lift its eyes beyond the short-term political considerations to the major questions.

It was a powerful speech and the arguments carried a great deal of weight. But of course it was defiant – an arrogant and an élitist speech. A demonstration had been prearranged afterwards and people banged and hammered and shouted. Roy's speech was of course a direct attack on Harold Wilson and also on Healey and Crosland, who had climbed off the fence against the Market, and it changed the political situation in the Party at one stroke.

Afterwards I went down to the smoking room and sat with the Left where Barbara was saying, 'We must organise, we must fight.' Michael Foot was shaken by it and I think it would certainly confirm Michael's determination to stand against Roy as Deputy-Leader. It took you right back to 1951 or 1961 – the Party at its worst. Harold has undoubtedly been damaged by Roy's speech in the long term. But Roy won't succeed him because, by splitting the Party in the way he has done, I think he will find that people won't forgive him; certainly the Left will never forgive him. Although he has picked up some support from the Centre, because it was a powerful argument and he emerged as a man of character, I think he is going to be in difficulty. Jim seems to me to be down and out now because of his manoeuvring. Denis and Crosland are weakened and even if they climb back on the bandwagon, I think the position will be difficult for them.

At the moment, of course, Harold is the hero of the Left and clearly entrenched for a period, at any rate for a year, because there is going to be no threat to his leadership this year – Roy can't and Jim wouldn't get any support. This is the position that we find ourselves in.

Tuesday 20 July
Went to the Trade and Industry Group meeting at the House which had been summoned to consider the employment situation: while I was there a message was brought over to me to go and see Harold Wilson. So I walked over to 5 Lord North Street and found Harold in his shirtsleeves, pacing up and down the room.

He told me that he intended to make a statement at the Party meeting later today. He was extremely agitated about Roy Jenkins's great speech at the Party meeting last night. He said he was going to lay down the law and while he remained Leader he would handle the Party as he thought right: one of his real 'smack of Government' or 'dog-licence' type speeches. Finally the text of his statement came over, he having written it and Marcia having made amendments. The first draft, which Marcia had cut down, was even more self-justificatory and obsessed with his leadership and referred to the number of weekends he had addressed meetings since the Election. He said to me, 'I don't know, I may just give up the Party leadership, they can stuff it as far as I am concerned. I pay out of my own pocket £15,000 a year to be Party Leader. I finance my own office. I have got an overdraft with my bank. All the money from my memoirs has gone. I don't know why I go on. But I'll smash CDS (the Campaign for Democratic Socialism) before I go,' and I'll do this and I'll do that. He was full of boasts but underneath was desperately insecure and unhappy.

I read the text and I said, 'Why do you raise the leadership question? I thought it was a mistake when you raised it at Newtown recently.' He said, 'Then it was a reference to Callaghan. Now it's a reference to Jenkins, and to warn them off.' He asked me who I thought would be elected if he gave up. So I said I didn't think the Party wanted any of the available candidates and that the Left was strongly with him, and so on. I tried to reassure him but I don't think I had any influence. He was dead set on putting the statement out to the press.

I walked back from his house – I didn't particularly want to be seen with him in his car. But it was interesting that he called me in, which he only does when there is trouble.

I went over to the House and to the PLP meeting, where the statement was presented and it was received with acute embarrassment by the Party. One or two people at the end sort of pretended to applaud but it was very uncomfortable and nobody – except for a few middle-of-the-road people who thought it was necessary to straighten the Party out – could understand why he had made it.

I had a brief talk with one or two of the journalists, then had a meal in the Tea Room with Roy Mason and Frank McElhone. The position really is this: by making the leadership an issue and by using phrases like 'whoever is Leader after October', Harold has put himself in the most vulnerable position of all and I think it not impossible that somebody will stand against him: it might be Jim, it could hardly be Roy Jenkins or any of the others, but I think there is just a possibility.

I don't myself see much chance for the deputy-leadership because I think Roy's honesty will win him support and the Left is almost bound to nominate Michael Foot, as the most direct attack on Roy that it can make. Michael is not an ambitious man. He is getting on himself (he is fifty-eight) and never having been in the Cabinet, he would be very much a stop-gap candidate and would probably be defeated by Roy: so there may be some pressure on me.

I am almost ashamed to talk about this in my diary because it makes it seem that I am mainly concerned with that, which I hope I am not. But egoism eats up all politicians in time, which is probably the case for getting rid of them.

Wednesday 21 July

To the House to hear Heath open the debate on the Common Market in which he quoted copiously from Harold and bored us all. I dozed off part of the time. Then Harold spoke and he bored the House as well which, in the circumstances, was probably the only way he could tackle the situation.

At 5.30 we had the Shadow Cabinet and we had to wait till 6 for Harold who was listening to Jeremy Thorpe who had followed him in the debate. I moved that we take up the suggestion that there should be a select committee to look at the White Paper. Roy was opposed to it of course. Tony Crosland raised the point that there had been no decision in the Shadow Cabinet about the line we should take on the Common Market and he very much hoped there would be some opportunity of doing this before the Executive on 28 July. This broadened out into a general discussion on the state of the Party.

I said I thought this was all part of the problem of trying to squeeze an issue which wouldn't fit into the Party system and that consulting the public was the right line to take, because on that you simply couldn't lose. There was great anxiety, which I shared, that we had gone back to 1951, and Roy's trouble was that in effect he had appealed to the Party to revolt against the Conference decisions.

Harold wound up quite moderately but the poor man is under tremendously heavy personal attack and I have some sympathy for him. But I don't trust him as a person and his position is curious now because Roy has isolated himself from the main stream of thinking, Denis and Tony Crosland are contemptible figures, Jim is thought to be so devious it isn't true, so Harold has no really credible rival. On the other hand, his personal standing has fallen sharply.

Thursday 22 July

Had a phone call from Gordon Farnsworth who told me that there was a story in the *Telegraph* saying that anti-Market MPs had decided to put me up against Roy Jenkins for the deputy-leadership. So Lucille Clark went out and bought the *Daily Telegraph* and there it was on the front page – 'Benn v Jenkins. Anti-Marketeers find a candidate', and so on, and describing the rage with Roy Jenkins, the desire to topple him, the fact that I had done a lot of work and built up my reputation with the trade unions and was active at Transport House, I had lost my undergraduate image, I was working hard and had a lot of energy. It was generally predicting the battle. Of course, I haven't been specifically approached by anti-Market people to stand against Roy although over the last few weeks this question has become a real one. But this is a new development in the situation and the real question is whether Michael Foot is going to stand.

I saw Michael in the House this afternoon and he said he should tell me that he was making it clear in *Tribune* this week that he was going to stand against Roy Jenkins. The position is that if Michael wants to stand he has a prior claim. He is a senior figure and the Left would certainly support him against me. But it is also clear that I would get more votes than him in different areas because I would appeal to people who were more widely spread.

I sat through most of the continuation of the Common Market debate and Mother came to listen to my winding-up speech, which began at 10. I had prepared it with enormous care but I must confess it did not go down well. The Marketeers were there in force on the Labour side and didn't at all like what I said. The Tories didn't like my case for the Market, which was to control the multinational companies, and of course they didn't like my case against going in without a Referendum or an Election. So by the time I sat down I felt quite uncomfortable. When I looked at the speech in *Hansard* afterwards and made a few minor corrections, it read better than I expected. The radio picked it up at midnight and said I had argued strongly for a Referendum or an Election. I think this is the right line to continue to take, but it is not popular with the Party at the moment on either side and I am in the difficulty of arguing very much a minority view. There is no doubt that the Conference will vote against the Market. But when we come to legislation in the House on 28 October, it is just possible that there will be a narrow majority in public opinion polls in favour of entry; then we shall have trouble. However, I am absolutely clear in my own mind that Party unity is my cause over the next twelve months, if for no other reason than that I am Chairman of the Party.

Friday 23 July

Up early and went to Cromford near Matlock to take part in the 200th anniversary celebrations of Richard Arkwright's first textile factory powered by water. I was fascinated by the old factory which was still in position and by the textile machinery designed by Arkwright. For the first time I understood how spinning was done. The beauty of the machinery and equipment was quite breathtaking. We have many cultural roots in the arts and architecture but we are rarely reminded of the origins of our industrial society and to see everything set out clearly in a way that was easy to understand gave me a homely, comfortable feeling. I realised that when you have seven generations of people who have worked in an industry it gives a certain unity to a community.

Sunday 25 July

Harold has announced in the papers that he has an overdraft, which he told me when I went to see him on Tuesday. I think he is falling to pieces at a time when his position as the best Leader, in comparison with Jenkins and the others on the Market side, should be pretty strong. I would not be surprised to find that by the end of the year he was no longer Leader.

Monday 26 July
The Common Market argument is building up to fever pitch in the press as a result of the events of the last few days and everybody is waiting for the Executive on Wednesday. Tonight Denis Healey made the most awful speech. The thing that aroused the greatest contempt was him saying that we were entering the Market on the basis of information as false as that which had led the Americans into the Vietnam War. This created a frozen reaction among those who were pro-Market and among those who knew that Denis supported the Vietnam War more than any other Minister.

Tuesday 27 July
At 10 the UCS shop stewards arrived at the House – Jimmy Reid, Jim Airlie, Jimmy Ramsay, Willie McInnes and Bob Cook. I got them in to the Gallery and there was a late-night debate on unemployment in Scotland with special reference to UCS.

Wednesday 28 July
To the Executive this morning for the major discussion on the Common Market. Jim said that far from feeling sad about it he thought that the Treaty of Rome was an awful thing the more he knew about it. Denis said he didn't think we wanted a split and Walter Padley said he thought it was tragic. Harold said that everybody should be absolutely free, certainly up to the Conference, to say what they thought. Then I moved my resolution calling for a campaign for an Election to give the British people an opportunity to pronounce on the whole range of Government policies, including Europe, and it was carried nem con. Jim moved that there be a tremendous campaign against the Market between now and the Conference and that was carried by 16 to 5.

Thursday 29 July
The UCS statement, and the Government published a pessimistic White Paper by the so-called Four Wise Men,[2] of which Robens was a member. There was extreme dismay in the House.

We had an immediate meeting with the shop stewards who had been in the House – Jim Airlie and Jimmy Reid – and I spelled out a sort of strategy which they found reasonably effective, in which we would ask for an immediate debate in the House under Standing Order No 9 and I would go back with them to Scotland. We would then push for some sort of official enquiry and later there would be demonstrations and political campaigns. I must report that Willie Ross was cautious, like most Scottish MPs who have been trained to believe that industrial affairs have got nothing to do with politicians and dislike the Scottish Communists. Frank McElhone is always pointing out that one is up against an extremely conservative group in the Scottish MPs.

I ought to mention that Harold had called me in before the UCS statement was made and said that he would like to come to Scotland next week. He was particularly keen to do this because he wanted to expose Heath who was sailing in the Admiral's Cup on Wednesday, and Harold had this idea, which he himself described as a gimmick, of sailing up the Clyde in a boat, visiting the doomed shipyards while Heath was yachting in the Admiral's Cup. He even suggested he might wear his outfit as an Elder Brother of Trinity House, which is the honorary title all Prime Ministers have. I must admit my contempt for Harold, which has been pretty high this last week, reached a peak. He said he would neither condemn nor condone the occupation. Well, that's no good, and I told him so. I was rather worried that he would wreck it all, but clearly he was getting on my bandwagon while being a bit more cautious about it.

Caught the train to Glasgow with Frank McElhone, Willie Ross and Norman Buchan, and the shop stewards and we sat up late into the night talking. They were candid and saw this as a dramatic gesture. I don't know how far, as Communists, they are keen on workers' control because the CP has always wanted a rather stronger centralised direction in society and has never been in favour of the Trotskyite ideas of decentralisation which I find make an awful lot more sense, having seen the Stalinist system in operation. I told Jimmy Reid and Jim Airlie that the possibility of an inquiry gave them an opportunity to get off the hook, if they wanted to end the occupation or the work-in failed.

Friday 30 July

Jimmy Jack, General Secretary of the Scottish TUC, was waiting at the Central Hotel in Glasgow and I had breakfast with him. There was a curious man sitting at the next table writing notes, who claimed to be the Rome correspondent of the *New Statesman*, which was most improbable and I have no doubt he was a security officer. We talked about the inquiry and how it might be handled but Jimmy Jack is worried – it might be because he thinks the shop stewards have got too much power and the full-time trade union officials want to play a larger part.

I went to the Clydebank yard, had lunch in the canteen. Talked to the press and said this was a historic moment and Scotland should be proud of these people, I supported them 100 per cent, it was the stuff of which great events were made and I gave them whole-hearted encouragement. This was taken, of course, to be a full support for illegality.

Then I met the shop stewards and said there was a long struggle ahead of them. I went round the yard and had a look at the work.

To the STUC meeting, and there was an interesting clash. The STUC have no alternative but to support the shop stewards; the shop stewards want to play a leading part in this but this brings them up against their full-time union officials – Danny McGarvey and Hugh Scanlon and the other national trade union leaders have said nothing so far. This is a difficult area in which one is operating. Undoubtedly the real battle in Britain today is between the powerful shop stewards' movement coming up underneath and the bureaucratic national trade union movement. I have seen and felt this for some time. But anyway the STUC accepted the idea of the enquiry. They said they would take responsibility for Harold Wilson's visit.

I returned to London exhausted.

Monday 2 August

I opened the House of Commons UCS debate which we had demanded, and my speech was perfectly all right. I got the case on the record but against bitterly hostile Tory benches and a certain amount of anxiety on our Back Benches as to whether I had gone too far in my support for the occupation.

John Davies called me an 'evil genius'. Heath had cancelled his Admiral's Cup racing for the day and was sitting looking sour. It was a short debate but certainly worthwhile. There is no doubt that the press think the Government was right to wind up UCS and are critical of the line I have been taking.

Tuesday 3 August

I worked at home this morning and all the papers put headlines such as 'Benn, Evil Genius of Shipbuilding', so that the Government clearly have got their case over, although there are the usual ritual objections to unemployment. However, I wrote a letter to *The Times* comparing the generous treatment of Lockheed by Congress with the ungenerous treatment of UCS by the Government.

I went to the House and saw the industrial correspondents on the workers' control issue, which I am going to write about in *Tribune* this week. Yesterday I talked to Norman Atkinson, to Johnny Prescott [MP for Hull] and one or two other young left-wing trade union MPs who are very much afraid, as I am, that I might appear to be misleading the men.

Wednesday 4 August

I went to talk to Harold who had been deeply affected by his visit to Scotland, which had been a great success, and he called all the Scottish Members in. He made a speech of twenty-six minutes to them, which bored them stiff. But he said it had moved him as much as his visit to Aberfan and Hugh McCartney confirmed that it had been a great success. Some Scottish Members, Willy Hannan of Glasgow Maryhill, and one or two others, were critical of what Harold had done.

Then back to the House at midnight and voted from 12 to 2 and came home via the West London Air Terminal, where I picked up the papers.

Friday 6 August
The papers carried a great deal about the *Oz* trial in which Richard Neville, the Editor, and two of his colleagues have been jailed for publishing an 'obscene' edition. Yesterday in the House, when the sentences were announced, Bill Hamling the Labour MP for Wolverhampton West, who is a member of the Humanists Group, handed me a motion condemning the sentences as being contrary to British justice, signed by Dick Taverne, who is a QC, Tom Driberg and Frank Allaun. I signed it too.

When I rang Frank McElhone today in Aberdeen where he is on holiday, he was worried about this and said there had been a lot of criticism in Scotland of my signing the motion and I would lose fifty votes for the leadership. I said I felt deeply that it was wrong to jail these young people. This is the difficulty, if you are going to go out simply for high office, then you have got to be cautious and I am not sure that I want to be. I would rather stand up for what I believe. Frank was worried and I tried to reassure him.

Then I sat down and thought about how one would deal with criticisms of the line that I had taken. The truth is that middle-aged parents are the last to criticise the young because we were the war generation and the young are fighting against the obscenity of racial hatred and poverty and war. I jotted this down and showed it to Hilary but he thought it was too apologetic and I had better simply stick by what I had done.

Monday 9 August
Today the men at Govan yard returned from their holidays and they supported the line taken by the shop stewards at Clydebank. There is going to be a big gathering of shop stewards from all over Scotland tomorrow, Tuesday, and a great demonstration is planned for 18 August.

The other news today was that the Ulster situation has got a great deal worse and the Government have agreed to Faulkner's request for internment so that from now on Ulster will be pushing UCS out of the headlines.

Wednesday 18 August
At 8 I was at the yards at Clydebank and had a talk with Jimmy Reid,
Jimmy Airlie and the others. I put to them the outline of my speech in
which I made it clear that shop stewards were not trying to create a little
pocket of revolution in a capitalist world but were trying to engage in a
serious industrial and political campaign. They fully accepted that. I
went and had a quick look around and then went to see the Provost of
Clydebank, Bob Fleming, briefly.

Gave a press conference, then immediately after lunch I went out and
joined an enormous demonstration. The numbers of people involved
varied in estimate from 50,000 in the *Guardian*, to over 70,000 in *The
Times*: there were probably 70,000 to 75,000. It was massive and I
marched in line in the front with Vic Feather, Danny McGarvey, Hugh
Scanlon, the shop stewards and Willie Ross and we linked arms and
marched right to Glasgow Green. Then there was an entertainment and
the speeches were made. Jimmy Reid absolutely dominated the
platform; Vic Feather was not bad; Hugh Scanlon was serious; the
Scottish Nationalist was booed; the Communist Secretary Alex Murray
made a brief speech of support. I was last but one and while I was
speaking, someone threw a piece of lighted paper on to the platform
which looked a bit like a smoke bomb. I warned in my speech of the
danger of the Clydeside Development Authority being a cover for the
murder of UCS and I think that rather pleased the shop stewards.

I came back on the plane and Hugh Scanlon dropped me at home.
Hugh is not the revolutionary figure that he was once made out to be. He
is a quiet chap who wants above all to be popular and to be taken
seriously, and this is one of the ways in which great left-wing radical
leaders ultimately get mellowed in the process of promotion.

Thursday 19 August
The unemployment figures came out today: 904,000 for the United
Kingdom as a whole.

I went to Transport House and met David Bleakley who is the
Northern Ireland Labour Party Minister for Community Affairs in
Brian Faulkner's Cabinet. He gave the most hair-raising account of the
situation, which he said was getting worse and worse.

I find Bleakley's account worrying. He said that the Catholics were
being withdrawn from the Protestant areas and vice-versa and the
Catholics were now living in sort of tribal encampments with the
barricades removed and the houses around them burned. When the
whistle blew, the Protestants would just march in and murder them by
the thousands and there would be the most appalling civil war and
carnage in Northern Ireland, in which the Southern Irish might become

involved willy-nilly. Lynch, the Irish premier, might well fall if Faulkner fell and this was a situation that had to be avoided.

It was intensely depressing.

I issued a statement about the unemployment figures and came down from London to Stansgate. In the car Melissa addressed a blistering revolutionary argument to me.

Wednesday 8 September
To the House of Commons to pick up Harold Wilson's letter to Chou-en-Lai, which I hoped would get me an interview with him.

Then I dictated a letter to the children in case anything happened to us.

Caroline and I were visiting China in the wake of the 'Great Proletarian Cultural Revolution' which began in 1966 and raged on in different stages until 1969. The Revolution was actively supported by Chairman Mao Tse Tung and it brought with it fundamental changes and involved a period of turbulence and violence between the old regime and the forces of radicalism, which rocked the country.

Mao's famous 'big character' poster BOMBARD THE HEADQUARTERS *constituted official approval for the action of the young Red Guards who took over the universities, colleges, schools and factories and began a purge of the bureaucracy. The main objective of Mao and the Red Guards was to prevent the old functionaries from dominating the country, and to re-educate them by sending them into the countryside, in line with Mao's teaching that theory and practice must go together.*

In the end calm was achieved by the intervention of the People's Liberation Army which re-established order while defending the aims of the revolution.

While we were there, though we did not know it until we had left China, Marshal Lin Piao was killed when the plane in which he was believed to be fleeing to the Soviet Union crashed in Mongolia. Lin Piao, formerly a close friend of Mao, was Vice-Chairman of the Communist Party, and was a leading figure in the war against the Japanese and in the reconstruction of China. But after the Cultural Revolution the two men fell out and Lin was implicated in a plot to undermine the Chinese Government. The dramatic circumstances of his death explained the cancellation of internal flights which affected us and also threw light on why the Chinese were so interested in the conversations I pursued with them, particularly the Deputy Foreign Minister, about the possibility of a military coup in China.

On our return, I immediately described my impressions and my discoveries about Chinese life and political thinking in an article for the Sunday Times, *and this is reproduced below. My diary of the first two days of the visit is also included to give a brief glimpse of the unique effect on the people's day-to-day activities of the Cultural Revolution.*

Friday 10 September

We went by train from Kowloon to Lowu where we arrived at 10.26. There we got off the train, walked along the platform through the Hong Kong border post which didn't look, to me, to be under any sort of strain or stress and we crossed the border into mainland China. It was a very remarkable feeling crossing from one world into the other towards the Red Flag, with the Chinese soldiers standing there in their drab khaki cotton uniforms.

There was a health check carried out on the platform, then passports and tickets were inspected and we went into the waiting room where we were invited to help ourselves to the works of Chairman Mao in several languages.

While we waited, we saw children coming back from school waving their red flags, and the big black steam locomotives with red painted wheels glistening with oil.

There were inscriptions on the walls of the station in Chinese and English. One particularly which read, 'The Japanese revolution will succeed if it follows Marxist/Leninist principles and pursues its own practice correctly' was put there at the request of the China Friends of the Japanese Workers' Delegation.

A Mr Sung, from the Institute of Foreign Affairs in Canton, arrived to take us to Canton. In the train he told us that Stalin had made mistakes but that today, the Soviet Union was, in effect, Fascist because it repressed criticism, Brezhnev was more cunning than Khrushchev. It was basically a revisionist regime. He stressed that the Chinese were only critical of the leadership and not of Party members. He thought that even in Russia, they must be yearning for a Marxist/Leninist Party. He also said that 90 per cent of the world wants revolution and particularly Asia and Africa though circumstances in Western Europe and America were slightly different. He thought that Mao would be remembered mainly as a teacher, a poet and as a man of letters.

At 3, we arrived in Canton and were met by a member of the Institute of Foreign Relations. From 4.30 to 6.15 we drove around Canton, visiting the Yuesuh Park where we saw the old Krupps guns which had been used against the British in the Opium Wars. Over a stadium was the statement: 'Be vigilant – defend the motherland. Be prepared for war and other calamities.'

At the People's Hotel we met Mr Sun, the Chairman of the Revolutionary Committee of the Hotel. He told us that the Revolutionary Committees were made up of members of the People's Liberation Army, the cadres and the mass of the workers. They had ten hours' study of Mao Tse Tung each week and three monthly self-criticism meetings. The hotel's Revolutionary Committee had removed the feudal decorations from the hotel; they had decided to admit workers and peasants which the hotel had not done before; and they had 'put politics in command'. The Revolutionary Committee was selected by continuous consultation.

We had dinner with Mr Chen Yu, aged sixty-nine, the Vice-Chairman of the Provisional Revolutionary Government of Canton. He said that by coming we had contributed to understanding. When I asked him what his greatest problem was, he said that it was to learn to use the thoughts of Mao Tse Tung, that the masses were right and that science must serve the people. The Chinese intended to expand agriculture first, light industry second and heavy industry third, and then electronics. As we later learned, electronics had become somewhat controversial at the time of Liu Shao-chi and the idea that electronics could solve everything had been rejected by Mao during the Cultural Revolution. I asked one or two questions about China: whether the tactics of cooperation with the Kuomintang in the past might be used again to bring Taiwan back to mainland China and whether Mao could ever be wrong. I was told that he could not be because what he said came from the masses.

Saturday 11 September
At 9.30 we went to the 7th Middle School in Canton where there are 3,800 pupils and were met by the First Deputy-Chairman of the Revolutionary Committee. The school had been opened in 1888 as a mission school run by Americans. After the liberation it became the 7th Middle School and in 1958 Mao had visited a nearby commune and the school, and this was a great event.

Before the Cultural Revolution the school had been run according to the bourgeois intellectual views copied from the old world but in the Cultural Revolution teachers and pupils had rebelled against this old line and had put 'politics in command'. We were told that the students were sent to factories and communes and railway workshops and had much to learn from the noble characteristics of workers.

The school had rejected the idea of marks and knowledge as a basis of selectivity.

The curriculum comprised politics, literature, maths, history, geography, revolutionary art, physics and chemistry. We were told that the main authors were Mao Tse Tung and Lin Piao, from whose work all literature was taught, and they also studied articles written by workers and peasants who had been learning Marxist and Leninist thought. They also studied military training and students went with the army units to learn how to fire guns.

An old teacher said that he preferred the new educational line and that in the old society, education had simply been taught to help pupils on step-by-step to university, to look for personal fame and glory, to put technology first. The exams were designed to catch the students out and really involved treating them like animals. Students didn't see their work as part of the general political development of society. But now they hoped they were more integrated with the masses. The leadership of the school was now under the firm control of the working classes and it was always asking, 'Whom do we serve?' Before, only 30 per cent of the places had been occupied by workers and peasants.

After lunch at 2.30, we went to the Canton school for deaf mutes. This had been opened in 1946 as a private, fee-paying school where there were forty students, and they were taught finger language. Now the school has been expanded and is based upon acupuncture. In the old days, nobody had cared much about deaf mutes, but in 1968 the PLA medical team had come, having learned acupuncture and having first experimented on themselves, and began to apply acupuncture to deal with the problems of the deaf mute.

At the beginning of the treatment many of the children were able to hear but not to speak. But after three or six months' treatment some began to regain their power of speech quite quickly. The treatment consisted of starting and stopping the acupuncture over a period of six months. They had secured about an 80 per cent success rate in speech and within that a fairly high success rate with hearing.

Back to our guest house and had supper alone. Then to the huge airport and boarded the plane, an Ilyushin, which took us to Peking in three and a half hours.

Sunday Times, 26 September 1971

'It should have been no surprise to find my hosts were so immensely knowledgeable about the world, so amusing and so ready to be amused. Twenty years of arm's length relationship with China has hardened our expectations: we have come to think of each other as stone images, like silent sculptures facing each other without the possibility of real communication. The least expected feature of my talks with Chinese leaders in Peking was the relaxed atmosphere in which they were conducted. We could – and did – laugh uproariously, without them worrying that the phrases that made us laugh might look very different in cold print.

'We had agreed that all our talks should be informal, and my hosts were glad to forgo official transcripts in which every dot and comma would have had to be checked and rechecked. On that basis they were eager to exchange views on a whole range of subjects – world problems, trade, technology, education, and the political situation in China itself, though I did not hear, and did not expect to hear, news of the real arguments that go on in the higher reaches of the Government.

'The longest conversation I had (with the banquet that followed, it

Team spirit: Soviet Prime Minister Kosygin at a Kilmarnock–Rangers match, 1967.

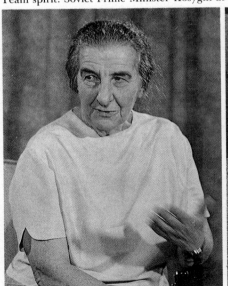

Israel's Iron Lady: Golda Meir in Britain for the Socialist International Meeting in January 1969, shortly before becoming Prime Minister; and Gough Whitlam, leader of the Australian Labour Opposition in 1972, later dismissed as Prime Minister by the Governor General of Australia.

President Pompidou embraces Britain: with Heath after discussions at Chequers to prepare British entry into the Common Market, March 1972.

European partners: Willy Brandt with Ted Heath at Downing Street, April 1972.

With Alec Issigonis, 'father' of the Mini, at the National Engineering Laboratory, East Kilbride, February 1969.

Supporting Lockheed Airbus at Palmdale, California in April 1970 after the agreement to power it with Rolls Royce RB-211 engines.

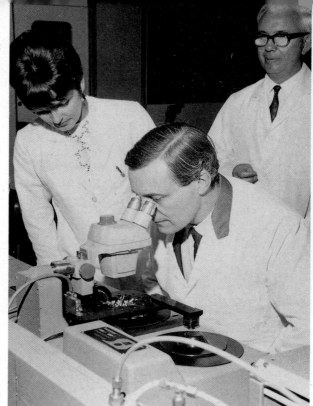

Microchip Minister: visiting Marconi's micro-electronics factory, Witham, Britain's first microchip production unit, July 1968.

Those Magnificent Men in their Flying Machines: with Brian Trubshaw, Concorde's Chief Test Pilot, after one of the first supersonic flights from RAF Fairford, April 1970.

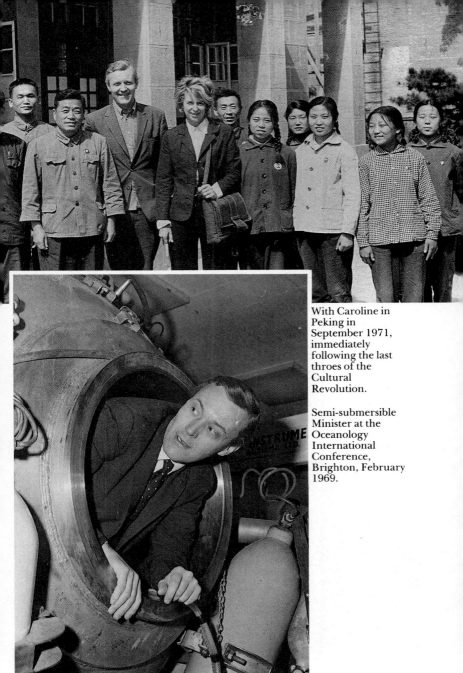

With Caroline in
Peking in
September 1971,
immediately
following the last
throes of the
Cultural
Revolution.

Semi-submersible
Minister at the
Oceanology
International
Conference,
Brighton, February
1969.

Mirror Magnates: Hugh Cudlipp v Cecil King (right) at the IPC Annual General Meeting, July 1968.

Press Barons: Robert Maxwell taking notes and Rupert Murdoch looking contemplative during *News of the World* shareholders' meeting, January 1969.

On her bike: Joan Lestor campaigning in Eton and Slough during the June 1970 General Election.

Enoch Powell on home territory during the 1970 General Election.

Alf Robens, NCB Chairman-turned-industrialist, pictured in July 1972.

Lord Rothschild, who chaired a committee to examine nuclear policy during the 1964–70 Labour Government: subsequently Director General of Ted Heath's 'Think Tank'.

Frank Kearton, a dedicated and influential public servant, one time Chairman of Courtaulds and of the Industrial Reorganisation Corporation.

Denning Pearson of Rolls Royce, the driving force that took Rolls Royce into the big engine business with the launching of the RB-211.

Pat Blackett, one of Britain's most distinguished physicists, wartime founder of operational research.

Bill Penney, wartime pioneer of atomic power, later Chairman of the Atomic Energy Authority.

lasted nearly six hours) was with Mr Chiao Kuan Hua, the Vice-Minister of Foreign Affairs, a close associate for thirty years of Chou-en-Lai and thought to be responsible for Chinese policy towards Western Europe and the United States. He is a delightful man who has travelled widely abroad, and like so many Chinese leaders at that level was prepared to pursue every subject wherever it should lead, referring me back to Cromwell, quoting Bernard Shaw, or telling me that he had been re-reading the physics he had learned at university because he was interested in the role and control of science in a modern society. Genghis Khan, he reminded me, had won his battles by combining the use of gunpowder (learned from the Chinese) with the horse as a delivery vehicle.

'Mr Li Chang, the Vice-Minister of Foreign Trade for the last eighteen years, and a man with an engineering background, was similarly ready to enter into a completely flexible discussion about every possible development of trading relations. He asked detailed questions about the operation of the COCOM embargo as it affected microwave equipment and wanted to know all about my flight in Concorde and its exact range and other capabilities.

'The final talks I had in Peking were something of a surprise. Late on Saturday evening when my wife and I were packing for an early start for Shanghai on the following morning, there was a tap at the door to say that the Vice-Premier, Mr Li Hsien-nien, wished us to come over and see him in the Great Hall of the Peoples, where all the senior Ministers have their offices and which has a banqueting hall capable of seating 5,000 people.

'The entrance was brightly floodlit and at the top of the steps between two Chinese soldiers in their plain green khaki uniforms with red collar tabs, holding fixed-bayoneted rifles loosely in their hands, the Vice-Premier was waiting to greet us with six senior Foreign Office officials and three interpreters.

'Inside, a semi-circle of armchairs awaited us and we sat with the usual porcelain cups of tea, talking to a man who had served as a Divisional Commander in the Red Army fighting the Japanese, and for nearly twenty years had been Vice-Premier, Minister of Finance and a Vice-Chairman of the State Planning Commission. Apart from Mao himself, Lin Piao and Chou-en-Lai and three largely inactive veterans, Li was the only full member of the Politburo as constituted before the Cultural Revolution to be re-elected in 1969. Our discussions with him went on well after midnight last Sunday morning. They were the frankest of all.

'Almost everyone we met from the Vice-Premier to the primary school teachers in Shanghai made the Cultural Revolution the starting point of their discussion. The defeat of Chiang Kai-shek is occasionally used as an historical reference point, but it took place in 1949, almost a generation ago. The Cultural Revolution, by contrast, is real and immediate and significant in every aspect of life and this has to be understood in order to understand China.

'The Cultural Revolution – a phrase almost unintelligible by definition to British minds – was a real revolution involving a major political conflict of ideas, marked by some violence, leading to the removal of a powerful group of top Chinese Communist leaders and the adoption of a dramatically new political course, the internal repercussions of which have almost certainly not subsided.

'Before comprehension becomes possible, the crudity of Western views of Chairman Mao portrayed among a crowd of Chinese waving their little red books must be broken down. And there is more than a simple language barrier: the images and concepts need to be translated as well. But once you get accustomed to the jargon of the Cultural Revolution it gradually ceases to be impenetrable; the outline becomes clearer of real issues of enormous importance (in all countries) that have been hotly debated and apparently settled in China during the last few years.

'These issues are what illuminate Chinese thinking as they observe the outside world. The role China is now playing and will play in the United Nations will certainly be shaped directly by the momentous events of the last few years at home.

'Behind the invariably courteous modesty with which Ministers and others draw attention to their own shortcomings it is important to realise that China is now deeply self-confident and that this self-confidence underlies her diplomatic strategy and tactics.

'China's first objective is, of course, membership of the United Nations, but only on the basis of the complete and final expulsion of Chiang Kai-shek's Taiwan regime.

'Peking is warily watching every single move being made by the United States to find a way of retaining a place in the General Assembly for Chiang Kai-shek. Only a vote that seats the Peking Government as the sole representative of China is acceptable to them.

'The Taiwan issue is the key to the central question of Sino-British relations: the elevation of the two missions to full ambassadorial status. It was often pointed out to me – and when it wasn't, I pointed it out myself – that it seemed absurd that Britain, one of the very first countries to recognise China in 1949, should now be badly lagging in having representation only by Chargé d'Affaires. As the Canadians, Italians and others appear to have succeeded in moving to full diplomatic relations by merely 'noting' the Chinese Government's declaration about its sovereignty over Taiwan, it is important to understand why Britain should still be having difficulty.

'Britain as a signatory of the wartime Potsdam and Cairo Declarations put its name to clear pronouncements about Formosa [Taiwan], then of course at the insistence of Chiang Kai-shek. Moreover as co-recipients of the Japanese surrender, we reiterated – as the Chinese see it – our attitude on Taiwan's place as a province of China. China therefore asks of Britain more than a "noting" of her position. She insists upon a clear British reaffirmation of the juridical right of China's sovereignty.

'The British Government's unwillingness to do this in the terms proposed by China is based upon a postwar statement made by Ernest Bevin 'that the status of Taiwan is undetermined', a phrase since repeated by successive Foreign Secretaries. It is this alone that is delaying the agreed statement.

'With things moving, at last, her way after twenty-two years of intervention, isolation and blockade, China will not sacrifice her rights in the present talks with Britain, even though I am sure both Governments genuinely want to reach an agreement. But the Chinese emphasised that they were in no hurry.

'Of course there are still several thousand US troops and advisers on Taiwan; and it is possible that Nixon is keeping a clear and unequivocal statement of intent to remove them all, at an early date, for his visit to Peking; or just before. After they have left, the Taiwan authorities and people may find it easier to accept what must inevitably happen one day – namely, the reuniting of the lost province under Peking authority.

'Now to the broader questions of China's attitude to foreign Governments. Their formal position can be gleaned from a study of official pronouncements, the long exchange of messages which are quoted in full in Chinese publications, supplemented by the occasional press interviews given by Chou-en-Lai. What was most pleasant was to have the opportunity of getting behind these statements and in meetings with senior policy-makers to realise that Chinese policy is made by men of enormous knowledge of the world who study events in great detail and are practical in approach and as diplomatically skilled as the very best negotiators in the world. One of the prices we have paid for isolating China all these years is to allow ourselves to forget this fact.

'People sometimes wonder how much China knows about the outside world. It was interesting, therefore, for me to be able to read from the Chinese news agency a full report of the TUC accounts of the industrial dispute involving BAC in Bristol and to be asked about the latest news on Upper Clyde Shipbuilders. Perhaps most shaking of all was to be mildly criticised for an article on Nehru I had written in the *Guardian* in 1963.

'One of the most important areas of discussion was that of the Chinese attitude to the United States. The contrast between the huge posters attacking "US Imperialists and their running dogs" which stare at you in airports, factories and hotel lobbies and the obvious interest and satisfaction over Nixon's intended pilgrimage to Peking is inevitably fascinating. The Chinese must have calculated in advance the domestic and international political risks in inviting President Nixon – the personification of US imperialism – to visit China. Fear of the Soviet Union must have been one factor in agreeing to his visit and another their assessment that President Nixon would need to make a success of the mission as part of his presidential campaign in 1972.

'They assume that with so much at stake he would not want to prejudice his chances of success by reversing his Vietnam rundown meanwhile; and so, to that extent, by agreeing to his suggestion that he should come, they have locked him tightly into his own timetable of withdrawal.

'One minor aspect of Nixon's visit which I raised, *en passant*, caused a small flurry of interest. I pointed out that every American President made a great thing of having to be in continual 24-hour contact with the Pentagon as Commander in Chief of American Forces; and that the black box communication system, which could activate a nuclear attack, will have to be with Nixon in China wherever the talks with Chairman Mao and Chou-en-Lai are held.

'The thought of an American nuclear button being situated in China, let alone pressed from there – were the balloon to go up – is more than faintly ironic.

'Sino-American contacts have obviously complicated the crisis in relations between Peking and Moscow. From the famous occasion in July 1960, when Khrushchev shouted intemperately at the Chinese delegation at the Sino-Soviet talks following the Rumanian Party Congress, the divisions have widened and become far graver. In ideological terms they are now irreconcilable.

'I was variously told that the Soviet Union was now capitalist, imperialist, and on one occasion actually Fascist. I was asked how I felt about Sovet imperialism having moved in to fill the vacuum left by the disintegration of the British Empire – presumably a reference to India and the Arab world. The gravest charge of all – revisionist – was used to compare Krushchev and Brezhnev to the disgraced Chinese leader, Liu Shao-chi, whose name is raised in virtually every discussion, be it in university, factory, commune or school, or with Ministers, all of whom speak about him as the arch traitor.

'The Chinese are very proud that during their long ideological exchanges they always published Soviet criticism in full and even invited Khrushchev to Peking to lecture on Marxism, a fact that was told to me more than once, and with more than a hint of a smile.

'But it was hard to escape the conclusion that Sino-Soviet hostility is in a way more bitter even than either's hositility to the West. The West,

the Chinese may argue, and seem to believe, will collapse in due course
from its own internal contradictions. But for China the Soviet Union has
committed the gravest sin of all. It has had its socialist revolution and
betrayed it – or, to be more accurate, has allowed its leaders to betray it
and then repressed those who have discovered what has happened.

'Grave risks lie in wait for the unresolved border dispute with the
USSR, which could flare up again at any time and which must have the
effect of making the military both anxious and influential.

'Since security rather than political doctrine normally dictates foreign
policy, it would be surprising if even the ideologically pure Chinese were
not at least as much influenced by their practical problems with Russia
as by the infinite evil they see in Soviet revisionism. But all that points to
the likelihood of a worsening rather than an improvement in their
relations with the Kremlin.

'China is also having to think out some of the political consequences
that have begun to flow from the limited American withdrawal imposed
by her failure in Vietnam and her economic difficulties. They seem to
have woken up rather slowly to the role that Japan may plan to assume
in these new circumstances.

'They do not like at all what they see as Japanese economic
imperialism and the thought that this might raise once again the
problem of containing Japanese power is intensely disturbing.

'As far as Europe is concerned, China appears to be far more relaxed
about the recovery of Germany and even about its Ostpolitik drama-
tised by the Brezhnev-Brandt talks which took place while I was there.
Her attitude to the enlargement of the Common Market, which she
favours, appears to stem from her pleasure at seeing both American and
Soviet influence reduced in Western Europe.

'In a deliberate probe I asked whether China thought of herself as a
superpower. "After all," I pointed out, "you are the largest nation on
earth, are developing your economy rapidly, you have nuclear weapons
and a rocket capable of launching an orbital satellite. It is impossible not
to think of you as a superpower."

'This intentionally provocative comment immediately drew a re-
solute denial. I was reminded that China was still a developing country,
technically behind the West and Russia. Her nuclear programme was
small, almost in the experimental stage, and though she had no
intention of abandoning it, nor of giving up nuclear tests, she did not
intend to join the nuclear arms race (which she thinks will go on), still
less a full-scale space programme. But more than that she understood
the phrase "superpower" to refer to the policy pursued by the Americans
and Russians brandishing their weapons and bullying other countries to
gain and hold spheres of special influence.

'So far as foreign policy is concerned, it is clear that China is anxious that she should be seen as a medium power, working with other medium powers – Britain, for example – and with the small nations. This reassuring assertion of future policy underlined by specific references to her good state relations with Yugoslavia and Pakistan – about neither of whose regimes she has any ideological illusions – does of course superficially conflict with her own open support of world revolution.

'This contradiction is likely to be sharpened with the increased international contact of UN membership. It would be a mistake to suppose that she will not want to play a constructive UN role, though at the UN itself in February I was told at a high level that the arrival of China was expected to lead to two or three years of unprecedented – but potentially beneficial – conflict, perhaps beginning with a volley of vetoes.

'China seems to see herself offering a third course to countries that reject the idea of a world divided between American and Russian imperialism. This is, in a sense, the re-emergence of de Gaulle's dream with the difference that de Gaulle could never convincingly speak for the developing nations, nor build on such a massive growth potential.

'Odd as it may seem to think of Peking, which is ideologically so far to the Left of both Washington and Moscow, as being a third force, the idea is not so improbable. The long guerrilla background which bred China's leadership and her self-reliant economic development may well prove more relevant to the Third World than anything that the two super-powers can offer.

'Indeed, it is in this background that Chinese strength is really grounded. No country that suffered a century of humiliation, a quarter of a century of invasion and civil war and then moved into twenty years of vigorous development without foreign help could possibly fail to have been strengthened by the experience. It has bred leaders of exceptional toughness and resilience and integrated them deeply and personally with their people in a way that is hard for outsiders to understand. The result is what one can only call moral force based on a cultural and psychological revival of a kind that simply cannot be ignored as a source of China's internal cohesion and energy.

'What is being constructed there is a society that poses more than a potentially long-term economic and military challenge. It is the only real working alternative society to that which in the West, and maybe now Russia, draws its inspiration from the ideas released by the Industrial Revolution (which produced both capitalism and *Das Kapital*). Marx is for China an Old Testament prophet and Mao has written a sequel – a New Testament that forecasts class struggle continuing within socialist societies and taking perhaps two or three centuries to resolve – and his ideas are accepted and taught throughout the oldest civilisation and largest nation in the world. This is a fact of life which we would do well to understand and we may find it is not at all as frightening as China's enemies would have led us to believe.'†

Friday 1 October
Went early to Brighton for the Conference. It is quite clear that the Common Market issue will absolutely dominate it.

In the afternoon I had a talk with journalists John Graham and James Margach: I admitted to them that I would consider standing for the deputy-leadership if nominated and so my hat is almost in the ring.

There are huge security precautions at the hotel and my flat is wired into an electronic screen because I am so near Harold.

Dinner which Mik had laid on at one of the hotels in Brighton for Bill Simpson, Gwyn Morgan, Terry Pitt, Tom McNally, Ron Hayward and me to discuss what the Party could do over the next twelve months – Mik laying down his mantle as Chairman at this Conference and me picking it up* and wanting to have some continuity. I said I thought the great new theme was Party democracy.

Saturday 2 October
I went to see Harold to tell him I was thinking of standing for the deputy-leadership. I don't think he was surprised and I told him I didn't expect him to give me support of any kind but he ought to know.

Sunday 3 October
The *Sunday Express* reported that I would be standing for the deputy-leadership and hoped to topple Roy Jenkins.

Monday 4 October
The Conference began. Ian Mikardo gave a very good Chairman's Address. Then there was the EEC debate and the entry to the Market was defeated by 5 to 1. It wasn't anything like as good a debate as we had at the special conference in July because Mik decided he wouldn't call anyone to speak who had been called on that occasion. But it was a foregone conclusion anyway.

At 5.15 I went to the Labour Parliamentary Association where, as Chairman, I was the host for Roy and Jennifer Jenkins. I made a particular point of being friendly to Roy in my speech, how I had known him for years, and so on.

Then he made an amusing speech. He is the figure dominating this Conference; there is no question about it. The press are determined that

---

* The man or woman who chairs the National Executive each year begins office at the end of each Conference and chairs the following year's Party Conference.
† © *Sunday Times*, 26 September 1971.

we shall enter Europe and they are not interested in anything except that. Harold is presented as the guy who has avoided the difficulty, and Roy as the great hero.

Tuesday 5 October

The National Executive election results. I came second with 407,000 votes. Harold Wilson bitterly attacked the Tories and the Conference loved it. I thought it was a cheap speech – most of Harold's speeches are – but he gets away with it and he is the old entertainer, the Archie Rice of the Labour Party. He knows how to press the right buttons and his position is strong.

We had dinner with the Townsends, David Butler and Peter Shore. Peter Townsend is bitter about the Labour Party and Peter Shore is depressed: the Common Market dominates his thinking more than anything else.

Wednesday 6 October

The economic debate was opened by Barbara and Roy spoke at the end of the morning. The UCS shop stewards appeared in the gallery, and when I spoke at the end of the debate they cheered like anything.

I was elected Chairman of the National Executive Committee for the coming year. I thanked Mik and gave him the gavel.

Thursday 7 October

During the day, Gerald Kaufman asked me if it was true that I was going to stand for the deputy-leadership because he was not prepared to vote for Michael Foot.

I went to the Mayor's reception and had dinner at the hotel with Judith and Tony Hart. Decided to postpone my Chairman's message which I was going to put out this week because Frank McElhone thought it would affect my campaign for the deputy-leadership. He thought it went too far in suggesting that there should be further opportunities for constituencies to replace their Labour MPs, that the Leader and Deputy-Leader of the Party should be confirmed at Conference and for raising the possibility that the Cabinet should be elected. But these are my ideas for democratisation and I am anxious to get them out.

Friday 8 October

The last session of Conference. Everyone said the Conference had swung heavily to the Left, which I think it did and I hope it has.

Wednesday 13 October

Caroline's birthday.

I sent my Chairman's message to *Labour Weekly*, the new Party paper, in which I began spelling out the extension of Party democracy. We had the Shadow Cabinet meeting at 4 – the first meeting after Conference on the Common Market. The Chief Whip reported on the business of the House, telling us that the European Communities Bill would begin to be debated on 21 October. Harold moved that the PLP did not support entry into the Common Market on the present terms.

George Thomson then moved to enter the Common Market after taking account of the resolution at the Conference. Shirley Williams supported. Jim Callaghan said if we flouted the Conference, we would immolate the Party and thoroughly upset the constituencies which would have consequences for the Shadow Cabinet elections. Harold Wilson summed up against George Thomson's motion and his motion was finally agreed. The Parliamentary Party will be recommended by the Shadow Cabinet, taking account of a decision of Conference to oppose the Tory Government's proposal to enter the EEC. That was the main motion.

As to speakers in the debate, Harold said that he proposed to end the present portfolios, and the speakers would be Harold, Denis, Jim, Barbara, Michael, myself and Willie Ross. Roy said that there should be a free vote in the House and we must discuss this. I said, 'Is there anyone intending to vote for the *Government*?' Harold said, 'We must take a step at a time. Don't discuss the Whip, because there will be a leak.'

Monday 18 October
We had the Shadow Cabinet at which we resumed the discussion on the Common Market. Roy put forward a resolution that we should have a free vote. Immediately after the meeting we heard that the Tories were going to be given a free vote – Heath had announced it himself. This was an absolute bombshell and so at 2.15 the Shadow Cabinet was called again. Harold said, 'If Heath gives a free vote, we shall have to have a free vote.'

I lost my temper with Harold, and I said, 'I don't know what game you are playing but we cannot have a free vote when the Party has decided its view.' I said, 'The line we take is that there must be a free vote of the *British public*. This is the right thing to happen, not a free vote of the House of Commons which excludes the public from any right of choice.' The position was more or less held after that.

I was beginning to have second thoughts then about whether I would stand for the deputy-leadership.

Tuesday 19 October
Another Shadow Cabinet this morning at 10.30 because Roy very much objected to a meeting being called at 7.15 the previous evening without

any notice of what was going to happen. He moved a resolution for the
Parliamentary Party meeting on these lines: recognising the deeply held
differences of view on the Common Market, this House has no
confidence in the ability of the Government to deal with the circumstances arising after entry. He tried to get this through and allow us to
have a vote, not on the question of entry but on the handling of matters
afterwards. But the decision was that we would have a straight vote
rejecting the present terms and we wouldn't vary our decision.

Next we had the PLP meeting itself, where there were two votes: for
Michael Stewart's amendment that we should enter Europe were 87 –
with Roy Jenkins, Shirley Williams, Tony Crosland and George
Thomson and Harold Lever all voting in favour – 151 against; and for
the Shadow Cabinet's motion in favour of rejecting the present terms
159, and 89 against.

Frank Allaun talked of the untold misery if the Government went in.
The Tory Government needs Labour to win and to give MPs a free vote
would save Heath. Heath is on the ropes and we can't behave like little
gentlemen. He has given way on the free vote not for the love of tolerance
but out of weakness. This was the best way of getting Labour votes.
Frank was in favour of a three-line whip but not, of course, of expulsion
afterwards.

Charlie Pannell said he could speak only for himself. His service to the
European Movement was as long as Roy's. He said, 'I can't turn
overnight; Europe is an act of faith which has grown and never more
strongly than now. It is not for those who have ratted on three-line whips
to try and impose one now.' He wanted to go into Europe with Harold
Wilson. 'Life has decisions that go to the centre of one's being,' he said,
'and I couldn't respect myself if I voted against Europe.'

Judith Hart said, 'Heath's Government is in deep trouble. Why don't
the pro-Marketeers let the record speak. We are bound to respond to the
views of our supporters. Integrity and credibility are at stake and we
could end up destroying the credibility of the Party.'

After all the speeches were over, in favour of a free vote were 111 and
against, 140. So at this stage the Party was committed against Europe
and against a free vote.

We had a further Shadow Cabinet in the evening and Harold tried a
new form of words. He said, 'This House, recalling the words of the
Prime Minister in the General Election that no British Government
could possibly take this country into the Common Market against the
wishes of the overwhelming majority of the British public, calls on the
Government to submit to the democratic judgment of a General
Election.'

Bob Mellish intervened to say, 'Look, Harold, it's all over. Leave it.'
Denis said, 'Leave it.'

Then Shirley tried to raise the question of the free vote and the argument started all over again.

By the end, the whole Shadow Cabinet was in a state of uproar and we were all set for a straight clash.

I had dinner with Eric Heffer, then phoned Judith, Joan Lestor, and Peter Shore to see how we could contain what had emerged, namely a European Social Democrat wing in the Parliamentary Party led by Bill Rodgers which was a minority but intended to defy the decision. I stayed talking until 1 am and the atmosphere was tight. When I heard Charlie Pannell say that for him Europe was an article of faith, he put it above the Labour Party and above the Labour Movement, I was finally convinced that this was a deep split.

Wednesday 20 October
I talked to Michael Foot and Fred Peart about the deputy-leadership. Fred was discouraging. I had a brief talk to Michael who made it clear that he intended to stand in any case. I must record here that Caroline is very doubtful about whether I should stand.

Wednesday 27 October
Worked until 5 this morning on my Fabian lecture and then I went to the National Executive, the first time I had taken the chair, and I had developed a new layout which I liked but which members of the Executive didn't.

Judith Hart put a motion that she and I had worked out together. 'The NEC welcomes the decision of the PLP to oppose entry into the Common Market. It believes that the British public are entitled to a vote on this issue in a General Election and calls upon the whole Party, inside and outside Parliament, to campaign for an immediate General Election. The NEC believes that the overwhelming will of the Party is to end the present economic and social evils of this Government and expresses the hope that this will be regarded as the absolute priority on 28 October. There are strong feelings and there would be grave consequences if the PLP ignored Conference decisions.'

Walter Padley said that although he was in favour of Europe he would vote for the Party.

Joe Gormley said, 'We must work for an Election – that's all-important.'

Jim Callaghan said he would vote against it because of the relationship between the Executive and the PLP. He said, 'Don't split the National Executive on this.'

Judith said it was imperative that the appeal be made, and the motion was carried by 15 to 8.

There was another resolution by Alex Kitson that had been tabled without proper notice, strongly welcoming the decision of the PLP to apply a three-line whip against entry into the Common Market. It concluded that in those cases where Labour MPs act contrary to the collective decisions of the Annual Conference and the PLP, this be drawn to the attention of the constituency Labour Parties. It called upon the small minority of MPs who have indicated an inclination to support entry on the terms now known to recognise that their action could only cause long-lasting division and conflict with constituency Labour Parties at a time when maximum unity is necessary to rid Britain of the Conservative Government.

Well, I had to rule on this and I simply decided that the main issue had already been discussed, the rest was long-term and wasn't constitutional, and I ruled it out of order.

Then to the Commons in the afternoon where Barber spoke in the Common Market debate and I came after him. I began by saying that I had never taken an absolutely clear view on this, but had developed my argument on the consent of the British people. On the whole the speech went well and the *Guardian* wrote a friendly piece about it.

Ken Coates of the Institute of Workers' Control contacted me to give his support to my standing for the deputy-leadership and said he would try to help me by ringing his left-wing friends. I said, 'Well, do it discreetly.' I am sure Ken Coates's telephone is tapped regularly by MI5 and I should think that my MI5 file is now full of the most extraordinary reports. They must think I have suddenly gone sharply to the Left. It may well be that some of the hostile press is coming from that source: I say that without any real evidence and it indicates what a state of paranoia one can get into.

At any rate, the Party is now on the eve of the great split when voting takes place and is absolutely dreading the situation. One of the factors that has made it a great deal worse is that Douglas Houghton, the Chairman of the PLP, has announced that he intends to vote for entry and this, of course, makes the revolt against the Whip respectable.

Thursday 28 October
I received a letter from Enoch Powell – now that was a surprise – congratulating me on my Common Market speech yesterday, 90 per cent of which he had agreed with.

Harold opened the last day's debate on the Common Market and he hedged so cleverly that it was clear that if a Labour Government was elected when he was Prime Minister, he would simply accept the Common Market. We had the vote and 69 Labour MPs voted for the Market, giving Heath a majority of 112. It was terribly tense and there had been rumours of people fighting after the vote; in fact, they were just shouting at Roy Jenkins as he went through the Lobby. It was awful.

Friday 29 October
I began drafting a statement on the Party crisis and I rang around and checked it with Frank McElhone, Ron Hayward and others, then put it out. The evening papers had a huge headline: 'Benn Stabs Roy'. The press is absolutely full of what is called 'Europhoria'.

Saturday 30 October
Frances Morrell came in from 10.30 in the morning to 8.30 in the evening, advising me on the deputy-leadership campaign and drafting my statement saying first of all, the Party was entitled to expect that its view would be represented in Parliament; second, that the public was entitled to expect Parliament to take some notice of what it thought; and third, on a constitutional matter of this importance (the Common Market), there must be some consultation with the public.

Mark and Val Arnold-Forster joined us in the evening and Mark was hostile to the idea of my standing. He took the more cautious Jim Callaghan view. Val said to me very significantly, 'In 1960 you tried to save the Party by resigning from the Executive and now you are trying to save it again. You are wrong in both cases.' I launched into a violent attack on her which I rather regretted, but I was in a tense state.

Later, I rang around the political correspondents and in effect decided to take the plunge. Then of course, I had instant doubts and I knew that there would be two weeks of absolute hell.

Monday 1 November
The Queen's speech was discussed and we were told that the Government would shortly be signing the Treaty of Rome followed by detailed legislation. There were various other items in the speech: legislation on monopoly, consumer protection, shipbuilding.

Wednesday 3 November
I gave my Fabian lecture tonight, 'Labour Party in Democratic Politics', in Caxton Hall. It was not well attended and I was depressed.

Thursday 4 November
The press comment on my Fabian lecture this morning was unfavourable. I had always thought that Harold Wilson was paranoid about the press but I can understand now how it can affect one.

The nominations had to go in today for the deputy-leadership. I went to the Commons where support was slipping away. I could just feel it. People didn't come up to me and I felt isolated. I talked around and went to the PLP meeting where Roy Jenkins, Michael Foot and I, as candidates, had to make statements. Roy made it absolutely clear that he did not commit himself, if elected Deputy-Leader, to vote with the Party throughout the year. Michael Foot spoke next.

I said that I thought that an organisation like ours had to be able to reach common decisions. We have important talks with the trade unions in the coming winter and unless they felt that our agreements, embodied in Conference resolutions, were to mean something, the whole coalition that constitutes the Party would break down.

I was interviewed later by Robert Carvel of the *Evening Standard* on my Fabian lecture, and I had a long talk to him afterwards and asked him why I had such bad relations with the press. He said, 'You shouldn't take any notice of what the Lobby says.' The Lobby liked people they could see through and the sea-green, incorruptible, teetotaller annoyed them; they didn't care for that type at all. He was quite friendly in a funny sort of way.

Then I came home and I was extremely depressed at the prospect of a serious defeat.

Tuesday 9 November
Roy Jenkins opened the unemployment debate in the House and I wound up. I tried to broaden out the issues a little bit and the Tories laughed at me. Caroline came to listen, and she said I was years ahead of my time. But I haven't got command of the House of Commons at the moment, and that's another thing that is worrying me. It is all rather a catalogue of gloom at the moment.

Wednesday 10 November
Hans Janitschek came to lunch and during it the results of the deputy-leadership were announced. Jenkins got 140, Foot 96 and me 46. Quite frankly by this stage 46 seems to me a very good vote and I was pleased. Douglas Houghton was re-elected to the Chairmanship of the PLP. It is obvious now that the Common Marketeers have been able to defy the PLP and get re-elected and there is something very interesting in that. It means that the Bill Rodgers's CDS group have got a majority in the PLP and that is something one will have to accept. But politically as well as personally, I am most depressed.

Thursday 11 November
Went to Belfast early with Jim Callaghan, John Chalmers, Gwyn Morgan and Terry Pitt, representing the British Labour Party. We had meetings at Dunardy Inn Lodge with Mora Walshe, Rod Connolly, Conor Cruise O'Brien from the Irish Labour Party; Gerry Fitt, Ivan Cooper and Paddy Devlin from the SDLP; and Vivian Simpson, Norman Kennedy and Douglas McIldoon from the Northern Ireland Labour Party.

While we were there 15,000 Protestants demonstrated against us. We decided we wouldn't put out a statement but we would survey the situation. I was put in the chair and we agreed that it was a good sign that all four Parties were now around a table to discuss the problems. I asked each of them to give their assessment.

It was clear that people thought it could get worse and Conor Cruise O'Brien said that he had in his mind a possible complete tragedy developing there which would have to be taken seriously as it could engulf North and South in the most appalling civil war. The Irish Labour Party would like to see the SDLP brought into the discussions. Internment was a major problem and we kept coming back to this. It became clear to me that the only way around the problem would be to try to transfer the whole of security from Stormont to Westminster, including the control of the police, which would create a difficult new situation.

There was a press conference at the airport and it was really awful. We were surrounded by paratroopers with Sten guns, looking in every direction and at any moment there might have been a bomb thrown. One felt as if one were in Hanoi or Saigon at the height of the war. Jim gave a very successful press briefing.

Saturday 13 November
Hans Van Den Bergh of the Dutch Socialist International Bureau came to interview me. He is another of these professional communicators – young middle class, articulate, liberal minded – who really have just taken over the Social Democratic Movement in Western Europe. It has nothing to do with the working class any more. I find it pretty unattractive. Indeed, I find myself getting more and more out of sympathy with the Labour Party which I think is just a sort of professional, Fleet Street type of Party. This feeling is all reinforced by the fact that the PLP has really only succeeded in escalating the crisis by re-electing the Marketeers.

Monday 15 November
In the evening, Caroline and I went to a party given by Jack Jones for Victor Ruether of the United Auto Workers. I was glad I went because I want to keep in with the Transport and General Workers' Union.

To the Commons and chatted to a lot of Labour MPs – John Silkin, John Prescott, Neil Kinnock, Jim Sillars, Hugh Brown, Charlie Loughlin, Neil Carmichael, Michael Foot, and to Dick Clements. They all want to talk to me now because, of course, they realise that Michael is going to have a job beating Roy in the second ballot and this is the great moment when we've got to try to get together again. I was pleased in one sense at the prospect of a united Left.

Tuesday 16 November
Frank McElhone came home and talked to Caroline and me. What he was really saying was, 'Look, you really must drop some of this forward-looking stuff which is damaging you with Labour MPs who think you are an extremist. You must concentrate on getting a good press and building up a solid block of support.' I was wondering at this stage if I would even be re-elected to the Shadow Cabinet.

Thursday 18 November
Went with Peter Shore to Toynbee Hall for the opening of Attlee House by the Queen. I found myself standing in for Harold who is in Northern Ireland on his week's mission. It was the first time the Queen had met Profumo since the scandal in 1963. I found the whole thing awful except I had a chance to talk to the Attlee children – Felicity and Alison.

Had a meal with Dennis Skinner and John Prescott. Came home still pretty depressed.

Friday 19 November
To Wesley College in Bristol where I talked to the theological students, and discovered that they shared the anxieties of everybody else about theology, not just unbelievers like myself. I found this rather encouraging because for some time my theological view has been that the mythology of Christianity is unnecessary, but that the ethics of Christianity are important. Indeed, if the ethics were presented as man's accumulated wisdom of how to learn to live with other people, it would be marvellous, but the authoritarian presentation of God's plan for the world I find quite unacceptable.

I watched the Transport and General Workers–Harlech TV film *My Brother's Keeper* which had arisen out of my May Day speech at Glasgow calling for the trade unions to demand programmes of their own. I only saw the rough cut without the commentary but, even so, it was excellent, really moving.

Monday 22 November
The Shadow Cabinet meeting. Harold is back from Northern Ireland and is furious to discover that no debate on Ireland has been fixed for him this week and it can't be next week because he is going to be in America selling his book and giving lectures. Harold is trying to get the debate restored so that he can make his great speech.

Tuesday 23 November
To the Industrial Society Conference at the Albert Hall, where there were two or three thousand 11-Plus successes, gathered there by the Industrial Society, which is a sort of boy scout, middle class, Christian

responsible-leadership type organisation. I don't like it. It seems very liberal and friendly but it is really financed by big business and it plays the role for big business here that Moral Rearmament does in America.

Caroline and I then had dinner with the Chilean Ambassador, with Judith and Tony Hart.

Thursday 25 November
Went to the Commons. Harold Wilson made his major speech on Ulster which he hadn't consulted anyone about. It was a remarkable success. It was much too long but it was the first time for over fifty years that a political leader had raised the question of re-unification between the North and South. He did it well. Where he was weak, from the point of view of the Catholics, was that he didn't condemn internment or come out with anything very relevant in the short term, but it was a major political initiative which completely defused Ireland as far as the Party was concerned and made Maudling seem defensive and inadequate.

We had a Shadow Cabinet just afterwards, then a Party meeting at which the Left was clearly not satisfied with the way in which Harold had dealt with internment and the immediate issues; Paul Rose moved a resolution calling for the end of bi-partisanship.

After the Party meeting it was evident that we would have to draft something else. I went along to see Harold and he said, 'I have got to go and do a television programme about my speech. You draft it.' So I went to see Jim Callaghan who was cross to have been upstaged by Harold on Ireland and he said, 'You'll have to do it. I'm going. I'm late for seeing my grandchild.'

So I drafted a resolution which was tabled later that night in the House of Commons, on which I said we declined to support the continuation of internment. We paid tribute to the British troops and the difficult work they were doing, but we did not support the use of the methods of interrogation which should not be accepted in any civilised country – the Compton Report had revealed most appalling methods of interrogation, forcing people to stand with black hoods over their heads and their arms against a wall for hours on end with a disorienting noise used against them. I discussed the resolution with Douglas Houghton briefly and he agreed, so it was tabled in the name of the Parliamentary Labour Party. This was a very important statement because it did break bipartisanship.

Friday 3 December
To meet the Bristol Council of Churches who were steamed up about Rhodesia. The trouble with liberally-minded middle class people is that they are concerned about matters of high principle but it is the immediate injustices and practical matters right close at home and

under their noses that they don't like to tackle. This is why working class people suspect middle class liberals like myself. I can see it now and I get a sort of mirror image of myself when I meet people like the Industrial Society people or the Bristol Council of Churches. That's just by-the-by, but one can understand these class tensions and why they build up.

Sunday 5 December
In the evening I had drinks with Peter and Liz Shore and Judith and Tony Hart. I said what I thought about the current state of the Labour Party. Peter had never heard me sound so bitter. I am depressed and I am bitter and I am gloomy, and I think it is largely my own fault. This November and December have, in many ways, been the lowest political period in my life.

Tuesday 7 December
I haven't recorded in my diary the result of Shadow Cabinet elections but I was re-elected with 122 votes, 13 less than last time. Denis Healey dropped to bottom place.

Friday 10 December
Today we heard that Concorde had got Government backing. So that's the end of that particular anxiety. Bristol would be in a terrible state if it was not going ahead.

Sunday 12 December
In the evening I had dinner with Elizabeth and Wayland Young, who gave tremendous warnings about the Labour left wing, and the possibility that we might all be overcome by feeling for the Russians, drop our defences, then Labour foreign policy would simply be seized by the Left. This was a curious warning and I wondered why it had been given to me; Wayland Young, I suspect, may have links with the Intelligence Services, and I think Mark Arnold-Forster is also a security officer. They probably keep an eye on me. I replied to Elizabeth that this was astonishing and that I had never heard of such an idea. I said Frank Allaun was a well-known pacifist and he wanted defence cuts but I didn't know anyone who was particularly sympathetic to the Russian regime, particularly since Czechoslovakia; Russia had lost all moral appeal with the British Left, which now looks to China. But, even so, they had obviously invited me over to plant this thought in my mind and then no doubt to report on my reaction.

Tuesday 14 December
Jim Callaghan asked me today why I didn't vote for him as the Home Policy Committee chairman. I said, 'Well, why didn't you vote for me for the deputy-leadership?'

'I've never said who I voted for.'

'I don't regard this as personal. I think the Party has got to shift a bit to the Left, Jim.'

He said, 'So do I. I retain my view that in the long run, you will be the Leader of the Party.' But that, of course, suits his book nicely because 'in the long run' means after he's given up and he still sees himself, I think, as replacing Harold. Frankly, I think his prospects are not very bright.

Wednesday 15 December

The Jordanian Ambassador was machine-gunned near Holland Park School about three minutes before Melissa and all her friends were going down to get their fish and chips in the lunch hour.

Monday 20 December

Another meeting of the four-Party Irish Commission. I was put in the chair again and Jim was there, having said beforehand we had to be careful not to be committed to the SDLP, or tied with the Catholic minority when there was a Protestant majority to be thought of. These were perfectly valid points but he meant he didn't want these meetings to be too important and he didn't want the thing transferred from the Parliamentary Party to the National Executive where presumably he felt he had rather less influence. He would rather be talking to Maudling informally than talking too much to the Irish representatives.

Vivian Simpson said the situation had deteriorated seriously. There was no hope until the violence could be stopped and therefore they wanted inter-Party talks with everyone joining in. Faulkner thought that the Unionists were more united, but Paisley is going ahead and Stormont is ready to support the unarmed vigilantes.

Brian Garrett of the Northern Ireland Labour Party said he thought Wilson's speech had started discussions. Paddy Devlin said he thought that Provo, the Provisional, activity was diminishing. The military have restricted their movement and therefore there would be more selective violence, it would be more dangerous and it would force activity over the whole board. The risk of assassination was very great. Military activity by the troops was driving people towards the Provos and they suspected that the McGurk's pub bombing, which killed fifteen people, and other attacks were the work of the Ulster Unionists trying to stir hatred against the IRA.

Ivan Cooper said the Provisionals were seeking confrontation, perhaps by shooting Ulster Unionist politicians, and the possibility of civil disobedience being escalated to extend to total paralysis couldn't be ignored.

Gerry Fitt said the situation had so deteriorated that we've come to a road-block. He welcomed Wilson's speech which legitimised long-term unity, and short-term transfer of security was of absolutely key importance to them. He couldn't see all-Party talks taking place because Faulkner wouldn't accept discussions about constitutional developments and transfer of security, and had no faith in the impartiality of the British army. The Paras had insulted him in a recent incident and all those interned were potential recruits into the Provisionals.

Jim murmured to me that of course the Foreign Office and the Ministry of Defence had wanted internment and cratering when *we* were in power, which I remember well.

Gerry Fitt repeated that the SDLP position was clear: they couldn't talk while internment lasted. If they did talk, the Provos would simply take over. But he thought the Government and the Opposition should go on talking.

We then had Michael O'Leary from the Republic. He reported on the position in Dublin. There is a strong swing of public opinion against the British, a massive confrontation is imminent and there must be an urgent re-examination. A unilateral release of internees over the Christmas period and a military pull-back of some kind would help because, he thought, hundreds of soldiers would be killed over the next three months and the troops would be put in an impossible position under Faulkner who is just fighting his own war.

We had lunch from 1 to 4, at which Harold spoke and he undoubtedly helped by indicating that he fully understood the SDLP position and that sovereignty was, for him, the transfer of security. This obviously made a big impression on them.

At the end there was the great question of whether there should be a statement or not. So I went away and drafted a unilateral Labour Party statement which I hoped they would assent to. I drew attention to the things the Labour Party had done, the Wilson speech, the initiative for talks, and the vote in the House of Commons against internment. I said we fully understood the decision of the other two Parties who had to make up their own minds, but that as far as we were concerned we would persuade the Government on their behalf that this was an open-ended commitment to talk.

This was argued over line by line; Jim didn't want a reference to internment that didn't contain praise for the British troops. But finally we worked out a formula and it was agreed, although it wasn't wildly acceptable. I couldn't go right against Jim because he is the parliamentary spokesman.

Friday 31 December
Played ping-pong and went out with the boys in the evening. Got home just as midnight struck and 1971 came to an end. It was the first full year of Opposition. As trade and industry spokesman I played a leading part

in the big debates on Rolls Royce and Upper Clyde Shipbuilders, and the Government's industrial policy, which was very much the 'lame duck' policy. I was under heavy attack from the Tories: they wanted to make me the scapegoat for the failures at Rolls Royce and UCS and, although I fought back hard in the debates and won some support, undoubtedly the Tories and the Government did succeed in associating me with failure. In supporting UCS I came up against another group of people, namely the right wing of the Labour Party, which is opposed to my support of shop stewards, many of whom are Communists.

I got drawn closely into the Common Market argument and I spoke out frankly. My position on this was slightly ambivalent because I wasn't hostile to the Common Market, indeed I made speeches broadly in support of it as a Minister, but I did think there should have been a Referendum and this was a difficult argument to get across. I certainly learned one thing – that the British public just isn't in favour of participation. It is told by its liberal élites that it shouldn't be interested in these things, and I am not sure how easy it will be to get people to accept participation at the moment. This intervention in the Common Market argument certainly cost me some support. I can't visualise myself having taken any other line because this is what I believed in, but it was a difficult period.

At the end of 1970 Frank McElhone had come to see me and had said that in his opinion I would be the next Leader of the Labour Party. For the first time I had a strong campaigner working for me. Frank McElhone is a very able political organiser, and without him I might have done much worse. But on the other hand, I think when it came to it, it would have been better if I hadn't stood; or, having stood, not to have spoken so frankly, been a bit more cautious in presenting views. But that is contrary to my own instincts.

At the end of the year the bitter press attacks on me for standing had done me a lot of damage, there is no question about that, and they had affected my self-confidence. I felt I had had something of the stuffing knocked out of me.

I never remember politics being quite as unpleasant as this before; but maybe this is what life is like at the top.

I very much want to improve relations with the trade unions where I think there has been deep damage done by the Common Market split, although the Government is so unpopular that the Party and the country don't want to see a split. We have got to handle this with great care.

The Party is in a bad way. I think the sourness left by the Common Market business, which is not by any means over yet, will remain for some time. I don't think Harold Wilson will ever be Prime Minister again, although I could be wrong. I have to improve my relations with the Labour MPs and with the Shadow Cabinet, and be a success as Party Chairman which is not going to be easy this year.

Caroline's book on comprehensive schools *Half Way There* is already required for a second edition. My admiration for her is quite unbounded.

The children are all doing well: Stephen at Keele, Hilary at Sussex; Melissa and Joshua at school.

The climax this year will be the Labour Party Conference in Blackpool and it will be a difficult one. I think the preservation of the British Labour Party as an effective alternative instrument of government is of supreme importance but, at the same time, I want to be sure that when we do get back to power (which I don't think we will for two Parliaments) we have got something distinctive to offer, something different from the Conservative philosophy that has now established itself quite firmly.

However much one may dislike Heath – and I personally find him a very unattractive person – he has emerged as a strong and tough Prime Minister who is prepared to face battles and fight them out. The economy, after having gone through a difficult eighteen months, is going to pick up and will look good and although unemployment won't drop to acceptable levels and prices won't be held in check, the position won't be too bad from Heath's point of view. He has settled the Rhodesian question by selling out to Smith. He has got us into Europe by accepting conditions that maybe are not ideal. He has emerged as a competent man who can deal with America – so he would claim – meeting Nixon in Bermuda and ending the special relationship. These are things which represent a historic trend and I think after Wilson, who appeared as rather a trickster, the public quite like the feeling of Heath as the strong Prime Minister under whom Britain can hold her head up again.

I have never felt more like one of Yesterday's Men than I do at this particular moment. I think an outgoing Government, eighteen months after it has disappeared from office, is bound to look a failure. We have to plod away and we shan't get returned to power until the Government's policies have clearly and more obviously failed and the Tories, though right wing, will be sensible enough to swing back to the Centre when it comes to the next Election period. I see nothing in Labour policies at the moment that is distinctive. A little bit of this and a little bit of that which is more liberal and fair: it is this connecting theme that I am searching for, and I believe that there should be more participation, which is the key to democracy and acceptability.

Of course the British Labour Party is not very democratic in its instincts either in its relations between the Parliamentary Party and the Party outside or in its attitude towards the voters. It is still rather bossy and dictatorial and I don't know how far these radical liberal instincts which I have are going to find acceptance in the Labour Party. I shall write and make speeches and lectures about these ideas to see whether I can get my thoughts accepted as a teacher, not as an academic in the dull and remote way, but as somebody who injects his values into society and in a way that people understand.

Well, there we are. It is the end of 1971. Politics is full of ups and downs: I just need that little bit of extra energy in 1972.

NOTES
Chapter Four

1. (p. 320) In 1969 the Kenyan Government passed legislation which had the effect of forcing Asian traders in Kenya out of business, and it was estimated that 20,000 British passport-holders would come to the United Kingdom. The Labour Party was generally sympathetic to the plight of the Kenyan Asians. But in their 1970 General Election manifesto the Conservatives had given an assurance that there would be 'no further large-scale permanent immigration', and in February 1971 enacted legislation limiting immigration to Britain from Commonwealth countries.

2. (p. 362) The 'Four Wise Men' appointed by John Davies to report on the UCS crisis were Forbes McDonald, Chairman of Distillers, David Macdonald of Hill Samuel, Sir Alexander Glen of Clarkson's shipbroking firm, and Lord Robens, former Chairman of the NCB.

The report concluded that UCS was doomed from its inception in 1967 and that 'any continuation of UCS in its present form would be wholly unjustified'. It recommended a new shipbuilding outfit concentrated at Govan and the disposal of Clydebank and Scotstoun by the Liquidator, with the consequent severe loss of jobs. The Government accepted the recommendation and Govan Shipbuilders was established.

5
Chairman of the Party
January–October 1972

Tuesday 4 January 1972
It was a horrible, cold, miserable day and I worked at home in the morning.

This evening I telephoned about fifteen members of the NEC to ask them what they thought about Harry Nicholas. Every single person I spoke to – twenty in all, including people I consulted before Christmas – was of the opinion that he should go now. So I will see him in the next few days and say that I have been taking soundings and there is a pretty unanimous view that the time has come when he should announce his retirement. But I am determined to do it delicately. I'll go and see Jim Callaghan in hospital tomorrow, I think, and get his assent because as Treasurer, it is very important to carry him with me.

Wednesday 5 January
In the evening I watched the BBC Ulster Television *Tribunal* – which had caused such a tremendous row and which Maudling had tried to stop – from beginning to end without moving from my seat. It was a major breakthrough in television because it gave access to the air to Ian Paisley,* Bernadette Devlin, Gerry Fitt, the Alliance Party and Neil Blaney from Dublin, the ex-Minister in Fianna Fàil, who is thought to be a supporter of the IRA. The Tribunal was made up of Lord Devlin, Lord Caradon and Sir John Foster, QC, Conservative MP for Northwich. There were various experts. It was serious, balanced and long, a remarkable programme.

Wednesday 12 January
I went to the colour studios to see the preview of Harlech Television's *My Brother's Keeper*. I found it deeply moving – terribly effective. They showed the clip at the beginning of my May Day speech and there were

---

* Ian Paisley, Protestant Unionist MP for Antrim North, and founder of the Free Presbyterian Church.

one or two rather scornful correspondents, Nancy Banks-Smith, Elkan Allen and others. But on the whole, I think it went over well. Jack Jones came to see it and he was delighted.

To the Shadow Cabinet where Peter called for the Government to publish and lay before Parliament the Treaty of Accession to the Common Market for debate and consideration. Roy said that if this motion was carried, it would mean that we were really asking for another debate on the principle before the legislation and that would divide us and have the same effect as 28 October. After the inevitable round of discussion, it was agreed but modified to say that it should be laid before Parliament 'for consideration'. That was as far as we went. Peter was optimistic that Tory rebels might come in on this and we might reduce Heath's majority from 128 to about 20.

Thursday 13 January

Got up at 5.30 and caught the plane out to Barbados and Trinidad for the Business International Conference. Business International is a postwar organisation providing big business companies with a central intelligence service and my contact with it comes through Richard Conlon, the European executive operating from Geneva. The founder and chief is a former American Ambassador and Orville Freeman, Kennedy's former Secretary of Agriculture, is also involved in it. The participants are the chief executives of about fifty or sixty of the world's multinational companies, eg IBM and the Chase Manhattan Bank, and ICI and Pilkington from Britain, and the average income would probably be £30,000–£40,000 a year – a very high-level group.

When I arrived in Trinidad I just had time to have a bath at the Trinidad Hilton before the first discussion group. The session concentrated upon the 'social responsibility' of multinational businesses and the general feeling was that the less that was spent on social causes the better. Executives complained that 'one man, one vote is no good – we can't even mobilise our workers to follow our line of thinking' and that 'the demands of the people were unlimited'.

But the challenge of pressure group influence had to be tackled. They thought that there was an anti-business prejudice in schools and colleges and among the young which had to be defeated. It was even suggested that they ought to consider financing lecturers to teach about capitalism.

The discussion about profitability was also revealing. People talked about the need to educate the public to believe in profit; one business had set up a 'committee of corporate responsibility'. The environment particularly they saw as a profitable area for corporations to tackle: they felt they got a very bad press over pollution from 'goddam intellectuals' and that there was long-term profitability in environment issues.

Friday 14 January

I went to the plenary session in the afternoon, which was infinitely the most interesting one. The more they listened to some of the criticisms that were being made – notably from me – the more frightened they seemed to become and there was a motion that after the conference no papers of proceedings be published. Orville Freeman, who was in the chair, kept trying to reassure participants.

To the challenge that was made to the power of the multinationals they responded by saying that many of the critics were 'abysmally ignorant' about the nature of business. They argued that attacks came from an 'over-abundance of highly-educated youth' – the Labour youth challenge has obviously worried them, in part, I think, because many of them have children who take this view. They were afraid that the pressure of unions would lead to protectionism.

They went on to consider Government representatives on the boards of multinationals and concluded that 'Government representatives on boards usually act in a most conservative business fashion, do no harm, and enhance the prestige of the boards'.

They recognised the need to accommodate change from below but the feeling was that they shouldn't recognise international labour unions.

Then the session attempted to produce a policy statement and this led to some disagreement. They wanted to state that multinationals shouldn't meddle in internal politics, but it became clear from other suggestions that they intended to interfere significantly by stepping up their case for business education in schools and universities.

There was one passage on South Africa in which they rejected appeals for the withdrawal of American business because they could have a 'greater influence from within' but discussed the possibility of a four-point policy: equal pay for equal work; the hiring of more blacks; the training of more blacks; and maximising employment opportunities for the blacks and Asians. There was great anxiety when this was proposed in case it became known and was interpreted as an invitation for wage demands which would antagonise the South African Government.

They were desperately worried about unemployment and recognised that unemployment in the United States and Europe could increase the protectionist threat.

They then considered the disclosure of information and made bitter complaints about the mass media again – the point raised at the plenary session earlier today. They were united in discouraging the less developed countries from prestige investments in high capital-intensive projects, and they argued that they should make it clear to less developed countries that high-risk investment required high profits and therefore these countries should make conditions for business very favourable. This was thought to be dangerous to put in the policy statement. Somebody had put in a reference to the practice of threatening to move plants from one country to another, and this was also deleted.

Somebody said, 'International businesses shouldn't deal with dictatorships,' and one of the executives retorted, 'The multinationals *love* dictatorships and a proposal not to deal with them should not be included in the statement.'

I had to leave just before the end and I took my papers with me; but Richard Conlon came specially to my hotel room to get them back. He was embarrassed and I was cross. I was just leaving when Orville Freeman came up to me and he was also embarrassed at what had happened and reassured me that the attack on the critics as being abysmally ignorant had not applied to me; he said my speech had been 'a smash hit' but he was trying to butter me up. I told him I felt as if I had dropped into a meeting of the Central Committee of the Communist Party in the Kremlin and had only been discovered at the end. Freeman said that Business International was trying to educate business and get it to realise the need for change.

I left under a cloud and angry, caught the plane and was so tired that I slept almost the entire way to London.

Saturday 15 January
Rang Nicholas Faith of the *Sunday Times* and I am going to write a piece on the Trinidad conference because undoubtedly, I have got access to the collective thinking of the multinationals of a unique kind at the moment.

Tuesday 18 January
To the Commons, for the coal debate. Harold Lever opened well and was followed by John Davies, who was poor. Then the miners' MPs spoke with great passion and Eric Varley wound up well. As a Party, we are now committed to the miners and it is a very interesting example of a return to the spirit of 1926.

When I came out there was Bill Rodgers, who said he had been sacked by Harold from the Aviation spokesman job. I said, 'How do you know you've been sacked?' He said, 'Somebody else has been offered my job.' I said, 'How do you know you aren't going to be offered another job?' He said, 'Well, I don't exactly.' 'Have you discussed it with Harold?' I asked. 'No.' I later learned from Gerald Kaufman that he has been sacked: I must say, if I were Harold, I would have done the same thing, because Bill Rodgers is an intolerable man – but he is also a great fighter.

Came home with £147 worth of documents – forty-four volumes in all – representing the statutes and regulations of the European Common

Market to which we shall adhere. It is an outrage that this country should be taken into commitments of this kind without any discussion.

Wednesday 19 January
Went to meet Gough Whitlam, the Australian Labour Party Leader, whom I had met before at Number 10 and whom I didn't much like. He said the unions were a shrinking element in Australian Labour politics and on balance an embarrassment; that law and order in industry and appalling urban conditions were the main things on which we would be fighting the election; that foreign policy would not be much of a factor and he thought that attacking the White Australia Policy would have to be considered. In response to a point from Shirley Williams, he said he would take up the question of women's rights.

Thursday 20 January
I had a talk to Terry Pitt about unemployment, in preparation for the debate on Monday in which I am supposed to be speaking, and while I was there the unemployment figures of 1,023,000 were announced – the highest figure for thirty-two years. I put out a statement saying it was a black day for Britain, that the Heath Government was responsible and calling for an Election.

Then I went back to hear Peter Shore open the EEC debate on our motion condemning the Government for signing the Treaty of Accession without publishing the Treaty. He did well but the debate was low key. I think the plain truth is that the European matter is settled and cannot be re-opened.

Saturday 22 January
Up early at Keele, where I stayed the night with Stephen. Had breakfast on the motorway at a services restaurant overlooking this fast road, a twenty-four-hour restaurant which has all the drama of the modern world about it – rather a tinselly, glittering attraction but full of vitality.

The MP for Newcastle-Under-Lyme, John Golding and his wife Thelma, picked me up and we went to one of the pits where I addressed a meeting of striking miners. Then I talked to one of the pickets outside a nearby power station. These miners, who have got a tremendous battle on their hands, I think appreciated an indication of Party support. One picket, who was a Geordie from Durham, was on his own in front of a brazier, talked about the cooperation of the police and how they helped them to maintain the picket lines.

Then John Golding drove me down to London and I got home about 1.45. I was so tired that I slept for a couple of hours.

In the evening I went to dinner at the New Ambassadors Hotel with the New Socialist International Research Council: the French, the

Germans, the Danes, the Swedes and the Italians were there. They had been meeting to talk about multinational companies and industrial relations. We had an interesting discussion, particularly about how the socialist parties could confront the real challenge of the ecologists, who are now saying that there must be a major cut in the population, a major reduction in growth, if humanity is to survive. The traditional social democratic view that if we are going to get socialism now, we must have growth and distribute it fairly, has got to be re-examined in the light of a possible ban on growth. This will drive us towards redistribution without being able to give us the excess that would make that redistribution painless. This certainly is a great challenge to our thinking.

Monday 24 January

We had the unemployment debate. Harold opened with a terrible speech. It lasted an hour and six minutes and ended with a violent attack on Heath. Then Heath gave a lecture on the causes of unemployment, to slip out of his responsibility, with a tough but patchy speech. It wasn't perfect but was a great deal better than Robert Carr from the Government Front Bench who was pitiful.

Tuesday 25 January 1972

Had lunch with Smirnovsky, the Soviet Ambassador. It was rather a painful meeting. They are hurt at the expulsion of all the Soviet diplomats in September* which they think was a Government measure to create an outside scare in order to build up anti-Soviet feeling and get Britain into the Common Market. There may well be something in that. They said it had entirely destroyed the expertise that the Russians were building up about affairs in Britain and that it would be bound to have an effect on trade and relations.

We went on to discuss the Common Market and the proposed European Security Conference, which they very much hoped would stimulate East-West relations. But they were extremely hostile on the Chinese. We talked about how to get a rather better Anglo-Soviet relationship developing. I said candidly that the treatment of the Jews and the problems of Soviet re-armament were causes of anxiety, and I would try and find a forum for opening all this up.

It wasn't as pleasant a lunch as it might have been. They are bureaucratic, they are growing in military strength and I don't have the same feeling about them as I did some years ago. I don't dislike them particularly, but I find them less attractive.

* Ninety Soviet diplomats and trade officials 'concerned in intelligence activities' were asked to leave Britain in September 1971.

Wednesday 26 January

To the Shadow Cabinet, where we discussed the Common Market. The European Communities Bill has been published, containing a clause which simply says that all Common Market legislation – past and future – will apply in Britain, and there was a fierce argument about this. Michael Foot said it was intolerable. Harold Lever argued interminably and violently and said it was inevitable and, speaking as a lawyer, said it was right.

I raised the question of consent and said this was the destruction of the parliamentary system. It was the central question and far from Harold Lever having given a legal argument, no lawyer would allow any change in the Common Law without legislation. This reversed the whole position between Parliament and the Government, and you couldn't undo it even if you changed the Government in an Election.

It exposed the Common Marketeers who desperately want Heath to stay in power and desperately want the Common Market legislation to go through in its present form. It does raise in one's mind the whole question (as I said in my contribution) not just of the future of the Labour Party, but the future of parliamentary democracy in this country. This is actually what the issue will be. There may have to be a battle for the soul of the Labour Party and this could be the issue.

Came home and had a long talk on the phone to Peter Shore, who is beginning to think along similar lines. If we abandon these central themes, we are not the British Labour Party, whatever else we are. We may be good, kind and liberally-minded people but we are not the British Labour Party, wedded to democracy and socialism.

Friday 28 January

Drove to Bristol on the M4 for the first time today. It took me two hours from home to the centre of Bristol. I must say it is a beautiful road and I began to feel that the whole geography of England had been altered by it.

Saturday 29 January

Did a surgery at Unity House.

I had lunch with Herbert Rogers who is still full of vitality, considering he is about seventy-eight, and is really an old revolutionary who wants to see the whole system break down. I don't frankly because I don't think it is practicable and I don't think we would be able to avoid the sort of authoritarian regime they have in the Soviet Union.

To Transport House to speak in the pensioners' rally with Will Wilkins. I decided I would sit instead of stand because I am fed up with making great orations, and so I sat and read some of the letters I have received from pensioners. It was very successful.

Then I had a deputation from the PTA in Perry Court in Whitchurch who objected to the fact that the two Merrywood schools are to be built as single-sex schools and they want them co-educational. Caroline came down for the meeting.

We went to the Brislington supper, left for London at about 10.45 and were home at about 12.30. An amazing journey.

Monday 31 January

There was a statement on the Bogside massacre yesterday in which thirteen Catholics were killed by troops, following the illegal march which had been undertaken by the Civil Rights people against a ban. I think it is the largest number of people killed in the United Kingdom by British troops for 200 years or more. Bernadette Devlin was not called by the Speaker so she had to speak on points of order. At one point, she stamped down the gangway and went over and attacked Maudling physically, an extraordinary sight. She smacked him and pulled his hair. People took her away and she was fighting with them. Poor old Hugh Delargy, Labour MP for Thurrock, is very shaky and sick, and being a devoted Irish Catholic he looked as though he would have an apoplectic fit and there would be a fight on the floor of the House. At any rate, she did withdraw, but came back again shortly afterwards. The Speaker, very wisely, didn't do anything about it.

Wednesday 2 February

Dick Clements came to see me and told me that he was going to apply for the general secretaryship of the Labour Party and would be running on a programme of Party reform in organisation.

Shadow Cabinet, and we came on to the European Communities Bill.* Peter Shore simply said that he moved that we oppose the Bill with no amendment. Roy said that he was in favour of the Bill, and he was critical that when we had last met, just after Christmas, to decide to oppose the Government, somebody had given a press briefing saying we were unanimous. He said, 'We were not unanimous.' He also strongly objected to the Common Market being seen as the central strategy of the Party because he thought this was not what people cared about.

Harold Wilson then launched into a typically long piece of self-justification. He said that Roy had been away and if he had been here, he would have known that the Common Market had not been central to our strategy. We had had tremendous debates on unemployment, Ireland, Rhodesia, and that he, Harold, was the victim of terrible briefing done against him and that as to the Bill itself, the last

---

* See p. 312 for the background and timetable of the protracted Common Market legislation which continued throughout 1972.

Government was certainly not committed to this sort of a Bill. He favoured a vote against the Bill with no amendment.

Then Roy said, 'But it is not unanimous and it had better be made clear that it is not unanimous.'

Denis Healey said he agreed we should oppose and Harold said, 'Are we agreed then that we should oppose?' and nobody muttered though it was quite clear that Roy, Shirley, Harold Lever and George Thomson were not opposed to the Bill.

Sunday 6 February

Today I went to the miners' demonstration in Trafalgar Square in support of their wage claim, marching from Hyde Park with Jack Jones, Lawrence Daly and Alex Kitson. I had a word with Jack Jones who said that he hoped the first meeting between the Labour Party Executive, the PLP and the trade unions would confirm a total repeal of the Industrial Relations Bill.

It was a marvellous demonstration although it was chilly and looked as if it was going to rain. I made my short speech which lasted about two and a half minutes and they were shouting at me part of the time. But I did get across that Heath was a cold, hard man and we ought to have an Election.

Monday 7 February

At 3.15 the UCS shop stewards came to see me with Jimmy Reid, Jim Airlie, Sammy Barr and Willy McInnes. What they were really saying was that they were on the eve of success and they wanted us to lay off John Davies so as not to make it politically difficult for him to put money into the new Govan Shipbuilders. Jimmy Reid stayed behind afterwards and asked me if I would attend his installation as Rector of Glasgow University on 28 April. I can't make it, but I was touched he should have invited me.

Thursday 10 February

To Imperial College to talk about China. I managed to get across some of the impact of their educational changes which run absolutely counter to the whole philosophy of Imperial College itself, which is the most élitist post-graduate institution in Britain.

Then to the Commons briefly, and came home where there was a power cut. The miners' strike is beginning to have quite serious effects now, since a state of emergency was declared yesterday.

Friday 11 February

Arrived early at Manchester University for the symposium on broadcasting policy organised by Professor George Wedell. It was a formidable conference, with all the best-known people in the media there, including its sternest critics, Brian Magee, Caroline Heller of ACTT, the film and television union, Stuart Hood, Mary Whitehouse* and others.

The first speaker said that accountability mattered less because as technology opened up more and more channels, and you moved towards a two-way telephone communication, accountability wouldn't be relevant.

Brian Magee said he thought the programmes that were produced were good and he wanted to defend the mystique of the professional broadcaster, and ensure that the oceans of dullness that were unwatchable and unwatched should not be allowed to seep over the television screens.

Mary Whitehouse asked to whom the broadcasting stations really belonged and how we were to monitor them.

There were many other points made but I felt as I often do that one was up against the master group of controllers of information who could always think of marvellous reasons why they should remain in control. They are in effect the new bosses of modern society. It confirmed my endorsement of the Chinese theory that private ownership of knowledge is what really seems to be determining our society.

Davies made a statement today in the House announcing the most drastic cuts in power for homes and industry on a rota basis, and this has knocked people absolutely sideways.

Later, Tom Holliday of the National Union of Mineworkers in the Northumberland area collected me to drive me to Newcastle. He is a short, quiet man who inspires a great deal of confidence. This miners' strike is for him a most dramatic moment in the history of the industry.

On the way to Newcastle, Tom told me that the soup kitchens were out again and that many of the old retired miners and others were coming along and collecting soup, which was being made available to them and to other pensioners because of the difficulties that people were having with power cuts. As a result of this young miners on the picket lines were hearing the stories of the earlier strike in 1926 and in this way one generation had an opportunity to convey its experience to another. This inspired and encouraged the older men and gave the younger miners a feeling of historical continuity.

Saturday 12 February
Tom Holliday drove me over to the Northumberland miners' meeting in the City Hall where Joe Gormley and I both had a tremendous

---

* Brian Magee, journalist and Labour MP 1974–81; joined SDP in 1981. Stuart Hood, sociologist and writer, formerly of the BBC; Mary Whitehouse, journalist and honorary secretary of the National Viewers' and Listeners' Association.

reception. It was a very curious occasion because this huge hall was filled with working miners in their working clothes and the general impression was one of greyness with no colour, because of the dark browns and blacks and greys of their clothes, but they were in terrific heart even though beginning to experience some hardship themselves as a result of the strike.

The power cuts are now widespread and on alternate days we lose power for about three hours so that the whole economy is beginning to feel the effects of the strike. One aspect of this is that it set into being a tremendous emergency system of help for old people which had not existed before. I discovered that in my own constituency in Bristol, about 80 per cent of the streets are now covered by street wardens and street committees brought into being by the strike. The other remarkable thing about the strike is the extent to which the wives of the miners have supported their men and the extent to which the public – although gravely inconvenienced – are in sympathy with the miners.

Monday 14 February

To Transport House this morning, where we had a special meeting of the NEC on the miners' strike. Judith Hart spoke first and said we must support the miners without equivocation and she asked whether we should demand the resignation of the Government. She also thought it necessary to say something about the old and the sick and the need for local authorities and Labour Parties to help.

John Cartwright, who is also the leader of a Labour local authority, thought we should have to try to register those who were in difficulty living in high blocks of flats and should make use of voluntary organisations, and fifth and sixth formers at schools.

Harold Wilson also commented on the need to coordinate the work of local authorities and Ian Mikardo thought we might try to get a list of Labour Party members in constituencies who would help.

Frank Allaun said he was suspicious of the Government's motives and wondered whether the situation was quite as serious as they were making out. Harold Wilson said he thought that it was not, and that they had miscalculated.

Joe Gormley came in late and said that if the latest offer had been made at the outset, the issue might have been settled without a dispute and the Government could have helped at an earlier stage. They had forced the country into a serious situation and the long-term effects would hinder production for four to five months. He said that even if the pickets were taken off today, the situation was going to remain difficult. As far as he was concerned, he felt bound to consult the membership on the Wilberforce* findings and the ballot would take place in about ten days. Joe has had a tremendous success with his extended picketing and he said that plans for this had been developed for months.

Jim Diamond said that political capital was not enough and that the steel workers had suffered as a result of the strike: the extended picketing, the miners opting out of safety work and the donations for the pickets had raised problems of presentation with the public, which had to be taken into account. The link between the miners, the TUC and the Party might be damaging politically.

Joe Gormley pointed out they could have forced a general strike, but if they had had one, Heath would have gone to the country. 'We have never argued,' said Joe Gormley, 'that we were a special case and we want a return to normality as soon as possible.'

At the end of the meeting the resolution which I had drafted was accepted. 'This emergency meeting of the National Executive Committee fully supports the miners and their struggle to defend and improve their living standards, which has won wide public sympathy. It condemns the Government and the Prime Minister for their gross mishandling of the dispute from the outset and their incompetence in tackling the industrial consequences which should have been foreseen and which have led to panic measures that have inflicted additional damage on the whole economy. It supports the initiative taken by the Leader of the Party in calling on the Prime Minister to assume his personal responsibility to bring the dispute to a fair and rapid conclusion. It calls on local authorities to take the initiative at once to coordinate the work of voluntary organisations to safeguard the old, the sick, the disabled and all those most likely to be affected and invites Labour Party members throughout the country to cooperate with them in this work.'

Tuesday 15 February
We had miners' meetings in the House this afternoon. A mass lobby took place. People were very critical of the previous Labour Government which, they felt, had let them down and I think that they were right. Looking back on it, I think our policy towards the mining industry was very short-sighted: stimulating nuclear power before we were really ready and running down the mines.

The theme of anarchy and unmanageability is beginning to emerge now in the Tory press and indicates that they may be thinking of turning this to political advantage. I think Ronald Butt in the *Sunday Times*

---

* The Court of Inquiry under Lord Wilberforce to consider the miners' wage claim accepted the argument for a 'general and exceptional increase' and recommended an approximate 30 per cent rise in basic weekly rates.

began it, and Hailsham and others are on the same tack. The fear of anarchy is something that drives people to the Right and this undoubtedly is what Heath wants.

Thursday 17 February

Today we had the vote on the second reading of the European Communities Bill. Heath won by eight votes with four Liberals voting with him. There were fantastic scenes in the House and great rage that some Labour people who had abstained would have carried Heath absolutely to the brink of defeat if they had voted.

I looked in afterwards to see Harold. He was immensely depressed. The fact that he had held the Party together right through to the second reading of the Bill was a great achievement and he couldn't understand why people weren't grateful to him. Of course, in practice, the situation is that everyone is thinking of Heath's humiliation, and nobody thinking of Harold's success.

But understandably, he being human, the terrible experiences he has had over the last few months on Europe have made him obsessed with his own position and he wanted a boost. I tried to cheer him up.

Friday 18 February

I went to the House of Commons and there was a further statement at the end of the day on the miners' dispute. The Wilberforce recommendations came out with a 30 per cent increase in pay. Right-wing Labour people like David Ginsburg and Shirley Williams and others were terrified that the miners wouldn't accept the Wilberforce award. I realised as well as anyone that if they didn't it would put them in a very difficult position with the public. But you do have to trust the common sense of people, and they knew quite well what they were doing.

In the evening, Caroline and I went to Mark and Val's party. Somehow the middle class Sunday supplement liberal consensus of professional communicators is not quite my cup of tea!

Sunday 20 February

Melissa's birthday. There was a power cut.

Monday 21 February

At 11 we had the first meeting of the Joint Liaison Committee between the NEC, the PLP and the TUC to discuss industrial relations. This meeting arises out of the complete breakdown between the Parliamentary Leadership and the Trade Union Movement during the period that we were in office and it has taken about eighteen months to get these talks set up. In practice their long-term significance is in the attempt to restore confidence between the two wings of the movement.

Harold Wilson was in the chair and we agreed to rotate the chairmanship.

During the course of my year as Chairman of the Party, the TUC–Labour Party Liaison Committee was established. It represented a turning point in Labour's relations with the TUC which had completely broken down as a result of 'In Place of Strife' and the rigid incomes policies adopted by the 1964–70 Government. From the June 1970 Election defeat until early 1972 there had been no effective contacts between the Party and the unions and at this new Liaison Committee there were echoes of the past conflicts between the trade union General Secretaries and ex-Ministers representing the Parliamentary Party.

The essential question was: would the next Labour Government agree to repeal the Tory Industrial Relations Act? The TUC representatives were adamant that it should. But some leading Parliamentary figures were reluctant to give such a pledge at least until the TUC accepted in advance the need for an incomes policy. My original diary records in Hansard-like detail the Committee's discussions which are necessarily reduced or omitted altogether in this volume. However, the outcome of these protracted negotiations will emerge clearly in the next volume, as the deliberations resulted in the document 'Economic Policy and the Cost of Living' which formed the basis of the February 1974 manifesto and which had enormous, unforeseen implications for the next Labour Government.

Vic Feather introduced the TUC document and Jack Jones referred to the Conference resolutions calling for immediate repeal of the Industrial Relations Act.

Douglas Houghton then reminded us of the PLP statement that he had made, that we must have a new Bill on the statute book before we could repeal the existing Act. He called on the Trade Union Movement to underwrite the next Labour Government. This was an immensely provocative comment and it had its effect. Roy Jenkins said he agreed with Douglas Houghton. Vic Feather said, 'We know we shall need legislation and at the same time we are absolutely determined to see this Act repealed,' to which Roy Jenkins replied, 'This may be a semantic difference.'

So Jack Jones read out the Party Conference resolution and Hugh Scanlon said that Douglas's statement did not constitute a *pledge* to repeal, and they were not prepared to talk with the sword of Damocles hanging over their heads.

Harold Lever asked what we were arguing about. Harold Wilson said, 'We are committed to the repeal and we hope to work out a replacement. We would want to have the repeal in the first session.'

Jack Jones said that this was the beginning of the accord he sought and Harold Wilson said, 'Let's get an agreed document between us.'

But Hugh Scanlon repeated, 'There must be an unqualified pledge for a repeal.'

Then we moved on to economic policy generally and Vic introduced the TUC Economic Review; Harold Wilson said there was no incompatibility between that and Party policy.

Harold asked how the industrial scene looked after the Wilberforce recommendations and Vic said that the General Purposes Committee of the TUC was meeting this afternoon and the ballot among the miners was still taking place. He thought the pay norm of 7–9 per cent had been destroyed and that the Tories were deliberately bringing about long strikes. He believed that the Government probably advised the Coal Board to withdraw the offer.

Hugh Scanlon thought that something positive must be said soon because we haven't highlighted the policy of Government confrontation and hostility to the unions as much as we should and we must speak up.

Harold Lever said he didn't want to be obsessive about it but we couldn't dismiss our political responsibilities. If the 10 per cent inflation rate came back, Labour couldn't win an Election. He thought we might be entering a period of strong-arm tactics, and did the TUC want a tougher period?

Harold said Heath would probably do a broadcast and ask the unions to accept an 8 per cent norm, and that we had to be ready for the possibility of an Election this year with 'the policeman's mandate' (which was the phrase I had mentioned in my paper to him), ie on law and order. We would have to offer a socialist 'doctor's mandate'. We must be ready to move fast.

This evening Harold Wilson, Peter Shore, Roy Jenkins, Harold Lever and myself went to dinner with the CBI. On the CBI side were Sir John Partridge, Campbell Adamson, Michael Clapham of ICI, Sir Hugh Weeks and Alex Jarratt. It was an interesting meeting for a number of reasons.

First of all, we discussed the coal strike, its aftermath and what effect this would have on the price restraint introduced by the CBI. Campbell Adamson said they would like to get closer to the TUC and get back to real tripartite talks.

Harold Wilson said it was a scandal that the CBI had had to take the initiative in proposing price restraint while the Government had backed out.

We got back to discussing whether there was such a thing as technological unemployment, which is something of an intellectual argument at the moment.

In the course of the evening, Harold Wilson attacked Jack Jones and Hugh Scanlon and said, 'The Government have big ears, and we know what these two men are up to, which was an absolutely unequivocal statement that he was using the knowledge acquired as Prime Minister, through the Intelligence Services, to say that Jones and Scanlon were

Communists. Since we had met with them that very morning and they were political colleagues, I thought that was a pretty scandalous thing to say to one's political opponents. I discussed it with Peter afterwards and he was equally shocked.

Tuesday 22 February
We had the first Policy Coordinating Committee between the NEC and the Shadow Cabinet with me in the chair, and it was rather a crabby meeting. We looked at the pledges that had been given on future policy by Front Bench spokesmen and at the NEC policy statements.

Wednesday 23 February
I went to the NEC and congratulated Joe Gormley on the success of the miners' strike and moved a resolution congratulating the miners.

On the Home Policy Committee we had a long debate about the Housing Finance Act* tactics, with Frank Allaun leading from among those who were in favour of a much tougher line of non-implementation, and others, of whom Terry Pitt played a leading part, arguing against non-implementation. In the end we agreed that we would pledge ourselves to change the law, but meanwhile the responsibility rested with the local authorities and we didn't feel able to tell them what to do. They had to safeguard the interests of their own tenants.

I came over to the House and there was a meeting of the Shadow Cabinet this afternoon. We had only just heard today that some anomaly in the law had appeared which made it necessary for the Government to rush through an immediate bill to indemnify the Armed Forces for taking part in actions in Northern Ireland which it was now apparent from the judgment given by the High Court were *ultra vires*.

Elwyn Jones said that the powers of searching and arresting and crowd dispersal only validated what we had assumed to be the case. Eddie Shackleton thought there should be a select committee to examine the matter. Harold Wilson said he thought it all might be handled by the United Kingdom Emergency Powers. I didn't rule out appeals by people who were arrested, but said, are we not accidentally underwriting internment? Then Harold said nobody should be convicted of an offence that was not an offence at the time that it was committed. Elwyn Jones said he thought this did have retrospective elements in it.

---

* The Housing Finance Bill, enacted in July 1972, introduced compulsory 'fair rents' into the public housing sector over 1972–3. It was extremely controversial legislation, requiring a drastic rise in weekly rents in some areas and its implementation was opposed by several Labour local authorities, notably in Clay Cross, Derbyshire.

Thursday 24 February

Had lunch with Bruno Kreisky, the Chancellor of Austria, and his Private Secretary, Jankovic, who is about to be appointed Ambassador to the United States. Denis Healey was there among others. Kreisky had been with Harold and Roy this morning and must have indicated his anger and disappointment at our attitude towards the Common Market. I tried to emphasise that we did feel strongly about it and that the Party really had to stand by its Conference decisions. This, of course, is not a view likely to appeal to the middle-of-the-road European Social Democrats.

Sunday 27 February

I went this morning to the Industrial Policy Conference at the Bonnington Hotel attended by about a hundred people. Before lunch there was a discussion on industrial democracy. Geoff Bish had written a good paper on the real democratisation of industry by a process of election.

Frank Welsh from Greenwich said we had the power in nationalised industries for industrial democracy but the British Steel Corporation, for example, was entirely authoritarian and Byzantine in its nature; but we might not need legislation to put this right. Jim Mortimer, formerly of the Prices and Incomes Board, said that trade unionism was industrial democracy and the shop stewards' movement should be its basis. Safety and training and discipline should be the next things to be transferred to democratic control.

Jim Tinn said we couldn't impose industrial democracy from above and direct democracy is what we want, not representative democracy, but it must relate to the individual work experience. We had got to be careful of disillusionment.

I said I thought Geoff's paper was excellent and it ought to be published. I shared Geoff's feeling that we must make progress. Why hadn't we? The workers' veto had developed in industrial disputes through political power and shop floor power, and intelligent management had sensed this and tried to develop programmes of job enrichment and supervisory boards, Government nominees and better Government communication programmes. 'This doesn't really alter the power balance,' I said and the unions really had to tackle this problem more vigorously. Perhaps the best thing would be to go for permissive legislation, with a test of acceptability of management, and the role of the shop stewards could be brought into play for this purpose. I thought there was a risk that we would develop a managerial approach to all our problems and this wasn't acceptable.

I got home and watched Heath on television, talking about the miners' strike.

Monday 28 February
Davies announced a £35 million grant for Govan Shipbuilders at UCS.

Harold was on television tonight. He is going through a bad patch, though how anyone can tolerate being Leader of the Labour Party I just don't know. It is an almost impossible position. No one likes leaders, and though Harold seems unattractive, I can't think of anyone who would be better.

Thursday 2 March
Went to Bristol, dozed a bit in the Grand Hotel because I was so tired and went to the Bristol constituency Party where we have to face the problem of Party organisation. We have got practically no organisation in St George's East and West wards, a shaky one in Brislington ward: generally the whole constituency is in a bad way. I have resolved that I am going to put a lot more effort and time into it.

Saturday 4 March
To Leeds to speak at Yorkshire Regional Conference; Ron Hayward was there. He sees these regional conferences as part of his campaign for the general secretaryship, and I am strongly in support of Ron, though I have got to be careful about it. I have had a brief word with Harold: Harold wants to keep out of it but is also keen that Ron should get it, mainly to keep Gwyn, who is a Roy Jenkins man, out.

There is a tendency to think of Gwyn, who is an agreeable person, as being quite harmless, whereas he is actually a Marketeer and supporter of the right wing. Ron Hayward is straight as a die, rather a sergeant major. Not as attractive superficially as he might be, but a person of sterling quality.

Monday 6 March
I had lunch at Malborough House with Dom Mintoff, who is in London for one of his meetings with Lord Carrington [Defence Secretary] about the Malta settlement. Barbara was there with one or two others. I had never met him before and he was grateful that the Labour delegation had gone over to Malta at the Party's suggestion at a time when everything appeared to be breaking down. He was full of vitality and new ideas of one kind and another.

He is an absolutely direct oriental bargainer which puts the stiff-upper-lipped British in a great difficulty. At the back of his mind he had the thought that at the last minute he should demand a guarantee against de-valuation as a way of getting more money for allowing the British to retain their naval base. The real value of Malta to the West, that is to say to the NATO thinkers, is to keep the Russians out, and Mintoff is using his bargaining power absolutely to the full to get every penny he can.

I sat next to Manzini, the Italian Ambassador to NATO. We talked for some time about the Roman Catholic view of marriage and annulment. He told me his own marriage had been annulled about two or three years ago. He had been married in 1936 and after about thirty years of marriage he got it annulled on the grounds that he had entered it with reservations about its permanence, or something of that kind. In fact it is easier to get an annulment than a divorce and Italy is deeply divided on the divorce law at the moment.

I also talked to Joseph Luns, Secretary-General of NATO, whom I had got to know when I was negotiating the centrifuge arrangement. He has been Foreign Secretary of Holland for about twenty-five years and has enormous experience: a big tough Western European with a tremendous sense of humour, telling vulgar jokes. He told me that he had been to Japan and talked to a number of Japanese and that when they were very drunk late at night, they had said what a pity it was that they hadn't had a second strike at Pearl Harbor and finally defeated the Americans. He felt at the back of his mind that Japan was on the eve of becoming a great military power and that we would have to watch it. He's not by any means left wing, so from him this story was especially interesting.

At 8.30 this evening, Thomas Kanza, who was former Prime Minister Patrice Lumumba's Secretary of State for Foreign Affairs in the Congo in the early Sixties, came to see me. He is working at St Anthony's College, Oxford, now and is just going to America. Kanza is a highly cultivated man, very wealthy – he comes from one of the principal tribes in the Congo – and is apparently trying to overthrow President Mobutu. Mobutu was a corporal at one stage under Lumumba and although Lumumba was assassinated, he now pays official tribute to Lumumba's memory. Kanza told me he was going to America to see Kissinger, hoping to get the support of the American Government to go back to the Congo and perhaps replace Mobutu. Mobutu actually wants him to return to the Congo but he is afraid that if he goes back under Mobutu's auspices he may be arrested.

He also had in mind becoming Secretary-General of the Organisation of African States and he has been running a big campaign to get support from various African leaders, but he feels he must have the Congo's support as well. Clearly Kissinger is backing Thomas Kanza and he wants Kissinger's advice before he makes his next move. The whole thing is very mysterious and one got a view of a tribal society with pretenders fighting for control and with no principle of any sort or kind involved. As Kanza works at St Anthony's, which is well known as an Intelligence centre in Britain, it may well be that he is actually working for the CIA, although he is superficially left wing. I found it a fascinating discussion.

Wednesday 8 March

At 4.15 I went to Harold's room with Jim and Roy to meet a deputation from the Women's Advisory Council. They said they wanted a clear statement of the Party's policy. They wanted a teach-in at the Blackpool Conference on the Women's Movement. The number of women candidates in the movement is falling and they want more women appointed on public bodies.

Friday 10 March

Up at 5.45 and flew with Frank McElhone to UCS. Jimmy Reid was away, resting after the strain of the last few months but Jim Airlie was there and so were some of the others. They told me that Marathon, who manufacture oil-rigs, wanted about £12 million for Clydebank which would work out at about £4,800 per job. The shop stewards were quite prepared to support the Marathon bid within reason; the men would hold together even if Marathon fell through.

Jim Airlie said he would prefer a new set-up to be run like a private company because if it was in the public sector, it might be subject to a public sector wage freeze – an interesting comment. He told me that he was prepared to reach a procedure agreement but they were not prepared to sign a no-strike agreement. They all asked that I should hold off criticism until the Marathon deal was fixed.

Then I had coffee with Jerry Ross, who is one of the old Communist shop stewards, Roddy MacKenzie, who has been the Treasurer, Bob Dickie and Willy McInnes who is a Labour Party shop steward. We talked about the next stage and in fact what these great revolutionaries want is simply joint production committees to share decision-making with the management. When I said, 'Surely you want more than this,' they replied, 'No – you must let the workers learn before you give them added responsibilities to carry. You must let them learn.' And so, far from this being a great Trotskyist plot (not that I ever thought it was), it turns out the most modest demands are being made by these people. I was much impressed to hear Jerry Ross, for example, saying, 'If we had a joint production committee, we should want to sit down when we made a profit and say "Now look, let's share some of it out in dividends, some to the state in payment of interest for the money they have loaned us, some in wages and some in investment."'

This is where you do have to rethink the propaganda that you get poured at you suggesting that the shop floor is irresponsible. In fact, the shop floor is not only responsible but painfully modest in the demands that it makes and I must try to get this point across in future speeches.

While I was with them, they told me that the *David Frost programme* had invited them to take part but in fact it was all planned to be a punch-up on the air. When they handed around a lot of drinks to the men before they took part, Jim Airlie had said, 'If anyone has more than a single beer, I won't let him on the programme.' Very impressive.

Wednesday 15 March
A big issue today was the Special Branch raids in Liverpool on the International Socialists: some friends of Stan Orme [Labour MP for Salford West] and Eric Heffer have been arrested and there is a great row about it.

Harold opened the Shadow Cabinet at 5 by saying he was thinking of the possibility of having a censure debate on Northern Ireland.

Then we discussed the European Communities Bill and I moved my paper on the Referendum. The discussion went on for some time and in the end I got only four supporters. I must say when I left the meeting, I really did feel for the first time like resigning from the Shadow Cabinet. I know I have to control my instinct but it was all immensely depressing to me and I thought if the Party is going to make an issue of not permitting the public to be consulted, one does wonder if this is the right Party to be in. But I resolved a long time ago that I would never resign again, but just go on campaigning in favour of what I believed from whatever position of power I occupied.

Stephen came in and we talked till about 4 am. He is such a friend. He was up from Keele for the weekend.

Thursday 16 March
This afternoon there was an absolute bombshell: President Pompidou announced there would be a Referendum on whether the French wished to have the Community enlarged. I put out an immediate statement and went and talked to a lot of people. This is the opportunity I have been waiting for and I am so pleased that I raised the issue at the Shadow Cabinet last night, before the French Referendum was announced, so nobody could say that it was the French Referendum that had led our debate to be re-opened. It does make the Government look absolutely ridiculous, given they are prepared to consider the possibility of a Referendum – or plebiscite – on the Northern Ireland situation: if the French are to have one on *our* entry, if the Irish, the Danes and the Norwegians are to have one on *their* EEC entry, and we are not.

At the PLP I spoke briefly and said that the implications of the French calling a Referendum were important. It indicated a complete break-down of confidence between Heath and Pompidou, since Heath had not been informed in advance. It was a continuing problem and we would *have* to look at the whole issue again. The Executive would look at it next week and the Parliamentary Committee would have to interpret it. I thought that a Referendum would bring about Party unity. There was a general sort of air of congratulation and I was cheerful today.

I came home and worked on a paper on the Referendum for the Executive.

Tonight Dick Crossman was fired from the *New Statesman*. I think they had hoped he wouldn't recover from his illness over the winter, but he did. They then tried to get him to withdraw on grounds of health, and he wouldn't, so they just fired him.

Friday 17 March
Went to see Clive Jenkins and tried to win his support for the Referendum. He is a shrewd guy, very bright. He runs his union rather like an American political machine with a lot of bosses who work round him. His driver is a former Communist. It is a left-wing union but is appealing to a right-wing group of people – the white collar workers. I say right-wing, but that is not quite true – people who, *if* they are politically interested, are left-wing, but who are normally thought of as being in the centre of politics. He told me about the amazing growth of the union and I asked him what he would like to be doing in 10 years' time. Would he like to be in a Labour Government? He very quickly assumed that I was offering him a job in my Cabinet. He then said, 'Of course, when Harold goes we'll have to have a chap who's just on the Left of Centre, like you.' It was like talking to someone at an American convention without any pretence of principle.

Monday 20 March
I went to the TUC at Congress House for the second session of talks on industrial relations.

Douglas Houghton was provocative, Barbara just can't help annoying people, and Harold Lever, although very skilful, was still touching on sensitive spots. But, in fairness, we have to sort this out because it is an important series of discussions that we are now having, and there is no point in concealing the fact.

I went to the House of Commons where the Referendum argument is still raging. We had a meeting on the general secretaryship and I insisted we should decide exactly how we handled the voting. I said, 'Do we have an exhaustive ballot?'

'Yes.'

'If there's a tie, what do we do?'

On my insistence we went right through the whole procedure. If there was a tie we would have a short adjournment, followed by a second vote. After the second vote, if that was a tie, the chairman would have a casting vote. Although it was burdensome to take them through this, I said I thought it was absolutely necessary to get it right. I think they agreed.

Tuesday 21 March
Budget day, I went to the House of Commons and Barber certainly carried through the most dramatic tax changes. In terms of taxation changes he has been the most creative Chancellor we have ever had. Of course the Tories are all in favour of the rich but it was an impressive speech and there were tremendous cheers from the Tories. He gave away about £1.5 billion, but Harold predicted that the euphoria would quickly disappear and like all Budgets, it did.

Percy Clark told me the latest predictions on the general secretaryship were 18 votes for Gwyn Morgan and 10 for Ron Hayward.

I know I have a killing weekend ahead, I have taken on much too much and greatly regret it.

Wednesday 22 March
National Executive Committee this morning, and an important meeting it was. After the usual business, we came to the appointment of General Secretary, where we agreed the recommendations made earlier this week – namely the six who were shortlisted and the job specification. I forced the Executive to confirm exactly how we would handle it in the event of a tie. Nobody took it very seriously but I reiterated it mattered to me to get it straight before the interviews next week.

Then we came to my Referendum resolution: 'This meeting of the NEC, recalling that the Labour Party Conference passed a resolution on the Common Market which called on the Prime Minister to submit to the democratic judgment of an Election, and noting that whilst the Prime Minister has refused to permit such a General Election to take place, President Pompidou is insisting that a Referendum be held to allow the French people to decide whether they want Britain in or not, congratulates the PLP on the amendment it has moved to the European Communities Bill calling for a General Election and invites the PLP to consider the desirability of moving or supporting other amendments which would make a Referendum necessary before entry, a proposal which, though rejected by Conference in favour of an Election, might well, in present circumstances, offer the only practicable means of meeting the spirit of the main Conference decision that the people must have a say in this historic decision.'

I said in introducing it that the resolution was quite clear and that I wouldn't make heavy weather of it. It was not a matter of principle that was being raised by this resolution; it was a practical matter. I had brought it here because the Shadow Cabinet, to whom I had taken it last week, had felt, in view of the Conference decision, it was something that had to be looked at by the Executive. The campaign we had built up on the Market over the last year had been based on the question of popular consent; an Election had been refused and the Bill was much more restrictive in its character than we thought when the Conference met. Pompidou, the Danes, the Norwegians and the Irish were all going to have Referenda and if we refused to consider one, people simply wouldn't understand our reservations. I said the Referendum and a General Election were linked. The best prospects of defeating the Government would be by voting to hold a Referendum and if there was then an Election called, we would offer a Referendum as part of our manifesto.

John Chalmers seconded my resolution. Walter Padley was opposed to it, or doubtful. Judith admitted that the circumstances had changed. Barbara said that after last October we had to face up to the need to fight the Market more effectively. Fred Mulley was against, as were Bill Simpson, Andy Cunningham and Joe Gormley. It was put to the vote in the absence of Harold Wilson, Jim Callaghan (who would have voted for it) and Denis Healey (who would have voted against it). The result was 13 votes to 11. It was a notable victory and I was extremely pleased at the way things had gone, particularly remembering that last year the Executive had not found a single member who was prepared to support either an Election or a Referendum.

I had lunch at the Connaught Hotel with William Rees-Mogg, who was very friendly. I had wanted to talk to him about the future of the press but we talked more about Roy Jenkins's campaign for the leadership of the Party – he said that Heath was very much afraid of Jenkins – and he tried to build up the idea that the Labour Party's best prospects of success were with Roy as Leader. Then I asked him to take a new view of the Referendum and said, 'Look, you mustn't assume that anyone who's in favour of a Referendum is opposed to entry; I am not opposed in principle, but this is a tremendously important matter.' He was surprised when he discovered the Executive had come out for it.

The Shadow Cabinet met and considered the Referendum. My resolution from the National Executive was read out, as I had to be in the House to listen to John Davies's speech. It was agreed to refer it to a working party under Michael Foot and Peter Shore, and wasn't actually discussed this afternoon.

John Davies made a great 'U-turn' speech on the Budget in which he totally withdrew everything he had ever said about lame ducks, and the House just roared with laughter.

Friday 24 March
Today, Heath announced that he had imposed direct rule on Northern Ireland and that there would be a plebiscite to decide whether they wished ever to join with the Republic. This is another confirmation of the need for consulting the public issues and it all helps with the Common Market Referendum campaign.

Saturday 25 March
Got up at 5, drove to Heathrow, flew to Inverness, addressed the Scottish Party Conference and then flew back to London. Found the car battery flat at London Airport because I had left the car lights on – absolute curse.

In the evening Caroline and I went to Frances Morrell's party from about 10.30 to 3.30 am, and talked to all the education correspondents.

Monday 27 March
To Merthyr Tydfil for the by-election. Old S.O. Davies recently died and Ted Rowlands, a young former Welsh MP and Minister in the last Government, who lost his seat in 1970, has been put in. He is very vigorous and bright. The fear there is that the Welsh Nationalists will gain a lot of votes because Labour have controlled the local authority for so many years that there is now a violent anti-Labour Establishment sentiment.*

Tuesday 28 March
I read this morning that Dr Mansholt, the President of the European Commission, an old socialist and the founder of the Common Agricultural Policy, had given a press conference yesterday in which he had denounced Harold Wilson and the British Labour Party for rejecting the Common Market. So I dictated a sharp letter criticising Mansholt and released it to the press. I showed it to Harold who read it but didn't want to be particularly committed.

The latest estimate I can make of tomorrow's special meeting to choose a new General Secretary is that Gwyn Morgan will win by 18 to 10.

There was marvellous coverage today of Caroline's press conference yesterday on her new school survey.

Wednesday 29 March
My letter to Mansholt was published.

I went to Transport House for the NEC meeting to select the new General Secretary.

We agreed to interview the candidates in alphabetical order, although, in the event, Stutchbury went for a walk and therefore had to be interviewed after Reg Underhill. I told them the questions I was going to put, and I reminded them that if there was a tie, there would be a short adjournment, a second vote and then I would use my casting vote.

* Rowlands won back the seat for Labour, after it was held by S.O. Davies (Independent Labour), 1970–72; Davies had sat for Merthyr Tydfil for Labour from 1934–70 but was not readopted in 1970 and fought and won the seat as an Independent.

In their own way, the candidates all made extremely interesting contributions.

The strongest impression was from Ron, in terms of his power and strength, but I was convinced that Gwyn had given all the sort of answers the Committee wanted to hear.

After they had all gone out we had the first ballot and the highest votes cast were Gwyn Morgan, 14, Ron Hayward, 11. The second ballot, omitting Dick Clements, Underhill and Stutchbury, was Hayward, 14, Morgan, 14. I voted, of course, for Ron Hayward. On the third ballot the results were the same – both candidates received 14 votes. By this time, it was about 12.20 and I announced that, in accordance with the decision of the Executive, I intended to give my casting vote. But Roy Jenkins said we should come back later and look at it in a month's time. Somebody else pointed out that in the event of us postponing the decision, there would be a month of fiendish canvassing and you might get the same result. Alternatively, an NEC member might be away – it so happened that this morning, every single member of the Executive was present. Well, the discussion went on and on. Despite the earlier agreement, Joe Gormley raised the question of whether the Chairman had a casting vote under our procedures. I pointed out that Harry Nicholas had told me that although there were no standing orders of the Executive this had been the normal practice; Harold Wilson said, 'Well, there are a lot of former Chairmen here,' and they all confirmed this.

After a while John Chalmers moved and Tom Bradley seconded that the Chairman's ruling not be accepted and the result was 14 for that motion and 13 against. I voted, obviously, in favour of my own ruling. Then Mik said he couldn't understand this, there must have been a mistake and he wanted a recount – thinking the recount would produce 14:14 and I would then use my casting vote in favour of my own ruling. What had happened was that one of the Executive members present, nobody knows who it was but it was thought to be George Chambers, had actually voted for Ron Hayward but did not want it to be known.

Well, there was a great fuss about a recount – which we did eventually have – and this time it was 15:13 for the Chairman's ruling.

Then John Chalmers moved a motion that we proceed to a final ballot on the general secretaryship and in the event of a tie in this ballot, the Chairman would give his vote forthwith. I put this to the meeting, making it absolutely clear that if this motion were accepted, there would be a further ballot immediately without any debate, and if necessary my casting vote would be used. That went through with nobody opposing it, so we proceeded to a further ballot: 14:14. I therefore announced publicly, 'I give my casting vote in favour of Ron Hayward.'

I went to Ron Hayward's room afterwards with Harry Nicholas.

Harry made it clear that he intended to be General Secretary until the last day of Conference. Then I put my head in Gwyn Morgan's room and said, 'Gwyn, I just want to say a word to you.' He was with Tom McNally and obviously his whole world had collapsed around his ears. He only said, 'Well, everyone's entitled to their own opinion.' That was that.

Then to the Shadow Cabinet where we had Michael Foot and Peter Shore's working party report recommending a Referendum.

Shirley said the public did want a Referendum but the Party would not survive if this precedent was created.

I said that we had to consider to what extent a Referendum was a constitutional innovation as compared with the provisions of the European Communities Bill. I said that I supported the Government policy on a plebiscite in Northern Ireland. You could have a situation in the future, when we were in the Common Market, whereby a series of French Referenda developed and changed the Market policy, while we were denied any chance – even in Parliament – of saying anything. A Referendum would get it out of our system and leave the Party united; the Party was divided at this stage and we should accept the fact that this would resolve it.

Well, the debate went on. Harold Lever was passionate. He said he had the deepest objection to a Referendum, that it was a fraudulent practice and that it would enormously damage Harold Wilson. Harold chipped in to say that anyone who thought that he might be damaged by what was going on might help him when he was attacked, and he wasn't having Harold Lever say that. Bob Mellish said there was a swell of opinion in favour of it and he would welcome it. Douglas said we did support the principle of the Common Market, there was no parallel for such a Referendum and that it would split the Left. Tony Crosland said he was against a decision in favour of a Referendum now because it was an innovation, it would involve another somersault, it would upset the morale of the Party if we reopened the issue and we shouldn't break the present position.

Harold said that whatever Pompidou's motives were – and he thought they were to split the French popular front – the situation had been changed by the Executive decision and we should support it. Roy said he wouldn't rule out a Referendum in the event of an Election manifesto requiring one, but he didn't want one now. Michael Foot said we couldn't have a sham fight; we must destroy the Bill and the pro-Marketeers want us to do nothing so we'll get in, but if we defeat the Government in the House it will be a stunning defeat for the Market and could lead to a General Election. If there were a Referendum, the people would see it as a victory for democracy. He said, 'You can't assume we'll go in. This must be a real fight or nothing,' and that the Party would never forgive us if we lost this opportunity.

George Thomson said he was against the Referendum on principle. He didn't think we should change our view; the situation was not new; Pompidou's point was irrelevant; the Northern Ireland plebiscite was a millstone around our neck; the Executive decision had been wrongly affected by Pompidou.

Jim said he thought it would be an important psychological victory if we could win in Parliament on the Referendum question. Conference resolutions admittedly were against the Market but they would have voted for a Referendum if it had been proposed and he would vote for it to get the Government out. He was influenced by Harold Wilson's wishes.

Ted Short said he couldn't understand the passion against a Referendum. He personally wanted to enter the EEC on the present terms and the public, he thought, might well vote to enter. Constitutional arguments were being overstated. This was a case on its own, it would get us off the hook and would be a real chance of defeating the Government.

By 8 to 6, the Shadow Cabinet voted for a Referendum: Peter, Michael, Fred, Harold, myself, Jim, Ted and Bob Mellish for; Roy (though mildly), Shirley, Harold Lever, Tony Crosland, Douglas Houghton, George Thomson against. So it was agreed to put a recommendation to the Party meeting that when the Market was debated again in April, we should vote on a two-line Whip in favour of a Referendum.

Well, that was a tremendous victory. I have never had a day like today for sheer success.

Friday 31 March
We cleared up all morning and then we went off to Stansgate in the evening. Hilary went to stay with a friend. Stansgate was wet but warm and it was really very nice to get away from London.

Tuesday 4 April
Southminster, shopping. Worked up in my little office. I was then diverted on to my carpentry. Mary Lou Clarke, my new secretary, started working at home today for the first time and we talked on the telephone getting everything straight.

I phoned Rupert Murdoch about the Referendum, thinking it was about time I got some press support. Ian Aitken phoned and I tried to contact Alastair Hetherington of the *Guardian* to win him over as well.

Friday 7 April
Went to see Ruper Murdoch who was with Larry Lamb, Editor of the *Sun*, and the editor of the *News of the World*. Murdoch is just a bit

younger than me. He is a bright newspaper man who has made a humdinger success of the *Sun*, which nobody else was able to do anything about, and the *News of the World*, although it has been declining in circulation, is now fairly stable. He was opposed to the Referendum, because he is in favour of entering Europe, so his two editors were opposed to it as well. But I used all the arguments I could and they asked if I would write about it.

Then I went to the Reform Club to see Hetherington to try to persuade him to change his opinion about the Referendum and I said he just couldn't refuse on the basis that it would embarrass Roy Jenkins and Dick Taverne as he had told me yesterday.

Monday 10 April

In the afternoon, just as I was leaving the Organisation Committee, Peter Carver, the *Bristol Evening Post* Lobby Correspondent, caught me, saying 'Come with me,' and began running through the corridors. I sort of pursued him. 'It's urgent,' he said, as he dashed downstairs and told me the rumour was that Roy Jenkins, George Thomson and Harold Lever were going to resign from the Shadow Cabinet because of the Referendum. So I went to see Harold and he said that it was true. I think he was actually quite pleased.

Then we went to the Home Policy Committee and a statement was put out by Roy in which he said he couldn't accept this further somersault, and so on. As his attitude towards the Referendum had been extremely relaxed at the second Shadow Cabinet, I don't believe it was that, but more the fact that he realised he couldn't go on as Deputy-Leader of a party when he disagreed with a central part of the Party's policy. I think that is really the position. Of course what he has been able to do is to put the blame on me for the Referendum.

I was interviewed in a hostile way on the *News at Ten* by Douglas Stewart. Then I went on *24 Hours* with Harold Lever: he was most arrogant about the public and denounced the Referendum. Although I like Harold personally, he really is a Tory – there is no question about it: a nice, kind, generous, humane, liberal Conservative. Brian Faulkner, the former Prime Minister of Northern Ireland, was also there, having been interviewed by Bob McKenzie. He got entirely brushed aside by this row. I felt it was a bit discourteous until I remembered that the Prime Minister of Northern Ireland is just like the Chairman of the London County Council, nothing more.

All of a sudden, I realised that the Referendum campaign had gone wrong on me because it made me out as a splitter, whereas it had originally been brought forward as a peace move. But you are judged by results and this is the price I'm paying for that.

Tuesday 11 April
The Labour crisis is the main headline news story. I got the blame, as I expected. I had to go off early to Dusseldorf for the International Metalworkers Conference: the President of the Republic was there; Olaf Palme, Prime Minister of Sweden; Bognar, Minister of Scientific Affairs from Hungary, and Ken Coates.

I flew home in the afternoon because of the crisis in the Party, cancelling a visit to Lausanne.

Wednesday 12 April
PLP meeting at 10.30. Bob Mellish introduced it and said he wanted to give the background to the debate next Tuesday. There would be a three-line whip on our amendment calling for an Election before entry; and the Shadow Cabinet had decided to have a two-line whip in support of the amendment by the Conservative MP for Banbury, Neil Marten, calling for a Referendum. He recommended support by the Party for this course of action.

Peter Shore spoke. He said that the Conference resolution had called for a General Election to decide the Common Market question, that this was a constitutional issue and although we ideally wanted an Election, if we couldn't get one, the best thing was to have a Referendum. Joel Barnett [MP for Heywood and Royton] said the Constituency Labour Parties wanted to see the Government defeated but people didn't care about the Common Market; the Referendum would be a major constitutional change and it would destroy the Party; he called for a free vote of MPs.

Charlie Pannell said he had had an understanding with the Chief Whip last October that he would vote for the Party at this point but he would not vote for Neil Marten's amendment; he would not vote for a Tory amendment. He wanted to know whether this was just a gimmick or a precedent. He attacked me and said I was a bad Chairman of the Party, and he was sorry that Roy Jenkins had resigned.

Then Reggie Paget [MP for Northampton] said the traditional British constitutional solution to problems of this kind was to have an Election and we must consult the people. He said he would prefer an Election, but the deal for the pro-Market MPs was that they would follow the Labour Party so long as it didn't defeat the Tory Government. This was quite unacceptable and the time for resignations was last July. This time, said Reggie Paget, we really could defeat the Government if we stayed together.

Harold Lever then made a speech explaining why he had resigned. He believed he had performed a service to the Party and quoted Nye Bevan, saying, 'When you kick a man in the testicles, you can't expect immediate gratitude for what you have done to him.' He said parliamentary government was respected as it was and not as Tony Benn would like to improve it. He said the Conference had voted against the Referendum and he quoted Harold Wilson's clip on television in which he said, in answer to Robin Day's question 'Would you change your mind about a Referendum if public opinion built up in favour?', 'On this I will never change.'

I should have mentioned that in my discussion with Harold Lever on television a few days ago, they actually showed that clip of Harold Wilson on the Referendum and it did create a tremendous wave of hostility to Harold among the pro-Marketeers. Then Harold Lever went on to say that he thought I should speak in debate.

Jack Mendelson reminded us that in his *24 Hours* interview, Lever had said that Britain would be in the Common Market and he thus implied that the fight against the Common Market was a charade. He thought that the resignations had not been ineptly timed, that the pro-Marketeers had wanted to help the Government to get into Europe.

Then Roy Jenkins said he wanted to speak calmly. This was not a tactical matter and he wanted to know whether a political party could turn around as quickly as this without damaging parliamentary government. He said that a two-line whip was no good on this, and that a Referendum would be damaging to the Party in the long term. He couldn't vote against Party policy. He was born and brought up in the Party and this was a deep but narrow divide.

Stan Orme believed that it was impossible for a Party of our kind to be frightened of the people. He thought the Conference would ask for complete opposition to the Common Market and the Labour Movement would welcome any vote against it. Maurice Edelman said a Referendum was a major constitutional change and there had been no real debate about it. De Gaulle was a demagogue and had used Referenda for demagogic purposes, the future of parliamentary democracy was at stake and he was surprised that Michael Foot, who was a parliamentarian, should support it. We must not surrender parliamentary rights to the people because Referenda would be used against the liberties of the people. He was in favour of a free vote in the House.

Douglas Jay made two points: that the nature of the Bill which we were debating transferred political power to Brussels and not to the public, and that there was a distinction between ordinary legislation and constitutional changes. He favoured an Election but was prepared to support a Referendum.

Speaking from a Scottish viewpoint, Dick Douglas, the MP for Stirlingshire East and Clackmannan, warned against the danger of Scottish Nationalism and said there were reactionary tendencies in Scotland. He had been to prison for his conscientious objection to the

War and as a free man he was not going to be told what to do by the Party.

George Wallace [MP for Norwich North] said the Party was already divided and we were here because of the sacrifice of the Party. He said, 'Speaking as a member of the Party for forty years,' and at this point he almost broke into tears: he recommended the Party to stick together.

Brian Walden was opposed to a Referendum, and thought the resignations were a tragedy for the Party since they had created great difficulties for the leadership. He was against what he called 'fancy ideas in democracy' and attacked me particularly for that. He said, 'We are a coalition. We cannot weaken the legislative authority of Parliament.' He thought there would be great bitterness in a Referendum.

Michael Foot wound up and said this was a big matter. He said he had spoken in the constituencies for pro-Market MPs and had tried to protect them from the consequences with their own angry local Parties, that he had concentrated on the European Communities Bill and tried to make a success of the fight against the Bill. He said the Bill was a usurpation of power. He didn't agree with Tony Benn on everything, but to vote against the Referendum would be to make a sham of the fight against the Bill. 'The Marketeers say it's all closed but it is not closed and this year the Conference will vote and will give its view on the Market.' He said we could win in the House of Commons if we voted for a Referendum and against the guillotine, and this would easily precipitate an Election. He said we could defeat the Government, but if the Party connived to help Heath to evade his pledge to obtain the full-hearted consent of the British public, it would be a terrible thing. Michael finished by saying this was the recommendation the Shadow Cabinet made; he understood the feeling but we must fight and should fight to win.

Well, then there was a vote and for the Shadow Cabinet recommendation there were 129, and 96 against – which was only a narrow victory for the Referendum, and therefore something of a disappointment. Frank McElhone was discouraged: he has been saying to me for a long time and even more so afterwards, 'You must drop this Referendum completely.' I detected a great deal of coolness by the Party and the general feeling was that the Referendum should now be dropped as too divisive.

I suppose in a way it's amazing that it got as far as it did, considering the fact that it went absolutely against the élitist thinking of the right wing of the Party and also worried the Left, which has a sort of authoritarian flavour about it and is afraid that if you do have a Referendum, then the leadership of the trade unions and political leadership of the Left will in some way be undermined. At any rate we had got it brought forward and somehow I don't think that this, as an issue, will ever die away.

I went to the Smoking Room and talked to Jim Callaghan, who said that we needed a new policy on Europe and if the Party comes out against the Market at the Conference, Harold's position will be impossible. I thought it was rather interesting that Jim should be putting Harold's head on a block as if to say, 'If you do this, Harold will have to resign.' The only possible explanation of that would be that Jim had his eye on the leadership as well.

The Times today had a centre-page report of my speech to the International Metalworkers and David Wood predicted that I might be in the leadership of the Party in 1980; a curious comment, but it cheered me up a bit.

At the Shadow Cabinet this evening, we went on to plan the elections for the deputy-leadership to replace Roy. I decided not to stand for the deputy-leadership, so it will be between Michael Foot, Ted Short and Tony Crosland.

Monday 17 April

I have been trying to analyse who is against Referenda and why. I've studied a lot of historical work on the nineteenth century and discovered to my surprise that opposition to the extension of the franchise had been fought in exactly the same way, at every stage, by people who said it would create a precedent, that it was contrary to our parliamentary traditions, and that it would open the door to all sorts of dangerous practices. The same sort of arguments were used against votes for women. But one thing that occurred to me was *why* were people against an extension of democracy? One conclusion I came to was that it was minorities who were opposed to it. That is to say the rich were opposed to it, because they were afraid that the mob would take away their money; immigrants, racial minorities, were opposed to it because they felt they were only nesting in a foreign society by the good will of the leaders and that the mob really disliked them. The left-wing minority was against it because they were afraid that if the public was consulted it would never go along with what they wanted to do, and you would never get socialism – this is the argument advocated by Jack Mendelson and Stan Orme, and is Jack Jones's case against ballots of workers. It is also the argument Roy Jenkins uses, though whether he really believes it I don't know. In this particular case the 'European minority' – the people who are in favour of entering Europe, and suspect the public don't agree with them – are against a Referendum.

Tuesday 18 April

Worked all morning on my contribution to the European Communities debate this afternoon. First of all we had the amendment on the General Election – a very powerful speech by Michael Foot – then I interposed on the Referendum by agreement with Michael and Peter Shore. I made my speech* which was detailed and long, and of course I got the absolute anger and hostility of the pro-Marketeers.

It wasn't a successful speech because frankly, every time I talk about the Market I just annoy people. The anti-Marketeers don't trust me because I am not anti-Market on principle, and the pro-Marketeers loathe me because I have pinpointed the thing that they find hardest to get away with, namely that they haven't got the support of the public for this. I do think I have suffered very much over the Referendum argument. Anyway, a number of Labour people abstained on the Referendum, enough for Heath to win the day. So once again, the coalition has worked and Labour MPs have saved the Government: everything the Government has done this year has been done with the consent of the pro-Market Europeans in the Labour Party.

Tuesday 25 April

Today we heard that Ted Short was elected Deputy-Leader. Michael didn't do as well as he hoped and Crosland's votes went largely to Ted Short, reminding one yet again that the PLP is a right-wing body. It may be anti-Market because of the unions but it is fundamentally on the right. It is extremely difficult for anyone who has any left-wing instincts ever to be elected to anything.

Friday 28 April

I went to the Textile Factory Workers' Association Conference in Blackpool. I was very struck by a woman trade unionist who demanded maternity leave for women textile workers. She said that up to now, if women textile workers had babies, they were sacked, lost their pension entitlement, and also redundancy payment entitlement, and if they went back to the factory after the child was born, they had to start all over again as newcomers. This was quite unacceptable. She said she was quite ashamed, as a member of the TUC Women's Advisory Committee, to hear what arrangements they had in other industries. She simply said, 'We won't accept it any more.' She put it so toughly and the men looked so shifty that all of a sudden it focused my mind on what the things are that change society. The moment in time when history changes is when people stand up and say – and mean – 'We won't accept it any more.'

Saturday 29 April

I went to Carlisle for the May Day meeting and I was so exhausted, I thought I was going to collapse during my speech. In the afternoon, I

* See Appendix VII.

was driven to Newcastle and I stayed in the Northumbrian Hotel, where I went to bed at about 8 o'clock and slept for 12 hours to recover.

Sunday 30 April
I went to the East Newcastle Action Group to speak for Ben Pimlott. He is a lecturer in politics at the University of Newcastle and was one of the authors of the Fabian pamphlet on Party organisation last summer for which I wrote the preface. He is a Marketeer, a *Socialist Commentary* chap. But he set up this Action Group to get intellectuals to work with the Party, and it is quite an active little group. I talked about the role of the Party and tried to develop some of my ideas about democracy.

Wednesday 3 May
Barbara Castle returned to the Shadow Cabinet today, having been elected over Eric Heffer by 111 to 89. I voted for Eric on the principle that we needed more trade union people, and Barbara really has no future although she is a very vigorous and active woman. Eric was terribly bitter about it: I didn't tell him I'd voted for him because first, I didn't think he'd believe me and second, I didn't think there was any point in doing so.

Tonight the *Tribune* Group went to see Harold Wilson to say that they were very dissatisfied with his leadership. Stan Orme said it was like punching cotton wool.

I went to see Harold late. I was very upset at the way things were going and unless we could get the Referendum incorporated into the Conference resolution, I was going to vote against the Common Market. Harold said that to be committed to come out would be impossible for him and that he would have to resign. About the sixth time he had referred to resignation.

Morale is completely undermined by the fact that we have had five votes on the European Communities Bill, all of which we could have won if all the Labour MPs had voted: but they were abstaining all over the place.

I talked to Frank McElhone this evening. He was very candid and said, 'Frankly at the moment, you have only got two friends in the Parliamentary Party – myself and yourself.' I think this is probably an accurate account of how things stand.

Thursday 4 May
The solemn conclusion I have reached is that my support for UCS and the shop stewards, and my support for a Referendum and my line on the Common Market have really alienated everybody. Put quite crudely, I have got to mend my fences.

We won control in the local elections in Bristol – Stockwood, Windmill Hill, Brislington, St George's East and West.

Friday 12 May
This evening I went to the Asian dinner – the Standing Conference of Asian Organisations – at the National Liberal Club. There were a number of speakers including David Lane, the new Minister at the Home Office, Peter Shore, Fenner Brockway and Dora Gaitskell. It was an enjoyable evening, though the National Liberal Club is an absolutely funereal mausoleum of a place and the surroundings were very British Empire.

I argued that we mustn't think of immigration as a problem since it enormously enriched our lives. My views on what was called a multiracial society had altered because I thought certain groups – for example Indians – would always remain different and it would be silly to try to assimilate them. I listed some of the contributions I thought the Indians had made, including non-violence, concern for the environment. All these things had been injected through immigration into our society and I welcomed it.

Saturday 20 May
I have had a message from Hugh McKay and others indicating that I am thought to be out of touch with the Labour group in Bristol. So I wrote to every one of the ward secretaries saying I would like to attend a ward meeting, and to every one of my councillors saying I would like to keep in touch, suggesting a meeting. The plain truth is that I don't make enough contact with people; I do things on my own and I ought to wait a bit and get people to support me.

Caroline went to a comprehensive schools conference at London University, which was absolutely crowded.

Monday 22 May
We had the Industry Bill second reading today and John Davies made a speech in which he totally reversed the position that he had adopted over the last two years; he made no reference to the fact that he had ever taken a different view so I pointed to this change of view and opened up the alternatives that would now have to be considered. The House was pretty empty.

My cousin Margaret Rutherford, the actress, died today, aged eighty.

Wednesday 24 May
Went to the Commons and spoke in the debate on EEC industrial policy. I had prepared the speech only briefly and hadn't gone into any great detail. The Government won by only 5 votes with 12 Labour

abstentions so that, once again, we lost the chance to defeat the Government: it really is disgraceful that Members are just cooperating with the legislation.

Thursday 1 June
My car broke down and was towed away, which made it difficult for me to get to Bristol. But I did manage it and I had a three-and-a-half hour surgery at Wick Road School – the longest and most complicated, I think, I have ever had. I had seventeen cases, including two doctors, who came to complain about a local chemist who practised as an abortionist and who used a drug that produced congenital malformations. It came to light through a young research doctor at Bristol General Hospital. I telephoned the police about it.

Then to the General Management Committee, where the Regional Organiser told us quite plainly that the constituency was now marginal. He pointed out that we had practically no members: there are about 250 real members as compared with 2,500 in 1935.

Friday 2 June
Went to the headquarters where Herbert Rogers made work impossible because he talked all the time. He told me of his attempts to get a popular front set up with the Communist Party. He also talked about his anti-Common Market work by trying to get anti-Market Tories to put up against pro-Market Tories in a number of constituencies – and he is even trying to get a Labour man who supports Labour policy put up against Arthur Palmer who is pro-Market. I am wholly against that. He drew my attention to the immensely expensive Europe Left propaganda which is being pumped out and he said he had ten copies of *Socialist Commentary* with Roy Jenkins's speech in it for distribution to the Party sent to him free.

I made enquiries at the Housing Department about the number of people who want transfers. My enquiries into local social issues, which I started systematically in May, have already produced a hundred and seventy replies, of which twenty-five were housing transfer cases. The accommodation officer at the corporation told me that there were between seven thousand and eight thousand people wanting transfers in Bristol and that a major policy decision was required before he could do anything: at the moment, the official policy is to discourage transfers.

Monday 5 June
Went to the House of Commons where there were tributes paid to the Duke of Windsor. I haven't referred in my diary to the death of the Duke of Windsor and the odious hypocrisy with which the royal family and the press and the Establishment handled it. Somehow, yesterday, this

reached a peak. I didn't hear the debate but the Government motion forgot to offer condolences to the Duchess and it was only as a result of a Back Bench enquiry that the amendment was made. The Trooping of the Colour was not cancelled and Parliament didn't adjourn on the day of the funeral of the former king. Tonight on television there was a marvellous programme about the Duke of Windsor which told his whole life story up to his abdication. Really, a lot of people are rediscovering how unattractive the monarchy is through the story of the Duke of Windsor.

I took the chair at the working group preparing amendments for the Industry Bill. After that, had a talk to Frank McElhone and Eric Heffer, who was very amusing about being expelled from the Communist Party. He said one of the people who clamoured for his expulsion was Les Cannon of the ETU, who was then an active and vigorous Communist. When Les left the Communists and joined the Labour Party, which Eric had already joined, he clamoured for the expulsion of Eric Heffer from the Labour Party on the grounds that he was too left wing. Eric is a free-thinking guy in the best non-conformist tradition.

Tuesday 6 June
This morning Caroline went off to the Rhondda for her visit to schools and education offices.

I met Harry Mitchell today and he told me that on Friday, when the Government produced its motion of condolence to the Queen on the death of the Duke of Windsor, he had raised a query as to why the Duchess of Windsor had not been mentioned. This means they knew about it and it did not take them by surprise on Monday when the motion was moved and amended by the House. Indeed Charlie Pannell said he went to see Heath about it to protest and Heath said that the motion was agreed with the Opposition. So Charlie felt he had been let down again by Harold, whom he really does dislike. It proves to my satisfaction that the Palace, who must have been consulted, did not want Parliament to take official cognisance of the Duchess of Windsor, and that is the end of a very shoddy story.

Sunday 11 June
Harold Wilson made a speech yesterday on the Common Market, in which he came out for the Referendum. It was the big news in today's *Sunday Express*. So my campaign has succeeded now and the Party will commit itself to renegotiation and to putting the issue to the public, after the renegotiation, in a Referendum.

Tuesday 13 June
At 3.30 Mr Vidac, the Yugoslav Ambassador, and Mr Drulovic, former editor of *Politika* in Belgrade and a former Yugoslav MP, came to see me

about self-management. Drulovic said that my pamphlet 'The New Politics' did contain within it all the issues that needed to be discussed in modern politics and he said it was the right approach, although it was short and lacked analysis.

In the evening I went to the dinner for Lester Pearson, the former Canadian Prime Minister. Robert Grant-Ferris, the Conservative MP for Nantwich, was in the chair. It was the first time I had been to dinner in the Speaker's House in twenty-two years in Parliament. There was a little speech by Grant-Ferris on the occasion of the presentation of the Victor Gollancz Humanity Award to Pearson. Macmillan was also there. I hadn't heard him speak since he left the premiership in 1963; he had an affectation of senility even when he was younger but he has grown into the part, he was just a bit more florid and a bit more shaky in his manner. He began by saying how Britain had never been a big country when it was the most powerful in the Middle Ages, and therefore influence didn't depend on size; he saw a great future for 'England', he said. He spoke about the Common Market and how our 'little differences' (the political arguments in the House of Commons) were unimportant compared with this great challenge. It was Mac the politician speaking with great emphasis; his mind is as bright as can be. It was impressive and I enjoyed it, but what he was saying simply had no bearing on the problems of our times.

Later I had a word with Harold Wilson. We discussed how to handle the Common Market at Conference and how to head off a possible attack on the whole principle of the Market. I said, 'Well look, Harold, if the Conference won't have the Common Market, it won't have it and as far as I am concerned, I am going to accept the Conference decision even if I disagree with it.' He seems terrified that it will down him and remove him from the leadership.

Wednesday 14 June

I went to the BBC and had a fascinating discussion with Sir Hugh Greene, the former Director-General, Robert Kee and a Swede from the International Broadcasting Institute. The intention was to discuss my paper for the Manchester symposium on broadcasting, access and workers' democracy in the media. Hugh Greene said democracy in broadcasting was impracticable, but apparently they had been doing it in Sweden for three years. The thing that came out of it was the aristocratic and élitist attitude of Greene himself, who said that communication was to give people the information upon which the decisions that affect their lives were made – no question of consulting them. And on workers' participation Robert Kee said contemptuously, 'What, consult the second cameraman about the content of the programme!'

Saturday 17 June
Our twenty-third wedding anniversary and in the evening Caroline and
I had a meal in Notting Hill Gate.

Monday 19 June
Stephen started work in the office today and will do two or three weeks
before he goes away. He began tackling the constituency jobs,
particularly the statistics for all the Election results in the constituency
over the last twenty years.

Tuesday 20 June
We had the first meeting of the Campaign Committee this morning: I
simply put myself in the chair as Chairman of the Party and this was
broadly accepted. We agreed on the terms of reference of the Campaign
Committee and that the minutes would go both to the National
Executive and the Shadow Cabinet. This was a very important
statement because what it said, in effect, was that Harold Wilson would
not be running the next Election by himself as he did the last one. This is
something we have been working on for a long time.

Wednesday 21 June
Peter Blackstein of the German SPD came to see me at the House of
Commons. He is a former German Ambassador in Yugoslavia, a very
senior diplomat. Willy Brandt had sent him to Britain to find out what
attitudes were being adopted by the Labour Party and others towards
the Common Market and I tried to put him in the picture. He was
polite, gentle and courteous and I think he took it on board.

    The difficulty with all these SPD people, and indeed all the
Continental socialists, is that the only Labour MPs that they ever meet
are Michael Stewart, Roy Jenkins, George Thomson and Fred Mulley,
who continually assure them that we shall be in the Common Market
and they don't have to bother about the Labour Party because it will
simply have to accept it; Heath will take us in. This causes a great deal of
ill will for others of us when we meet them, so it is worth taking a little bit
of trouble over them.

    Later this evening was a debate on the United Reformed Church Bill.
This was a Bill to provide for certain financial arrangement following
the merger between the Congregationalists and the Presbyterians, and
Mother had been active with one or two others in trying to form a
continuing Congregational Association that would resist this merger,
which she felt would completely destroy the Congregational principle.
Now, John Huxtable, the General Secretary of the Congregationalists,
had got this Private Bill through a committee of the House of Commons
and the House of Lords making a provision under which all the

Congregational Church property would accrue to the United Reformed Church.

Nigel Spearing, the Labour MP for Acton, moved an amendment saying that if a church wished to come out and become independent again, it could take its property with it. He and I had discussed it and we agreed we would both speak in the debate. We had another ally in Ian Paisley, who also spoke for the amendment which was somewhat embarrassing.

Mother was in the Gallery. When I got up somebody objected to the fact that I was speaking from the Opposition Front Bench, and although I had checked with Bob Mellish that that was the thing to do, I went on to the Back Benches and I made my speech. I never felt such absolute hostility in the House. The Archbishop of Canterbury had written to all the Anglicans and others telling them to go along and support the Bill. The Roman Catholics were there; Norman St John Stevas spoke and it was the whole Establishment gathered together against dissent.

In the end it was so clear that there was no support for us that Ian Paisley, Nigel Spearing and I agreed that we simply would not push it to a division, so the debate ended. But the extent to which managerial solutions to all our problems have become accepted like the entry into the Common Market is rather frightening. It's a winding up of the Reformation, a winding up of British political traditions. These are battles that have got to be fought and won all over again.

Friday 23 June

Bristol for a surgery, then went up to Kingswood for a meeting on the Housing Finance Bill. The Kingswood Council are pretty militant and the Tenants' Association had turned up and were pressing me hard to 'give a lead', by which they meant, 'Tell us not to implement the law if it becomes an Act'. I was trying to explain that it was not my job to tell people to break the law but that if they decided on their own discretion that they felt they could not go along with it, then quite a different situation would arise. This whole question of one's attitude to the law has become dominant this summer, indeed over the last year, with UCS, the sit-ins, the work-ins, the flying pickets, the railwaymen, and so on. It was an interesting opportunity to test out the arguments at a meeting, but I must be absolutely clear in my mind that although I have broken the law (as when I stood as a disqualified candidate) and I hope I would break the law myself again under certain circumstances, it is not for me to tell other people to do so.

Sunday 25 June

In the evening I flew to Vienna with Jim Callaghan, Walter Padley and Joan Lestor, for the Socialist International Congress. Stayed in the

Royal Hotel in the Singerstrasse. At the reception at the Rathaus Judith Hart greeted us by saying that the British delegation was being treated extremely coldly because of our attitude towards the Common Market. We were being cold-shouldered and not given our proper place on the top table, and so on; not an argument I, personally, found convincing but that is because the glamour of it all doesn't much affect me.

Monday 26 June
The conference began at 9 with the Vienna Symphony Orchestra and there were more musicians than delegates. The hall was only about 20 per cent full and after the opening ceremonies there was a long break and I had the opportunity of having a talk to Betty Lockwood* and some of the other women about my speech for the women's session tomorrow. They were rather critical of the self-help line that I was plugging because the women want to call the men in to assist them with their battle. Of course I sympathise with that and understand it. But I was not keen on omitting this element of self-help which, I think, is the secret of all success. It is only when women won't accept things, or when the blacks won't accept things, or when the poor won't accept things, that the moment comes when circumstances begin to change, and there is no substitute for this in political action.

Jim was very tired and he hasn't entirely recovered from his prostate operation early this year. I had a talk to him while I sewed a button on his coat in his room. He was anxious to make clear to me that as far as he was concerned, his own political ambitions were satisfied. He said, 'I wish Harold well and I think he knows it.'

I told him that Harold kept threatening to go if he didn't get his way on the Common Market and Jim said, 'Ah well, if the vote went the wrong way, it would create great difficulties in the Party and things would become impossible for Harold.'

Jim himself thinks the Referendum is nonsense. He thought it would unite the Party but when it showed it didn't, he wanted to drop it.

Dinner at the Chancellor's residence, where I was greeted by Kreisky, a very shrewd politician who keeps himself to himself but is very skilful at his job. The Finnish and Austrian Foreign Ministers were also there.

After dinner I was summoned over to sit next to Golda Meir, the Prime Minister of Israel. I told her that I had met Martin Buber and she was scornful of all that group in Israel who had thought that you could solve the problem of peace with the Arabs by being conciliatory. I told her that Martin Buber never served food to his guests because it diverted

---

* Assistant National Agent of the Labour Party 1967–75; subsequently Chairman of the Equal Opportunities Commission, 1975–83.

from the conversation. As we were talking Willy Brandt gave me a friendly nod.

I said, 'How do things look now? Do they look peaceful?' She said, 'Well, whatever peace there is, is due to the US Phantoms. The Arabs are terrified of the Phantoms and the Russians keep telling them that although they are not ready, if they want to attack, the Russians won't stop them and that's what we have got to be careful about.'

At this stage in our discussion a piece of paper was handed to her by a man whom I didn't recognise. She asked him something, sent him away and then laughed. She said to me, 'Do you know what was on that piece of paper?' I said, 'No, of course not.' She said, 'Well, that man who brought it over was my Chef du Cabinet and he had seen you talking to me, didn't know who you were, thought you were a Belgian and wanted to remind me that Belgium was on the Security Council this year and I was to take the opportunity of making any points that would be helpful in the Security Council discussions.' We roared with laughter.

Then I asked her about Sadat: was he better or worse than Nasser? I reminded her that when I was in Israel four years ago, the Foreign Office believed everything would start to improve.

Golda Meir said that Sadat was terrified of coups against him and that nothing would happen until an Arab came forward who really cared about his own people.

Then a man came up and bowed to her. It was the Dutch Ambassador and she thanked him for the Dutch representations on behalf of Israel in Moscow.

After that – we talked for about an hour and a half – I felt it was time for me to move on and I had a talk to Olaf Palme. Harold and Mary had arrived with Joe Haines: Harold declined to say what would be in his speech although it was known it was going to be about the Common Market.

Tuesday 27 June
I got up early this morning and made my speech at the women's session. I have been absolutely horrified by the Socialist International. It is entirely without roots in the working class movement and is just an international Fabian Society, with people like those in the Campaign for Democratic Socialism: intelligent, agreeable people, some of whom, of course, do have a long record of struggle behind them: but they have more or less eliminated the ideology of socialism from their vocabulary, and have got no formal links with the trade unions. This is something I referred to in my speech.

I got a taxi to the airport and arrived home at 4, pretty glad to be away from Vienna, which I must admit I didn't find very attractive.

Thursday 29 June

Stephen, Hilary and Mary Lou worked in the office all day. Stephen has completed the graphs of the Election results in Bristol South-East broken down by wards, and the turnout broken down by polling districts, right back to 1951. So I have got an understanding in depth of my constituency which I have never had before. The outstanding feature of it is the 13 per cent fall in turnout at Elections. I have no doubt that this has contributed to the fall in my majority, but undoubtedly the Tories suffer from it too. If you take turnout as an index of political interest and confidence in the system, it is a pretty gloomy picture. When there was mass confrontation of opinion in 1951, with Attlee *v* Churchill, you got the maximum turnout. But the more you moved towards the centre and looked for the middle ground, the lower the turnout becomes. Also, a lot of other changes have occurred and people don't think Parliament matters.

Caroline and I went to Number 10 for a dinner given by Heath for a Senegali delegation including musicians. I was standing in for Harold. Caroline liked the music and talked to Heath about it. I find it difficult to talk to him, but I asked him about Sir Francis Chichester, the yachtsman. He told me that Chichester was dying from leukemia and that was why he had had to come back from his trip. I did make him laugh by saying that at the Labour Conference, we sang 'The People's Flag is deepest red . . .' while the people at the back, the right wing, would sing, 'The People's Flag should be forgot, And never brought to mind again.'

Heath made a mad, impassioned speech about Europe and Africa and how now the imperial period was over, Europe was united and it could work with Africa to be an influence in the world. It was nineteenth-century imperialism reborn in his mind through status within the Common Market.

Caroline and I talked to Sir Patrick Reilly, the ex-Ambassador in Paris. He was the man who had written a sensational farewell despatch which was read everywhere in Whitehall and which included some frank comments on George Brown.

Wednesday 5 July

This was the day that we had the Executive to discuss the Green Paper.* It was an enormously long meeting and the most interesting part of the whole thing was undoubtedly the acceptance of the Referendum.

A lot of people didn't vote, but it was the culmination of a long period of campaigning and I was pleased.

---

* 'Labour's Programme for Britain' which contained the National Executive statement made at the 1972 Conference on the Common Market.

Tuesday 11 July
Michael Meacher, the Labour MP for Oldham North, came to my room for a talk. He has been interesting himself in regional policy and he is by way of being a bit of a friend and admirer. I liked him very much.

Wednesday 12 July
Lunch at Esso's offices, with Harold and Tony Field, who works in Harold's private office and who used to be in the oil business. The big oil companies are as well informed about the world – if not better – as any Foreign Office. They wanted to get across to us the need to conserve North Sea oil resources because they would run out soon and that gave me the impression that they didn't want to find that their imports from other parts of the world would be affected. Maybe they were preparing us for the idea that the price of North Sea oil was wrong, or something. I am not absolutely sure.

Larry Grant of the National Council for Civil Liberties came to see me, asking me if I would give evidence in support of Peter Hain. This summer Hain is to be the subject of a private prosecution for conspiracy for his work on the 'Stop the Seventies' tour, preventing the South African rugby team, the Springboks, from playing here. Peter is looking for allies and I had been asked if I would take part. I said I would but that I didn't think it would help very much.

Saturday 15 July
To Durham last night for the Miners' Gala and up early to go to the Bear Park to see the band march around the village. It was very moving. There were old miners, youngsters, women in their curlers and working miners coming out.

Came back to the hotel for breakfast, then watched the march past. It was the biggest and best I had ever attended although the number of pits involved has diminished sharply, with between 130,000 and 170,000 people, according to the police estimates. The weather was superb and morale high and it was terrific. Michael Foot made an impassioned speech of the old kind, stirring people to socialism.

Saturday 22 July
The five dockers have been imprisoned in Pentonville.[1] I think it all happened yesterday and I understand that Reg Prentice, who is our spokesman on industrial relations, made a statement saying he had no sympathy with the dockers at all. This incensed me. Tomorrow is the celebration of the Tolpuddle Martyrs' meeting down in Dorchester, so I drafted a statement saying that millions of people would respect the dockers for sticking to their beliefs. I then rang Reg Prentice and read it to him. He was angry and so I modified it slightly. But I said I felt I must

put it out; it is what I believe. Of course, the public at the moment is being whipped into an absolute frenzy of hostility to the dockers particularly to the five militants – Bernie Steer, Vic Turner, Derek Watkins, Tony Merrick and Cornelius Clancy. Jack Jones, who has been trying to get a settlement, is the great hero of the day for the Establishment: the moderate Mr Jones, as compared to the mindless militant of a few weeks ago.

The position is complicated. Even though the Government are trying to whip up great feeling on law and order, we must be quite clear in our own minds that we are not going to be stampeded on these lines. I am afraid Reg Prentice showed some signs of being a sort of Ray Gunter – that is his danger. Anyway I put the statement out.

Sunday 23 July
The *Sunday Times* carried my statement on the dockers in full. They accompanied it, of course, by a great attack on me in their leader.

Monday 24 July
Went over to the Commons: there is considerable hostility by the Left against Reg Prentice and considerable discontent with me from the Right for saying that millions would respect those who had gone to jail for their opinions.

Had a talk to Frank McElhone, who feels at the moment that he is riding a tiger because the events of the last few days, particularly the dockers, have thrown me back into the centre of public controversy and worried the Establishment figures and he wonders whether this is going to damage me.

Tuesday 25 July
To the House of Commons, where we had a great discussion of the special Organisation Sub-Committee about Dick Taverne.[2] Although the enquiry had reported that the rules had been fully carried out by the Lincoln Party, it suggested that there was some breach of natural justice and recommended that in this case Dick's appeal be upheld. Well, there was a tied vote of 4 to 4 on whether we should uphold the Enquiry Committee report. In the end, John Chalmers, who is a completely weak vessel and for whom I have no time – he talks tough and always moves to the Right – voted for the Enquiry Committee (on which, in fairness, he had sat). So Dick Taverne's appeal was upheld with a recommendation to the National Executive to accept the appeal.

I went to do *Panorama* with Robin Day and Robert Carr on the Pentonville Five, as the dockers are now being termed. I must say I was pretty tense and Robin Day was very rough. But I survived.

Wednesday 26 July
At the Executive the Taverne appeal decision was overturned by 12 to 8.

I moved a resolution, 'That this meeting of the NEC condemns the imprisonment of the five dockers by the National Industrial Relations Court and calls upon the Government to secure their release immediately,' which was carried *nem con.* Then we later heard that the General Council had passed a resolution calling for a one-day strike unless the imprisoned dockers were released before Monday. So I then moved that we supported the TUC call for a general strike and this was also carried *nem con.*

Later, at the Shadow Cabinet we heard that the dockers had been released which is a marvellous outcome for our persistence in supporting them.

Thursday 27 July
At the PLP meeting this evening, Denis Howell [MP for Birmingham Small Heath] raised the Taverne case, which had nothing whatsoever to do with the Parliamentary Labour Party. But since it was raised, I did not try to stop it being discussed. Will Griffiths [MP for Manchester Exchange] wanted the discussion deferred, so did Eric Heffer and Hugh Jenkins but Dennis Howell pressed on. He said that he was worried about the way the decision had gone, saying that the Parliamentary Party is a constituent element of the Labour Party, and we should have a code of conduct on these things. The issue before the Executive was the behaviour of an MP, and that a small caucus could capture a whole constituency Party and make trouble for the MP. It would be raised at the Annual Conference, and would damage our image.

Reggie Paget said we shouldn't interfere between an MP and his constituency, and Roy Jenkins intervened and said we should discuss it and we must be tolerant.

Eric Heffer said we shouldn't have been having this discussion at all.

And so it went on: it was quite a tough meeting in many ways and difficult because the suggestion that Dick Taverne is a little man being sat on by the Party is a difficult one to destroy. Actually he is a man trying to sit on the rights of the British people to decide whether they want to go into the Common Market or not.

Sunday 30 July
Did *The World This Weekend* on Lin Piao, whose death has now been officially announced. I was in Peking the day he died, so they asked me in.

Michael Meacher came home for a talk on his way to Sweden to study Labour Party policy; he is a very intelligent man who has done well – highly regarded by the Left, Right and Centre of the Party. He is a warm ally to have.

I phoned Alastair Hetherington to complain about the awful treatment of the present industrial situation by the *Guardian*. I also rang the Editor of the *Daily Mirror* and tried to get on to Hugh Cudlipp because I felt – and I was encouraged in this by Geoffrey Goodman – that an absolutely major counter-attack against the general Establishment line was necessary at this moment. Otherwise, if we lose this battle or appear to be in retreat, we are never going to be able to assert ourselves on law and order or industrial relations or anything else.

Monday 31 July
A really unpleasant meeting of the Shadow Cabinet. Crosland attacked me over the docks for supporting an unofficial strike. I pointed out it wasn't unofficial, that I had checked with Jack Jones, and that more or less blew him out of the water.

Shirley said that really the time had come when Harold Wilson had to be tough and override opposition from different views that might be being expressed on the whole question of industrial relations.

Denis Healey said the Tories were dividing the nation on this as they were on Northern Ireland, with a majority dominating a minority; they were politicising the judges; the Industrial Relations Act had destroyed the common ground; there were deep divisions in the Tory leadership; but we did not want middle class Robespierres (that was a reference to me). The general theme of his speech was the same as the leading article in *The Times* this morning: 'Back to Rees-Mogg – Men of Power Move into the Consensus'.

Reg Prentice pointed out that the railwaymen had kept the law and won their fight and that, in his view, the five dockers' case was nothing like Tolpuddle, with which I had compared it.

So Michael Foot said you didn't have to go as far as Reg had done. The dockers *did* command sympathy and the proof of that was to be seen in the TUC General Council and the National Executive. 'We can't be negative or neutral or defensive. We must demand an Election. The Law Lords rushed into a decision on this: the Act is unworkable, the people will disobey it and when they do we can't blame them. We must be confident.'

Bob Mellish said that the dockers are unpopular; but they have lost a third of their workforce and yet they have achieved a 200 per cent increase in productivity. The scandal is that the cold storage works are part of the Vestey combine. Lord Vestey sells the docks when they become redundant and buys cold storage sites and then claims that the dockers are trying to ruin his business in cold storage. Bob Mellish said we would get a bad press but we can't survive without the trade unions.

Peter Shore thought that we were fighting for public opinion. The Act is unworkable, it hasn't got a broad consent and that is not because of the militants. We shouldn't attack the courts, but the law is part of our national property.

Elwyn agreed with Peter. He attacked the Government and its law. 'We are a law-abiding people. Why has the mood changed in this country? The judgment of the Law Lords now makes the situation impossible. It puts responsibility for everything the shop stewards do on to Jack Jones and therefore the TGWU would either become a totalitarian union or it would fragment. The law is impossible and it is restrictive.'

The discussion went on and I couldn't resist saying that I had listened carefully but I didn't need to be lectured by some members of the Shadow Cabinet about my attitude to the Trade Union Movement. I said my father went to the 1889 dock strike on his father's shoulders. I was always taught to believe that the dockers were the best workers of the lot. 'And,' I said, 'You might be interested to see the address on which my father fought the Election in 1906: cheap food, reform and prosperity for the port of London, freedom for the trade unions and justice for Ireland, and it doesn't seem as if we have made any progress in any of them.' I said that there was an atmosphere of folk festival over the Pentonville Five, and it wasn't frightening. We ought to read the signs and see what was really happening.

That was almost the end of the discussion and I felt the hot breath of disapproval.

Immediately after that, I went to see Hugh Cudlipp and the Editor of the *Daily Mirror*, Tony Miles, was there with him. I said to him, 'Hugh, for many years when I went to my constituency or round the country, I found your leading articles repeated to me as the opinions of the people I met. That is not true any more. You do not speak for your readers. You write all these things about the present situation. But it is not what people think. Something important happened last week. Something new and different and important.'

In the end, he said to me, 'All right, you can have the centre pages. I decided that before you came and you can say what you like.'

I promised him he would have a piece by tomorrow.

I went back and did a first draft straight on to the typewriter. The House sat all night and I got the second draft finished by 6.30 am. It is a real breakthrough.

Tuesday 1 August

Came home, retyped the final draft, went in to vote again. Frances Morrell came in and helped me with the article and in the evening, at about midnight, I sent the text over to the *Mirror*, cut and shaped. Frances has played a large part in structuring it.

Wednesday 2 August
I worked at home this morning. An awful lot of letters began pouring in about the dockers; most of them were against, I must be fair. The *Mirror* piece was approved and set in type.

Today I had the idea that I would resign my Privy Councillorship, my MA and all my honorary doctorates in order to strip myself of what the world had to offer but whether this would be a good idea, I don't know. It might be ridiculed. But 'Wedgie Benn' and 'the Rt Honourable Anthony Wedgwood Benn' and all that stuff is impossible. I have been Tony Benn in Bristol for a long time.

Thursday 3 August
The 'Citizen Benn' piece went out to the *Mirror*'s full readership – six or eight million people.

Monday 7 August
I went to the Commons for Department of Trade and Industry questions. Afterwards had tea with George Thomas who told me about his dealings with the Prince of Wales, which will amuse me when I read my memoirs. He said that during the course of the Investiture proceedings, when George had said something about Powell, Prince Charles had said he didn't understand why people attacked Powell. And Charles and the Duke of Edinburgh were angry when George described Charles I as a scoundrel!

Tuesday 8 August
The *Mirror* published the response to my piece last week. They had had well over 1,000 letters, 8:1 in support for my article. It was a remarkable response and it surprised me. Frances Morrell will be delighted. I know it has had some effect on the *Mirror* editorial policy. They asked Jack Jones to write for them almost immediately afterwards and I think they realised they had gone off on the wrong track. It was something of a breakthrough and even if it is no more than that, at least the arguments I have been putting forward are being taken seriously.

Thursday 10 August
At Stansgate.

Fixing up portable filing cabinets for my Bristol records. Took Father's old 1918 wooden card index cabinets, which he had used in his Parliament Street office, fitted them all up, varnished them and they look nice. Carpentry is my relaxation on holiday.

Friday 11 August
Played chess with Stephen. The Fischer and Spassky world chess championshps in Reykjavik have created enormous interest all over the place.

Wednesday 16 August
I began again to knit the scarf that I started for Stephen before he was born and which I never finished. Since he is twenty-one in a few days, I decided I would knit another ball and a half of wool and give his finished scarf to him.

The dock strike is over. The dockers have accepted the latest offer.

Sunday 27 August
Caroline is hard at work. I don't put much about her in this diary but researching and writing books occupies all her day. She has just finished the book on the education of women and the second edition of *Half Way There* is coming out from Penguin in a month's time.

Tuesday 5 September
I gave my fraternal greetings to the TUC Conference and was given the gold TUC badge. In my speech I looked back at our record and our relations with the trade unions:

'The last Labour Government, in which I was proud to serve, faced and surmounted some appalling economic difficulties and it carried through a formidable programme of socialist reforms.

'It also made some mistakes. One of those mistakes was in our approach to industrial relations and as a result, we lost the confidence of many of our own people. I accept my full collective responsibility for that decision.

'It is not pleasant to have to say you were wrong. But we must, if we are to learn from that experience. And may I add this, that even so, history will be much more generous, I believe, about the achievements of that Government than were our critics at the time. It is simply not good enough to blame the Labour Government or the Parliamentary Labour Party entirely for our defeat in 1970. The Trade Union Movement, with all its virtues, must also accept its share of responsibility.

'Until very recently, the unions have hardly made any serious effort to explain their work to those who are not union members and not even very much to the wives and families of those who are. You have allowed yourselves to be presented to the public, very often, as if you and the General Council actively favoured the Conservative philosophy of personal acquisitiveness. The fact that the Trade Union Movement came into being to fight for social justice, as well as higher wages, has simply not got across. If the public opinion polls prove nothing else, they certainly prove that.

'Finally, neither the Party nor the TUC has perhaps given sufficient support to other movements of legitimate protest and reform, I think particularly of those led by women, by the old and by the young and by others who are, in reality, engaged in our common struggle. If we want them to be more interested in us, we must first be more interested in them.

'We have not yet agreed – it is very evident – how we should respond to these challenges. But, you know, these are not new problems at all. There is nothing that I can say today that has not been said before at past Congresses, facing far greater difficulties than this Congress faces, at a time when workers, for example, did not even have the vote to use in self-defence, a vote we won and have so often wasted.

'Our whole history tells us how to work together for the transformation of Britain, by our own direct efforts, combining industrial and political action, peacefully, by persuasion, using Parliament as an instrument to serve the people.'

Wednesday 6 September
There was an awful massacre yesterday at the Munich Olympic Games – an appalling thing to have happened. Eleven Israeli athletes were killed by Arab terrorists from the Black September organisation.

Thursday 7 September
Telephoned Harold to tell him that he must recognise the distinct possibility that the Conference will vote for a resolution that is in principle against the Common Market. He's just got to get it clear that this could happen and he mustn't make this a vote of confidence in him. I'm sure I didn't persuade him because he is very pro-Europe. He keeps saying this will be the breaking point and, of course, if that did happen and he felt he couldn't lead the Party any more, then it would create a frightful crisis because it would divide the Party into the Marketeers plus Wilson against the rest. Harold is worried about the possibility that Chris Mayhew might stand against him as a man of straw, but I don't think this will happen. He wanted me to move an amendment to the rules of the Parliamentary Party that ten people had to nominate a person to be Leader and not just one.

Sunday 10 September
Some shop stewards from Aldermaston came to see me this morning to describe the strike in the nuclear weapons centre there. There are about fifty people working in Site A11, where the warheads are actually machined and they have been on strike since June; it is pretty remarkable that this should have been going on and there should have been nothing reported in the papers. I thought they had a strong case and promised I would write to John Davies about it.

A family lunch in Holland Park.

Monday 11 September

Home Policy Committee. Another row over the Asians,* although to be fair to him Jim Callaghan does recognise that we must have the Asians but just thinks we should limit the numbers. He was very open about it. I have some sympathy with those who say that it is easy for the people who live in Hampstead and Holland Park to say that the Asians should be admitted, but what are they themselves doing about helping the immigrants.

Thursday 14 September

There was headline news today concerning the *Elecon*, a Greek ship which came into Bristol a month ago. National Union of Seamen representatives went on board and found out that the crewmen were owed a lot of back pay; the officers' association found the same and the International Transport Federation discovered that the agreement with the shipowners had been broken. So the three unions appealed to the Board of Trade who refused the ship a certificate of sailing until the arrears were paid and until the crew was up to proper manning levels. The Board of Trade then sent down a surveyor who refused to prevent the ship sailing and gave it a clearance certificate. So then the three unions appealed to the dockers at Bristol who blacked the ship, declined to open the dock gates for it and in effect imprisoned it there.

In the afternoon, I had an urgent call from the NUS organiser, Derek Tedder, who told me that the Industrial Relations Court was being summoned tomorrow on the initiative of the owners in Cyprus to bring an action for unfair industrial practice against the dockers. I immediately rang John Davies's office and tried to get him to intervene and send the surveyor back again to cancel the ship's clearance, but without success.

Friday 15 September

I heard today that negotiation have begun over *Elecon* and the Industrial Relations Court action has been suspended.

Saturday 16 September

I had a telephone call from Derek Tedder saying the owners had capitulated and come up with £8,500 in back pay, had flown two extra crew over from Rotterdam, that the dockers had lifted the ban and the ship had been released by the dockers and allowed to sail. Well, that is the best story I have heard for a long time. International trade union

---

* In August 1972, President Amin of Uganda announced the expulsion of thousands of Asians living in the country, who were holding British passports. Most were settled in Britain over the following 3 months.

solidarity through the ITF; cooperation between four unions; total failure of the Government to care at all; dockers engaging in an 'unfair industrial practice' and winning their case. I was so impressed that I rang the *Evening Post* and told them they must give it a big boost. I also rang Harry Evans of the *Sunday Times* personally and said, 'Look, you panned the dockers. Here's a marvellous story: you ought to print it.' He said he would.

Tuesday 19 September

Douglas Jay telephoned to say he had just come back from Denmark where he had been studying the Referendum campaign and had attended an enormous meeting of something approaching 7,000 people. He said the campaign was going extremely well, by which he meant it was moving against, and that they would like me to go over. I thought it would be difficult, as Chairman of the Conference, to go and talk about Party policy a week before that policy was to be further clarified at Conference, but I promised to keep in touch with him.

I think, myself, that given an absolutely free hand, what the Conference would say would be, 'Look, we are opposed to entry on the Tory terms in principle. We don't like the Treaty of Rome; we don't like the Common Agricultural Policy; we don't like the terms negotiated by Rippon; we don't like the legislation. We want to be shot of the whole thing and if a future Labour Government were to try and reach an arrangement with the Community of some kind or another, we are not opposed to it in principle but we would insist that any change they proposed would have to be put to the British public.' I have a feeling that is really what Conference wants to say, so we must find resolutions that allow it to be said.

Thursday 21 September

Looked in to the House of Commons in the morning to meet a group from the Kingswood Townswomen's Guild.

In the evening Ken Coates of the Institute of Workers' Control telephoned me. The first time I heard of him was when he was expelled from the Party for writing a tremendous attack upon Harold Wilson. He got in touch with me because I came out in favour of workers' control. He is a naïve person in many ways, too ready to see good in me, but at any rate he has been a great supporter and when I stood for the deputy-leadership a year ago, he rang up one or two other people, such as John Prescott, and recommended they support me.

He rang to say he thought I was in some danger at this Conference because I was not on the *Tribune* list of candidates (they have picked seven candidates for the Executive) and he thought also that there was going to be a great move against me by the Campaign for Democratic

Socialism constituencies – the Jenkins, Taverne, Rodgers crowd – and that I might find myself squeezed and lose some votes. He said could he speak for me, could *Tribune* help in any way? I thanked him, but didn't think it would help.

I have never been on the *Tribune* list. But it did turn my mind to the question of how the list was worked out and who votes for it. The answer is, I think, by a few Labour MPs who are members of the *Tribune* Group, and Dick Clements. I don't think it is voted upon by *Tribune* readers, or anything. I did say to him that I thought that there might have to be a showdown in the Parliamentary Party and that I might have to say candidly what I thought about Party democracy, even though it would be very unpopular. It might be that I would have to be thrown out of the Shadow Cabinet in order to establish that there was a real argument going on about this, to improve my credibility with the people in the Party who think I am having it too easy – which, in a way, I am.

Friday 22 September
Submitted the speech I intend to make in Tiverton tomorrow to Transport House and all hell broke loose. Percy Clarke rang up and said that I couldn't make any reference to the leadership in my speech without clearing it with Harold – because I had said in it that the leadership of the Party should accept the Conference decision on the Common Market. Had I consulted with Harold? I sent a message back saying I hadn't, so I did authorise the removal of all references to the leadership.

Then Harry Nicholas saw it and struck out a passage in which I said that Conference had disagreed with the Labour Cabinet in the past and that Conference had sometimes been right – a thing I have said publicly on many occasions. Harry said it sounded like a bid for the leadership by me, which it certainly isn't. But I have absolutely no doubt that if Harold were to do a 'fight and fight and fight again', the Party would be split down the middle and he would carry a lot of people in the Centre and Right with him. Then the Left would come up with its candidate and there would be an attempt to find a compromise.

Saturday 23 September
I went by train to Exeter and I was taken to Tiverton for the rally. David Owen was there. I delivered my speech in which I made the case for Party democracy and argued that we should accept the EEC decision of Conference. Came back on the train. Read the whole of the Lord Longford Report on pornography, which was very poor stuff.

Sunday 24 September
The papers had large headlines: 'Benn-Wilson on Crash Course', 'Benn Warns Wilson', 'Benn Warns Jenkins'. Yesterday's speech, even as

corrected carefully by Percy Clark to delete all references to the leadership, was taken as a warning to the parliamentary leadership not to think they could disregard Conference decisions on the question of Europe. Harold had briefed Terry Lancaster saying, 'Mr Benn's advice to the Party is to stand on your head.' Harold may well feel more threatened by me than by anybody else at this moment and he is a very dirty fighter – he can get an awful lot of stuff out if he wants to.

Anyway, Eric Heffer rang up and said he was glad I said it. He said *Tribune* was being very cautious on anything that might endanger Harold's position; I said I didn't want to endanger Harold's position but we had to get the ground rules right as to how you settled an argument in the Party.

The *Daily Mirror* rang me up and asked me if the interpretation put upon my words was correct. I said it certainly was not correct. The speech is not directed at Harold. It is not a bid for the leadership. It is an attempt to get the Party to see that this issue, which is deeply divisive, has got to be settled democratically.

Monday 25 September

I had a telephone call from Michael Zander this morning, saying he hoped we wouldn't drive the European minority out of the Labour Party. I said to him that I have never voted to expel anybody or to withdraw any whip of any kind but we had to accept Conference decisions.

Watched *Panorama*, where they had an extract from my speech in Tiverton. I must say, I looked very wild with my hair all over the place. Then Roy Jenkins came on, all very smooth, attacking my views. Roy, of course, is the hero of every drawing room but whether he speaks for British people or not, I don't know.

Tuesday 26 September

The Norwegian Referendum result came out today and it was substantially against entry. Bratelli, the Norwegian Social Democratic Prime Minister, announced that he would resign, as he had pledged he would if the vote went against entry.

I dashed off from there to do a Thames Television interview with Llew Gardner in their *Today* programme. This was scheduled for six minutes but in fact they let it run for nine and a half and I was asked by Llew Gardner how it felt to be the most hated man in Britain, to which the answer was, of course, that I was only hated by Fleet Street. I didn't think it was true that I was universally loathed, and I said that nothing would ever change in Britain if people weren't prepared to disregard pressure and criticism. He was trying to nail me on the relationship between the Conference and the Parliamentary Party.

Friday 29 September

Blackpool. Woke very early and read the papers. The campaign on democracy in the Party is building up. Maurice Edelman in the *Daily Mail* wrote 'Wilson's fight'. Harry Boyne in the *Daily Telegraph* said that Denis Healey or Tony Crosland will have to take over from Harold and David Watt, predictably, in the *Financial Times* said that Party Conferences are just a charade, a fraud and nobody needs to take any notice of them.

At 10, with some quaking, I sat in the chair at the Executive in the suite at the Imperial. The television cameras were allowed in and we began what I thought might prove to be an extremely difficult meeting. After preliminary announcements, we came on to the three National Executive Committee statements to the Conference. First was the question of the Common Market and John Chalmers moved that no special statement be issued by the Executive; Lena Jeger seconded this.

Fred Mulley said, 'Surely we should at least prepare a statement because we might need it.' Harold Wilson said he was in favour of sticking where we were but the question was, where were we? So long as the National Executive could commend the statement in the Green Paper to Conference, he would be happy. Lena Jegar, Mik and Joe Gormley agreed with Harold. Harold Wilson said he hoped that I would not be too upset if the Referendum question wasn't specifically put. This was a dig, although I was expecting a great deal more.

Denis said that the main issue was of Party unity and we should seek to get endorsement if we could; we should keep the option open as to whether or not we had a statement.

We moved on to the Ugandan Asians, the whole Common Market issue really being completely over. Mik proposed there should be an NEC emergency motion and Joan Lestor and Tom Driberg agreed. In the end we decided we would set up a little drafting committee of appropriate people to produce a statement.

Then Northern Ireland. Should we have an emergency statement on that? I explained the background and John Chalmers said we should have a statement, and so it was decided that Harold and Jim would do a draft.

We finished at about 12.20. Quite amazing – no votes, no disagreements, a sweet atmosphere.

I took the press conference and I told the press this, which they found very hard to take.

Saturday 30 September

At 12.30 I went to see Harold. He was pacing up and down in his suite, in shirtsleeves. When I got there Marcia was with him. I hadn't seen her for ages. Her book has just been sent to me with two or three very friendly pages about me, and I said to her, 'How nice to see you – I haven't seen you for a year. Thank you for sending me your book: I must say your references to me in it were much kinder than in Harold's book,'* pointing at Harold but not looking at him. As a matter of fact, it is a nice book. It recreates the confidence we had in 1964 when we all thought a great deal of each other.

We talked around a bit and then I said, 'You know, Harold, I have read all these silly things about a row between you and me but I'm the only one of your colleagues who came out publicly in your support in the summer and you know very well that I have never made things difficult. I was looking back over my papers for 1960 . . .'

'So was I,' he interrupted. 'I sent for photocopies of everything that happened in 1960.'

'Well,' I said, 'I had them in my files and I read your statement when you stood against Gaitskell, and I read my statement when I supported you and we have both been saying the same thing for many years.' We talked about the Common Market resolutions, and it was altogether a friendly chat.

The remaining events at the Labour Party Conference and for the following three weeks were not dictated for my diary until the end of October, from detailed notes made throughout the month. There is therefore a retrospective element in the diary entries as I looked back on the last month of my chairmanship of the Party and Conference.

Sunday 1 October

This morning Caroline and I went to the church service where Harold read one lesson and Ted Short the other. From the point of view of the folk culture of the country, I felt it washing over me with familiarity, and the ritual was very steady and reliable and comfortable; but the actual political message of the prayers is appalling and this is the great difficulty of the Christian faith at this moment.

Donald Soper gave a very good sermon.

The press coverage this morning continues to suggest that the clash lies between Harold Wilson, who is trying to defeat the extreme resolution on the Common Market, and me, trying to tie the whole of the Party to the AUEW resolution calling for us to withdraw if we are in the Market when we come to power. That actually is not my view and never has been but I am determined to make clear to the Conference before it begins that we shall take seriously what it says, and in that case

---

* *The Labour Government* by Harold Wilson, 1971. Marcia Williams's book was *Inside Number Ten*. She subsequently published a second autobiographical account called *Downing Street in Perspective*, 1983.

we are more likely to get delegates to vote seriously instead of engaging in the overkill which Peter Shore wants.

I went to the Executive – the last full Executive over which I was to preside. It was dominated by the resolutions on the Common Market, but was nevertheless an even-natured meeting. My chairmanship was good, to be honest, and I was complimented on it. We settled our line on everything. The question now is, will the AUEW support the Boiler-makers' resolution, calling for opposition to the Market on the present terms and for the assent of the British people to renegotiated entry arrangements, as well as their own resolution. And will Jack Jones support the AUEW, which declares total opposition and demands withdrawal from the Market in future, as well as the Boilermaker's resolution? This is really what the voting is all about.

I went to the National Executive reception in the evening and spoke briefly. Then on to the Transport and General Workers' Union reception.

I went back to my suite to complete work on my Chairman's Address. Finally, at 2 am, I took it to Percy Clark to get it typed.

Stephen and a friend turned up and spent the night on the floor of the hotel room.

Monday 2 October
We had the formal opening of the Conference and I made my Chairman's speech. After the expectations the press had built up following Tiverton, my speech was thought to be a slight anti-climax. That is one of the difficulties about press coverage: the Tiverton speech was meant to say that we must accept the whole policy-making role of Conference but the press had built it up as a challenge to Harold and were preparing themselves for Harold's great triumph, in which he would emerge as the man who saved the Party from extremism. So the Conference was worried because it had seen all this and began recalling the 1960 days.

Jim Callaghan, in a long and enormously boring speech, moved 'Labour's Programme for Britain' and took an hour and five minutes – he had been allowed about thirty-five. It was an absolute abuse of Executive privilege.

In the afternoon we had the housing debate and there was an uproar because I had announced that the Executive had put certain reserv-ations forward and when the vote was taken and the resolution was carried, the mover and seconder wanted to know whether the reserv-ations were binding or not. I said this was a very important matter on which I would like to give a ruling the next day.

Went to the *Labour Weekly* reception and there was a big cake for their first anniversary. I said to Harold, 'You stick the knife in for a change,

Harold.' Harold laughed, mainly because he thought it was an incredible piece of effrontery to make such a joke. At any rate, he did, and the story appeared in *Labour Weekly*.

That was the end of the first day of Conference. Clearly it got off to a reasonably good start but people are inevitably waiting for Wednesday's debate on the Common Market. I now see, after my first day as Chairman, that there is a very great deal of scope for democratising the Labour Party through democratising its procedure at Conference, and I intend to pursue this and write a paper for the Executive.

Tuesday 3 October

At 9.30 I gave my ruling on the Executive's reservations and explained that the mover of the resolution had to be asked whether he approved of these reservations: if he did not approve them, then the Executive automatically asked Conference to reject the resolution in question. I applied this to the whole question of the housing resolution which related to the compensation for Councillors, following their possible non-implementation of the Housing Finance Act. Since the mover did not accept the reservation, I had to ask the Conference, on behalf of the Executive, to reject the resolution but the platform was overturned by about 4 million to 1 million.

Harold made his great Parliamentary Report speech – enormously long, terribly carefully prepared, with forty-four references to Heath in it, and not a single idea to present to the Party. But the Conference liked it as they always do. It was a set piece which is what the press like and what the Party is used to and it appears to show his command of the situation. I think it offers very little that is constructive but still it was very funny and we gave him a standing ovation, which is also all part of the ritual.

In the afternoon we had the private session, which, without the television lights and in the quietness of the hall, seemed very dull and unimportant.

I went to the UPW-POEU party. Innes McBeath, who is the Industrial Correspondent of *The Times*, told me that the NUJ chapel, I think, at *The Times* had protested to the Editor at the way in which I had been treated in the last week or two – but it had no effect. Still, it was interesting that this should have happened.

Clive Jenkins was there and I remarked to Clive that I inevitably felt inadequate for the job I was doing. He said, 'What do you mean inadequate?'

'Well, I don't feel I am as good as my job requires.'

'I never feel inadequate.' he said.

I said, 'Well, I make mistakes.'

'We all make a few mistakes, but I don't feel inadequate.'

So I replied, 'Well, the credibility of a man who admits his mistakes is slightly greater if, in advance, he has confessed he was inadequate.'

He laughed, 'Oh, I must write that down.' Then he turned to Ray Buckton, General Secretary of ASLEF, and asked Ray, 'Do you feel inadequate?'

Ray said, 'Yes, of course I do.'

He asked Muriel Turner, ASTMS's National Officer, if she felt inadequate and she answered, 'Of course I do.'

Clive got very agitated. He repeated, 'I don't feel inadequate.'

I had a talk to Jack Jones about the block vote. Jack is very remote and hard to get through to. I respect him very much but I think he is hard pressed, he's tired and he doesn't easily open up to people. I said we would have to look at the block vote one day, not with a view to reducing trade union influence but to see that it is exercised more democratically. He doesn't really dissent from that.

Wednesday 4 October

We had the debate on the Common Market. I formally moved the statement and then we had Composite 43, moved by Clackmannan and East Stirlingshire, the Boilermakers' resolution, moved by Danny McGarvey, and the Engineers' resolution. The debate was thrown open and we got through it very well. I said at the beginning of the debate that I didn't intend to call many MPs but I knew that the Conference would obviously want to hear from Roy Jenkins and Michael Foot.

I had not actually had a 'request to speak' card from Michael Foot but I had had a hand-written note and I had not had a card at all from Roy; indeed, I had heard rumours that Roy didn't wish to speak. So I asked Gwyn Morgan, who was sitting next to me, whether he'd send a message to Roy. He said he didn't know whether he wanted to speak, so I said, 'Well, that's entirely up to him, but would you send a message, to ask him when he would like to speak, and I will call him.' A message came back saying he didn't want to speak. I said to the Conference, 'As Roy has indicated that he doesn't wish to speak, I will call Willy Hamilton to speak against the resolutions.'

Apparently at that moment people who were sitting near Roy shouted, 'Chicken, coward,' and he was absolutely furious. This became quite an issue – had I done it deliberately or not? Well in fact, I did decide in the morning that I would do this because Roy had been attacking me all week for new levels of censorship, for trying to shut him up and for intolerance. So I decided I would put that to the test by making it clear that I had offered to call him to speak and let him face the consequences of not speaking. I knew his line – the 'low profile' which means you are afraid of the mass audience and you just want to talk in private little groups about your principles and integrity. Also Roy has been attacking me for a total failure of leadership. I had failed, he argued, to give leadership to the Conference of the Party; he by contrast was always giving leadership. The plain truth is that he hasn't spoken at Conference about the Common Market for years, certainly not since he got anywhere near the top, and whatever people may say about me, I have certainly never lacked the guts to say what I thought. So, in fact, it was a prepared manoeuvre if you like; it's a crude way of putting it but it was a prepared decision – if he refused to be called – to expose the fact that he wouldn't speak. I wasn't absolutely sure that he didn't want to; that is the plain truth for the history books, in case anyone wants to know. And I am not at all sorry.

Anyway, I called Willy Hamilton instead, and he delivered an attack on me but it made a friend of him for life, so Frank McElhone assured me!

In the end the Executive statesman and the Boilermakers resolution* were carried and the AUEW was defeated. Jack Jones had been to see Harold and Harold had given him some assurances about this and that, and no doubt twisted his arm. So Jack had agreed not to vote for the AUEW, there being no love lost between him and Hugh Scanlon at the moment.

After the morning session, Glyn Williams, Chairman of the Conference Arrangements Committee, came up to me and said that the Committee had received a number of complaints from delegates about the 'request to speak' cards which I had introduced and the Committee wished to recommend to Conference that I should discontinue the practice. I said, 'That's up to you to recommend it but who is called is entirely up to me as Chairman; make a statement at the end of the lunchtime session.' This was the way in which the trade union leadership was boiling up against me. So he did make a statement and recommended the ending of the 'request to speak' cards. I replied to the delegates, 'Well, it's for Conference, obviously, to decide but I hope we can go on with it because otherwise the only people who write to me are people who know me or have got some influence, and this is a way of helping the rank-and-file delegates to be called.' On a show of hands the Conference turned down the Conference Arrangements Committee

---

* 'This Conference declares its opposition to entry to the Common Market on the terms negotiated by the Tories and calls on a future Labour Government to reverse any decision for Britain to join unless new terms have been negotiated including the abandonment of the Common Agricultural Policy and the Value Added Tax, no limitations on the freedom of a Labour Government to carry out economic plans, regional development, extension of the public sector, control of capital movement, and the preservation of the power of the British Parliament over its legislation and taxation, and, meanwhile, to halt immediately the entry arrangements including all payments to the European Communities, and participation in their Institutions in particular the European Parliament, until such terms have been negotiated, and the assent of the British electorate has been given.'

recommendation. A great achievement, because normally the Chairman represents the Executive and the Conference Arrangements Committee represent the rank-and-file delegates. But the rank and file had by this time come to trust me sufficiently to support me.

I announced at the end of Wednesday that I would be available from 8.30 in the morning for any delegates who wished to raise points of order with me to save time and sort out difficulties. This was another innovation – the Chairman's surgery – and was welcomed. I must add that the only problem I was running into at this stage of the Conference was that people were angry that there had not been an opportunity to debate the question of MPs' behaviour and Party democracy. I had said on Monday that this would come up at the private session and it hadn't been reached.

I had a talk to Jimmy Reid and the UCS people who were down. They were meeting Wayne Harbin, President of Marathon oil-rig builders, that night. I had an amusing exchange with them. We were talking and I was advising them as best I could; they were all my old buddies. Then Jimmy Airlie said, 'There's a photographer here, do you want a photograph?' So Jimmy Reid said, 'We're seeing Chataway tomorrow and it might be embarrassing if we were photographed with you.' I said, 'That's fine. A year ago I was wondering whether it was respectable to be seen with you but if now it's the other way round and you don't want to be seen with me, that's a very great tribute that I shouldn't be respectable enough for you.' They saw the point immediately and they laughed, and they got the photographer.

Friday 6 October
We had Harry Nicholas's farewell speech in which he meant to be friendly but it came out in a way that revealed him for the male chauvinist pig that he is – with all the cheap jokes about women. Made Caroline cringe.

I had heard rumours of Taverne's imminent resignation and so I had asked various journalists to keep their eyes open and Mary Lou to feed me immediate information on the platform in case Taverne did make a statement before the end of the Conference. I waited anxiously all morning. Tony Banks, a Labour Councillor, moved his point of order asking whether the changes I had made in Conference procedure would continue in future years. I said that was a genuine point of order but it was not for me, it was for the next Chairman. This was designed to boost my chairmanship, which had come in for a lot of criticism.

Then at about 12.15 I began getting news that Taverne had called a press conference. All the press lobby had gone to London to listen to it. He announced that he would be standing as a Democratic Labour candidate, and he attacked the Party. Mary Lou sent me a garbled

"My patience is exhausted! If you dare to praise the Tories or criticise our great National Socialist Party, my stormtroopers will burn down Fleet Street, the B.B.C. and ITV!"

typed account of what he had said but it was enough to indicate that his plan had been to see the Labour Conference end on a phoney vote of unity and then wreck it all by his statement. So I decided – without telling Caroline or anyone else – that I would make this the occasion for a comment on Taverne and also on the role of the mass media; because last weekend *The Times* had published its survey showing that there would be tremendous support for a new Centre-Left-Liberal type party, and I knew that John Torode was involved in helping Taverne in preparing a television programme this weekend.

So when it came to me to speak, I made my proper Chairman's remarks of thanking everybody and then I said the Conference had wanted socialism; wanted unity; wanted us to work hard together and wanted an Election. I said by chance, not of our making, the opportunity for the latter had come with the announcement this morning, a few minutes ago, that there would be a by-election in Lincoln. 'I say nothing about our departing colleague except for a tinge of sadness; but others have tried to damage us before and haven't succeeded.' They cheered and cheered at all this. Then I said, 'This is more than that because it is the first time that the mass media has actually put up a candidate in the election. I wish the workers in the media would sometimes remember that they are members of the working class and have a sense of responsibility to see that what is said about us is true.' This led to another great wave of cheering. Then I went on to say that the mass media was difficult to deal with when it was selling their papers or producing their programmes but if they actually put up a candidate, then we should have a chance of defeating them.

Then I brought the Conference to its feet to sing 'The Red Flag'.

It was quite clear to me that the people on the platform were absolutely livid at my speech. Harold apparently had been smoking his pipe furiously and everyone else was angry that I had raised the temperature by mentioning Taverne. What I gathered was that they still regarded Taverne as a member of the Party and an attack on Taverne was reopening inner Party splits, which they wanted to play down. Also they were annoyed about the reference to the mass media because they don't want trouble with the media and they are all gutless.

We packed up, and caught the special train home. When we got to London, the *Evening Standard* was already running my 'amazing' outburst against the press and my 'savage personal attack' on Taverne.

We were very tired. Caroline thought that a period of silence was required. She thought I had really perhaps made a mistake in ending the Conference in the way I had done. I think that was also the view of Mary Lou, Frances Morrell and one or two others.

Saturday 7 October
There was tremendous coverage this morning of my Blackpool speech, the *Telegraph* charging me with inciting workers to strike against the press.

Sunday 8 October
I did *The World This Weekend* and I was asked about my views. I said I was certainly against censorship by striking but there was a question of moral responsibility.

The *Sunday Express* had a big headline: 'Benn Must Go – Move Gathers Force' and a nasty cartoon of me. Really enormous press attacks.

The massive press criticism which was directed at my final speech continued unabated for some days. The media generally were particularly enraged at my urging journalists and printworkers to consider carefully their position when invited to write or print lies about the Labour Movement. This was seen as a direct attack on the freedom of the press, although it was a reference to the role of the proprietors. Nevertheless, Harold Wilson was acutely embarrassed and made it clear that he wished to be dissociated from it.

The Common Market argument raged throughout the remaining three months of the year and beyond. One interesting footnote to it is contained in a letter I received from a correspondent enclosing another from Lord Fisher, former Archbishop of Canterbury, who turned out to have been very much opposed to the Common Market.

I am very glad you approved of my letter in *The Times* of 18 April. I feel as strongly as you do about the need to save the nation from being deprived of its sovereignty, its identity, its self-possession. This is not selfishness at all; it is self respect. *The Times*' reports from Europe in the last two weeks warn us against 'going to Europe for our politics and even for our business'.

In no sense do I have the ear of the Queen now except, I suppose, as a member of the Privy Council.

Yours sincerely,
Fisher of Lambeth

NOTES
Chapter Five

1. (p. 438) The Industrial Relations Act of 1971 included penal sanctions against trade unions if they failed to comply with the judgments of the National Industrial Relations Court which was set up under the Act and over which Sir John Donaldson presided.

In 1972 a major dispute arose over 'containerisation', the process by which cargo was stored in containers at inland depots instead of at the dockside, and as some of the employers owning these container depots were the same people who owned the old docks, London dockers naturally felt that their jobs were being stolen.

This led to a strike in the London Docks in June 1972, as a result of which the employers sought and received an interim order from the Industrial Relations Court restraining picketing. However, the picketing continued and as a result of the defiance of the court order, five dockers were imprisoned at Pentonville. There was an uproar in the Labour Movement, with the TUC calling for general strike action if the men were not released. The NEC, under my chairmanship, reinforced this demand.

The Government, clearly worried by the reaction to this imprisonment, introduced a figure called the Official Solicitor whom very few people outside the legal profession had ever heard of before, and whose functions were wholly unclear, but he made representations to the Court on behalf of the prisoners which led to their quick release.

They were carried shoulder-high from the prison gates and it was regarded, quite properly, as a great victory.

2. (p. 439) Dick Taverne, QC, was elected as Labour MP for Lincoln in 1962. He had assisted me during my peerage battle and I had therefore known him for many years. A pro-Marketeer, he voted in October 1971 against the three-line whip, along with other Labour MPs, in favour of Common Market entry. This action incensed his local constituency Party, which decided to call on him to retire to clear the way for the selection of a new parliamentary candidate.

Taverne was the only one of the pro-EEC rebels to run into this difficulty with his local Party and he appealed to the National Executive to uphold him against the Lincoln constituency, which the NEC refused to do. He therefore decided to resign from the Labour Party and from Parliament and stand for Lincoln as a 'Democratic Labour' candidate. At the by-election in March 1973 he was returned but lost the seat to Margaret Jackson (Labour) in 1974. Taverne subsequently joined the SDP.

Principal Persons

(I) Political and Official

Each person is named according to his or her status as the diaries open. A full list of Government Members as at January 1968 and January 1970, some of whom do not appear here since they do not feature prominently in this volume, is given in Appendix I. The terminology here and throughout the main text conforms to usage at the time.

ADAMSON, Campbell. Industrialist. Director General of the Confederation of British Industry and member of the National Economic Development Council, 1969–76. Seconded to the Department of Economic Affairs as industrial adviser, 1967–9. Subsequently Chairman of Abbey National Building Society.

ALLAUN, Frank. President of Labour Action for Peace since 1965. CND activist. Chairman of the Labour Party, 1978/9, and Labour MP for Salford East, 1955–83.

ALLEN, John Scholefield. Political and economic research assistant to the Labour Party before the 1964 Election. Subsequently attached to the Cabinet Office, 1964–70.

ARMSTRONG, Sir William (1915–1980). Head of the Home Civil Service and Permanent Secretary of the Civil Service Department, 1968–74. Joint Permanent Secretary of the Treasury, 1962–8. Created a life peer in 1975.

ARNOLD-FORSTER, Mark (1920–1981). Senior journalist and political commentator on the *Guardian*, the *Observer* and ITN, 1946–81. Distinguished service with the Royal Navy while engaged on secret missions during the Second World War. Married to Val Arnold-Forster, journalist. Family friends.

ATTLEE, Earl (1883–1967). Clement Attlee, Leader of the Labour

Party, 1935–55 and Prime Minister, 1945–51. MP for Limehouse, subsequently West Walthamstow, 1922–55. Created an Earl in 1955.

BACON, Alice. Minister of State in the Home Office, 1964–7 and Education and Science, 1967–70. Labour MP for Leeds, 1945–70. Chairman of the Labour Party, 1950/51. Created Baroness Bacon of Leeds and Normanton in 1970.

BALOGH, Thomas (Tommy) (1905–1985). Oxford economist of Hungarian birth, close adviser to Harold Wilson in the 1950s and early 1960s, and Economic Adviser to the Cabinet, 1964–8. Created a life peer in 1968. Minister of State at the Department of Energy, 1974–5, and Deputy Chairman, British National Oil Company, 1976–8.

BARBER, Anthony. Chancellor of the Exchequer, 1970–74, replacing Iain Macleod who died in July 1970. A former PPS to Harold Macmillan, Financial Secretary to the Treasury, 1962–3. Conservative MP for Doncaster, 1951–64 and Altrincham and Sale, 1965–74. Created a life peer in 1974.

BARKER, Dame Sara (1903–1973). National Agent for the Labour Party, 1962–9.

BERKELEY, Humphry. Conservative of liberal views, MP for Lancaster, 1959–66. Left the Conservative Party in 1970; in 1974 unsuccessfully fought North Fylde for Labour. Joined the SDP in 1981.

BESWICK, Lord (Frank Beswick) (1912–1987). Government Chief Whip in House of Lords, 1967–70. Minister of State for Industry, 1974–5, subsequently Chairman of British Aerospace. Labour Co-operative MP for Uxbridge, 1945–59. Created a life peer in 1964.

BLACKETT, Patrick (1897–1972). Chief Scientific Adviser at the Ministry of Technology. Pre-eminent nuclear scientist. President of the Royal Society, 1965–70. Created a life peer in 1969.

BONHAM CARTER, Violet (1887–1969). Leading Liberal, President of the Liberal Party, 1945–7. Active in the League of Nations and United Nations. Daughter of Liberal Prime Minister, Herbert Asquith, mother-in-law of Liberal Leader, Jo Grimond. Created a life peer in 1964, as Lady Asquith.

BOWEN, Gordon. Permanent Under-Secretary, Ministry of Technology, 1966–9, formerly at the Board of Trade. Director of the Metrication Board. 1969–74.

BRADDOCK, Bessie (1899–1970). Labour MP for Liverpool

Exchange, 1945–70. Long-standing member of the National Executive.

BRAY, Jeremy. Joint Parliamentary Secretary at the Ministry of Technology, 1967–9, dismissed by Harold Wilson in 1969 for writing a book, *Decision in Government*. Labour MP for Middlesbrough West, 1962–70, for Motherwell and Wishaw, subsequently Motherwell South, since October 1974.

BROCKWAY, Fenner (1888–1988). Life-long campaigner for peace and founder of the Movement for Colonial Freedom in the 1950s. Labour MP for East Leyton, 1929–31, and for Eton and Slough, 1950–64. Leading member of the Independent Labour Party between 1922 and 1946. Created a life peer in 1964.

BROWN, George (1914–1985). Deputy-Leader of the Labour Party, 1960–70, and in that capacity member of the National Executive and Chairman of the Home Policy Committee. Held office in the 1945–51 Government, finally as Minister of Works. First Secretary of State at the Department of Economic Affairs, 1964–6, and Foreign Secretary, 1966–8. Ardently pro-Common Market: tried to negotiate Britain's entry in 1967. Labour MP for Belper, 1945–70. Created a life peer, Lord George-Brown, in 1970. Resigned from the Labour Party in 1976 and later joined the SDP.

BROWN, Sir Stephen. Industrialist. President of the Confederation of British Industry, 1966–8, and member of the National Economic Development Council, 1966–71.

BUTLER, David. Political scientist and broadcaster, whose special subject is the study of elections; the first person to coin the term 'psephology'. Has published study of every British General Election since 1951. Life-long friend. Married to Marilyn Butler.

CALLAGHAN, James. Chancellor of the Exchequer, 1964–7, Home Secretary, 1967–70, Foreign Secretary, 1974–6, Prime Minister, 1976–9 and Leader of the Labour Party until 1980. Held junior posts in the 1945–51 Labour Government. Chairman of the Labour Party, 1973/4 and Labour MP for South, South-East and again South Cardiff, 1945–87. Father of the House, 1983–7. Made a Knight of the Garter and a life peer in 1987.

CASTLE, Barbara. Minister of Overseas Development, 1964–5, Minister of Transport, 1965–8, First Secretary of State at the Department of Employment and Productivity, 1968–70. Chairman of the Labour Party, 1958/9. Secretary of State for Social Services, 1974–6, dismissed by James Callaghan when he formed his Government in

1976. Labour MP for Blackburn, 1945–79. Leader of the British Labour Group in the European Parliament, 1979–85.

CATHERWOOD, Fred. Industrialist and Chief Industrial Adviser at the Department of Economic Affairs, 1964–6. Member of the Advisory Council on Technology and Director-General of the National Economic Development Council, 1966–71.

CHAPPLE, Frank. General Secretary of the Electrical, Electronic Telecommunications and Plumbing Trade Union, 1966–84. Member of the National Economic Development Council, 1979–83. Created a life peer in 1985.

CHATAWAY, Chris. Minister of Posts and Telecommunications, 1970–72, and of Industrial Development at the Department of Trade and Industry, 1972–4. Former Olympic athlete. Under-Secretary of State at Education and Science, 1962–4. Conservative MP for Lewisham North, 1959–66; Chichester 1969–74.

CLARKE, Lucille. Private secretary in Tony Benn's parliamentary office for many years from 1968. A South African, moved to London for political reasons. Died in 1987.

CLARK, Percy (1917–1985). Director of Publicity of the Labour Party 1965–79.

CLARKE, Sir Richard (Otto) (1910–1975). Permanent Secrtary at the Ministry of Technology. Formerly a senior Treasury official. Retired 1970.

CONSTABLE, Douglas. Curate at the Church of Christ the Servant in Stockwood, Bristol; a member of Bristol South East Labour Party. Later became Vicar of St Thomas' Church, Derby.

COUSINS, Frank (1904–1986). General Secretary of the Transport and General Workers' Union, brought into the Labour Cabinet as Minister of Technology in 1964. Resigned in 1966 over the wage freeze and returned to the Union until his retirement in 1969. Labour MP for Nuneaton, 1965–6.

CROSLAND, Anthony (1918–1977). Minister of State for Economic Affairs, 1964–6, Secretary of State for Education and Science, 1965–7, President of the Board of Trade, 1967–9 and Secretary of State for Local Government, 1969–70. In the 1974–9 Labour Government he was Secretary of State for the Environment till 1976 and then Foreign Secretary, in which post he died suddenly in February 1977. Labour MP for South Gloucester, 1950–55 and

Grimsby, 1959–77. Married journalist Susan Barnes in 1964. A personal friend since the war years.

CROSSMAN, Richard (1907–1974). Minister of Housing and Local Government, 1964–6, Lord President of the Council and Leader of the House of Commons, 1966–8, Secretary of State for Health and Social Security, 1968–70. Chairman of the Labour Party, 1960/61. He published three volumes of diaries describing his years as a Cabinet Minister. Labour MP for Coventry, 1945–74. An Oxford academic, he wrote *Government and the Governed*, 1939. Became Editor of the *New Statesman*, 1970. Married to Anne Crossman.

CUDLIPP, Hugh. Succeeded Cecil King as Chairman of Daily Mirror Newspapers, 1963–8. Deputy Chairman, then Chairman of International Publishing Corporation (IPC), 1964–73. Created a life peer in 1974.

DALYELL, Tam. PPS to Richard Crossman 1964–70. Labour MP for West Lothian, 1962–83, and Linlithgow since 1983.

DAVIES, John (1916–1979). Director-General of the Confederation of British Industry, 1965–9. Elected as an MP in June 1970 and went direct into Cabinet as Minister of Technology from July to October 1970, when Mintech was abolished. Secretary of State for Industry, 1970–72, Chancellor of the Duchy of Lancaster with responsibility for Europe, 1972–4. Member of the National Economic Development Council, 1962–72. Conservative MP for Knutsford, 1970–78.

DELL, Edmund. Joint Parliamentary Secretary at the Ministry of Technology, 1966–7, Joint Under-Secretary of State at the Department of Economic Affairs, 1967–8, Minister of State at the Board of Trade, 1968–9, and at Employment and Productivity, 1969–70. Secretary of State for Trade in the 1974–9 Government, resigning in 1978 to take up an appointment as Deputy Chairman of Guinness Mahon; later joined the SDP.

DIAMOND, Jack. Chief Secretary to the Treasury, 1964–70. Labour MP for Blackley, 1945–51, Gloucester, 1957–70. Chaired the Royal Commission on the Distribution of Income and Wealth, 1974–9. Created a life peer in 1970 and became Leader of the SDP in the House of Lords.

DONOUGHUE, Bernard. Senior member of staff at the London School of Economics, 1963–74. Senior policy adviser to the Prime Minister 1974–9. Created a life peer in 1985.

ENNALS, David. Secretary of the Labour Party's International Department, 1958–64. PPS to Barbara Castle, 1964–6. Under-

Secretary of State at Defence, 1966, and at the Home Office, 1967. Minister of State at the Department of Health and Social Security, 1968–70. In the 1974–9 Government he was Minister of State at the Foreign and Commonwealth Office and Secretary of State for the Social Services, 1976–9. Labour MP for Dover, 1964–70 and Norwich North, 1974–83. Created a life peer in 1983.

EVANS, Ioan (1927–1984). PPS to Tony Benn as Postmaster-General. A Government Whip, 1968–70. Labour MP for Yardley, 1964–70, Aberdare, 1974–83 and Cynon Valley, 1983–4.

FEATHER, Vic (1908–1976). Assistant General Secretary of the TUC, 1960–69. General Secretary, 1969–73 and member of the National Economic Development Council. Created a life peer in 1974.

FOOT, Sir Dingle (1905–1978). Solicitor-General, 1964–7. Labour MP for Ipswich, 1957–70, previously Liberal MP for Dundee, 1931–45. Brother of Michael and Hugh Foot.

FOOT, Michael. Back Bencher during the 1964–70 Labour Government. Held posts in 1974–9 Government as Secretary of State for Employment, 1974–6, Lord President of the Council and Leader of the House of Commons, 1976–9. Deputy-Leader of the Labour Party, 1979–80, and Leader, 1980–83. Member of the National Executive, 1971–83. Labour MP for Devonport, 1945–55, Ebbw Vale, 1960–83, and Blaenau Gwent since 1983. Author and journalist; close friend and biographer of Aneurin Bevan.

GARDINER, Gerald. Lord Chancellor, 1964–70. Created a life peer in 1963. Former Chairman of the National Campaign for the Abolition of Capital Punishment and from 1973–8 Chancellor of the Open University.

GOFTON, Eunice. A senior private secretary in Tony Benn's office at the Ministry of Technology, 1966–70, responsible for planning engagements and meetings.

GORDON WALKER, Patrick (1907–1980). Foreign Secretary, October 1964–January 1965. He was defeated in the 1964 Election as Labour MP for Smethwick, a seat he had held since 1945, and was therefore a Cabinet member without a constituency. Fought and lost Leyton, 1965 but elected Labour MP for Leyton, 1966–74. Returned to Cabinet as Secretary of State for Education and Science, 1967–8. Created a life peer in 1974.

GORMLEY, Joe. President of the North West area of the National Union of Mineworkers, 1961–71, and subsequently of the NUM,

1971–82. Member of the National Executive, 1963–73. Created a life peer in 1982.

GREENE, Sir Hugh (1910–1987). Director-General of the BBC, 1960–69. *Daily Telegraph* correspondent in Germany in the 1930s, appointed Head of BBC German Service in 1940.

GREENWOOD, Anthony (1911–1982). Colonial Secretary, 1964–5, Minister for Overseas Development, 1965–6, and Minister of Housing and Local Government, 1966–70. Chairman of the Labour Party, 1963/4. Labour MP for Heywood and Radcliffe, subsequently Rossendale, 1946–70. Son of Arthur Greenwood, a Labour leader of the 1930s and 1940s. Created a life peer in 1970.

GRIERSON, Ronald. Director of Warburg, Deputy Chairman of the Industrial Reorganisation Corporation, appointed by the Labour Government, 1966–7.

GRIMOND, Jo. Leader of the Liberal Party, 1956–67. Liberal MP for Orkney and Shetland, 1950–83. Created a life peer in 1983. Son-in-law of Lady Violet Bonham Carter.

GUNTER, Ray (1909–1977). Minister of Labour, 1964–8, and Minister of Power for two months in 1968 before resigning from the Government. Member of the National Executive, 1955–66. Labour MP for Essex South East, 1945–50, Doncaster, 1950–51, Southwark, 1959–72. Resigned from the Labour Party, 1972.

HAILSHAM, Lord. As Quintin Hogg sat as Conservative MP for St Marylebone, 1963–70, after disclaiming his peerages in 1963 during the contest for the Conservative Party leadership. Previously sat as MP for Oxford City, 1938 to 1950, when he succeeded his father as 2nd Viscount Hailsham. Held ministerial posts in the House of Lords during the 1951–64 Conservative Governments, including Secretary of State for Education in 1964. Returned to the Lords with a life peerage in 1970. Lord Chancellor, 1970–74 and 1979–87.

HARRIMAN, Sir George (1908–1973). Chairman of the British Motor Corporation from 1961 and of British Motor Holdings, 1967–8. President of British Leyland Motor Corporation, 1968–73.

HARRIS, John. Labour Party's Director of Publicity, 1962–4. Special Assistant to Michael Stewart, 1964–5, and to Roy Jenkins, 1965–70. Created a life peer in 1974, and was Minister of State at the Home Office, 1974–9. Joined the SDP in 1981.

HART, Judith. Joint Under-Secretary of State for Scotland, 1964–6, Minister of State for Commonwealth Affairs, 1966–7, Minister of

Social Security, 1967–8, Paymaster General, 1968–9, Minister for Overseas Development, 1969–70. In the 1974–9 Government she was Minister for Overseas Development, 1974–5 and 1977–9. Chairman of the Labour Party, 1981/82. Labour MP for Lanark, 1959–83, Clydesdale, 1983–7. Married to Tony Hart, scientist and leading anti-nuclear campaigner.

HEALEY, Denis. Secretary of State for Defence, 1964–70. Chancellor of the Exchequer, 1974–9. Deputy Leader of the Labour Party, 1980–83, member of the National Executive, 1970–75, and as Deputy Leader. Labour MP for Leeds South East, 1952–5, and Leeds East since 1955.

HEATH, Edward. Succeeded Alec Douglas-Home as Leader of the Conservative Party in 1965 and continued until his defeat by Margaret Thatcher in 1975. Prime Minister, 1970–74. Back Bencher since 1975. Minister of Labour, 1959–60, Lord Privy Seal, 1960–63, and Secretary of State for Industry and Trade and President of the Board of Trade, 1963–4. Conservative MP for Bexley, subsequently Old Bexley and Sidcup, since 1950.

HELSBY, Sir Laurence (1908–1978). Joint Permanent Secretary to the Treasury (with Sir William Armstrong) and Head of the Civil Service, 1963–8. Created a life peer in 1968.

HILL of Luton, Lord (Charles Hill). Chairman of the Independent Television Authority, 1963–7, moving to the BBC as Chairman of Governors, 1967–72. Physician, the original 'Radio Doctor', and Liberal and Conservative MP for Luton, 1950–63. Created a life peer in 1963.

HILL, John. Chairman of the UK Atomic Energy Authority, 1967–81, and of British Nuclear Fuels, 1971–83. Member of the Advisory Council on Technology, 1968–70.

HOME, Lord (Sir Alec Douglas-Home). Foreign Secretary, 1960–63, in the House of Lords. Before inheriting his peerage in 1951, the Earldom of Home, he was Conservative/Unionist MP for Lanark, 1931–51, using his courtesy title of Viscount Dunglass. He succeeded Macmillan and renounced his title in 1963. Prime Minister from October 1963 until October 1964, and MP for Kinross and West Perthshire, 1963–74. In 1974 he was created a life peer and re-entered the Lords as Home of the Hirsel.

HOUGHTON, Douglas. Chancellor of the Duchy of Lancaster, 1964–6, Minister without Portfolio, 1966–7. Chairman of the House of Commons Public Accounts Committee, 1963–4. Labour MP for Sowerby, 1949–74. Created a life peer in 1974.

JAY, Douglas. President of the Board of Trade, 1964–7. 'Resigned' in the reshuffle of August 1967 and returned to the Back Benches. Leading anti-Common Marketeer in the Labour Government. Labour MP for North Battersea, 1946–83. Created a life peer in 1987.

JEGER, Lena. Labour MP for St Pancras and Holborn South, 1953–9 and 1964–74 and for Camden, Holborn and St Pancras South, 1974–9. Chairman of the Labour Party, 1979/80. Created a life peer in 1979.

JENKINS, Roy. Minister of Aviation, 1964–5, Home Secretary, 1965–7, Chancellor of the Exchequer, 1967–70, Home Secretary, 1974–6. In 1976 he became President of the European Commission. Deputy Leader of the Labour Party, 1970–72, in which capacity he sat on the National Executive. Labour MP for Central Southwark, 1948–50, for Stechford, 1950–76, Leader of the SDP, 1981–3, and SDP MP for Glasgow Hillhead, 1982–7. Created a life peer in 1987.

JONES, Sir Elwyn. Attorney-General, 1964–70. Labour MP for Plaistow, 1945–50, for West Ham South, 1950–74 and for Newham South, February to May 1974, when he was created a life peer, Lord Elwyn-Jones, and appointed Lord Chancellor, a post he held until 1979.

JONES, Jack. Assistant General Secretary of the Transport and General Workers' Union, 1963–9, succeeded Frank Cousins as General Secretary in 1969. Member of the Labour Party National Executive, 1964–7, when he went on the Trades Union Congress General Council. Vice-President of Age Concern since 1978.

JOSEPH, Sir Keith. Secretary of State for Social Services, 1970–74, for Industry, 1979–81 and Education and Science 1981–6. From 1959–64 served as Parliamentary Secretary and as Minister of Housing and Local Government and of Welsh Affairs. Conservative MP for Leeds North-East, 1956–87. Created a life peer in 1987.

KAUFMAN, Gerald. Labour Party press officer, 1965–70. Previously journalist on *Daily Mirror* and *New Statesman*. Minister of State, Department of Industry, 1975–9. Labour MP for Manchester Ardwick, 1970–83, and Manchester Gorton since 1983.

KEARTON, Sir Frank. A distinguished public servant. Chairman of Courtaulds, 1964–75, and served on the Atomic Energy Authority, and the Central Electricity Generating Board, 1955–81. First Chairman of the Industrial Reorganisation Corporation, 1966–8. Member of the Advisory Council on Technology. In 1975 he became the first Chairman of the British National Oil Corporation. Created a life peer in 1970.

KEITH of Castleacre, Lord (Kenneth Keith). Industrialist and banker. Member of National Economic Development Council, 1964–71. Chairman of Hill Samuel 1970–80, of Rolls Royce Ltd 1972–80, and of Standard Telephones and Cables since 1985. Created a life peer in 1980.

KING, Cecil (1901–1987). Chairman, International Publishing Corporation (IPC), 1963–8. A director of the Bank of England, 1965–8. Chairman of Daily Mirror Newspapers Limited, 1951–63.

KNIGHTON, William. Principal Private Secretary to Tony Benn at the Ministry of Technology, 1966–8. Subsequently became a Deputy Secretary.

LEE, Jennie (1904–1988). Parliamentary Secretary at the Ministry of Public Building and Works, 1964–5. Under-Secretary, then Minister at the Department of Education and Science, 1965–70 during which time she was responsible for establishing the Open University. Chairman of the Labour Party, 1967/8. MP for North Lanark, 1929–31, and Cannock, 1945–70. Widow of Aneurin Bevan, Deputy Leader of the Labour Party. Created a life peer in 1970.

LESTOR, Joan. Under-Secretary at the Department of Education and Science, 1969–70; at the Foreign and Commonwealth Office, 1974–5 and at the Department of Education and Science, 1975–6. Chairman of the Labour Party, 1977/8. Labour MP for Eton and Slough, 1966–83, and Eccles since 1987.

LONGFORD, Earl of (Frank Pakenham). Lord Privy Seal and Leader of the House of Lords, 1964–8. Colonial Secretary, 1965–6. Created a peer, Lord Pakenham, in 1945 in order to hold office in the 1945–51 Labour Government but subsequently succeeded to his brother's title, Earl of Longford, in 1961.

McELHONE, Frank (1929–1982). PPS to Tony Benn, 1974–5. Under-Secretary of State for Scotland, 1975–9. Won Glasgow Gorbals in a by-election in October 1969. Labour MP for Gorbals until 1974, Glasgow Queen's Park, 1974–82.

McGARVEY, Dan (1919–1977). President of the Amalgamated Society of Boilermakers, Shipwrights, Blacksmiths and Structural Workers, 1965–77. Member of the National Economic Development Council, 1975–7. Knighted just before his death.

MACLEOD, Iain (1913–1970). Leader of the House of Commons, 1961–3, and Chairman of the Conservative Party during that period. Served in the 1951–64 Conservative Governments as Minister of

Health, Minister of Labour and Colonial Secretary. Chancellor of the Exchequer, June-July 1970. Conservative MP for Enfield, 1950–70.

MACMILLAN, Harold (1894–1986). Prime Minister from 1957 until his retirement in October 1963, previously Minister of Defence, 1954–5, Foreign Secretary, 1955, and Chancellor of the Exchequer, 1955–7. Created Earl of Stockton, 1984. Conservative MP for Stockton-on-Tees, 1924–9, 1931–45, and for Bromley, 1945–64.

MADDOCK, Ieuan. Atomic scientist who worked at the Atomic Weapons Research Establishment, Aldermaston, and directed the research programme for the Nuclear Test-Ban Treaty, 1957–66. Controller at the Ministry of Technology, 1965–71, and subsequently Chief Scientist at the Department of Trade and Industry.

MALLALIEU, J. P. William ('Curly') (1908–1980). Minister of State at the Ministry of Technology, 1968–9. Previously a Minister at the Ministry of Defence and the Board of Trade. Labour MP for Huddersfield, then Huddersfield East, 1945–79.

MANLEY, Ivor. Principal Private Secretary to Tony Benn at the Ministry of Technology, 1968–70. Deputy-Secretary at the Department of Energy since 1982. Member of UK Atomic Energy Authority, 1981–6.

MARSH, Richard. Parliamentary Secretary at the Ministry of Labour, 1964–5. Joint Parliamentary Secretary at the Ministry of Technology, 1965–6, and Minister of Power, 1966–8. Minister of Transport, 1968–9, when he was dismissed by Harold Wilson. Labour MP for Greenwich, 1959–71. Resigned his seat and became Chairman of British Railways Board, 1971–6. Created a life peer in 1981, and left the Labour Party.

MARSHALL, Walter. Director of the Atomic Energy Research Establishment at Harwell, 1968–75. AERE scientist since 1954. Chief Scientist, Department of Energy, 1974–7 and Deputy Chairman then Chairman of the United Kingdom Atomic Energy Authority, 1975–83. Chairman of the Central Electricity Generating Board since 1982. Created a life peer in 1985.

MASON, Roy. Minister of State at the Board of Trade, 1964–7. Minister of Defence, 1967–8, and of Power, 1968–9, and President of the Board of Trade, 1969–70. In the 1974–9 Labour Government he was Secretary of State for Defence, 1974–6 and Secretary of State for Northern Ireland, 1976–9. Labour MP for Barnsley, 1953–87. Created a life peer in 1987.

MAUDE, Angus. Conservative MP for Stratford-on-Avon, 1963–83, and for Ealing South, 1950–58. Paymaster General, 1979–81. Director of the Conservative Political Centre, 1951–5, and appointed Deputy Chairman of the Conservative Party in 1975. Created a life peer in 1983.

MAXWELL, Robert. Owner of Pergamon Press and Labour MP for Buckingham, 1964–70. Chairman of the Mirror Group of Newspapers since 1984.

MAYHEW, Christopher. Appointed Minister of Defence for the Royal Navy in 1964, resigned in 1966 in protest against naval cuts. Labour MP for South Norfolk, 1945–50, and for Woolwich East, 1951–July 1974, when he resigned from the Labour Party to join the Liberal Party. Sat as a Liberal MP for Woolwich East for three months. Created a life peer in 1981.

MELLISH, Robert. Joint Parliamentary Secretary at the Ministry of Housing, 1964–7. Minister of Public Building and Works, 1967–9. Government Chief Whip, 1969–70. Opposition Chief Whip, 1970–74. Labour MP for Bermondsey from 1946 to 1982, when he resigned from the Labour Party and sat as an Independent until the by-election in March, 1983, which was won by the Liberals. Created a life peer in 1985.

MELVILLE, Sir Ronald. Permanent Secretary in the Ministry of Aviation, 1966–7, when it was absorbed into the Ministry of Technology. Secretary (Aviation) in the Ministry of Technology, 1967–70. Permanent Secretary, Aviation Supply, for its year of existence, 1970–71. Previously held appointments in the Air Ministry, War Office and Ministry of Defence. Retired 1972; subsequently a director of Westland Aircraft.

MIKARDO, Ian. Labour MP for Poplar, 1964–74 and for Bethnal Green and Bow, 1974–87. MP for Reading and South Reading, 1945–59. A distinguished leader of the Labour Left, he was Chairman of the Labour Party, 1970/71. A close associate of Aneurin Bevan and sometime chairman of the Tribune Group of Labour MPs.

MOON, Derek. Tony Benn's senior press officer, Ministry of Technology, 1966–70; formerly with the *Bristol Evening Post.*

MORRELL, Frances. Press officer for the National Union of Students and the Fabian Society, 1970–72. Previously a schoolteacher, 1960–69. Political adviser to Tony Benn, 1974–9. Leader of Inner London Education Authority, 1983–7.

MOUNTBATTEN, Admiral of the Fleet, Earl (1900–1979). Chairman, National Electronics Research Council. First Sea Lord, 1955–9.

Chief of Defence Staff, 1959–65. Supreme Allied Commander, South-East Asia, 1943–6, appointed last Viceroy of India, 1947. Created Earl Mountbatten of Burma, 1947.

MULLEY, Fred. Deputy Defence Secretary, 1964–5 and Minister of Aviation, 1965–7. Minister of State, Foreign and Commonwealth Office and Disarmament, 1967–9, Minister of Transport, 1969–70, and again in the Department of the Environment, 1974–5. Secretary of State for Education and Science, 1975–6 and for Defence, 1976–9. Chairman of the Labour Party, 1974/5. Labour MP for Sheffield, Park, 1950–83. Created a life peer in 1984.

NELSON of Stafford, Lord. Industrialist, Chairman of the English Electric Company, 1962–8, and member of the Advisory Council on Technology.

NICHOLAS, Harry. General Secretary of the Labour Party, 1968–72. Joined the Transport and General Workers' Union as an officer in 1936. Assistant General Secretary of the TGWU, 1956–68. Treasurer of the Labour Party, 1960–64.

PADLEY, Walter (1916–1984). Minister of State for Foreign Affairs, 1964–7. President of the Union of Shop, Distributive and Allied Workers, 1948–64. Chairman of the Labour Party, 1965/6. Labour MP for Ogmore, 1950–79.

PANNELL, Charles (1902–1980). Minister of Public Building and Works, 1964–6. Labour MP for Leeds West, 1949–74. Created a life peer in 1974.

PEARSON, Sir Denning (Jim). Chairman of Rolls Royce, 1969–70. Joined Rolls Royce in 1932. Member of the NEDC, 1964–70.

PENNEY, Lord (Sir William Penney). Chairman of the Atomic Energy Authority, 1964–7. A wartime pioneer of nuclear weapons. Director of the Atomic Weapons Research Establishment, Aldermaston, and Rector of Imperial College, London, 1967–73. Created a life peer in 1967.

PITBLADO, Sir David. Permanent Secretary at the Ministry of Power, 1966–9, and Permanent Secretary (Industry) at the Ministry of Technology, 1969–70. Previously Principal Private Secretary to Clem Attlee, Winston Churchill and Anthony Eden respectively. Comptroller and Auditor-General, 1971–6.

PITT, Terry (1937–1986). Head of the Labour Party's Research Department, 1965–74. Special Adviser to the Lord President of the Council, 1974. Later elected to the European Parliament.

POWELL, Enoch. Minister of Health, 1960–63. Resigned as Financial Secretary to the Treasury in 1958 in protest at the Budget. Conservative MP for Wolverhampton South-West, 1950–74. Resigned in 1974 over Conservative policy. Ulster Unionist MP for Down South, 1974–87.

PRENTICE, Reg. Minister of State, Department of Education and Science, 1964–6. Minister of Public Building and Works, 1966–7, and of Overseas Development, 1967–9, and again 1975–6. Secretary of State for Education and Science, 1974–5. Labour MP for East Ham North, 1951–74, Newham North East, 1974–9. In October 1977 Reg Prentice crossed the floor and sat on the Conservative benches until 1979. In 1979 he was elected Conservative MP for Daventry and sat for Daventry until 1987; he was Minister for Social Security, 1979–81 in the Conservative Government.

REYNOLDS, Gerry (1927–1969). Under-Secretary of State for Defence, 1964–5, and Minister of State for Defence, 1965–9. Former head of Local Government Department of the Labour Party. Labour MP for Islington North, 1958–69.

RIDLEY, Nicholas. Parliamentary Secretary to Minister of Technology, 1970 and Under-Secretary of State at the Department of Trade and Industry, 1970–72. Minister of State at the Foreign and Commonwealth Office, 1979–81; Financial Secretary to the Treasury 1981–3; Secretary of State for Transport 1983–6 and for the Environment since 1986. Conservative MP for Cirencester and Tewkesbury since 1959.

ROBINSON, Kenneth. Minister of Health, 1964–8. Minister for Planning and Land, 1968–9. Labour MP for St Pancras North, 1949–70. Later Chairman of London Transport Executive. Chairman of the Arts Council, 1977–82.

ROGERS, Herbert. Election Agent for Tony Benn, 1951–79. Secretary of the East Bristol Independent Labour Party from 1912. Agent for Sir Stafford Cripps, MP for Bristol East, and after wartime work in the Government became Secretary of the Bristol South East Labour Party.

ROSS, William. Secretary of State for Scotland, 1964–70, and 1974–6. Labour MP for Kilmarnock, 1946–79. Created a life peer in 1979.

ROTHSCHILD, Lord. Scientist and Chairman of Shell Research Ltd, 1963–70. Member of the Central Advisory Committee for Science and Technology, 1969. Subsequently Director-General of the Central Policy Review Staff ('Think Tank'), 1970–74.

RYLAND, William (1913–1988). Director of Inland Telecommunications at the GPO, 1961–5. Deputy Director-General, 1965–7, Managing Director, Telecommunications, 1967–9. In the reorganised Post Office Corporation Ryland became Chairman, 1971–7.

SCANLON, Hugh. President of the Amalgamated Union of Engineering Workers, 1968–78. AEU organiser, 1947–63. Member of the National Economic Development Council 1971–8. Created a life peer in 1979.

SCHON, Sir Frank. Industrialist. Member of the Advisory Council on Technology 1968–70, of the Industrial Reorganisation Corporation, 1966–71 and Chairman of the National Research and Development Corporation, 1969–79. Sometime Chairman and Managing Director of Marchon Products and Solway Chemicals, and Director of Blue Circle Industries. Created a life peer in 1976.

SHACKLETON, Lord. Minister of Defence for the RAF, 1964–7. Leader of the House of Lords, 1968–70. Created a peer in 1958. Former Labour MP for Preston, 1946–50, and Preston South, 1950–55.

SHINWELL, Emmanuel (Manny) (1884–1986). Chairman of the Parliamentary Labour Party, 1964–7. Minister of Fuel and Power and Minister of Defence in the 1945–51 Labour Government. Labour MP for Linlithgow, 1922–4 and 1928–31, for Seaham, 1935–50, and for Easington, 1950–70. Chairman of the Labour Party 1947/8. Created a life peer in 1970.

SHORE, Peter. Head of Research Department of the Labour Party, 1959–64. PPS to Harold Wilson, 1965–6. Joint Parliamentary Secretary at the Ministry of Technology, 1966–7, Secretary of State for Economic Affairs, 1967–9. Minister without Portfolio, 1969–70. Became Secretary of State for Trade in 1974. Secretary of State for the Environment, 1976–9. Labour MP for Stepney, subsequently Stepney and Poplar, and then Bethnal Green and Stepney since 1964. Married to Dr Liz Shore who after leaving general practice rose to become a senior medical officer at the Department of Health and Social Security.

SHORT, Edward. Government Chief Whip, 1964–6. Postmaster General, 1966–8. Secretary of State for Education and Science, 1968–70. Deputy Leader of the Labour Party, 1972–6. In the 1974–9 Labour Government he was Lord President of the Council and Leader of the House of Commons. Labour MP for Newcastle-on-Tyne Central, 1951–76. Created a life peer, Lord Glenamara, in 1976.

SILKIN, John (1923–1987). Government Whip, 1964–6 and Chief Whip, 1966–9. Minister of Public Building and Works, 1969–70. In the 1974–9 Labour Government he was Minister for Planning and Local Government, subsequently Minister for Agriculture, Fisheries and Food. Labour MP for Deptford, 1963–87.

SIMON, Brian. Professor of Education and subsequently Emeritus Professor at the University of Leicester since 1966. Has published a large number of books on education including *Half Way There: Report on the British Comprehensive School Reform* (1970) with Caroline Benn.

SIMPSON, Bill. General Secretary, Amalgamated Union of Engineering Workers (Foundry Section), 1967–75. Chairman of the Labour Party, 1972/3. Chairman of the Health and Safety Commission 1974–83.

SLATER, Harry. Senior civil servant in the Ministry of Technology. Responsible for International Technological Agreements during Tony Benn's tenure of the Department.

SMITH, Charles Delacourt (1917–1972). General Secretary of the Post Office Engineering Union, 1953–72. Formerly Labour MP for Colchester, 1945–50. Created a life peer in 1967, and was Minister of State at the Ministry of Technology, 1969–70.

SOSKICE, Frank (1902–1979). Home Secretary, 1964–5. Lord Privy Seal, 1965–6. Served in the 1945–50 Labour Government as Solicitor-General. Labour MP for Birkenhead East, 1945–50, for Neepsend, 1950–55, and for Newport, 1956–66. Created a life peer, Lord Stow Hill, in 1966.

STEWART, Michael. Secretary of State for Education and Science, 1964–5, Foreign Secretary, 1965–6, Secretary of State for Economic Affairs, 1966–7, Foreign and Commonwealth Secretary, 1968–70. Held junior office in the 1945–51 Labour Govenment. Labour MP for Fulham East, subsequently Fulham and then Hammersmith and Fulham, 1945–79. Created a life peer in 1979.

STOKES, Sir Donald. Managing Director and Deputy Chairman, subsequently Chairman, of Leyland Motor Corporation from 1963, and after the takeover of British Motors Corporation became Chairman and Managing Director of British Leyland in 1973, President in 1975. Created a life peer in 1969.

STONEHOUSE, John (1925–1988). Parliamentary Secretary, Ministry of Aviation, 1964–6. Under-Secretary of State for the Colonies, 1966–7. Minister of Aviation, 1967. Minister of State at the Ministry of Technology, 1967–8. Postmaster General in 1968 and Minister of

Posts and Telecommunications, 1969. Labour Co-operative MP for Wednesbury, 1957–74, and Walsall North, 1974, until his resignation in 1976.

THOMAS, George. Minister of State at the Welsh Office, 1966–7, and Commonwealth Office, 1967–8. Secretary of State for Wales, 1968–70. Speaker of the House of Commons, 1976–83, (Deputy Speaker 1974–6). Since 1983 Chairman of the National Children's Home. A former Vice President of the Methodist Conference. Labour MP for Cardiff Central, 1945–50, Cardiff West, 1950–83 (sat as Speaker from 1976). Created a hereditary peer, Viscount Tonypandy, in 1983.

THOMSON, George. Minister of State at the Foreign Office, 1964–6 and Chancellor of the Duchy of Lancaster, 1966–7 and 1969–70. Secretary of State for Commonwealth Affairs, 1967–8. Minister without Portfolio, 1968–9. Chairman of the Labour Committee for Europe, 1972–3, appointed an EEC Commissioner, 1973–7. Chairman of the Independent Broadcasting Authority (IBA) since 1981. Labour MP for Dundee East, 1952–72. Created a life peer in 1977.

THORPE, Jeremy. Leader of the Liberal Party, 1967–76. Liberal MP for North Devon, 1959–79.

TREND, Sir Burke (1914–1987). Secretary of the Cabinet, 1963–73. Created a life peer in 1974.

UNDERHILL, Reginald. Labour Party Assistant National Agent, 1960–72. National Agent, 1972–9. Labour Party official since 1933. Created a life peer in 1979.

VARLEY, Eric. PPS to Harold Wilson, 1968–9. Minister of State at the Ministry of Technology, 1969–70; Secretary of State for Energy, 1974–5, exchanging Cabinet jobs with Tony Benn to become Secretary of State for Industry, 1975–9, while Tony Benn was responsible for Energy, 1975–9. Labour MP for Chesterfield, 1964–84. Retired in 1984 to become Chairman of Coalite Group.

VAUGHAN, Ron. Official driver to Tony Benn at the Ministry of Technology, 1968–70, and at the Departments of Industry and Energy, 1974–9.

WEINSTOCK, Arnold. Industrialist. Managing Director of GEC since 1963, of Radio and Allied Industries, 1954–63. Created a life peer in 1980.

WHITE, Eirene. Minister of State at the Foreign Office 1966–7, Welsh

Office, 1967–70. Chairman of the Labour Party, 1968/9. Labour MP for East Flint, 1950–70. Created a life peer in 1970.

WHITTY, Larry. Assistant Private Secretary at the Ministry of Technology, 1965–70. Since 1985 General Secretary of the Labour Party.

WILLIAMS, Bruce. Economist and academic. Economic adviser to the Minister of Technology, 1964–7. A member of the Advisory Council on Technology until his appointment in 1967 as Vice-Chancellor of the University of Sydney.

WILLIAMS, Sir Len (1903–1973). General Secretary of the Labour Party, 1962–8. Formerly Assistant National Agent, National Agent and Deputy General Secretary, 1946–62. Governor-General of Mauritius, 1968–73.

WILLIAMS, Marcia. Personal and Political Secretary to Harold Wilson since 1956. Created a life peer, Lady Falkender, in 1976.

WILLIAMS, Shirley. PPS to Minister of Health, 1964–6. Parliamentary Secretary at the Ministry of Labour, 1966–7. Minister of State, Education and Science, 1967–9, and the Home Office, 1969–70. In the 1974–9 Labour Government she was successively Secretary of State for Prices and Consumer Protection, for Education and Science, and Paymaster General. Member of the National Executive, 1970–81. Labour MP for Hitchin, 1964–74, for Hertford and Stevenage, 1974–9. Founder of SDP in 1981, President in 1982 and SDP MP for Crosby, 1981–3.

WILSON, Harold. Leader of the Labour Party, 1963–76. Prime Minister, 1964–70, and 1974–6. Resigned in 1976 and did not hold office again. President of the Board of Trade, 1947–51, when he resigned with Aneurin Bevan. Chairman of the Labour Party, 1961/2. Labour MP for Ormskirk, 1945–50, and Huyton, 1950–83. Created life peer, Lord Wilson of Rievaulx. Married to Mary Wilson, poet and writer.

WOODCOCK, George (1904–1979). General Secretary of the TUC, 1960–69. Assistant General Secretary, 1947–60. Member of the National Economic Development Council, 1962–9.

ZANDER, Michael. Lecturer, subsequently Professor in Law at the London School of Economics. Gave great assistance to Tony Benn during the peerage campaign, 1960–61. Left the Labour Party to join the SDP.

ZUCKERMAN, Sir Solly. Zoologist. Long-time Government adviser.

Chief Scientific Adviser to Harold Wilson, 1964–70, and to the Secretary of State for Defence, 1960–66. Chairman of the Central Advisory Committee for Science and Technology, 1965–70. Created a life peer in 1971.

(II) Personal

BENN, Caroline. Born in Ohio and graduated from Vassar College with post-graduate degrees from the Universities of Cincinnati and London. Founder member of the main comprehensive education campaign group in Britain, and editor of *Comprehensive Education*. Author of many educational publications including *Half Way There* with Professor Brian Simon (1970) and *Challenging the MSC* with John Fairley (1986). President of the Socialist Educational Association. Adult education lecturer since 1965, currently teaching an Open University preparation course. Former member of the Education Section of the UNESCO Commission and of the Inner London Education Authority, and governor of several schools and colleges. Married Tony Benn in 1949. Four children: Stephen, born 1951, Hilary, born 1953, Melissa, born 1957, Joshua, born 1958.

BENN, David Wedgwood. Younger brother, a barrister, worked for the Socialist International and later for the External Service of the BBC. Head of the BBC Yugoslav Section, 1974–84. A writer specialising in Soviet affairs.

BENN, June. Former lecturer; novelist writing under the name of June Barraclough. Married David Benn in 1959. Two children, Piers, born 1962, and Frances, born 1964.

CARTER, Peter. Close family friend. Architect who worked in Chicago under Mies van der Rohe.

FLANDERS, Michael (1922–1975). Actor and writer. Contemporary of Tony Benn at school. Family friend who, with Donald Swann, formed the duo well known for its musical stage entertainments.

GIBSON, Ralph. University contemporary, a barrister who was later made a judge. He and his wife, Ann, are close friends of the family.

KHAMA, Sir Seretse (1921–1980). Founder and President of the Bechuanaland Democratic Party from 1962, becoming Prime Minister of Bechuanaland (Botswana) in 1965, and President of the Republic of Botswana in 1966. A barrister educated at Oxford, Seretse had become chief of the Bamangwato tribe in 1925, aged four.

He was removed from the British protectorate by the Labour Government in 1950 over objections to his marriage to Ruth Williams, a white British woman, in 1948. Became close friends with the Benns who lent support in the 1950s. Seretse Khama was godfather to Melissa Benn, and Tony Benn godfather to Anthony Khama.

LAMBERT, Phyllis. A Canadian architect, a college contemporary of Caroline Benn, and long-time friend of the family.

RETEY, Rosalind (1953–1979). A contemporary of Hilary Benn at Holland Park School graduated from Queen Mary College, London; they married in April 1973. Rosalind contracted cancer in 1978, and died at home in June 1979 after much suffering which she bore with immense courage. A fund in her memory has been established at Holland Park School which is under the control of the students.

STANSGATE, Lady. Margaret Holmes, born in Scotland in 1897, the daughter of Liberal MP, D. T. Holmes. Married William Wedgwood Benn in 1920. They had three children (the eldest son, Michael, was killed while serving as an RAF pilot during the war). A long-standing member of the Movement for the Ordination of Women, the first President of the Congregational Federation, served on the Council of Christians and Jews, and of the Friends of the Hebrew University. Fellow of the Hebrew University. Joint author of *Beckoning Horizon*, 1934.

STANSGATE, Lord (1877–1960). William Wedgwood Benn. Son of John Williams Benn, who was Liberal MP for Tower Hamlets and later for Devonport, and Chairman, 1904/5, of the London County Council of which he was a founder member. William Wedgwood Benn was himself elected Liberal MP for St George's, Tower Hamlets, in 1906. Became a Whip in the Liberal Government in 1910. Served in the First World War and was decorated with the DSO and DFC, returning in 1918 to be elected MP for Leith. Joined the Labour Party in 1926, resigned his seat the same day, and was subsequently elected Labour MP for North Aberdeen (1928–31) in a by-election. Secretary of State for India in the 1929–31 Labour Cabinet. Re-elected as Labour MP for Gorton in 1937. He rejoined the RAF in 1940 at the age of sixty-three, was made a peer, Viscount Stansgate, in 1941, and was Secretary of State for Air, 1945–6, in the postwar Labour Government. World President of the Inter-Parliamentary Union, 1947–57.

SWANN, Donald. School contemporary and family friend who wrote the music for and performed in many shows, including *At the Drop of a*

Hat, which he and Michael Flanders staged in London and took on a world tour. Composer of church music.

WINCH, Olive (Buddy). Miss Winch was with the family as a children's nurse from 1928 until 1940, when she left to undertake war work. A life-long friend.

APPENDIX I
Her Majesty's Government
Complete List of Ministers and Offices

The Cabinet, January 1968

Prime Minister and First Lord of the Treasury	Mr Harold Wilson
Secretary of State for Foreign Affairs	Mr George Brown
First Secretary of State	Mr Michael Stewart
Secretary of State for the Home Department	Mr James Callaghan
Lord Chancellor	Lord Gardiner
Chancellor of the Exchequer	Mr Roy Jenkins
Lord President of the Council and Leader of the House of Commons	Mr Richard Crossman
Secretary of State for Defence	Mr Denis Healey
Secretary of State for Scotland	Mr William Ross
Secretary of State for Education and Science	Mr Patrick Gordon Walker
President of the Board of Trade	Mr Anthony Crosland
Secretary of State for Commonwealth Affairs	Mr George Thomson
Secretary of State for Economic Affairs	Mr Peter Shore
Minister of Housing and Local Government	Mr Anthony Greenwood
Minister of Labour	Mr Ray Gunter
Minister of Agriculture, Fisheries and Food	Mr Fred Peart
Minister of Transport	Mrs Barbara Castle
Lord Privy Seal and Leader of the House of Lords	Lord Shackleton
Secretary of State for Wales	Mr Cledwyn Hughes
Minister of Power	Mr Richard Marsh
Minister of Technology	Mr Anthony Wedgwood Benn

Ministers not in the Cabinet, January 1968

Minister of Overseas Development	Mr Reg Prentice
Chancellor of the Duchy of Lancaster	Mr Frederick Lee
Minister of Health	Mr Kenneth Robinson
Minister of Social Security	Mrs Judith Hart
Postmaster-General	Mr Edward Short
Minister of Public Building and Works	Mr Robert Mellish
Chief Secretary to the Treasury	Mr John Diamond
Ministers of State for Foreign Affairs	Mr Frederick Mulley
	Lord Chalfont
	Lord Caradon
	Mr Goronwy Roberts
Minister of Defence for Administration	Mr G. W. Reynolds
Minister of Defence for Equipment	Mr Roy Mason
Minister of State, Home Office	Lord Stonham
Minister of State, Scottish Office	Dr J. Dickson Mabon
Ministers of State, Department of Education and Science	Miss Alice Bacon
	Mrs Shirley Williams
	Mrs Jennie Lee
Ministers of State, Board of Trade	Mr George Darling
	Lord Brown
	Mr J. P. W. Mallalieu
Ministers of State for Commonwealth Affairs	Mr George Thomas
	Lord Shepherd
Minister of State, Ministry of Housing and Local Government	Mr Niall MacDermot
Minister of State, Ministry of Transport	Mr Stephen Swingler
Minister of State, Welsh Office	Mrs Eirene White
Minister of State, Ministry of Technology	Mr John Stonehouse
Attorney-General	Sir Elwyn Jones
Lord Advocate	Mr H. S. Wilson
Solicitor-General	Sir Arthur Irvine
Solicitor-General for Scotland	Mr Ewan Stewart

The Cabinet, January 1970

Prime Minister, First Lord of the Treasury and Minister for the Civil Service	Mr Harold Wilson
Secretary of State for Foreign and Commonwealth Affairs	Mr Michael Stewart

Chancellor of the Exchequer	Mr Roy Jenkins
Lord Chancellor	Lord Gardiner
Secretary of State for Social Services	Mr Richard Crossman
First Secretary of State and Secretary of State for Employment and Productivity	Mrs Barbara Castle
Secretary of State for the Home Department	Mr James Callaghan
Secretary of State for Defence	Mr Denis Healey
Lord President of the Council and Leader of the House of Commons	Mr Fred Peart
Secretary of State for Local Government and Regional Planning	Mr Anthony Crosland
Minister of Technology	Mr Anthony Wedgwood Benn
Secretary of State for Scotland	Mr William Ross
Minister without Portfolio and Deputy Leader of the House of Commons	Mr Peter Shore
Secretary of State for Education and Science	Mr Edward Short
Chancellor of the Duchy of Lancaster	Mr George Thomson
President of the Board of Trade	Mr Roy Mason
Minister of Agriculture, Fisheries and Food	Mr Cledwyn Hughes
Lord Privy Seal and Leader of the House of Lords	Lord Shackleton
Secretary of State for Wales	Mr George Thomas
Chief Secretary to the Treasury	Mr John Diamond
Paymaster-General	Mr Harold Lever

Ministers not in the Cabinet, January 1970

Minister of Housing and Local Government	Mr Anthony Greenwood
Minister of Overseas Development	Mrs Judith Hart
Minister of Transport	Mr Frederick Mulley
Minister of Public Building and Works	Mr John Silkin
Minister of Posts and Telecommunications	Mr John Stonehouse
Ministers of State for Foreign and Commonwealth Affairs	Lord Caradon
	Lord Chalfont
	Lord Shepherd
Parliamentary Secretary to the Treasury (Chief Whip)	Mr Robert Mellish
Financial Secretary to the Treasury	Mr Dick Taverne
Minister of State, Treasury	Mr William Rodgers

Ministers of State, Department of Health and Social Security	Mr David Ennals
	Baroness Serota
Minister of State, Department of Employment and Productivity	Mr Edmund Dell
Minister of State, Home Office	Mrs Shirley Williams
Minister of Defence for Equipment	Mr John Morris
Minister of Defence for Administration	Mr Roy Hattersley
Minister of State, Home Office	Mr T. W. Urwin
Ministers of State, Ministry of Technology	Mr Eric Varley
	Lord Delacourt-Smith
Ministers of State, Scottish Office	Dr J. Dickson Mabon
	Lord Hughes
Ministers of State, Department of Education and Science	Miss Alice Bacon
	Mrs Jennie Lee
	Mr Gerry Fowler
Ministers of State, Board of Trade	Mr Goronwy Roberts
	Lord Brown
Minister of State, Welsh Office	Mrs Eirene White
Minister of State, Ministry of Housing and Local Government	Mr Denis Howell

Parliamentary Committee (Shadow Cabinet), October 1970

Leader	Mr Harold Wilson
Deputy Leader	Mr Roy Jenkins
Chairman, PLP	Mr Douglas Houghton
Chief Whip	Mr Robert Mellish
Trade, Industry and Aviation	Mr Anthony Wedgwood Benn
Home Office	Mr James Callaghan
Employment	Mrs Barbara Castle
Environment	Mr Anthony Crosland
Power	Mr Michael Foot
Foreign Affairs	Mr Denis Healey
European Affairs	Mr Harold Lever
Parliamentary Affairs	Mr Fred Peart
Education and Science	Mr Edward Short
Defence	Mr George Thomson
Health and Social Security	Mrs Shirley Williams
Scotland	Mr William Ross

Leader, House of Lords   Lord Shackleton
Chief Whip, House of Lords   Lord Beswick
Labour Peers' Representative   Lord Champion
Secretary   Mr Frank Barlow

APPENDIX II
Labour Party National Executive Committees 1968 and 1972

1967/8

Mrs Jennie Lee, MP	Chairman
Mrs Eirene White, MP	Vice-Chairman
Mr James Callaghan, MP	Treasurer
Mr Harold Wilson, MP	Leader of the Parliamentary Party
Mr George Brown, MP	Deputy-Leader of the Parliamentary Party
Mr L. Williams	General Secretary

Trade Unions' Section
Mr T. G. Bradley, MP (Transport Salaried Staffs' Association)
Mr J. Chalmers (Amalgamated Society of Boilermakers, Shipwrights, Blacksmiths and Structural Workers)
Mr F. J. Chapple (Electrical Trades Union)
Mr A. Cunningham (National Union of General and Municipal Workers)
Mr J. Diamond (British Iron, Steel and Kindred Trades' Association)
Mr J. Gormley (National Union of Mineworkers)
Mr P. Hanley (Amalgamated Engineering Union)
Mr F. Lane (National Union of Railwaymen)
Mr F. W. Mulley, MP (Clerical and Administrative Workers' Union)
Mr H. R. Nicholas (Transport and General Workers' Union)
Mr W. E. Padley, MP (Union of Shop, Distributive and Allied Workers)
Mr W. Simpson (Amalgamated Union of Foundry Workers)

Socialist, Co-operative and Professional Organisations' Section
Mr A. Skeffington, MP (Royal Arsenal Co-operative Society)

Constituency Organisations' Section
Mr F. Allaun, MP
Mr A. W. Benn, MP
Mrs B. Castle, MP
Mr T. Driberg, MP
Mr Anthony Greenwood, MP
Miss J. Lestor, MP
Mr I. Mikardo, MP

Women Members
Miss A. Bacon, MP
Mrs E. M. Braddock, MP
Mrs M. Herbison, MP

1971/2

Mr Anthony W. Benn, MP	Chairman
Mr William Simpson	Vice-Chairman
Mr James Callaghan, MP	Treasurer
Mr Harold Wilson, MP	Leader of the Parliamentary Party
Mr Edward Short, MP	Deputy-Leader of the
Mr Roy Jenkins, MP	Parliamentary Party
Sir Harry Nicholas	General Secretary

Trade Unions' Section
Mr T. G. Bradley, MP (Transport Salaried Staffs' Assocation)
Mr J. Chalmers (Amalgamated Society of Boilermakers,
   Shipwrights, Blacksmiths and Structural Workers)
Mr G. W. Chambers (National Union of Railwaymen)
Mr F. J. Chapple (Electrical Trades Union)
Mr A. Cunningham (National Union of General and Municipal
   Workers)
Mr J. Diamond (British Iron, Steel and Kindred Trades'
   Association)
Mr L. Forden (Transport and General Workers' Union)
Mr J. Gormley (National Union of Mineworkers)
Mr A. Kitson (Scottish Commercial Motormen's Union)

Mr F. W. Mulley, MP (Clerical and Administrative Workers' Union)

Mr W. E. Padley, MP (Union of Shop, Distributive and Allied Workers)

Mr W. Simpson (Amalgamated Union of Foundry Workers)

Socialist Co-operative and Professional Organisations' Section
Mr A. Skeffington, MP (died February 1971) (Royal Arsenal Co-operative Society)

Constituency Organisations' Section
Mr F. Allaun, MP
Mr A. W. Benn, MP
Mrs B. Castle, MP
Mr T. Driberg, MP
Mr Denis Healey, MP
Miss J. Lestor, MP
Mr I. Mikardo, MP

Women Members
Mrs Judith Hart, MP
Mrs Lena Jeger, MP
Mrs Renée Short, MP
Lady (Eirene) White
Mrs Shirley Williams, MP

APPENDIX III
Technology and the Quality of Life

Extract from Royal Society lecture to the Manchester Technology Association, 25 February 1970

As economic standards rise, there is an increasing fear that technology is being misused, that we are pursuing production of goods and services too singlemindedly and without regard for the general quality of life. People are becoming increasingly concerned that this general quality of life will be damaged because the wider effects of technological change are either not thought about or disregarded.

In its most extreme form this reaction sometimes seems to be in danger of becoming a campaign against technology. To read some of the wilder comments made one would imagine that technology had produced a steady reduction in the quality of life over the last fifty years; and that we are all being actively poisoned to the point where the immediate survival of the species is now in question. This of course is a ludicrous overstatement of the nature of the problem. And it leaves out of account the fact that it is only by the application of technology that we can cope with the consequences of technological change that has already occurred. In fact, the application of technology has noticeably raised not only the standard and quality of life, but the length of life as well.

For example, the generation of electricity by nuclear or hydro power is immensely cleaner than any previous method of providing light and heat. Domestic technology has liberated millions of women from hideous drudgery. Communications technology has given us all a wider range of experience, either by extending our capacity to move freely or to enjoy a fuller range of experience from our own home.

Medical technology – in the form of drugs and appliances, surgical and other equipment – has not only lengthened the expectation of life but is making life itself more tolerable for the old, the sick and the disabled.

Computer technology, too, has opened up possibilities of managing complex systems without which we could not hope to control the power we have created.

No one wants to turn his back on all this. But what is now, quite rightly, under direct challenge is the tendency for an unthinking acceptance of everything that is scientifically exciting and technically within our capability; regardless of its social consequences.

Technology, like all power, is neutral and the question is how do we use it. It is the decision-making process that we are concerned with and how it can be improved. This is indeed one reason why the Ministry of Technology itself was set up.

The timescale of technological development is so long and the costs so high that, if there is no discussion during the formative stage, people may wake up one day and find that major technological changes are well advanced and it is too late to stop them because so much money and effort has already been committed.

This, more than almost anything else, gives people the feeling that their views count for nothing and drives them to the extremes of obscurantist opposition against technology itself or, worse still, against scientists and engineers in general. It is therefore to the decision-making process that we must look for improvements. As far as Government is concerned the process of analysis must be widened at the very outset. Everyone working on, or promoting new projects or processes must be actively encouraged to think much more widely about the social implications of what they are doing while they are actually engaged in their work, and so must all those in responsible positions in industry and society, who are concerned with the advocacy of technological changes. The wider responsibilities which need to be opened up for managers, engineers and scientists could help to liberate them from the restrictions which may have hitherto limited their scope. Most of them are highly qualified, with a deep knowledge of and concentration upon, their field of work or responsibility. No one wants to restrict the specialist. Quite the reverse.

What we want is what Dr Paine, the NASA administrator, calls T-shaped men. The vertical stem of the T reflects the deep knowledge of a special subject in which a man may study and work throughout his life. The horizontal cross-bar at the top of the T symbolises his wide and general interest over the whole range of human activities.

We shall have to devise some more comprehensive interrogation to which we can subject new industrial processes, new methods or new projects as they emerge from Government and industry.

In addition to that we shall now have to push some fairly basic questions down the line and require them to be answered at the point of initiation, by the initiators.

1. Would your project – if carried through – promise benefits to the community, and if so what are these benefits, how will they be distributed and to whom and when would they accrue?

2. What disadvantages would you expect might flow from your work; who would experience them; what, if any, remedies would correct them; and is the technology for correcting them sufficiently advanced for the remedies to be available when the disadvantages begin to accrue?

3. What demands would the development of your project make upon our resources of skilled manpower, and are these resources likely to be available?

4. Is there a cheaper, simpler and less sophisticated way of achieving at least a part of the objective that you have in mind; and if so what would it be and what proportion of your total objective would have to be sacrificed if we adopted it?

5. What new skills would have to be acquired by people who would be called upon to use the product or project which you are recommending, and how could these skills in application be created?

6. What skills would be rendered obsolete by the development you propose and how serious a problem would the obsolescence of these skills create for the people who had them?

7. Is the work upon which you are engaged being done, or has it been done, or has it been started and stopped, in other parts of the world and what experience is available from abroad that might help us to assess your own proposal?

8. If what you propose is not done what disadvantages or penalties do you believe will accrue to the community and what alternative projects might be considered?

9. If your proposition is accepted what other work in the form of supporting systems should be set in hand simultaneously, either to cope with the consequences of it, or to prepare for the next stage and what would that next stage be?

10. If an initial decision to proceed is made, for how long will the option to stop remain open and how reversible will this decision be at progressive stages beyond that?

The answers provided would have in major cases to be considered by a wider interdisciplinary group including those whose special knowledge will allow them to consider the implications in greater detail.

They may find it necessary to have further studies done and recommend that these be set in hand either before the project is approved or in parallel with its development.

Why a 'think tank' is not enough

This group would not be a 'think tank' upon whom to off-load the full responsibility for assessment. What is wrong today is that too few people are encouraged to think for themselves outside their own field.

The assessment group, to be effective, has got therefore to be made up of people who are themselves also regularly engaged in their own work and who have been drawn out of it part-time to work with others for the purpose of the assessment. What we want is sabbatical groups, made up of people who take part in the problems of inter-relationships without losing their contact with reality. It should be a changing group, whose membership is selected according to the problem that is to be thrown to it, always changing while maintaining its fundamental inter-disciplinary character.

This whole process that I have been describing has, in fact, a much wider significance than may at first appear. It represents the demand by an ever-growing number of thinking people that the power of technology, whoever exercises it, be brought more effectively into the arena of public affairs and made subject to democratic decision.

Just as in earlier centuries the power of kings and feudal landowners was made subject to the crude and imperfect popular will as expressed in our primitive parliamentary system; and just as the new power created by the Industrial Revolution was tamed and shaped by the public which demanded universal franchise, so now the choices we make between the alternatives opened up by technology have got to be exposed to far greater public scrutiny and subjected more completely to public decision, especially by those whose interests are most intimately affected.

The development of the Ministry of Technology, which has brought most industrial sponsorship and the control of many public research resources together under a single Minister accountable to Parliament represents a significant shift in the right direction.

The establishment of a Select Committee on Science and Technology in the House of Commons in recent years marked an important step forward and it has significantly altered the balance of power in favour of elected MPs and it has quite properly kept my own Department's work under close examination.

It has helped to educate Parliament in the new problems that confront us all and has brought the House of Commons more directly into contact with the decision-making processes in this field.

Another important development has been the innovation of Green Papers through which the Government now shares its thinking with the public before it commits itself to a firm policy decision.

The first objection will be from those who believe that the decisions that have to be made require such expert knowledge that it would be foolish, dangerous and wrong to allow ordinary people to have a say in them.

They will argue that it would be disastrous if a nation, the majority of whom, by definition, have, as it were, 'failed the 11 Plus' should be allowed to decide things which can only be understood by PhDs or the chairmen of big corporations or Ministers, together with their highly qualified teams of economists and technologists.

However superficially persuasive this argument may seem, it is in fact exactly the same argument as was used in the last century – and in this – against both universal suffrage and votes for women.

For our policy towards technology is now the stuff of government and that is either to be under democratic control or not. There is no middle course.

To argue for the exclusion of these issues from popular control is not only fundamentally undemocratic but is also completely impracticable. The doctrine of limiting democratic control is based upon a complete underestimation of the general level of public intelligence and knowledge.

Even with all its present, and unacceptable defects, the educational system and the mass media have enormously raised the level of public education and understanding in the course of a single generation.

The genie of human genius has got out of the bottle and it cannot ever be put back in again and the cork replaced.

The next obstacle – and it is a far more formidable one – lies in the minds of people themselves.

Far too many ordinary people still believe that they have not got the knowledge to make independent judgments on these matters or that if they tried to do so, their efforts would be doomed to failure, because nobody really cares what they think.

This combination of lack of self-confidence and defeatism – both self-generated – must be overcome.

You may have to be a brilliant surgeon before you can do a heart transplant but you don't have to have any scientific qualifications at all to be able to reach a view as to whether the largest sums of money and the medical research teams involved would do more good by transplant-ing a few hearts each year or by establishing say more health centres, or developing a better industrial health service to cut down the thousands of preventable deaths and disabilities that occur each year.

You may have to be a brilliant aerodynamicist to design a space capsule that will land on the moon, but you don't have to have any qualifications before you express the view that some of the money spent in space research might be better employed in improving the quality of public transport and the development of quicker, quieter, cleaner and more comfortable bus services or commuter trains.

But if we are able to persuade people that they ought to be able to influence decisions and are qualified to do so we still face the much more difficult job of overcoming their suspicion that, even if they were to make the attempt, it would be bound to fail because nobody cares two hoots what they think.

This defeatism is born out of past frustration, before the wider assessments were made, or public discussion was encouraged.

As people realise the significance of what has been done public confidence in their ability to have an influence will slowly return.

We have also got to identify the main problems facing society and find ways and means of converting these needs into real demands which can be met best by the use of technology.

There are already many thousands of human pressure groups or action groups now in existence with proposals to do just this. Unless we can provide better facilities for these people to have access to those who might be able to solve their problems we could miss one of the most important ways in which technology could be used for human benefit.

Indeed I suspect that the political leadership that has the most lasting effect exists not in the confrontations so beloved of Fleet Street, but in the stream of analysis, exploration, interpretation and argument that slowly but surely changes the collective will.

What I am really saying is not at all new.

It is no more than that the method we use to reach our decisions is at least as important as, if not more important than, the decisions themselves, and the expertise that lies behind them.

But this, of course, is exactly what the parliamentary system is all about. It is based upon the belief that how you govern yourself – by argument, election and accountability instead of thought control, civil war and dictatorship – is what really matters.

I am, therefore, simply arguing that the methodology of self-government based on the concept of talking our way through to decisions must now be clearly extended to cover the whole area, at all levels of the development of technology which is in our century the source of all new power, just as ownership of the land or the ownership of early factories was in the nineteenth century.

If we don't succeed in doing this we shall run the risk of becoming robots.

It won't be the machines themselves that make us robots but the fact that we have subcontracted our future to huge organisations backed by their own resources of managerial, scientific or professional talent.

Whether we do this or not is, I believe, one of the most important single issues in the whole area of public policy.

APPENDIX IV
Learning to use Power

Extract from the Roscoe Lecture, delivered to the University of Manchester, 25 April 1970.

The thing that struck me most forcibly when I visited the United States recently, and I have been there regularly over a period of twenty-five years, was the tremendous debate now going on there (as it is here) about the proper uses of technology; the side effects that it produces; the problems of pollution and the environment; and the role of human beings in an age of technology. It is my belief, and this is my argument, that the significance of this debate goes far deeper than is yet fully realised. Quite apart from the specific campaigns that have come to the forefront during this developing debate; about, say, the use of nuclear weapons, or chemical warfare, about the effects of pesticides; or in favour of a better environment, we are now pinpointing crucial and central questions affecting the whole nature of our society and touching upon its essential character.

The problem that lies at the heart of this issue can be expressed in a paradox: here we, all of us in industrialised societies, live in a period of history when the material options open to man, both personally and collectively, are wider and greater than they have ever been; and yet, more and more people feel they count for less and less. This is the paradox. This is the problem. This is at least in part the explanation of the alienation, the protest, the apathy, to which we, as mature citizens, have to direct our attention.

Why is it that this has happened? Is it the fault of the scientists? Is it the fault of technology? Is it the fault of our economic system? Is it that we have all suffered, by some historical mischance, from a general bankruptcy of leadership? These are the questions that are now seriously being posed. There are some people who believe that we are now going back, as a result of these developments, to authoritarianism, or are moving on to some sort of anarchy. In an attempt to get this debate into focus, because it is very difficult, and the problems are very complex, may I try briefly to set it into its historical perspective? Of course all these questions have been debated before, and we are, to some extent, misled by the change of terminology we use, into thinking that these are really new issues.

I would like to look back for a moment at this very same debate as it occurred during the first Industrial Revolution. Although the development of steam for the factory and for transport was very primitive as compared to the technology that we have today, it still produced a new economic system: capitalism. It altered the social structure of society and it also altered, as we all know very well, the balance of world power. And during the first Industrial Revolution of course we also had demonstrations about the quality of life and a demand for participation. All these things occurred in the nineteenth century, but we used different names for them.

May I show you a picture of men re-enacting a nineteenth-century demonstration. They are carrying a banner on which are inscribed the words, 'Educate, organise and control'. Those are some very revolutionary words, still carried each year by the Durham miners. I took the picture myself a few years ago. Nowadays there is a Scots band in the front, because the occasion has slowly changed from being a fierce demonstration into a folk festival; and the police, instead of being there to disperse the demonstrators, are there to protect the marching miners from the throng of admiring people who stand and cheer them. But that is basically the sort of demonstration which still looks threatening in other contexts and on other issues, as perhaps over Vietnam in Grosvenor Square.

Next may I show you a nineteenth-century monument to what we now call participation, the Houses of Parliament. People come from all over the world nowadays to see the quaint old parliamentary customs of our time. But the struggle to get control of that place, from the days of the 1832 Reform Bill through to the time when we got one man, one woman, one vote, at eighteen (which was about four weeks ago) was a hard-fought struggle for participation, a great nineteenth-century human response to the first Industrial Revolution. We must never forget that these are a part of the very same struggle we are seeing again.

The capitalist system, which developed in the nineteenth century, also led to some serious questioning at the philosophical level. There was one philosopher (I suppose today we would call him a sociologist) who thought deeply about the relationship between technology and politics and I quote what he wrote, 'Technology discloses man's mode of dealing with nature, the process of production by which he sustains his life and thereby lays bare the mode of formation of his social relations and the mental conceptions that flow from them . . .' He was the first political philosopher ever to link technology directly with human relations and his name of course was Karl Marx. Marx worked away in the British Museum, and he produced a theory of society which was based upon the idea that this new industrial power could only be controlled through national ownership and that the right way forward for mankind was by a collective leap from poverty to plenty.

A few years later, on the other side of the Atlantic, there was another man who was a sort of industrial philosopher, even though he is remembered for saying that 'history is bunk'. His name was Henry Ford and he had another conception of the way in which technology could help people out of poverty, and it was by mass producing automobiles. He offered to the individual American, and ultimately, because the mass-produced car went all over the world, he offered to the individual everywhere a chance to escape from poverty not by collective action, but by energetic personal enterprise and thrift. Each individual could, he seemed to argue, escape from poverty, one by one, like men using the Davis Escape Apparatus in a submarine. In this way Ford thought technology could be harnessed to the new purposes of man.

Ford *v* Marx, Marx *v* Ford. The two men reflect in a very rough and ready way two approaches to the development of technology and the use that man could make of it; and the two means of control that man could adopt to shape his destiny by the use of technology. Broadly speaking American and Soviet societies have developed one by following Ford, the other, Karl Marx. It is perhaps quite appropriate that, in the very month when Henry Ford II has been in Moscow, discussing with the Communist leadership there the development of the motor car industry in Russia and when simultaneously American students have been burning automobiles in Detroit as a protest against their pollution of the environment, we should be having another look to see what is actually happening, in the light of the experience we have now had of these two societies wedded to these two different conceptions of how technology might be controlled and used.

What is technology? The best and simplest definition that I have ever heard is one given by the American professor Buckminster Fuller, for whom I have a great admiration, who said technology simply means getting 'more out of less'. If the central problem of the world, overall, is shortage, which it is, the need to get 'more out of less' is a rather more accurate way of describing the challenge facing us than can be deduced from the more limited and mechanical words that are used to describe technology.

I have tried to measure the extent to which technology has really developed over the years, and the 'more' that we have got out of 'less', and I want very briefly to describe it to you.

I have taken four sorts of machines and sought to measure their historical development; travelling machines, communicating machines, killing machines and calculating machines. You could not be simpler than that. I am not concerned with how these machines do what is done, simply in what they do.

Take first, travelling machines. You start at four miles an hour, man's speed on foot. Then men achieve greater speed by riding animals and later use the wheel. In the nineteenth century came transport on rail using the steam engine and in 1900 the fastest speed reached was 80 miles an hour. In 1920 an aircraft first achieved a speed of 100 miles an hour; by 1945, which is only twenty-five years ago, jets had got to 700 miles an hour. Today the speed at which an Apollo space craft returns to earth is 25,000 miles an hour.

The picture looks just the same for communicating machines. A small audience for the human voice, a larger one for the mechanical megaphone, a far bigger one with the development of radio. No satellites for world TV audiences came until the Fifties. And then, last year, 1000 million people heard and saw Armstrong land upon the moon.

Killing machines have developed in the same way. People killed one by one in the Old Testament, using the Cain/Abel method. Later people threw things and that increased very slightly the number you could kill at one moment. Then the Chinese discovered gunpowder and forgot about it again. Later still you get the development, in the nineteenth century, of the first instrument of mass destruction, the machine-gun; in 1945 the atom bomb killed 90,000 at one go, and if a hydrogen bomb landed on Central London, up to 8 million would be killed by one machine.

Take calculating machines: very little is possible using your fingers. The abacus speeded it up. Babbage's analytical engine, built on a Government grant in about 1830, was the forerunner of computers. Mechanical calculating machines came later. There were no computers in 1945, but today computers are in use that will do one million calculations in a second.

Those then are some of the indices of the power we are talking about and are learning to control, and when you look at them, they do pinpoint some very interesting problems. First of all, the technological gap, so called, is the difference in performance between what rich societies are capable of achieving and the level at which the majority of mankind now lives. This is not only the difference between say America and India. One of the tensions even inside industrial societies, which we all experience, is that the gap between our full technological capability and the actual experience of ordinary people is enormous.

Still in the academic, educational world in Britain we most admire the man who sits in his laboratory trying to solve the problems of say high-energy physics, and we rate him higher than the person struggling to make sense of the administration of say a school, or a community, or a city, where the full complexities of human relationships have to be faced and where the real problems of application arise.

The important thing about the generation gap is that it shows how much parents have to learn from their children. I, personally, do not find it difficult to learn, I find it extremely hard to forget what I was taught as a child. Yet we now do have to forget about the nature of the world of our childhood if we were born between 1900 and 1945. That is the real challenge if we are going to take advantage of the possibilities and avoid the dangers of technology. Karl Marx was writing about the first Industrial Revolution – and his ideas inspired the Russian Revolution and the Chinese Revolution. It does really make you wonder what the philosophers will make of today's power and what revolutions the second Industrial Revolution will trigger off.

All these technological developments have occurred in the Northern hemisphere and what we call the colour line between white and non-white can be drawn exactly along the same lines, to reflect where technology has happened and where it has not. If I am going to set the argument about technology into its global framework I must just remind you that the whites who have technology live in the North, and the non-whites who have not got it live in the South. You could redraw the map of the world in terms of its production. It would show a huge America, a huge Britain, and Western Europe, and Russia, all in the North. But in the South, where there is not enough technology, you would see a small Latin America, a tiny Africa, and India. If for comparison you drew that map again in terms of population, you would see a huge South (without the technology), and the small North (with the technology).

The organisations which control modern machines divide into three main groups. There are Governments, there are defence forces (which control military technology), and there are firms (which control industrial technology). If you compare some of these organisations according to how much money they spend, you will find – not surprisingly – that the biggest organisation in the world is the American Federal Government, with a budget of more than £25,000 million a year. The next biggest organisation controlling and creating technology is the Soviet Central Government. The third is the Pentagon. The American Defense Forces spend more than the entire British Government spends in the course of the year. The British Government spends more than General Motors worldwide but General Motors spends more money than the Japanese Government every year. Japan is the fourth industrial power in the world. Ford is a bit bigger than the French defence budget, which ranks above and is quite substantially bigger than the ICI turnover. Last in line is the Norwegian Government. These are some of the human organisations which actually control contemporary power. These are some of the bodies which create power and control the use of power and, as they grow they employ more and more people. The sense of impotence, the sense of powerlessness that many people have today is, in part, caused by the fact that these organisations employ so many of us as well as controlling the use of so much power.

Some people, of course, accept all this quite uncritically. Other people, when they consider the magnitude of the task of trying to control big organisations, just get frightened off and give up. Others who make the attempt and meet with the sort of resistance that you meet whenever you try to change anything, are driven into protest and, sometimes under certain circumstances, into violence. I am not speaking of this country alone. Indeed, in respect of violence I am thinking of the way in which people react worldwide to this accumulation of power, which is the distinguishing characteristic of our society. We have now got to consider, and this is really what I came here specially to talk about, how we, in this generation, can develop the means by which we can control this power.

We have already begun to make some decision-making work at a world level. This is quite new. The League of Nations was a first attempt, an institutional response to the military technology of the First World War, which then seemed terrible. The United Nations in 1945 was a second attempt to find a worldwide institutional means by which we could secure peace. We have also recognised that global communications have got to follow the old model of the Post Office, where you have a technically imposed monopoly. Satellite communications systems really cannot compete against each other. We have therefore through COMSAT and INTELSAT now got a world communication system going. World poverty, the first demand, if you like, of the poor in the world for a world welfare state is now reflected by the creation of the FAO and various other world organisations. These are some examples of the globalisation of decision-making, or at any rate, an attempt to make it work.

Below the world-scale institutions you now have a large number of international organisations, for example the Common Market, COMECON in Eastern Europe, GATT and the IMF, set up because you cannot run a modern industrial system effectively unless certain economic decisions are taken internationally. Similarly it is impossible today to seek to defend yourself on the basis of national frontiers, because modern military technology crosses national frontiers as if they didn't exist. NATO, the Warsaw Pact and other military arrangements are an attempt to internationalise defence. Similarly, multinational companies have internationalised industrial decision-making.

At the national level the responsibility of Government today, quite unlike Government of fifty years ago, includes a responsibility for national prosperity (which means evolving a whole range of economic and industrial policies), and for security, which in a technical age means the security of having redundancy payments, retraining, a Health Service, and a Welfare State. Modern national Governments are also responsible for where a nation puts its efforts in science and technology. Government today is also the custodian of the nation's cultural identity, in the face of many pressures tending to erode it.

Now let us see what technology is doing for the individual person. It is in practice devolving power upon him to a quite remarkable degree. First of all, higher living standards made possible by technology mean an absolute transfer of newly created wealth and hence a command over material resources on a rising scale, to the individual. These resources, and the machines they buy, increase our freedom of action. This is perhaps best reflected by the motor car. Instead of using national public transport systems like the old railways which limit movement to existing lines, transport decisions are decentralised for the man who has a motor car; he can go where he likes. The individual use which people make of the power which technology has given them; the individual use they make of electricity, electrical appliances, transport mechanisms, telephones, and so on, when it is all added up creates community problems which are already forcing themselves to the attention of those at the centre in Government, and compelling action.

The 'new citizen' has now begun to organise himself, not, as in the nineteenth century, in very few sorts of groups like the Trade Union Movement, or the Co-operatives, or early Trades Associations, but into literally thousands of human action groups; community groups, environmental protection groups, consumer groups, educational action groups, amenity groups, the shop stewards' movement, housing groups, world development organisations, Black Power, student power, and so on. These are all part of the organisation of the human response from the bottom upwards.

The new action groups operating within industrial trade unions have now acquired a great deal of new power. As technology makes production more interdependent, any group which has any control over any part of the system can by withdrawing its labour now dislocate the whole or vast parts of the system. The people who work say in a ball-bearing plant in the Midlands, which supplies the Western European motor industry, can dislocate production on a continental scale. Thus some of the most significant decentralisation that has occurred producing a real transfer of power from the centre to the individual has come about because technology has made us all interdependent.

These major shifts in the level at which decisions are now taken – some being centralised and some decentralised – are extremely confusing and have created something like a crisis of national identity. In 1900 it was obvious what being British meant. You were defended by the Queen's Army, you communicated through the good old General Post Office, the economy was far more self-sufficient in a national context, the farms and firms for which workers worked were small and local. The official moral code of the land was embodied in legislation. Censorship was very strong. Unpleasant as life may have been, you knew where you stood and who was in charge. That is what it meant to be British. But today? British policy is discussed at the United Nations, you watch your football game from Mexico, over an American satellite, you are defended by NATO, you work for Ford, whose export practices have to conform to GATT and whose home market is studied by the IMF, permissive legislation has almost eroded censorship, you are metricating, decimalising, and have even abandoned Greenwich Mean Time. Technology appears to be changing everything and producing a sense of loss of cultural identity. This I am sure is the explanation of much of the new nationalism of our time. I am responsible for metrication, and metrication is in line with Joseph Whitworth's arguments about the interchangeability of components. But I got a letter the other day, an absolutely sizzling letter, against metrication, enclosing a pamphlet called 'The Battle for the Inch'. It said that the inch had been mentioned in the Bible and it was British and best. I never quite understood how those two things were achieved. It accused me of treachery in moving Britain from the inch to the metre. I wrote back to say that there would be nothing to prevent anyone keeping an old ruler and measuring anything at home in inches. We are simply concerned to see how we can put the measurement decision on the right level, the world level. Just as the world has adopted the Greenwich Meridian for navigation and timekeeping so we are adopting the metre. We cannot underestimate the extent to which this whole business of change is profoundly unsettling to people and it is one of the reasons why they feel impotent. They do not realise how quickly power is moving upwards and inwards, and downwards and outwards. The nightmares that people have are either that this centralisation will lead to a police state run by NATO, or Washington, or Brussels, or alternatively, if it is the crowds that frighten you more than the military-industrial complex, that we are all heading towards anarchy, with law and order and moral values collapsing in a welter of protest tolerated by a spinelessly permissive society.

All these developments provide a new insight into the Ford v Marx argument which I described. Fifty years after the Russian Revolution, which was presented as the great liberation of ordinary people through permitting them to gain control of the ownership of their industry, you find that in the Soviet Union they have not succeeded in creating the wealth fast enough to meet the needs of ordinary people and have

burdened themselves with an enormous bureaucratic structure caused
by the centralisation of most of the decision-making in the name of
Marxism. In the United States, with Ford's philosophy of pumping
consumer goods in at the bottom, they have created almost insoluble
problems of urban planning, of pollution, of congestion, of health, which
are now leading to a demand there for far greater state intervention than
Karl Marx, who believed in the withering away of the state, would ever
have contemplated. So you get this complete contrast, after fifty years of
experience, between what both solutions to the problem of technology
were expected to achieve, and what has actually happened.

There is much to learn from Marx and from Ford, and much to learn
from others as well. I have had the privilege recently of travelling to
Russia and Eastern Europe, the United States and many other
countries, and I see a convergence in practice between the differing ways
in which people with differing ideologies are tackling the same problems
created by technology. We should learn as much as we can from the
experience of others.

After four years as Minister in charge of technology and machines, I
have become even more convinced, if I ever needed convincing, and I do
not really think I did, that machines are of far, far less interest than
people; and that the only way in which we may control this new block of
power, which we have made and inherited, is exactly the same way as we
controlled other blocks of power in other periods of history, and that is
by educating ourselves so to do. When I think of the problems thrown up
by some of the factors that I have put before you, it seems to me the need
for relevance in education is the critical need. It is all very well doing
your BA, and MA, and your post-graduate work and your doctorate,
and your post doctoral and post-post doctoral research. One day I shall
open a funeral parlour, as the Americans call it, named 'Post Doctoral
Services Incorporated', because by the time most people have got two
doctorates they will be ready for the mortuary. The real priority must be
to re-establish a real relationship between education and real life,
throughout the whole of life. To raise the school leaving age to seventy-
five is the only sensible objective of educational policy.

I do not believe that any education that does not integrate with life, as
extra-mural part-time education does, can really claim to be contributing to our urgent need for skilled people to solve the problems of our
society. In 1926 during the General Strike my parents were in Moscow,
and they were invited to stand on the rostrum in the Red Square as
Labour visitors, to watch a demonstration by the Russians in support of
their British trade union colleagues. The procession went by with
banners, rather like the Durham Miners' Gala. They were carrying
pictures of Marx, Lenin, and Stalin and hideous cartoons of the British
capitalist leaders. One banner came by with a lot of words in Russian on

it and my father turned to the interpreter, Andrachin, and asked him to translate the slogan, fully expecting it would say 'Death to the British capitalist class' or something of that kind. Andrachin replied, 'I will translate that for you. It says "Workers of the electrical trade, improve your qualifications".' It was a splendid reminder that in a moment of great crisis and difficulty, it is to ourselves and what we can contribute to solving our own problems that we must turn for an answer and only thus can we ultimately find the means of controlling the power that we have created.

APPENDIX V
The New Politics: A Socialist Reconnaissance

Extracts from a Fabian Tract published in September 1970.

Parliamentary democracy and the party system have, in recent years, been criticised not only for their inability to solve some of our problems but also for their failure to reflect others adequately. It is not sufficient to congratulate ourselves on having avoided some of the tragedies that have beset other countries. We cannot be so very certain, as events in Ulster have proved, that we shall be able to cope with human and community tensions better than anyone else has done.

It is not only some members of the public who are disenchanted. There are people inside active politics, of whom I am one, who have long begun to feel uneasy, and to believe that the alienation of Parliament from the people constituted genuine cause for concern.

Political debates concentrating on economic and other management issues between Government and Opposition (whether Labour or Conservative) sometimes appear to blank out everything else, especially on the mass media, while a number of other issues are not sufficiently discussed because they have not been fitted into the current pattern of political debate.

Since the war the underlying problems of Britain's economic performance have occupied a central position in all political argument and Government competence in handling them has been regarded as of over-riding importance. Important as these issues are, and will continue to be, they are not the only ones that matter, and the public may have sensed this more quickly than the political parties. Fewer people now really believe that the problems of our society can be solved simply by voting for a Government every four or five years. More people want to do more for themselves, and believe they are capable of doing so, if the conditions could only be created that would make this possible.

If the Labour Party could see in this rising tide of opinion a new expression of grass-roots socialism, then it might renew itself and move nearer to the time when it is seen as the natural Government of a more fully self-governing society. Unless we succeed in doing this there is a danger that the Labour Party might get bogged down in stylised responses and fail to attract the support of those, especially among the young, who want to see more real choices in politics, and less of a personal contest between alternative management teams.

If we want to make the Labour Party more relevant, we must, as socialists, begin with an analysis of the underlying changes which are now taking place in our industrial system.

The process of re-equipment of the human race with an entirely new set of tools, for that is what has happened, has produced two trends – the one towards interdependence, complexity and centralisation requiring infinitely greater skills in the management of large systems than we have so far been able to achieve – the other, going on simultaneously, and for the same reasons, towards greater decentralisation and human independence, requiring us to look again at the role of the individual, the new citizen, and his place in the community.

In this country our parliamentary, political party, Civil Service, trade union, educational and legal systems, all of them now under stress, were developed at a time when the machine capability was infinitesimal compared with what it is today. Many of our problems stem from institutional obsolescence. We live at a time in history when both the personal and collective material options open to us, and the expectations we have, are far greater than ever before. Yet a large number of people feel that they have progressively less say over the events that shape their lives, because the system, however it is defined, is too strong for them.

Interdependence, complexity and centralisation

The growth of machine capability in all advanced societies whether capitalist or communist, has been made possible by the adoption of techniques of production which have allowed a degree of specialisation of labour only attainable in very large units. Henry Ford's revolution has now spread worldwide and no nation wishing to industrialise and raise its living standards, and no firm competing for markets, has been able to avoid following the same pattern of production. With the arrival of true automation the scale of production has increased still further and the optimum return on investment in research, manufacturing and marketing is now only possible when the whole process can be kept near its capacity.

It is widely assumed that the dominance of the multinationals will continue and will be extended in the years ahead. These are the very firms that generate most new technology, use new technology and control new technology. They will almost certainly employ more and more people by growth and takeover and will increasingly be making heir key investment, research and design decisions on a global scale to gain the benefits of low labour costs and good industrial relations in one country, high skills content in another, good market prospects in a third, and advantageous tax measures wherever they exist.

Seen as a political phenomenon these tendencies represent the emergence of an entirely new type of economic organism, more akin to the chartered company of the first Elizabethan era and later, than to the early type of capitalist firm that emerged in the nineteenth century as a result of the adoption of laissez faire economics. They also represent a new source of real power no longer anchored to the geography of a particular nation state, and greater than many states. For the people who work for the multinationals the problem is one of remoteness from the centre of authority in organisations whose real managers they might never meet in a lifetime of service within the vast bureaucracy of the firm.

Another aspect of this centralisation, complexity and interdependence, which also stems from technological development, arises in the military field. Joint intelligence work, standardised specifications and interdependence for equipment and spares, joint targeting of weapons with double-key safety devices, have made defence integration almost complete.

The third great new power centre that technology has directly and indirectly built up is of course Government itself. This growth is partly in response to the growing demands of people for collective action either to promote, control, or deal with the social consequences of change; and partly because, as the level of power elsewhere rises, the management and regulatory function in Government grows, just as it does in business or the armed services.

All these tendencies towards big industry, big defence forces and big governments – national and local – have occurred in all developed societies whether capitalist or Communist. Interdependence, complexity and centralisation are functions of technological development not ideology.

We have to turn our minds to ways of acquiring more power to modify, improve, influence, democratise, restructure and ultimately gain greater control of the system to make it serve human ends. There are no instant Utopias and even revolutionary socialism has proved only to be the starting point for those countries forced by circumstances to adopt it.

One of the underlying causes of Labour's defeat in 1970 could well have been that we did not appreciate the changing nature of our relationship with the people, and that in our preoccupation with exercising our authority we failed to give leadership on some of the issues that required, above all, vigorous public education, if they were to be successfully tackled.

More and more people are coming to understand that, if we want to make politics, Parliament and Government relevant again we have got to speak about them more realistically. For we are dealing with a new sort of citizen, nowadays, who is far more intelligent than most people in positions of authority yet accept that he is. It is to the nature of the new citizen that I now want to turn – because his new power derives exactly like the new power of big organisations – from the impact of technology upon society.

Decentralisation and the emergence of the new citizen

Let me briefly describe the powers enjoyed by the majority of new citizens as I understand them, here in Britain.

1. He has the vote and hence shares the power to destroy the Government of the day.
2. He enjoys a steadily rising real income or more leisure or a mixture of both.
3. He has access to far better education, training, re-training and further education for himself and his family, all of which improve his analytical capability.
4. He has access to a mass of information about current affairs which was almost entirely denied to his father and grandfather; and he hears something of the alternative analyses of events – capitalist, Marxist, Socialist, Freudian, Christian, Maoist or Buddhist, and has the time and opportunity to broaden the range of his own direct experience and his relations with wider groups of people.
5. His bargaining power in industrial negotiations is immensely greater than it was, and is the greatest in those advanced industries where interdependence has gone furthest, and the cost of dislocation is greatest.
6. He can and does make increasing real demands on Government for action to deal with industrial and community problems and social spending to provide the infrastructure he thinks he wants.

People today – these new citizens with this new power – have responded to the pressure of events by banding themselves together with others of like mind to campaign vigorously for what they want, and thousands of such pressure groups or action groups have come into existence.

They are producing a new style of political leadership committed to a cause rather than the search for elected authority. The relationship that develops between this new structure of issue politics and the political parties, especially the Labour Party, is of crucial importance. Some such groups will be working for causes hostile to our own objectives. But the majority, being the expression of human values against oppression by authority and the system of centralised power would be natural allies if only we can discover the right sort of relationship with them. We must not mistake their criticism for hostility, nor resent the fact that those who work in them have chosen such a role in preference to work exclusively within the Party. Each side has its own part to play in the process of socialist construction, and this is, in practice, recognised by the fact that many individuals work both in the action groups and in the Party. Their importance lies in the proof they offer, by their existence and their success, that people do have more power than many of them realise in achieving change from below.

The new citizen, despite his fears and doubts and lack of self-confidence, is a far more formidable person than his forebears. Increasingly he dislikes being ordered around by anyone, especially if he suspects that those who exercise authority underestimate him.

A growing number of them – everywhere – are just not prepared to accept poverty, oppression, the denial of human equality, bureaucracy, secrecy in decision-making, or any other derogation from what they consider to be their basic rights – and are gradually acquiring the power to enforce that view upon the societies in which they live.

In sketching in the changing relationship between democratic politics, the huge new organisations on the one hand, and the new citizen on the other, there is a common thread of argument. It is this. Authoritarianism in politics or industry just doesn't work any more. Governments can no longer control either the organisations or the people by using the old methods. The fact that in a democracy political authority derives from the consent of the electorate expressed at an Election instead of by inheritance, as in a feudal monarchy, or through a coup d'état, as in a dictatorship, makes practically no difference to the acceptability of authoritarianism. Except in a clear local or national emergency when a consensus may develop in favour of an authoritarian act of state, or if imposed it is accepted, big organisations, whether publicly or privately owned, and people, whoever they are, expect genuine consultation before decisions are taken that affect them.

It is arguable that what has really happened has amounted to such a breakdown in the social contract, upon which parliamentary democracy by universal suffrage was based, that that contract now needs to be renegotiated on a basis that shares power much more widely, before it can win general assent again.

The alternative philosophy of government, now emerging everywhere on the Right, takes as the starting point of its analysis the argument that modern society depends on good management and that the cost of breakdowns in the system is so great that they really cannot be tolerated and that legislation to enforce greater and more effective discipline must now take priority over other issues. The new citizen is to be won over to an acceptance of this by promising him greater freedom from Government, just as big business is to be promised lower taxes and less intervention and thus to be retained as a rich and powerful ally. But this new freedom to be enjoyed by big business means that it can then control the new citizen at the very same time as Government reduces its protection for him.

A socialist, by contrast, should never forget that he is in office in a representative capacity, regarding Government as the people's instrument for shaping their own destiny. He must remember that it is management in trust working through information and communication. Legislation may confirm a victory in argument already won; occasionally be used to educate, more often to protect, regulate or organise, but only as a last resort to enforce settlements that cannot be reached in any other way. This theme of continuing responsibility by leaders to the people, and by the people to each other, runs throughout the issues next identified for a further socialist reconnaissance.

Human dignity through development and diversity

Traditional socialist concern, with money as a measure of inequality, remains of fundamental importance, but it must also be seen as a problem of power. Where ownership is, or can be, separated from the power of management in industry, ownership loses its capacity to dominate; where, through social action, money can no longer purchase advantages in health and education, it loses some of its capacity to maintain privilege at the expense of the many. In recent years socialists have concentrated so much on the financial aspects of politics that they have underestimated the problems of power, and have allowed themselves to be deflected from effective policies to control it directly, by supposing that nothing could be done until ownership was communal, and that when it was communal nothing remained to be done.

If we are to make human dignity our first objective, not only have we got to eliminate poverty by using technology; secure the best possible management of our resources; eliminate old economic inequalities and guard against the creation of new ones; construct new safeguards against the abuse of new power; but we must also see that our new-found capabilities do in fact permit human dignity to express itself in diversity. This aspiration is not a new one – but it happens that this generation has acquired the power to make it possible.

Towards a new view of world affairs

Of all the semantic tyrannies that make serious analysis difficult the use of the phrase 'Foreign Affairs' is one of the most absurd. Technology started to abolish foreign affairs when the first real travellers conquered man's geographical imprisonment at the place of his birth, and by the time Marconi's radio message first crossed the Atlantic and international aerial bombardment started in the First World War, foreign affairs had outgrown their old diplomatic definition. In a world where colour television pictures, carried by satellites, can reach us from anywhere in less than a second, and where missiles with nuclear warheads can be targeted to any city, from any place in the world, it is meaningless to regard the cliffs of Dover as being of anything but scenic, cultural and nostalgic significance to the British people, as a frontier against foreigners and the rest of the world.

The idea that all the meaningful relations of any people with others who live in other countries can be squeezed through a network of narrow channels called Foreign Offices is at least a hundred years out of date.

There are world affairs, full of problems which affect the whole world. To help solve these problems we have many resources, technical and material, human and financial, ideas and people and information that can be brought into play. There are multilateral organisations of which every country is a member which cover as wide a field of human activity as government – or life itself. There are bilateral relations with other peoples that extend equally widely. Finally, there are those diplomatic and political contacts between Governments which have traditionally been handled through the Foreign Office. It would be foolish to minimise their importance, but they now represent a tiny sector of the interface between nations. Moreover, intergovernmental political relations necessarily concern themselves mainly with clashes of supposed national interest, ideological differences, and all the points of friction which, emphasised to the exclusion of other considerations, can blind all peoples to the reality of their common interest in cooperation in the war against hunger, oppression and indignity.

We shall never discover the full potential for the unity of mankind through foreign policy or diplomatic talks. Our best hope may well lie in trying to bypass our differences by opening up new areas of cooperation. Trade and technology, the transfer of knowledge and know-how, the freer movement of ideas, these are what we should seek to promote.

Across a world communications network, once it is established, we must also seek to pass accurate information about each other's problems and achievements and transfer more of the teachings of the world's greatest thinkers, so that we can all gradually come to share the same sources of human inspiration as we educate ourselves and our children to realise that we live in a world no bigger in real terms than the television screen on which we observe each other's doings every day.

An intensive study of organisational problems

It is clear that unless the world as a whole can find better means of managing all its many organisations, and unless more efficient means of creating and developing new resources can be devised, the technological revolution will take too long to realise its full potential; and will not deliver the goods necessary for the material improvement in living standards of millions of people, now living in poverty, within their own lifetime. For a socialist in a non-socialist society to speak approvingly of the key role of management makes him, for some people, suspect, because management is associated automatically either with private industry, authoritarianism or bureaucracy, or most likely all three. But this cannot blind us to the fact that management skills are of the greatest importance and are in critically short supply. In any case, ownership has long been becoming separated from management, at least in large corporations, and that process of disentanglement can be assisted by, among other things, vigorous action by the workers.

The overwhelming majority of managers are, in effect, salaried workers, able to be hired and fired like those they supervise, even if their pay and conditions of service are vastly better. To the extent that the ownership function of control can be weakened still further, the manager and the workers should be able to identify a greater common interest in the wealth-creating processes, or else, in non-industrial enterprises, in a partnership to achieve whatever social, communal or service objectives the organisation in which they work is there to serve.

The old crude industrial authoritarianism of the past is now being attacked as directly by modern management thinkers as it is by the trade unions who are determined to change it. For management, like modern government, is simply not practicable on an authoritarian basis any more. It just won't work without a high degree of real devolution and a most sophisticated information network that feeds back continuing reports on how the human, as well as the mechanical and financial parts of the system are coping with their work.

Towards workers' control

Here in Britain the demand for more popular power is building up most insistently in industry, and the pressure for industrial democracy has now reached such a point that a major change is now inevitable, at some stage. What is happening is not just a respectful request for consultation before management promulgates its decisions. Workers are not going to be fobbed off with a few shares – whether voting or non-voting. They cannot be satisfied by having a statutory worker on the board or by a carbon copy of the German system of co-determination.

The claim is for the same relationship between government and governed in factories, offices and shops as was finally yielded when the universal adult franchise brought about full political democracy, or what it might be more helpful to re-name 'voter's control', first advocated by the Chartists, and finally conceded in 1970 when eighteen-year-olds won their rights.

On the face of it the perils of yielding 'production by consent' when we have already survived the far riskier experiment of 'government by consent' would seem less daunting. It would have been, on the face of it, more logical if the experiment in democracy had begun with industry; and only then, when proved successful, extended to Government.

Certainly there is no more reason why industrial power at plant or office level should be exclusively linked to ownership of shares, than that political power should have been exclusively linked to the ownership of land and other property as it was in Britain until the 'voter's control' movement won its battle.

Nor, and this is the important point, is there any reason why the new demands should be any more revolutionary, in the sense of paving the way for violence, than were the old demands. It is true that some of the advocates of workers' control are believers in the violent overthrow of the existing order. But then so were some of the advocates of the wider franchise. In the event, by one of these characteristically skilful and long-drawn-out withdrawals in the face of the inevitable which is the genius of the British – that mixture of realism, laziness, decency and humanity that has given us 300 years free of violent revolution – the powers that be, in the end, granted the demands in full.

It is important that those who advocate workers' control, or are sympathetic to it, should not mislead anyone about its likely effect. It will prove to be no more, and no less, a panacea for industrial workers than parliamentary democracy has been for the electors. With real power will come real responsibility for dealing directly with some of the outer realities of our competitive world, including the inescapable market mechanisms and other interconnections which will set severe limits on the freedom the new power will bring. This is not to say that there will not be real gains in self-respect, self-fulfilment, improved working conditions, better management and productivity. There will be. But there will almost certainly be failures too. These could hardly be worse, in their human consequences, than those experienced by many thousands of workers who become redundant every year under the owner-imposed management system of today. One of the real potential beneficiaries will be the community itself, since an effective workers' control system probably stands the only real chance of creating the sort of responsibility in industrial affairs that is now lacking and that the legislative proposals for dealing with prices and incomes or industrial relations seemed or seem unlikely to achieve.

It must also be noted, in passing, that some of the problems of control of the mass media would be easier to solve if such a radical change as the one implied by workers' control could be made to work constructively in the press, radio and television.

A frontal assault on secrecy in decision making

If a mature and more self-regulating society is to have a real chance of success, people must know much more about why and how the decisions that affect them are actually made. Unless this information is made available people will never discover what the alternatives are early enough to have any influence on which of them to support and which to oppose.

As far as Government is concerned this must mean a completely fresh look at all the many barriers that exist to ensure that ordinary people do not know what is going on in Government. The practice of secrecy that has grown up over the years, in Britain and all other countries, goes back to the very distant past. The medieval Privy Councillor's oath pledging utter secrecy and administered to each new Minister on his knees when assuming office is a symbolic, but interesting example. It was written centuries before democracy was even contemplated, at a time when the only responsibility of a Minister was to the Crown. The Official Secrets Act of 1911, to which each official is also sworn, entrenches secrecy in statute.

The justification given for secrecy is usually based on a complete and deliberate confusion of the national interest with the political convenience of Ministers, buttressed by the natural preference of civil servants for the full protection of their role as completely anonymous ministerial advisers.

A move towards much more open Government would not need amending legislation. A clear policy decision in favour of a progressive relaxation of secrecy, in practice, would be quite sufficient to deal with the problem. It would constitute a real gain for the community and would also be good for Government, in that Ministers and officials would be in a position to receive more relevant comments and advice from those outside, who would know more accurately what was at issue and when the matter concerned was due for decision.

I have put the Government's responsibility to provide more information first because it lies directly within its own power to change its practice. But the same arguments apply with equal force to the publication of much more information by industry. The case for this is so very well known, and has so often been argued, that it does not need labouring. But since knowledge is power, a more general statutory requirement to publish information would be a very important way of seeing that the power of private corporations is shared and they thus become more accountable.

This theme of publicity versus secrecy should be a major one for a future Labour Government and the onus of proof should be squarely placed on those who want to preserve the mystique of secrecy rather than on those who want to lift it. To do this would almost certainly slow down the process of decision-making because of the lengthy consultations that would take place – but it would provide a more effective means of considering in advance the interaction of decisions on each other and on the community, and without it we cannot hope to change the balance in favour of the people.

The democratisation of the mass media

Parliament exercised significant power in Britain long before it was democratic, deriving from its freedom to assemble, to discuss and debate. These rights were so important in the struggle for political power that the nineteenth-century popular battle for participation concentrated on the right of access of ordinary people to Parliament.

Today, the freedom of debate and discussion remains central to the control of power. But unless this freedom is amplified by high-speed printing presses or powerful transmitters it need not amount to very much more than the right to set up on a rostrum at Speakers' Corner in Hyde Park. Regular access to the public at large is virtually the prerogative of publishers, newspaper proprietors, the massive BBC, commercial TV programme companies and those business organisations that use the mass media to advertise their products – and their values. That about sums up the list of those with *effective* power to publish, apart from organisations which issue their own material.

The public, as a whole, is denied access or representation in these new talking shops of the mass media as complete as the 95 per cent without the vote were excluded from Parliament before 1832. The real question is not whether the programmes are good, or serious, or balanced, or truthful. It is whether or not they allow the people themselves to reflect the diversity of interests, opinions, grievances, hopes and attitudes to their fellow citizens and to talk out their differences at sufficient length.

The democratisation and accountability of the mass media will be a major issue for the Seventies and the debates on it are now beginning. The press and broadcasting authorities have a responsibility for providing enough accurate information, at the time when it really matters, to allow people to acquire greater influence.

New priorities in education

Education, like information and communications, is moving into the centre of political controversy. Indeed it has already become the focal point of debate and political controversy. Education is the key to the development of the individual; it equips him to work and earn; it allows him to share in the world's richest treasures of wisdom and art and it offers him some of the keys to political power. The denial of access for the many, by an élite, has proved to be a most powerful instrument for long-term popular subjugation. The majority of children have been – and still are being – branded as failures at eleven, then told they do not merit real secondary education; only to discover later that, as a result, they cannot qualify for higher education. Then, for the rest of their lives, they are kept out of many positions of responsibility, which are reserved for graduates.

The battle for comprehensive education is only half-way won at the secondary level, and is only just beginning at the level of higher and further education, where the massed ranks of the élitists are already in position to repel the expected assault by the many, with the familiar cry of 'more means worse'. It will be just as hard, but just as necessary, to win that battle and the sooner it is won the better.

At the moment we still accept a wastage of human ability which is so massive that if we could only tap a small proportion of the reserves of talent that exist, we could raise both our standard of life, and the quality of it, much more rapidly than now seems possible. But we can only achieve this if we concentrate far more attention on raising the level of the average in both people and performance rather than continuing to focus so much of our effort on the so-called best; and if we are also prepared to see the potential of education in helping us to overcome the hard-core problems of the poor, the sick and the deprived. A real programme for education that set itself these new objectives would be bitterly resisted, but without a change in our existing educational priorities we shall go on exploring the frontiers of knowledge as brilliantly as we have done; and then wonder why the problems of application and community organisation seem so insoluble.

Beyond parliamentary democracy

The main theme of this pamphlet is that the new citizen wants and must receive a great deal more power than all existing authority has so far thought it right, necessary or wise to yield to him.

This demand for more real power by people is slowly but irresistibly building up on every front here and in every country in the world. Some people want it to replace the power of the tyrants who oppress them, others to protect existing rights or to assert new ones which they believe their dignity and self-respect require.

The British Parliament cannot expect to be exempted from this general demand for greater participation both from within and without. The welcome erosion of the power of the Whips has gone much further than most people outside politics realise in restoring to MPs the power to limit the automatic exercise of executive power by Cabinets.

The next stage in public participation in Government is bound to come from the first serious reconsideration of the possibility of adding some direct decision-making, or at any rate comprehensive opinion-testing mechanism, to that of the ballot box, on specific issues.

The most discussed form of direct decision-making has been the idea of holding nationwide Referenda on specific issues – either those which transcend party loyalties and are of supreme importance – or those on moral questions which are now by general consent left to a free vote of the House.

The arguments against adopting such a course are too well known to need elaboration: it would undermine representative Government, pave the way for dictatorship sustained by plebiscites; frustrate all liberal reform; pander to the worst instincts of the public, and so on. Both Front Benches and the overwhelming majority of Back Bench MPs – either because of their intimate knowledge of politics, or possibly from an understandable reluctance to see their representative status eroded by being shared with their constituents – are wholly opposed to any concession whatsoever on this score, and anyone who even raises the subject is immediately made aware of the fact that he has broken one of the unwritten rules of the club.

But quite apart from the intrinsic merits or demerits of Referenda as a means of decision-making in a democracy, we have to face the fact that a demand for a Referendum has begun to emerge over the Common Market issue where there are such sharp differences of opinion within each party that it would not be possible to decide the issue at a General Election even if the leadership of the two major Parties were taking contrary views. A decision taken by the House of Commons that committed Britain to membership of the EEC might or might not conform to the popular view as ascertained by the (somewhat discredited) public opinion polls. But if it did not, and those who were opposed to entry refused to accept the reasons given for joining (or vice-versa) something like a breakdown in the social contract might occur.

Some demand for a procedure for a national consultation on this, or some other issue, is bound to be strongly pressed at some stage, and if it is to be rejected, and its rejection made acceptable, far stronger and more compelling arguments than those hitherto advanced against it will have to be produced and argued convincingly.

If Government has now got to accept that many of its functions are being taken over by international institutions beyond its shores, or are to be devolved, or hived off, or shared with the people below who are claiming greater rights as new citizens, we shall have to consider afresh exactly what the role of national Government is to be. In short, it should concern itself mainly with the big decisions within the state, concentrating its attention on its major objectives; adjusting the system and the organisation structures to allow their realisation at various levels; and interacting intelligently and professionally with all those parts of other systems that touch upon Government's own broad range of responsibilities for promoting the human welfare and dignity of its citizens.

It naturally follows from this argument that the role of political leadership is likely to change in a number of significant ways in the years ahead. New-style political leaders at national level will need to establish a new sort of relationship with the people. They will have to recognise that the real limitation on their power to shape events will be the extent to which they can connect themselves through proper information, and communications systems, with the two new realities of our time – the managements of other centres of power, and the new citizen with his developing organisations.

They will have to be leaders, rather more in the Moses tradition, drawing their power less from the executive authority they have acquired by election and more from influence, helping people to see what they can achieve for themselves, and acting as a consultant, equipped with all the necessary support and facilities, to allow them to do so. This is not a charter for anarchism, nor a dream of creating a wholly self-regulating economic and political system. Leadership there must be, but not all from the top. Leadership is inseparable from responsibility and responsibility is inseparable from power, and if, as I have argued, power is now being disseminated more widely, leadership will have to be more widely shared too. Indeed, in a world bulging over with new power, the sheer volume of work for leaders to do is so great that unless far more men and women take their share of the load of leadership and management, and become responsible, the whole system will break down through sheer unmanageability. No one could possibly be wise enough, or knowledgeable enough, or have the time and skill to run the world today even if he had all the authority and all the expert advice he asked for to do the job. Individual people have got to do it themselves and argue it out as they go along.

More than five hundred years before the birth of Christ, Lao-Tzu, the Chinese philosopher, had this to say about leadership: 'As for the best leaders, the people do not notice their existence. The next best the people honour and praise. The next the people fear, and the next the people hate. But when the best leader's work is done the people say, "We did it ourselves".'

To create the conditions that will allow the people to do it themselves is the central task of leadership today.

People who want to change the community in which they live, the conditions under which they work, and the world in which their children will grow up, are now everywhere engaged in a struggle to get the power that will allow them to do all these things. It must be a prime objective of socialists to work for the redistribution of political power to allow them to acquire more of it to work out their own destiny in their own way. Strong Government to control the abuse of power will certainly be necessary; strong leadership too to articulate clear object-ives, but above all the creation of a strong and responsible society in which more people exercise more responsibility than those in authority anywhere yet seem ready to yield to them. In the Seventies the debates inside the Party and between the Party and the public will increasingly need to centre around this key question.

Appendix VI
Upper Clyde Shipbuilders Bill, June 1971

Upper Clyde Shipbuilders
(Public Ownership)

A

BILL

To make provision for and in connection
with the continuation of the undertaking
of Upper Clyde Shipbuilders Ltd. under
public ownership, the development of
the management structure thereof, and
the carrying on of the undertaking;
and for purposes connected therewith.

Presented by Mr. Anthony Wedgwood Benn
supported by
Mr. William Ross, Dr. J. Dickson Mabon,
Mr. William Hannan, Mr. Bruce Millan,
Mr. Hugh McCartney, Mr. William Small,
Mr. John Rankin, Mr. Richard Buchanan,
Mr. Frank McElhone, Mr. John Robertson
and Mr. Dick Douglas

Ordered, by The House of Commons,
to be Printed, 22 June 1971

LONDON
Printed and Published by
Her Majesty's Stationery Office
Printed in England at St. Stephen's
Parliamentary Press

3p net

[Bill 195]   (385972)   45/1

A

BILL

T O

Make provision for and in connection with the continuation of the undertaking of Upper Clyde Shipbuilders
Ltd. under public ownership, the development of the
management structure thereof, and the carrying on of
the undertaking; and for purposes connected therewith.

A.D. 1971

WHEREAS it is desirable for the workers by hand and by
brain in Upper Clyde Shipbuilders Ltd. that the assets
of the Company should be secured upon the basis of
common ownership under the best obtainable system of popular
5 administration and control:

Be it therefore enacted by the Queen's most Excellent Majesty,
by and with the advice and consent of the Lords Spiritual and
Temporal, and Commons, in this present Parliament assembled,
and by the authority of the same, as follows:—

10 **1.** The management and workers in Upper Clyde Shipbuilders
Ltd. shall jointly prepare, in consultation, a plan for the development of a new company under public ownership designed to
ensure the viability of the undertaking at an early date, including
details of the management pattern and structure of the company
15 accepted by the management and workers as a whole, and shall
submit such a plan to the Secretary of State.

Preparation of plans for public ownership.

  2. *There may be defrayed out of moneys provided by Parliament
any expenditure which a Minister of the Crown, may with the
approval of the Treasury, incur—*

Expenses.

20   (*a*) *with a view to or in connection with the acquisition for
the benefit of the Crown (whether by a Minister or his
nominee or by a company in which the shares are held
for the benefit of the Crown) of the whole of the undertaking and assets of Upper Clyde Shipbuilders Ltd.; or*

    (*b*) *with a view to or in connection with the carrying on of the
undertaking acquired in pursuance of this Act;*

*including expenditure in subscribing for shares in or securities of,
or making loans to, any company so acquiring any undertaking or
assets.*

5

Short title.   **3.** This Act may be cited as the Upper Clyde Shipbuilders
(Public Ownership) Act 1971.

APPENDIX VII
European Communities Bill

Extract from House of Commons debate on 18 April 1972 in which an amendment sponsored by Neil Marten and five other anti-Market Conservative MPs, calling for a Referendum, was supported by Labour's Shadow Cabinet.

Mr Benn: I ask the indulgence of the Committee to intervene briefly to convey officially the support of the Opposition for the Amendment moved by the hon Member for Banbury (Mr Marten).

Turning to a practical argument that has not found much space in the debates we have had so far today, the House of Commons is divided on Europe. Both parties are divided on Europe. Indeed I would go further and say that the House is fragmented on the European question, for I agree with the hon and gallant Member for Lewes (Sir T. Beamish) that there are many different views.

It cannot have given much pleasure to my right hon Friend the Member for Birmingham Stechford (Mr Roy Jenkins) or our right hon Friends who resigned with him to have parted company with their colleagues on a matter of this kind. It cannot really give much pleasure to hon Gentlemen opposite, including the hon Member for Banbury, who like most Members of this House have tried to give devoted service to their Party, to find themselves in a position in which they might prefer to see the other side in power to avoid the consequences they fear would be so serious for the country. When Members of Parliament on both sides who have a long record of service to their Parties find themselves in the position in which we find ourselves put, this is not a moment to mock, to laugh, to trade quotations that may somehow help our short-term interests.

Mr Thorpe: If the right hon Gentleman is right, and I think he is, in his thesis that the House of Commons is fragmented and if he feels compassion for those in all parts of the House who find themselves in disagreement, does it not make it sheer hypocrisy for him to have supported throughout the whipping system being applied to the vote in October and still more in February?

Mr Benn: My concern throughout has been a free vote of the British people. The right hon Gentleman cannot get away with that. He knows very well that the effect of the vote of 18 October and the effect of the votes tonight will be to deny to the British public the right he claims as a Member of Parliament.

Mr Thorpe: Let us hear about this place first.

Mr Benn: That is no recommendation for the parliamentary system. I will deal with the right hon Gentleman's points as they come. The British parliamentary system cannot survive if we are to have distinguished parliamentarians saying 'Let us think about this place first', because if that is what Parliament is about there is no reason why anybody outside should support it.

Mr Thorpe: Freedom starts here.

Mr Benn: Now we have it. Freedom began before the House of Commons was set up. Freedom was forced on the House by people outside it. Freedom is defended by the ballot box and not by the Division Lobby. If the Liberal Party now says that freedom rests in Parliament instead of seeing itself as the guardian of freedom outside Parliament, no wonder it is a tiny minority. I began with a pledge to be conciliatory and it is not my wish that I should provoke the one Party in the House that has consistently supported the view of entry from the beginning.

There are factors in this debate which the House of Commons must take seriously. I believe the first such factor to be that neither side will accept the verdict of the House of Commons on the European question. Those who favour entry will never give up their advocacy of entry. We have seen that from those who have separated themselves from my colleagues and myself on this question. Similarly, they must learn that those who will not support entry without consent will *never* support entry without consent. Even if that entry is forced through the House of Commons, forced to Royal Assent, and the celebrations in Brussels take place in January, that will not be accepted. This is the difficulty which we face. We could cope with our own disagreement if it were this place first. We could cope with our disagreement in the ordinary parliamentary way. What we cannot do is to cope ourselves, in the ordinary parliamentary way, with deep differences reflecting deep interests that have been wholly shut out from the decision we are asked to take.

Mr Maclennan: My right hon Friend has rested his argument on the inflexibility of those who are committed in favour of the Common Market and those who are against it, but some of us remember very clearly – indeed, his own example speaks loud in this matter – how flexible some politicians are able to be.

Mr Benn: I take my hon Friend's point. I am not one of those – and I have made this clear every time I have spoken in the House – who have been committed at all costs to our joining the Common Market or to our staying out. I have been consistent in saying for many years that this issue must be decided by the people, and I will accept the popular verdict, whichever way it goes. But if flexibility in response to a developing situation is an offence, there is not one man, including my hon Friend, who will be able to claim that he came down the motorway of life without turning the steering wheel to left or to right to take account of changing circumstances.

The vote on 28 October was a majority that was not normally reached. It was reached before the treaty was published and before the Bill was published. It was reached by a coalition of people voting together who had never sought together the mandate which they claimed they had in the Lobby that day. It is a constitutional change. It is an irreversible decision. I heard the hon and gallant Member for Lewes say on television that it was not irreversible, but that cannot easily be said by Leaders on the Front Bench. If our Continental partners-to-be thought that we were lighthearted about our attitude to entry, they would not have us in. So the case must be presented as being a solemn, irreversible decision.

I should like to see the British public, on a free vote, decide the matter on the basis of a recommendation which came from a free vote of the House. What I will not accept is the House, on a free vote, using that vote to deny the electors the right to say whether they wish Britain to join. That is the alternative which the right hon and learned Gentleman proposes, and it is not acceptable.

Another respect in which public anger will be caused is this. If there is further development of the Community, if we have an economic and monetary union, if we have a defence community and political reunification, and if every time the French proceed by Referenda we are hogtied by Clause 2, the public will not understand it. People will not accept that the Government, without consent, have put a statutory straitjacket on parliamentary debate in advancing the Community, whereas France is allowed to proceed by popular vote.

Although Referenda in France have been the agents of Presidents, they have also destroyed Presidents. President de Gaulle disappeared, hoist on his own petard. There are safeguards in a Referendum for the French which are utterly denied us – not just now, but in any development of the Community.

I do not want to sound alarmist, but we should be very foolish if we supposed that there were not people in this country who cared as much about being subordinated to Brussels without consent as so-called loyalist Protestants in Northern Ireland care about being subordinated to Dublin without consent. They may be a small minority, as minorities are everywhere when violence errupts, but if the feeling that the independent right of the electors, through the ballot box, to decide constitutional questions is as deeply entrenched as the feeling of Ulster loyalists, as I believe it is, there could well be trouble following a decision to enter. No doubt the Government, with their police and perhaps a little advice from the French police in Calais, could put it down. It is better to say it now than wait until it happens and then wonder why it has happened. [HON MEMBERS: 'Stir it up.'] I am not stirring it up.

I say this to the Government. The capacity to put down that sort of thing, if it arises, depends upon one's being able to say to the man whom one is putting down, 'Change your Member of Parliament, change the law, and you can have your way by peaceful means.' However, if some power, some law – the power to tax, for example – is put outside the control of the British electorate, one destroys at any rate a part of the moral authority that allows one to deal with those who struggle against what has been done.

The Government cannot, on the one hand, stand on the issue of law and order and, on the other hand, themselves deliberately fracture the delicate social fabric of the social contract upon which our system of government has been founded.

How does the House of Commons settle the issue? A General Election is the traditional way, if it is to be that way. I personally would accept unhesitatingly, as I think that the whole House of Commons would, a Conservative re-election at any Election now, settling the European question. Of course it would settle it, because the country knows the Bill, it knows the terms and it knows the treaty. If the Government were to be re-elected, we would accept that.

However, the Government would not be re-elected. An hon Member can get a round of cheers by mocking his constituents in the Chamber. Today I have heard many hon Members laughing at the ignorance of their constituents. Hon Members have asked, 'Who knows what a Referendum is?' By God, the miners won the right to strike and their battle in the recent dispute on a Referendum. The British people know the meaning of the right to choose through the ballot box. Hon Members can mock their electors with impunity from the safety of the Chamber, but when the battle is taken to a General Election the Government would be utterly defeated if they were to deny the British public the right to decide the matter. I warn hon Members not to be surprised if the British public laughs at the British Parliament if hon Members are so quick to laugh at the British public when debating its rights.

I therefore believe that a Referendum must and will be offered in a General Election. After all, if the Labour Party is to offer a Referendum in its manifesto, why wait? We can do it tonight. We have a parliamentary majority tonight if the Opposition support their colleagues for a Referendum tonight. If the Government will not accept a

Referendum, we get an Election, which is what all my hon Friends want. Therefore, the issue of a General Election and that of a Referendum are inextricably bound up together.

If the arguments that I have summarised are invalid, the case against the Referendum is overwhelming. I cannot hope in one speech to deal with all of these arguments against the Referendum. What I can do is to show the Committee the historical origins of these arguments.

Sir Robert Peel, in opposing the Reform Bill, said this in 1831: 'I am convinced that it is not founded on the acknowledged principles of the constitution – because it does not give security to the prerogative of the Crown – because it does not guarantee the legitimate rights, influences, and privileges of both Houses of Parliament.' Peel said this first when he opposed the Reform Bill. This argument about its being contrary to our parliamentary traditions has been used in opposition to any extension of the people's rights which has been proposed over the past 140 years.

The second argument is that it establishes a precedent. I invite hon Members to listen to this quotation from Asquith on votes for women in 1910: 'In the long run, if you grant the franchise to women, you will have to grant it on the widest possible basis, and with all the consequences to which I have referred . . .' [OFFICIAL REPORT, 12 July, 1910; Vol. 19, c. 250.]

Asquith was against votes for women because it would open the way to votes for everyone. That is exactly the argument that we have had in the course of this debate.

Lord Cranborne, later Lord Salisbury, attacked Disraeli's Reform Bill in 1867 on the same grounds.

The third argument is that the public are not equipped to reach decisions. Bagehot is the man to listen to here. He said this in 1872: 'In plain English, what I fear is that both our political parties will bid for the support of the working man; that both of them will promise to do as he likes if he will only tell them what it is, that, as he now holds the casting vote in our affairs, both parties will beg and pray him to give that vote to them. I can conceive of nothing more corrupting or worse for a set of poor ignorant people than that two combinations of well-taught and rich men should constantly offer to defer to their decision, and compete for the office of executing it. *Vox populi* will be *Vox diaboli* if it is worked in that manner.'

That is the case against the Referendum. If it is looked at in one way, of course it is the case against the Referendum. If it is looked at in another way, this having happened, it is our traditional parliamentary way of life that we are being asked to defend.

Britain is different. Asquith explained why votes for women in Australia were all right because Australia had such a sparse population, but Britain was different.

The fifth argument is that the advocates are not sincere. The arguments against the Referendum are the very same arguments as have been used against every extension of the people's rights for 140 years. It follows the same pattern. First, the argument is ignored. It is described as a fringe issue. It is then described as trendy. Then it is mocked. Then it is laughed at. Then hon Members who do not support the Referendum laugh at their own constituents and laugh at those who advocate the Referendum. Then they warn against the Referendum and against its dangers. Then they denounce it. Then they capitulate. Then they forget and hope that everyone else forgets too. It is always the same process – ignore, mock, laugh, warn, denounce, capitulate, then forget and then hope that everybody else forgets that one has gone through the process.

That was how the British Empire became decolonised and there were just as many humbugs, according to *The Times*, voting for freedom in the colonies as there will be voting for the Referendum tonight because there were many people who wished that the public, the people, would go away. But when they did not go away, they found it more advisable to accommodate themselves to what the public wanted. The arguments are always the same. They are always wrong and when they are brought up again they are always supported by certain minorities.

They are supported by the rich because, of course, the rich are afraid that the public, if they had a vote, might be interested in the redistribution of wealth. They are opposed by racial minorities because all racial minorities are a bit nervous and this is why we hear about immigrants. They are opposed by a particular section of the Left who are afraid that if they had to convince the public that socialism was right they would never succeed. Therefore they would rather sneak into Parliament to do it before the public discover.

Tonight will not settle this matter. Even if the Amendment fails by the vote of the Government and by some abstentions from my hon Friends, the clamour of those outside the House of Commons will continue to grow until it is heard on this and, if I might add, on other issues in which they believe that Parliament pays too little attention to their needs.

I would venture to prophesy that hon Members who vote against or abstain will later live to hide today's HANSARD from their grandchildren, particularly its Division List, because they will want to avoid the embarrassment of explaining why they voted as they did. I believe they will be ashamed at their blindness in failing to see that what they opposed in the name of parliamentary democracy was the floodtide of popular consent without which parliamentary democracy cannot survive. Trust between Parliament and the people must be a mutual trust. If we do not trust them, then not for long will they trust us.

APPENDIX VIII
Abbreviations

ACAS	Advisory Conciliation and Arbitration Service
ACTT	Association of Cinematograph, Television and Allied Technicians
AEA	Atomic Energy Authority
AEI	Amalgamated Electrical Industries
AERE	Atomic Energy Research Establishment
AGR	Advanced Gas-cooled Reactor
ASSET	Association of Supervisory Staff, Executives and Technicians (subsequently merged with ASTMS)
ASTMS	Association of Scientific, Technical and Managerial Staffs
AUEW	Amalgamated Union of Engineering Workers (formerly AEU and AEF)
AWRE	Atomic Weapons Research Establishment
BAC	British Aircraft Corporation
BBC	British Broadcasting Corporation (BBC1 and BBC2)
BCV	Bristol Commercial Vehicles
BEA	British European Airways
BMC	British Motor Corporation
BMH	British Motor Holdings (formerly BMC, subsequently British Leyland)
BP	British Petroleum
CANDU	Canadian Heavy Water Reactor
CBI	Confederation of British Industry
CEGB	Central Electricity Generating Board
CERN	Conseil Européen de Recherche Nucléaire
CIA	Central Intelligence Agency
CLP	Constituency Labour Party
CND	Campaign for Nuclear Disarmament
COCOM	Coordinating Committee for Multilateral Exports
COMECON	(East European) Council for Mutual Economic Assistance

CSC	Comprehensive Schools Committee
CSEU	Confederation of Shipbuilding and Engineering Unions
DEA	Department of Economic Affairs
DEP	Department of Employment and Productivity
DES	Department of Education and Science
DHSS	Department of Health and Social Security
ECGD	Export Credit Guarantee Department
EDC	Economic Development Committee
EEC	European Economic Community
EETPU	Electrical, Electronic, Telecommunications and Plumbing Union
EFTA	European Free Trade Association
EMI	Electric Music Industries
ETU	Electrical Trades Union (subsequently part of EETPU)
EURATOM	European Atomic Energy Community
FAA	Federal Aviation Agency
FBI	Federal Bureau of Investigation
GEC	General Electric Company
GLC	Greater London Council
GMC	General Management Committee
GOC	General Officer Commanding
GPO	General Post Office
IBM	International Business Machines
ICI	Imperial Chemical Industries
ICL	International Computers Ltd (formerly ICT)
ICT	International Computers and Tabulators
ILEA	Inner London Education Authority
IMF	International Monetary Fund
IPC	International Publishing Corporation
IRA	Irish Republican Army
IRC	Industrial Reorganisation Corporation
ITA	Independent Television Authority
ITN	Independent Television News
ITT	International Telephones and Telegraph
ITV	Independent Television
KGB	Soviet Intelligency Agency
LCC	London County Council
LEA	Local Education Authority
LSE	London School of Economics
MLF	Multi Lateral Force
MOD	Ministry of Defence
NASA	National Aeronautical Space Agency

NATO	North Atlantic Treaty Organisation
NCB	National Coal Board
NEC	National Executive Committee
NEDC	National Economic Development Committee (Neddy)
NHS	National Health Service
NOP	National Opinion Poll
NPT	Non-Proliferation Treaty
NRDC	National Research and Development Corporation
NUJ	National Union of Journalists
NUM	National Union of Mineworkers
NUR	National Union of Railwaymen
NUS	National Union of Seamen
NUS	National Union of Students
OAU	Organisation of African Unity
OECD	Organisation for Economic Cooperation and Development
O&M	Organisation and Methods
OPD	Overseas Policy and Defence Committee (of Cabinet)
OPEC	Organisation of Petroleum Exporting Countries
PIB	Prices and Incomes Board
PLP	Parliamentary Labour Party
PMG	Postmaster General
POEU	Post Office Engineering Union
PPS	Parliamentary Private Secretary
PTA	Parent Teachers' Association
PWR	Pressurised Water Reactor
QEII	*Queen Elizabeth II* (Cunard liner)
RTZ	Rio Tinto-Zinc
RUC	Royal Ulster Constabulary
SBAC	Society of British Aircraft Constructors (later Aerospace Companies)
SDLP	Social Democratic and Labour Party
SDP	Social Democratic Party
SEP	Economic Policy Committee (of Cabinet)
SET	Selective Employment Tax
SGHWR	Steam Generating Heavy Water Reactor
SHAPE	Supreme Headquarters Allied Powers in Europe
SIB	Shipbuilding Industry Board
SST	Supersonic Transport
STC	Standard Telephones and Cables
STUC	Scottish Trades Union Congress
TASS	Soviet News Agency
TGWU	Transport and General Workers' Union

TUC	Trades Union Congress
UCS	Upper Clyde Shipbuilders
UDI	Unilateral Declaration of Independence
UN	United Nations
UPW	Union of Post Office Workers
USDAW	Union of Shop Distributive and Allied Workers
WEA	Workers' Educational Association

Index